TWITCH UPON A
STAR

The Bewitched
Life and Career of
ELIZABETH
MONTGOMERY

TWITCH UPON A STAR

HERBIE J PILATO

TAYLOR TRADE PUBLISHING
LANHAM • NEW YORK • BOULDER • TORONTO • PLYMOUTH, UK

Published by Taylor Trade Publishing
An imprint of The Rowman & Littlefield Publishing Group, Inc.
4501 Forbes Boulevard, Suite 200, Lanham, Maryland 20706
www.rowman.com

10 Thornbury Road, Plymouth PL6 7PP, United Kingdom

Distributed by National Book Network

British Library Cataloguing in Publication Information Available

Library of Congress Cataloging-in-Publication Data

Pilato, Herbie J.
Twitch upon a star : the bewitched life and career of
Elizabeth Montgomery / Herbie J Pilato.
p.   cm.
Includes bibliographical references and index.
ISBN 978-1-58979-749-9 (hardback)—ISBN 978-1-58979-750-5 (electronic)
1. Montgomery, Elizabeth, 1933-1995. 2. Actresses—United States—Biography.
I. Title.
PN2287.M69335P55   2012
791.4302′8092—dc23
[B]
2012017147

Printed in the United States of America

For the highest good of all those concerned . . .

Also by Herbie J Pilato:

The *Bewitched* Book
Bewitched Forever
The *Kung Fu* Book of Caine
The *Kung Fu* Book of Wisdom
The *Bionic* Book
Life Story: The Book of *Life Goes On*
NBC and Me: My Life as a Page in a Book

"Win, lose, or draw, I'm going to keep
on being Elizabeth Montgomery."

—Elizabeth Montgomery, 1965

"Lizzie didn't want to walk around for the
rest of her life being *Samantha*."

—Ronny Cox, friend and co-star of Elizabeth Montgomery's

"I ain't never met another woman I wanted to be like."

—*Belle Starr*, as played by Elizabeth Montgomery in the
1980 TV-movie of the same name

CONTENTS

PREFACE

In 1979, Elizabeth Montgomery appeared in the NBC TV-movie *Jennifer: A Woman's Story*, in which she played *Jennifer Prince*, the widow of a wealthy shipbuilding executive. In this backdoor pilot for a new series (that Montgomery chose not to pursue), *Jennifer* battled the highbrow board members of her late husband's company that she struggled to control.

On *Bewitched*, which originally aired on ABC from 1964 to 1972, Elizabeth portrayed the beloved nose-wriggling house-witch *Samantha Stephens*. In an episode from 1969, "The Battle of Burning Oak," *Samantha* and her feisty mother *Endora* (Agnes Moorehead) forged one of their rare but sturdy alliances, and set out to discredit the braggart members of a private mortal club. With this and every segment of *Bewitched*, Elizabeth played *Samantha* not so much as a *witch-with-a-twitch*, but as a woman who *just so happens* to be a witch who just so happens to twitch. How she machinated the magic was secondary to the sorcery itself; the supernatural acts were not nearly as pertinent as the distinguishing and ironic essence of *Samantha*: her humanity.

In like manner, Elizabeth eagerly utilized her benevolence with an extraordinary life and career, relinquishing an arrogance that could have easily evolved by way of her prestigious upbringing. As the liberal daughter of film and television legend Robert Montgomery, a staunch Republican, and Broadway actress Elizabeth Allen, an elegant Southern belle, she became disillusioned with the loftiness of Hollywood. She retained an unaffected demeanor on the set of any one of her nearly 500 individual television and film performances, or when approached on the street by some random fan. In either scenario, she relished the simple treasures of life, just as *Samantha* embraced the "everyday, mortal way."

Elizabeth, however, was not immortal in real life. Her light was dimmed

xi

too soon. On May 18, 1995, she died a victim of colon cancer—only two months after completing production of *Deadline For Murder*, her second CBS TV-movie as true-life Miami crime reporter Edna Buchanan (her first, *The Corpse Had a Familiar Face*, aired in 1994).

The shining star, the iconic actress, the outspoken political activist, the kind and loving mother to three children (with *Bewitched* producer/director William Asher: William, Jr., Robert, and Rebecca), and the very private and all-too-human woman was gone. It was devastating news for those within her intimate circle and to the millions of fans who continue to worship her from afar.

More than fifteen years after her painful demise, countless Facebook pages are adorned with her name; over 800,000 readers of *TV Guide* once voted her more popular than Barbara Eden, the star of classic TV's other supernatural blonde-led sitcom, *I Dream of Jeannie* (a blatant replica of *Bewitched* that infuriated Elizabeth); and her TV-movies remain classics.

In 1974, she received an Emmy nomination for *A Case of Rape*, which originally aired on NBC (a decade before the network aired the similarly themed film, *The Burning Bed* starring Farrah Fawcett). *Case* became the first issue-oriented TV-movie of its time, helped to change human rights and legislation for rape victims, and registered itself as one of the highest rated TV-movies in history.

In 1975, Elizabeth received another Emmy nomination for ABC's *The Legend of Lizzie Borden* (a namesake and alleged distant sixth cousin that she took a particular delight in portraying), which will soon be remade for the big screen.

Her feature films remain revered as well: 1955's *The Court-Martial of Billy Mitchell;* 1963's *Who's Been Sleeping in My Bed?* (in which she co-starred with Dean Martin and good friend Carol Burnett); and *Johnny Cool*, also released in 1963, directed by William Asher (who died in Palm Desert, California, on July 16, 2012, at age 90, due to complications from Alzheimer's disease), whom she met and fell in love with on the set.

Approximately one year later, on September 17, 1964, *Bewitched* debuted and was party to the escapist entertainment that America sorely needed amidst the upheaval of the era. Elizabeth, like her contemporary, actress Jane Fonda (to whom she was frequently compared in appearance and talent), protested the country's involvement with Vietnam. Her father was none-too-pleased with his daughter's political view. Such opposition was an earmark for their entire relationship until the day he died, in 1981, succumbing to cancer, like Elizabeth.

A few years later, she delivered the chilling narration for two controversial feature film documentaries: *Cover Up* (1988), which detailed the murky circumstances surrounding the Iran-Contra affair, and *The Panama Deception* (1992), about the American invasion of Panama (which won the Oscar that year for Best Feature-Length Documentary). Into this mix she, along with Elizabeth Taylor, another legendary actress and good friend, became one of the first courageous few to lend support in the mid-1980s to those suffering from AIDS, then a widespread and misunderstood disease affecting mostly homosexual men.

Subsequently, among her multitude of enthusiasts are those within the gay community. Her appeal and notoriety with this portion of the population is unparalleled thanks in part to her humanitarian efforts for research into AIDS (no longer just a "gay disease"). In 1992, she sealed that acclaim when she served as Co-Grand Marshall for the Los Angeles Gay Pride Parade with former *Bewitched* star Dick Sargent (who had recently exited the closet).

Through it all, the central message of *Bewitched*, as she suggested, believed, and trumpeted, was prejudice. *Samantha* was a sorceress isolated in a mortal world, a *witch out of water*, a repressed housewife instructed by an overbearing human husband (*Darrin*, played by Dick York, later replaced by Sargent) to never reveal her true identity.

Despite what critics perceived as confinement, *Samantha* was a free spirit, an independent soul. It was her choice to live the mortal life, and Elizabeth sought to convey the significance of that directive. Liberated women embraced her contributions with *Bewitched* and beyond, and *Samantha* became the first independent and *powerful* woman of the television age. She reflected the progress womanhood had made in the eyes of the public at large. This on the heels of Betty Friedan's blockbuster book, *The Feminine Mystique* which, when released in 1963 (one year before *Bewitched* debuted), documented more than any other single factor the launch of women's lib.

Like many raised in the glare of Hollywood, Elizabeth lived a life that was sprinkled with stardust and littered with trauma. She had loving but disparate relationships, including a core-shaping and life-shifting association with her father, who objected to her liberal views and her initial decision to become an actress.

She loved life and life loved her back, although not always as evenly, particularly in the form of marriages to first husband New York blue-blood Fred Cammann, and her second husband, the troubled and alcoholic actor Gig Young. Her third and fourth husbands, William Asher and actor Robert Foxworth (best known as *Chase Gioberti* on CBS-TV's *Falcon Crest*), were equal lights in her life, but like all true love affairs, even these relationships proved uneven.

Eight years after her divorce from Asher, she appeared in the 1982 TV mini-series *The Rules of Marriage*, which co-starred Elliot Gould. They played *Joan* and *Michael Hagen*, a successful suburban couple who found new partners after separating on their fifteenth wedding anniversary. Like much of Elizabeth's work, *Marriage* broke the rules, when its characters "broke the fourth wall" and periodically talked to the camera, documentary style, as on contemporary shows *The Office* and *Modern Family*. But *The Rules of Marriage* was not a comedy, and no one was laughing on stage or off.

Joan Hagen was a seemingly happy affluent wife, and so was Elizabeth when wedded to Asher during the original reign of *Bewitched*. *Marriage* showcased the disintegration of a seemingly perfect marriage, as both husband and wife became involved in a series of affairs. Asher strayed from Elizabeth throughout their marriage and into the final years of *Bewitched*, which ultimately led to her two-year affair with *Bewitched* producer/director Richard Michaels and to their subsequent divorce and business dissolve. *Bewitched* was cancelled in 1972 and the Asher marriage ended in 1974, around the time she met and fell in love with Foxworth on the set of her TV-movie *Mrs. Sundance*. She didn't leave Asher for Foxworth; she fell in love with Foxworth after her marriage ended.

Foxworth was to have played *Michael Hagen* in *The Rules of Marriage*, but when cast as *Chase* on *Crest* he was replaced by Gould (formerly married to Barbra Streisand, another high-powered, strong-willed independent female force in the entertainment industry).

Elizabeth now sought work diametrically opposed to *Bewitched*, but periodically opted to play characters that represented her role in real life. She gave 100% to each character she portrayed, but savored parts that were leaps and bounds from *Samantha*. Unsuppressed ambitions may have taxed at least her first marriage (to Fred Cammann), but beyond that her career took a backseat to family. There was no stopping her always forthright but elegant manner; while the parallels between her and twitch-witch *Samantha*—her most famous role (for which she was Emmy-nominated five times)—were undeniable:

Elizabeth was born to two actors not of the ordinary (screen idol Robert Montgomery and Broadway thespian Elizabeth Allen). *Samantha* was born to two extraordinary beings (*Endora* and *Maurice*, played by acting legends Agnes Moorehead and Maurice Evans).

Elizabeth was raised in privilege with mansions, movie stars (like Bette Davis and James Cagney) as good friends, the best schools to attend (including Harvard-Westlake School in Los Angeles and the Spence School for Girls in New York), and traveled the world. *Samantha* was raised in opulence, had the best teachers the witch world had to offer, and enjoyed other-worldly travels.

Elizabeth shunned the arrogance of her elitist background and retained an approachable demeanor. *Samantha* rejected the arrogance of her supernatural heritage and remained down-to-earth.

Elizabeth's first upper crust New York husband (Cammann) was thrown out of the social register because he married an actress, a profession frowned upon by his aristocratic family. *Samantha's* clan believed her mortal husband *Darrin* disgraced their aristocratic family heritage, and just as Cammann wanted Elizabeth to give up her craft of acting, *Darrin* wanted *Samantha* to give up witchcraft.

Elizabeth made frequent attempts to stop acting but failed. Her talent was her destiny. Despite *Samantha's* earnest attempts to embrace the mortal life, she never quite stopped using her powers to assist *Darrin* and friends. Her magic was her birthright.

Elizabeth deeply loved each of her four husbands. *Samantha* deeply loved her two *Darrins*.

Elizabeth embraced her theatrical gifts and challenging marriages. *Samantha* embraced her special powers and mixed marriage.

Elizabeth raised her family in the traditional manner. *Samantha* raised her children in again—the "everyday mortal way."

Elizabeth played childhood games with her look-alike cousin Amanda

Panda Cushman. *Samantha's* adult life was challenged by her fun-loving look-alike cousin *Serena* (played by Elizabeth, but billed as *Pandora Spocks*).

Elizabeth became a beloved celebrity worldwide and *Queen of the TV-movies. Samantha* was elected *Queen of the Witches.*

Elizabeth was a political activist who defended her rights and the rights of others, from Vietnam to the Reagan era and beyond. *Samantha* fought city hall in the mortal world, defended her rights to the *Witches Council*, and decried arrogance in both realms.

Elizabeth represented the grassroots movement of the day: women's liberation. *Samantha* defended her personal *witch's honor.*

Elizabeth cherished her family and home life beyond Hollywood, and ultimately accepted her immortal legacy as *Samantha. Samantha* treasured her family and human life, and ultimately accepted her mortal existence.

This book is about Elizabeth's mortal existence. From the day she was born, she had a nervous facial tic that was destined to inspire *Samantha's* magical mugging twitch. It was a mere spec in a vast list of traits and characteristics, characters, and performances that appealed to a mass group of people; that's also what this book is about . . . and everything else in between.

INTRODUCTION

Elizabeth Montgomery welcomed me into her hushed world. I was enamored with the rise, demise, and rebirth of *Bewitched*, and she was intrigued. She marveled in my appreciation of not only her most famous show, but her varied accomplishments, talents, and charitable ways. Initially reticent then unrestrained she, for the first time in twenty years, offered in-depth conversations about her life and career. She explained during the first of what would become four interviews in the spring and summer of 1989:

> It's a strange thing . . . I loathe to chat away about me. I've never liked it. I always hate interviews. I just want to act, and do the best job I can. Hopefully people will appreciate it. That's what my job is. It isn't sitting down and talking about me. If I were a gardener (which she fancied herself as around her home in Beverly Hills), I would be out there trying to make gardens as pretty as I could, and not expect people to come up to me and ask a lot of questions. What it boils down to is this: It's always easier for me to talk about other things than it is to talk about me.

She described our conversations as "cathartic." She spoke about her famous father, film and TV idol Robert Montgomery; her childhood; years of education; early motion pictures, stage, and television appearances. She addressed what it means to be an actress; her friendships with President John F. Kennedy (assassinated on November 22, 1963—the day rehearsals began for *Bewitched*), Carol Burnett, and her *Bewitched* co-stars, including Agnes Moorehead and Paul Lynde; her TV-movies and feature films and, of course, *Bewitched* itself. She discussed all she did and didn't understand about herself and her massive following; all she gave, all she became, all she hoped to be, all she was: a wife, a mother, a friend, a TV legend, a pop-culture icon, a courageously bold endorser of human rights.

My *Bewitched* books concentrated on her most renowned performance, but a more expansive magical story was yet to be told. *Twitch Upon a Star: The Bewitched Life and Career of Elizabeth Montgomery* tells that story. The unpublished memories she shared with me in 1989 are now interspersed with her commentary from other interviews, before and after we met. Only following our chats did she allow for lengthier conversations with regard to *Bewitched* after she ended the show in 1972. She then seemed more comfortable discussing her career, specifically her days on *Bewitched* from which she had long kept safe distance. She later gave interviews to *One on One with John Tesh, The Dennis Miller Show, CBS This Morning*, and *The Advocate* magazine as well as to acclaimed film historian, preservationist, and author Ronald Haver, who for twenty years (he died in 1993) served as the curator and director for the Los Angeles County Museum of Art's film center. The latter interview transpired for a commentary track accompanying the fiftieth anniversary documentary 1991 laserdisc release of *Here Comes Mr. Jordan*, the 1941 film classic starring her father, Robert Montgomery.

Elizabeth and I also talked about her dad; as well as her mother, former Broadway actress Elizabeth Allen; and her maternal grandmother Rebecca Allen; all of whom played substantial roles in the development of her life and work; a career that she sometimes felt was overshadowed by *Bewitched*.

Yet she had little choice but to address her immortal link to *Samantha*. By the time we met in 1989, twenty-five years after *Bewitched's* debut, she and the show's popularity reined steady, expanded by way of nostalgic-oriented networks like Nick at Nite, TBS, and WGN. The series flooded the airwaves, she was finding a new audience, and original and novice fans were falling in love with her all over again. When I asked if she understood just how happy she makes viewers, how classic and contemporary fans adore her just as much, if not more as when the show premiered in 1964, she replied:

> Well, I do now. I mean, you've pointed it out to me certainly. I know they like the show and everything. But it's never been anything that's kind of been bounced in my face as much as it has now with your focus on it. And

I tell you something if only one person feels as you do then that's fine with me. Something was accomplished, because your dedication to this has been absolutely extraordinary. It's the work that is to me its kind of own reward. I know that sounds terribly Pollyanna, but I don't care because that's true for me. And it's the same with you. To put that much energy into what you have done and for us to be sitting here is very good for both of us. It's good for you on every level that you have explained to me, and it's fun for me to sit down and talk about it with somebody who enjoys it that much because I've done so much since *Bewitched*. While doing something you're so concentrated on it, you don't get a chance to sit back and say, *Wasn't that or isn't that fun?* I'd like to think that the stuff that I've done since has meant something to somebody on various different levels. Because I've tried to be real diverse in the work that I've done since I left *Bewitched*.

Her post-1989 interviews with others proved insightful from a personal standpoint; one in particular stands out from the pack. In 1990, veteran television journalist Ann Hodges, mother to a dear friend, talked with Elizabeth for *The Houston Chronicle* about her CBS Hallmark Hall of Fame TV-film *Face to Face*. After the interview, Ann put down her pen and paper and said, "I just have to tell you. My daughter is very good friends with one of your biggest fans." Before Ann had a chance to finish her sentence, Elizabeth blurted out the name, "Herbie!"

There are countless individuals and fan-based groups who assuredly know the more minute trivia related to Elizabeth's entire body of work, but that she would think of me amidst a random reference remains a cherished memory and not insignificant praise. I was honored to hear of that interchange which I will forever humbly embrace. I can do nothing less. Elizabeth was one of the kindest people I ever met, and one of the least arrogant in or outside of Hollywood. I admired her lack of pretension and strive to meet that standard every day.

That said, she was also one of the most complicated individuals on the planet—a conundrum that makes her story so compelling—and one in turn that I felt driven, dare I say, *bewitched*, to explore and share within these pages. This book is also filled with collected reflections from her family members and friends, and coworkers from her TV-movies, feature films, TV guest-star appearances, and other performances and, of course, *Bewitched*. Thoughts from interviews that she and others granted to me appear alongside selected commentary previously published in studio bios, press releases, newspaper and magazine articles, books, TV talk shows and news programs, and online sources.

There are new memories from my exclusive interviews with her friend and fellow actress Sally Kemp (whom Elizabeth met while attending the New York American Academy of Dramatic Arts and who offers some of the most profound insight into Elizabeth's young life); Florence *The Brady Bunch* Henderson (also from the Academy); her TV-movie co-stars and friends, including David Knell (who played her son on *Belle Starr*); Ronny Cox (from *A Case of Rape* and *With Murder in Mind*); the Oscar-winning actor Cliff Robertson (who died only two weeks after granting his interview); *Bewitched* guest star Eric Scott (who would later be cast in *The Waltons*); Peter Ackerman—son of *Bewitched* executive producer Harry Ackerman; *Bewitched* writer Doug Tibbles; Emmy-winning actor and Elizabeth's fellow political advocate Ed Asner (*The Mary Tyler Moore Show*); actress, comedienne, women and children's advocate, and political blogger Lydia Cornell (*Too Close For Comfort*), among many others.

Also included are never-before-published commentary from my original *Bewitched* interviews in 1988 and 1989 with Harry Ackerman, William Asher, Dick York, and Dick Sargent (the two *Darrins*); David *Larry Tate* White, and others associated with the series, including *Bewitched* director Richard Michaels who, in 2006, went on *Entertainment Tonight* and admitted to his affair with Elizabeth. It was an affair that contributed to the downfall of the show and Elizabeth's marriage to Asher (as well as Michaels' nuptials to Kristina Hansen).

When I interviewed Michaels in 1988, I was not aware of his liaison with Elizabeth, but you'd think I'd have had a clue.

We met in Santa Monica for lunch at The Crest, then a new, but very regular eatery, along the lines of Perkins or Denny's, if maybe just slightly upscale. Michaels was cordial, informative, intelligent, and his memories of *Bewitched* and all that it entailed were astounding. But as we finished our interview, he started to tear up. "When you talk with Elizabeth," he instructed me, "you be sure to tell her that I said there will never be anyone else like her in the world. Never!"

Originally taken aback by the statement, especially when he made me vow to relay it, I ultimately agreed, and upon meeting Elizabeth, kept my promise.

After hearing Michaels' message, she looked at me and said, "That's very sweet." And that was that. With hindsight being 20/20, it appeared that Michaels was still in love with Elizabeth, and most likely remains so. (Who wouldn't be?)

Another unexpected event occurred when, upon my second interview with Elizabeth, she surprised me by having invited *Bewitched* actor David White to join us. He and Elizabeth had not seen one another since the series ended in 1972. At the time, that was approximately eighteen years. Portions of their individual and interlocking commentary from that day, all never before published, now appear in this book.

Who would have thought that Elizabeth and David, along with so many other *Bewitched* luminaries, Dick York, Dick Sargent, Harry Ackerman, Alice Ghostley (who portrayed *Samantha's* bubbling witch maid *Esmeralda*), et al. would be gone only a few years later? White died in 1991; York in 1993; Sargent in 1994; and Elizabeth in 1995; the latter three of which while only in their sixties.

Unfortunately, I was unable to attend Elizabeth's memorial service at the Canon Theatre in Beverly Hills on June 18, 1995. I was also unable to attend a ceremony in her name, when finally, if posthumously, she received her designated star on the Hollywood Walk of Fame, January 4, 2008.

Fortunately, my good friend and radio journalist Jone Devlin managed to at least attend the star ceremony, and shared with me what transpired at the event. In addition to what was reported in the press, and from further research, I learned that it was an illustrious event.

Unfortunately, Sally Kemp, Lizzie's best friend from their youth, was also unable to be present at the *star* ceremony, at which the name *Elizabeth Montgomery* was so elegantly chiseled in glittering stone on that famous walkway. While pleased that her friend was immortalized in exactly that manner, Sally was puzzled as to why her friend would later answer to anything but her formal birth name.

"It's strange for me to hear Elizabeth referred to as *Lizzie*," Kemp told me in 2012. "Never while I knew her was she called that. She didn't like *Liz* either . . . only *Elizabeth*. *Lizzie* must have been born after she and Gig (Young) decamped to L.A. I just wonder where it came from."

At the Walk of Fame ceremony the answer was provided by Liz Sheridan, best known as *Helen Seinfeld*, Jerry's mother on NBC's iconic 1990s non-sitcom *Seinfeld*. Sheridan is also known as *Mrs. Ochmonek*, a *Mrs. Kravitz*-type neighbor on NBC's 1980s alien-com *Alf* which like *Bewitched* was an otherworldly, fish-out-of-water sitcom (*Samantha* was a witch in a mortal world; *Alf* was an alien in a human world).

Best friends in their later years Sheridan was introduced to Elizabeth through writer William Blast, who in 1974 penned *The Legend of Lizzie Borden*. From what I learned Sheridan explained at the ceremony, Elizabeth wanted to be called *Lizzie* from the moment she played *Borden*. It was a nice play on a name, especially when Sheridan was around, because Sheridan's younger sister could never quite pronounce the name *Elizabeth*, the formal first name she and Lizzie shared. According to what Sheridan explained, it always came out *Dizabeth*.

In the event, Sheridan became Dizzie and Montgomery became Lizzie, and there they were . . . *Lizzie* and *Dizzie*.

So, however serious Elizabeth was about her life and career she knew when not to take herself seriously. She imbued a playful spirit towards *Borden* that stemmed from her childhood. "I used to get teased all the time about the childhood rhyme, *Lizzie Borden took an ax*, etc," she said in 1989.

Robert Foxworth and I were apparently then slated to reap the brunt of that teasing, so to speak, as when Elizabeth revealed to me a memory she had of the two vacationing at her summer home shortly after the *Lizzie Borden* movie aired. At one point during the getaway, it was raining, and he was kneeling in front of the fireplace, attempting to ignite a flame. "And I had an ax in my hand," she remembered, "because we had just chopped some wood."

Foxworth had then turned toward her, pointed to the ax, and made a request: "Would you please put that thing down?"

The ax was making him nervous and she knew it, but with a devilish smile belying what she recognized as the truth, Elizabeth asked, ever so innocently, "What?"

He reiterated: "Would you please put that thing down?!"

She finally complied, and once they cozied up to the fire, he made an admission: "I have to tell you. That ax really gives me the creeps."

She told me this story in 1989 at her Beverly Hills home, while holding the prop ax from the *Borden* film, and standing next to another fireplace. So I knew exactly how he felt. "You see," she said with utter delight, as I sat squirming. "This is the actual ax. It used to have hairs on it, and I keep telling people not to dust it, but they do. And they've taken some of the blood off it. It's not very sharp. But it would do the job."

She had a wicked sense of humor, a measure of which I had already experienced.

In the early part of 1989, and upon her permission, Bill Asher had given me her phone number. I called her, and did not hear back from her until four months later. Or at least that's how long it seemed.

This occurred about ten years before cell and smart phones hit the mainstream market. At best I stayed close to my old-fangled answering machine, but I still missed her call—on several occasions; although she later confessed to hanging up many times without leaving a message.

Why? She didn't know how to respond to the *Bewitched* theme and "twitching" sound effects from the show's opening credits that I had taken great pains to strategically record on my machine (again, in a pre-high-tech-phone-apps-ring-tone era).

We finally did connect while I was living in Santa Monica and had one day temporarily stepped away from the phone to place a load of towels in the wash. I later noticed the flashing message light on my machine; pressed *play*, and heard: "Hi! It's Lizzie Montgomery. I keep missing you, you keep missing me. This is crazy!"

Like Sally Kemp, not only was I surprised to hear the nickname *Lizzie* being voiced by the actress herself, but I was somewhat frazzled in general that *Elizabeth Montgomery* had just telephoned my house and left a message on my machine. In any event, I collected my thoughts, waited a few moments and then called her back. She picked up the phone, we exchanged *hellos*, and I apologized for missing her call.

"I was doing my laundry," I said, as if talking with an old friend, which in a way I was. I had been watching *Bewitched* nearly my entire life and easily recognized Elizabeth's voice and mannerisms.

Upon hearing of such a humble task, she responded with her trademark giggle and said, "And so you should."

It was so typically Elizabeth to put me or anyone else at ease. Our conversations continued and she was nothing less than charming and dis-arming with each subsequent visit, either by phone or in person.

At our first meeting, we were both nervous. I tripped over her coffee table, and she carefully weighed her words. During our second meeting, we considered the signatory roles she played in my life, and she was slightly more relaxed and free with her phrasing. At one point, we took our conver-sation from her living room to the kitchen so she could feed her dog Zuelika. A small countertop TV was blaring in the background, set on a PBS cooking show.

I picked up our conversation: "You know . . . whatever critic has reviewed you in the past . . ."

"I know," she interrupted, "because forget it . . . *you're worse than my father*, right?"

I smiled, but at the time, did not fully grasp the assumption. Only later did I comprehend what she meant. In researching this book, I realized just how muddled her relationship was with her father. As individuals, they were each complicated. In combination, they were confounding.

But whenever she spoke of him, in our conversations or with others, there was an underlined air of respect. He and her mother, actress Elizabeth Allen, had raised her well, in tandem with Allen's mother, Elizabeth's beloved grandmother, Rebecca "Becca" Allen.

Becca also had a positive influence on Elizabeth's brother, Robert "Skip" Montgomery, Jr., whom I had the privilege of speaking with shortly after she passed away in 1995.

A few years later, I was saddened to learn of Skip's own passing in 2000. When Bill Asher told me, I wanted to call Skip's wife Melanie, but never did. I regret that, and not speaking with Skip more often. But I'll never forget our first conversation. He was so cordial and down to earth, just like Elizabeth. As much as they were blessed in life, neither possessed an ounce of arrogance.

He called to inquire what I wanted to do with the crystal unicorn I had given to Elizabeth upon our first meeting. *Samantha* liked unicorns; and so did Elizabeth; and she loved presents and appreciated gifts, even in the most token form.

Yet the crystal unicorn was no small token. At the time, I had little extra cash to spend on so extravagant a gift. Elizabeth, of course, was worth it, but she was stunned when she saw it. She turned toward me, gave me a big hug, and said in that lyrical voice of hers, "Oh my . . . you know, don't you? You know!"

Skip had the same kind of upbeat, chipper, affable voice.

"Hey, Herbie!" he said that day when I picked up the phone. "How ya' doin'? This is Skip Montgomery. . . . Listen, I have the unicorn that you gave Elizabeth. Do you want it back?"

"No, no, no," I replied. "You keep it. I wanted her to have it—and I want you to keep it in her memory."

We talked a little more, exchanged addresses, and the following December, I received a Christmas card from him and Melanie, a special memento I cherish to this day more than I could have ever treasured the return of that unicorn.

The entire Montgomery family has always been kind to me, including Elizabeth's children, as well as Robert Foxworth, who I had profiled for *Sci-Fi Entertainment* magazine in 1996. And certainly, too, Bill Asher.

One day, in between interviews with Elizabeth, she telephoned me out of the blue, just to see how I was. That morning, I was upset. The strings were broken on the guitar my father had purchased for me when I was a young boy. I was desperate to fix them, not because I played the guitar so well—which I never properly learned to do—but because the instrument held sentimental value. (Like that Christmas card from Skip would years later.)

For some reason, I explained all of this to Elizabeth and to my surprise she in turn told me that Billy Asher, Jr. would fix my weeping guitar.

"Why don't you bring it to my son?"

"Uh? What do you mean?"

"That's what he does. He owns a music shop in Santa Monica."

"You're kidding? I live in Santa Monica."

"Where?"

"On 17th and Santa Monica Blvd."

"I'm going to make this real simple for you. His shop is at 17th and Wilshire Blvd."

"That's just up the street."

"Then you better get going."

We said goodbye, I hung up, packed my guitar and was out the door.

By the time I reached Wilshire, Lizzie had already called Billy to tell him on was on my way. When I arrived at his shop, he was standing at the counter. I shook his hand, explained about the guitar, and a few days later, it was like new again.

We chatted about his Mom, and I immediately noticed he had inherited her down-to-earth demeanor. When I told him so, he shared a few stories of what it was like growing up as not only her son, but the son of the legendary director Bill Asher.

He recalled a time in 1968, when he was just eight years old, and a certain bewitching "screen transfer" proved somewhat confusing for him.

One Thursday night at around eight o'clock, he was at home watching his Mom on TV. It just so happened that Thursday night was the one day a week when the *Bewitched* cast and crew worked later than usual. Elizabeth did not usually arrive home until about 8:15 or 8:30 PM, but this one night she walked in the Asher's front door, just as *Samantha* popped out on *Bewitched.* Eight-year-old Billy was startled. "Geez, Mommy," he said, ". . . you really *are* a witch."

Elizabeth offered a careful explanation: "No, Honey . . . I just play one on TV."

Another time, when Billy was a teenager, circa 1977, he was again in the Asher living room but this time with a friend who was unaware of his heritage. At one point, Elizabeth walked in the room to get a magazine off the coffee table.

His friend screamed, "Oh, my gosh! It's Elizabeth Montgomery!"

"Naw," Billy said, ever carefree. "That's just my mom."

Not one to boast about position or social status, Billy, along with his brother Robert (named for Elizabeth's father) and daughter Rebecca (named for her grandmother Becca) always chose to walk with dignity and integrity, as they do to this day.

Rebecca has always been cordial in the few phone conversations we've shared, displaying her mother's sense of humor each time. When I first talked with her, it took her a few weeks to call me back—just as it had been with Elizabeth. When I mentioned this to Rebecca, she laughed and said, "It must be genetic."

Genes had everything to do with it, especially when it came to Elizabeth's grandmother Becca, for whom her daughter was named—and whom she brought up at the close of our third interview in 1989—following my confession.

"You know who I really am, don't you?" I posed, if somewhat cryptically.

"No," she said, followed by a cautious pause, ". . . who?"

"I'm your guardian angel."

Surprised and relieved, she smiled sweetly and said, "The last person who referred to themselves that way was my Grandmother Becca. And if it's true—that you are indeed my guardian angel sent to replace her—well, then you better do one hell of a good job."

More than twenty years after that exchange, I make an earnest attempt to do just that with this book, which could be described as part biography, part media history guide, part psychology book, part mystic primer, part political dossier, all trustingly compelling.

But Lizzie placed high expectations on biographies, in particular, referring here to the one-page actor profiles that publicists for the studios and networks put together to promote the TV show or film in which a given actor is currently starring:

> I've always found them very self-conscious and they've always bothered me. I've never found one that somebody's written that I've liked. I always think they are dry and stupid, and don't really mean much to anybody.

Hopefully, *Twitch Upon a Star: The Bewitched Life and Career of Elizabeth Montgomery*, will mean something to someone—be it a member of Elizabeth's family, a friend, a fan—because it's a real story, a human story, an honest story—because sincerity was one of the many virtues which Elizabeth held dear. It's a profile in humility and generosity because such traits shaped who she was, strived to be, and became, and who she remains in the hearts and minds of millions. It's a portrait painted with reminiscences of her playful spirit, intelligent mind, and expansive resume; it's the sum of her intricacies and complexities.

I agonized over whether or not to present particular passages in this book; some may be disturbing to read; they certainly proved challenging for me to report. I'd type in specific paragraphs and then delete them; I'd paste them back in and then cut them out again. Finally, I decided to buckle down and include them because it was time to address the elephants in the room. The previous books were fan letters about a fantasy TV show, written as though seen through rose-colored glasses. With this book, I had a job to do. This time, it's not a fairytale, but a true love story, and all true love stories are earmarked with happy and sad elements. As a human being, I was forced to ponder those elements; as a journalist, I couldn't ignore what I heard, some statements of which were glaring. In previous books, as Elizabeth's "angel," confident, friend, or fan, I regret ignoring those statements; had I found the courage to reveal them, *this* story may have had a different ending.

I also sensed that if I had not elected to write an honest biography about Elizabeth, eventually someone else might do so and not as delicately as I believe the material is presented within these pages.

In either case, it was clear to me that Elizabeth was multitalented, multifaceted and multi-complex; reclusive and protective; generous to a fault but private. She was anything but easy to figure out, certainly more challenging to analyze than any of her performances, and she delivered diverse interpretations of a myriad of characters with what appeared to be total ease.

One of her more off-beat roles was that of private detective *Sara Scott* in the 1983 CBS TV-movie *Missing Pieces*, a mystery story that was adapted from Karl Alexander's novel *A Private Investigation*. Similarly, this book detects and connects the missing pieces of a clandestine and extraordinary existence as it expounds on the amazing journey of a public figure who employed her widespread image for a better world. It's for the multitudes who remain charmed by the contrasting work of an actress before, during, and after her superstar-making twitch as a witch named *Samantha*, a beloved character who retained a fiercely independent spirit amidst other unique roles that were brought to life by a majestic, courageous, and real-life heroine named Elizabeth Montgomery.

At its core, *Twitch Upon a Star: The Bewitched Life and Career of Elizabeth Montgomery,* is about a celebrated individual who, for the sake of clarity, simplicity, and intimacy, and in tribute to her unaffected demeanor, will from here on be mostly referred to as either "Elizabeth" or "Lizzie," both which she so modestly and endearingly insisted on being known as at different times throughout her life and career.

PART I

Prewitched

"I just never had the desire to be a star."

—Elizabeth Montgomery, *Look Magazine*, January 26, 1965

One

~

Once Upon a Time

"I like to grow naturally instead of being pruned into formality."

—Elizabeth Montgomery, *TV Radio Mirror*
Magazine, November 1969

Elizabeth Montgomery literally grew up on television, making her small screen debut on December 3, 1951 in "Top Secret," an episode of her father's heralded anthology series, *Robert Montgomery Presents*, which aired on NBC between 1950 and 1957. She'd appear in a total of twenty-eight episodes, but it was in "Secret" that she played none other than the apple of her father's eye. Written by Thomas W. Phipps and directed by Norman Felton, this episode also featured Margaret Phillips (as *Maria Dorne*), James Van Dyk (*Edmund Gerry*), John D. Seymour (*Dawson*), and Patrick O'Neal (*Brooks*):

> Foreign service agent *Mr. Ward* (Robert Montgomery) brings his daughter *Susan* (Lizzie) on a mission to a country on the brink of revolution with spies on all sides complicating the matter at hand.

The "Secret" title may have represented Elizabeth's off-screen desire for privacy, while other *Presents* headings also proved significant, such as "Once Upon a Time," written by Theodore and Mathilda Ferro; airing May 31,

1954. This time, Elizabeth played a newlywed who contemplates how different life might have been had she married someone else.

In real life, Lizzie didn't just contemplate that notion, she lived it . . . four times, with Fred Cammann, Gig Young, Bill Asher, and Robert Foxworth.

Ten years after the "Time" episode of *Presents* aired, *Bewitched* debuted with the Sol Saks pilot, "I *Darrin*, Take This Witch, *Samantha*," narrated by Jose Ferrer. The show opened with his first line, "Once upon a time . . ."

Whether represented on *Robert Montgomery Presents* or recited on *Bewitched*, it was a fairytale phrase that Lizzie adored and which ignited her interest in both projects, especially *Bewitched*. As she recalled in 1989, Bill Asher was in the room when she first read that term in the initial *Samantha* script.

"Okay, I love it!" she said.

"That's it?" Bill wondered. "*Once upon a time*, and you love it?"

"Yeah!" she mused. "Anything that starts out that way can't be all that bad."

It was a spontaneous decision that intrinsically represented the essence of her carefree spirit which, in turn, contributed in no small measure to the show's enormous success.

In fact, before Jose Ferrer got the job, she had asked her father if he would narrate the *Bewitched* pilot. In 1991, she celebrated the fiftieth anniversary of his 1941 classic film *Here Comes Mr. Jordan* by granting an interview to Ronald Haver for a special laserdisc release of the movie. It was here she revealed her father's decline to speak life into *Bewitched*, calling his response, "very strange":

"No . . . I don't think so."

"Why not?"

"It's your show."

"Ah, ok. All right."

Elizabeth was disappointed, and she later told him so. She would have enjoyed him kicking off *Bewitched*, her new series in 1964, just as he had given a jumpstart to her TV career when she made her small-screen debut on *Robert Montgomery Presents* in 1951.

For Lizzie, success was at times a burden, especially when it came to public revelations. For one, her age was a sensitive issue, cloaked in a chicane. But as author and genealogist James Pylant explains, "Celebrity genealogies are always hard to trace." In 2004, Pylant authored *The Bewitching Family Tree of Elizabeth Montgomery* for genealogymagazine.com. "Biographical data abounds," he said, "yet there's no guarantee of accuracy."

Elizabeth played into such wriggle room. Various studio and network press bios document her birth year as 1936 and 1938. In reality, it was 1933, as recorded in the State of California, California Birth Index, 1905–1995, published in Sacramento by the State of California Department of Public Health, Center for Health Statistics.

When she died in 1995, a few obituaries listed her age as fifty-seven, trimming five years off her birth date. Others offered conflicting details about her marital status: some said she was single at the time of her demise; some said she was survived by her fourth husband, Robert Foxworth.

But the "marital mystery," as Pylant put it, was orchestrated by the self-protective Lizzie, who kept a step ahead of the press. She viewed her relationship with Foxworth as confidential. Even their marriage in 1993 was shrouded from the media. The event took place at the Los Angeles apartment of her manager Barry Krost and not a soul knew about it until after the fact.

Nevertheless, she appears on the Social Security Death Index as "Elizabeth Asher," the surname of her third ex-husband, *Bewitched* producer/director William Asher. There, at least, her birth date is correct—April 15, 1933—although "Elizabeth A. Montgomery" is the name listed on her death certificate. The "A" is either for "Asher" or "Allen," the maiden name of her mother, actress Elizabeth Allen.

According to A&E's *Biography, Elizabeth Montgomery: A Touch of Magic* (which originally aired on February 15, 1999), Lizzie's middle name was "Victoria," a moniker sometimes linked with royalty, as is the name "Elizabeth" itself.

But that fits. From the mid-1970s until her demise in 1995, she was known as *Queen of the TV-Movies*. On *Bewitched*, *Samantha* was crowned *Queen of the Witches* (in the episode, "Long Live the Queen," September 7, 1967); before that *Aunt Clara's* (Marion Lorne) bumbling magic mishaps forced Sam's introduction to *Queen Victoria* (Jane Connell in "Aunt Clara's Queen Victoria Victory," March 9, 1967).

Before Lizzie basked in the sparkle of stardom as *Samantha*, she was born in the shadow of Robert Montgomery's fame. The story of who she was begins with him; the seeds of who she became were indelibly planted by this versatile actor and political idealist—a father who was just as complex as his daughter; a daughter who had a father complex.

Five years after his marriage to Broadway actress Elizabeth Allen on April 24, 1928, Lizzie was born into her privileged childhood, at the peak of his film popularity.

Talented, handsome, athletic, rich, and famous, Robert had the right social credentials, coupled with a solid intellect. Before his stable career on the small screen of the 1950s, he was a feature film legend of the 1930s and 1940s.

Although he was a Republican, and she a Democrat, Lizzie followed in his social advocacy. It was difficult for her to fathom and accept the scope of his notoriety before she ever began to question her own. She would later ponder the harvested influence over a legion of *Bewitched* buffs, because she had seen the role celebrity played in her father's life. Once she glittered with fame, it was hard for her to embrace praise even from those whose lives she helped improve.

A political promoter rooted with a conservative outlook, her father held a stoic position in moderate contrast to her liberal stance; but both believed in the American dream (and the freedom that goes along with it).

In 1935, he was elected to the first of four terms as president of S.A.G., the Screen Actors Guild. It was here his political agenda began to take shape. In this capacity, he gained publicity in 1939 when he helped expose labor racketeering in the film industry. He went on to become a lieutenant in the U.S. Navy Reserve, an assistant naval attaché at the American Embassy in London, an attendant at a naval operations room in the White House, a commander over a PT boat in the Pacific, and an operations officer during the D-Day invasion of France. He was awarded the Bronze Star and later decorated as Chevalier of the French Legion of Honor.

In 1947, he headed the Hollywood Republican Committee to elect Thomas E. Dewey as President. That same year he testified as a *friendly witness* in the first round of the House Un-American Activities Committee, denouncing communist infiltration in Hollywood. Following President Eisenhower's 1952 campaign, he was called on by the Principal Head of State to serve as a special staff consultant to television and public communications—the first individual to hold such a media post for the White House.

Robert came to Eisenhower's attention because of his affiliation with *Robert Montgomery Presents*. During the 1960s he was engaged in a futile campaign against the practices of commercial TV, which he summarized in the book *An Open Letter from a Television Viewer* (J. H. Heineman, 1968). Also in the 1960s, the decade in which his daughter would begin to turn the world on with her twitch, Robert served as a communications consultant to John D. Rockefeller III and a director of R. H. Macy, the Milwaukee Telephone Company, and the Lincoln Center for the Performing Arts. From 1969 to 1970 he was president of Lincoln Center's Repertory Theatre.

Steven J. Ross is the author of *Hollywood Left And Right: How Movie Stars Shaped American Politics* (Oxford University Press, 2011). On April 22, 2012, Ross appeared on C-SPAN at the Los Angeles Festival of Books. When asked what role Robert Montgomery played in the Hollywood/political game, he replied:

> Robert Montgomery actually had gone to prep school with George Murphy and the two of them were very close friends and Murphy . . . during the late '40s and '50s was a very prominent Republican activist. In fact, he was Louis B. Mayer's [MGM executive] point man going around the country and when in 1952 Eisenhower wanted some help from Hollywood, or should I say the GOP got Eisenhower help, the two people who advised him on media strategy were Montgomery and Murphy. And Eisenhower liked the two of them so much that he basically told his Madison Avenue firm that had been hired to do the TV, "You can keep writing the ads, but they're going to show me how to appear on TV." Afterwards, Eisenhower asked both men to come to Washington with him. Murphy kindly deferred and Montgomery still kept his career but he actually had an office in Washington to help Eisenhower for eight years with sort of media appearances and helping him stage his presence. Remember . . . this is a period when TV is just really emerging as a national phenomenon and politicians don't

really know how to deal with television. They were teaching them things like how to use makeup, what color glasses to use, how to face a camera . . . how to do sound bites . . . how to hold your body, camera angles . . . everything that a sophisticated actor would learn, they taught to Eisenhower.

As recorded in James Pylant's expertly researched *Bewitching* article Robert Montgomery was born Henry Montgomery, Jr. on May 21, 1904 in Duchess County, New York.

Beacon is commonly given as his birthplace, though he was actually born in Fishkill Landing. (Beacon was formed from the adjoining towns of Fishkill Landing and Matteawan in 1913.) Metro-Goldwyn-Mayer (MGM) promoted Robert Montgomery's movie persona as a sophisticated, well-bred socialite by embellishing the elite family background of its handsome star. And while the actor was *born in a large house on the banks of the Hudson River,* and his father served as an executive of a rubber company, the 1920 Federal Census leaves a somewhat different impression. Fifty-two-year-old Henry Montgomery, the vice president of a rubber factory, and Mary W., age forty-seven, with sons Henry, Jr., age sixteen, and Donald, age fourteen (all New Yorkers by birth), boarded in a Beacon hotel kept by William Gordon. Henry, Sr., was a first generation American, his father being Irish and his mother was Scottish. Mary W.'s father was a Pennsylvanian, while her mother was from the West Indies. Twenty years earlier, the 1900 Federal Census shows the newly wedded Montgomerys ("years married: 0") boarded in William Gordon's hotel, then in Fishkill. Private secretary Henry Montgomery (Sr.), age 32 (born in May of 1868) and 'Mai W.,' age 24 (born in March of 1876) were among the hotel's many boarders. Mrs. Montgomery's birthplace is listed as New Jersey and her mother's birthplace is Jamaica. Robert Montgomery's mother is named in biographies of her son as Mary Weed Barnard, but her maiden name was actually *Barney*. At the time of the 1900 federal census, the Montgomerys had been married a little over six months, their marriage date being 14 December 1899. Mrs. Montgomery appears twice on the federal census in 1900, the second instance being as 'May W. Barney,' age twenty-five, born in March of 1875 in New Jersey. Her marital status was indicated as single, then written over to read *married*. She is named as a daughter of eighty-one-year-old Nathan Barney, who rented a Third Street home in Brooklyn, wife Mary A., age fifty-six (born in October 1843), sons George D., age thirty-four (born in October 1865 in Connecticut), Nathan C., age twenty-seven (born in June 1873 in New Jersey), and Walter S., age eighteen (born October 1882 in New Jersey). A twenty-three-year-old Irish servant also made her home with the family. Mr. Barney was born in Pennsylvania, and Mrs. Barney was born in 'Jamaica, W. I.,' a fact consistent with what May W. Montgomery supplied in 1900. According to *Genealogy of the Barney Family in America*, Mary Weed Barney was born on 30 March 1875 in Bayonne, Hudson County, New Jersey, to Nathan Barney, Jr. and his second wife, the former Mary A. Deverell. The Barney genealogy identifies the parents of Henry Montgomery, Sr., as Archibald Montgomery and the former Margaret Edminston of Brooklyn. Henry Montgomery, a one-year-old, is found in the household of Irish-born Archibald Montgomery—a prosperous shipping merchant—and Margaret (born in Scotland) on the rolls of the 1870 Federal Census in Brooklyn.

In 1970, Robert Montgomery gave an interview to Richard Lamparski for his book, *Whatever Became Of . . . ? Volume III* (Ace Books, 1970). He explained how he had to support himself after his father, "an executive with a rubber company," died and left the family without an income.

As Lizzie expressed to Ronald Haver in 1991, "Daddy had to quit school and go to work, to help support the family; and his father just kind of fell apart."

That's putting it lightly. According to Pylant, Henry, Sr. was depressed, suffered a nervous breakdown, and subsequently committed suicide:

Not only did Robert Montgomery have to cope with the tragedy of his father's death, he had to face a financial crisis as well as the social stigma of having a suicide in the family. Henry Montgomery's nervous breakdown was also a public reminder of the scandal that unfolded in newspapers a generation earlier when Archibald Montgomery, Robert's grandfather, was accused of being an insane alcoholic. The charges against Robert's grandfather were dismissed, yet the damage had been done to the family name. Whispers of a nervous breakdown, insanity, alcoholism and suicide were devastating to a prominent family's social standing. Wire reports of Henry Montgomery's suicide caused the story to be spread in newspapers across the country.

On October 25 and 28, 1884, respectively, *The Brooklyn Eagle* published the articles, "Is He Insane? The Predicament of a Well-Known South Brooklyn Man" and "The Montgomery Suit: Withdrawal of the Suit at the Insistence of the Family," both about Archibald.

On June 25, 1922, *The Philadelpia Inquirer* published the item below titled "Man Jumps To Death From Brooklyn Bridge: Hundreds See Suicide From Trolley To Rail":

> A man believed to be Henry Montgomery, of Brooklyn, leaped to his death from the Brooklyn Bridge this evening, in the view of hundreds of pedestrians and surface car and elevated train passengers. He leaped from a passing car to the bridge roadway, stepped to the rail without looking back and jumped.

On June 26, 1922, *The Denver Post* published the following item under the heading "Wealthy N.Y. Rubber Firm Head Drowns Himself In River":

> Henry Montgomery, 45 years old, of Brooklyn, wealthy retired president of the New York Rubber company, committed suicide late Sunday afternoon by jumping into the East River. Montgomery, who had been suffering from a nervous breakdown which forced his retirement ten months before, had apparently planned to take his own life, and left instructions for notifying his relatives.

Either way, Henry (Sr.) left his family penniless, and his son Robert (Henry, Jr.) was forced to pick up the slack—as a railroad mechanic and oil tanker deckhand—and he was none too pleased about it. Fortunately, by the late 1920s, and following ineffectual attempts to become a writer, he became an established Broadway actor, joining his stage peers in the mass migration into film as *talkies* came into play.

But his subsequent tumultuous relationship with Lizzie may have been ignited by the resentment and the frustration he experienced in his pre-acting days. No doubt those years helped to foster a strong work ethic that he would later instill in Lizzie. But initially, it was no pleasant experience. What's more, a future family tragedy would further loosen and then only entangle the father-daughter link between Elizabeth and Robert Montgomery.

Elizabeth and her father did not always see eye to eye, and they were definitely on opposite ends of the political spectrum, but their lives were in many ways similar. He was educated at exclusive private schools, as she would be later (at his instruction). She made her theatrical stage debut at six years old in *Red Riding Hood's World* (a French language stage production at the aristocratic Westlake School for Girls in Los Angeles); his theatrical film premiere occurred much later in life (with the comedy, *Three Live Ghosts*, in 1929); but they both loved acting (after his initial objection to her vocational choice).

Contracted with MGM, Robert would later be pigeonholed as that carefree leading man; just as Lizzie would later be typecast as a lighthearted leading witch. And just as she would later distance herself from *Samantha* (with a list of edgy TV and motion picture roles), Robert tried to break the happy-go-lucky mold and waxed *psychotic* in several feature films, including: *The Big House* (a prison movie released in 1930 that set the pattern for similar future films) and *Night Must Fall* (a 1937 thriller in which he played a mysterious brutal killer who terrorized the countryside).

The latter earned him an Academy Award nomination. He received a second Oscar nod in 1941 for *Here Comes Mr. Jordan*, this time, portraying an angel.

On a flight to his next fight, boxer *Joe Pendleton's* (Robert) soul is prematurely snatched from his body by the newly deemed *Heavenly Messenger 7013* (Edward Everett Horton) when his plane crashes. Before the matter can be rectified by *7013's* supervisor, the celestial *Mr. Jordan* (Claude Raines), *Joe's* body is cremated; so *Jordan* grants him the use of the body of wealthy *Bruce Farnsworth* (original character unseen), who's just been murdered by his wife (Rita Johnson). As *Joe* attempts to remake *Farnsworth's* unworthy life in his own clean-cut image, he falls for *Betty Logan* (Evelyn Keyes).

Lizzie failed to win an Emmy for playing a witch on *Bewitched* (for which she was nominated five times, with a total of nine nominations throughout her career); her father failed to ace any formal acting award for playing a seraph (or a psycho).

In 1945, legendary film director John Ford became ill on the set of *They*

Were Expendable, and Robert stepped in as his replacement, making his first mark as a director. After receiving this initial tech credit, he turned out an unusual, controversial production titled *Lady in the Lake* (1947), a Raymond Chandler mystery thriller told in the first person through tricky subjective camera angles (much like Lizzie's *Missing Pieces* 1982 TV-movie). Playing the hero (private eye *Philip Marlowe*), he was seen on the screen only twice—once in the prologue, then within the body of the film, when he briefly crossed in front of a mirror. All other scenes were shown from his point of view, as if seen though his eyes. Robert went on to direct and star in several other films that received varied response before retiring from the big screen, and turned his attention to politics, TV, and the stage.

On Broadway in 1955, he won a Tony Award for best director for the play *The Desperate Hours*. He later formed Cagney-Montgomery Productions with early screen idol James Cagney to produce *The Gallant Hours* (1960), his final effort as a film director. Cagney was fond of Lizzie, and later became a mentor of sorts, maybe something even closer.

As she told Ronald Haver for the 1991 laserdisc release of *Here Comes Mr. Jordan*, Cagney was one of her dad's closest friends who was like a second father to her, and it never occurred to her that Cagney was a big star.

Another larger-than-life celebrity who both Elizabeth and Robert Montgomery befriended was film legend Bette Davis. Lizzie would later take the lead in the 1979 TV-movie, *Dark Victory*, a remake of Davis' 1939 motion picture; Bette had co-starred with Robert in 1948's *June Bride* (directed by Bretaigne Windust). In time, Lizzie and Bette became closer friends than Bette and Robert, and he became jealous; not so much of Bette, but of Lizzie. But as Bette recalled to author Charlotte Chandler in *Bette Davis: A Personal Biography—The Girl Who Walked Home Alone* (Simon and Schuster, 2006), Robert left little to be desired or envied. She even went as far as to describe him as "a male Miriam Hopkins," a reference to her arch rival on the big screen.

Actress Hopkins had well-publicized arguments with Davis (who reportedly had an affair with Hopkins' then-husband, Anatole Litvak) when they co-starred in the films *The Old Maid* (1939) and *Old Acquaintance* (1943). Davis admitted to very much enjoying a scene in the latter movie in which her character forcefully shakes Hopkins' character. There were even press photos taken with both divas in boxing rings with gloves up and *Old Acquaintance's* director Vincent Sherman standing between the two.

Davis never came to such blows with Robert Montgomery on the set of *June Bride*, but she came close. She explained in Chandler's book:

> He was an excellent actor, but addicted to scene stealing. He would add business in his close-ups which didn't match mine, so that there would only be one way to cut the film—his way. Mr. Montgomery understood films. (Director) Windust, who was not a film man at all, never noticed, and I couldn't have cared less. Montgomery was welcome to all the close-ups he wanted. I act with my whole body.

In 1991, Elizabeth told Ronald Haver that her father and Davis didn't get along. After Lizzie had moved out of the Montgomery homestead, Robert would call and invite her to dinner.

"I can't," she'd reply. "I'm going over to Bette's."

"Oh," he'd say, and hang up.

After meeting at various social events in New York, Davis became somewhat of a mentor for the young ingénue. In fact, while only in her late teens, Lizzie was invited by Davis to her home in Maine on a street named, "appropriately enough," Elizabeth said, "Witch Way." That name represented Davis' reputation and not *Bewitched*, which was years from creation. But for the moment, the *witch* reference seemed to fit Davis and, as Lizzie told Haver, "She knew that."

One weekend on Witch Way, Lizzie and Bette picked beans from Davis' garden and later strung them inside the house, while sitting in front of her fireplace. Shortly after, an argument ensued between the two, Davis stalked out of the room, and then stopped in her tracks. She turned to face Lizzie and said, "*Betty*—when they do the story of my life, you should play me, and I'm not sure that's a compliment." Lizzie thought that was funny; Bette Davis was the only person Elizabeth Montgomery ever allowed to call her "Betty."

According to James Pylant's *Bewitching Family Tree*:

> Elizabeth Montgomery's death certificate gives her mother's maiden name
> as Elizabeth Allen, a Kentucky native. The 1930 federal census of Los
> Angeles County, California, shows Robert Montgomery, age twenty-five,
> born in New York, *Actor, Motion Pictures*, and wife Elizabeth A., also
> twenty-five, born in Kentucky, and a fifty-year-old servant lived on Black-
> wood Drive in Los Angeles. The *age at first married* for both was twenty-
> three. The couple had married on 14 April 1928 in New York, and the
> following year they moved to Hollywood when Robert signed a contract
> with M-G-M. Elizabeth was the couple's second child. Tragically, their first
> born, Martha Bryan Montgomery, died at age fourteen months in 1931.

In May 1965, *Movie TV Secrets* magazine published the article, "Witches
Are People Too," by Jackie Thomas. It explained how Robert was devastated by the loss; how tiny Martha's death left him in a state of severe
depression that immobilized him for months. A friend who knew the
Montgomerys described his condition:

> I don't think I've ever seen anyone as shaken as Bob. All his life seemed to
> be invested in that child; when she died something in him died with her. I
> don't think he has ever really recovered. Something inside him was twisted
> and destroyed by Martha's death.

Lizzie was interviewed for that same article. She addressed her father's
strict reign over her youth, one that seemingly increased with time, as if in
gradual reaction and retaliation to her little sister's death, a young sibling
she never knew. Little by little, her father's stern rule nibbled away at her
self-esteem until the day she died in 1995. But thirty years before in May
1965, it was a different story.

She said she was too sure of a great many things. Being the daughter of
a star had its effect on her. Not that her father went out of his way to make
things easier for her, because he didn't. In fact, she said, at times he bent
over backwards to go in the opposite direction. "Maybe that was his problem," she thought. "He gave me the best of everything—clothes, education, things like that, but he demanded a lot, too. Dad is a very complex
man. I don't think I've ever been able to come up to Martha in his eyes."

However, five months prior to that she told *TV Radio Mirror*:

I never replaced Martha in his heart, but I did help to soothe his grief.

As was explained in Richard Lamparski's book, *Whatever Became Of . . . ? Volume III*, between 1928 and 1950, Robert Montgomery was married to "actress Elizabeth Allan" (with an "a"), an actress best known for her 1936 pairing with Ronald Coleman in the 1935 film, *A Tale of Two Cities*. But this Elizabeth Allan, born British in Skegness, England, in 1908, was not Lizzie's mother, nor was she ever married to Robert.

A little over two decades later, the American actress Elizabeth Allen (with an "e") was born "Elizabeth Ellen Gillease" on January 25, 1929 in Jersey City, New Jersey. In 1972, she co-starred on ABC's *The Paul Lynde Show*, playing Lynde's on-screen wife in this series that was executive produced by *Bewitched's* Harry Ackerman, and William Asher and Elizabeth Montgomery under their banner production company, Ashmont Productions. But this Elizabeth Allen was not Lizzie's mother either, nor was she ever married or related to Robert Montgomery.

However, a second American actress named Elizabeth Allen (with an "e") arrived on the scene before Gillease. James Pylant provides the details in his *Bewitching* article:

> Elizabeth Daniel Allen was born on 26 December 1904 in Louisville, Jefferson County, Kentucky, to Bryan Hunt Allen and the former Rebecca Lowry Daniel. Elizabeth Montgomery's maternal grandparents—like her paternal grandparents—were newlyweds at the time of the 1900 federal census enumeration. Fifty-seven-year-old widow Ellen W. Daniel, born in Indiana in February of 1843, owned a house on Brook Street in Louisville, Kentucky, which she shared with daughter Lizzie W., age twenty-five; son William A., age thirty-five, daughter-in-law Mollie, age thirty-six, and daughter Rebecca Allen, age twenty. Except for Ellen Daniel, all were born in Kentucky. Rebecca Allen's marital status is given as married, with *o* given for the number of years married. Bryan H. Allen is listed elsewhere in Louisville, although his marital status is recorded as single. An inspector for a gas company, he was born in November of 1877 in Kentucky to a Missouri

father and a Kentucky mother. Rebecca Lowry Daniel Allen—Elizabeth Montgomery's beloved *Becca*—was born in June of 1879 in Kentucky (as per the 1900 census), but her death certificate gives 5 June 1886 as her birth date. Her death certificate also identifies her mother's maiden name as Wright. Daniel family genealogists show that Ellen Wright was the wife of Coleman Spencer Daniel, who died in Louisville on 8 June 1898, two years before Mrs. Ellen W. Daniel is shown on the rolls of the twelfth federal census as a widow. Daniel family records show Ellen Wright Daniel died two years later on 7 June 1902. The same record gives 16 February 1843 as her birth date, which agrees with what is found on the 1900 census. Coleman S. Daniel and Ellen Wright wedded in the bride's native Switzerland County, Indiana, on 20 May 1864. The daughter of John W. Wright, who represented Switzerland County in the state legislature, Ellen Wright was only six months old when her mother, Ellen (Lowry) Wright, died at age 36. Her father remarried the following year to Rebecca D. Saunders. Clearly, when Ellen (Wright) Daniel named her daughter Rebecca Lowry Daniel, she did so in honor of her mother and stepmother.

It was Lizzie's grandmother Becca with whom she formed a special bond (and who eventually introduced her to the potentially lighter side of life, like horse racing and gambling.)

Becca moved with her daughters Elizabeth Allen and Martha-Bryan to New York City in the early 1920s where Martha-Bryan had a role in the Broadway play, *He Who Gets Slapped*, which played at the Garrick Theater. In all, Martha-Bryan, mother to Lizzie's first cousin, Amanda (a.k.a. "Panda," a childhood playmate), was in two dozen plays at one point before she met her husband-to-be Arthur Cushman.

Into this mix, Elizabeth Allen also performed in several live stage productions until she married Robert Montgomery on April 14, 1928. She received superb reviews for many of these plays, such as with *Revolt*, of which *The New York Times* said, "The lovely Miss Allen is poised for leading lady status anytime soon. She always brings freshness to her roles."

Allen and Robert were married at the Episcopal Church of the Transfiguration also known as "The Little Church Around the Corner" on 29th Street between Fifth Avenue and Madison Avenue. The church was also the home of the Episcopal Actors' Guild, of which she and Robert were members.

She retired almost immediately at Robert's request for her to concentrate only on being his wife. Lizzie chatted about Elizabeth Allen to *Modern Screen* in May 1965:

> Mother is a marvelous person. Just great. It's her attitude toward people that's so marvelous. She's a very warm, outgoing, generous human being. She'd acted on Broadway (that's where she met Dad); so did her sister, Martha-Bryan Allen. Both of them got reviews that are so extraordinarily good, they make you sort of proud. Mother did light comedy; she co-starred with Lee Tracy and Elizabeth Patterson. But she gave up her career when she married Dad and I don't believe ever regretted it for a moment. She loves her house and she and Dad gave my brother and me a wonderful childhood. It just couldn't have been happier, healthier or more fun.

When Lizzie was a stage-struck teen, Robert tried to sway her decision from acting by using his wife a prime example. According to the August 1967 edition of *Screen Stars* magazine, Robert told Lizzie that her mother was wise to forfeit her career to marry him and raise a family. He went on to tout his wife as the toast of Broadway, but that she knew her career would be detrimental to raising children. "It's difficult to know who your real friends are," Robert added. "Worst of all, acting requires the constant rejection of your real self. Sometimes you don't even know who you are anymore. Imagine what that does to a family!"

Lizzie wouldn't have to wonder about the consequences; she'd experience them first hand.

Two

~

Grim

"There's a little bit of a displaced person in everybody, and it's
nothing to be ashamed of."
—Elizabeth to Ronald Haver, 1991

Elizabeth's young life was divided between her parents' massive estate in
Patterson, New York, and their elegant home in Beverly Hills. It was there
they hosted various dinner parties and Sunday brunches that were attended
by the conservative likes of James Cagney, Bette Davis, Rosalind Russell,
Irene Dunne, Frank Morgan, and George Arliss. Her parents moved in
A-list circles, and were considered Hollywood royalty. They were well-
groomed, poised, and intelligent leaders of the community. They were
quiet, private, and peaceful in their everyday lives and, like many of their
friends (and later, Lizzie), rejected exhibitionism and screwball conduct.

On October 13, 1930, Robert Montgomery and Elizabeth Allen gave
birth to the little girl they named after Allen's sister Martha-Bryan, the
infant-child whose subsequent tragic death in December 1931 at only fourteen months (due to spinal meningitis) would forever change the Montgomery family dynamic.

Elizabeth's parents resided in a small house in Los Angeles until 1932,
when they moved to Beverly Hills. Approximately one year later, little
Lizzie arrived at 4:30 AM on April 15, 1933 (and not 1936 or 1938). However, after her brother Skip was born on February 15, 1936, the family

moved to Holmby Hills, an affluent neighborhood in West Los Angeles just north of Sunset and east of Beverly Glen, in a custom-built sixteen-room mansion with an Olympic-sized swimming pool. They lived there until they all moved to New York.

Franchot Tone, a substantial star in Robert Montgomery's league at the time, then purchased the Beverly Hills home. Elizabeth later attempted to buy it back when she married Bill Asher, but Tone wouldn't budge. Subsequently, the Ashers purchased their Beverly Hills estate on Laurel Canyon Drive from Howard Hawks (the legendary director of westerns, along the lines of John Ford), where Lizzie remained after her divorce from Bill, through her marriage to Bob Foxworth, and until her demise.

Elizabeth told Ronald Haver in 1991 that her childhood was "all very kind of abnormally normal." As Foxworth explained on A&E's *Biography* in 1999, the upscale world that she grew up in did not contribute to a regular childhood. She was expected to dress properly and to have good manners and behave in a certain way. She took that as an act, Foxworth believed, because it failed to mirror her own true feelings. So, in a sense, he said, "she was always an actress."

In March of 1939, Robert Montgomery told *Collier's Magazine* that his farm in the Towers section of Patterson, New York, near Brewster was his refuge from acting. He lived there three months a year and any visitor to the farm who mentioned the entertainment industry in any way was reportedly "apt to be slugged."

Robert Montgomery's love-hate partnership with Hollywood would mirror his personal relationship with Lizzie. She didn't get along with her father because, as Foxworth also surmised on A&E's *Biography*, to some extent her father was envious of Elizabeth's popularity.

Billy Asher, Jr., the first of Lizzie's three children with William Asher, blamed the ongoing rift between his mother and grandfather on their opposing political views. He, too, appeared on *Biography*, and said, "They just didn't see eye to eye."

In later years, she and her dad seldom spoke. But if she phoned him, at least he'd answer, as he did when Hollywood called him abroad in May of 1939.

It was then he traveled to England to make *The Earl of Chicago*, which would become Lizzie's favorite of his films:

A Chicago gangster (Montgomery) learns he has inherited an earldom in England, and he travels to London in order to claim it; he does so, even though he remains involved with mobsters back in the States. Ultimately, he transforms from a two-bit gangster and ends up living in an English castle with this wonderful old valet (Edmund Gwenn) who proceeds to tutor him in the ways of being an earl. Unfortunately, his previous life continues to haunt him; he commits murder, is tried by a jury of his peers in Parliament, and ends up in prison. In the end, his valet brings his best clothes, knickers, silk stockings, and patent leather shoes, coat with lace collar, ultimately dressing him for his execution.

In 1991, Elizabeth expressed to Ronald Haver just how impressed she was with this movie:

It's just a gem, and it's not because he's in it. I could see anybody in it, as long as they were as good as he was in it. It is imaginative, it's beautifully directed, it's cleverly acted. Edmund Gwenn is so fabulous. It builds to such a point where they had the courage to do what they did at the end, instead of somebody saying, *You're kidding, you can't do that. How can you possibly end it this way?* I was just flabbergasted the first time I saw this. (You think) *Superman will swoop down and take this man away.* But he doesn't, and by God, the guy walks out of the prison, down to the guillotine, starts to walk up the steps and there's a wonderful cut of Edmund Gwenn in the window, looking down, where *The Earl of Chicago* is totally panic-stricken at this point. The look on his face is just the most horrendous thing. I mean, he's just scared to death, and quite rightly, when he realizes (that) nothing (is) going to save him. And he turns around and he looks as if he's about [to be] ready to run, and looks up at the window, and sees the valet at the window, and the valet bows to him, and he realizes, *Oh, God, it's just a killer.* He realizes he's gotta go through with this. Oh, I was in tears. I almost am now thinking about it. It was just extraordinary.

Lizzie then elaborated on the scene during which the Earl was tried in front of Parliament, how her father decided not to see the set before filming, or that scene's dialog. He knew his character was on trial; he had a vague concept of the questions and answers; but he had no idea about protocol:

He just didn't want to make himself familiar with the script at all. And I think when you watch the movie, you can tell, because when those doors open onto that room, it's like (he thinks), *My God, this sure isn't like any little courtroom in Chicago that I've ever seen before.* It's just this kind of awe-struck kind of almost childish thing that happens to this man. I love that movie. Can you tell?

Although Elizabeth's adult relationship with her father was strained, she never stopped loving him, and he never stopped loving her or her brother Skip. Family-oriented, Robert, unlike *The Earl of Chicago*, refused to go to Britain unless his wife and children accompanied him, and they did.

But while the Montgomerys journeyed to the United Kingdom, the Nazis invaded Norway, World War II began, and Robert promptly joined the American Field Service Ambulance Corps and was attached to the French army as an ambulance driver. A young Lizzie and her even younger brother Skip were then shipped back to the United States on an Arandora Star steamship bound for New York City.

Due to the radio silence of the time, it was eight days before their parents learned of their safe arrival under the care of Lizzie's grandmother Becca, who was there to greet and take them back to California.

In 1991, Elizabeth offered a concise description of her father to Ronald Haver for the fiftieth anniversary laserdisc release of *Here Comes Mr. Jordan*:

> . . . primarily self-educated . . . well, brilliantly . . . with a very kind of quirky sense of humor, very stubborn . . . arrogant . . . pompous to a point where I wanted to slap him sometimes . . . could be extremely understanding one minute and just irrational the next . . . I don't mean irrational, I mean to someone that disagreed with him, irrational, obviously . . . very obviously right-wing, politically . . . but . . . he was terrific with little children, and they seemed to adore him, which is always a good sign [she laughed], and he loved animals . . . he adored my mother . . . he adored my stepmother . . . he was very hard on my brother, much more so on him than me . . . he loved pretty things, like antique stuff, or modern even. He loved Andrew Wyeth, who was also a friend of his . . . he loved) Daumie, Max Beerbohm. I loved the way he dressed . . . There were times when he'd be kind of tweedy . . . Maybe that was his pompous wanting to be

33

King of England department . . . I always remembered too, when I was little, how handsome he looked in a dinner jacket. He always seemed very at home when he was dressed up a lot. Very relaxed; so it just suited him very well; as did . . . riding a horse. He had his own kind of style . . . and he had a great voice, really nice voice. He used to read Dickens' *A Christmas Carol* every Christmas and I used to love that. It was wonderful.

Robert Montgomery was clearly a larger-than-life figure in Lizzie's eyes, but she still referred to him as just plain "Daddy" in much the same way that *Samantha* called to her warlock father named *Maurice* (pronounced as *More-eese*) played by the late Maurice (pronounced *More-iss*) Evans.

In fact, before Evans was cast as *Maurice*, Lizzie asked Robert to play the role. "Unfortunately," she recalled in 1989, "he said no. But I would have loved him to do it. He would have been divine in the role."

She couldn't help but feel despondent about the ordeal. She was already disappointed that Robert had declined to narrate the *Bewitched* pilot in 1964; now he rejected the chance to play his daughter's father on-screen, as she had played her father's daughter on that "Top Secret" episode of *Robert Montgomery Presents* in 1951.

Robert, however, had been ill when she asked him to portray *Maurice*, so he may not have been able to do the role even had he so desired. And while Lizzie believed Evans was "perfect" for the part of her majestic TV father, that's how she also had described her real "Daddy."

As a child, Elizabeth had not realized her father was a star. He just worked for a living, like everyone else's dad; he just so happened to be an actor and worked at a movie studio. That didn't seem out of the ordinary. As she explained to *Photoplay Magazine* in 1968, his work never entered their home and she rarely saw him on the job. She visited one of his sets once, maybe twice, when she was growing up, but she didn't discover his occupation until someone told her at Westlake.

As she lamented in 1992 to John Tesh on his short-lived TV show, *One on One*, it was kind of like finding out there was no Santa Claus. It never occurred to her that he was "doing something odd . . . or wonderful . . . or not so wonderful" with his career.

However, in August 1967, Jacqueline Starr wrote in *Screen Stars* magazine:

Robert Montgomery tried everything in his power to keep his daughter from confusing the Robert Montgomery—suave movie hero—with Daddy, the loving gentle man who was, nevertheless, human and capable of error. But Liz saw only a bigger-than-life father, the one on the screen. And when he tried to tell her about all the everyday problems of being an actor she just wouldn't listen. She was convinced that everything Daddy did was perfect and she intended to follow suit herself. That's when she ran into genuine trouble.

However wonderful or not so wonderful Robert Montgomery was, he could not prevent his legal detachment from Lizzie's mother Elizabeth Allen. In turn Lizzie, like other children of dysfunctional households from any era, was forced to become what was then referred to as a "product of a broken home."

Her parents divorced on December 5, 1950 after Robert had an affair with yet another Elizabeth in the fray, this one Elizabeth "Buffy" Grant Harkness, who was married to William Harkness, one of the wealthiest socialites in New York City. Buffy was also heiress to the Standard Oil fortune and she married Robert on December 9, 1950, a mere four days after his divorce from Elizabeth Allen.

At the time, it was noted that not only did the second Mrs. Montgomery have the same first name as her predecessor but she bore a striking resemblance to her as well. But according to the January 1965 edition of *TV Radio Mirror*, the first Mrs. Montgomery's only comment about her former husband's new marriage was:

Moving East wasn't the best. Usually, Hollywood gets the blame for divorces, but in this case, it was the reverse. I had hoped we could work out our differences, but now I realize it can't be.

In the same article, Lizzie insisted:

I felt no bitterness when my parents parted. There was no spite or name-calling. There was no open quarreling that I knew of. They separated with the same dignity and mutual respect I had come to expect from them.

Yet, how could she feel anything but devastated by her parents' dissolve? At this early stage in their relationship, she had worshipped her father and the divorce most probably contributed to the wedge between them; and feeling worse for her mother didn't much help matters. She and her brother Skip may have moved to Manhattan with Mrs. Montgomery to help ease the traumatic transition, but Lizzie continued to put up a less traumatized front to cover her disillusionment.

"When you think everything's fine, this comes as a blow," Elizabeth admitted to *Modern Screen* in May 1965. "But we saw Dad all the time."

She was proud that her parents had remained together for so long. Childhood friend Billie Banks explained as much to MSNBC's *Headliners & Legends* in 2001. The sense of united family was "extremely important" to her, Banks said.

As Lizzie herself told *TV Guide* in 1961, her "wonderful feeling of security" had stemmed from her mother and father. In describing her and Skip's relationship with them, she unabashedly added: "Our parents protected us from too much Hollywood stuff, but it seeped through."

How could it not? Robert Montgomery expected a great deal from those in his inner personal and professional circles and, as time marched on, Lizzie fit into both those categories. On a subconscious level, she may not have even allowed herself to fully grieve her parents' divorce, which could have added to the emotional burden of it all, further widening the already significant gap between them.

As Liz "Dizzie" Sheridan revealed to *Headliners & Legends* in 2001, Elizabeth once told her, "I don't think my father liked me very much." On that same program, *Bewitched* director Richard Michaels claimed Elizabeth wanted praise from her father more than anyone else in the world, but it wasn't as forthcoming as she desired, at any stage of the game.

Five years later, Michaels appeared on *Entertainment Tonight* and dropped a bombshell: he and Elizabeth had an affair, one that ultimately contributed to the end of *Bewitched* in 1972 and, in 1974, the end of her marriage to Bill Asher, Michaels' mentor.

For Lizzie three times was not the charm in the marriage department, at least not as she had once hoped. Although her nuptials with Asher at first seemed ideal, she disengaged from him, sadly, just as she had from Fred Cammann and Gig Young. But she remained loyal to Asher, partially in respect of his talent, but mostly because of their three children.

It was the same sense of loyalty she retained for her parents when *they* divorced, despite her distress at the disintegration of what she viewed as the perfect family. She still kept a stoic upper lip during their separation proceedings and decades later mourned their demise. When Robert Montgomery passed away at age seventy-seven in 1981 in Manhattan, she refused to speak with the press, especially the tabloid press.

"I hate those magazines," she said in 1989, one of which contacted her not more than two days after her father died, asking, "How does it feel, now that your father's dead? You never agreed with him anyway. We'd like your comments because we know you never got along with him politically."

She hung up without dignifying the call with a response. "And that was the last time I spoke to that magazine," she acknowledged, "and haven't since."

In the long term, Lizzie was proud of her ancestry, as was evidenced by the names she and Bill Asher would later bestow upon their children. As *Bewitching* genealogist James Pylant chronicled:

> Their third child was named Rebecca Elizabeth Asher. *I knew . . . another Becca had arrived*, the actress said when she gave birth to her daughter. Rebecca Lowry Daniel Allen died in 1964, just as her actress-granddaughter launched the first season of (*Bewitched*). Elizabeth Montgomery and husband William Asher had given family names to their two older children, with William Allen Asher bearing his father's first name and his maternal grandmother's maiden name, while Robert Deverell Asher carries the first name of his maternal grandfather and the middle name of his great-great-grandmother, Mary A. (Deverell) Barney.

As Lizzie explained to *TV Radio Mirror* magazine in November 1969, she named her daughter in tribute to her grandmother as well as a childhood friend:

> With Rebecca Elizabeth, it's been legitimate to call her *Rebel*. I sort of hope that happens. I went to school with a hellion named Rebecca whose nickname was *Reb*—not *Becky*. If the baby had been a boy he'd have been called *John*. I kind of like Adam—but *Adam Asher*?! That's too *cutesy pooh*.

The latter distinction never came to fruition, except partially.

On *Bewitched*, *Darrin* and *Samantha* named their son *Adam* who was born in the sixth season of *Bewitched* (and played by David and Greg Lawrence, who were fathered by Tony Curtis in real life); but Lizzie and Bill Asher never had another child after Rebecca.

Then, after Elizabeth ended *Bewitched*, there was another relative, if distant, who played into the fold: an accused ax murderess whom she portrayed in the 1975 TV-movie *The Legend of Lizzie Borden*, based on the real-life woman who was accused of murdering her father and stepmother in 1893. James Pylant's research revealed that Elizabeth and Borden were sixth cousins once removed, both descending from seventeenth-century Massachusetts resident John Luther.

Author Rhonda R. McClure originally documented the relative connection in her book, *Finding Your Famous (And Infamous) Ancestors* (Cincinnati: Betterway Books: 2003); in which she asked, "I wonder how Elizabeth would have felt if she knew she was playing her own cousin?"

Retro curator Ed Robertson is the host of *TV Confidential*, one of radio's most renowned showcases of nostalgic television talent and discussions. He's also the author of a number of acclaimed classic TV literary companions, including guides to *The Rockford Files* and *The Fugutive*. He weighs in on the Lizzie/Borden relative link: "Whether that's true or not, I don't know. But I'm not sure whether Elizabeth would have taken on the role, or at least allowed Borden to be characterized the way she was in the role, had she known she was in fact playing one of her cousins."

Years after playing *Borden*, Elizabeth finally learned of her lineage with the character. Entertainment historian Thomas McCartney, who has archived Elizabeth's career since 1994, puts it all in perspective: "She was bemused by the idea, but never said anything else."

That sounds about right; *no response* was a typical Lizzie response.

Several decades before Elizabeth played *Borden*, her grandmother Becca was born "Rebecca Lowry Daniel Allen" in 1886. Seventy-eight years later, Becca succumbed to cancer in Los Angeles, approximately ten days before *Bewitched* debuted on September 17, 1964.

Lizzie's mother Elizabeth Allen passed away at age eighty-seven on the Montgomery farm in New York, June 28, 1992, the same day Lizzie served as Co-Grand Marshall with her former *Bewitched* co-star Dick Sargent in the Los Angeles Gay and Lesbian Pride Parade.

Elizabeth Allen's cause of death was never documented, but she had been in poor health for quite some time, then died suddenly and quite unexpectedly. Shortly thereafter, Lizzie's childhood landscape was sold.

In the short period between that time and her own passing in 1995, Elizabeth continued to view the big picture of her parents' influence as she always had, especially the impact made upon her by her father. She followed his pathway to a successful and prestigious career and, in the process, learned to handle the good with the bad, the advantages and the obstacles that went along with being born the child of a star.

Three

Elizabeth Montgomery Presents

"Our hope was that she would turn out to be a good actress and
not just the daughter of Montgomery."

—Robert Montgomery, *TV Radio Mirror Magazine*, January 1965

Rebecca Allen wasn't an actress, but Elizabeth thought she should have
been. Next to her parents, Becca was the greatest influence in Lizzie's life;
she provided a sense of safety and comfort in her youth. As Lizzie recalled
to *Modern Screen* magazine in 1965, "It was a feeling only grandmothers
know how to give."

Whenever Robert Montgomery and Elizabeth Allen were away on
business or vacation, Lizzie and her brother Skip never felt rejected. Becca
was always there, Lizzie said, to offer encouraging words, to make sure she
and Skip held their parents close at heart, and "prayed every night."

"It was really too bad," she told *TeleVision Life* magazine in January
1954. "I mean, Mother and Dad being on the road so much and missing
my birthdays. But it didn't bother me too much . . . I wasn't a neglected
child."

Little Elizabeth didn't see as much of her father as she would have liked,
but she and Skip had a nurse for years. She claimed to have "had a wonderful
childhood," but at school, she'd have to watch her words. When classmates
mentioned a dinner out with their parents, Lizzie would join in with,

"Daddy took me to Romanoff's." But they'd offer blank stares and, suddenly, she said, "I'd be all alone."

But Becca was waiting in the wings, ready to pick up the pieces, particularly when it came to her granddaughter's "play-acting." According to the article, "The Girl Behind the Twitch," published in *Modern Screen* magazine, May 1965, Becca watched everything performed by Lizzie, who described her grandmother this way:

> . . . such a lovely lady . . . a small woman with enormous brown eyes and a lovely kind of auburn hair. Up until the day she died she was the youngest looking thing, terribly young and vital. She adored California and was a one-woman Chamber of Commerce . . . She had such a love of life . . . an extraordinary imagination . . . and . . . such warmth. There wasn't a soul she ever met who didn't adore her. She loved children and was so good with us. She wrote a lot of songs and poems I would love to see published. Maybe someday I'll illustrate them and send them off to a publisher.

That never happened. But Lizzie was busy with other endeavors, namely, Billy Asher, Jr., whom she had just given birth to and who she said was "one of the biggest thrills" of Becca's life. "I'm just sorry he's going to miss having her for his audience. She was only the greatest audience I ever had." And she wasn't kidding.

When she was about eight years old, Lizzie's flare for the dramatic was already in bloom. She and her cousin Amanda "Panda" Cushman would play detective, foreshadowing characters Lizzie would depict in TV-movies like 1983's *Missing Pieces* and the Edna Buchanan films from the mid-1990s (including her final performance in *Deadline for Murder*).

When Panda wasn't available, Lizzie's little brother Skip would pinch-hit. Although his chances for getting the juicy roles were slim to none because his older sister would always win out—even if she was not right for the part.

According to what Elizabeth told *Modern Screen* in 1965, she and Skip once performed in their own edition of Walt Disney's classic animated feature, *Snow White and the Seven Dwarfs*, released in 1937. The pre-production dialogue went something like this:

"I'll play the king," Skip would say.

"No," Lizzie countered. "I'm going to play the king."

"Then can I be the princess?"

"No, you're a boy. You can't be the princess."

"Then, I'll be the prince."

"No, I'm going to be the prince, too."

"But how can you be the prince, when you're a girl?"

"Well, just because . . . I'm the director."

Lizzie ultimately cast Skip as the announcer, hidden *off-stage* in a closeted area, from where he spoke into a wastebasket, which added a grand reverberation to his voice.

Before their first performance, for which Lizzie naturally tapped herself as the lead, she'd tell Skip, "Go out and announce me."

Ever the loyal young sibling, Skip walked into the middle of the Montgomery living room, their stage, and declared to the audience, only Becca, "I am presenting . . . Elizabeth Montgomery!"

But Lizzie protested from behind the invisible curtain.

"No, no, Skip," she interrupted, "the *great* Elizabeth Montgomery."

"I am presenting the *great* Elizabeth Montgomery," he then said, adding, "but I don't know what she's going to do!"

"*Don't know what she's going to do?!*" Lizzie yelped from the sidelines. "Of *course* you know what I'm going to do!" Turning to her grandmother, she said, "Clap, Becca, clap!"

Becca consented, and then sat patiently and watched whatever production Lizzie presented (and she'd keep watching through the years).

Elizabeth's creative control of this pubescent *Snow White* production offered telling signs of her early confidence and ambition which diminished over time, while the "presenting" part of Skip's intro foreshadowed the title of their father's TV series, *Robert Montgomery Presents*, on which Lizzie would make her professional debut playing her father's daughter.

According to *Cosmopolitan Magazine*, July 1954, Mr. Montgomery was there, beside Becca, for Lizzie's *Snow White* re-do, somewhere in the proverbial bleachers, cheering her on, at least during the *wishing-well* moment that transpired in Disney's original *White* film. As Robert recalled, his daughter's rendition was somewhat scaled down:

> If you remember the scene, *Snow White* would sing a line of that song, "I'm Wishing," and then an echo would sing it back to her. Well, Elizabeth was

apparently all by herself in her room, singing the song in front of (that) wastebasket, which she was using as a wishing well. And sure enough, an echo was coming from somewhere in the room.

Further investigation identified the echo as Skip's voice, but the father Montgomery was impressed nonetheless:

How hammy can you get? Anybody who at the age of five would go to all that trouble to set up a scene could never be anything but an actress in later life. So I wasn't surprised when Elizabeth came to me a few years later, when she was around fourteen, and announced she was planning to go on the stage. I never discouraged her, because I think being an actress is as good a life as any if you really work hard at it, and Elizabeth is a hard worker. She asked me if I would appear with her in her first play, and I said I would.

In 1951, Lizzie made her social debut at New York's Debutante Cotillion and Christmas Ball, and her father kept his promise: that same year, she made her TV acting debut on his show. But she never doubted his word; she believed her parents empathized with aspirations of all shape and color, specifically theatrical endeavors. As she told *Modern Screen* in May 1965, "They certainly understood Skip and me and never ever discouraged either one of us about the theater."

But her acting bug stung deeper than Skip's. She'd go on to perform in a variety of roles and mediums for fifty years; he appeared in TV westerns for about four years. Then he retired from the entertainment industry, and began working at the Hayden Stone brokerage firm.

Elizabeth was terribly proud of him. As she explained to Ronald Haver in 1991, her father was "very hard on my brother, much more so on him than on me. But I think Skip turned out to be a much better person, maybe in spite of it, I think, because he's a terrific guy. My brother's really neat."

"There's only a two-year gap between my brother and me," she said in 1965, this time, in August to *TV Radio Mirror* magazine. "I can't recall an instance of jealousy between us as we grew up. Oh, I guess there were occasions when kid brother got in big sister's way. But jealousy? Not a bit of it."

"Well," as *Samantha* might have said, except maybe only once, although the incident had more to do with sexual discrimination than sibling rivalry.

"A Second Baby, A Special Problem" was published by *TV Radio Mirror* in November 1966 which profiled the birth of Lizzie's second son, Robert, named for her father—and her brother. In the article, Lizzie recalled a childhood moment when Skip was allowed to cross the street by himself whereas she wasn't.

"Why can't I do that?" she asked her mother.

"Don't forget," she replied. "Skip is a boy."

That seemed most discriminatory to Lizzie, but she kept her mouth shut:

> I knew Mom did not make her decisions lightly and, once made, she stuck to them, without discussion. Of course, once I reached my teens, she'd sit down and talk such things over, explaining why she had come to certain judgments, and she would listen carefully to my arguments on why I deserved fewer restraints.

Certain restrictions may have inhibited Skip's career in acting aspirations, but not his life in general. Lizzie was right. He was a "neat" person.

According to Montgomery archivist Tom McCartney, www.bobsbe witchingdaughter.com, and www.earlofhollywood.com, Skip was born Robert Montgomery, Jr., in Los Angeles on February 15, 1936. Although his birth year has been incorrectly reported as 1930, Skip was actually three years younger than Elizabeth and six years younger than their late sister Martha Bryan.

Though Lizzie and Skip were raised in Hollywood, they enjoyed their summers at the Montgomery country estate in Patterson, New York or in the U.K. where their father worked in films.

In 1939, Skip became the youngest Lifetime Honorary Member of the Screen Actors Guild, over which his dad presided as president. In 1945 he attended school in Arizona. Five years later, when their parents divorced, Skip remained with Lizzie in the family's Upstate New York home with their mother and attended St. Mark's School in Southborough, Massachusetts in 1952. In 1958, Skip, then twenty-two, formally joined the family business by becoming a working actor. That same year, he also became a father when his wife, socialite Deborah Chase, gave birth to a son, Robert Montgomery, III.

The following year, he won small roles in movies such as *Say One for Me* and *A Private's Affair* as well as on TV shows such as *The Loretta Young Show* (NBC, 1953–1961), in which his sister performed, and *Gunsmoke* (CBS, 1955–1975), the latter in which he made his TV acting debut. Here, he appeared in the macabre episode "Lynching Man" which originally aired November 15, 1958.

Directed by Richard Whorf and written by John Meston, this segment also featured an overacted performance by guest star George Macready (who had played Elizabeth's father in NBC's *Kraft Television Theatre* production of "The Diamond as Big as the Ritz" in 1955):

A mild-mannered *Hank Blenis* (O. Z. Whitehead) doesn't stand a chance in the Old West. He owned an apple farm back in Ohio, but now he's not even sure how to ride a horse. Unfortunately, he won't soon have to worry about learning to do so; when his healthy stallion is stolen, and he's left for dead, hung by a tree. Meanwhile, one man vigilante *Charlie Drain* (Macready), whose father was lynched when he was a child, sets out to find *Hank's* killer. This infuriates *Marshall Matt Dillon* (star James Arness), who along with his sidekick *Chester* (Dennis Weaver), sets out to find the real culprit. They soon meet the kindly farm hand *Billy Drico* (Skip), shortly before uncovering the mystery, while losing *Charlie* in the process.

While Macready over-projected his part, Skip appeared to underact. Although his was a minor role, Skip could have made the part of *Billy Drico* something more. It was his TV acting debut. Understandably nervous, he made every attempt to live up to his father's great expectations. But his anxiety appears to have got the best of him. Skip did not give the role his all; he appeared awkward and uncomfortable on camera. Unlike Lizzie, unfortunately, his performances were not given a chance to be properly modulated; he never quite attained the opportunity to hone his craft under his father's watchful eye. By the time Skip started to legitimately pursue acting, *Robert Montgomery Presents* had completed its run.

But, happily, Robert Montgomery, Jr. had other things on his mind.

Nine months after *Gunsmoke*, on July 10, 1959, he and his wife welcomed a daughter into the family when Deborah Elizabeth Montgomery was born.

He continued acting on television with minor roles in such popular fare as *Sea Hunt* (in two episodes, one in 1959, the other in 1961), the anthology show *Death Valley Days* (hosted by future president Ronald Reagan), and a series called *The Tall Man*, which was created by Samuel Peeples (of *Star Trek* fame), in which he played a character named *Jimmy Carter* (precursing at least the name of yet another future president).

Skip also acted on the big screen with in 1960: a small part in *The Gallant Hours*, a feature his father both produced and directed, and enjoyed a larger role in the science fiction film, *12 to the Moon*.

But correctly sensing that his career was going nowhere fast, in 1962, he left the world of acting and became a Wall Street stockbroker with Hayden Stone & Co. where he enjoyed a lucrative career for the next two decades.

He spent his golden years in Tallahassee, Florida, where he became the community liaison for Florida State University's Graduate Film Conservatory. He also established the Sleepy Actors Group, which provided housing for students working on their thesis films and hosted a database listing production related services and locations.

In 1998, he served as executive producer on the independent film, *Roses*.

On February 7, 2000, he underwent surgery for lung cancer and the outlook seemed positive. But on April 28, that prognosis turned grim, and he died suddenly at the age of sixty-four, leaving behind his third wife, Melanie, son Adam, and daughter Meghann.

Years before, "kid brothers" was one of the many commonalities Elizabeth shared with her friend Sally Kemp, whom she met while attending the New York American Academy of Dramatic Arts. Kemp had few memories of Skip when they were all young and didn't recall much of Skip's relationship with his father. But what she did recall is noteworthy:

> I too had a brother Skip's age, two years younger than I. Elizabeth and I were starting our adult lives and careers; our brothers were still in school when we first knew each other and I seldom saw them together. She seemed fond of him; he was cute, blond, curly haired, choirboy face but our paths at that age didn't meet very often. Little brothers weren't foremost in our minds. Whenever I was with Bob (Sr.) and Elizabeth it was in a more

adult situation. Skip would be doing whatever it is young boys do. Bob seemed very proud of Elizabeth when I was with them and Buffy (Harkness, Bob's second wife), too, was proud of her. It was all, from my point of view, very warm, funny, and delightful. Bob often made Elizabeth and I sing Broadway songs for him and any guests around. I saw only a privileged, affectionate family. One I envied at times. Buffy was always gentle, gracious, and perfectly lovely to everyone. If there was any trouble underneath I never saw it.

After Robert Montgomery passed away in 1981, Kemp on several occasions spent time with Skip and his family and found him to be "a charming man, very like his father." She was sad when he died "far too young," succumbing to lung cancer at age sixty-four on April 28, 2000. She still has infrequent contact with his widow, Melanie Montgomery, their daughter Meghann, and son Adam.

Bicoastal from birth, in their youth, Lizzie and Skip were at home among Hollywood stars and the East Coast upper crust. They both attended elite private educational facilities that provided solid preparation for their adulthood. But while Skip left Hollywood behind, Lizzie delved right into the mix of it, helped along by that refined academic background.

From September of 1939 to June of 1950, she attended the Westlake School for Girls, an exclusive elementary academic hall in Beverly Hills. From September 1950 to June of 1951, she was enrolled at the aristocratic Spence School for Girls (where she played field hockey) in New York City.

The following information for both facilities was gathered from their respective websites:

> In October 1989, the Boards of Trustees of both the Westlake School for Girls and the Harvard School, a military school for boys that was established in 1900, agreed to merge the facilities. Today, Harvard-Westlake School is an independent coeducational college preparatory day school, grades 7–12, that ultimately commenced in September of 1991. In 2010, 566 of its students took 1,736 A.P. tests in 30 different subjects, and 90% scored 3 or higher. The school ranks among the top high schools in the country in

number of National Merit Semifinalists. In the class of 2011, there were 90 students who received National Merit Recognition, with 28 students as National Merit Semifinalists.

Clara Spence, a visionary educator, founded her Spence School for Girls in 1892, welcoming ten students to a brownstone on West 48th Street in New York City. The outside world of politics, the arts, and the community was embraced in her school and from the beginning Spence girls developed a keen sense of self-confidence and assumed their roles as significant members of the community. The facilities motto, "Not for school but for life we learn," has defined a Spence education throughout its long history. Or as Spence herself once said of her renown facility it was "a place not of mechanical instruction, but a school of character where the common requisites for all have been human feeling, a sense of humor, and the spirit of intellectual and moral adventure.

All of which describes Lizzie in spades.

Actress June Lockhart, best known for her iconic roles as the intergalactic mother *Maureen Robinson* on TV's *Lost in Space* (CBS, 1965–1968) and the kindly country physician, *Dr. Janet Craig* on *Petticoat Junction* (CBS, 1963–1970), played an integral role in Lizzie's life.

Before her stops in *Space* and at *Junction*, she was guest-star on *Bewitched* in a first-season episode called "Little Pitchers Have Big Fears" which co-starred Jimmy Mathers, brother to Jerry Mathers, better known as *The Beaver* on *Leave It to Beaver* (CBS/ABC, 1957–1963).

Years before her *Bewitched* guest-spot, Lockhart made nine appearances on *Robert Montgomery Presents*. She is the daughter of actors Gene and Kathleen Lockhart who portrayed *Mr.* and *Mrs. Bob Cratchit* in the 1938 film edition of *A Christmas Carol*, in which June played one of the *Cratchit* children. Reginald Owen who, decades later guest starred on *Bewitched* as *Ockie*, boyfriend to Marion Lorne's *Aunt Clara* (and *Admiral Boom* in 1964's *Mary Poppins* movie), played *Scrooge*.

What's more, June's father Gene was good friends with Lizzie's father Robert, both of whom were instrumental in the founding of the Screen

Actors Guild (S.A.G.). Gene also made four appearances on *Robert Mont-gomery Presents*, of which three were with June (and directed by Grey Lock-wood). Meanwhile, Kathleen Lockhart had a small role in Robert Montgomery's 1946 film, *The Lady in the Lake*.

Although June did not appear with Lizzie in any episodes of *Presents*, she recalls,

> I used to watch her work. And I remember seeing her once in rehearsal. She was very professional, and her reputation for always doing live TV was legendary. And the directors that I worked with, who had also worked with her, said she was just a joy and lots of fun. And that was my experience with her when I did *Bewitched*. Both she and Bill Asher were fun to work with. We shot the episode at the Rancho Golf Course on Pico Blvd and Motor Avenue [in West Los Angeles]. There wasn't a dressing room for Elizabeth or me. So I joked with her and asked, *What are we supposed to do? Change in the front seat of the car?* But then a short time later, the crew brought in a few portable dressing rooms. I was just glad I didn't have to change outside on Motor Avenue.

However, June's stint on *Bewitched* is not her most vivid recollection of Elizabeth. That part of her memory is savored from another time, decades before, when they both attended the Westlake School for Girls in Beverly Hills. Although June was a senior and Lizzie was just in kindergarten, the two crossed paths one very special morning when only four people in the world—June, Elizabeth, Miss Carol Mills, the Westlake principal, and a very uniformed Robert Montgomery—were there to experience what June now reveals for the first time anywhere:

> In the middle of World War II, Robert Montgomery was in the South Pacific, I believe as Lt. Commander or higher. So, one day, there we were, Elizabeth and I, both at Westlake. I was coming back from the Borders wing on campus, back over to the classrooms and Miss Mills was standing next to Elizabeth, outside where the circle driveway was. I greeted them both and Ms. Mills said, *Wait here a minute, June.* So I stood with them and asked, *What's going on?* And she said, *You'll see.* And within a few moments a car pulled up and out got Robert Montgomery in full uniform, back from a very long trip overseas in the South Pacific. Upon seeing her father get

out of the car Elizabeth, with screams of delight, ran towards him. And he picked her up in his arms and hugged her so tight. He then came over to Miss Mills and I, greeted us, and then got back in the car with Elizabeth and drove away. Of course there were tears on our cheeks after seeing this great reunion between Elizabeth and her father. And he came to pick her up in the middle of the school day . . . and there was nobody else around . . . there were no other students milling about; no one. Just Miss Mills, me, and Elizabeth. And I remember that day clearly, even so vividly I can remember where the sun was at the time. It must have been maybe 11:30 or 12 noon. And of course no one was let out of school in the middle of the day unless it was really very important. So Miss Mills and I just looked at each other and it was a sweet wonderful warm moment that we had just witnessed. A very exciting moment, too, because we later learned that Robert Montgomery had just returned not only from the South Pacific but [that] it was a very important business. He did not just come back on leave, where he would be home for a month or so, and then have to go back. It wasn't like that. He was back for good. And whatever work he was involved with in the South Pacific was very top secret.

After revealing this story, June laughs in irony upon learning that Lizzie's first episode of *Robert Montgomery Presents* was titled "Top Secret," in which she played none other than the daughter to her father's character, a spy, who teamed together for a covert adventure in a foreign land.

In January 1965, Elizabeth talked to reporter Eunice Field and *TV Radio Mirror* magazine for the article, "Elizabeth Montgomery: You Know Her as a Witch, Now Meet Her as a Woman." "I'm afraid I gave my teachers gray hair," she said, "because all I could think of was *Dramatics*."

But it was her mother who saved her from getting Ds in every subject; she'd permit little Lizzie to take part in school plays only if her daughter maintained a B average. Miss Mills, Lizzie's headmistress at Westlake, would call the Montgomery child into her office and say, "You're not stupid. You need to apply yourself and you can get all As." Lizzie would curtsy and reply, "Yes, Ma'am," and then go to the drama department instead of the library as she had promised, all of which became a weekly ritual.

"I spent half my time in the headmistress's office," she admitted to *TV Guide* in 1961, "and the other half," she said, in the drama department. Her classmates included the distinguished daughters of actors Spencer Tracy, Herbert Marshall, and Alan Mowbray, and classical pianist Arthur Rubenstein (father to actor John Rubenstein, who later co-starred with *Bewitched* guest-star Jack Warden on the 1980s CBS series, *Crazy Like a Fox*).

But Lizzie was unimpressed. She was bored with school, and always knew that *she* "wanted to be actress."

Beyond her homebound performance as *Snow White*, her first public theatrical performance would be at Westlake, when she was just 6, in that French language production of *Little Red Riding Hood*. "Naturally," she had said of this early endeavor, "I already knew enough to go to Daddy for professional advice."

According to *TV Radio Mirror* in January 1965, he told her, "Forget about acting, Honey. Just think you really are the wolf and act the way you think a wolf would act." It was her introduction to *method acting*.

Slightly less appreciative may have been the faculty of Westlake. Miss Mills may have been correct. Lizzie was a good student but she didn't always work as hard as she could have. It didn't help that she had a penchant for bringing unusual pets to class. According to *Modern Screen* magazine in 1965, one Easter she received a pig which, "horribly enough," she called *Pork Chop*. Her instructor was not too sure how to cope with that and was even more perturbed when Lizzie arrived in class with Chinese hooded rats.

The rodent business began when her mother once traveled east by train to see her husband, Robert Montgomery. Lizzie accompanied Mrs. Montgomery to the station, where she noticed a little boy walking around the station with one of the Chinese hooded rats on his shoulder. Lizzie announced that it was just the thing to have as her mother boarded the train. But Elizabeth Allen's last and very definite word was *no* . . . until, of course, the following Christmas when her daughter received two tiny animals as gifts she named Connie and Otis.

From there, *the things* just multiplied like crazy, she said, and at one point she owned approximately fifteen rats at once. "They used to get out of their cages and we were always counting noses, tails, and whiskers to be sure we had them all."

On one of those days when Connie and Otis were let lose in the Montgomery abode, Allen asked Lizzie to place her new playthings back in their cage. To which Lizzie replied, "But I want one to sleep on my bed."

"You can't sleep with the rat, Elizabeth."

"The dog sleeps on the bed."

"That's different."

"Why?"

"Well, you might roll over on it."

The wise Lizzie child was finally convinced to place her pet rat, be it Connie or Otis, back in its gilded environment, although not for long.

One evening the Montgomery family was entertaining guests, as they were prone to do, and little Elizabeth came down from her room for a meet and greet. She did everything expected of a young lady of her stature: curtsied and politely introduced herself, saying, "How do you do?"

Then the unexpected happened, causing one unsuspecting female guest to let out a shriek and drop her martini. Two little rat heads peeked out from behind Lizzie's hair bows and two skinny rat tails were protruding on either side.

"Elizabeth, try to keep the rats upstairs," murmured Mrs. Montgomery.

Her poor mother! At one point they had three dogs, two cats, a white duck called "Pittosporum," some alligators, and a cockatiel named "Nankypoo." The problem was Nankypoo, which her parents had given her. As Lizzie remembered in *Modern Screen*, 1965, her mother was always saying, "Will you please make sure the bird stays upstairs?" If that sounds like a wild thing to say about a bird, it's because Nankypoo was never in his cage. He was always walking around, following some unsuspecting individual. In fact, he never flew; he walked. "He'd get up on top of doors but he wouldn't fly," Lizzie said.

If that wasn't enough, another time, Nankypoo walked into the living room, walked up to the coffee table, hopped up on the edge of the table, and then onto a certain female visitor's glass and proceeded to drink it nearly dry. Lizzie always thought it might have been the same woman who dropped her martini over her rats, because this time she and all the other women in the room screamed loudly. Nankypoo had walked across the table, hopped to the floor, walked two feet and fell flat. "He must have had a dreadful hangover next day," she mused.

A few years after those early spirited days at Westlake, Lizzie, at 17, embarked on her final semester with the school and faced a tough decision. Her family was leaving Los Angeles, and she could either remain at Westlake or enroll for a year at the Spence School for Girls in New York. The thought of being separated from her family was one she could not imagine. So she left Westlake and went to Spence where, she said, they were "very dear" to her, and where she enrolled in various courses in French and architecture that she called "interesting."

After attending the Spence School, she spent two years studying acting at that same city's renowned American Academy of Dramatic Arts. Her charismatic charms were surely visible to audiences at this early stage, but her student performances drew the most stringent commentary from her father. He would send her curt, disapproving notes for performances that he deemed less than worthy. "Not good enough," he would scribble. "Try again."

"Daddy listens to my ideas, and then criticizes," she told *TV People and Pictures Magazine* in October 1953. "It's all impersonal and constructive."

According to *People Magazine* in 1995, Lizzie once said, "Like Daddy, I try to be neat, concise in my work, and in anything else for that matter."

In 1989, however, she laughed and said her father's response to her chosen profession was, "Oh, shit!"

"That was the first time I had ever heard that word. And I was no more than six years old."

But they were still chums, at least from when she was a child until she became a star on her own and of her own show. As she conveyed to *TV People and Pictures* in 1953, "We're terrific companions and are so much alike. We love to Charleston together. And Daddy is the only one who can tire me out. Usually, I sit out the Charleston at a dance. It's too strenuous for my dates."

According to "Our Name Is Montgomery," published in *TeleVision Life Magazine*, January 1954, Elizabeth dated her first boy at fourteen, when she and her family lived in an elegant white home in the Bel Air district of Beverly Hills. "Dad sort of scrutinized each young man when he came to call for me," she said. "It was really sort of sad; they were all terrified of him. Sometimes he was a little cold, when he really disliked the boy, but most times he tried to make them feel at home."

By the time she was twenty, she was on her own. Sometimes her mother asked her about the boys she dated, sometimes she didn't. "I was brought up to be trusted," Lizzie said.

In either case, Mrs. Montgomery didn't wait up for her daughter to arrive home from a night out on the town. And as for marriage, it was far from Lizzie's mind at the time. She wanted to first start her career. As if mimicking the plot of *Bewitched* that would debut ten years later, she added, "I really don't think it's fair to the man if he doesn't know what he's getting—an actress or a housewife."

As played out in the pilot of *Bewitched*, *Samantha* didn't reveal to *Darrin* that she was a witch until after they married.

Lizzie's relationship with her parents, specifically, her father, was passive-aggressive, to say the least. Robert and his friends, like James Cagney, eventually assisted with her theatrical pursuits, but also became her toughest critics, even when it came to how she dressed and carried herself. According to the Ronald Haver interview in 1991, Robert's primary acting advice to Lizzie was to listen to the other actors in a scene, while Cagney cautioned her about the way she walked. "Be sure you're listening to what the other person is saying to you," her father would tell her. Cagney advised, "Just learn your lines and just don't bump into anything."

Cagney once went as far as to say, "Elizabeth, you are the clumsiest person for a graceful person I've ever met in my life." And she agreed. "I could ride (horses) like the wind," she said. "I was very athletic. But trust me, to walk from here to that door I'd probably fall down three times. It was awful."

But at least she'd fall gracefully, and looked good on her descent.

In 1988, Byron Munson, *Bewitched's* costume designer, always said Lizzie had "horrible taste in clothes." Maybe that's because her father was never around. He had only visited the *Samantha* set a few times, and it was only once documented with a photo-op.

Ten years before *Bewitched*, however, he was there to adjust her sense of fashion. According to *TV People and Pictures*, October 1953, he'd tell her, "Never get flamboyant and always dress well."

But at the end of that same month in 1953, she told *TV Guide*, "I like to fuss and primp before (a) party. Clothes have to fit right and be right so that I can concentrate on my date and not what I'm wearing."

"Some parties are just impossible to figure out in advance," she added. "Whenever I show up with shoulders bared, someone else is covered up to the neck. And then, when I cover up, no one else does."

It all sounded like a plot on *Bewitched*. In fact, it was. Namely, the pilot episode in which *Darrin's* former girlfriend *Sheila Summers* (Nancy Kovack) invites him and his new bride *Samantha* to a party *Sheila* claims would be "casual." It ends up being nothing of the sort, and Sam is embarrassed in her less-than-formal wear. Then, in "Snob in the Grass," from the fourth season, *Sheila* tricks her again. This time inviting the *Stephenses* to a formal party, but upon arrival in their finest duds, they see the other attendees in casual wear.

In both episodes, *Samantha* lets *Sheila* "have it." She twitches to her heart's content, at one point twirling *Sheila* into a frenzy of wardrobe malfunctions, leaving her emotions frazzled and her clothes unraveled, while *Darrin* stands by in amusement and somewhat guarded approval.

But Lizzie's wardrobe approval rating with her father wasn't as flexible as *Sam's* nose wriggle. So she'd keep things simple. He liked her in suits and thought blue jeans were acceptable only in the summer, as long as they were clean. She wore little makeup, liked pearl chokers, face veils, and poodle haircuts. Her father also insisted that she watch her posture. "I get a slap on the back if I don't stand up straight," she told *TV People and Pictures*.

Unphased, Lizzie would merely get annoyed when in her youth her schoolmates and her dad called her "Betta," just as when Bette Davis called her "Betty." More than anything, her ambition, at least at this acting stage of the game, was her true calling—to become as accomplished and respected a performer as either Davis or her father, despite her wardrobe or lack there of.

Bill Asher directed her second feature film, Paramount's 1963 release *Johnny Cool*, the year before they combined their powers to be on *Bewitched*. As author Ronald L. Smith observed in his book, *Sweethearts of the '60s* (S.P.I. Books, 1993), the studio had been grooming Lizzie as a "sultry, super bewitching sex symbol, five foot eight in heels." *The New York Times* deplored the "flaccid direction of William Asher," but not the scenes featuring Lizzie, especially when she does her soul searching wearing nothing but a lap robe. "Miss Montgomery, without the benefit of wardrobe, attracts more attention then the entire uncomfortable cast," all of whom remained clothed.

Four

~

Brush with Fame

"My art belongs to Daddy."

—Elizabeth, to *Screen Stars* magazine, August 1967

Both of Lizzie's parents were very talented and artistic individuals. They were also wise in other ways of the world, and she trusted them for counsel in all areas, specifically when it came to her choosing a vocation.

According to *TV Radio Mirror*, April 1970, her mother once told her not to be "foolhardy" or "back away from obstacles . . . enjoy everything you do to the fullest or don't do it. There's nothing worse for the people around you than if you're doing something which makes you miserable."

And in Lizzie's jubilant and advantaged youth, acting made her the happiest, although it was merely first on her list of four main potential career choices. The remaining three were: a jockey, a criminal lawyer, or an artist for Walt Disney. Of the last, she mused in 1989, "For some reason he never asked me. Can you imagine? The poor thing . . . certainly ruined his career."

As *Modern Screen* magazine pointed out in May 1965, the walls of Lizzie's dressing room were lined with some quick sketches of a child named Annabelle about whom Elizabeth was writing a book. Annabelle had pigtails with polka dot bows but she also had ragamuffin eyes, "round, listening eyes, full of warmth and love like Elizabeth's."

Today, her friend Sally Kemp says Elizabeth was very serious about her artistic endeavor:

> She always wanted to draw for Disney. She drew all the time. We would get in trouble in class at the Academy because she was always drawing little creatures and caricatures, and she'd sometimes get caught. I knew she was talented, but I didn't know how seriously she thought about it. We never talked about it. That was just one of the things that Elizabeth did . . . was draw charming pictures. I pretended to be a ballerina. And Elizabeth would draw pictures.

Soon, Elizabeth would be *starring* in *moving* pictures, including *Bewitched*, the opening animated credit sequence of which featured the cartooned caricatures of her first with Dick York and then later with Dick Sargent. But she wasn't impressed. As she explained in 1989,

> I didn't like *those things*. They were real *stick-figury*. They didn't look right to me. It was a cute idea. If that had been a basic storyboard, I would have said, "Great! Now, where can we go from here to make it a little more *snappier* and sophisticated" because I thought (the way it was) was too simple.

She said the *Bewitched* animation didn't have to be as elaborate as in the 1988 animated feature film *Who Framed Roger Rabbit?* but, in another nod to Walt Disney, she smiled and suggested, "I'm talking *Bambi*, maybe." Meanwhile, her own artwork looked right to *Bewitched* director by R. Robert Rosenbaum, who was later crowned Head of Production for Lorimar Television (which produced shows like *Falcon Crest*, starring Lizzie's future husband, Robert Foxworth). But while still guiding *Samantha's* live-action adventures, Rosenbaum praised not only Lizzie's on-screen abilities but her off-screen artistic talents. "One gift I'll always treasure," he said in 1988, "is the painting of a man in a director's chair that Elizabeth created for me."

As was detailed in *TV Guide*, May 13, 1967, Lizzie had dabbled in watercolors and in quite effective pen-and-ink sketches. Her art had a fetching quality. "I'd love to do watercolors like Andrew Wyeth," she said, but added firmly, "I know I never can." A friend then theorized, "Liz is not sure of herself artistically. She is not willing to put herself on the line until she is damn sure she is the best artist in the whole world." The friend likened all this to *Bewitched*. "The show is fun, but no challenge. Liz is too happy being *Samantha* to try anything truly difficult."

All of that would later change with her post-*Bewitched* TV-movies like 1972's *The Victim* and 1974's *A Case of Rape*, both of which explored the darker themes that Lizzie had experimented with in pre-*Samantha* TV guest appearances like *Kraft's Theatre '62* rendition of "The Spiral Staircase" (NBC, October 4, 1961) and the *Alcoa Premiere* episode, "Mr. Lucifer" (ABC, November 1, 1962).

According to the August 1967 edition of *Screen Stars* magazine, Lizzie once said, "My art belongs to Daddy." And although she was an artist of many colors, she wasn't referring here to her painting and drawing ability, but to her talent as an actress. In her heart, she knew she inherited her theatrical abilities from her father. She appreciated that talent and she ultimately credited him for helping her to hone it, whether that guidance took the form of general advice over the years, for example, by his insistence that she attend the New York American Academy of Dramatic Arts, or actual hands-on experience during early TV performances on *Robert Montgomery Presents*. Either way, Lizzie received formal dramatic training, although sometimes *melodramatic* training by way of *Presents*. As she told Ronald Haver in 1991, that show became an outlet for her dad's need for "control . . . the desire to thin-line." She wasn't sure how well-liked her father was as a person, but *Robert Montgomery Presents* was liked by the audience. It became one of television's pioneering live dramas.

Her initial performances on *Presents* elicited excited responses from various producers. So much so, she eventually made her Broadway debut as the ingénue in *Late Love*, which ran from October 13, 1953 through November 7, 1953 at the National Theatre (today known as the Nederlander), and from November 9, 1953 to January 2, 1954, at the Booth Theatre, for a total of 95 performances.

Love also starred Arlene Francis, and Cliff Robertson who, after prolonged failing health, died at age eighty-eight on September 10, 2011 (the day after his birthday and two weeks following his interview for this book).

In his prime, Robertson was a handsome actor with a stellar resume and even more fascinating life, one worth noting if only because it peaked and somewhat mirrored Lizzie's life.

Born on September 9, 1923, in La Jolla, California, he was two years old when he was adopted by wealthy parents who named him Clifford Parker Robertson III. After his parents divorced and his mother passed away, he was reared by his maternal grandmother, whom he adored. He later gained attention for his second marriage to actress and heiress Dina Merrill, daughter of financier E. F. Hutton and Marjorie Merriweather Post, heiress to the Post Cereal fortune and one of the world's wealthiest women. (The two would periodically work together, notably in a two-part episode of the ABC/Screen Gems 1960s camp series, *Batman*, in which he played a villain named "Shame" to her "Calamity Jan.")

In 1963, he portrayed John F. Kennedy (who was good friends with Lizzie via Bill Asher) in the feature film *PT-109*, and would go on to win an Oscar for his lead performance in *Charly*, the 1968 feature film in which he played a mentally challenged man who undergoes an experiment that temporarily transforms him into a genius. Although never elevated to the top ranks of leading men, Cliff remained popular from the 1950s into the twenty-first century with roles such as the kindly "Uncle Ben" in the first *Spider-Man* feature film (released in 2001).

Like Elizabeth, he did not shun controversy or tolerate injustice. In 1977, he blew the whistle on a Hollywood financial scandal. He discovered that David Begelman, president of Columbia Pictures, had forged his signature on a $10,000 salary check, and contacted the FBI and the Burbank and Beverly Hills police. Hollywood insiders were none too pleased with the unattractive publicity and Robertson said that neither the studios nor the networks would hire him for four years.

But decades before, in 1953, he worked with Lizzie in *Late Love*, an experience he recalled in 2011 if only for the appreciation she had for their co-star Arlene Francis:

> Arlene was a big TV star at the time, and she had been in the theatre in her earlier days. She brought a humanistic element to the play. She was also a very down-to-earth person, who was bright, quick, and witty. And Elizabeth admired and respected that. Liz was very young and, therefore, not too experienced. But she was quite ambitious and very professional. She had that respect for her craft that she garnered from her father, I'm sure. He was from Brooklyn, but as he got older he went into theatre and then on

to Hollywood, where he became quite a successful film star. From there, he went into television.

Cliff's relationship with Lizzie never waxed romantic, but as he said, they became those "good pals." Meanwhile, her sophisticated family, particularly on her mother's side, took a shine to him, partially due to his Southern roots and possibly due to his cosmopolitan upbringing.

"Her family was very nice to me," Robertson said. "They used to invite me up to their place in New York. She had an elderly aunt, a wonderful lady who lived in Beverly Hills. And I used to see (Becca) for a number of years, and then she passed away."

But her maternal relatives were not particularly fond of her father or his profession. "I don't think the Southern tier of her family was completely impressed by Robert Montgomery, or any actor." As Robertson acknowledged, Lizzie still became enamored with acting, but with provisions.

> She was determined not to be thought of as just a social actress, and she was also determined to be recognized as a professional. She knew she had to work hard to earn that respect. She was well aware that her father was a fine and respected actor, and a well-known producer. And she knew and respected that difference as well. She in no way ever wanted to be treated special because she was his daughter. She was very democratic that way, and I don't mean (just) politically.

The "political" relationship between the liberal Lizzie and her Republican father may have at times proved a challenge, but Robertson described the association as "very good," with reservations:

"I would say Elizabeth was always politically aware, not oriented. And I suspect her marriage to Bill Asher had something to do with that, at least later on. I don't know that for certain, but I suspect that." When reminded that it was Asher who directed President Kennedy's birthday celebration at which Marilyn Monroe sang a breathy "Happy Birthday, Mr. President," the near-ninety-year-old Robertson exclaimed, "Yes, of course. Because he knew JFK. That fits!"

Equally surprised to learn that *Bewitched* began rehearsals on November 22, 1963, the day President Kennedy was assassinated, Cliff went on to explain how much Lizzie's particularly bright appeal contributed to the success of that series during what became a very tumultuous and dark time in American history. "She was most certainly the main ingredient that was brought to that show. What you saw on the screen was pretty much who she was . . . that was her personality. She was delightfully up. She was smart. But she wasn't smart-ass."

In the *TV Guide* article, "Like Dad, Like Daughter," published July 24, 1953, Lizzie expressed hopes of one day finding fame by way of her famous father. Although she refused to ride that road on his name only, he sought to simplify her path as much as possible. That summer she became a member of his select acting company and, despite the nepotistic boost, they both insisted that she, then only twenty, would ultimately have to make it on her own.

"I have a standing offer with Liz," Robert Montgomery said. "Any time she wants to discuss her career with me, I'm available. But the decisions are hers."

"I grew up with Dad's acting, which probably raised my hopes of becoming an actress," she added. "But I think I'd have wanted that even if Dad had never acted."

She had looked forward to winning a role in *Eye Witness*, a 1950 film her father was making in England. She asked for a screen test and Robert consented. "The only trouble with that," she said dolefully, "was that another actress (Ann Sheldon) got the part."

The following year, she finally won her father's approval for that now famous *Montgomery Presents* episode, "Top Secret," the last line of which Robert called "the best one in the script. It was originally to have been mine," he said. "But Liz wanted it, so I had to give in. What else could I do?" Fall prey to her charms, it would seem; just as her mother did on many an occasion. As Lizzie explained in 1965:

> They were both sweet enough to point out some of the difficulties of a show business life, especially for a girl. The difficulty is actually the matter of exposing yourself to a series of rejections. It isn't like any other business. You're selling yourself, offering yourself, and if you don't get a part, it's you

who are being rejected. It's something you have to learn to live with if you're really serious about acting.

She was clearly very serious about her theatrical pursuits and her parents, specifically her father, were willing to support the task at hand. He promised her when she was fourteen years old that she could make her professional debut with him, and with the "Secret" episode on *Presents*, he kept that promise. "He knew me well enough to know that being an actress would never interfere with me," she said in 1953. "Actually working with him gave me an enormous respect for the business."

But in July 1954, she told *Cosmopolitan* writer Joe McCarthy a different story. According to the article, "The Montgomery Girl," she wasn't at all happy with working in her father's summer stock TV theatre:

> *What will people think?* People will say I'm working on this show because I'm Daddy's daughter. That bothers me. I don't want anyone to think I'm not standing on my own two feet. Golly, at times like this I wish Daddy were a laundry truck driver or a certified public accountant.

Then for *TV Guide*, August 7, 1954, she added:

> The trouble is that if Daddy were driving a laundry truck, I'd probably be washing shirts in his laundry instead of acting on Summer Theatre.

Meanwhile, her father, interviewed for the *Cosmopolitan* piece, had a less intense view of the scenario:

> I'm sure the only person who is sensitive about our father-daughter relationship is Elizabeth herself. Actually, I've gone out of my way not to push her along. Partly because nobody helped me when I was young and I think it's better that way, and partly because Elizabeth is a strong-willed girl with a mind of her own and she doesn't need help.

Robert claimed Lizzie didn't ask him to make even a phone call on her behalf when she was trying to land the ingénue role in *Late Love*, the live stage production in which she made her Broadway debut in the fall of 1953. "She never discussed the play with me before she took the role," he relayed to *TV Guide*, "and she never talked with me about how she should handle her part while she was in rehearsal. As a matter of fact, she didn't show me the script of *Late Love* until a few days before the played opened."

She may have simply wanted to wing it alone this time. As she told *TeleVision Life Magazine* the following January, 1954:

> You have two strikes against you when you're a movie star's child. There are some people who are waiting for you to do something wrong. If a director tells you to do something you really don't agree with, you're not in a position to object. The extras would just love it if Montgomery's daughter argued with the director.

But no one showed her any animosity. "Everybody's been just so wonderful and kind," she said. Her father's company excluded.

According to *TV Radio Mirror* in January 1965, when a preparatory edition of *Late Love* was performed in Hartford, Connecticut, a proud if judgmental papa was in the audience. He went backstage after the curtain fell and said, as she hung on his every word, "Well, my girl, naturally, I hope you'll improve before you get to Broadway."

To which she dutifully responded, "You're right, Daddy. I'll try harder." And she did. *Late Love* hit Broadway on October 13, 1953, and before its season (of 95 performances) was up on January 2, 1954, Lizzie had won the coveted Daniel Blum Theatre World Award. A note of congratulation arrived from her dad. It said simply, "Good."

Upon receiving it, she sighed and said, "That one word from my father was equal to a volume of praise from anyone else."

Later on *Bewitched*, an affirmative "Good!"—with an exclamation point—became one of the popular one-word catch phrases that Lizzie incorporated into *Samantha's* speech pattern whenever she approved of some random magic or mortal occurrence on *Bewitched*.

As opposed to when *Sam* would squeal "Well?!" whenever she was unable to answer one of *Darrin's* spastic queries of "What's going on?!"

On August 7, 1954, *TV Guide* published the article, "Biggest 'Barn' On Earth: Summer Stock Was Never Like This"; it profiled *Robert Montgomery's*

Summer Theatre (also known as *Robert Montgomery's Playhouse*), which was a summer replacement series for *Robert Montgomery Presents*. At the time the show was in its third hit season. Robert Montgomery was proud of the series, which he conceived in 1952 as what *TV Guide* called, "a sound way to hold onto his network spot during the dog days of July, August, and early September." Or as he further explained, the program gave "a group of young actors a chance to put on a show of their own, undominated by big names and formidable reputations . . . this week's star may be next week's butler." *Presents* always aired live (only Robert's intros and farewells were on film), and the scripts had "nearly always been reasonably lively," *TV Guide* said.

After her affair with *Late Love* ended, Lizzie was seduced by a role in *A Summer Love*, which aired as a critically praised episode of her father's summer series on July 20, 1953:

> An egotistical actor many times married (John Newland), falls hopelessly in love with a young ingénue (Lizzie) in his theatre troupe. But upon meeting her family, he enlists the assistance of a former wife (Margaret Hayes) to help him secure happiness with his new love.

She also received high marks from her co-star, the reputable John Newland who, according to *TV Radio Mirror*, said, "Elizabeth is one of the most flexible actresses I've ever known."

Robert, meanwhile, was more subdued with his review. "Elizabeth," he remarked, "always remember that, if you achieve success, you will get applause; and, if you get applause, you will hear it. But my advice to you concerning applause is this: Enjoy it, but never quite believe it."

The following May, Lizzie continued to address whether or not her prestigious lineage helped or hindered her career. In the article, "The Girl Behind the Twitch," published by *Modern Screen*, she said, "Celebrity offspring or no celebrity offspring, it's one thing (to have a name) to open doors and another to keep them open. Nobody will take a second chance on you unless you're good, no matter who you are."

Or as she reiterated to John Tesh in 1992, "A name will open doors."

But when she wed senior actor Gig Young in 1956, Elizabeth Montgomery considered changing her name to "Elizabeth Young," if only out of respect to her new husband, and maybe as a tiny jab to her dad. "I gave it to him good," she mused to *TV Guide* in 1961.

Robert, however, recoiled at the notion and responded with a "real pathetic look," she recalled. He was unhappy with her choice to marry a "father-figure" of a man more than half her age. What's more, he was concerned that the public would think she was the daughter of rival actor Robert Young who, during the reign of *Robert Montgomery Presents*, was the star of the hit family show, *Father Knows Best* (CBS/NBC, 1954–1960). Not only would Robert Young have another hit series (*Marcus Welby, M.D.* on ABC, 1969–1975, debuting in *Bewitched's* sixth season); but like Lizzie's father, he had been a film star of the 1930s and 1940s at the same studio, MGM.

In effect, Mr. Montgomery wondered if Lizzie was "ashamed" of him and their family name. And even though she at times enjoyed confounding him, a brief press item about actress Lee Remick's wedding may have offered at least a measure of relief.

Lizzie was a dear friend of Remick's and served as matron of honor at her marital ceremony, held at the Church of St. Vincent Ferrer in New York. As archived in the Thomas Crane Public Library, the wedding announcement/press release, dated August 3, 1957, was titled: "Lee Remick, Quincy Star of TV and Movies, Bride of William A. Colleran in New York City." It described Lizzie as:

> Mrs. Elizabeth Montgomery Young of New York City, daughter of Robert Montgomery, film star, TV actor, and producer. Mrs. Young will wear a ballerina gown of pastel mint green chiffon with a harem skirt, matching accessories, velvet coronet, and will carry a nosegay of white carnations and pink sweetheart roses.

Despite such intermittent clarifications, Lizzie's lineage was always in question, as when George Montgomery, another contemporary of her father's with whom she shared no relation, was added to the name game. (Additionally, George, Lizzie, and Robert were no relation to actor Earl Montgomery—born 1894, died 1966—who is periodically albeit inaccurately linked to Robert Montgomery's film, and Lizzie's favorite of her father's movies, *The Earl of Chicago*.)

Film historian Rob Ray co-hosts the esteemed weekly Friday Film Forum at Long Beach School for Adults in Long Beach, California. As he sees it, George Montgomery was more of a common man who came to prominence in the early 1940s as the more established stars like Robert went off to war. George was a Twentieth Century Fox contract player who made minor hits like 1942's *Roxie Hart* (*Chicago* without the music), "but he never really became a star. He usually supported the female star in a list of films and had the lead in B movies."

George also went on to support and marry TV legend Dinah Shore, and lived somewhat in her shadow when she became a hugely popular star of her own show. While she devoted all her time to a successful television career and entertained millions, he became a talented carpenter and wood-worker (a role he later popularized in Pledge TV commercials of the 1970s).

Eventually, he became bored and "started dallying with the hired help and other available women," Rays says. "She caught him and divorced him in 1963, but they remained friends and had children together; and he was at her side when she died, long after her very public relationship with Burt Reynolds. He died sometime later in the nineties. But he was always just another average vendor selling his wood pieces at those home craft festivals around the country back in the '80s and '90s. You'd never guess he had been a star, except that he still had the star charisma.

Robert Montgomery's life was quite a different story. He came from money and entered films around 1930 at MGM as what Ray calls "a suave, Cary Grant–type in the days before Archie Leach (Grant's real name) became Cary Grant." He worked largely at MGM, which is now owned by Ted Turner, and remained a star into the forties. But as they aged, Grant garnered the suave roles and Robert moved into films noir and war movies in the 1940s and went behind the cameras directing and producing espe-cially on television in the 1950s. During the Red Scare of the late 1940s and early 1950s, he was considered a loyal, conservative old-money establish-ment Republican, which Ray says, "Elizabeth rebelled against."

Just as her career took off with *Bewitched*, Robert's started slowing down. He largely stayed out of the limelight for the rest of his life until his death in 1981. "I never, ever saw him appear with Elizabeth anywhere after she became a star," Ray intones. "I suspect she always feared being known as "Robert Montgomery's daughter" and did everything she could to downplay that relationship, including not casting him as her father in *Bewitched*."

Actually, she did cast him, but he said no. By the time *Bewitched* became a hit—which was immediately after it debuted in 1964—it was Robert Montgomery who became known as "Elizabeth Montgomery's father." Fact is, she became a bigger star than he ever was. As Lizzie's friend Sally Kemp revealed on MSNBC's *Headliners & Legends* in 2001, she encountered people who knew of Elizabeth, but were unfamiliar with who her father was.

In 1999, Billy Asher, Jr. told A&E's *Biography* that post-*Bewitched*, people would approach Robert Montgomery and identify him as Elizabeth Montgomery's father. That just tickled Lizzie to no end. At such times she responded with a triumphant "Yes!" because as Billy saw it, she had a very strong sense of who she was as a person.

The label, "Robert Montgomery's daughter," was an albatross around her neck. "And boy did she want to get past *that*," Billy added. Indeed. As reported in Elizabeth's interview with *TV Radio Mirror* in January 1965,

> "After ten years as an actress, you'd think people would have stopped asking me how it feels to be Bob Montgomery's daughter," she grumbles, but without losing the twinkle in her eyes. "How the devil do people think it feels? I'm deeply fond of my father, he feels the same about me. Just like any father and daughter. What else is there to be said about it?"

With that in mind, and although a reserved actress, Lizzie did not shy away from the public life created first by her father's name and then her own. In the end, her charismatic father trusted his dynamic daughter to follow her own career path. In the early days, pre-*Bewitched*, and upon her request, he remained accessible to her, but was sure not to play favorites. She would still have to "prove herself," he said, which she certainly would do, time and again.

Elizabeth's relationship with Robert Montgomery, however, also helped to build her character and strengthen her spine in an industry that many times takes no prisoners. As Bill Asher, Sr. told *Screen Stars* in August 1965, "She is perhaps a little overly conscientious, in short, a worrier. But that's a good way to be in a demanding profession."

However, he concluded, "I think she gets her professional attitudes, her capacity for taking infinite pains, from her father."

Bottom line: Elizabeth wasn't all that interested in following her father onto the big screen. She felt more comfortable on TV and the Broadway stage, venues that for her boded well. By the time "Top Secret" aired, she had just graduated from the American Academy of Dramatic Arts (with Sally Kemp, and June Lockhart of *Lost in Space* fame, herself the daughter of esteemed actors Gene and Kathleen Lockhart). Lizzie had also served a summer internship at the John Drew Memorial Theater, in Easthampton, Long Island. Because of her youthful appearance, she was placed in ingénue roles at this theatre and was already concerned about being typecast, some thirteen years before immortalizing *Samantha* on *Bewitched*. "Even though I'm twenty now," she bemoaned to *TV Guide* in 1953, "everybody thinks I'm about fifteen. If this keeps up, I'll probably be playing ingénues until I'm forty."

Of a liberal mindset with no interest in making a mark in feature films, Lizzie preferred to play comedic parts, which were at the very least a staple of her dad's career. She was also interested in pursuing musical comedy but confessed, "I can't sing." Or at least she believed she couldn't carry a tune, which she would later disprove as *Serena* in a few peppy musical episodes of *Bewitched* and as the guest-hostess in 1966 on ABC's *The Hollywood Palace* variety show. For the moment, however, she only danced, with training in ballet, in case a Broadway musical ever materialized. But that opportunity never presented itself.

Except for her initial "Top Secret" segment of *Robert Montgomery Presents*, she had not yet even acted on TV, mostly because the American Academy of Dramatic Arts frowned upon students performing in any manner outside its walls. But she held no ill will against the school. In fact, she was grateful to it for teaching her how to read lines, something her father had prodded her to do for years. As she continued to tell *TV Guide* in 1953, "Dad taught me to read everything since I was a little girl."

Despite and during her privileged upbringing, she developed a daring sense of humor, which later contributed to an approachable persona that was unaffected by the various Hollywood machinations. As she explained to *TV Radio Mirror* in 1965:

The parents of Hollywood children really do try to protect them from acquiring too much of the glamour stuff too soon. But, of course, some of it is bound to seep through. Still, it was only in rare cases that the kids got a lopsided view of their position in life. Take me, for instance. I never felt special because my father was a star. Most of the people who came to our house were important in one phase of the industry or another. Many of the kids I went around with at school came from richer or more renowned families than the Montgomerys. I'd say my environment was more likely to teach me humility than the feeling of arrogance.

In 1989, she once more attributed her kind demeanor to her family's guidance. Had she behaved with even the slightest trace of pretention, she said her father would have "picked me up by the feet and slammed me against the wall. And I probably would have deserved it. So, it's no credit to me how I was raised. But it's an enormous credit to my Mom and Dad."

As previously noted, when Robert Montgomery served in the Navy from 1940–1945 during World War II, Lizzie's maternal grandmother Becca Allen became a member of the Montgomery household, contributing a great deal to both Lizzie and her brother's Skip's non-pretentious character.

Out of all the adults who supervised Lizzie as a child, her grandmother Becca certainly seemed to be the one who, more than the others, had it all together. She was young at heart, carefree, and knew how to enjoy life beyond the rigid underpinning of her conservative Southern upbringing. She was supportive of Lizzie's life and career, encouraging, worldly, but unaffected and open-minded. In short, she was *hip*, long before that word was introduced into the vernacular. No wonder Lizzie loved her so much. They bonded on so many levels and were on much more common ground than Lizzie ever shared with her parents.

As Lizzie acknowledged in 1989, had she behaved insolently, Becca would have objected with a sardonic "Oh, please!"

But still, Lizzie looked back and pondered, "Who knows what a *value* is? When you're a tiny child, you really don't know."

To her credit, she admitted to not being "the easiest child to get along with. I was stubborn. I had a very bad temper that I have since learned to control because Daddy had a worse one." But her mother used a different strategy in reprimanding her. "Mom had a habit of becoming very quiet," she recalled. "She would let Dad do the heavy-duty, very articulate disciplining. And I tell you, it was better to raise a hand than an adjective, a verb, or a noun."

"Boy," she added of what could be her father's periodic stern ways, "he could really give it to you." Yet she took it all in stride. In the era in which she was raised, the 1930s–1940s, parents were taught not to spare the rod, or they would spoil the child. "I can barely think of a time when I resented getting in trouble," she said in 1989.

Not one to shirk responsibility, she kept herself in check. If she fell from any particular grace under her parents' close watch, then she stepped up to the plate and took the blame. "If it was my fault, it was my fault," she intoned with unabashed honesty. But she resented getting punished, as much as getting caught. "Because that just meant that I wasn't as clever as I thought I was."

Lizzie believed her parents were rarely incorrect in the way they raised her and she had no complaints. Although she admitted her parents and Becca were "very strict," they made certain she retained her own sense of values. Homework had to be done. Grades were expected to be good. "There were always choices within choices," she explained. "It wasn't just totally regulated. They gave me a lot of freedom to a point."

Despite that latitude, there were specific restrictions that she termed "weird." For one, her parents forbade her from going to the movies, which was unfortunate because for her so simple an excursion was "an amazing treat." That isn't to say her parents denied their daughter the joyful pastime that millions around the world continue to embrace unto this day. They did not put their collective foot down and demand that she never step foot in a movie theatre. "It was much subtler than that," she said.

"Oh, now, Elizabeth," she recalled her father saying, "you have something a hell of a lot better to do than on a Saturday afternoon than sitting in a movie theatre."

"But everybody else gets to go," she would protest.

"We don't care what everybody else is doing," would be the response. "This is what *you* are going to do." She said such exchanges were "fairly regular," and in time, she became intrigued with not attending the cinema, a media-sensitive prohibition that may have seemed odd, particularly due to her father's movie stardom. But she didn't think they were trying to *protect* her. "That might not be the right word," she said. Instead, she viewed the prevention measure as a modus by her parents to steer her from temptation. "I was a mad enough child that I would want to jump into it immediately," she concluded in 1989 of the movie-going experience.

However, in 1991, during her conversation with Ronald Haver, she explained how her father's film *Here Comes Mr. Jordan* played into the game of her non-movie-going experience when she was as a child. She began by explaining an early scene in the movie in which the plane carrying her father's character, *Joe Pendleton*, was falling apart. It became a particularly traumatic sequence for her to watch as a child:

> When I saw that strut, or whatever that's called, on the plane snap, and plane suddenly started to go, I was just a mess. I hated that. I hated it when I was little. That's probably why they never let me see movies because I just reacted so badly to everything. I didn't see (Disney's) *Snow White (and the Seven Dwarfs)* until it was like rereleased for the fortieth time or something because I swear I was like fifteen or sixteen . . . They would never let me see it because of the witch.

Sally Kemp recalls things differently. "We'd go to the movies all the time." But this was in their teen years, when they met as students at the prestigious American Academy of the Dramatic Arts in New York. Somewhat more independent by then, it was Lizzie who now set the rules, if only to confuse Sally with the provisions. Lizzie would take her cousin Panda to Walt Disney pictures, but Sally was only allowed to see horror movies, and she never understood why. "It was like she had some kind of catalogue," Sally says, mimicking her friend's logic in the situation: "*Sally goes to horror movies and my cousin goes to Disney films.*"

Sally found the cinema segregation particularly puzzling, mostly because Panda, with whom she remains good friends today, seemed better suited for viewing horror films. "She had more of a macabre streak than I did."

Ever unpredictable, Lizzie surprised Sally one day, inviting her to see the classic 1953 feature film, *Lili*, starring Leslie Caron, Mel Ferrer, Jean-Pierre Aumont, and Zsa Zsa Gabor. Though a few of the characters may not always be on their best behavior, this delightful romantic comedy with a dash of fancy could hardly be classified as a monster movie:

A circus troupe in France takes under their wing a poor 16-year-old girl named *Lili Daurier* (Caron). After her father dies only a month before, *Lili* finds herself stranded in a strange town. *Marc the Magnificent* (Aumont), a magician in a local circus, takes a particular interest in *Lili*, though not romantically, for he views her only as a troubled child. Rejected, *Lili* turns to the circus puppets with whom she sings away her troubles, oblivious to the puppeteers behind the curtains. Upon her initial chorus with the puppets, a crowd gathers. The circus almost immediately has a new act, and the little girl lost is found, even though she's not at all fond of the angry *Paul* (Ferrer), the carnival's owner, who is also the main puppeteer. In time, *Lili* realizes *Marc* the magician is married (to his assistant, Gabor), and that her feelings for him were mere fancy, for it is *Paul* who she truly loves. It's a fact she learns almost too late if not for the indelible mark *Paul* makes by infusing his heart and soul into the beloved puppets, which at the film's conclusion, have seemingly come to life.

Upon close inspection of the film, it may be clear as to why Lizzie held it so dear—and why she chose to share it with a good friend like Sally.

Lili had lost her father when she was only sixteen. Sally's father had died when she was young. *Lili* tells a joke early on in the film that references horses, which both Lizzie and Sally adored.

Lili to Marc: When is a singer not a singer?
Marc: When?
Lili: When he is a little horse.

Other quotes from the film are more reflective: "A little of what you want is better than large quantities" and "Refusal to compromise is a sign of immaturity."

On screen, *Lili* was seeking answers to life's biggest questions. Off screen, in the 1953 reality of her youth, and with an adventurous, if short, life ahead of her, so was Lizzie. With her good and generous heart, she may have then felt Sally was also seeking the same answers. Instead of viewing the beastly images of the horror movies they all too frequently attended, Lizzie may have wanted her good friend to gaze upon the simple beauty of *Lili*—a film that Sally would later view sixteen times. "I love it," she says.

"And I think of Elizabeth each time I see it" (as will probably anyone who reads this passage). The similarities are significant between *Lili* and Lizzie's return to comedy with the CBS TV-movie, *When the Circus Came to Town*, which originally aired on January 20, 1981.

> *Mary Flynn* (Lizzie) lives a middle-aged existence that is tedious and empty. When the circus arrives in her small town, she decides to leave home and join its ranks. In the process, *Mary Flynn* is rejuvenated with a new life purpose. She ultimately finds happiness and love with circus ring leader *Duke* (Christopher Plummer), if fleeting.

A tender and happy story, filled with hope and promise for change, the movie (which was filmed at the Coastal Empire Fairgrounds near Savannah, Georgia) might have been equally pleasing to *Bewitched* fans, providing them with an opportunity to see their beloved Elizabeth Montgomery in a lighter role that most would find fitting to her comedic forte. What's more, *Circus*, like much of Lizzie's work, was filled with lines that could have easily been pulled from the dialogue of her real life. At various points in the film, her character, *Mary Flynn* said:

> "I don't believe in age discrimination."
> "My father just passed away." (The movie aired in 1981—the year Robert Montgomery died.)
> "I have often been complimented on my appearance."
> "I'm deathly afraid of heights" (which Lizzie was in real life).
> "I could never do anything in front of a crowd."
> "I read a lot of Shakespeare myself" (which Robert Montgomery instructed Lizzie to do as a child).
> "Southerners have a long tradition of taking care of their own."
> "Maybe I'll bleach my hair. I used to see all the blond ladies walking around like someone told them it was all right to be sexy. But not me."
> "I always wanted to marry the man I felt close to in bed."
> "I always wanted for somebody else to tell me that things were okay."

Although a few other lines weren't entirely true to Lizzie's form, they came close. At one point in the movie, Lizzie's *Mary* tells Plummer's *Duke*,

"I have guts," which was true of Lizzie. But then *Mary* added, "I also have bad posture," which was not true of Lizzie. Her father wouldn't have allowed it.

In another partially true-to-life moment, *Duke* quizzes *Mary*:

Duke: So you were a *Daddy's girl*?
Mary: I was a Momma's girl until she died. *Then* I was a Daddy's girl.

Off-screen, Lizzie's mother died in 1992, approximately nine years after her father.

In general, however, *When the Circus Came to Town* still spoke to Lizzie's reality, as did many of her performances through the years, including *The Awakening Land*, which, like *Circus*, was also directed by Boris Sagal. More significantly, *Land* was filmed on vast country landscapes in Ohio, many of which played into Lizzie's memory of her youth growing up on the expansive Montgomery homestead in Patterson, New York. In *Land*, Lizzie portrayed a pioneer woman named *Sayward Luckett Wheeler*, and she was surrounded by a plethora of animals for which she had a great affection, especially horses.

Five

~

The Equestrians

"I have a pair of jodhpurs that look like they belong on a Madame
Alexander Barbie doll."

—Elizabeth Montgomery to Ronald Haver, 1991

Lizzie's early life was a relative age of innocence, one in which she strived
to appreciate the simple pleasures, significantly helped along by her love for
animals. As she explained in 1989, "I've had dogs, cats, crickets, crocodiles,
alligators, deer, goats, pigs, horses, chickens, and anything else you could
name."

Consequently, she frequently performed on screen with nonhumans
such as a chimpanzee in the 1963 feature film *Johnny Cool*, a seeing-eye dog
in the 1984 CBS TV-movie, *Second Sight: A Love Story*, and any number of
minions from the animal kingdom on *Bewitched*. Due to her realistic theatrics, the audience was made to believe that she was bonding with the given
goose or frog, etc. As *Bewitched* writer Richard Baer asserted in 1988, "This,
I believe, is a very difficult thing to do. Yet, there wasn't any question as to
whether she could pull it off."

In fact, according to the March 1965 issue of *TV Picture Life* magazine
and the January 1965 edition of *The Saturday Evening Post*, a special cat
named "Zip Zip" later played into Bill Asher's direction of Lizzie on
Bewitched. Whenever he was looking to pull a particular emotion for her to
utilize as *Samantha*, he would say, from the sidelines, "Zip Zip!"

But all other creatures aside, it was Lizzie's particular affection for horses that stood out, a bond which her son, Billy Asher, Jr. said was influenced by her dad. "My grandfather was an equestrian," the young Asher relayed in 2001 on the televised *Headliners & Legends* profile of his mom. "When she was very young he had her on a horse and she was drawn right to it."

When she was three years old, Lizzie's father sat her on a pony and said, "Ride!" and so she did; whether around the Montgomery homes in Beverly Hills/Bel Air and Patterson, New York, or in Britain, where she spent school vacations while her father produced films there. To help pass the time, she took horse-jumping lessons and frequently rode with him in the English countryside and London's Hyde Park. She even won a number of ribbons for horsemanship.

As she told Ronald Haver in 1991, "I'll always remember him on horseback . . . and teaching me to ride. I remember him being very athletic . . . on horseback is how I . . . immediately think of him. That and like polo, and jumping."

Their shared love for mares was one of the non-Hollywood pastimes that contributed to their strong bond in Lizzie's youth. Although Robert at first objected to his daughter's chosen profession, investigative journalist and best-selling author Dominick Dunne told A&E's *Biography* in 1999 that Lizzie and her father thought very highly of one another. According to Dunne, Robert embraced the idea of Lizzie as an actress. "She was a thoroughbred," Dunne assessed [no comparison to horses intended], which Sally Kemp confirms both she and Lizzie "adored. I think she even had a pet llama. And if she didn't, then she always wanted one."

In time, her art once more would imitate her life—in fact, a few times more. Lizzie rode a variety of mares in her twin TV-movie westerns, *Mrs. Sundance* (1974) and *Belle Starr* (1980), while horses came into play on two episodes of *Bewitched*.

As she explained to *TV Radio Mirror* magazine in November 1969:

> Lord, I *adore* horses. We go to the track every Saturday. I even named a character in *Bewitched* after a horse. There's a horse named John Van Millwood, a great big thing that can't get his legs straightened out until he's halfway around the track. And once when a script had a character—I think it was an old boyfriend of *Endora's*—he had some plain old name so I asked if we could call him *John Van Millwood*.

In 1989, she correlated working on *Bewitched* to playing the horses:

There wasn't a moment when I thought, *Oh, I'd rather be someplace else.* First of all, the only other place I'd probably have rather been was the race track and there was always that on the weekends . . . or the tennis courts, right? So that was cool. It's ever so amazing to be paid for something you really enjoy doing," she went on to say. "I still feel that way about acting. I mean, in general, it's a grind. I think physically you pace yourself and that's the way it goes. Horses do that . . . so can people . . . well, jockeys kind of help.

The two *Bewitched* episodes that showcased her love for horses—as well as the race track—were "The Horse's Mouth," a black and white segment from the second season with Dick York that aired March 3, 1966, and "Three Men and a Witch on a Horse," a color episode from the last season with Dick Sargent, airing December 15, 1971.

In "Mouth": A race horse named *Dolly* feels neglected and flees from her owner and into *Samantha's* backyard, while her sister *Adorable Diane* keeps winning races *Dolly* helps to set up. To fully understand her quandary, *Sam* transforms *Dolly* into a woman. When *Darrin* objects to the magic manifestation, *Samantha* says it's a special opportunity to fully understand a horse's day at the races.

In "Three Men": *Endora* transforms *Darrin* into a gambler, after which *Sam* insists the spell be broken. Ignoring her daughter's plea, *Endora* has *Darrin* bet on a horse named *Fancy Dancer* who is bound to lose—and on which he convinces *Larry* and a client to place all bets. As a result, *Sam* pops over to the stables to have a motivating chat with *Dancer*, who ultimately wins the race for fear of ending up at the glue factory.

In 1968, writer Rick Byron interviewed Lizzie for a *Photoplay* magazine article called "The Lady Gambles." Here, she expressed her fondness for horse racing by comparing two views from abroad, most assuredly influenced by her periodic summer vacations in England with her father. "I'm about as thoroughly American as anyone can be," she said, and yet she felt that the United States was missing some of the ceremonial aspects of the

British who, she believed, knew how to "do things in a beautiful, pageant-like manner. "That's one of the reasons I love the races. They're so ceremonious, so steeped in tradition." Whenever she heard the song "My Old Kentucky Home" at the famed Derby, she was driven to tears. "That is how wonderful I think the tradition is," she decided.

At one point in the interview, Lizzie apologized for what she considered to be a boring life, but in the process revealed more insight into her personality than she have may realized or intended. "I'm sorry that I haven't given you much," she said. "I'm afraid I'm a pretty dull interview. The fact of the matter is that I'm not really wild about talking about myself (which is also what she had said in 1989). I'd much rather talk about books or movies or . . . horses."

Her love of horses may have been ignited by her father, but her penchant for the real life race track was instilled in her by her grandmother Becca. According to what Robert Foxworth said on A&E's *Biography*, it was Becca who introduced Lizzie to horse racing. When Lizzie was a little girl, Becca one day walked into her room and said she would not be attending school that morning. Instead, little Lizzie would be accompanying Becca to the races. "You'll learn much more about math at the track than you ever will in class," Becca said.

In a 1993 interview with magazine journalist Bart Mills, Lizzie professed, "I love the track." She didn't own any race horses herself because, "I can lose money perfectly well on other people's horses." Although, she wasn't doing too badly at the time; the Santa Anita Race Track had been "very good to her." "I go as often as I can," she explained, "and when I can't go, I send my bets with my friends . . . There's nothing like a day at the races. There are no phones and if you're lucky, you come back richer."

However, Lizzie's mother was reportedly not at all fond of the equestrian creatures and vice versa. According to Montgomery archivist Tom McCartney, Robert Montgomery had named his polo pony after his wife. Lizzie once recalled the day the two *Bettys* met for the first time. Apparently, they both took a strong dislike to one another. As Elizabeth recalled at the time, her mother was the only person she knew who could fall off of a polo pony that was "standing perfectly still."

79

Next to her affection for horses, Lizzie's second favorite member of the animal kingdom had to be dogs, various breeds of which she owned through the years.

In 1989, it was the beautiful female canine, Zuleika, named after the heroine *Zuleika Dobson* from the book of the same title written by Max Beerbohm whose entire literary collection Lizzie inherited from her father.

As she explained to Ronald Haver in 1991, Robert Montgomery had instructed her to read Beerbohm, Dickens, Thackeray, and Shakespeare since she was six years old.

> I was really weird as far as that was concerned. (If) you saw a funny little boney-kneed scrawny kid sitting down with Hamlet, at the age of about six, wouldn't you think she was kind of odd? Yes. It's true. It's absolutely true. I was very peculiar. And I guess nothing changes. And I am so really grateful to him for all that and forcing me . . . certainly not against my will . . . to be an avid reader when I was little, so of course I still am. But I think that's why he was so hell-bent on wanting to read everything and (owning) collections of authors . . . because (learning) meant a great deal to him.

Originally published in 1911, *Zuleika Dobson* was a shameless parody about what happens when an enticing young woman enrolls at the elite all-male Judas College, Oxford. A conjurer by trade, *Zuleika Dobson* can only love a man who is immune to her allure: a circumstance that proves ruinous, as many of her love-sick beaus lose the will to live due to her cold-shoulder. Filled with notable catch-phrases ("Death cancels all engagements," utters the first casualty) and inspired throughout by Beerbohm's robust creativity, this rhapsodic take on Edwardian undergraduate life at Oxford has, according to [literary great E. M.] Forster, "a beauty unattainable by serious literature."

"*Zuleika Dobson*," Forster had also said, "is a highly accomplished and superbly written book whose spirit is farcical. It is a great work—the most consistent achievement of fantasy in our time."

Beerbohm, who lived between 1872 and 1956, and whom George Bernard Shaw once dubbed "the incomparable Max," was an essayist, caricaturist, critic, and short story writer who endures today as one of Edwardian England's leading satirists. *Zuleika Dobson* was Beerbohm's only novel, but a particular favorite of Robert Montgomery's.

Upon subsequently reading the adventures of *Dobson*, Lizzie so loved the character's first name that she gave it to what would become one of her many household pets. As she explained in 1989, the *Zuleika* character in Beerbohm's book was "so beautiful that the statues that she drove by in her carriage broke into cold sweats when she went by. So I thought, 'Well, if I ever get a real pretty dog, I'm going to give her that name.'"

Approximately five years before Zuleika came into Lizzie's life, there was "Emma," a Labrador retriever and her co-worker, as it were, on the TV-movie, *Second Sight: A Love Story*, which originally aired on CBS, March 13, 1984. Here, Lizzie portrayed *Alaxandra McKay*, a stoic, reclusive blind woman who must come to terms with her disability and the subsequent need to utilize the services of a seeing-eye dog. Lizzie in 1989:

> I became very attached to that dog. I always get very attached to every pet I work with. But there was something special about Emma. I think it's because I worked with her for such an extended amount of time (three weeks) before I even started shooting the film. Her trainer, Lee Mitchell, is the most wonderful, gentle person for seeing-eye dogs, and he worked so hard with me with this dog. So I got attached to her, and she got attached to me. And that was it, and the way it should be.

Lizzie and Emma shared nearly every scene together in *Sight* and, at the film's wrap party, found it difficult to detach from one another, so much so, Mitchell at one point turned to Lizzie and asked, "Would you like to have Emma?"

Lizzie was shocked. "It never occurred to me that they would want me to keep her."

She tried to talk herself out of it, if only because she thought the gifted canine would be better placed with someone who was visually impaired. "Emma was totally trained as a seeing-eye dog and I thought she could at least be used as a companion for someone who really needed her," Lizzie said.

But Mitchell was persistent. Emma was too strong for any disabled candidate. His remaining list of specially trained dogs had already been paired with clients and continuing sessions with Emma would not have been a practical business decision. "Aside from that," he said to Lizzie, "she's attached to you."

"Oh, no—she's not!" Lizzie protested, hoping to convince herself of what she knew in her heart was simply not true. She also found it especially hard to dissuade Mitchell, because during their conversation, Emma remained right by her side, panting, with an eager joyful gleam in her eyes.

Lizzie melted. "Oh, shit!" she thought. "I don't believe this!"

Although she still needed time to decide, Mitchell would not take *no* for answer, and pressed her further. "You know you want that dog!"

In the end, Elizabeth finally consented to keep Emma, but unfortunately this story does not have a happy ending. The dog later developed tumors and died.

"It was just the most heartbreaking thing," Lizzie said. "I was just a wreck. It took forever for me to get over losing her."

Long after Emma was gone, the pang of her loss certainly haunted Lizzie with each viewing of *Second Sight*, once even while working on another of her movies, *Face to Face*, which aired on CBS in 1990, but which she filmed with Bob Foxworth in Africa in 1989. For some reason, *Sight* was being screened on the closed circuit monitors on the *Face* set. For those who have not seen the film, be warned, here is a spoiler alert:

At the end of *Sight*, Elizabeth's character, *Alaxandra*, no longer requires Emma's assistance and the two are forced to part ways. Consequently, *Alaxandra's* heartbreak became Lizzie's heartbreak in reality, and she was reminded of it every time *Sight* was seen, particularly on the set of *Face to Face*. It didn't much help matters that *Alaxandra* cried in those last aired moments in the movie.

When reminded of that scene in 1989, Lizzie explained how that moment between *Alaxandra* and Emma became intolerable for her to watch and experience, even in rehearsals:

I don't like to cry. In fact, I hate it. I mean, I really hate it. So for me, having to cry when I'm working in a scene, well . . . I really have to *do a number on myself*. It's just not a pleasant thing to go through. It's a lot of hard work for me to get to that point. Yet, when an actor performs in certain scenes, you have to do it, and it's yucky. After going over it the first time, I turned around to say something to the director, and noticed that half the crew had disappeared. They each went off to their own little corners and cried, including the cinematographer, Frances Hayes, my wardrobe assistant, and Adele Taylor, the hairdresser. No one stuck around. They were all sobbing and they just left. They couldn't handle it.

It was the kind of emotional effect Lizzie's performances would have on fans and friends alike. Her talent and persuasive personality was evident from a very early age. According to what her former schoolmate Billie Banks revealed on MSNBC's *Headliners & Legends*, even as a child Elizabeth commanded a star-like charisma and respect, and that she at times would wriggle her nose for "good luck" during school exams.

Another childhood friend Deborah Jowitt appeared on *Legends* and said Lizzie had a "mischievous . . . happy-go-lucky nature" and was known for her humorous comments and "funny faces."

Sally Kemp today recalls the particular facial expression—an animal imitation—that would later prove quite fortuitous. "We called it her 'bunny nose,'" she explains in reference to Elizabeth's inevitably famous proboscis wriggle. "And we all tried to do it, but nobody could."

By *we*, Sally means herself and cousin Panda, who were both Elizabeth's inseparable sidekicks in their youth. A good portion of that friendship was spent riding horses and roaming the endless acres of the Montgomery homestead in Towners, New York—a sprawling landscape located within Patterson, New York, and near Brewster, a place Sally remembers as a "Kennedy-like compound."

At the turn of the twentieth century, Towners was one of Patterson's major population centers, particularly while it was a junction of the New York Central's Harlem Division and the New Haven's Maybrook Line. The commercial vicinity included a blacksmith shop, a meat market, hotel, grocery store, and hardware store. There were rumors of a reservoir project and cessation of passenger rail stops that contributed to the decline of the community as a vital commercial spot.

In short, and at least geographically speaking, Towners was to Patterson what Beverly Hills is to Los Angeles County. Elizabeth talked about the area to *Modern Screen* in May 1965.

Every summer she and her entire family, including her various aunts, uncles, and cousins, would travel back East to stay. There were three lakes in the area and, as she said, "We swam like crazy." With rowboats and horses, "It really was the most wonderful life a child could have. We had such freedom, and such good discipline. We were taught never to go off on our own. We were taught to have respect for horses and guns (her family enjoyed shot-putting and hunting, the latter of which she later deplored). The older kids looked after the smaller kids and it was just a great big happy sort of world with no such thing as competition or any feeling of being left out. My whole life we went there, every summer. I loved the place so."

The "left out" line was an omen of sorts. At the time of that interview, Lizzie had received her first Emmy nomination for her 1960 performance in *The Untouchables*, and would later garner a total of eight more nominations, collectively, for *Bewitched, A Case of Rape, The Legend of Lizzie Borden,* and *The Awakening Land.* But she never won.

Also, too, as will later be delineated, she loved to play games, whether it was with friends at home or behind the scenes, or on camera for game shows like *Password* or *The Hollywood Squares.* And although she later claimed indifference to her lack of Emmy victories, it was clear that, in some venues, she retained a competitive spirit throughout her life, sometimes less productive than others.

By the time Lizzie and Sally Kemp were playing with horses in Patterson, New York, Robert Montgomery and Elizabeth Allen had divorced, and he was living with his second wife, Buffy, in what Sally describes as "a beautiful home," which was located near an equally attractive home owned by Lizzie's Aunt Martha-Bryan, sister to Elizabeth Allen, and mother to Panda.

A little more background on Martha-Bryan Allen proves bewitching:

She was born on April 30, 1903. In 1925, she met her future husband Arthur Cushman. The couple had two children: Arthur, Jr., born in 1927, and Amanda, born in 1932.

Rebecca raised her two daughters, Elizabeth Allen and Martha-Bryan, with the help of her brother William, as father John Allen was not a consistent presence in their lives.

In the meantime, the affluent Cushman family also lived in Patterson, close to the Montgomery brood in Duchess County, where their ancestors had dwelled over several generations. Arthur Cushman owned a large farmhouse in which their daughter, Elizabeth's cousin Panda, resides to this day.

The Cushmans were so affluent, they lived on Cushman Road, which was named for Lizzie's Uncle Arthur—a moniker that she would later bestow upon the beloved *Bewitched* character played by Paul Lynde.

In fact, the crossroads between Patterson and *Bewitched* were manifold. Lizzie exhibited a special love for the area that was later reflected in the characters and places mentioned on the show. But most probably only viewers from the Patterson area would understand the various references to Towners and Patterson that would appear in the show's scripts. For a 1968 interview with the New York *TV Time* magazine, Lizzie revealed, "Our life in Patterson was a paradise for us. That's why I placed *Darrin* and *Samantha* in the town. If I can't be there year-round, than at least *Samantha* can."

In the intervening time, *Samantha* and *Darrin's* last name of *Stephens* may have served as a nod to the members of the Stephens family who have represented Patterson in the New York State Assembly for several decades. The TV couple's daughter, *Tabitha*, attended the *Towners Elementary School*. Flowers within the premise of the series were delivered by *Patterson Florist* and *Mrs. Phyllis Stephens* (*Darrin's* mother played by Mabel Albertson, sister to Jack *Chico and the Man* Albertson) shopped at the *Patterson Department Store*.

Further still, real-life Towners/Patterson street names were often utilized on *Bewitched*. In the *Bewitched* episode "Sam in the Moon," *Samantha's* pharmacist was named *Max Grand* (played by Joseph Mell), after a long time Patterson resident.

The Grands and the Montgomerys were close friends and neighbors. The Montgomery home was the second house on the left on Cushman Road off NYS Route 311. The Grands lived on the first house on the right on NYS Route 164, off Route 311. For many years, the only house in between was the Ludkin residence, which was at the start of Cushman Road at Route 311. The Ludkins operated a turkey farm and factory for many years, while most of the property in the area was owned by members of the Montgomery and Cushman families.

As the years passed, and as both of her daughters grew into adulthood, Lizzie's grandmother Becca would later divide her time every year between the homes of Elizabeth Allen and Martha-Bryan, and her own abode three thousand miles away in Malibu, California.

Training Days

"School bored me and I always knew I wanted to be an actress."
—Elizabeth in *TV Guide*, August 19, 1961

In the core of her *Bewitched* years, Lizzie shared a home in Malibu with her husband Bill Asher and their three children. Years before that business and family foundation was developed and secured, she paved the groundwork for her career. After graduating from finishing school, otherwise known as high school, she attended the American Academy of Dramatic Arts in New York.

According to the October 1953 edition of *People and Pictures* magazine, Robert Montgomery had instructed Lizzie to attend the Academy, and to play summer stock in preparation for a professional career:

> Last summer she was an apprentice in summer stock. She graduates from the academy this summer. This doesn't make her a finished actress, of course, but it does give her preparation. Actually, there's no school that can imbue anyone with talent, but a school can give technique and knowledge of the job to be done. My advice to all young people [who are interested in acting] is not to quit school. Finish college if possible and major in dramatics.

Either way, Lizzie attended the Academy, where she befriended Sally Kemp. Like Lizzie, Sally did not attend college, but was a good student. So her mother gave her a choice. She could rise to her debutante ovation, receive an education in Paris, attend Sarah Lawrence College in the States, or enroll at any other upper-crust educational facility that would accept her. She also had the option of attending the Academy in New York. "And as soon as that became a possibility," Kemp says, "that's where I was going."

As fate would have it, Sally had already bonded with Panda Cushman, Lizzie's first cousin by way of her Aunt Martha-Bryan. The two had been acquainted in boarding school, and to this day, Sally says Panda remains one of her "closest friends."

But years before today, near the end of their shared educational tenure, there was Sally's enrollment at the Academy, and Panda was delighted. Lizzie would attend the same school, and Panda encouraged Sally to make the new connection. Shortly thereafter, Sally says she and Elizabeth became instant friends, and sat next to each other in every class.

Once in the fold, certain traditional and universal school laws did not escape the halls of the strict Academy. "We weren't allowed to chew gum or anything like that," Sally recalls. However, such classic constraints did not prevent her new best friend from playfully breaking the rules. Ever of the avant-garde mindset, Lizzie soon discovered what Sally recalls as "little violet candy, which you can still buy today. They're similar to little lifesavers, but they smelled like perfume."

While in class at the Academy, the then teen girls would keep that smelly candy moist in their mouths, and not in their hands. "We figured nobody would know it was candy," Sally intones.

At the time, the Academy was still located at Carnegie Hall. Classes were held in different studios, and large portraits of great actors and opera singers, who were either alumni or present teachers, donned the walls of each studio, which they rented to teach classes.

"Elizabeth was always a bit more rebellious," Sally admits. When it came to rambunctious scheming to while away the hours, Lizzie would take the lead. "This is what we have to do," she'd tell Sally, and they would commence one exciting endeavor after another.

One especially adventurous day, Lizzie had a particular plan in mind. "As soon as we break for lunch," she told Sally, "I have found a way to get into the balcony of Carnegie Hall through a special door."

Sure enough, when the clock struck twelve, the two brave young souls journeyed through that secret passageway and, once on the other side, they came across none other than the one and only musical maestro, Arturo Toscanini, rehearsing with his famous orchestra.

In time, the two young women would sit mesmerized before the music master on a near-daily basis. "And of course, we would also be late for class," muses Sally, the daughter of the famous bandleader Hal Kemp who, in 1940, was voted along with Glenn Miller and Tommy Dorsey as one of the top three dance bands in America (although, tragically, Hal was killed that year by a drunk driver on his way to play an engagement at the Coconut Grove).

So, whenever the opportunity arose, the daring duo of Lizzie and Sally would sneak away through that secret door to that hall of Toscanini, whom Sally says they perceived as "a very little man."

One afternoon, however, a sour note was heard in the massive musical camp of the tiny Toscanini who became displeased with an orchestra member's performance. As Lizzie and Sally stared from the dark trenches, Toscanini halted his ensemble, pointed to the unfortunate musician in question, shouted in Italian something they assumed was quite derogatory, took his baton, broke it in two, tossed it across the room, and marched off the stage. As Sally remembers it, the mischievous Lizzie then whispered to her asking, "Ok, what's gonna happen now?"

Finally, one of the violinists in the orchestra deadpanned, "I think we're breaking for lunch."

"It was all such fun to watch," Sally chortles. "And Elizabeth and I would do things like that all the time."

A kinder, gentler *Thelma and Louise* of their day, the dynamic twosome of Lizzie and Sally would later become a daring trio, when they befriended yet another young classmate at the Academy named Jarmila Daubek. Jarmila was the daughter of Czech baron George Daubek and Jarmila Novotna, the celebrated Czech soprano and actress who, from 1945 to 1956, was a star of the Metropolitan Opera. According to Sally, both Jarmilas were extremely attractive, but the younger Jarmila, the close chum to both girls, "was even more beautiful."

"She arrived at the Academy a few days after Elizabeth and I did," Sally explains. "But as soon as we caught sight of her, well, we both shrank. She was taller than we were. She had stunning chestnut hair, and the most beautiful skin we had ever seen, along with these huge brown eyes. She was just exquisite."

"We have to make friends with her," Sally remembers Lizzie saying.

When Sally wondered why, Lizzie mused, "Because she's prettier than we are, and we have to keep her on our side."

But according to Sally, Jarmila had a gentle disposition, and was embarrassed when people found out that she was a baroness.

Just as when a shy Lizzie during these Academy days never touted herself as the daughter of a famous movie star, or as when years later on the *Bewitched* set, she remained accessible to the cast and production team. As the show's star, she could have easily adopted a condescending approach, but instead took the high road, discouraging brass and presumption. She may have lacked confidence at times, but she was replete with courage and conviction. She was equally cool and self-reliant. She embraced every opportunity to shock with subtlety those who may have felt even the slightest intimidation by her heritage or very presence.

Case in point: a certain fellow classmate at the Academy named Florence Henderson who would also later become a classic TV icon by way of an ABC sitcom. Henderson played mom *Carol Brady* on *The Brady Bunch*, which debuted in the Fall of 1969, *Bewitched's* sixth season (the year Dick Sargent replaced Dick York as *Darrin*).

When I first met Elizabeth at the American Academy of Dramatic Arts, I thought she was so beautiful and elegant. But she was also always sweet and friendly. And Sally Kemp was also so nice and friendly with a great smile. I thought they were the best dressed and most sophisticated girls in the school.

"She had a beautiful singing voice," Sally says of the multitalented and ever-youthful Henderson who, when Lizzie and Sally knew her, was set to audition for the 1952 Broadway musical, *Wish You Were Here*, which was an adaptation of *Having Wonderful Time* (both of which were directed by Josh Logan). "But the show's producers needed to see how she would look in a bathing suit."

So, their fellow classmate Candi Parsons lent Florence swimwear from her wardrobe. Now outfitted with the perfect look, the future *Mrs. Brady* went on to win the part. Billed as "the new girl" in *Wish You Were Here* (which also featured Jack Cassidy, Tom Tryon, Phyllis Newman, Reid Shelton, and Frank Aletter, Lizzie's co-star from *Mr. Lucifer*), Florence enjoyed a healthy run of 598 performances in the show.

Years after they graduated from the Academy Florence, as opposed to Lizzie, seemed more at peace with the sitcom character that brought her fame. While Florence would continue the role of *Carol Brady* in countless *Bunch* sequels, Lizzie literally began to fight her way out of her most recognizable TV persona with very non-*Samantha* roles, post-*Bewitched*, in TV-movies like *A Case of Rape*, (NBC, 1974), *A Killing Affair* (NBC, 1977; with O. J. Simpson), or *Act of Violence* (NBC, 1979). She'd come to terms with playing *Samantha* only decades after she first played the role. "But she was a terrific actress and a fascinating person," Henderson intones.

The *Brady* TV parent also thought the *Bewitched* star must have been "a wonderful mom" in real life, which she decided after meeting Rebecca Asher, Lizzie's daughter. Though Florence never appeared on *Bewitched*, she did a guest spot on another high-concept ABC comedy titled *Samantha Who?* on which Rebecca was hired as script supervisor. "She was lovely, and we had some wonderful talks," she concludes.

When Lizzie attended New York's American Academy of Dramatic Arts it was a breeding ground for future stars-in-the-making. Past graduates included the likes of Grace Kelly (who would ultimately leave Hollywood and become Princess Grace of Monaco) and Anne Baxter (who played royalty of a whole other kind in 1965's classic film *The Ten Commandments*).

There were additional students of the Academy and other similar institutions who paid tuition with funding from, for example, their G.I. Bill, namely actor James Arness. A contemporary of Lizzie's, Arness would later become a legendary TV star in his own right, taking the lead in *Gunsmoke* (CBS, 1955–1975) on which Lizzie's brother Skip ultimately made his TV debut. Meanwhile, too, Arness was brother to another soon-to-be-popular actor, Peter Graves, future star of *Mission: Impossible* on CBS, 1966–1973/ ABC, 1989–1990). In either case, Arness utilized his military assistance to join an acting program at the Bliss-Hayden Theatre, a small established theatre school in Lizzie's future city of Beverly Hills (where he was ultimately discovered by an agent).

Other Academy graduates would periodically assemble for training or observation purposes, sometimes even after they graduated. As Sally Kemp recalls, one day in the green room there prowled a certain young charismatic man who left a year or so before she, Lizzie, and Jarmila. "But he was always lurking around there."

Many of the thespian alumni would "make the rounds" following graduation, she says. "In those days, you could do that." It was one of many traditions that allowed for aspiring actors to pay random first visits to producers' offices. "I never had the courage to do that. But it was possible."

"We were more privileged than many of the other students," Sally says of the fortunate young life she shared with Lizzie and Jarmila. "There were those who had worked for years as waiters and waitresses to make money in order to attend the Academy."

In any case, the newfound male dramatic arts alumnus who frequently concealed himself and his perceptions in the distance was just about to spark Sally Kemp's interest.

During his periodic peeks from inside the Academy green room, the relatively new graduate remained clandestine and silent until one day, when he stopped Sally and said, quite unabatedly, "You're one of the three graces, aren't you?"

Sally was flustered and a little annoyed.

"Yeah," the young man affirmed. "You, Montgomery, and the baroness—we call you the three graces."

Now flattered and somewhat embarrassed at how she and her dear friends were perceived by a few of their former, present, and maybe even some future schoolmates, Sally said, "Oh . . . well, that's lovely. Thank you so much." Then added, "But who are you?"

"My name is John Cassavetes," the young man answered.

"How do you do," she replied in turn. "I'm Sally Kemp."

Almost urgently, she then walked away, and thought sadly, "That boy's just never going to amount to anything. He's always in the green room."

She was dead wrong, of course, as the young Cassavetes would go on to become one of the greatest actors and directors of their generation. In the article, "A Second Look: John Cassavetes' touch is clear in 'Too Late Blues'" by Dennis Lim, Special to the *Los Angeles Times*, May 27, 2012, Cassavetes was dubbed "the original Method actor turned DIY [do-it-yourself] filmmaker." As Lim went on to explain, "For that reason his early forays into studio directing . . . 1961's *Too Late Blues* for Paramount and 1963's Stanley Kramer-produced *A Child Is Waiting* for United Artists—are usually thought of as footnotes at best, or compromised failures at worst (a view that has been ascribed to Cassavetes himself)."

Before dying too young at fifty-nine in 1989, he was featured in a list of celebrated big and small screen appearances. Those included the occult theatrical film, *Rosemary's Baby*, about an evil coven of witches, which was released in 1968. The latter part of that year also marked the fifth hit season of *Bewitched*, two episodes of which ("The Battle of Burning Oak" and "*Samantha's* Shopping Spree") made a reference to *Rosemary's Baby*, which also happened to feature Maurice Evans.

As fate would have it, Cassavetes was linked to Lizzie via a few TV appearances. First, in 1954, for an episode of *Robert Montgomery Presents* titled "Diary," and then on his own show, *Johnny Staccato*, for an episode called "Tempted" (which aired November 19, 1959):

> *Faye Lynn* (Lizzie) literally runs into *Johnny* (Cassavetes), seeking his protection while delivering a valuable diamond necklace. They share a brief romance and a sensual moment in his living room. *Faye* at first seems sincere, but in the end, her obsessive hunger for the finer things in life reveals her true intentions.

Robert B. Sinclair directed this *Staccato* segment, in which Lizzie has some memorable lines as *Faye Lynn* that, if they don't quite reflect her reality off-camera, certainly reference it.

For example, regarding her failed and insincere relationship with *Johnny*, *Faye* tells him: "We tried to make a go of it. It's just one of those things!" He says, "Faye—you've seen too many movies," and she replies: "That's right, Johnny . . . too many movies with too many glamorous people, wearing glamorous clothes and going to glamorous places. But that's what I want, Johnny. I want it so very much."

In reality, of course, Lizzie could not have cared less about those things . . . except attending movies, at least when she was a child. She always wished she could have seen more films in her youth, something her parents prevented her from experiencing.

Meanwhile, Lizzie as *Faye* shares a passionate kiss with Cassavetes as *Johnny* in one scene, probably the most passionate scene from her entire body of work.

$\mathscr{S}\!even$

$\sim$

The Europeans

"Only then in Europe could she begin to see Robert as a father, a
person separate and different from the famous star."
—Writer Jacqueline Starr, *Screen Stars Magazine*, August 1967

In 1979, Lizzie appeared in two very different TV-movies: *Act of Violence*
and *Jennifer: A Woman's Story*. *Violence* was in keeping with her post-
Samantha traumatic plot choices (a woman is assaulted and turns bitter);
Jennifer's story was somewhat more uplifting (a wealthy woman loses her
husband and takes over his successful company).

That same year, Lizzie's friend Lee Remick was featured in a film called
The Europeans which was the initial presentation of Merchant Ivory Productions, headed by producer Ismail Merchant of Bombay and American director James Ivory, who later directed such acclaimed and stylish films as
Howards End (1992) and *The Remains of the Day* (1993).

The Europeans was the first in this series of movies to address the pertinent balance of social graces and reserved emotions—the kind Elizabeth had
been addressing her entire life, as instructed by her parents, most certainly
her father.

Remick was born in Quincy, Massachusetts, the daughter of Gertrude
Margaret Waldo, an actress, and Francis Edwin "Frank" Remick, a depart-
ment store proprietor. She appeared on six episodes of *Robert Montgomery
Presents*, during which she and Lizzie developed their friendship.

93

Although the two young actresses never performed together on *Presents*, Remick made her Broadway debut with *Be Your Age* in 1953, the same year Lizzie debuted on Broadway in *Late Love*. They later appeared in a fanciful rendition of F. Scott Fitzgerald's novella *The Diamond as Big as the Ritz*, adapted by William Holdack for an episode of NBC's *Kraft Television Theatre*. Airing September 28, 1955, the story was broadly played by all cast members including Lizzie as a seemingly pre-*Serena*-esque character named *Jasmine*, who's unimpressed with her family's wealthy status.

Remick played her sister *Kismine*, alongside Lizzie's future TV-movie co-star William Daniels (from 1974's *A Case of Rape*) as her brother. Rounding out the cast was Signe Hasso and George Macready, as Lizzie's on-screen parents, and Mario Alcalde as Remick's boyfriend.

Lizzie has a free-for-all as *Jasmine*, reciting biting dialogue with such flare to her arrogant pretend mother and father, as if hoping her off-screen prestigious real parents would take a listen.

Here's a sample, regarding *Jasmine's* father:

"There's a look about not feeding the animals all over Father's face"
"It would just take a twist of Father's wrist to put you back in the pit again"
"Oh, now Father, you're just getting yourself upset about nothing"
"You mustn't mind Father. He's a bit theatrical"
"That would be a good one on Father."

To *Jasmine's* mother:

"Mother, why do we always have to have wealthy people visit us? They're such bores"
"Mother, why don't you send *Kismine* to college?" ("It's only for boys, dear.")

In several scenes, *Jasmine* is seen reading *Cinderella*, one of many fairytales, Disney-related or otherwise, that Lizzie loved; and at one point *Jasmine* says to her mother:

Mother, don't you think *Cinderella* is divine? It's the only book that is worth anything, well except the one about the little girl who has to sell matches to support her father [*The Little Match Girl* by Hans Christian Andersen]. Oh, I love that one.

And then:

I think *Cinderella* is the best. Only I think everybody ought to be poor in the end instead of rich. I think it would be much better that way.

To her sister *Kismine* near the end of the episode:

You don't expect me to go on living in this house, doing stupid things and meeting stupid wealthy people, while you're out in the world, poor and having fun, do you?

And later, when she wants to accompany her sister and Alcalde:

I won't be a nuisance. I'll help all I can. And we will be poor, won't we . . . like the people in books. And I'll be an orphan, and utterly free. Free and poor. What fun!

Dialogue from the other characters also must have proved compelling for Lizzie upon her first read of the script. Remick's boyfriend says: "Everybody's youth is a dream," to which Lee adds, "How pleasant to be young." The most telling non-*Jasmine* dialogue that might have hit a nerve in Lizzie's father/daughter dynamic was voiced by Macready's parental TV role: "Cruelty doesn't exist where self-preservation is concerned."

In January 1954, *TeleVision Life* published the article, "Our Name Is Montgomery" by Norma Gould, in which Elizabeth talked about her how her parents viewed her career. She had expressed how much her father tried to discourage her from acting, painting the bleakest possible picture of the entertainment industry. "He said it was the most heartbreaking field you can go into," she recalled. However, her father added that it could also be quite satisfying.

These comments were voiced the year Elizabeth debuted in "Summer

Love," an episode of *Robert Montgomery Players*, the summer replacement series for *Robert Montgomery Presents*. It was in "Love" that she co-starred with John Newland, who spoke glowingly of Lizzie, who called him a "wonderful performer." When asked if they had ever dated, she replied, "Well, we've had drinks together after rehearsals at the Barberry Room. We're just good friends."

Her ideal man, as explained in the article, was one with personality, character, ease, and a nice wardrobe. "She also prefers older men," Gould wrote, as was later more than evident when Lizzie married Gig Young and then Bill Asher.

But at the moment, her father was the only older man in her life; and for the most part, he approved of her life and career. He kept a close eye on each of her performances, including those on *Robert Montgomery Presents* and the *Robert Montgomery Summer Theatre* shows. As for her mother, "Well, I guess she's pleased," Elizabeth said. "You know how it is; she's never actually sat me down and said, 'Elizabeth, I want to tell you how pleased I am with what you're doing.'"

In September of 1967, *TV Radio Mirror* magazine published the article, "An Old Beau Tells All about Liz Montgomery's Past," by Jane Ardmore. It profiled a former boyfriend of Elizabeth's from New York, a physician who—because the American Medical Association apparently then frowned upon the personal publicity of its members—was clandestinely identified as "Bud Baker."

Baker used to dance at various high society balls with Elizabeth; he had attended St. Mark's High School in New York with Lizzie's brother Skip and then later went to Harvard with a young sophisticate named Frederic Gallatin Cammann, who graduated in 1951.

In 1950, after her parents divorced, Lizzie moved with her family to New York. Her father was despondent over the lack of Hollywood roles for forty-something men his age and he had high hopes for a lateral career move on the East Coast. He was also now married to the socially prominent Elizabeth "Buffy" Harkness, an heiress who just happened to be close friends with Cammann's mother, who according to Tom McCartney, was known as Mrs. H. Thomas Richardson; Cammann's father was Frederic Almy Cammann.

While it is uncertain as to who exactly introduced Lizzie to Frederic, who would in time become her first husband, it was most likely Buffy, who was slightly class conscious. But Lizzie and Cammann had many mutual professional and personal connections, and they saw one another at various social functions and dances in New York, the same debutante gatherings that were periodically attended by Bud Baker. As Baker told *TV Radio Mirror* in 1967, "I'd always be on the stag line," where he would see Lizzie whom he described as "very, very pretty, very popular."

"You couldn't dance with her one minute straight without some other guy cutting in," he said. "And she always seemed so above it all; bored stiff, really." Or so she appeared. In reality, the high society game wasn't Lizzie's style. Only later did Baker understand that she was a country girl at heart, someone who loved horses and dogs, any animal, and the wide open spaces of the Montgomery compound in Upstate, New York.

"The social game was new to her," he said. Her entrée was, he confirmed, by way of her stepmother Buffy Harkness, "and of course, everyone knew she was Robert Montgomery's daughter. But Liz was a bright light in her own right. She had this built-in radiance."

Bud had first met Lizzie when his cousin escorted her to a prom at St. Mark's—a cousin who apparently still treasured her picture in his year book. "And let me say," he clarified, "that my cousin wasn't any big romance of Elizabeth's. He was a *fun* friend. That's what I was, too."

That's how dating was defined in those days; you attended dances and proms with platonic friends, most of the time never sharing the slightest kiss or even holding hands. At least such was the case for this younger wealthier set . . . from the outside looking in.

Baker then recalled another dance, this time at the River Club, down by the water on New York's East End Avenue. The summer before, he had met Lizzie's father and brother. His family owned a home on the shore and someone invited the Montgomerys, including Robert and Skip, to join them. Bud said they were both "great . . . easy-going," Skip, in particular, "always was."

Bud hoped such associations would have proved fortuitous, if only so he could cut in line to dance with Lizzie at the River Club, approach her and say, "Hey—you know, I met your dad and your brother this summer."

More times than not, however, and to his great disappointment, she would be unimpressed, which made him think, "*She's really snooty.*"

Bands headed by Meyer Davis (who died in 1976), or Lester Lanin (who died in 2004, but was still going strong into his nineties) would be playing in the background, and Bud would try again. "Great band, isn't it?" Still, Lizzie would give him that "above-it-all look."

"To tell you the truth," he said in 1967 at the height of *Bewitched's* popularity, "she wasn't as much fun as she is now." And apparently, she wasn't as attractive to him then as she had become. "Her figure was always okay, but her face was sort of babyish and kind of pouty, especially when you mentioned her father. It wasn't from any lack of love for him, though. Through the years I've discovered that. She adores her dad. But who wants to talk about a famous father?"

Probably not Lizzie; but Bud wasn't "hung up" on those dances. He didn't get carried away and he never thought Lizzie did either. The only reason he attended those dances was to dance with her and a few other gals.

Although Lizzie was very reserved, and more insecure than she let on, according to Bud, she danced like a dream. She was a coordinated athlete who looked and was totally feminine. She wore lovely discreet clothes, in excellent taste. "You figured she'd marry young . . . someone with a great family name behind him and become one of the social set on the East Coast."

She did. Frederic Gallitan Cammann, Baker's upper-class Harvard acquaintance whom he said came from "a great family," namely Albert Gallatin, Cammann's maternal great grandfather, and a former Secretary of the Treasury. According to the U.S. Department of the Treasury:

> Born to an aristocratic Swiss family, Albert Gallatin (1761–1849) emigrated from Switzerland to America in 1780. Elected to the House of Representatives in 1795 and serving until 1801, Gallatin fought constantly with the independent-minded first Secretary of the Treasury Alexander Hamilton. He was responsible for the law of 1801 requiring an annual report by the Secretary of the Treasury, and he submitted the first one later that year as Secretary. He also helped create the powerful House Ways and Means

Committee to assure Treasury's accountability to Congress by reviewing the Department's annual report concerning revenues, debts, loans, and expenditures. Appointed Secretary of the Treasury in 1801 by President Jefferson and continuing under President James Madison until 1814, Gallatin was in office nearly thirteen years, the longest term of any Secretary in the Department's history.

In the meantime, Fred Cammann became friends with Lizzie and the Montgomery brood before his service to the United States. After graduating from Harvard, he enlisted in the army and was stationed in Korea. Once discharged from the service, Cammann was reintroduced to Lizzie in 1953, when he was hired as a stage manager-turned-casting director for *Robert Montgomery Presents*.

It has been suggested that Cammann was drawn to Lizzie primarily because of her entertainment affiliations, as his career interests leaned toward the industry, specifically in the casting department. But *why* they got together didn't matter to Robert Montgomery. According to Dominick Dunne, Elizabeth's father was just plain "thrilled" that his daughter was interested in as well-bred a man as Cammann. At least that's what Dunne told MSNBC's *Headliners & Legends* in 2001.

Like Cammann, Dunne started out in show business as a stage manager on *Presents* and the two were friends. Robert Montgomery had also befriended Dunne and placed a great deal of trust in him, and held him as a confidant. As Dunne explained it, Robert told him that Cammann was "the kind of guy I want my daughter to marry."

This time, Lizzie was all too eager to bend to her father's will. She and Cammann started dating and then, according to *Newsweek Magazine*, March 29, 1954:

> Engaged: Elizabeth Montgomery, 20, actress, daughter of movie actor and TV producer Robert Montgomery, and casting director Frederic Gallatin Cammann, 24, obtained a marriage license in New York, March 18.

The wedding was held on March 27, 1954, at St. James Protestant Episcopal Church in New York. When asked in 2011 about his life with Lizzie, Cammann was cordial, but brief: "I'm in my eighties now, and that was a long time ago. It's in the past, and that's where I'd like to keep it."

Sally Kemp, however, remembers Lizzie's wedding to Cammann as if it happened yesterday. It was a not-so-great marriage that was at least preceded by a happy and reverent ceremony, and an elegant and festive reception. Lizzie had been a bridesmaid at Sally's first wedding, and when Lizzie decided to marry Cammann, Sally returned the favor. She recalls:

It was a beautiful wedding. We all arrived at her mother's apartment. Our dresses had been purchased for us, along with the petticoats that went under them, pearl necklaces, all exactly alike. White kid gloves all exactly alike . . . the little headdresses that we wore, and white satin shoes . . . because it was a white wedding. I had never seen a totally white wedding before, but we were each adorned with these beautiful ivory dresses. We all dressed together, and usually bridesmaids have to pay for their own way, but not this time. Everything including the underwear was paid for—including the stockings! And we all had the same shade of nylon stocking. I was very nearsighted, but too vain to wear my glasses. So I really didn't see a whole lot. (But) She was an incredibly beautiful bride. She was always both enchanting and adorable, but not like Jarmila (their fellow student from the New York Academy). Elizabeth did not have that kind of beauty. She was like a pixie . . . a little gamine when she was young, even as she got older. She had beautiful eyes, a beautiful mouth, and that cleft chin. But she didn't have that grand kind of beauty. But she was the most beguiling and amazing looking bride. I thought Freddie was going to faint when he saw her. He really loved her. But they all did (men in general). I couldn't imagine how they couldn't.

Academy Award–winning actor Cliff Robertson loved Lizzie, too, but as a platonic friend. The two performers remained close through the years and, like Sally, Cliff was there when Lizzie married Cammann:

It was very festive. St. James Church was on the upper Eastside in New York, and I specifically remember her walking down the aisle, because I had an aisle seat. And right after when she and Freddie were pronounced man and wife, she walked passed me, and with that ring on her finger, gave me a big ol' wink, as if to say, *I got the man I wanted!* It was fun to watch. Everyone was there, including her brother (Skip), who was dancing the Charleston. Freddie was a nice guy. He was brought up in the East. He was very ambitious to learn the TV production work and he utilized his assets rather wisely on Madison Avenue. But they weren't married too long.

Robertson had "no idea" why Lizzie's first marriage failed, but he detected it might have had something to do with her theatrical ambitions. Cammann's career choices were periodically described as a stage manager, TV producer, casting director and/or executive; he wanted an old-world wife and Lizzie wanted to be a newfangled actress. That was something she worked hard to achieve, and not by exploiting her father's famous name. According to Robertson, she was determined not to be labeled a society actress. "And I think that came from her mother's side," he said. "Her mother was a Southerner, and her aunt (Martha-Bryan), who was a dear friend of mine as well, was from I think Tennessee, and she had all the graces of a Southern lady."

In other words, Lizzie had a strong sense of pride and wanted to succeed as an actress on her own merit. "Freddie was very upper crust and old-fashioned," Sally Kemp says. "The marriage probably would have lasted had Elizabeth decided not to become an actress."

If anything, Elizabeth's marriage to Cammann proved to be benchmark in her friendship with Kemp. They were moving in different directions. By the time Lizzie married Freddie, she and Sally did not see one another that often anymore. In the pre-Cammann days, the two women would have dinner, lunch, or get together somehow several times a week. "When we each married," Sally laments, "things changed."

To anyone who knew Lizzie, the idea of her being identified as a stay-at-home wife, minus any form of career, was slightly absurd, at least at this time in her life. Only later would she more readily embrace the sequestered home life, and sometimes crave it. But that transpired after she became a star on *Bewitched*, when she was able to better balance and appreciate the finer and simpler things in life.

In the beginning, Cammann made an effort to support her theatrical endeavors. According to *Cosmopolitan Magazine* in July of 1954, he was in the service when she made her TV debut on that "Top Secret" episode of *Robert Montgomery Presents* (December 1951). She explained:

To be specific, he was in the Army and he had been on KP for eighteen hours. He was so anxious to see me on television that he sneaked out of the kitchen to see our show in the recreation room. The mess sergeant caught him. And thanks to me, he had to stay on KP for the next two days.

When he was relieved of the KP duty, and upon eventually leaving the Army, he and Elizabeth were busy with decorating their new apartment on New York's Upper East Side. When asked if he objected to Elizabeth continuing her acting career now that they were married, he replied, "Not at all. How else can we pay for all the furniture she's ordered?"

Certainly, no one on either side of their family had to worry about meeting such payments. The main concern, at least for Lizzie and Cammann, was meeting eye to eye on the marriage in general, which just simply never came to be. As one of their mutual friends concluded in an article for *The Saturday Evening Post* in 1965, "Freddie just couldn't measure up to her father." But it wasn't all Robert Montgomery's fault.

Lizzie's marriage to Cammann was unstable from the onset. Although wired for show business, Cammann cut such ties away from the set. In Lizzie, he envisioned a stay-at-home wife, much like *Darrin* hankered for *Samantha* to remain earthbound on *Bewitched*. But the actress, unlike her most famous TV counterpart, wanted a full-time job, outside of the home, specifically, an acting career. And she wanted to take it to the next level . . . in California, but he didn't want to leave New York, so the marriage went south.

Had the two met later in life, the bond may have stuck. Instead, their wedded bliss unraveled, commencing with his ousting from the elite social circles to which he had become accustomed. Close colleagues and friends were aghast at his alliance with Elizabeth, whom they incorrectly labeled as a common actress. It was not a personal attack on her, but rather a general displeasure with her profession. His peers were simply unimpressed with the theatrical world, even when such a world revolved around so endearing a performer as Lizzie.

On the home front, the two bickered constantly, with their first major disagreement proving to be nothing less than outright jarring. He apparently became so upset he packed his bags and went home to mother. *Samantha* had at times threatened to do the same on *Bewitched*. In such a case *Darrin* would exclaim, "What for? Your mother's always here!" *Samantha* was usually supportive of her mortal husband, but would be appalled at his attacks on her mother.

In contrast, Lizzie was stunned at Cammann's inaugural retreat to his mother's.

Following each minor or major altercation, he would storm out only to return to his newlywed wife, time and again. After what ultimately became the final intense bout with his packing ritual, Lizzie allegedly—and we can only assume, gently—placed her derriere upon his suitcase in order for it to lock properly, which paved the way for his final exit. Immediately following, she purportedly filed for divorce.

At least this is what Gig Young, her second husband, apparently told his sister, according to Young's biography, *Final Gig: The Man Behind the Murder* by George Eells.

That said, a brief item in the press, "Star's Kin Asks for Divorce," appeared in a Las Vegas newspaper on August 10, 1955, stating that Lizzie, now 22, and referred to as "Robert Montgomery's daughter," had obtained a divorce from Cammann, now 26, whose profession was listed as "a television executive." Although terms of a property settlement were not disclosed, she charged cruelty and was granted restoration of her maiden name.

Lizzie's break-up with Fred Cammann was coined a *quickie* Nevada divorce, the criteria for which was met by her fulfilling a residency requirement in that state for thirty days. After that, she left for Hollywood to work with Gary Cooper on *The Court-Martial of Billy Mitchell*, her big screen debut.

In an interesting twist, this film shared several aesthetic similarities with *The Rack*, a motion picture from 1956 starring Paul Newman, Walter Pidgeon, Cloris Leachman (*The Mary Tyler Moore Show*), Robert F. Simon (who played *Darrin's* father on *Bewitched*), and a fair-haired Anne Francis.

Mitchell was based on a true story of the American general (Cooper), and his court martial for public complaints about High Command's dismissal and neglect of the aerial fighting forces during World War I. *The Rack* was a fictional account of *Captain Edward Hall* (Newman) who returns to America after two years in a prison camp during the Korean War. But both films dealt with the military and alleged insubordinate behavior of its lead screen soldiers.

About a decade after working on *Mitchell*, Lizzie would star in *Bewitched*, which debuted on ABC in 1964. Some years following her work in *The Rack*, Francis would find TV fame with another ABC show called *Honey West*, which debuted in 1965 (if only running one season to *Bewitched's* eight). In *The Rack*, Francis played a troubled woman struggling with the death of her solider husband, a successful brother to Newman's ultimate poor soul. In *Billy Mitchell*, Lizzie portrayed an emotionally torn woman struggling with the loss of her husband at the apparent misguided hands of the Navy Brass.

The Rack was a superior film, with Newman delivering an A-list performance at the on-set of his career. In *Billy Mitchell*, Cooper gave a tired performance near the end of his career. (Four years later, he would appear with Lizzie's *Bewitched* co-star Dick York in the 1959 film, "They Came to Cordura," during which York suffered a permanently damaging back injury that ultimately forced him to be replaced by Dick Sargent as *Darrin* in 1969).

In either case, Elizabeth was gripping as the grieving wife in *The Court-Martial of Billy Mitchell*, potentially pulling emotions (via her preferred training in "method acting") from the turmoil she was experiencing off-screen with her failed union to Fred Cammann.

For the time being, too, there was a rumor circulating that Cooper, well known in Hollywood as a Lothario of sorts, went chasing after her on the *Mitchell* set. According to Montgomery archivist Tom McCartney, Cooper was "driving pretty hard to the hoop." The actor frequently flirted with Lizzie and was "on the make." At one point, "Coop," as he was sometimes known, was nowhere to be found, even after a stage manager completed an extensive search on the set. The stage manager finally knocked on Cooper's dressing room door, which was locked. Finally responding to the interruption, the actor popped opened the door—with Lizzie reportedly in view inside his room. Although it appeared that she was ultimately seduced by Cooper's various charms, the hearsay of their alleged affair was just that and never was substantiated.

There was additional supposition of a potent off-screen romance between Lizzie and the historically womanizing crooner Dean Martin when they co-starred in 1963's *Who's Been Sleeping in My Bed?*, a salaciously titled film with a slightly daring plot for its time:

Actor *Jason Steele* (Martin) is not a doctor, but plays one on TV. He's so convincing in the role, women of all shapes and sizes, including the alluring

Toby Tobler (Jill St. John), find him irresistible. His poker buddies (some played by Louis Nye and Jack *Barney Miller* Soo) may envy him, but his fiancée, art teacher *Melissa Morris* (Lizzie), isn't the least bit impressed. In fact, she's quite upset; although she eventually learns to hold his attention by implementing an inventively affable bedside manner of her own, which she partially introduces with a seductive dance sequence.

In 1989, Lizzie remembered that sequence with a smile, and posed, "Wasn't that funny? And that was strangely enough one of the more difficult things I had to do." The actual dance moves were not an issue. She was always athletic and had studied dance for years. But it was the precise choreography that forced her to face the music. She clarified:

It wasn't like dancing today, which is freewheeling. And Jill St. John (who also danced in the film) did it better than I did. But my character was supposed to be a wonderful dancer, so that was cool. If they had me out there riding a horse or playing eight sets of tennis I would have been much better. Or if we filmed it today, I'd have been out at some disco dancing. That would have been no problem either. But it was difficult for me because you get so kind of confined when you have to do it and the *clicks* (dance measurements) are going and the music starts and stops, and the dialogue starts and the music stops. But it was fun. I enjoyed it. I enjoyed being pushed into the pool at the Beverly Hills hotel. That was really funny because there were a couple of people who couldn't swim, and I found myself in this bridal gown which must have weighed 900 pounds, saying, "It's okay. I can swim. And I'll be right here." It was a very nice experience. It was a feature, which was fine—and it was one of those things that you did.

Elizabeth would work with Martin one other time, in another feature film, but to a much lesser and somewhat odder extent, in 1960's *Bells Are Ringing,* directed by Vincente Minnelli (once married to Judy Garland and father to Liza):

A Brooklyn phone service operator (Judy Holliday) seeks to improve the lives of her clients by relaying between them various bits of information. In the process, she falls in love with playwright *Jeffrey Moss* (Martin), whom she is determined to meet. Problem is: he only knows her on the phone as "Mom!"

Lizzie's credited role? *Girl Reading Book*, one of the strangest cameos in big screen and small screen history; one of the oddest appearances of any performer on record, anywhere; she's seen with her head down, collapsed over a table in a tavern. It may have had something to do with her love for reading, a practice her father had instilled in her ever since she was a child. Either way, entertainment historian Ken Gehrig tries to make sense of it all:

> Having already made *The Court-Martial of Billy Mitchell*, and many guest-starring roles on television, it's a mystery that Liz would appear in this wordless role where she virtually seems a mannequin. In a very long take at an actor's hang-out in New York, Judy Holliday's character is trying to convince the Brando wannabe actor played by Frank Gorshin to drop *the method*. Liz is in the foreground screen left; no dialogue, no movement, no expression; very much concentrating on her reading matter. What? Was it the opportunity to work with Oscar-winners: actress Judy Holliday, director Vincente Minnelli and/or producer Arthur Freed? Sadly, this was Judy's last film appearance and the last MGM musical of Minnelli and Freed. So unwittingly this was Liz's only opportunity to do such a film. Also, it's unlikely anyone knew that in hindsight this film is early exposure for future TV people: Jean Stapleton (*All in the Family*), Frank Gorshin (*Batman*), Hal Linden (*Barney Miller*) and Donna Douglas (*The Beverly Hillbillies*). Ironically, Liz has less to do onscreen than all of these others—and yet, her concentration on her actor's *goal* seems relentless. None of the posturing of Holliday or Gorshin distracts Liz from her book!

As to any alleged affair with Martin, during production of this film or *Who's Been Sleeping in My Bed?* Lizzie mentioned not a word. However, Montgomery archivist Tom McCartney points out that various revealing documents from the files of famous Hollywood gossip columnist Hedda Hopper are now accessible online. Among the papers is a transcript of an alleged telephone conversation between Lizzie and Hopper during which Hedda threatened to expose the alleged affair that Lizzie had with Dean.

Into this mix, actor J. Anthony Russo, who had a small role in *Bed*, chronicled his own observation about a Montgomery/Martin connection in his book, *Creativity and Madness: The Passion of a Hollywood Bit Player* (BookSurge Publishing, 2005). According to Russo, one day at lunch between filming scenes for *Bed*, Lizzie apparently jumped onto Martin's lap and began to smother him with kisses. When she left, Martin turned to all of those who would listen and supposedly intoned, "Don't mind her. She's a little stunod," which is Italian for "a little drunk."

That said, if the rumor of Lizzie's purported affair with Martin had been addressed elsewhere, which it has not, she may have been on the rebound from Gig Young just before falling in love with and later marrying Bill Asher, whom she met on the set of *Johnny Cool* (which was filmed the same year as *Bed*). By then, her relationship with Asher was her only real documented affair, a dalliance that transpired after she and Young separated.

Concurrently, according to George Eell's book, *Final Gig*, Young was having a very public—and one could only assume also a very wild—fling with Sophia Loren. He and Lizzie then reunited for approximately six months, after she which she divorced him for good.

On February 15, 1954, Lizzie appeared with Sally Kemp and Cliff Robertson in "Our Hearts Were Young and Gay," an episode of *Robert Montgomery Presents*. The episode was based on the book by actress Cornelia Otis Skinner and journalist Emily Kimbrough. Originally published in 1942, the book is about their European tour in the 1920s when they were fresh out of college at Bryn Mawr. It spent five weeks atop the *New York Times* Best Seller List in the winter of 1943, and was adapted for the big screen in 1944, starring Gail Russell as *Cornelia*, Diana Lynn as *Emily*, and Charlie Ruggles (a future *Bewitched* guest-star) as *Otis Skinner, Emily's* father.

In the TV version on *Presents*, Lizzie played *Cornelia*, Kemp was *Emily*, and Robertson was *Paul Smith*, a romantic interest for *Emily*. Each actor brought youthful buoyancy to their roles.

Lizzie, Sally, and Cliff made many appearances on *Robert Montgomery Presents*, and appeared in the show's first summer stock theatre group that included an orchestra conducted by Al Kemp (not *Hal* Kemp, Sally's father). Cliff enthusiastically recalled it all in 2011:

One summer, Robert decided to form the *Robert Montgomery Playhouse* with a particular number of actors, and I was one of the few lucky ones to join in. And we got to do a number of shows. It was very nice, if a little bit isolated and insolated from Hollywood. Bob preferred the East, as it were. But we all worked so well together, and it was a romp! We never took each other too seriously. We just plain had a ball performing in a play called *Our Hearts Were Young and Gay*, written by a very good writer named Rod Crawford [although sources document Nathaniel Curtis as penning the teleplay]. Both Elizabeth and Sally were a delight to work with. They were very close, like sisters. And Sally was a lovely friend . . . to both of us.

Sally adds:

Our Hearts Were Young and Gay was a surprise. We were all so young and *green!* And sweet Cliff Robertson; I saw him again a couple of times when I moved back to New York City; sad to lose him last year (2011). At least there were glimpses of talent on all our parts. I went on to specialize in classical roles, Shakespeare, Shaw, Wilde, etc., mostly in theatres in L.A. and New York, keeping me in non-luxury, but great satisfaction; Elizabeth and Cliff achieved a far wider audience.

From 1962 to 1993, whenever a young comedian impressed Johnny Carson during an appearance on *The Tonight Show*, the heralded late-night king of talk shows would invite them over to his famous sofa. In the same way, Robert Montgomery would periodically invite key players from a given episode on *Presents* to join him at the show's end to bid farewell to the home audience until the following week. After they performed to their *Hearts* desire, a very young and bubbly Lizzie and Sally joined Robert at the end of the show. All three were beaming. Robert was proud of their performance, which pleased Elizabeth, but also surprised her. Robert spoke directly to the camera, but she did not, nor did Sally, who recently had a chance to see the episode nearly sixty years after she appeared in it:

It was good to see Elizabeth (in her interviews) looking lovely and warm and charming. She seemed to be at ease in spite of confessing to nerves. But that's what we do. Not just as actors, but for the backgrounds we were both from. You try to make your guests (or interviewers) feel at home.

If anything, it's pleasing to see Lizzie interact so honestly and joyfully with her father and her best friend. The latter dynamic, unfortunately, would later change.

In the days before she met and married Fred Cammann, Lizzie's friendship with Sally was solid enough for Robert Montgomery to consider Kemp a member of the family. "He treated me as though I were his other daughter," she says. "I absolutely adored him and his (second) wife Buffy. From the day Elizabeth and I met, she didn't live with her father. And he and Buffy had the most beautiful duplex penthouse on East 72nd Street, not far from Fifth Avenue."

Lizzie lived with her mother during the week and would visit her father for regular weekend trips in the country, and Sally tagged along. The Montgomery East Hampton abode "was always very impressive," she says in recalling a playful interchange that usually transpired between the two prior to such excursions:

> The phone would ring. My mother would answer, and this voice on the other line would say, "This is Robert Montgomery's secretary. I'm calling for Mr. Montgomery. Can Miss Kemp come out to play in the country for the weekend?"

It was Lizzie, of course, on the other end of the line, disguising her voice.

Sally's mother was always frustrated that she never had the chance to meet Robert Montgomery, but gave her consent: "Well, of course Sally can go to the country."

"I practically lived with them when I wasn't at home," Sally recalls of the Montgomery visits, which periodically expanded into trips abroad.

After Lizzie married Fred Cammann, her father and Buffy would go sailing, or take summer European excursions. Along for the ride would be Annie, Buffy's daughter from a previous marriage, and a random classmate of Annie's. Both were about 18.

Then in 1954, when Lizzie and Sally were both 21, the Montgomerys planned a trip to Europe that ultimately proved a milestone in their relationship. According to Sally, Lizzie called her and said, "Daddy and Buffy are leaving for Europe and they're having a bon voyage party on this huge ship. Let's go to the party.'"

Sally had never traveled on a great ocean liner, although she was supposed to have done so on an earlier trip with her mother and stepfather that never transpired. "So, I went with the Montgomerys," she explains. "I adore the old luxury liners. But not those great big things like the new Queen Mary or the Queen Elizabeth. They're too big. But the old ones are heavenly."

Sally arrived on this one particular classic luxury liner, the kind of which she was so fond, and there were the Montgomerys "in their beautiful suite, with champagne and lots of elegant people and some press standing around." She and Lizzie remained over in one corner, taking all of it in, hoping, "Someday, we'll get to do this, too." Much to the surprise of both young ladies, that day and moment had arrived—when Robert, minutes later, walked up to Sally, startled her, and asked if she was 21.

"Yes. I just had a birthday a few months ago."

"And do you have some money of your own?"

"Yes."

"All right, then . . . why don't you fly to London and join us and come on the trip?"

Upon viewing this interchange between Kemp and her father, Lizzie naturally assumed that she, too, would be joining her parents and her best friend on the trip. "Oh, Daddy," she said. "What a divine idea!"

At which point Robert looked at her and said, point-blank, "Elizabeth—you just got married a few months ago. You are *not* coming with us to Europe for six weeks. You're going to stay with your husband." Lizzie was stunned into silence. Sally, however, was putting a call into her parents who were out of town.

"Mommy . . . may I go to Europe with the Montgomerys?"

"Of course, Darling, but what are you going to wear?"

When it came time to depart, Sally made certain to find the proper attire, then packed it all into a suitcase, and flew to London. Her plane landed in the U.K., and the Montgomerys, who arrived beforehand, sent a customs official to greet Sally before any passenger was allowed to exit the aircraft. A man dressed in uniform approached her, and said, "Miss Kemp . . . I've come to escort you through customs."

As the two deplaned, Sally was carrying her mother's treasured Elizabeth Arden alligator make-up case. She and the customs representative made their way across the walkway, where Robert and Buffy Montgomery were waiting at the entrance. Upon running to greet them, she triggered loose the handle on her mother's make-up case, and out onto the ground rolled various crystals and other cherished items. "I was so embarrassed," she recalls. "I tried to pick them up and fit them into the hem of my skirt. It was terrible." That is, until she reached the Montgomerys, who eased any minor mortification. "Never mind," Robert told her. "We'll get another make-up case for you."

"They were just lovely," Sally recalls of Lizzie's parents, who were waiting for her in a Rolls Royce, driven by a chauffeur wearing a uniform with boots, a tunic, and a cap. They drove the long way in order for Sally to see Buckingham Palace and places like the Connaught, one of the great, elegant London hotels which, though reasonably small is still her favorite.

And it was at the Connaught she stayed, along with Buffy's daughter Anna and her friend Jill—all expenses paid by the Montgomerys, another gift, this time as a gesture to encourage a sense of freedom for three young girls on an exciting trip abroad. Sally remembers:

> We went all over Europe. And everywhere we'd go, everybody knew who Bob was. We had dinner with people like the American Ambassador of Paris, and attended parties where we were the only people who did not have *titles*. We went to Sutherland and saw the incredible mansion of the Duke of Sutherland, which was later purchased by J. Paul Getty. And I had the great opportunity to be there when the Duke was home. It was an extraordinary time.

Yet not so much for Lizzie, who remained back in the States while her parents vacationed in Europe with her best friend. "I don't think Elizabeth ever forgave me for that," Sally intones. They were still friends, but that vacation slight ever lurched in Lizzie's memory. The two never broached the subject until decades later during what became their final meeting. "The last time I saw Elizabeth was the only time she talked about that trip," Sally explains of an awkward encounter that took place in Los Angeles sometime in the 1980s.

A decade or so before that landmark day, Sally portrayed *Nurse Ratched* in the 1970 first revival of the play, *One Flew Over the Cuckoo's Nest*, directed by Lee Sankowich at the Little Fox Theatre in San Francisco, where it ran for five years. By this time, Sally had divorced her first husband Bob Grant and was now married to actor Paul Jenkins, who was playing *McMurphy* in *Cuckoo's Nest*. A few years passed and a production of the play, with Sankowich back as director, was presented at his proprietorship, the Zephyr Theatre in Los Angeles, where Sally and Jenkins had relocated. Only this time, circa 1980s, the role of *McMurphy* was played by Robert Foxworth, who had been with Lizzie since their meeting in 1973 on the set of the ABC TV-movie *Mrs. Sundance* (which debuted in 1974; Foxworth would perform in 1975 with *Star Trek: Deep Space Nine* actor Salome Jens in yet another production of *Cuckoo's Nest*, this one at the Huntington Hartford Theatre in Los Angeles).

Sally never had the chance to see the 1980s edition of *Cuckoo's Nest*, but her husband did. And on closing night after the curtain came down, there was an on-stage party for all present and previous cast members. "But we arrived late," Sally recalls. "And I found myself walking into this dim theatre, where there wasn't much light. I approached the stage where the party was taking place, and all of sudden, I heard this voice from the shadows saying, 'Well, as I live and breathe, it's *Scary* Kemp.'"

That was Lizzie's nickname for Sally, who immediately recognized her old friend's voice. As such, she replied in kind, with a pronounced Southern accent, posing into the dark hall, "Elizabeth Victoria Montgomery? Is that you in the corner?"

They both ran into the middle of the stage, fell into each other's arms, and stood there for what Sally approximated as about 15 to 20 minutes, catching up on the twenty or so odd years since they had last seen each other.

Lizzie opened the chit-chat: "I've had three children."

"I know. I've heard from your cousin. I only have one. My husband died."

And on they went, until an awkward pause froze the memories of times gone by.

"We were still holding one another, face to face," Sally intones. "But then Elizabeth pulled back a little bit and said, 'My father always loved you more than he loved me.'"

Now, it was Sally who was stunned into silence, as was Lizzie decades before, when Robert Montgomery insisted that she remain in the States with her then-new husband Fred Cammann (while her best friend gallivanted throughout Europe with her parents).

"I thought I was going to die," Sally says, upon hearing Lizzie's statement. She was hurt when Lizzie said that, and protested, "Elizabeth, you are so wrong. Your father adored you. You were so like him in so many ways."

But such sounds fell on deaf ears, which as Sally explains, was par for the course:

> Even though she embraced me that day on the stage, and we ran into one another's arms on that stage, she still resented that I went to Europe all those years before, while she did not. But there were a lot of people who Elizabeth eliminated from her life. She kind of had a way of dropping people. There were no second chances with her. And this also even happened with her cousin Panda, who had grown up with Elizabeth like a sister. I don't know what that was in her. As young girls, we couldn't have been closer. I never really had as close or as loving and supportive a relationship as I had with Elizabeth. That's why it was so strange when she was no longer in my life. I never even heard from her when Gig died, and certainly not when her father died. Nothing. The last conversation we had was when she dropped that bombshell on me about her father, which I called ridiculous, because he did love her so much. And we still loved each other.

While the two women stood face to face on that dark stage in 1980s with their arms wrapped around each other's waists at the after-party for the final curtain call for *One Flew Over the Cuckoo's Nest*, the situation was if not *crazy* then certainly strange. "Who's your agent?" Lizzie asked.

"*Oh, Elizabeth,*" Sally thought to herself. "*You don't want my personal phone number? And you won't give me yours. You just want to know how to contact me, should you ever need to.*"

So, instead, she said, "Elizabeth—don't worry about it. We'll see each other again."

"I suppose so," Lizzie added.

"We then embraced one last time," Sally recalls. "And I never saw her again." In hindsight, it appears Lizzie never stopped loving those whom she had ever cared about, but she was so sensitive a human being that if she felt offended or possibly threatened by someone, even in the slightest, unintended way, a defense mechanism would kick in, ensuring that she would not place herself in that vulnerable position again. "I think, too," Sally surmises, "it was a little bit of the *out of sight, out of mind*" train of thought. Her life was very busy, especially when she first went out to California and started doing *Bewitched*. Then she had three children. That's an awful lot to deal with and it's certainly understandable that we drifted apart at least for those reasons."

Meanwhile, Lizzie eventually traveled abroad, if not with her father. Ironically, on May 19, 1967, *TV Guide* later compared her and Bill Asher to world-renowned foreign royalty in explaining the great power they amassed in Hollywood by way of her *Samantha* success. After *TV Guide* reporter Arnold Hano noted, "The Ashers run *Bewitched*," the studio spokesperson declared, "They are like the crowned heads of Europe!"

Eight

~

Spirits and Demons

"Are you starting a rumor, or merely repeating one?"
—*Ann Evans*, as played by Elizabeth in "Patterns,"an episode of
NBC's *Kraft Television Theatre*, January 12, 1955

Ghosts played an integral role in Lizzie's life, long before she'd encounter them as *Samantha* on *Bewitched* ("*Tabitha's* Cranky Spell," 3-28-68; "The Ghost Who Made a Spectre of Himself," 10-27-71). As she explained to *TV Photo Story* magazine reporter Laura Wayne in June 1971, she had apparently seen a real live ghost in a hotel, shortly after arriving in England where she was visiting her parents. Here's how it went:

She was about to open her hotel room door, when she became conscious of someone hurrying down the hall. A few days later the same thing happened. Again, she was just vaguely conscious of feeling someone hurry by her, but by the third time it happened, she "definitely saw a foot and the bottom of a skirt as it disappeared around the corner." Swiftly, she rushed to the corner and looked down the hall. There was no one there and, as she assessed, it would have been impossible for anyone to have reached and entered one of the doors in that hall in so short a time.

She returned to her room, and contemplated what had transpired. She then became certain that whoever, or whatever, she had seen was not dressed in the fashion of the day. The "ghost's" skirt was long and full, and the foot and ankle which had disappeared around the corner were clad in a high-buttoned shoe.

The housekeeper entered her room a few minutes later and when Lizzie relayed what she had experienced, the housekeeper said, "Oh, you've seen her. She has been here for many years, ever since this house was new," and passed the incident off casually.

Lizzie concluded, "I never learned the name of my ghost or her story."

Author and professional namedropper Dominick Dunne had befriended Elizabeth when he served as a stage manager on *Robert Montgomery Presents*. In his book, *The Way We Lived Then: Recollections of a Well-Known Name Dropper* (Crown, 1999), he recalled, among other things, working on *Presents*, her marriages to Fred Cammann and Gig Young, and his developing friendships with Cliff Robertson and Arlene Francis, both of whom starred with Lizzie in the hit Broadway play *Late Love* (from October 1953 to January 1954). Dunne was delighted with *Love's* success, and intrigued by the bond that formed between Lizzie and his wife Lenny, a relationship that he said would have "twists and turns in years to come."

For the moment there were only ups and downs, as the newlywed Cammanns lived in the New York apartment above the space Dunne shared with his mother, who one night hosted a party to celebrate *Late's* success. Dunne claimed that he and his mother were good friends with Lizzie, as he had served as an usher at her wedding to Cammann, a fellow stage manager on *Presents*. Both Dunne and his wife Lenny were so close to Lizzie that, after the birth of his first child (actor Griffith Dunne), she would often babysit, a fact which Dominick said his son to this day takes delight in revealing. Yet those intimate proximities would soon contract and fade.

In time, the Dunnes moved to a larger apartment on East 76th Street, Lizzie disengaged Cammann in Vegas, and on December 28, 1956, in that same fast-paced, high-living Nevada city, she wed Gig Young of whom her father was not the least bit fond. As Dunne told *Headliners & Legends* in 2001, "Bob Montgomery hated Gig Young, and was . . . distressed" about Lizzie's romance with the older actor. "I think that put the first strain on their father-daughter relationship."

In the interim, the Youngs moved to Los Angeles, and Cammann married again (to Nora Franke) in yet a second ceremony for which Dunne served as an usher.

By the time all of this transpired, Lizzie's old friends, like Bud Baker, had lost track of her. She extricated herself from him and others as she had from Sally Kemp. Occasionally, after she married Young, Baker, for one, would run into her at waving distance in some mob scene when she and Gig were on the East Coast. But other than that, she was a no-show. She turned the page. Seemingly, with each new relationship came a new crop of friends, and a new era was born for the actress who liked to draw. A fresh canvas awaited her at each new brush with fame.

When Elizabeth was living with Gig Young in their rented furnished New York apartment, she fell in love with a white dishtowel decorated with blue butterflies. As writer Arnold Hano observed in the *TV Guide* article, "Rough, Tough and Delightful," May 19, 1967, "This was no doubt a climax in the life of Liz Montgomery. When she wiped something, it turned out to be with an item totally domestic, albeit festooned with butterflies."

In that same article, Hano made note of a poem Elizabeth composed when she was only in third grade:

> Creepy, crawly caterpillar
> You are very funny.
> You will be a butterfly
> When the days are sunny.

When Hano asked her about that poem, and which animal she most identified with, the caterpillar or the butterfly, she replied, indignantly, "Goodness, surely not the butterfly!" Meanwhile, her marriage with Young was at times like living in a cocoon.

She first met the actor, twice married and divorced, after he had recently ended an engagement to actress Elaine Stritch and began hosting the anthology TV series *Warner Brothers Presents*. According to George Eells' biography of Young, *Final Gig: The Man Behind the Murder* (Harcourt Brace Jovanovich, 1991), Gig's show was filming on the same Warner's lot that Lizzie was shooting her first motion picture, *The Court-Martial of Billy Mitchell.*

To celebrate signing contracts for Gig's new series, Warner Bros. staged a dinner at the Beverly Hilton Hotel at which studio executive Gary Stevens requested the actor's presence. Gig consented but was uncertain about his potential escort. Since she was on the lot, Stevens suggested Lizzie who was then all of twenty-two. Gig was born November 4, 1913, which made him forty-two, approximately, because like Lizzie he was known to tally his age with a minus-five-year span that was left open to the imagination.

In either case, Gig was apprehensive about the potential date. He simply did not want to give the impression that he was too old to be dating a young starlet. Assured by Stevens that such would not be the case, Gig invited Lizzie to join him for the studio dinner. As it turned out, she was excited about the idea. Apparently, she had seen one of his recent film performances and said to anyone who would listen, "I think he's the most attractive man on the screen and I intend to marry him."

While most shrugged off the remark, fate seemed to play against Lizzie's hopes for a romance, let alone a marriage. At the time of her first date with Gig, she was scheduled to return to New York shortly to begin rehearsing a play. More importantly, she was not totally legally free from her marriage to Fred Cammann.

That said, and as Eells explained in his book, it was obvious to many that Gig's appearance and mannerisms were oddly similar to those of Robert Montgomery. The two had met when Gig guest-starred in an episode of *Robert Montgomery Presents* called "The Sunday Punch," which aired October 19, 1953:

> One-time fighter *Tony Marino* (Young) is on his way down the boxing ladder but can still throw a mean "Sunday punch." After his manager (played by Frank Wilson) attempts to bribe him to "take a dive" in a fight with up-and-comer *Kid Walker, Tony* becomes infuriated and almost wins the fight, but then suffers a dangerous head injury that may have lasting repercussions.

Three years after *Punch* aired, and approximately twelve months after Lizzie met Gig, she performed in an episode of his show, *Warner Brothers*

Presents, titled "Siege," which aired on February 14, Valentine's Day, 1956. On camera, she played a country schoolteacher whose class is held captive by an escaped convict. Off-camera, her young heart was held captive by Gig and the two were married the following December 28, and her father Robert Montgomery was nowhere in sight. He would not attend his daughter's second marriage.

Meanwhile, Lizzie and Gig decided they wanted to have children of their own, immediately, if possible. But to alleviate certain health issues he had had a vasectomy when he was only twenty-five. He would later reverse the procedure but his relationship with Lizzie, which lasted six years, still did not prove fertile.

What it did produce was a lot of turmoil, largely due to the fact that Gig was a chronic alcoholic. What's more, it was challenging for him get over the loss of his second wife. In 1949 he and his first wife, Sheila Stapler, were divorced after nine years of marriage. In 1951, he wed drama coach Sophia Rosenstein, who died of cancer one year later.

Number three was up when Gig met Lizzie. He was immediately hypnotized by her sophisticated ways and flattered by the attention she showered on him. When she returned to Broadway to replace the ingénue in *The Loud Red Patrick*, they were constantly on the phone.

After finishing his stint on *Warner Brothers Presents*, Gig received an offer to go into the legendary Jean Dalrymple's revival of *The Teahouse of the August Moon* at the New York City Center. He wasn't as impressed with Dalrymple as he was with Lizzie. So, he leapt at the opportunity to be near the future *Bewitched* star. The *Moon* revival didn't spark any interest, but his romance with Lizzie was set afire.

Charismatic and confident, her charms were evident wherever she went. As author Eells uncovered in his book on Young, the actor found Lizzie alluring but somewhat intimidating. But she helped to fill a void and loosened him up socially. At times they were like two little kids, according to Bob Douglas, a mutual bystander and friend to the couple.

One weekend, for example, Lizzie took Gig and Douglas to her family's attractive country home in Patterson, New York. Upon arrival there, and after several drinks, Gig blurted out, "What about dinner?"

At which point, Lizzie ventured into the kitchen, returned and said, "Well, we really don't have much of anything." They discussed going to a restaurant, but apparently that wasn't an option. After a time, she appeared with three plates, on which were three hamburgers. Everyone tasted them, and Gig said,

"Mmmmmm, don't think much of these."

"What?" Lizzie wondered. "I don't think much of these," Gig repeated.

As Douglas recalled, the meat patties were "absolutely filthy." Lizzie had made them out of dog food!

Out of such shocking hijinks as this their romance increased and became serious. According to Douglas and his wife Sue, it was Lizzie who pushed to be married, but Gig was uncertain. Sharing the secret of his 1938 vasectomy with her was not easy. His wife Sheila had resigned to the information calmly and rarely made reference to it. With his wife Sophie, it wasn't an issue at all, since she had undergone a hysterectomy before they married. Elaine Stritch had assured him they would be together even it was not possible for him to father children. But with Lizzie, Young felt old. He became increasingly concerned about his masculinity which, as he viewed it, was diminished by the vasectomy. But he finally told her the truth, and she didn't care. They would breed dogs, she said. Sue Douglas in *Final Gig*:

> She went into the marriage with her eyes wide open. She was so nuts about him. I don't think anything would have made any difference. I think he was a little scared of the marriage, but not Liz. She adored animals and in some way believed they would take the place of children, which, of course, is ridiculous thinking.

According to an early studio bio, Lizzie and Gig did at least own a collie, which they named *Willie Grogan*, in honor of the principle character he played in 1962 Elvis Presley feature film *Kid Galahad*. They also had a goat named *Mary Chess*, which happened to be a trade name for a then-line of perfumes. At the time, they lived in Sunset Plaza, a fashionable mountain-side residential area above Sunset Strip, where Lizzie maintained her green thumb . . . for mint, which she grew in her backyard.

The two-page bio also went on to explain her principal hobby was painting. She had sold watercolor works of art and was working on an assignment to illustrate a children's book. She was a collector of antiques and had "no particular liking for modern art, although she respects it."

As Eells explained in *Final Gig*, a band of "loosely connected couples" from the entertainment industry surrounded Lizzie and Young in Manhattan, including the Dunnes, Howard and Lou Erskine, Betsy Von Furstenberg and Guy Vincent, and Bill and Fay Harbach.

Husband and wife actors William Daniels and Bonnie Bartlett were also part of that group. Married for over fifty years, Bartlett and Daniels had known Lizzie and Gig from their days in New York when they performed in guest-star roles on *Robert Montgomery Presents*. Although Lizzie made frequent appearances on her father's show, none were with Daniels and Bartlett. The two would not work with her until years later. Daniels, best known to classic TV fans for his regular stints on *St. Elsewhere* (NBC, 1982–1988) and *Boy Meets World* (ABC, 1993–2000), as well as being the voice of *K.I.T.T.* on the cult car show, *Knight Rider* (NBC, 1982–1986), appeared with Lizzie in her 1974 NBC TV-movie, *A Case of Rape*. Bartlett, a heralded actress in her own right with countless TV and film appearances under her belt, worked with Elizabeth in her 1975 TV-movie for ABC, *The Legend of Lizzie Borden*. "So Bill and I just happened to be in two of her biggest hits," Bartlett says.

Decades before, Elizabeth and Gig visited Daniels and Bartlett in their New York apartment:

"Gig was a rather elegant and charming gentleman," Bartlett recalls. "But he drank too much. *Everybody* drank too much. They were both drinking a lot, but I never saw her drunk, while he was pretty hopeless. She was good to get away from him."

Actor/author J. Anthony Russo had chronicled in his book, *Creativity or Madness*, that Dean Martin believed Lizzie to be intoxicated on the set of *Who's Been Sleeping in My Bed?*, and now Bartlett remembers Lizzie once revealing that her mother "drank a lot." "She had a nice way of saying it, so it wasn't coarse," Bartlett explains, "but she said, 'I told Mother I was going to cut her off at the bar.' And I believe at this point, her mother lived with her. She adored her mother."

Upon hearing this, Sally Kemp, has an epiphany: "My mother, I realize now, like Elizabeth's, was an alcoholic."

But while studies have shown that alcoholism is both a disease and hereditary, Sally questions if Lizzie had a substance abuse problem:

Elizabeth and I usually sat next to each other in classes at the Academy and always had lunch together. I *never* smelled alcohol on her and would have known instantly. I was very wary and conscious of it. I wasn't aware of her drinking much until she was trying to extricate Gig from Elaine Stritch. She had a tremendous crush on him and there was a big age difference between them . . . I don't know how many years . . . and [her father] was against the match. I saw less of her by then since I was pursuing my own life. I saw them occasionally once they were married and they seemed happy. Gig was very charming until he'd had too much, then he'd kind of blur. I think Elizabeth *did* try to keep up with him, partly to lessen the age difference. I think she was far more intelligent than he was. He had a suave, sleek surface, but I've no idea what was beneath it, or even if there was a beneath it. If she was unhappy or becoming unhappy, she never shared it and once they moved to L.A. all contact ceased and I know nothing of hers or their life together. When I heard the horror story of Gig's death, I was deeply grateful she was well out of it. I don't know about her life from then on except that she and Bill Asher had three children, which must have made her very happy . . . she always had a lovely childlike ability to create fun. I heard rumors of [her] drinking with [Bob] Foxworth, but they were only rumors and there are always rumors about celebrities. I knew as an actress myself that she couldn't keep up her work schedule, raise three children, and look beautiful if she was incapacitated by booze. I wish our lives hadn't gone apart, that's all I can say.

Biographer George Eells in *Final Gig*:

If the Young-Stritch affair played itself out as a bittersweet Neil Simon, then Gig and Liz's mad marriage radiated Noel Coward savoir faire: communal dashes to the martini fountain after screenings, croquet matches and other games. To those who knew them both, it seemed that Liz was intent on matching Gig's capacity for drink, as though it were some kind of contest.

Agent Martin Baum represented both Lizzie and Gig while they were together. Baum to Euell in *Final Gig*:

As a couple, Gig and Liz were a delight. There was a childlike innocence about him that was totally refreshing. There was little guile, no jealousy or resentment of others who were doing well. A dear person. Of course, that was the surface Gig. I noticed when we were out on an evening socially, he drank excessively by my standards, and Liz was drinking right along with him. But they seemed happy.

In late summer of 2011, Lizzie's good friend Cliff Robertson described her relationship with Gig as "very warm and passionate," adding:

They seemed to get along very well. He was a charming fellow and a good actor. I would see them out on the West Coast for a while, when she was spending most of her time out there. But then she and Gig split up and she called me in New York, where I was still living at the time. She'd call every once and a while [to] say, "Are you coming to town?" And I'd tell her when and we'd often meet at a restaurant to catch up. She would tell me about her latest exploits and what not. But I never had any indication of whether or not there was trouble in the marriage. And when they did split I was sorry to hear that. I knew that they had been very happy, though clearly not for a long period of time.

Loyal until the end, Robertson believed Lizzie handled every circumstance throughout her life with "grace and charm. She showed a lot of spunk for a girl who was brought up with creature comforts." Once more, it was Lizzie's unaffected demeanor that marked her appeal, specifically with Gig. "That was probably one of the main things that he saw in her," Robertson surmised. "That she was so well-grounded."

Montgomery archivist Thomas McCartney:

Her background helped to ground her, especially in that industry, which allowed her to survive where as so many other's within it perished, literally. Her inner strength allowed her to continue to focus on her work when all around her crashed and burned in her personal life, this again came from being fundamentally strong, stable, and secure within herself and who she was as a human being. She was able to float with ease from one to any other social interaction, no matter if it was a lunch-bucket crew member or someone with high social standing to the point of royalty itself. She mainly drank with Gig to be able to be close to him on an emotional level so he would not shut her out, this being to keep loneliness at bay and to make Gig emotionally available, otherwise he shut down emotionally and shut her out. All addicts like company and pressure those around them to take part in their addiction. In this case, the pressure to do so came from Liz herself to retain access to Gig, so he would take her along on his magic carpet rides rather than leave her behind. Drinking like they did, as with Liz's mother, was the norm then; in those days, no one would bat an eye at someone who drank a half a dozen hard drinks a day. Point being that the way Liz and her mother drank then was not noticeable. That's what people did and society almost expected [it] of one. It was the norm. Now, we know better, but then they did not, nor would they be aware that their actions would be taken with anything more than a shrug of the shoulders.

McCartney makes a valid observation: In the 1950s, 1960s, and 1970s, on-screen and off, daily alcohol consumption was considered socially acceptable and *cool*, as was smoking. But the devastating health ravages of such vices were not yet fully calculated.

As with many dramas and sitcoms in the 1960s, specifically, *Bewitched*, characters were frequently seen drinking or inebriated. Certainly, whenever *Darrin* felt overwhelmed by his wife's witchcraft, he made himself a *double* or a *triple*, once even asking *Sam* to fix him a *quadruple* (in the fifth season episode, "I Don't Want to Be a Toad; I Want to Be a Butterfly," where he says, "Make it a quadruple and finish the story after I pass out"). In fact, actor Dick Wilson, better known as *Mr. Wilson* from the famous Charmin bath tissue commercials, was considered nearly a semi-regular on *Bewitched* due to his more than fifteen appearances as a drunkard, either at *Darrin's* favorite bar, trying to pick up *Samantha* outside a restaurant (while *Darrin* fetched the car in "If They Never Met"), or as a neighborhood bum who thought *Endora's* down-sized version of *Darrin* was a leprechaun (in "*Samantha's* Wedding Present").

Consistent drinking also took place on 1960s shows like *That Girl*, *I Dream of Jeannie*, even on the daytime gothic soap, *Dark Shadows* (which Johnny Depp and director Tim Burton recently resurrected for the big screen), where a glass of sherry was the gothic drink of choice. Acting and song legend Dean Martin, Elizabeth's co-star in the 1963 film, *Who's Been Sleeping in My Bed?*, had a reputation as a chronic drinker and he brought that role to the party every week on his very successful TV variety hour, *The Dean Martin Show*. Additionally, one of the *Martin* program regulars was comedian Foster Brooks who, like Dick Wilson on *Bewitched*, became famous for making light of the drinking-man persona.

Later into the 1970s, drinking appeared regularly on sitcoms like *The Paul Lynde Show*, which just so happened to star a former *Bewitched* regular, which was produced by *Bewitched's* Bill Asher, who also just so happened to be Elizabeth's third husband. Lynde's anxiety-ridden attorney *Paul Simms* would frequently ask his wife *Martha* (played by Elizabeth Allen, but not Lizzie's mother) to fix his regular dose of martini.

However, the devastating health ravages of weekly if not daily inebriation were not fully explained because the statistics just weren't there at the time. It was an ignorant era and ignorance was bliss, or maybe just blind, even after 1964, when *Smoking and Health: Report of the Advisory Committee to the Surgeon General of the United States* was published. Unfortunately, before the 1970s, tobacco advertising was legal in the United States and most of Europe. In America in the 1950s and 1960s, cigarette brands frequently sponsored TV shows, from all-family fare such as *The Dick Van Dyke Show*, *I Love Lucy*, and *The Beverly Hillbillies*, to the celebrity-laden game shows *To Tell the Truth* and *I've Got a Secret*.

Flash forward to two interviews in the early 1990s, and Lizzie seemed to have made a startling realization of her own. Two times she was asked if she ever got tired of people asking her to do the twitch, and with both replies, she mentioned the topic of wine. In 1991, when she sat down with Ronald Haver for their *Here Comes Mr. Jordan* laserdisc conversation, she mused, "Well, it depends on how many people I ran into," then adding she'd be unable to nose-wriggle if she had a drink. "If I wanted to get sloshed on the (*Bewitched*) set," she continued with a laugh, "I would have never been able to [do the] twitch. So, I can't do it if I'm tired or if I've had a glass of wine. Isn't that funny?"

In 1992, during her chat with John Tesh for *One on One*, she laughed, and said:

> If I'm tired, if I've had one glass of wine, or if I'm inclined to get the giggles, there is no way to do it. Now, you can figure out which one is my excuse now. Obviously, I haven't had a glass of wine, I'm not tired—yet— and I mean, sitting here (trying to do it, when asked, on camera, and not in character as *Samantha*) . . . it's very hard.

☆

According to a variety of sources including the March 1962 issue of *Photo-play Magazine*, Thomas McCartney, and www.elvispresleynews.com, music superstar Elvis Presley, who certainly had his own issues with substance abuse, may have undermined the foundation of Lizzie's relationship with Gig Young. It appears that a tense situation developed on the set of *Kid Galahad*, the 1962 motion picture starring Presley, and a purportedly very agitated Young. Although *Kid* is considered some of Presley's best work on screen (1956's *Love Me Tender* and 1958's *King Creole* notwithstanding), it's startling to conceive how it ever completed filming considering Gig's antics.

Apparently, Lizzie was a daily visitor to the *Kid* set and while Gig was busy filming, she'd chat up a "storm" with Elvis, so much so that one time Gig became enraged and caused a scene. Green with "Elvis envy," he nearly physically attacked Young, while Lizzie was crushed at Gig's accusation and burst into tears. At which point Elvis reached out to comfort her, which only further infuriated Gig. The two men exchanged threats and then Elvis called Gig "an asshole" and ordered him to "grow up!"

At some point, Elvis had his fill of the daily Liz/Gig quarrels and he was not at all pleased with Young's unprofessional behavior. He was getting so fed up with Young, that he felt like it wasn't worth completing the movie. But he did. He would often hear Young verbally abuse Lizzie. But he didn't intercede. He just hoped that one day she would "come to her senses." Ultimately, he was relieved that the movie was over because as he saw it, "I never want to work with Gig Young again."

But such was not the case with Lizzie, whom Elvis attempted to cast in at least one of his films approximately one year after meeting her on the *Kid* set. But studio big-wigs kept passing on pairing the two, specifically in 1961's *Blue Hawaii*, in which Joan Blackman was cast instead, and which Lizzie later described as one of her favorite Elvis films.

There was also some talk that hip-twisting Elvis was indeed romantically interested in the future nose-twitching Lizzie. He was allegedly envious of Young's marriage to Lizzie. "If she was single," he was to have stated, "I would certainly pursue her."

When asked how she felt about Presley, Lizzie replied at the time:

I think Elvis is very attractive and yes, if I was single I would date him. Even though he isn't my type, I would have given him a chance and who knows what it could have led to? Let's face it, what girl wouldn't want to date Elvis? I do want to work with Elvis one day, if the studios would let me. But it doesn't seem likely at this present moment.

Three weeks after *Kid Galahad* completed filming Gig was still adamant that Lizzie had slept with Elvis and continued to argue with her about the alleged antics. At one point, the disagreements became so intense, Gig apparently left town for a few days to see a friend named Helena, a development he sardonically implied would allow Lizzie to spend time with her new "lover!" Now lonely and neglected, with tears turned to anger, Lizzie allegedly hurried to Elvis' side, stopping short of having the affair that would have manifested Gig's worst nightmare.

Around the same time, rumor had it that Lizzie found Gig in their bed with some random nimble naked young blonde. Upon viewing said scene, Lizzie apparently instructed the woman to dress and leave, and in the process tossed Gig out on his ear—without any nose-twitching assistance on her part. That would come later, when she wed herself to *Bewitched* and married Bill Asher, which was another relationship for which Elvis reportedly had a measure of envy. While Asher claimed in 2003, for an interview with Terry and Tiffany DuFoe (today of www.cultradioagogo.com), that such was not the case, because he "didn't know Elvis," he did have one issue with him. Apparently, Elvis was supposed to have starred in one of Bill's films. "It was a pretty good story," Asher recalled, "and he had agreed to do it." The motion picture would have apparently given the singing sensation the opportunity to play a "heavy," which was very different from the more carefree persona he created in most of his films. But right before he was scheduled to work on the movie, Elvis made his famous television debut on *The Ed Sullivan Show.* Consequently, his representatives advised against their client portraying the darker role, and the young superstar pulled out of the film.

Gig Young was four years older than Vernon Presley, Elvis' father, not to mention two decades older than Lizzie. As Sally Kemp has said, she believes her friend was attracted to Gig mostly as a father figure and recalls further how Robert Montgomery was none too pleased with his daughter's decision to marry the senior actor:

> I think he was very angry that she married Gig. He wasn't that much younger than Bob, who probably saw what Elizabeth couldn't see. And

what no one else really saw. It was a challenge to look past Gig's great charm. But he must of have hurt her, because she left him.

Indeed, according to various sources when Robert learned of Lizzie's intention to wed Gig, he became incensed. Their relationship somewhat mercurial, he was ardently against her marrying someone he once called "almost as old and not one quarter as successful as I am."

As time passed Robert's disdain for Gig did not subside, and Lizzie and her new love seemed to relish this fact, devising little schemes that incensed her father. As Dominick Dunne's wife Lenny explained in *Final Gig*, during one particular visit to Los Angeles, Robert invited the Youngs and the Dunnes to dinner. It was not the most tranquil of evenings, because neither Robert nor Gig was able to be cordial—sincerely or otherwise. "But after we finished dining," Lenny relayed, "Nick and I invited everyone back to our house for a drink. They came, some more eagerly than others."

But Lizzie had an early call the next morning for a TV show and, after a respectably lengthy visit with the Dunnes, she and Gig begged their good-byes, though not before approaching and kissing her father with a simple, "Goodnight, Daddy Bob." Mimicking the move, Gig swiftly leaned toward his father-in-law, smacked him right on the lips, and echoed Lizzie's words, "*Goodnight, Daddy Bob!*"

"Well," recalled Lenny Dunne, "I thought Robert Montgomery was going to have a stroke."

The cards may have held a similar fate for Gig. According to Eell's biography, he suffered from skin cancer and was Valium-dependent. His career failing, he was paranoid about the future and, as Lizzie's friends Bonnie Bartlett and Sally Kemp had assumed, he was an alcoholic.

Although Sally did not know Young "that well at all," it was clear to her that he did have a "huge drinking problem. And that was always a mystery to me how that horrible, horrible thing happened with him later. I was never around him that much and I never knew him that well. So I never saw that side of him. But anyone who drinks like that has to have major demons."

The "horrible, horrible thing" to which she refers here and to which she previously referred as the "horror story of Gig's death" was the murder/ suicide that involved him and his fifth wife, a thirty-one-year-old German woman named Kim Schmidt. Schmidt was hired as the script girl on Gig's final movie, *The Game of Death*, which was released in 1978. On September 27 of that year, the two were married. Three weeks later on October 19, 1978, in the Manhattan apartment they shared, Gig shot Schmidt in the head, killing her instantly. He then shot himself. The police theorized that it was a suicide pact, but were baffled by the additional three revolvers and 350 rounds of ammunition found in the apartment. After the investigation the police stated Gig had definitely acted on the spur of the moment and his actions were not planned.

Clearly, Elizabeth's marriage to Gig was troubling and trouble-making, but it could have ended much worse than it did. Because of Gig's vasectomy, the union did not produce any children. Finally and fortunately, and after repeatedly denying she was even estranged from Gig, Lizzie confessed in April of 1963 to what would become her second "quickie" divorce in Nevada. She met Gig in 1956 while she was filming *The Court-Martial of Billy Mitchell* and she left him while working with Dean Martin in *Who's Been Sleeping in My Bed?*

Nine months after his divorce from Lizzie, Gig married real estate agent Elaine Whitman who was pregnant with his first child, a daughter, Jennifer, who was born in 1964—the year *Bewitched* debuted. While Lizzie was making new magic as *Samantha* (and a baby of her own with William Asher, namely William Asher, Jr.), Gig proclaimed his first child's birth a "miracle," validating his reverse surgery as a success.

Although the Gig was up, the joy didn't stick. On November 23, 1966, Whitman filed for divorce. Frequent court battles over child support led him to publicly deny Jennifer was his daughter, claiming he was duped into his marriage to Whitman, but because he had claimed Jennifer as his own in the original divorce papers, he had no legal recourse in the matter.

According to George Eell's book, when Lizzie and Gig were still married, she envisioned having children who would have inherited his large gray eyes and dark wavy hair. When the issue of his paternity suit later became Hollywood news, she was purported to have then said to a friend: "(Jennifer's) not Gig's child. Believe me, if Gig didn't get me pregnant, he didn't get anyone pregnant."

In *The Way We Lived Then*, Dominick Dunne said Lizzie and Gig were "wildly happy" for a long while. Dating back to his days as script supervisor for *Robert Montgomery Presents* and shortly beyond, he and his wife Lenny were friends with the Youngs and then "something happened." But the Dunnes hadn't a clue as to what that was, as neither Lizzie nor Gig were the type to disclose private information. Apparently, she left their house in one direction and he went the opposite way, "furious with each other," Dominick said, and that was that.

Conversely, Lizzie dearly loved her fourth and final husband Robert Foxworth who once had his own take on her marriage to Young. As he explained on A&E's *Biography* in 1999, her relationship with Young was unpleasant and "some domestic violence" was involved. Fortunately, as Foxworth pointed out, Lizzie was intelligent and strong-willed enough to break away from Young's grip.

According to George Eells in *Final Gig*, Lizzie's marriage to Young was not the perfect union that was sometimes portrayed in the press. "The first hint that trouble was brewing came early on, back in the golden days in New York." Helena Sterling, Gig's old friend from the Louis Shurr West Coast office, had moved to Manhattan at the Youngs' request and found herself spending a great deal of time with Elizabeth, whom she at first considered as Eells put it, "scatterbrained." "Then," Sterling told Eells, "I realized she was lonely." Writer Lily Brandy offered this conclusion in the article, "I Hope This Spell Lasts," published October 1966, in *Inside Movie* magazine:

> Gig Young . . . gave Liz something of an inferiority complex. His career was riding high during their marriage . . . and he was much better known than she was. She tried to subordinate her own ego and ambitions to his. It didn't work. She was truly her father's daughter. The acting bug hit her hard and despite the setbacks, the false alarms, the disappointments, she determined to persist. Significantly, her star really began to rise after her divorce from Gig.

Nine

~

Two Plus Hundreds

"Precrassny."

—The Russian word for *pretty*, as spoken by Elizabeth as *The
Woman*, who has the only line of dialogue in *The Twilight Zone*
episode, "Two," airing September 15, 1961

Between Lizzie's "Top Secret" premiere segment of *Robert Montgomery Presents* (December 3, 1951) and her initial twitch in *Bewitched* (debuting September 17, 1964), she made over 200 diverse guest-star TV appearances.
Some of those shows include: *Boris Karloff's Thriller* (NBC, 1960–1962),
Alfred Hitchcock Presents (NBC, 1958, "Man with a Problem"), *Johnny Staccato* (ABC/NBC, 1959/1960, "Tempted"), *One Step Beyond* (1960, "The
Death Waltz"), *Wagon Train* (1959, "The Vittorio Botticelli Story"), *Rawhide* (1963, "Incident at El Crucero"), and *77 Sunset Strip* (1963, "White
Lie").

She also delivered stand-out performances in ABC's *The Untouchables*
(for "The Rusty Heller Story" episode that aired October 13, 1960, for
which she received her first Emmy nomination in 1961); the series premiere
of NBC's *Theatre '62* edition of "The Spiral Staircase," which aired October
4, 1961 (in which she starred as a mute, alongside a very vocal character
played by her then-husband Gig Young); *The Twilight Zone* episode two,
which CBS broadcast September 15, 1961 (and in which she delivered yet
another muted performance, this time with Charles Bronson, who also did

not speak a word of dialogue); and for the "Mr. Lucifer" segment of *Alcoa Premiere* that aired on ABC, November 1, 1962 (when she literally "danced with the devil," played by none other than famed hoofer Fred Astaire, who also hosted the series).

Produced by Everett Freeman, "Mr. Lucifer" was written by Alfred Bester and directed by Alan Crosland, Jr. who would years later helm episodes of *The Six Million Dollar Man*, *The Bionic Woman*, and *Wonder Woman*; among others. Not only is the entire episode classified as a fantasy comedy, which was a rare segment for any anthology series of the day, but it is laden with *Bewitched*-like special effects with items and props "popping in and out"; "Mr. Lucifer" even snaps his fingers and stops time as did *Samantha* many times on *Bewitched*.

As to the actual premise of the episode, and Lizzie's character, she played *Iris Haggerty*, the devil's assistant (a.k.a. "a legitimate moon goddess"). Apparently, *Iris* did her thesis (wherever that was) on moon goddesses: "I always thought it was rather unfair when the Christians turned her into a demon. But in mythology that's the way the banana splits."

Upon review of "Mr. Lucifer," it immediately becomes clear just how much Lizzie reveled in the performance, as she delivered what could be described as an early, energetic pre-witched take on *Serena*, *Samantha's* look-a-like cousin on *Bewitched*. *Iris* is hot, snippy, loose, fun-loving, free-spirited, and devious. We see her as platinum blond, a raven-haired beauty in elegant evening wear, and in a bikini. At one point, she even says it straight out, ". . . I'm on the loose, and I just may take off."

Other dialogue is as revealing, and somewhat more representative of Lizzie's real life. At one point, she begins a telling conversation with Astaire's *Lucifer*: "All I can say is they don't make men like they used to. When I was a moon goddess . . ."

But he interrupts her: "When they made *you* they broke the mold."

Another of *Iris's* lines which slightly bespoke Lizzie's life: "I always thought that every woman should marry, and no man"; "When you're independent it costs you."

But probably the most interesting sequence of "Mr. Lucifer" is when Lizzie as *Iris* and Astaire as the *Devil* are literally monitoring on screen the life of the mild-mannered *Tom Logan* (Frank Aletter), who they so very much want to bring over to the dark side. Here, the audience is introduced

132

to *Jenny Logan*, Tom's wife, on whom *Iris* and *Lucifer* set their sights to use as a pawn in his seduction.

When *Mr. Lucifer* wonders how to first seduce *Jenny, Iris* suggests summoning *Don Juan, Casanova,* and *Ben Casey,* the latter of which was a popular TV doctor of the time played by Vince Edwards. But *Lucifer* rejects the idea:

"You don't corrupt the young American girl with matinee idols."

"Oh," *Iris* replies, "you don't?" (a possible wink to Robert Montgomery).

What proves more provocative about this sequence is that the role of *Jenny* is played by none other than actress Joyce Bulifant who, years later would not only go on to star as Gavin MacLeod's spouse on *The Mary Tyler Moore Show* (CBS, 1970–1977), but would become William Asher's wife in real life after his divorce from Lizzie. As *Lucifer* and *Iris* discuss Bulifant's character, Iris looks none too pleased, if not downright jealous, and says of *Jenny*: "She's the kind of wife women hate. She designs and makes her own clothes, speaks three languages, she's a fine cook, a charming hostess; and she's writing a novel in her spare time."

An additional noteworthy, if not lengthy, appearances from this early era of Lizzie's career was when she performed in the "Patterns" segment of another live anthology series, NBC's *Kraft Theatre* (1947–1958). "Patterns" aired January 12, 1955, and was written by the prolific Rod Serling and directed with great skill by Fielder Cook. The episode, which was remade as a theatrical feature film the following year, proved so popular, it was first re-performed live on TV February 9, 1955, a rare development for the small screen at the time. Usually, live segments were broadcast only once; even recorded editions of the same episode never aired twice. But such was not the case with "Patterns," which also just so happened to be the five hundredth episode of *Kraft Theatre*.

Here, Lizzie played the small role of a secretary named *Ann Evans*, alongside a cast that included a young Richard Kiley (*St. Elsewhere*), Ed Begley (father to Ed Begley, Jr., also from *St. Elsewhere*), Everett Sloane, Joanna Roos, Jack Starter, Victoria Ward, June Dayton, Jack Livesy, and others.

Fred Staples (Kiley) is the newest executive in a large firm who befriends *Andy Sloan* (Begley). Staples is good at what he does, and the company's head *Walter Ramsay* (Sloane) is content with his performance on the job. But the situation soon becomes stressful, delicate, and then ultimately tragic, when *Ramsey* tells *Fred* he's been hired to replace *Andy*, who has dedicated his life to the company, at the expense of his family.

One of Lizzie's opening lines (to a fellow secretary) sets the stage for the entire premise. Even though we never hear too much from her again, she says: "No sign of the new genius, I suppose?"

Her most memorable line in the episode: "Wow . . . you never know when you're going to hit a nerve"; which, off camera, proved telling of her sometimes too frank conversations with her father—or anyone else who was in the room.

Other than that, she said little else to say or do in "Patterns," and although it was a small part, she made it her own. She was helped along, of course, by Cook's clearly defined direction and the densely written script by Serling, with whom Lizzie would work a short time later on her now famous "Two" episode of *The Twilight Zone*.

Arguably her most prominent and best known pre-*Samantha* TV spot, "Two" debuted on CBS September 15, 1961, and co-starred a young and pre-superstar Charles Bronzon as the only other cast member. Author Marc Scott Zicree summarized the episode in his excellent book *The Twilight Zone Companion* (Silman-James Press, 1992):

While searching for food, a young woman wearing the tattered uniform of the invading army encounters an enemy soldier—one intent on declaring peace. Initially, she is violently distrustful of him—a situation which only intensifies when they remove two working rifles from a pair of skeletons. Later, though, when she admires a dress in a store window, he removes it and gives it to her. She goes into a recruiting office to slip it on. Unfortunately, the propaganda posters within rekindle the old hatreds; she rushes out and fires off several rounds at him. The next day, the man returns, dressed in ill-fitting civilian clothes. To his surprise, the woman is wearing the dress. Finally having put aside the war, she joins him and the two of them set off, side by side.

As Zicree appraised, "Two" was penned and directed by the multitalented Montgomery Pittman (1920–1964). Pittman's first assignment in the *Zone* was helming "Will the Real Martian Please Stand Up?" But it was "Two" that demonstrated the full extent of his abilities. Here, he presented an optimistic story set in a substantially dark, post–World War III desolated town inhabited only by the dead, with the exception of two enemy soldiers. Zicree explains how fairly obvious it becomes that Bronson signifies an American soldier and Lizzie a Russian. "In fact," he writes, "her single line is 'precrassny'—Russian for 'pretty.' This is a gritty and realistic story of survival, told with a minimum of dialogue yet with the emphasis always on characterization."

The "Two" characters "go against the stereotype," Zicree goes on to say. It is Bronson's character, "broad and muscular, with a face like an eroded cliff, who is the pacifist." On the other hand, he labels Lizzie's character as "one who is suspicious and quick to violent action. Those who remember her from *Bewitched* might be shocked by her appearance here: long brown hair, smudged face, pretty in a peasant-like way, but not at all the glamour girl."

Pittman's widow Murita also comments in the book, saying Lizzie "was so dedicated to her art. Most girls want to look really pretty for the camera. Monty had to fight her, really, because she wanted to make her eyes really black. She got too much makeup on; she was making herself too haggard."

Maybe so, but her dedication to the role was more than evident. "It was not an easy part by any means," Zicree concludes.

And Lizzie embraced the challenge. "You find yourself reacting to things you never reacted to before," she said at the time. "You find it difficult not to exaggerate every look, every action. You think nobody will notice you unless you ham it up. You have to underplay every scene in a play of this type. But I must say I never enjoyed doing a show as much as I did 'Two.'"

According to *The Twilight Zone: Unlocking the Door to a Television Classic* by Martin Grams, Jr. (OTR Publishing, 2008), Lizzie thought making "Two" was "creepy. I couldn't help thinking what it would be like if I went around the corner and there actually wasn't anyone there—nothing but rubble, grass growing in the streets, the debris of a dead human race."

On September 18, 1961 *The Hollywood Reporter* offered its review of "Two":

> Some confusion at CBS as to whether Friday's *Twilight Zone* was the season's debut, the confusion caused by a sponsor change next week, methinks. . . . But this was the first new one of the season, starring only Charles Bronson and Elizabeth Montgomery in "Two," a tale of the only two survivors in an atomic war—Bronson, essaying one of us, and Liz, mute but effective as an enemy soldier . . . Seg was interesting but not as powerful as other short-cast *Zones*, particularly the one where Robert Cummings carried the show solo ("King Nine Will Not Return," 9-30-60).

As Grams pointed out in his *Zone* guide, *Variety*, the other industry trade, had a policy of reviewing all season premieres of television programs and was also confused. The magazine ended up reviewing next week's episode instead of this one.

Elizabeth made two appearances on yet another anthology series, this one titled, *Appointment with Danger*, which aired for only one season on CBS, from 1955–1956. Filmed live each week, *Danger* gave viewers a glimpse of drama and adventure from around the world and from the distant and not-so-distant past. Subjects of the weekly plays included the American wars, as well as conflicts of far-away countries, and were performed by a number of well-known stars of the time.

The episodes in which Lizzie starred were called "All Through the Night" (2-5-56) and "Relative Stranger" (11-20-55). In "Night," she performed with her friend John Cassavetes (an alumni of the New York Academy of Dramatic Arts) and actress Tina Louise (who would later play movie star *Ginger* on *Gilligan's Island*).

"Relative Stranger," however, stands out. Written by Irving Werstein and directed by Paul Stanley, the episode also starred William Windom, who would later take home an Emmy for his lead in the ground-breaking if short-lived sitcom, *My World and Welcome to It* (NBC, 1969–1970). He also appeared as *Commodore Matt Decker*, commander of the doomed USS *Constellation* in the famous 1968 *Star Trek* episode "The Doomsday

Machine," and in the 1980s–1990s portrayed the curmudgeonly *Dr. Seth Hazlitt* opposite Angela Lansbury's mystery-writing/solving *Jessica Fletcher* on CBS' *Murder, She Wrote.*

But for the moment, he was married to Lizzie, and found himself involved in the mysterious escapades of "Relative Stranger":

> After her father dies and leaves an inheritance, *Helen* (Lizzie), a young married American married woman, visits relatives in Copenhagen who prove to be more than unfriendly, if not downright corrupt and violent. Fortunately, her husband *Dan* (Windom) arrives at a dire moment, and just in the nick of time.

The anthology's main title (*Appointment with Danger*) was melodramatic, but it must have appealed to Lizzie's adventurous side, while the specific episode title ("Relative Stranger") was an ominous description of how Lizzie at times perceived Robert Montgomery in her youth (as she once admitted not knowing he was an actor until learning so from a fellow Westlake classmate).

The paternal dialogue in "Relative" was clear as a bell. *Helen* tells *Dan* things like: "I'm kind of nervous about meeting Dad's cousins for the first time. I hope they like me"; "I've never had a large family. There's just mother and dad and me"; and "I don't mind talking about Father. Of course it has been rather lonely without him" (which may have specifically echoed Lizzie's feelings as a child when her father spent months making movies abroad or serving in the Air Force).

Upon arrival in her relative's homeland, *Helen* loses a favorite necklace, explaining: "My grandmother gave it to me," mirroring the relationship Lizzie had with her grandmother Becca who gifted her with many things (like a cherished broach that Lizzie wore throughout her life), but most importantly the gift of understanding priorities.

In later, more violent scenes, Lizzie's *Helen* is seen tied-up with her hands behind her back, spread across a bed on her stomach. It's a scene that would be repeated, down to camera angles, in her 1992 TV-movie, *With Murder in Mind,* in which she played real-life real estate agent Gayle Wolfer who was assaulted and traumatized by a client.

But *Helen* in "Stranger" was the first of many victimized characters Lizzie played before Wolfer in *Mind.* Eventually, she played *Kate Wainwright* in

The Victim (1972), *Ellen Harrod* in *A Case of Rape*, and *Catherine McSweeney* in *Act of Violence* . . . . as well as *Helen Warren* in the *Theatre '62* segment, "The Spiral Staircase," in which Lizzie delivered one of her more outstanding performances from this early, pre-*Bewitched* television era.

"Staircase" debuted as part of NBC's *Theatre '62* in on October 4, 1961. In this small screen remake of the 1945 film (starring Lizzie's friend Dorothy McQuire), she plays *Helen Capel*, who, because of a childhood trauma, has not spoken a word in decades. It's an old-fashioned mystery with dark hallways, flickering candlelight, rain storms and lightning, and with it, Lizzie delivers one of her most riveting, pre-*Samantha* dramatic performances. Although the characters are different, the cinematic mood is the same when she plays the murderess *Lizzie Borden* in the 1975 TV-movie *The Legend of Lizzie Borden*. But little wonder, as both productions were directed by the talented Paul Wendkos who on "Staircase" also guides the likes of Lizzie's co-stars Lillian Gish, Edie Adams, Eddie Albert and Gig Young.

Playing a mute character is always a challenge and tour de force for any actor and Lizzie had the chance to do it twice. First, for "Two" on *The Twilight Zone* and in "Spiral." As with many of her other roles, the dialogue she heard in "Spiral" proved telling and insightful into Lizzie's life.

At one point, *Helen* is told: "Don't settle. Don't hide out." Lizzie never did the former, and infrequently performed the latter.

Elizabeth enjoyed gardening in real life. As *Helen*, she heard Eddie Albert's character tell her: "You like to make things grow, don't you?"

Lizzie had boundless energy, and yet she was one to pick and choose not only her friends but her topics of conversation. And if she didn't like what she was hearing, for whatever reason (mostly because it may have been negative), she'd switch topics (how Freudian!). That's why it proves so intriguing when Lillian Gish's character tells *Helen* on screen: "You change the subject faster than anyone I know."

Albert's character later tells *Helen*: "You're imperfect, and there's just no room in this world for imperfection."

Yet, Lizzie embraced the imperfect populace of the world. She campaigned for the downtrodden and disadvantaged.

But it's Gish that has the best "Lizzie-life" dialogue, even though she doesn't speak it to Lizzie. Rather, she says it to Gig Young's character,

Steven, whom Gish believes is a scoundrel. In the end, we find out otherwise. But before that she tells him:

"You're an insect, Steven . . . a carrier . . . a breeder of disease and
disorder. You should have stayed away."

Young, in real life, proved to have those similar traits. If only Elizabeth
had never met and married him. Fortunately, she found the courage to
divorce young and ultimately stayed away from him.

Even in these pre-witched television days, Lizzie had her choice of material,
many times receiving personal requests to work with top directors, including a young Sydney Pollack, who years later, went on to become a feature
film legend with, among other movies, romantic classics like *The Way We
Were* (1973), *Tootsie* (1982), and *Out of Africa* (1985).

As she expressed to *TV Guide* in August of 1961, she was uncertain
about one particular role Pollack had in mind for her.

> I don't know whether I want to do this script or not. It's a strange kind of
> a thing, really; Sydney Pollack's directing it. It's for *Frontier Circus* (a CBS
> series that debut the following September). But it's really incredible. I was
> telling (Pollack) today the last three things I've done have all come from
> directors. *The Untouchables* I got through Wally Grauman, and then last
> week I did a *Twilight Zone* ("Two," scheduled to open *Zone's* new season
> also on CBS in September). I'm absolutely mad (about writer and director)
> Monte Pittman. I don't know what it is all of sudden.

What it was was that she was "hot," and not only in her physical appearance. In spite of her good looks, which were a given, she had talent, and
everyone who was anyone in television wanted to work with her, including
Pollack for his episode of *Frontier Circus*, which was created by future *Star
Trek* writer Samuel A. Peeples. The series was about a one-ring circus that
traveled through the American West in the 1880s. The segment Pollack had
in mind for Lizzie, "Karina," was written by Jean Holloway, and broadcast
on November 9, 1961, and she may have decided to do this episode for
several reasons, possibly on a subconscious level:

Karina Andrews (Lizzie) becomes a fugitive after shooting *Jeff*, her abusive husband (played by Tod Andrews). A first, she hides out in a circus wagon. But owner *Col. Casey Thompson* (Chill Wills) later allows her to join his camp as the target in a knife-throwing act, just as a local lawman and his vengeful spouse are soon hot on her trail.

It's a stock and interesting entry in a series that held much potential, but it's more intriguing that Elizabeth would opt to perform in this episode about an abusive husband, while in the midst of an abusive marriage to Gig Young. In fact, Young was pictured and interviewed with her for the very same article in *TV Guide* in which she talks about this new *Frontier*. At one point during the interview, the doorbell rang; as Lizzie explained, albeit playfully, it was the "liquor store man. Mr. Young's been shopping."

Lizzie would later play out the "abused" aspect of the *Karina Andrews* character in future TV-movies like *The Victim* (1972), *A Case of Rape* (1974) and *Act of Violence* (1979), while the fugitive aspect of the *Karina* role becomes a precursor to similar plights of Lizzie's future parts in the post-witched TV-movies, *Mrs. Sundance* (1974) and *Belle Starr* (1980).

The parallels may have easily been made: Lizzie was in the midst of what ultimately turned out to be a failed marriage to Bill Asher, which was in the process of ending right around the time she agreed to star in *The Victim*. *Etta Place*, a.k.a. *Mrs. Sundance*, as well as *Belle Starr*, were "on the run," while Lizzie went into hiding with *Bewitched* director Richard Michaels upon learning of Asher's affair with actress Nancy Fox (during the eighth season of *Bewitched*).

A few years before she took the lead in *Karina*, Elizabeth had played *Millie* who was experiencing a "Marriage Crisis," in that 1959 episode of *The Loretta Young Show*, a dramatic anthology series hosted by the actress (who also appeared in various episodes). By the time of "Crisis," Lizzie had replaced one real-life marriage drama (with Fred Cammann) with another (Gig Young). What's more, also appearing with Lizzie in the "Crisis" episode of the *Loretta* show was future *Hawaii Five-O* actor Jack Lord playing her husband *Joe*, who was also her on-screen spouse in her first feature film, *The Court-Martial of Billy Mitchell* (1955). In that movie, Lord's character dies. In real life, Cammann is alive, but Lizzie leaves him, and later walks out on Gig, who later dies in a tragic murder-suicide.

However, beyond all of that dire news, Lizzie's involvement with the "Karina" episode of *Frontier Circus* further solidified her spirited interest in circus stories. One of her favorite feature films was the 1953 classic *Lili*, starring Leslie Caron (whose lead character joins the circus), and she starred in the 1981 TV-movie, *When the Circus Came to Town* (in which her character, *Mary Flynn*, a bored housewife, joins the circus).

Lizzie's most prominent pre-*Bewitched* TV performance is that of her Emmy-nominated lead as a prostitute in *The Untouchables* episode, "The Rusty Heller Story," which was directed by the aforementioned Wally Grauman, and which aired on ABC October 13, 1960. A little background on the series in general:

The Untouchables ran from 1959 to 1963 and featured Robert Stack as *Elliot Ness*. Stack went on to become the popular host of the documentary series, *Unsolved Mysteries*, (NBC/CBS, 1988–1999), while *The Untouchables* was adapted into a feature film in 1987 and then returned to television as a new syndicated weekly edition in 1991. But in 1959, its original version was considered shocking programming.

Authors Tim Brooks and Earle Marsh explain just how much so in their *Complete Directory to Prime Time Network and Cable TV Shows: 1946 to Present* (Ninth Edition, Ballantine Books, 2007):

> With the chatter of machine-gun fire and the squeal of tires on Chicago streets, *The Untouchables* brought furious controversy—and big ratings—to ABC in the early 1960s. It was perhaps the most mindlessly violent program ever seen on TV up to that time. Critics railed and public officials were incensed, but apparently many viewers enjoyed the weekly bloodbath, which sometimes included two or three violent shoot-outs per episode.

TV Guide observed that, if anything, *The Untouchables* was consistent:

> In practically every episode a gang leader winds up stitched to a brick wall and full of bullets, or face down in a parking lot (and full of bullets), or face up in a gutter (and still full of bullets), or hung up in an ice box, or run

down in the street by a mug at the wheel of a big black Hudson touring car.

Either way, Lizzie relished in the opportunity to appear in the "Rusty Heller" segment, which also happened to feature a guest stint with future *Bewitched* regular David White. On *Bewitched*, White portrayed the conniving ad-man boss *Larry Tate*. In *Heller*, he was *Archie Grayson*, right hand man/attorney to gangster *Charles 'Pops' Felcher* (played by Harold J. Stone). Ultimately, *Rusty* used *Archie* to get to *Pops*—who was the man with the real power. When Lizzie was reminded in 1989 that *Rusty* was responsible for *Archie* losing his tongue, she said, "Well, he got his tongue cut out, and I squealed on him so he could." She also remembered one of her favorite lines as *Rusty*:

"I'd rather walk barefoot through a snakepit."

With his tongue intact in 1989, White only praised Lizzie's performance in the episode, stating very simply and to the point: "She was very good in it." A synopsis of the episode reads:

> *Rusty Heller* is a nightclub performer who envisions a better life which, in her case, means attaining a lot more money. So she sets her eyes on mobster *Charles 'Pops' Felcher*, who has ambitions of his own. With the recent arrest of Al Capone on tax evasion charges, *Pops* seeks to become the top mobster in Chicago. But when he shows little interest in *Rusty*, she settles for his attorney, *Archie Grayson*. Although *Pops* eventually comes around, *Rusty* starts to live and play more dangerously; she ups the ante, as it were, and decides she can make more money by selling the same information to both *Pops* and the Capone mob.

In his biography, *Straight Shooting* (McMillan, 1980), *Untouchables* star Robert Stack said the "Rusty Heller" story was one of his favorite segments in the series, mostly because of working with Lizzie:

> One of the best episodes was "The Rusty Heller Story." When it came time to cast the lead, the producers drew up a list of actresses as possible stars. The last name on the list was Elizabeth Montgomery. I had known Liz's father Bob Montgomery; I went shooting with him, and took him to Dad's duck lodge when I was a kid. I'd only known Elizabeth as a young

socialite. When the girls at her finishing school talked about making a debut, I'm sure they weren't thinking about the kind Liz made in her first appearance on *The Untouchables*, in the role of a tough young southern hooker. I'd learned from parts I'd lost that you must be objective in your judgment; the fact that I knew this girl and her background was no reason to disqualify her from consideration for the part. The producers didn't always ask my opinion about casting, but in this instance, I'm glad they did. Anyway, she took the part and ran away with it; she got an Emmy nomination and, I think, should have won it. Dame Judith Anderson won the award for *Medea*, which was shot in Scotland on location over a thirty-day period. Liz turned in a smashing performance in six days. It was the only time that *Ness* got emotionally involved. The episode had a touching and gentle poignancy to it.

As *TV Guide* noted at the time, this *Untouchables* segment and Lizzie's Emmy-nominated performance doubled her "acting price." She also attained a feature film contract, was inundated with TV scripts, and, after a decade of hard work, all but established Robert Montgomery as "Liz Montgomery's father." But she, then married to Gig Young, was all but surprised by the attention. As she recalled at the time, Stack had approached her while working on the show and said, "Liz, if you don't get an Emmy nomination for this, I'll be surprised." She replied:

Oh, Bob, for heaven's sake. It was the last thing I did in 1960 before Gig and I left for New York (Young appeared on Broadway for six months in *Under the Yum Yum Tree*). Then last spring Gig and I were driving back from New York and we stopped in Arizona. Gig said, 'There's a Los Angeles paper,' and I said, 'Oh, I just can't wait to see who's been nominated for all those statues.' And I looked down and saw Ingrid Bergman—Judith Anderson—and me. I knew Judith Anderson would get it. It wasn't a wish. I just knew it.

Anderson won that year for "Outstanding Single Performance by an Actress in a Leading Role" for her interpretation of *Lady Macbeth* in the Hallmark Hall of Fame production of *Macbeth*, which aired on NBC. It was Hallmark's second version of Shakespeare's classic play with a different supporting cast, but the same two leads (Anderson and Lizzie's future *Bewitched* father, Maurice Evans), and the same director (George Schaefer).

Lizzie's other fellow contender that year was Ingrid Bergman, who was nominated for her role in CBS's *Twenty-Four Hours in a Woman's Life*. Bergman's *Clare* was grandmother to *Helen Lester* (played Helena de Crespo) who was in love with a man she had known only 24 hours, a playboy who spent time in jail for passing bad checks. Although the man has promised to change, most of her straitlaced relatives are up in arms. Bergman's *Clare* says the girl is free to join the man she loves on one condition: that she listen to the story of a day in *Clare's* own life and of a man she tried to change.

Bergman's *Clare* was a character of great texture, as certainly was Anderson's *Lady Macbeth*, and both actresses were stellar veteran performers, even then. Lizzie, however, was still somewhat of a newcomer and pigeon-holed as her father's daughter. Those were two strikes that may have worked against her in the eyes of Emmy academy.

What's more, the twitch ties to *The Untouchables* were manifold if not yet realized.

The Untouchables was produced by Desilu, the powerhouse studio run by Lucille Ball and Desi Arnaz, the latter of whom gave Bill Asher his big break in TV directing for *I Love Lucy* (CBS, 1951–1957). A few years after her *Rusty Heller* stint on *Untouchables*, Lizzie, coming off of two failed marriages, fell in love with Bill on the set of *Johnny Cool* in 1963, shortly before they worked together on *Bewitched*. It was a match made in magic, as two very different but somehow similar people were brought together to form what eventually became one of the most successful Hollywood business partnerships this side of Ball and Arnaz.

Not only did Bill direct episodes of *I Love Lucy* and *Bewitched*, but there were other similarities between the two shows. The famous *Lucy* episode, "Job Switching," was remade as a *Bewitched* segment called "*Samantha's Power Failure*." Just as *Lucy* squealed, "Well!" to her husband *Ricky* on *Love* at some impending doom, so did *Samantha* to *Darrin* on *Bewitched*; *Lucy* and *Ricky* were of different cultures as were *Samantha* and *Darrin*. Lucy employed her wit and special prowess to resolve any particular situation, as did *Samantha*.

In any case, Asher was the "third man in." Freddie Cammann had long been out of Lizzie's life; Gig Young, like Cammann, was not able to live up to the qualities of the idealized man Lizzie envisioned to be her husband. Now it was up to Asher, and everyone wondered if he'd be able to pull it off.

LITTLE TWITCH: A one-year-old Elizabeth Montgomery is held by her mother Elizabeth Allen in 1934. SMP—Globe Photos

EARLY ELEGANCE:
Elizabeth at age 2 in 1935.
Supplied by SMP—Globe Photos

SHIPPING AND NEAR-MISHANDLING: Lizzie and her brother Skip were in Europe when World War II broke out in 1939, the same year their father Robert Montgomery was filming *The Earl of Chicago* in England. He joined the American Field Service, and was attached to the French Army as an ambulance driver. Her mother Elizabeth Allen went to work as a volunteer for the Red Cross. The Montgomerys had booked Lizzie and Skip on the Athenia steam ship to go back to the States. But the reservations were jumbled, and the children were given passage on the Arandora Star steam ship leaving the same day. According to *TV Star Parade* magazine in October 1956, world headlines reported the sinking of the Athenia, and there was no word from the Andara. Under censorship the liner couldn't break silence at sea. For twelve frantic days, the Montgomery parents waited for news. Finally, the cable reported Lizzie and Skip's safe arrival home to their grandmother Becca. Courtesy of Everett Collection

DASHING, DEBONAIR, AND DAUNTING: Robert Montgomery strikes an intimidating pose in this publicity photo from 1932. It was a look and a "feeling" that would impress, haunt, and taunt Lizzie long after he died in 1981. Photographed by George Hurrell, courtesy of Getty Images

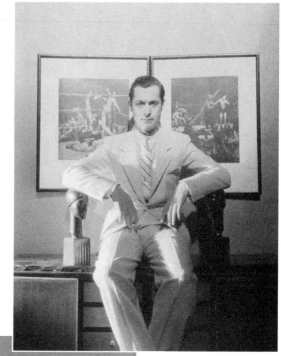

CLEAR AS A SOUTHERN BELLE: Elizabeth's natural beauty was as fresh as the country air in this, her first publicity TV photo from the early 1950s. Supplied by SMP—Globe Photos

TOP SECRET: Elizabeth and Margaret Phillips in a (behind-the) scene from the famed "Top Secret" episode of *Robert Montgomery Presents*, which aired on December 3, 1951, and which marked Elizabeth's television debut. Supplied by SMP—Globe Photos

THE EYES HAVE IT: Elizabeth, her father, and their famed matching "arched eyebrows" are ready for the cameras in this publicity still from 1953 for *Robert Montgomery Presents*. Supplied by SMP—Globe Photos

SUMMERY SMILES: Some of the Summer Stock Players of *Robert Montgomery Presents*: Elizabeth with (from left) Vaughn Taylor, Margaret Hayes, and John Newland in 1953. Supplied by SMP—Globe Photos

A SOPHISTICATED LADY AND GENTLEMAN: Elizabeth and her first husband, high-society roller Fredrick A. Cammann, on their wedding day in New York City, March 27, 1954. AP Photo—Tom Fitzsimmons

POISE AND POSTURE: Elizabeth was no "slouch." Robert Montgomery would never allow it. He always insisted she carried herself with class and distinction, all of which is evident here in this publicity shot taken for her first feature film, 1955's *The Court-Martial of Billy Mitchell*. Supplied by SMP—Globe Photos

NOT INTERESTED: Elizabeth rejected Gary Cooper's alleged romantic advances on the set of *The Court-Martial of Billy Mitchell*, 1955. Supplied by SMP—Globe Photos

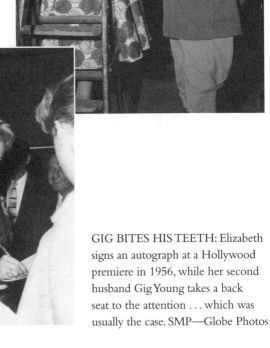

GIG BITES HIS TEETH: Elizabeth signs an autograph at a Hollywood premiere in 1956, while her second husband Gig Young takes a back seat to the attention . . . which was usually the case. SMP—Globe Photos

HER MAN PRE-TATE: Elizabeth was a romantic interest for future *Bewitched* actor David White (*Larry Tate*) whose character, attorney *Archie Grayson*, had it bad for her hooker-with-a-heart role in "The Rusty Heller Story," the 1960 episode *of The Untouchables.* For this she received her first Emmy nomination. ABC Photo Archives, courtesy of Getty Images

DANCING IN THE DARK: Elizabeth's dazzling *Iris Hecate* literally dances with the *Devil*, played by the ever-dashing Fred Astaire, in the 1962 *Alcoa Premiere* episode titled "Mr. Lucifer." As *Iris*, Lizzie delivered one of her finest and most versatile pre-*Bewitched* TV performances. The character also imbued shades (in hair color and personality) of *Serena*, *Samantha's* somewhat more mischievous cousin who Elizabeth would later play on *Bewitched*. Courtesy of Everett Collection

COOL LOOK: Lizzie displayed her "sexier side" in the 1963 big screen cult film classic *Johnny Cool*, where she met and fell in love with director Bill Asher, whom she would marry and later team up with for *Bewitched*. UA/Photofest

A VARIETY OF ROLES: Elizabeth embraces famous "Rat Pack" member Dean Martin, while real-life future best friend Carol Burnett awaits her turn in this publicity shot for their 1963 feature film *Who's Been Sleeping in My Bed?* Lizzie's blond look in this film offers shades of things to come for *Bewitched*, which debuts the following year. Meanwhile, both Martin and Burnett would go on to star in very successful TV variety shows, both in which Lizzie politely declined invitations to perform. She got her start in live theater and would return to the stage post-*Bewitched*, but she would make her only variety show appearance with a guest-host stint on *The Hollywood Palace* (with guest star Paul Lynde) in 1966. mptvimages.com

PART II

Bewitched

"This is Elizabeth Montgomery. Stay tuned
for *Bewitched*. Next! In color."

—Elizabeth Montgomery, in on-air promos for *Bewitched*

Ten

~

Lizmet

"There's one thing that makes *Samantha* easy to play . . . she's as
much in love with *Darrin* as I am with Bill (Asher)."

—Elizabeth Montgomery, *Look Magazine*, January 1965

In 1985, Bill Asher directed his final feature film, *Movers and Shakers*, written
by Charles Grodin, who also appeared on-screen in the movie, along with
Walter Matthau and many classic TV legends: Gilda Radner (*Saturday Night
Live*), Bill Macy (*Maude*), Tyne Daly (*Cagney & Lacy*), Vincent Gardenia
(*All in the Family*); with cameos provided by Steve Martin and Penny Mar-
shall (star of *Laverne & Shirley*, co-producer of 2005's *Bewitched* feature film):

> Hollywood studio president *Joe Mulholland* (Matthau) makes a slightly silly
> promise to his dying friend *Saul Gritz* (Gardenia), most of which involves
> making a movie using the title—if not the content—of a best-selling sex
> manual. *Joe* ultimately hires down-and-out writer *Herb Derman* (Grodin)
> and off-beat director *Sid Spokane* (Macy) to formulate a concept, but soon
> realizes he may have over-promised his friend *Saul*.

Twenty years before, in 1963, Asher was keeping promises to Lizzie on
the set of *Johnny Cool*, although it wasn't exactly love at first sight. In fact,
upon first meeting, they loathed one another. As Asher told *TV Circle* magazine in August 1970, "It was a case of instant hate. I was late for our appointment. She didn't like that and I didn't think it mattered whether she liked

it or not. So it was rocky going at first, until we began working. Then after a while, bam! There we were." As Asher concluded on MSNBC's *Headliners & Legends* in 2001, after he cast her, he was pretty well "gone," in other words, head over heels in love.

However, just prior to their mutual Cupid encounter, Bill and Lizzie were preoccupied with other relationships. As he expressed to *The Saturday Evening Post*, March 13, 1965, "We were both emotional basket cases when we met. Maybe Liz had never been loved, never been happy before. I don't know. I wouldn't want to speculate."

No speculation required. In 1951, Asher married actress Dani Sue Nolan, who made over thirty film and TV appearances between 1949 and 1988. (She played William Holden's secretary in his famous Asher-directed *I Love Lucy* episode, "L.A. at Last," in which *Lucy* burned her nose with a cigarette). They had two children: Liane (born 1952) and Brian (born 1954).

By 1963, they'd been separated for approximately two years, but feelings lingered. Elizabeth, meanwhile, had recently separated from Gig Young, feelings depleted.

In retrospect, Lizzie meeting Bill on the set of *Johnny Cool* turned out to be a blessing, if at first in disguise.

Compared to the previous men in her life, he was the opposite of the dashing Fred Cammann and Gig Young, not to mention her debonair father Robert Montgomery. Writer Joe Hyams explained it all that spring in *The Saturday Evening Post*. Asher was muscular, stocky, and tan, but he had bushy eyebrows and closed-cropped hair. He resembled more of a "retired prize fighter than a director." Although Hyams called Asher the "antithesis" of Lizzie's first two husbands, like Cammann, Young, and her father, he was also "a strong and dominating presence."

Also like Young, Asher was in his forties and Lizzie liked older guys, this older guy, in particular, whom she called "the greatest director I know, because he's a sensitive, compassionate person." Consequently, after smoothing the initial bump on the hot road to their *Cool* romance, they became inseparable. Lizzie liked the great outdoors. So did Bill. She loved to play tennis. So did he. In fact, it was one of the many things they had in common. They even shared the same sense of humor. They loved each other. They loved to work. They loved working together, and when they did so, it was magic. Asher, in particular, was a master of making it all work, on-screen and off. As a man, he knew how to please the ladies. As a director, he was one of the greatest conductors to orchestrate media magic in TV history. Before and after *Bewitched*, he was a heralded presence in the industry.

Born William Milton Asher on August 8, 1921, Bill is the son of Ephraim Asher, an associate producer of the classic 1931 horror films *Frankenstein* and *Dracula*, as well the original 1935 edition of *Magnificent Obsession* starring Irene Dunne and Robert Taylor (which was remade in 1954 with Jane Wyman, Rock Hudson, and *Bewitched's* Agnes Moorehead). His mother Lillian worked as a clerical assistant for MGM.

As chronicled in *Palm Springs Life* magazine December 1999, Bill lost his father when he was just eleven years old and "the excitement of a life in the new and daring film industry" was supplanted by the bottle for a Catholic mother whose Jewish associate producer–husband had died young and left her the burden of rearing children during the Depression. At fifteen, Bill enlisted in the Army, lied about his age, and forged his mother's consent.

After four years with the Signal Corps as a photographer during World War II, he left the service, which he said probably saved his life because he was one to fight authority.

Consequently, he headed for Hollywood where he approached "some guys" his father knew for help. They slammed the door in his face. At which point, he left Tinseltown for the low-rent, basic living of the Salton Sea area east of Palm Springs. There, he began writing short stories for magazines, which he had done in the army.

In 1948, he co-directed with Richard Quine the feature film *Leather Gloves*, starring Cameron Mitchell, Virginia Grey, and a young aspiring actor named Blake Edwards. Like Asher, Edwards would later marry an actress best known for playing a supernatural woman: Julie Andrews (*Mary Poppins*). (Also like Asher, Edwards would become one of the industry's most prominent directors; *10*, *S.O.B.*, *The Pink Panther*, *Victor/Victoria*, *The Man Who Loved Women*).

In addition to feature length movies, Asher also wrote short films, five-minute reels that were utilized as interstitials in theatres for a new growing sensation called *television*. This resulted in a call from CBS officials who were familiar with his work and seeking directors for this new small screen medium, then a foreign concept for all parties concerned. But within six weeks, Asher had returned to Hollywood, where he was directing shows like *Racket Squad* (1950–1953, syndicated CBS), and *Big Town* (1950–1954, CBS/NBC). He also completed a pilot for a new TV series called *Our Miss Brooks* (1952–1956), featuring big screen star Eve Arden, recreating her hit show from radio.

On the sound stage next to *Miss Brooks* was another infant CBS show called *I Love Lucy* which was about a relatively diverse married couple. He was *Ricky Ricardo*, a Cuban bandleader played by the multifaceted Desi Arnaz; she was his wife *Lucy*, daffy-but-crafty Hollywood-obsessed American redhead embodied in the one and only Lucille Ball. Despite such combined talent the show's immediate future was in doubt. But Lucy and Desi remained calm in the midst of the storm, preserved the honesty of their *Love* and, in the process, the series became the cornerstone for an entertainment empire called *Desilu* (a company title that combined its proprietors' first names).

One of the first bricks placed to solidify that creative foundation was by a vigorous Asher who, in 1952, was hired by Arnaz to direct a few *Love* episodes. By the end of its first season, *Lucy* was a monster hit and was renewed for an additional year. Bill was asked to direct the show for $500 per episode. "In those days if you were making $200 a month, you were doing well," he told *Palm Springs Life*. "I was in my mid-twenties, unmarried, working on *Our Miss Brooks* and *I Love Lucy*, making $1000.00 a week from both shows combined. I lived like a drunken sailor! You can believe I spent the money."

But he also spent time honing his craft, in the process blazing the trail for a new medium that would change the way the world communicated. Once turned away by his dad's false friends, Bill eventually connected with the TV greats of the era: Danny Thomas on *Make Room for Daddy* (ABC/CBS, 1953–1965); *The Dinah Shore Chevy Show* (1956–1963; for which he won an Emmy); Sally Field on *Gidget* (ABC, 1965–1966; for which he directed the pilot and several episodes); producer Sidney Sheldon on *The Patty Duke Show* (ABC, 1963–1966), and countless others.

By 1963, he ventured into directing movies first for TV (*Mickey and the*

Contessa), and then features, beginning with *Johnny Cool*, in which met and cast Lizzie, who shared the lead with actor Henry Silva. The film was co-produced by Asher's friend Peter Lawford, who was married to Pat Kennedy, sister to President John F. Kennedy, and party to the famous celebrity *Rat Pack*: Frank Sinatra, Dean Martin (Lizzie's co-star from *Who's Been Sleeping in My Bed*, which filmed that same year), Joey Bishop, and Sammy Davis, Jr., who both had supporting roles in the movie (while Davis performed the title song). Adapted from the novel, *The Kingdom of Johnny Cool*, by John McPartland, the movie follows this story:

> Gangster *Salvatore Giordano* (Silva), his future fortunes and misfortunes, were planted in his youth, growing up in the hard climate of World War II Sicily defying both the government and the mafia. When he was but a boy, his mother was shot in the crossfire—and from then, his gun was his only family. (At least, that's how the English subtitles translated the Sicilian dialogue in the film's prologue.) Years after his mother is killed, an adult *Salvatore* is crowned *Johnny Cool* by an ostracized American gangster named *Johnny Colini* (Marc Lawrence)—the *first* Johnny Cool—who in turns sends his replacement to America to whack those responsible for his exile. Upon arriving in New York, the new *Mr. Cool* proceeds with *Colini's* vendetta, and begins to make the required assassinations. But complications arise after he hooks up with divorced socialite *Darian "Dare" Guiness* (Lizzie).

While hardcore *Bewitched* fans may liken her character's name to *Samantha's* "what's-his-name" mortal husband, *Dare* was also the name Elizabeth once considered giving her first daughter. But that never panned out (she ultimately decided on *Rebecca*, after her grandmother).

As to the film itself, it's the kind of violent project to which Lizzie would later cling, post-*Bewitched*, with TV-movies like *A Case of Rape* and *Act of Violence*, both in which her characters were severely beaten—as was *Dare* shortly after meeting Johnny.

In fact, when *Cool* was released, an item in the press singled Elizabeth out as possibly the "most bruised actress in pictures as a result of her co-starring role opposite Henry Silva in the electric dramatic thriller."

The item went on to explain how in one day's filming Lizzie's *Dare* was beaten in a "frighteningly realistic violent scene," which was followed by another scene in which a car door slammed on her hand upon entering the vehicle (after fleeing a pool bombing). In the next day's filming, she was then called upon to leap from a pier to a small dinghy in Los Angeles Newport Harbor, and that's when things really turned ugly. Poor Lizzie failed to clear the pier and fell forward with a shuddering thud. Consequently, she received contusions on her arms and legs, and that last scene was cut from the final print of the film.

But as the press release stated further, "true to the acting heritage of her family name, Miss Montgomery, famed Bob's daughter, showed up bright and early for the next day's filming, and the shooting of *Johnny Cool* proceeded on schedule."

Into this mix, however, Lizzie's *daring* portrayal of *Guiness* continued to fit her choice of roles that somewhat resonated with her reality. For example, upon first meeting Silva's *Cool*, *Dare* offers this telling introduction:

> I'm twenty-seven. I grew up in Scarsdale with all the advantages . . . braces, dancing school, riding lessons . . . the whole bit. I've been divorced for about a year from a boy who grew up the same way.

Beyond the inconsistent age reference in 1963 (when the film was released that year, Elizabeth was thirty years old) and the braces (she always prided herself on her uniquely chipped front tooth), it was Lizzie all over, at least until she met, married, and then divorced Fred Cammann.

The same year *Cool* was released, Asher directed his first *Beach Party* movie, which spawned *Muscle Beach Party* and *Bikini Beach*, both in 1964, and *Beach Blanket Bingo* and *How to Stuff a Wild Bikini*, both in 1965, the latter in which Lizzie made a cameo doing her then newly famed twitch.

Through it all, there was additional *Cool/Rat Pack* intermingling involving Sammy Davis, Jr., Peter Lawford, and Frank Sinatra, who was then entertainment counsel to President Kennedy's Inaugural. Not only did Lizzie meet Bill on the set of *Cool*, she was introduced to the *Pack* via Bill's friend Lawford, who was Kennedy's brother. From there, she went with Bill to Washington for JFK's Inaugural on January 20, 1961. Approximately eighteen months later, on May 19, 1962, Asher produced, directed, and supervised the President's birthday bash at which Marilyn Monroe performed her sultry ditty "Happy Birthday Mr. President." Asher recalled in *Palm Springs Life*, December 1999:

Lawford was a good guy. Marilyn was a wonderful woman. She really cared about people. She also cared about the work. All she really wanted to do was be the best actress she could be . . . Jackie Kennedy didn't like many in the Hollywood crowd but she liked me. Actually she barely tolerated anybody else.

Suffice it to say, Elizabeth and Bill's friendship with the Kennedys was solidified at the President's Inaugural—and nearly two years before the tragic political incident that would send shockwaves around the world—just as a particular magical mayhem would step in to help ease the fray.

The pilot for *Bewitched* began rehearsals on November 22, 1963—the fateful day on which President John F. Kennedy was assassinated.

The night before, Elizabeth and Bill Asher were at home, wrestling with what in perspective was a minor frustration, but one that later became a major magic snag: they had yet to conceive of a unique and identifiable gesture with which *Samantha* could manifest her magic.

Fortunately, a creative spark provided a proverbial light when, Bill, from the living room, shouted to Lizzie, "That's it!" Upon hearing her husband scream, she rushed to his side to offer comfort during what sounded like a pressing tragedy. But that was yet to come. For now, upon her arrival at his side, Bill simply asked, "What's that thing you do with your nose?"

Clueless as to what he meant, she queried in return, "What *thing*?!"

"When you become nervous, you move your nose in a certain way," Bill prodded.

"He thought I just didn't want to do it or something," she remembered in 1989, and she was still confused, and downright aggravated. "The next time I do this (thing)," she told him, "let me know."

At that moment, Lizzie became so flustered she instinctively performed what has today transmuted into one of the world's most recognizable facial tics. Bill then went on to explain what he had seen, and what she had done and, in those joyful moments, *Samantha's* nose twitch was born, igniting the eventual birth of *Bewitched*—if on the night before a catastrophic incident that would change the world.

Elizabeth remembered that fateful November day in 1963, which began like any other, if at first unique only because she was preparing to leave for her first *Bewitched* rehearsal. As the early hours passed, the events of this new atypical day expanded. As she recalled in 1989, she was brushing her hair in the bedroom and heard Bill scream from the living room. But this time, it wasn't a good thing.

"No! It can't be true!" he said.

"For some reason," she said in 1989, "I felt it had nothing to do with family. But it's as if I inherently knew what had happened. The whole thing was very strange, but to keep on working did seem to be the right thing to do."

So, that's exactly what they did. Lizzie and Bill pushed forward, and went on to the set of *Bewitched*, which filmed at the Sunset Gower Studios in Hollywood. She remembered:

> We went ahead and had the first reading of the script. It was very interesting. There wasn't one person that didn't show up. There weren't any phone calls made. It was like everyone on the set just needed to talk with each other. We needed to be there, working. It was like a little memorial service that hadn't turned yet. Everyone was there supporting each other (during) this horrendous thing.

Essentially, Lizzie, Bill, and the rest of the *Bewitched* cast and crew did what should always be done in the midst of tragedy: realize that, for the living, life must go on.

On July 24, 1964, the summer before *Bewitched* debuted, Elizabeth and Bill welcomed a 7 lb. 6 oz. baby boy they named William Allen Asher, Jr. On October 5, 1965, Elizabeth gave birth to their second child, a 7 lb. 2 oz. boy named Robert Deverell Asher. On June 17, 1969, the Asher's youngest was born: a beautiful 7 lb. 13 oz. girl they named Rebecca Elizabeth Asher.

Through it all, on the other side of the screen, *Samantha* and *Darrin's* little *Tabatha* (later changed to *Tabitha* with an "i") was born on January 13, 1965 in the episode "And Then There Were Three." *Tabitha's* brother *Adam* later materialized on October 16, 1969 in the episode, "And Something Makes Four."

In reality, Billy Asher, Jr. arrived during *Bewitched's* first season which began production in the summer of 1964—some nine months after Lizzie filmed the show's pilot in November 1963. For that initial episode, she was showing slightly, and strategic camera angles and wardrobe choices were utilized to conceal her condition.

In June, July, and August of 1964, she was in a fully expectant/recovery/ rest period that forced her to miss most of the shooting schedule for the show's first full season. She then returned to the set the first week of September 1964, just in time to complete filming of the episode, "Be It Ever So Mortgaged."

Elizabeth became pregnant with her second child Robert (named for her father), around New Year's Day, 1965 (the second part of the first season of *Bewitched*), and worked through the following summer, taking maternity leave from September 10 to December 10, 1965.

She became pregnant with her third child Rebecca (named for her maternal grandmother) in mid-October 1968 during production of *Bewitched's* fifth season—and beginning with the non-*Darrin* episode, "Marriage Witches, Style," which began filming on January 20, 1969. To allow Lizzie some headway on this her third pregnancy, *Bewitched* filmed four episodes early in March and April 1969: "*Samantha's* Better Halves," "*Samantha's* Yoo-Hoo Maid," "*Samantha* and the Beanstalk," and "*Samantha's* Curious Cravings." Following Rebecca's birth, Lizzie returned to the *Bewitched* set on August 22, 1969 to film "*Samantha's* Caesar Salad."

Ultimately, Lizzie's first pregnancy (Billy, Jr.) was hidden from the TV viewers, while her second (Robert) and third (Rebecca) pregnancies were written into the show when *Samantha* became pregnant with *Tabitha* (Robert) and *Adam* (Rebecca). Although most people associate twins Erin and Diane Murphy with the role of *Samantha* and *Darrin's* daughter, there have actually been ten little witches on the show since 1966. Cynthia Black, who was two-and-a-half weeks old when she appeared on the series, played Tabatha in episode 54, "And Then There Were Three." Then, twins Heidi and Laura Gentry took over the part the following week. The Gentry girls were born on August 16, 1965.

A few weeks later the role of Tabatha was given to slightly older twins Tamar and Julie Young, and they stayed for the remainder of the second season. The Young girls were born on June 24, 1965. The last set of twins,

Erin and Diane Murphy, became cast members at the start of the third season. The Murphy girls (fraternal twins) were born on June 17, 1964, so the now-spelled Tabitha had physically aged more than a year between seasons two and three. This was necessary as the part would expand once it was announced that she was indeed a witch.

However, before all that transpired, the birth of *Bewitched* itself became just as intricate.

Resulting from an extended *affair* between several pertinent parties, the seeds of *Bewitched* were planted by Columbia/Screen Gems studio executives William Dozier and Harry Ackerman, the latter who had long-envisioned a supernatural sitcom that he titled *The Witch of Westport*.

In early 1963, Dozier and Ackerman, both of whom died in 1991, hired writer Sol Saks to write the pilot script, "I, *Darrin*, Take This Witch, *Samantha*," and *Bewitched* was born.

Dozier, then Vice President of Screen Gems West Coast operations, detailed *Samantha's* genesis for *TV Guide*, January 27, 1968, in the article, "The Man Who Helped Deliver a $9,000,000 Baby Tells How it All Happened."

With periodic meetings in 1963 Dozier and Ackerman discussed potential new TV projects, one of which was about a mortal wedded to a supernatural who did not reveal her persuasion until their honeymoon.

Shortly after these meetings with Ackerman, Dozier lunched with George Axelrod, the author of the 1952 play *The Seven Year Itch*, starring Vanessa Brown and Tom Ewell (who later reprised his role in the 1955 feature film adaptation starring Marilyn Monroe). It was then Dozier suggested the concept for a sorceress sitcom, the notion of which delighted Axelrod who very much wanted to write the pilot, which was not yet titled *Bewitched*.

An agreement was bartered with Axelrod's agent Irving Lazar and work was to commence immediately. But there was an issue. Lazar had also managed to cut a significant deal for his client to write, produce, and potentially direct several feature films for United Artists, which also wanted Axelrod to start work at once.

To alleviate the conflict a generous Dozier released Axelrod from his Screen Gems commitment and then met with writer Charles Lederer who, like Axelrod, immediately recognized the potential of a weekly witch series. But Lederer was also too involved with another job in this case, writing the screenplay for MGM's 1962 feature, *Mutiny on the Bounty* (starring Marlon Brando).

In stepped Sol Saks, with whom Dozier and Ackerman had both worked at CBS where he had penned *My Favorite Husband* for Ackerman and *Peck's Bad Girl* for Dozier. Now Saks was commissioned to write the pilot script he tentatively titled *Bewitched*.

Around the time Saks was hired, New York actress Tammy Grimes was under contract to Screen Gems. Then the star of Broadway's hit, *The Unsinkable Molly Brown*, Grimes had signed not only to do a series for Screen Gems, but one or more films for its feature film unit Columbia Pictures. Upon reading his witch script, Grimes requested changes from Saks, who sent along revisions after she returned to New York.

While that transpired, Dozier had separate business in that same city, where he was approached by an enthusiastic agent named Tom Tannenbaum who wanted very much to team his clients with a show for Screen Gems. Those clients were Lizzie and Bill Asher.

As fate would have it, Dozier was a friend to Elizabeth with whom he had long wanted to do a series and Ackerman, Dozier's Columbia colleague, was a CBS executive during the reign of *I Love Lucy*, countless episodes of which Bill had guided. Now with Screen Gems, Ackerman was executive producer for a host of the studio's very popular TV programs, not the least of which was *Father Knows Best*, co-starring Elinor Donahue, who would become his wife in real life.

Who would *Darrin* wed on *Bewitched*? That die was yet to be cast. For the moment, Dozier and Ackerman were working on finding *Samantha*.

By this time, the Columbia-contracted Grimes was considering the lead in playwright Noel Coward's new Broadway musical, *High Spirits*, which he had also signed to direct. Based on his previous hit play, *Blithe Spirit*, *High Spirits* centered around a female ghost, and like *Bewitched*, embraced a fantasy-comedy premise.

Grimes' choices were similar but different: Would she portray a sorceress or a spectre? She ultimately chose the latter and, like writer George Axelrod, was released from her contract with Columbia.

In 2007, she told writer Peter Filichia and *Theatre Mania's* online magazine, "I vetoed the script they gave me." In 1963, she told the studio, "This *Samantha* has all these powers? Well, then why isn't she stopping wars? Why isn't she fixing traffic in Los Angeles, saying to all of those drivers, '*Just a second—I'll soon get you all home.*'"

However, she said, Columbia didn't agree with her, so they "went to Elizabeth Montgomery."

When asked if she regretted the decision, Grimes replied: "No, but I used to wonder what would have happened if I'd done it. I probably would have done far more television and less theatre. So it's all right."

Yet as Harry Ackerman recalled in *The Bewitched Book* (Dell, 1992), Grimes did indeed regret not starring on *Bewitched* as *Samantha*, who when she read the script was named *Cassandra*. "I run into her every two or three years, and she's still kicking herself for not having done (the show)."

In 1989, Lizzie said she "met Tammy in New York when I was about fourteen." Although she years later decided to end *Bewitched*, and made every creative attempt to distance herself from the series after it ended, Elizabeth threw herself into the role of *Samantha* and felt "eternally gratefully" to Grimes for rejecting it. "I didn't get the part because I beat out hundreds of women in some huge casting call which was painstakingly narrowed down to me," she explained. "Tammy said *no*, I said *yes*, and I was simply at the right place at the right time."

That "right time" occurred shortly after she and Bill Asher completed production on *Johnny Cool*, in which she starred and he directed, and during which they fell in love. Enamored with him, she at that point became disinterested in acting, mostly because of the grueling schedules and distant film locations that meant extended periods of time away from the new love of her life. Bill, however, did not want her to disengage from her craft. "I felt that would have been a great loss," he said in 1988. "She had a lot to offer the industry, and she should be working, for herself, as well as for her contributions to the business."

Consequently, he suggested the possibility of working on a series with her during which there would be no periods of separation. "And Liz was all for that," he added.

Although Lizzie and Bill met for the first time on the set of *Johnny Cool*, she was well-aware of his work. As she recalled in *Modern Screen* magazine in 1965, she had rejected a number of series and always said if she did decide to do a show, "it would be wonderful to get William Asher."

Got him, she did. But initially Bill wasn't all that excited about "getting" Lizzie, as a thespian, that is. He always said the last thing he'd ever do was fall in love with an actress. Yet, as he too told *Modern Screen*, he soon realized that Lizzie was "special, very definitely special. She has none of the *personality* which usually goes with a personality. She doesn't possess the slightest affectation. She isn't affected by adulation. She's first of all what she is. Second, she's an actress."

"What he means," Lizzie chimed in at the time, "is that the only drive I have is to get home." Still, she often wondered if it was possible to be both a good actress and a happy woman. When she met actress Julie Andrews, whom she deemed "enormously talented," she knew it was possible. In her view, Andrews appeared "extremely happy."

Like Lizzie, Andrews would for years be associated with an iconic magical female role, this time, on the big screen as *Mary Poppins*, co-starring Dick Van Dyke, released in 1964, the same year *Bewitched* debuted on the small screen. It was produced by Walt Disney, for whom Lizzie as a youth had long desired to be hired as an artist.

"The Fun Couple" . . . that's what Lizzie and Bill were considered in and around Hollywood, and that's the title of the TV show on which they intended to work together when they first approached Screen Gems. *Couple* was based on the novel by John Haase, who later teamed with writer Neil Jansen to adapt the book for a Broadway play (that opened and closed within three days at the Lyceum Theatre in October 1962).

Bill's TV edition of *Couple* featured a character named *Ellen*, the world's wealthiest woman who falls for "an average Joe" actually named *Bob*, who was an auto mechanic. Fiercely independent, *Bob* was intimidated by *Ellen's* elite status. As Bill explained it in 1988, *Couple* was "a real Getty's daughter–type thing," which was set at the beach where "nobody really knows each other's last names." In this way, *Couple* was a kin to his *Beach Party* movies of the era and the *Gidget* series he directed for ABC, Columbia, and Acker-man. It also sounded an awful lot like Lizzie and Bill's reality, minus the auto-mechanic aspect.

Notwithstanding, somewhere between the first *Beach* movie and *Gidget*, Bill brought *Couple* to Dozier, who later gave the green light to high con-cept Twentieth Century Fox shows for ABC like *Batman* (1966–1968) and *The Green Hornet* (1966–1967). He liked the *Couple* premise, but suggested that Bill meet with Ackerman. "He's got something in mind that's very similar," Bill recalled Dozier saying, "and you might like it better."

Dozier, of course, was referring to *Bewitched*, which was an opposites-attract comedy that featured an attractive young woman who just so hap-pened to be a witch. *Couple* was an opposites-attract comedy that featured an attractive young woman who just so happened to be rich. Consequently, Dozier's instincts proved to be "on the nose." Bill not only favored *Bewitched*, he said he and Lizzie "flipped over it."

In retrospect, it appears Columbia merely stored the *Bewitched* pilot until Lizzie and Bill arrived on the scene. Due to Ackerman's *Lucy* affiliation with Bill, the studio was aware of his strength in directing TV female leads. The studio also respected Lizzie's artistic body of work, and as she perceived it, those in power merely saw the writing on the wall. "Columbia purely felt that Bill and I would work well together," she intoned in 1989 with a wink and a smile. "An extraordinarily good producer/director teamed with someone who at least looks like she could do the job."

While a few key players viewed the near "breech birth" of *Bewitched* with ease, creative conflicts continued to arise which almost thwarted the game. Beyond the basic script and casting decisions, the series was having issues with budget and the Writers Guild, the latter of which claimed the show's premise was lifted from the 1942 feature film *I Married a Witch*.

A revered fantasy comedy classic, *Married* is considered to be one of the best English-language motion pictures of its time. As directed by French film maestro Rene Clair, the ingenious story (based on a novel by *Topper* author Thorne Smith) cast the enchanting Veronica Lake as *Jennifer,* a sexy seventeenth century sorceress, who appears in modern day New England to haunt a gubernatorial candidate played by Fredric March, a descendent of the Puritan who condemned her. But she falls for him instead. Adding to the fun, March portrays various incarnations of his character through the years, which only adds to the film's style, wit, and inventiveness.

After the pilot for *Bewitched* was filmed, Bill Asher was asked if he had seen Clair's masterpiece. He had not. "And besides," Bill clarified in 1988, "there wasn't any valid comparison between the two concepts, certainly none which would have invited any legal ramifications. *Bewitched* began where the movie ended. Our story was about a married couple and the movie was about a courtship."

One bullet was dodged, at least until former child star turned studio executive Jackie Cooper came into the fold. According to what *Bewitched* director Richard Michaels said in 1988, "Bill was the unnamed producer of the show from the beginning." But when Jackie Cooper replaced William Dozier as a top executive for Columbia, the studio sought to avoid bestowing series control to husband and wife business teams due to a not-so-positive experience with *The Donna Reed Show*, which was produced by its star and her spouse Tony Owen.

"Jackie came in and saw me controlling things from a distance," Bill explained in 1988. "He tried to institute a policy which would prohibit Liz and me from working on *Bewitched*, and we damn near didn't do the show."

Cooper alluded to the derision in his autobiography, *Please Don't Shoot My Dog* (Morrrow/Avon, 1981), and learned rather quickly the "art of dealing with people, and specifically, how to be an executive." He also never doubted *Bewitched's* potential and was eager to work with Lizzie, whom he had met when she was just a teenager years before *Robert Montgomery Presents*. She was "already beautiful and already very strong and positive," he said; and she would remain so when they met on two future occasions: first, when she was married to Gig Young, and later when she was with Bill Asher whom Cooper, like Harry Ackerman and many other industry insiders, had known as the director of *I Love Lucy*.

In January of 1964, two months after filming was completed on the *Bewitched* pilot, Jackie and Lizzie reconnected, at her invitation. She wanted to discuss a business matter. He suggested they have lunch at the Beverly Hills Hotel. After the meal, her tone apparently became formal and she requested that Cooper honor the promises allegedly made by William Dozier, his Columbia predecessor:

She wanted Bill to be secured as *Bewitched's* core producer and show runner, with Harry Ackerman serving as executive producer. She had her own ideas of which direction *Bewitched* should go and she wanted those concepts incorporated into future scripts. She was to retain casting and director approval, and wanted Bill to direct the first eight or nine episodes.

Cooper thought such "promises" sounded quite unlike Dozier. In response, Lizzie apparently just glared at him with what he described as her "big blue eyes," which were actually green and could become "very steely when she wanted them to."

Lizzie's animated pupils merely added to her arsenal of unique facial expressions which, according to Cooper in this instance, emphasized a very straightforward decision not to do *Bewitched*. "It's too bad," she told him upon leaving their lunch/meeting. "It would have been a nice little show."

Back at his office, Cooper contacted her agent, Tom Tannenbaum, and said he'd have to inform Columbia's New York senior executive Jerry Harmon of the recent developments. Harmon would then be obligated to notify ABC which undoubtedly would cancel *Bewitched* before it hit the air—unless a mutually satisfactory lead replacement actress could be found, which Cooper assumed would be highly unlikely. Needless to say, Tannenbaum was concerned. "Please, hold the fort," he told Cooper. "Don't do anything until I talk to her."

A short time later, Tannebaum called back with what Cooper expected to be a mere confirmation: Lizzie was indeed quitting. But Cooper stood his ground. As he wrote in *Please Don't Shoot My Dog*:

> There were good reasons not to go along with her demands. Ackerman was a tried-and-true TV producer. He should be in charge. No way was Billy (Asher) going to direct the first eight or nine shows—nobody in his right mind did that. Casting and director approval? Not in my studio. And if she had ideas as to the direction in which the show was going, fine, but let her funnel them through the producer.

Cooper made further calls, next to Tom Moore, then head of ABC. "Tom was a good, level-headed person, not given to hysterics," he said. Cooper explained what had transpired, and despite the odds, Moore thought there was a possibility of finding another actress to play *Samantha*. Consequently, Cooper instructed his casting office to start looking for another actress who would fit Lizzie's age and type. He didn't tell the press of the recent developments, and neither did Lizzie, which he was pleased to learn. But still somehow there was a leak.

In those days, Hollywood gossip columnists had "moles" in every studio on the payroll. Consequently, the story seeped into the trades, stating that "Elizabeth Montgomery was unhappy at Screen Gems," and no one denied it.

During the casting search, the studio found three actresses who proved they could play *Samantha*. Screen tests were arranged, a director was hired, and Dick York, already signed to co-star, was brought in to work with the potential new replacements, all of which was funded by Screen Gems, at a not inconsiderable sum.

But the day before the screen tests were to commence, Cooper claimed a messenger appeared at his office door, bearing Lizzie's handwritten note of apology. Apparently, she realized that her demands were incongruent with her contract, and that she should have respected and trusted Cooper's discretion. She promised not to insist that Bill produce or direct, and she would work well with Harry Ackerman. She hoped Cooper would keep Bill in mind for the future.

In Cooper's eyes—and hands—Lizzie's note was a victory, but he wanted to officially secure her words. So he brought the note to the studio's legal department and integrated it as a new contract addendum, which she agreed to and signed.

From that day forward, and for the first five seasons that *Bewitched* was on the air, Lizzie never spoke to him again. "On the other hand," he explained in his book, "she was never late, she always knew her lines, she never caused anybody any trouble, she was a perfect lady, and she made the show a huge success." Also, too, Cooper ultimately agreed to Lizzie's previous creative "suggestions": Bill ended up directing the first fourteen episodes of the first season and, by the fourth year, was promoted to producer, ultimately supplanting producer Danny Arnold, who switched over to ABC's other popular female-driven sitcom, *That Girl*, starring Marlo Thomas. Arnold later created and produced *Barney Miller* for ABC in 1975.

On the other hand, Harry Ackerman was executive producer from day one.

During those early tense contract negotiations with Jackie Cooper and Screen Gems/Columbia, Lizzie and Bill Asher required at the very least a strong Hollywood player in their corner. Consequently, in stepped none other than Lizzie's father, Robert Montgomery. "I asked him if he'd back me up," Bill acknowledged in 1988. "I told him that Columbia didn't want me to do the show and that Liz wouldn't do it without me."

Without hesitation Robert consented to support his daughter and son-in-law in any way possible, which meant helping to schedule a meeting between Bill and Jerry Harmon. In that meeting, Bill promised Harmon that he would be financially responsible for all of *Bewitched's* production costs and that Columbia would own distribution rights and overhead. "I was accountable from a creative and financial standpoint," Bill said. "But from a logistical standpoint, the studio owned the copyright, which is something I really shouldn't have let happen" (though Bill later controlled even that).

That provision proved an attractive choice for Screen Gems, and it was not dismissed. With a final agreement signed and sealed, all parties were in accord, and as Bill acknowledged in 1988, "The studio backed off, I proved them wrong and, on a very precarious note, Elizabeth and I began to shoot the show."

Eleven

~~~

Remember the Mane

> "It's a gossamer thing; and there are so many factors involved. They just mesh . . . and I certainly appreciate his talent. He's incredible."
>
> —Elizabeth, describing then-husband Bill Asher,
> *Modern Screen Magazine*, 1970

In the second half of its first season on May 20, 1965, *Bewitched* aired an episode called "Remember the Main," directed by William D. Russell and written by Mort R. Lewis. It featured an actor named Edward Mallory who in 1967 married actress Joyce Bulifant (who later married Bill Asher after his divorce from Lizzie in 1974).

In the "Main" segment, the *Stephens* family gets involved with the political campaign of a local candidate running for office:

At *Darrin's* suggestion, hopeful *Ed Wright* (Mallory), challenges his opponent *John C. Cavenaugh* (Byron Morrow) to a public debate for a seat on the city council. The issue at hand: illegal fund allocations for a new drainage system. When a water main bursts, subsequently securing an easy win for *Wright*, *Darrin* suspects *Samantha's* handy witchcraft. Not so, she says. It's *Endora* who's to blame.

While the episode represents Elizabeth's political ideals off-camera, and certainly *Bewitched's* general message of democracy and equality on-camera,

"Remember the Main" invites a play on words with insight into Lizzie's emotional metamorphosis with each new marriage, signified by something as simple as the change in style and color of her hair.

For example, by the time she and Bill Asher became involved with *Bewitched*, their relationship was sealed. She appeared more at peace than ever, a contentment that seemed to coincide with her decision to go blonde. When she and Asher first met on the set of *Johnny Cool* in 1963, her hair was brunette. After *Cool* and before *Bewitched*, she had a very *Samantha*-like blonde hairstyle in a few episodes of *Burke's Law* (one in which, in fact, she subconsciously does her famous twitch—even before she brings it to *Bewitched!*).

In general, Lizzie's real hair color was best described as "ash blonde, dirty blonde, or on the blonde side of brunette."

As a young girl, she had very blonde hair—what they used to call *tow-head blonde*—but as she grew older, her hair grew darker, as is usually the case with tow-heads (although knowing Lizzie, her sense of humor, and her love for animals, she probably called herself a "toad-head").

At various intervals in her adult life, she experimented with different shades that seemed to somehow match not only her mood, but her professional objectives, and indeed sometimes her husbands.

During her first marriage to Fred Cammann, she was wet behind the ears and inspired, but restless and inattentive. Her hair was merely streaked with blonde, possibly signifying her ambivalence to this union to the wealthy sophisticate, which she ended after only a year.

For a good portion of the time she spent with second husband Gig Young—in what could certainly be described as a dark marriage—Lizzie dyed her hair a dark brunette in hopes of being cast for darker, more textured characters. The strategy worked as she went on to play the war-torn *Woman* from "Two" on *The Twilight Zone*, the prostitute *Rusty Heller* from *The Untouchables*, and the devil's assistant in *Mr. Lucifer*. Ironically, of course, for her role in *The Spiral Staircase*, in which she co-starred with Young, she was a lighter brunette. But her off-screen troubles with Young outweighed whatever professional strides she made, and this marriage ended after six years.

A decade or so later, when she appeared in 1975's post-*Bewitched* TV-movie, *The Legend of Lizzie Borden*, she had a darker shade of blonde, which distinguished her from playing an all-blonde *Samantha* while still adding a unique tone to help ease the transition from comedy to drama. She wanted to distance herself from *Bewitched*, but not from her audience.

By this time, too, she was living with a brown-haired Robert Foxworth. They weren't yet married and would not be for years to come, but he was then the love of her life, and her darker blonde hair was a better match for his brown locks.

But in that first season of *Bewitched*, back in 1964, shortly after losing her heart—and dark hair—to director Bill Asher on the set of *Johnny Cool*, it was if the all-blonde Lizzie had the best of all worlds. For her, at the time, blondes did have more fun.

Before that, non-actor Cammann wanted Lizzie to give up her beloved acting craft (like *Darrin* would ask *Samantha* to give up witchcraft). And although she viewed the thespian Young as a father figure—and he certainly respected their combined theatrical craft—it was director Asher who would guide her most succinctly, on and off camera. In short, she was bored with Freddie, exhausted by Gig, and the happiest with Bill.

As writer Joe Hyams pointed out in *The Saturday Evening Post*, March 13, 1965, with Bill, Elizabeth was leading a rich, full life without the stigma of being "a poor little rich girl." She still did all her favorite things—like ride horses, paint, and play tennis—which as previously mentioned Asher also enjoyed. But she found in *Samantha* a role that fit her like a glove—and a husband in Asher who, although slighter in physical stature, stood just as tall as her father in commanding a room.

As her old friend Bud Baker told *TV Radio Mirror* in September of 1967, at the onset of *Bewitched's* fourth season—and the fourth year of her marriage to Bill—Lizzie was "so alive now; so completely honest." There was no "above-it-all" attitude like when she was as "a kid at those parties. No faking the phony social stuff the way she had to with Freddie. No trying to adapt to Gig's very nice quiet reserve. She's Billy's girl, and absolutely honest; nothing to fear. Every actress has to have a pretty strong ego, but you can't overpower a guy like Bill."

Baker further explained:

> She's changed. She's really radiant, fulfilled. And it isn't just a matter of having found herself professionally. That's great, but she takes it in stride;

she has what most show business people I've met never have—perspective. She knows glamour for what it's worth, knows how many women scramble for careers because they aren't happy enough in other areas of their life. Acting is normal and natural to Liz—both her father and mother had the talent—and it is something fun to *do*, not something to sacrifice your life *for*. No, what changed Liz is this guy Bill Asher. He's the right kind of man for her; a gutty guy, a real man-type guy who is strong. They are ideally suited to each other, totally in love. He doesn't try to lock her up, he doesn't have to. They are both whole people with everything in the world in common, and it's great they got together.

"Together" is putting it mildly. They were joined at the hip, at home and at the office.

According to what *Bewitched's* publicist Harry Flynn told *TV Guide* writer Arnold Hano in 1967, Bill Asher was tough and tender for all the right reasons: "If you make a mistake, he can give you a rough time. He's especially hard on phonies"—as was Lizzie. "If an interviewer is not her cup of tea, she can't sit down and be pleasant. She loathes pretensions."

In effect, the Ashers were refreshing, direct, and honest. If they reminded you less of the crowned heads of Europe, Hano said, they reminded you more of the Kennedys. Like the Kennedys, they were brisk, businesslike, tireless, hard-nosed, competent, personable, pragmatic, and intelligent; and they liked to play touch football.

They were also in tune. When Lizzie performed as *Samantha*, she kept her eyes glued on Asher, who would feed her the cues. If he beamed, she beamed; he nodded, she nodded; he smiled, she smiled. Asher judged actors within a strict margin, and Lizzie was on his scale. "As an actress," he said, "there is nothing she can't do." Lizzie added, "Bill is the best director I've ever worked with."

More than anything, as Hano detected, they were two people in love. They also *liked* each other, and were subsequently perceived as a combined breath of fresh air in Hollywood—living proof that opposites attract.

Again, they were "the fun couple"—not the series idea, but the actual people. She was the rich Beverly Hills girl and he was the not-quite-poor boy from Manhattan. She was tall, slender, blonde, and beautiful, the cool-eyed girl who danced until dawn at all those New York balls in 1951. He was short, squat, thick-necked, and balding, like your friendly neighborhood wrestler. She went to swank finishing schools, danced with Andover boys and Harvard men, summered in England with her father, and began her career at the American Academy of Dramatic Arts. Asher never finished high school. But decades later on *Bewitched*, as far as Lizzie was concerned, Asher graduated at the top of his class, and they became an unstoppable team.

Once they got rolling on *Bewitched*, Lizzie and Bill had their life and art down to a science. Although she once said that her "art belonged to Daddy," that is, Robert Montgomery, Bill Asher was the new "daddy" in town.

According to *TV Guide* in 1967, their work day began at 5:30 AM and lasted until 7:15 PM, when they'd arrive home to see the kids: first-born William Jr., followed by Robert and then Rebecca. After play time Elizabeth would study lines while Bill planned the shooting schedule. From there it was dinner and bed.

On weekends they played golf, tennis, or both, they'd drive down to Palm Springs to party, and were usually the last to leave any festivity. Lizzie decided at one gathering to play the piano, just before dawn. "She does not really play the piano," a friend said. "She attacks it."

Early the next morning they romped through a game of that Kennedy-esque touch football on the lawn to loosen their muscles for countless sets of tennis.

"We work hard during shooting days, to have more free time in the evenings and on weekends," Asher said. "Our private life comes first."

Lizzie agreed. And although *TV Guide's* Arnold Hano described her as a "reasonably headstrong girl," she deferred to Bill in nearly all matters. Just as her old friend Bud Baker had concluded, her alliance with Asher created a new Lizzie. The one-time social butterfly now seemed to be locked in a cocoon.

Although they still enjoyed a night on the town, Lizzie and Bill were old-fashioned, maybe like Fred Cammann had once envisioned he and Lizzie might be during her first marriage. But now, with Asher, she was ready to settle down.

"If I am asked to make a publicity trip and Bill can't go along, I don't go," Lizzie told *TV Guide.* "It's all right for the man to go off by himself. The man is head of the family."

In short, Mr. Asher would never be known as "Mr. Montgomery." When explaining *Bewitched's* appeal to *TV Guide,* it sounded like he was tooting his own horn. But the fact was, he knew his stuff. "The show," he said, "portrays a mixed marriage that overcomes by love the enormous obstacles in its path. *Samantha,* in her new role as housewife, represents the true values in life. Material gains mean nothing to her. She can have anything she wants through witchcraft, yet she'd rather scrub the kitchen floor on her hands and knees for the man she loves. It is emotional satisfaction she craves."

When asked whether he was defining his own philosophy of life and marriage, Asher replied, "Completely."

While their material gains may have meant nothing to Lizzie or Bill, as was explained in *TV Guide,* neither was discarding the luxuries. By the spring of 1967, the close of *Bewitched's* third hit year, they had four vehicles: a Mercedes 220 SE coupe (his), a Jaguar XK-E (hers), a Chevrolet Corvette (his), and a Chevy station wagon (theirs). The latter two were company courtesy cars (Chevrolet was a *Bewitched* sponsor).

The Ashers' Benedict Canyon home (which Lizzie would later share with Robert Foxworth and retain for the rest of her life) was massive, and located directly across from Harold Lloyd's fabled estate.

They also owned land in northern California. But most importantly, they retained 20 percent of the profits of *Bewitched.* At the time, 20 percent of any television show going beyond the third season (as *Bewitched* certainly did) was worth approximately $2 million.

Lizzie was raised in wealth, but her newfound money was something else again. It would be a lot to expect for her to refrain from using it to ease even the slightest burden.

In today's world, statistics show that many marriages dissolve due to lack of money. Conversely, many stay together because of lots of money. It wasn't all that different during the reign of *Samantha* and *Darrin,* and Lizzie and Bill.

Bewitched was a success. They were in love. They had a happy marriage and a happy show. In the midst of it all, the *new* Lizzie had arrived. She had kowtowed to Asher's rule and found emotional satisfaction, at least in 1967.

In the later years of the series, she played a more active role in the business aspect of their relationship. The show became a co-production of Screen Gems/Columbia Studios and Ashmont Productions, which was initiated in 1965. Then in full swing, Ashmont rivaled the much larger Desilu Productions in name only. The title Desilu was formed by the first names of Desi Arnaz and Lucille Ball; the shingle "Ashmont" was shaped from the last names of Bill and Lizzie. Still, Ashmont—the company and the happily married couple—were a force to be reckoned with . . . at least until the "twitch hit the fan."

Twelve

~

Double Double . . .

"Every little breeze seems to whisper Louise."

—*Dr. Bombay* to *Samantha*, in the *Bewitched* episode, "Mixed
Doubles" (3-4-71)

Beyond the fact that there were two *Darrins* on *Bewitched*, there were several
twin aspects of the series that were concocted or just plain happened . . . on
camera and behind the scenes.

After Alice Pearce died in 1966, Sandra Gould stepped into the role of
nosy mortal neighbor *Gladys Kravitz*. Alice Ghostley's bumbling witch maid
Esmeralda replaced Marion Lorne's blundering sorceress *Aunt Clara* following Lorne's death in 1968. Kasey Rogers was hired to play *Louise Tate*, after
Irene Vernon exited the role in 1966. Multiple sets of twins played little
Tabitha over the years, notably sisters Erin and Diane Murphy, while twin
brothers David and Greg Lawrence played the part of *Tabitha's* younger
sibling *Adam*. And, of course, Elizabeth herself played both *Samantha* and
her look-alike cousin *Serena*.

Into this mix, a few episodes of *Bewitched* imbued a "doubles" premise,
such as "Mixed Doubles," which aired on March 4, 1971, and was directed
by William Asher and written by Richard Baer:

> *Samantha* can't sleep. She's concerned about *Larry* and *Louise* (Rogers), who
> are having marital troubles. But the next day, she has troubles of her own.
> She finds herself in bed with *Larry*, while *Louise* is at the *Stephens* home

with *Darrin*. Somehow, *Samantha* and *Louise's* souls have switched bodies. Consequently, *Sam* calls *Dr. Bombay* (Bernard Fox), who remedies the situation which, he says, was caused by something called "dream inversion."

"I always thought those [type of episodes] were kind of fun," Lizzie said in 1989. "I just hope that we didn't do too many of them. And I don't think we actually did, but they were fun because I think audiences enjoyed all that kind of nonsense. I always enjoyed watching stuff like that, too. It's fun to watch other people behaving like they shouldn't behave."

In 1980, music legend John Lennon released what would become his final recording: *Double Fantasy*, an album that in many music circles was labeled a love letter to his wife Yoko Ono, who by then was also a member of his band.

Years before, Lennon and his original "mates," The Beatles—Paul McCartney, George Harrison, and Ringo Starr—made their American television debut on CBS' *The Ed Sullivan Show*, February 9, 1964, approximately eight months before *Bewitched* debuted on ABC.

Bewitched and The Beatles offered entertaining escape from the turbulence that infested the 1960s. The Beatles wanted everyone to hold their hands to forget their troubles; *Samantha* made everyone wish they could twitch away their heartache. Off-screen, Lennon married an Asian princess in the form of Ono; on-screen, *Darrin* married the queen of the witches in the guise of *Samantha*.

Both were mixed marriages that fell victim to third parties who sought to create a great divide. McCartney, Harrison, and Starr blamed Ono for the breakup of The Beatles. *Endora* desperately desired *Samantha* to leave *Darrin*. The Lennons represented racial equality and sang to give peace a chance. *Samantha* advocated for conciliation among TV's top two races— witches and mortals.

Lizzie and *Bewitched*, and Lennon and The Beatles each strived for some sense of familial and universal tranquility. It was a double fantasy, and a dark reality. But somehow, we all came out of it a little better and none the worse for wear. We were delivered by a music superstar (who commented that The Beatles were more popular than Jesus Christ) and a supernatural TV series that delivered a fantastical solution for a subpar world.

Magic was welcomed wherever it could be found, and with Elizabeth and *Samantha, Bewitched* provided the perfect forum—a forum that still stands today, if born amidst the controversy of yesteryear.

When *Bewitched* debuted, September 17, 1964, certain network, studio, and advertising executives expressed concern as to whether or not the show would be perceived in the Bible Belt as a platform for Satanism. The notion may today seem absurd, particularly because at its core the series was a romantic comedy, certainly more human and humane than much of contemporary television.

But if *Bewitched* had any serious evil overtones, Lizzie's co-star, Agnes Moorehead, would have been the first to voice any objections. Passionately opinionated, the fiery redhead was the daughter of Dr. John H. Moorehead, a Presbyterian minister who, by present standards, would be considered a Pentecostal Christian Fundamentalist. Charles Tranberg, author of *I Love the Illusion: The Life and Career of Agnes Moorehead* (BearManor Media, 2005) explains:

> It seems a contradiction because Agnes was such a fundamentalist Christian in her upbringing and throughout her life. But she loved playing *Endora.* [She] even came up with the name of the character and liked to come up with all kinds of ideas. She also had played witches before, in an episode of *The Shirley Temple Playhouse* for example, and later on an episode of *Night Gallery.* She really never thought of *Endora* as "evil" but as mischievous, and somebody who was simply pointing out the foibles of mortal life.

Moreover, if anyone had the "right" to object to Lizzie's portrayal of *Sammy's* supernatural ways, it most probably would have been Britain's Sybil Leek, then the world's top-ranking self-professed, real-life witch.

Fortunately, as Lizzie explained in 1989, Leek had visited *Bewitched* set and granted her sorcery seal of approval. "Sybil gave us her blessing and was very sweet."

"Oh, Darling," Leek told her, "I've seen so many of these *things* (other media witches) and I really can't stand them. But I just love your show. You're so nice and have such a sweet way about you. You're doing everything just perfectly."

Had Leek not sanctioned her performance, Lizzie mused, "I would not have shown up for work the next day."

On September 13, 1970, reporter Lorraine St. Pierre profiled *Bewitched* for *The Boston Sunday Advertiser* to commemorate the show's first on-location filming in Salem, Massachusetts, a city that *TV Guide* once named "the witch capital of the world." The article was published in tandem with the airing of eight *Bewitched* episodes from the seventh season involving *Samantha's* trip to a witches' convention, and St. Pierre described Lizzie's *Samantha* as "a cute prankster."

In her *Book of Shadows* (Broadway Books, 1998), author and real-life Wiccan priestess Phyllis Curott wrote, "A witch is anyone who cultivates divine and sacred gifts." She also deduced that television programs like *Bewitched* are important because "they're showing witches are good."

Fortunately, while working on *Bewitched*, Lizzie agreed.

Exhibit A: She vetoed the name *Cassandra* which, inspired by the sorceress from Greek mythology, was *Samantha's* original name in the *Bewitched* pilot. Lizzie "hated that name. It's terrible; a real *doom and gloomer. Boo . . . boo. Hiss . . . Hiss,*" she said in 1989.

The other suggestion was calling her *Elizabeth*, but she was just as adamant about that not happening. "*No, thank you,*" she intoned. "I mean, isn't that the stupidest thing you ever heard? Having the character's name be the same as the actor's name? I find it distracting. It doesn't separate the character from the actor. And I think it smacks of a rather appalling ego."

Despite Lizzie's strong opinion on the matter, there was a kinship of sorts between *Samantha* and *Cassandra*. *Cassandra* and other gods of Greek mythology abided by a strict and specific mystical doctrine; *Samantha* and her supernatural peers followed a particular code of ethics found in the *Witches' Book of Rights* (as relayed in the *Bewitched* episode, "Long Live the Queen"). Both *Samantha* and *Cassandra* possessed the power to foretell the future (although the *Bewitched* creative team decided there would be no conflict if *Sam* chose not to engage this particular foresight).

That leaves one last *Samantha-Cassandra* affinity. In the Greek myth, the god *Apollo* places a curse on *Cassandra*. Eons later, it would seem *Samantha* got caught in the fall-out. Like *Cassandra*, she always knew of some forth-coming disaster but was helpless to avert it, namely, Agnes Moorehead's *Endora*.

Moorehead was part of the equally legendary Orson Welles and his esteemed Mercury Theatre group, a band that eventually transferred their unbridled talents into several classic films, not the least of which was 1941's *Citizen Kane* (considered in many a cinematic circle as one of the best mov-ies ever made).

In August of 1965, *Bewitched* entered its second hit season. Moorehead talked with reporter Earle Hesse of *Screen Stars* magazine about working with Lizzie, saying: "She keeps us all on our toes. I play a witch also on that show, and it takes some doing to out-witch and out-charm her. She's a born scene-stealer." And she was, literally, in two "double aspect" episodes of *Bewitched*, initially, in a first-season Dick York episode called "Which Witch Is Which," and then in "The Mother-in-Law-of-the-Year," during the middle of Dick Sargent's second year (but the show's seventh season). Sum-maries for each episode are as follows:

"Which Witch is Which?" (3-3-65) Written by Earl Barrett. Directed by William D. Russell: *Samantha* is unable to make a dress-fitting appointment, so *Endora* transforms herself into her daughter's double and shows up in her place. While being fitted, *Endora-as-Sam* catches the eye of *Bob Fraser* (Ron Randell), a friend of *Darrin's*. *Mrs. Kravitz* (Alice Pearce) sees the two together, and thinks *Samantha* is cheating on *Darrin*. In the end, *Endora* pops in at the *Stephenses* in her *Sam-guise* and leads *Fraser* to believe that she and *Samantha* are "identical twins."

"Mother-in-Law-of-the-Year" (1-14-71) Written by Philip and Henry Sharp. Directed by William Asher: *Samantha* is forced to impersonate *Endora* who in a unique display of emotion feels neglected by her son-in-law. To get on his good side, she creates and stars in an ad campaign called the "Mother-in-Law-of-the-Year" for *Bobbins Bon Bons*, his new client at *McMann & Tate Advertising*. At first, *Mr. Bobbins* (John McGiver) is smitten by *Endora's* creative charms, but the tables turn when she grows bored with the mortal festivities. At which time, *Samantha* replicates her mother's image, and literally inserts herself into the "Mother-in-Law-of-the-Year"

TV commercial. *Endora* then rematerializes in the commercial, and everyone sees double.

Off-screen, however, Lizzie sometimes saw red, as she and Moorehead, aka *Aggie*, were not always on the same page. Both were independent thinkers and rarely backed away from confrontation, although in 1989 Lizzie was quick to make clarifications:

> People were always trying to create fights between us and said that Aggie and I hated each other or that Aggie and Maurice (Evans) hated each other, or that Maurice and I hated each other. And none of that was ever true. Even Mabel (Albertson, who played *Darrin's* mother) and Aggie got along fine, mostly because Mabel wouldn't put up with any bullshit. And it was great because Aggie would always try to push it (the limits) with the women that would come on the show. And I would just sit back and say, "Well, let's see how this turns out."

Elizabeth believed Moorehead enjoyed the challenge of their relationship "because she knew I loved her dearly," and that "Aggie's bark was worse than her bite."

But Moorehead chomped at the bit when Dick Sargent was hired to replace Dick York as the new *Darrin* in the fall of 1969. Sargent's new term on the show began on a foot of edgy hostility. Set in her ways, Moorehead was not at all pleased his presence. She was fond of York and his talent, and respected his New Age-like spirituality. Even though such beliefs countered her conservative Christian viewpoint, Moorehead felt his presence was key to the show's success.

As was explained in *TV Guide*, May 29, 1965, with the article, "He's Almost Invisible in the Glare of Success," York many times invoked religious items into sculpting, an art he practiced in his spare time. He described one of his pieces as "four-dimensional":

> I try to incorporate all religious teaching, the Old Testament, the New Testament, Confucius, Buddha, The Agnostic, one figure representing all. In the front you see Adam, a cloud-like Adam. Eve is beside him on the ground looking into an empty cradle. As you revolved around it, the back of Eve's head becomes Woman. And Adam, from the back, is the crucified

Christ. Then Eve becomes the Virgin Mary from another angle. There are six different perspectives.

It seemed a convoluted concept, but Moorehead respected York's vision, which in her view, contributed to her understanding of the man behind the vision:

> I probably understand him better than others. He's rather profound, you know. He has a spiritual quality. I am a religious girl. I have a great faith. This creates a rapport between us. Actors who have this spiritual quality often understand each other without much communication.

Adds Moorehead biographer Charles Tranberg today:

> Aggie Moorehead absolutely loved Dick York! And this never wavered. They both had a deep spirituality. Aggie's was more of a conventional God-based spirituality which was developed from a childhood as a minister's daughter. She was a fundamentalist. Dick was not. He was spiritual, but he was more of a deep thinker. He was the type of guy who could find God anywhere. God is being outside looking at a beautiful mountain range. He was interested in all kinds of philosophies, not only the Christian faith. But still Aggie saw him as a fellow seeker of wisdom and somebody who felt that there was a supreme being. They had lots of conversations on the set, between scenes, on things like this. When Dick left the show, she was not happy. She felt he was a big part of the success of the show and even said that he had the hardest part of all because he had to make all these supernatural things happening to him seem real, and that took real acting, another thing she appreciated. She thought he was a superb actor.

With specific regard to the *Darrin* switch, Tranberg adds:

> Aggie didn't like the *Darrin* switch. She hoped it wouldn't happen, but she accepted it, because this type of thing does happen in the theatre all the time as she noted. She took out her disappointment on Dick Sargent, who was hired to play the new *Darrin*. For a while on the set she made his life difficult. He wasn't happy about the way she treated him either. She certainly didn't have the rapport on-screen that she had with York. Eventually as time went by, she did mellow somewhat, even inviting Sargent to her

annual Christmas-Birthday bashes, but there certainly wasn't the same bond with Sargent that she had with York.

Although Agnes Moorehead claimed no lack of communication between herself and Dick Sargent, or any personal objection to him replacing Dick York, David White, the irascible *Larry Tate* on *Bewitched,* recalled things differently.

In the fall of 1970, the *Bewitched* cast and crew traveled to Salem, Massachusetts (the show's first on-location filming) for an arc of episodes having to do with *Samantha* attendance at a Witches' Convention. On the plane-ride back to Los Angeles, White was seated next to Sargent, who he said, had a tear in his eye. Apparently, something Moorehead said had made him cry. "He was very upset," White said.

It was like that from the beginning. At the first table script-reading with Sargent the year before, in 1969, White said Moorehead rose from her seat, turned to all of those who would listen, and stated pointedly, "I am not fond of *change.*"

In 1992, Sargent granted an interview to author Owen Keehnen, which appears in Keehnen's book, *We're Here, We're Queer* (Prairie Avenue Productions, 2011). According to Sargent, Moorehead said, "They should never meddle with success."

> "Meaning," Sargent explained, "Dick York should never have been replaced, which I thought was a very cruel and unthinking thing to say in front of me. But that was her. She came to rehearsals with a Bible in one hand and her script in the other. She was certainly the most professional woman in the world, and she was so good [an actress]. Thank God we became friends eventually."

In 1989, Sargent only praised York's performance as *Darrin,* calling him "excellent!" In 1992, Sargent told Keehnen that he was set to play the famous *Mr. Stephens* before York, and even actor Richard Crenna (*The Farmer's Daughter*), who was in the running for the role. "I had the interview and by the time they got back to me, I had already signed on a series called *Broadside,* so Dick York got it. But I was the original choice."

One year before, in 1988, York assessed Sargent's take on *Darrin*. Although York wanted the summer of 1969 to "rest up" in order to continue playing the part through that fall and for the remainder of the series, he had nothing but kind words for Sargent: "The man had a job to do, and he did it well. He was an actor, and he did a fine job. I never held anything against him."

As to York's relationship with Elizabeth, *Bewitched* writer Doug Tibbles recalls:

> He was quiet, and now looking back, that was because of the pain he was in. He did not seem loaded the way people on pain medication [do]. It didn't seem that way at all. He just seemed like a nice quiet professional. He was semi-detached. Through my eyes, his relationship with Elizabeth was simply professional. I mean, they were kind of almost sweet. But you couldn't tell if it was just two polite people or two people just being polite. I didn't see tons of closeness and I didn't see tons of distance. It was somewhere in the middle.

That's kind of where Elizabeth found herself when she ultimately confronted Moorehead about her mistreatment of Sargent, of whom Lizzie was fond and enthusiastic about his joining the *Bewitched* cast. She made every attempt to keep peace on the set. At one point early on, she walked with Sargent to see Moorehead, who proved to be nothing less than unwelcoming. As Lizzie explained in 1989, upon greeting Sargent, Moorehead outstretched her arm and instructed him to kiss her hand, as if he was greeting royalty. Lizzie was stunned. "Oh, Aggie," she said with a ting of sarcasm. "How wonderful . . . I can always count on you to make people feel at home."

Moorehead responded with an icy glare, but Lizzie would have none of it. "Don't you look at me that way," she told her.

Lizzie thought "Aggie's response was great, because that meant we were really communicating."

Later that day, she walked into Moorehead's dressing room, something she rarely did, and communicated some more:

> Now, you know how you can be, and I know how you can be. So, I don't want you to be like you and I know you can be. Obviously you're being

difficult because you know what I'm telling you is true, and that I should have never come in here . . . and that we should have never had this conversation, because it may sound like I think you're stupid. And if that's true, well, then, I'm sorry. I do apologize. I didn't mean to hurt your feelings by telling you something that you already know.

As Lizzie went on to explain in 1989, Moorehead feigned ignorance. "She pretended as if she didn't understand what I meant and was a little aggravated."

A short time later, she and Moorehead were back on the set, and ready to shoot a scene. Suddenly, in the middle of rehearsal, Moorehead turned to her TV daughter and said, "You're right."

"That was all that was ever said about the incident," Lizzie recalled. She believed Moorehead enjoyed the challenge of their relationship because "she knew I loved her dearly. We really did have a mother daughter-relationship. I truly did adore Aggie. She was heaven."

A few graffiti artists in Hollywood would have agreed. Sometime in the mid-1980s, the phrase, "Agnes Moorehead is God," was canvassed across the side of a Tinseltown structure, once standing opposite the Capitol Records building on Vine Street. Upon learning this in 1989, Lizzie's eyes widened and smiled in bemusement. "Huh!" she said, "She finally made it, eh?"

In playing opposite two *Darrins* on *Bewitched*, Elizabeth shared unique interplays with Dick York and Dick Sargent. But off-screen, she may have considered Sargent more of a friend. According to what *Bewitched* third-season producer William Froug revealed to www.emmytvlegends.org, documented on September 14, 2001, Lizzie had issues with York. Froug said executive producer Harry Ackerman hired him on the show to "take the fall," to buffer any personal tension that transpired on the set—between Lizzie and York, as well as between Lizzie and Bill Asher. Froug explained:

> Asher and Liz were in a troubled marriage . . . They lived together, they drove [into work] together, but there was tension there that nobody but them could know about. So they needed someone in the [producer's] chair.

And I was the guy they chose. It was [a] perfect [fit]. Nothing to lose for them, and nothing to lose for me.

Consequently, Ackerman hosted an initial meeting with Froug, Asher, and Lizzie; and as Froug went on to explain:

The first thing out of Liz's mouth was, "We've got to get rid of *him!*" Now, I'm brand new, and I'm wondering, "Who the hell is *him?*" So, after the meeting . . . I finally had to say to Bill, "Who is *him?*" And he said, "Dick York. Liz can't stand him."

As Froug perceived it, "Dick was madly in love with Liz," and whenever York was forced to rest between filming, due to his severe back ailment, he would glance over to Lizzie, "longingly."

"It was pretty clear he was very smitten," Froug said, "and it was equally clear that she couldn't stand him because of that. Liz was the kind of woman that if you loved her, you were in trouble," Froug concluded. "She was a tough cookie!"

Beyond Froug's somewhat indiscreet personal opinion from behind-the-scenes, on-screen, Elizabeth and Dick York were pure magic.

Charles Tranberg profiled York for *Classic Images* magazine in October, 2011. As he sees it, Lizzie had veto power over casting the show's pilot. Had she not approved of York, he would never have made the initial cut, much less come to play the role. Tranberg explains:

I think she thought that he was a strong counterpoint to her, and certainly their scenes together were magical. They had on-screen chemistry from day one. Whatever problems they might have had off-camera never showed up on-camera—not even towards the end when York was increasingly ill due to his back problems and the psychological effects that the medication he was taking was causing. She probably became frustrated with him due to missing some shows, but when they worked together on-camera . . . the chemistry was spot-on.

Tranberg also says York recognized in Elizabeth a trace of his wife Joey, the former actress known as Joan Alt, and whom he had known since they were children:

184

I think that always had a great effect on him and how he worked with and perhaps acted around Elizabeth. He realized how good they were together on camera. I think her interpretation of *Samantha* appealed to him both as an actor and maybe a bit as a man.

No maybes about it. As York acknowledged in his memoir, *The Seesaw Girl and Me,* (New Path Press, 2004), he "first fell in love with Elizabeth Montgomery by leg distance," after seeing her perform with Tom Poston in the "Masquerade" episode of Boris Karloff's anthology series, *Thriller.* "My God," he thought, "what a pretty dark-haired girl. And those legs! Oh my God!"

A few years later he auditioned for *Bewitched,* and had a chance to get a closer look, when Lizzie was sitting outside the casting office that housed Bill Asher and Harry Ackerman. "She unfolded those gorgeous legs and looked at me," York wrote, "and I saw her in person for the first time. She had full lips and dark, soft hair. She was sex all over."

A few minutes later, he and Lizzie walked in to read for Asher and Ackerman. By this time, of course, Lizzie already had the part. This audition was for York, who told her right before they read together, "Oh, God, you'd be wonderful" for the part of *Samantha.*

York also noted in his book, "I've known Elizabeth Montgomery all my life, and she's kind of been my wife because she reminds me of Joey." He explained how he walked into the audition "more confident than I've ever been in my life."

At this point, he had his arm around Lizzie, and quipped to Asher and Ackerman, "I don't know about you guys, but this girl is perfect. Let's sit down and read this turkey and see if I'm the right guy for her."

York's confidence paid off. He was more than right for the part. He was perfect.

Off-screen, as Charles Tranberg assesses, Lizzie's relationship with York was also ideal.

At least, in the beginning, she reportedly invited the Yorks to play tennis and socialize every now and then. But they were a private couple, and when away from the set, he liked to spend time with Joey and their children. Tranberg explains:

I don't think Elizabeth resented this, because she was a strong believer in family first, too. But as the time went by something, and I'm not certain what it is, soured their off-screen relationship. Not to the point that Elizabeth was demanding that they get rid of Dick, she knew how important he was to the show, as did Bill Asher. I don't know what it was; that she was getting fed up with his illnesses and I'm not sure how much empathy she had for his pain. They accommodated him on the set, certainly.

I do know that she felt the show was stronger when it was focused on *Samantha-Darrin*, and that when he was sick and missed shows it affected the balance of the show. I recall Mrs. York telling me, and I don't think she would mind my revealing this, that when Dick was nominated for an Emmy . . . finally! . . . in 1967, the cast, as usual, had a table at the awards ceremony. Elizabeth was also nominated as was Agnes Moorehead and others associated with the show.

But Dick was not there, so, at some point, Elizabeth excused herself and called Dick's house to see if he was coming. Apparently she was told that the whole family was gathered around the master bed watching the telecast on TV, and they were having more fun doing that. My guess is that Elizabeth probably didn't think that was being a professional and showing support for the show.

Into this mix, David Pierce, author of *The Bewitched History Book* (Bear-Manor Media, 2012), assesses Lizzie's alternate interpretations of *Samantha* in playing opposite first York then Sargent:

Many fans of *Bewitched* have varied opinions of the chemistry between Elizabeth Montgomery and her TV husbands, Dick York and Dick Sargent. I think she she had more chemistry with the former but I think the reason for it wasn't so much because of him, but because of what was going on in her life at the time she worked with him. Liz had just recently married Bill Asher and they were just starting their family. By many accounts, Bill and Liz were very much in love and Liz had mentioned how much she loved being a mother. Being able to work with her beloved husband who worked her schedule to make it easier to be with the children made her very happy, and that I think that translated into her acting with Dick York. The show was successful which would also have contributed to her happiness. With Dick Sargent, I think she had great chemistry with him as well, at least at first. However, her personal life starting going into shambles with the breakdown of her marriage, and though I think she could've maintained the energy, she didn't have it in her. Therefore, though Dick Sargent gave it his all, I personally believe Liz didn't, and it shows in her performances toward the end.

In 1989, Elizabeth herself concluded of the dual *Darrin* days:

I don't know who anyone's first choice was [to play *Darrin*], all I know is that, Dick York, Dick Sargent, and Richard Crenna were there. And any one of the three I would have been totally delighted with. . . . It's really difficult to compare a couple of actors like that when you've been that close to them. But I felt that Dick Sargent was a more easy-going presence, actually. But don't forget, too, by the time he came in, that marriage was five-years gold. So the characters themselves changed automatically. The newness of the relationship was done, and the relationship matured. So, I felt that *Darrin*, in any case, was becoming more of an easy presence, which made the problems even funnier at times. And he would sort of lapse into this kind of complacency, whenever he could. It was almost as if *Darrin* grew in the relationship . . . he felt maybe he wouldn't have to be on his guard as much. So, when he was suddenly confronted with something . . . like five years into the relationship . . . he wasn't quite the nervous wreck [as when York played him]. It was a marriage that had worked for six years [by the end of spring of 1970, Sargent's first season]. I mean, how many of those do you find around, especially with a mother-in-law like *Endora*.

Beyond the *Darrin* debacle, Lizzie found it challenging to address other issues with Agnes Moorehead, *Endora's* alter ego. For one, she said it was "impossible to talk politics to her . . . so you'd stay [away] from all sorts of really complicated areas like ice cream and religion."

But Doug Tibbles rememberd Moorehead as "kindly and polite . . . removed and semi-serious. I don't think it was directed at Elizabeth. It was simply her carriage."

Lizzie remembered how such carriage led to a terse, if comical, interaction between her and Aggie when film legend Ida Lupino was hired to direct the *Bewitched* episode, "A is for Aardvark," the plot which Bill Asher once said represented the message of the entire series.

Darrin is home sick in bed. Tired of running up and down the stairs to cater to his every whim, she grants him the gift of witchcraft. At first he goes wild with the power, but ultimately discovers that having material things without working for them is meaningless. And once he's feeling better, he buys her a watch (with money he earned from *McMann & Tate*), that's inscribed, "I love you every *second*." *Samantha* cries real tears, and their love is stronger than ever.

However, as Lizzie acknowledged in 1989, there was no love lost between Lupino and Moorehead, nor herself and Moorehead while filming this episode. Lizzie thought Lupino was "terrific, and really liked her, but she had her hands full with Aggie."

Elizabeth recalled Moorehead standing up against the television set in the *Stephens'* living room, and having "one of her snits. She had that attitude," which Lizzie felt was exacerbated by Moorehead's heavy eye make-up, or "whatever it was that (make-up artist Ben Lane) used to paste on her eyelashes. I just never understood how she could (have) . . . all that gook in her eyes." So Lizzie finally asked:

"Aggie, can you take a nap?"
"What do you mean?"
"How can you close your eyes with all that shit up there?"
"Don't talk to me that way!"

"It was amazing, because she was giving Ida this really kind of weird look," Lizzie went on to remember.

But Lupino was legitimately concerned about Moorehead's well-being. "What's the matter, Darling? Are you okay?"

Elizabeth intercepted those questions and said, "I think she's got something in her eye."

"And Aggie was fuming," Lizzie mused. "She almost popped her eyes, because she couldn't say, 'How dare you?'"

The situation became progressively worse from there, especially with Moorehead backed up against that television. Finally realizing that Agnes was sincerely upset, Lupino was more desperate than ever to address her concerns.

"Is there anything we can do?!"

And Lizzie was "just sitting there on the sofa, trying to stifle a laugh."

At which point, Aggie turned around to leave the set and, as Lizzie said, "She looked like an owl . . . her head almost went in a 180 degree turn. And she looked at me and I just looked at her, and she stomped off, away to her dressing room and slammed the door. And boy those violets (Moorehead's favorite flower, based on her favorite color) in that dressing room just went *boooogoooogooosh*."

Another jolting conversation took place between Elizabeth and Moorehead on the *Bewitched* set during the potent Sylmar earthquake of 1971. "There were still aftershocks," Lizzie recalled. "So we were all still kind of nervous, and I asked her if she was scared."

"No, of course not!"

"You weren't the tiniest bit scared?!"

"No! Why should I be scared? God takes care of me! God protects me through anything!"

"Well, that's good. So, what was the first thing you did when you felt the quake?"

"I grabbed my Picasso plate and put it underneath the piano."

"I see . . . God would take care of you, but you wouldn't trust God with your Picasso plate, eh?"

"Oh, Elizabeth! Really!!"

At which point, according to what Lizzie recalled in 1989, Moorehead "flounced off into her dressing room!"

Elizabeth also remembered how Agnes would sometimes employ a slight affectation in her voice when reciting certain words. "It's like when she hit us that day with 'Meami' instead of saying 'Miami.' I said, 'You just came back from *Meami*?' And I thought, *If anybody says anything, I'm gonna' kill' em.* Because I didn't think I could handle that. I just went, 'Oh, give me a break!'" While filming the episode, "Double, Double, Toil and Trouble," on September 28, 1967, something or someone was going to *break* for sure. In this segment:

Samantha, now Queen of the Witches, has to hold court at her house. When *Darrin* arrives home and sees the unusual proceedings, he orders every witch and warlock, including *Endora*, to vacate the premises. Infuriated, *Endora* enlists *Serena's* help to rid *Samantha* of *Darrin* forever. So, while

Sam attends a church fundraiser, *Endora* and *Serena* impersonate *Sam* [making] every attempt to drive *Darrin* away. Later, when their plan fails, Endora and *Serena*, along with *Samantha* and *Darrin*, [each] receive a pie in the face, during a free-for-all that takes place after *Sam* brings home a few baked goods from the church fundraiser.

The pie-throwing scenes were ignited when *Darrin* mistakenly threw a pie at *Samantha* who he thought was *Serena*, and the mayhem just expanded from there. And when this episode is viewed closely, Lizzie, who received a pie in the face twice, first as *Samantha* and then as *Serena*, is seen laughing so hard, her lines had to be dubbed twice. She and York clearly enjoyed filming this episode, but as Lizzie recalled in 1989, Moorhead was none too pleased about receiving a pie in the face:

It was instant fury and amusement at the same time. It was totally beneath her dignity when it happened to her. She wasn't the least bit happy. She was seething, and not a happy camper . . . And yet it happened to everybody else and because she was an actress that's the only thing that saved it. But there was no reason she should have been happy *all* the time. We would accommodate her in the schedule when she really had something to do like her one-woman show. Even though she confessed to me once that when she first read for [*Bewitched*], she thought well, *It's a job. I'll take it. It's going to be a failure anyway.* And then of course she was kind of hoping that it wouldn't have been a success, and then [when it was] she said she only wanted to do seven episodes . . . Then after doing [those seven and more], she said, *What do you mean, only seven episodes?* I always knew that once she was hooked on it, she wasn't going to go away too much.

But that's exactly what Moorehead eventually would do with her cross-country one-woman stage show tour, and it ultimately annoyed Elizabeth.

We'd do the schedule around her and everything. And she was cranky. I used to think, *I can't believe this. Why are we accommodating this woman?! If I'd try to do this, everybody would say, 'What?! Get your ass on the set, and stop behaving like an ass!'* Right? And of course I wouldn't have done it anyway, but that used to bother me (that Moorehead did it). And then she would get really nasty about stuff sometimes. And Bill would say, *Oh, come on, now, Liz . . . she's lonely.* And I'd be like, *Dammit—it's her own fault!* She's lonely and feeling put upon. Because I always tried to really make her feel terrific. I mean, I'd argue with her and stuff like that. I mean, why not? . . . Because that was fun.

Clearly, there were highs and lows, bonds and gaps between Lizzie and Aggie. But more than anything, as Charles Tranberg confirms, the two women had a solid professional relationship. Lizzie, in particular, "did little things" for Moorhead, sent cards, flowers, etc. "But off the set, except for an occasional party, such as one of Aggie's lavish Birthday-Christmas parties, they really didn't hang out together. If anybody was the daughter Agnes never had it was probably Debbie Reynolds."

As Tranberg sees it, Lizzie's association with Moorehead could have been more competitive on Aggie's part:

> But Elizabeth took great effort to make sure that Aggie felt comfortable as a member of the *Bewitched* family. She would send her cards for holidays and birthdays and flowers and funny little notes, just to let Aggie know that she was thinking of her. Aggie, I think, came to like Elizabeth very much so. At first she might have been a little dismissive of Elizabeth's talents. She once, reportedly, told Elizabeth that she basically plays herself, while when Aggie was Elizabeth's age she was *always characterizing*.
>
> I think Elizabeth took that kind of comment with a grain of salt and as time went on Agnes came to revise her opinion of Elizabeth's talent. She would have been greatly impressed, had she lived long enough, to see the many diverse and different types of roles that Elizabeth took on after *Bewitched*—and how well she did in them.

Tranberg says Moorehead always perceived Lizzie as a refined woman with good manners and a funny bone:

> Aggie loved a good sense of humor and Elizabeth could have a wicked one—as could Aggie. Neither, I believe, suffered fools gladly. They were both professionals who came to the set on time and knew their lines; Aggie certainly appreciated this about Elizabeth. Certainly as people that they had a respect and certain affection towards one another. As artists, I'm sure that Elizabeth was proud to be on a series that included an actress of Aggie's

stature. Aggie could be a bit jealous, however, that she was not the *star* of the show. It's somewhat revealing that in her correspondence to her secretary, Aggie repeatedly refers to *Bewitched* as *my show.* It's kind of funny.

Lizzie and Aggie were at the very least strong-willed, if not competitive. The competition, Tranberg says,

> . . . would be mostly on Aggie's side. Elizabeth was proud to be associated on the series with her. In fact, she was the one who suggested Agnes for the role of *Endora* and actually approached her about doing it. Agnes, at least from her private letters, seemed to feel that at times her contribution to the show was less appreciated than say, [that of] Elizabeth and Dick York.

In 1968, both women were Emmy-nominated in the lead actress category, possibly leaving room for Moorehead's vindication because, as Tranberg goes on to explain,

> . . . she felt it was her rightful place to be; even though Elizabeth, quite frankly, was certainly the lead actress and appeared in every episode. Whereas Agnes, who was brilliant as *Endora,* didn't appear in every episode [only two-thirds] and in some of those in which she did, she might just 'pop' in and then 'pop' out again. My guess is that when Agnes was, afterward, nominated in the supporting category again, it was a disappointment to her."

Another interesting cross-tone between Lizzie and Aggie was Robert Montgomery, an actor for whom both women had a great deal of respect. In the 1940s, when Moorehead was new to Hollywood, a columnist, "perhaps it was Hedda Hopper or Louella Parsons," Tranberg suggests, asked her to name a few actors she admired and the elder Montgomery, a Republican, was on her list.

> Politically, Agnes grew more conservative as the years went by. Early on she had greatly admired Eleanor Roosevelt and even had provided the voice of ER on radio with *The March of Time,* but by the 70s Agnes was openly supporting Richard Nixon and Ronald Reagan. She had previously thought that actors shouldn't be publicly involved in politics, but she truly

MAGICAL: No other word better describes Elizabeth in this publicity still from 1962.
Frank Bez—Globe Photos

A NEW ADAM AND A NEW EVE: Lizzie's "The Woman" struggles with Charles Bronson's "The Man" in "Two," her famous episode of *The Twilight Zone*, which originally aired September 15, 1961. No dialogue was spoken in this apocalyptic story except for one word by Elizabeth's character: "precrassny," which is Russian for "pretty." CBS/Photofest

BELOVED: Like every aspect of her life and career, a modest Elizabeth never gave herself credit for being a loving, kind parent. But she was. Just ask her children, two of whom she is seen with here in 1966 (on the grounds of her Beverly Hills home), all of whom she had with William Asher: Robert Asher, named for Lizzie's father (sitting on her knee), Billy Asher, Jr. (playing with the grass), and her daughter Rebecca, the youngest (not pictured), who would come along in 1969. She would be named after Elizabeth's beloved grandmother Becca. Globe Photos

THE EYES AND EARS OF COMEDY: Elizabeth and Dick York struck gold with their on-screen chemistry in *Bewitched*. They are seen here in a publicity shot from one of the show's most *end-ear-ing* episodes, "My, What Big Ears You Have," which originally aired on December 7, 1967. ABC/Photofest

WITCH WAY IS UP: Elizabeth and Agnes Moorehead in the colorful witches wardrobe from the *Bewitched* episode, "If They Never Met," which aired January 25, 1968. Elizabeth designed her own black witch's garment. At first it was as it appears here. The following year it was replaced with a revised black gown with a green lamet breast plate, which she adorned for the remainder of the series. Moorehead's costume was first all violet and later changed to this light green/violet combination. (Violet was Moorehead's favorite color; she even decorated her dressing room with it and came to be known as *The Lavender Lady*). ABC Photo Archives, courtesy of Getty Images

THE EIGHT-YEAR WITCHES AND MORTALS: The *Bewitched* cast assembled for this rare pic from the show's eighth season (1971–1972). Top Row (from left): David White (*Larry Tate*), Kasey Rogers (*Louise Tate*), Robert F. Simon (*Frank Stephens*, Darrin's father), Alice Ghostley (*Esmeralda*), Bernie Kopell (*The Witch Apothecary*). Second Row (from left): Dick Sargent (*Darrin, Number Two*), Elizabeth (*Samantha/Serena*), Maurice Evans (*Maurice*), Agnes Moorehead (*Endora*), Bernard Fox (*Dr. Bombay*). Third Row (from left): Paul Lynde (*Uncle Arthur*), Erin Murphy (*Tabitha*), Diane Murphy (*Tabitha*), David Lawrence (*Adam*), Greg Lawrence (*Adam*). © 1978 Gene Trindl/mptvimages.com

SHE STOOD BY AND BEHIND HER MAN: When it was good, it was great, and when it was bad, it was terrible. But while it lasted, Elizabeth's marriage to Bill Asher was pure magic, on-screen and off. After they divorced in 1974, she retained respect for him as an artist and as the father of their three children. They remained friends, and Lizzie called upon his professional counsel on many of her post-*Bewitched* TV-movies. Roy Cummings Archive

LAUGHTER IN THE RAIN: Elizabeth finally received her much-deserved "star" on the Hollywood Walk of Fame, during a very stormy-weather ceremony, January 4, 2008. Those in attendance included (from left) Elizabeth's fourth husband Robert Foxworth, Hollywood's Honorary Mayor Johnny Grant, her children Billy Asher, Jr. and Rebecca Asher, and close friend Liz Sheridan. They each shared their memories of Elizabeth and mentioned how she would have found humor in the fact that it was pouring rain that day. Grant passed away only five days later, making Elizabeth's ceremony the last over which he presided. © Smith/Retna Ltd./Corbis

BEDEVILED: Many of Lizzie's post-*Bewitched* performances were much darker roles than *Samantha Stephens*. But none were as diabolically evil as her TV-movie characters from 1975's *The Legend of Lizzie Borden*, 1991's *Sins of the Mother*, and *Black Widow Murders: The Blanche Taylor Moore Story* (as pictured here), which aired May 3, 1993. Interestingly, in both *Mother* and *Widow*, Lizzie sported a very *Serena*-like hairdo, short and teased. In this photo from *Widow*, her hair is short and auburn. In *Sins of the Mother*, her hair was short and exactly *Serena*-black. Picture-Alliance/Newscom

WITCH UPON A MOON: A statue of Elizabeth as *Samantha* was commemorated by TV Land in Salem, Massachusetts (*the witch capitol of the world*), on June 15, 2005. The design combined the visual of the *Bewitched* animated opening credits sequence of *Samantha* flying on a broom past the moon through a starlit sky with the live-action sequences in which she was dressed in regular mortal clothes. TV Land

felt that America was on a moral decline and felt that people like Nixon and Reagan would implement policies that would turn this around.

In that way, she was probably closer to Robert Montgomery than to Elizabeth—who was a lifelong liberal. I doubt very much that Elizabeth and Agnes ever discussed politics. I can't really document it but I have a feeling somewhere along the line Agnes might have told Elizabeth, "You did a good job in that scene. Your father would be so proud!" But then again, if she felt that there was a hint of Elizabeth and Robert Montgomery having problems in their personal relationship—she might not say anything to Elizabeth about him.

Tranberg concludes that both actresses were bright, funny, strong-willed, and talented women who came to like each other a great deal and enjoyed working together. "Agnes probably thought that Elizabeth got a few more perks and consideration due to the fact that her husband, Bill Asher, was the director and later producer of the show. She alluded to it a couple of times in letters to her secretary regarding this." But in general, he concludes, Lizzie and Aggie complemented each other well. "You could see really in their performances that they could be mother and daughter. They brought a lot of affection and love to their scenes together."

Meanwhile, the following twitch-bit of information proves intriguing:

According to entertainment historian Rob Ray, the name *Endora*, bestowed upon Moorehead's *Bewitched* character, refers to the Biblical *Witch of Endor*. Ray says this sorceress, sometimes called *The Medium of Endor*, was "a woman who apparently conjured up the spirit of recently deceased prophet Samuel, at the command of King Saul of the Kingdom of Israel, in the *First Book of Samuel* (28:3–25)," although the witch is absent from the version of that event recounted in the deuterocanonical *Book of Sirach* (47:19–20). If anything, that seemingly fits Moorehead's religious personal profile (which also includes her coaching actor Jeffrey Hunter for his role as Jesus in the 1961 movie, *King of Kings*).

Ray further explains how William Shakespeare is nicely added into the witch's brew here, specifically Act IV, Scene 1 of *Macbeth*: "There's that infamously popular moment in *Macbeth* when those three witches cast a spell to bring a double amount of 'toil and trouble' to the king"—a moment that concurs with Lizzie and *Bewitched* in more ways than one, mostly because she caused her father a periodic measure of heartache, and vice versa.

Thirteen

~

. . . Toil and Trouble

"Do I look like *Mary Poppins* to you?"

—*Serena*, in the *Bewitched* episode,
"*Serena's* Youth Pill," February 5, 1972

Lizzie loved to watch science fiction/fantasy programs like the original *Star Trek* (NBC, 1966–1969) and the gothic daytime soap *Dark Shadows* (ABC, 1966–1970), the latter of which featured another blonde sorceress (*Angelique*, played by Lara Parker). After *Bewitched*, she delighted in shows like *The Incredible Hulk* (CBS, 1978–1982), which co-starred Bill Bixby and Lou Ferrigno in a double lead role.

To tone her own theatrical twin muscles on *Bewitched*, she'd don a black wig and some funky 1960s wardrobe to play *Serena*, *Samantha's* look-alike and somewhat wilder cousin.

The idea for Serena was generated early on in the series. In 1989, Lizzie explained the *Samantha-Serena* transformation process:

Melody McCord was my understudy. We would go into my dressing room and go over dialogue, so she could get the timing right, so there wouldn't be any gaps. She was exactly my height and looked very much like me. That's why we could do the wonderful crossover (scenes on camera). We were lucky that she worked out that way. There are times when you have an understudy that doesn't look anything like you at all, except for light coloring. She and I are built alike, same coloring. Then they would have to tie-off all the cameras and wait until we changed clothes and makeup. For her, makeup was no problem unless we were using ³/₄ of her face, and not just changing her wig. With me, it would be a complete makeup change. It was always easier to go from *Sam* to *Serena* than *Serena* to *Sam*. *Serena* wore a lot more makeup . . . that crazy person.

Whenever *Serena* showed up, Lizzie was billed in the credits as *Pandora Spocks*, a subtle nod to the famous Greek myth of *Pandora's Box*.

Pandora's Box was an artifact, taken from the myth of *Pandora's* creation as it is explained around line 60 of *Hesiod: Works and Days*. The "box" in question was actually a large jar given to *Pandora* (translated as "all-gifted") which contained all the evils of the world. When Pandora opened the jar, the contents were released, except for the virtue of hope.

Today, opening Pandora's Box means *to create evil that cannot be undone*. In *Serena's* world on *Bewitched*, it meant Lizzie's interpretation of *Samantha's* free-spirited cousin would be significantly hipper than her performance as the more conservative *Sam*. Lizzie played *Serena* to the hilt, further amusing herself with the *Serena/Spocks* billing.

"I just thought I was so clever when I came up with the name," Lizzie said in 1989, even though a *Bewitched* co-worker had another suggestion when doing the show.

"Why don't you just call her *Pandora Box*?"

"Um, I don't think so," she replied. "My choice is a little subtler and funnier."

She was also clear on another matter: Her real-life cousin Amanda did *not* serve as the prototype for *Samantha's* cousin *Serena*. She explained in 1989:

We had always been very close as kids. But she was not the inspiration for *Serena*. And instead of making *Serena* out to be *Samantha's* long lost sister, I thought to make her *Samantha's* cousin.

However, another *Bewitched* character, *Uncle Arthur*, played by Paul Lynde, had at least been named after Lizzie's real-life relative. "I always adored my Uncle Arthur," she acknowledged in 1989, while she also thought highly of Lynde. "I got along very well with Paul," she said . . . almost to a fault.

One morning on the set of *Bewitched*, the two shared a laugh so hard, director Bill Asher screamed, "I give up!" called for lunch at 10:30 AM, and walked off the set. That's when Lynde pointed to her and said, "It's all *her* fault."

"We were a mess, just an absolute wreck," Lizzie mused in 1989, recalling the incident during which they behaved like childhood playmates reprimanded by a grade-school teacher.

One of her favorite *Bewitched* episodes was the first season episode "Driving Is the Only Way to Fly," which featured Lynde in his first guest-star appearance on the show, not as *Uncle Arthur*, but as *Harold Harold*, a very nervous mortal driving instructor for *Samantha*. Lizzie recalled:

> "Driving Is the Only Way to Fly" was one of my favorites! I mean, I totally truly enjoyed that. When you're working with somebody who's totally off the wall like [Lynde was], it gives you a lot of [creative] freedom. And Bill having known Paul for a long time, trusted him a lot and vice versa. So stuff that we would do also bled over into [Paul's performance] . . . His instincts were fascinating. I wish he would have known. I wish he [had] understood how important he was despite all of his problems [alcoholism, manic depression]. I tried to help him. . . . It was wonderful because when you work with somebody really like that you find yourself kind of using another part of your imagination that you don't use with people that you [usually work] with. It was on a different level [with Lynde].

No doubt Lizzie laughed a lot with Lynde whenever he played opposite her as *Samantha*, be it as *Uncle Arthur* or *Harold Harold*. But he hardly cracked a smile whenever she portrayed niece *Serena* to his *Uncle Arthur*. "Paul couldn't stand *Serena*," Elizabeth admitted. "His attitude was very different when I played her as opposed to when I played *Samantha*. But so was everybody else's. I'd walk on the set as *Serena* and the crew acted entirely different toward me than when I was *Sam*."

Vi Alford, the wardrobe designer, not only functioned differently around Lizzie when she donned the *Serena* black wig and garb, she would periodically fail to recognize the actress. "There were times, when Vi would forget that I was playing *Serena*," Lizzie recalled. "I'd be standing right next to her, and she wouldn't even know I was there."

Former actor Peter Ackerman is a married Episcopalian priest with children who serves as Rector of St. Christopher's Episcopal Church in Springfield, Virginia. In the 1960s, he was the child of a TV star and a network executive who oversaw nearly every hit Columbia/Screen Gems series of the era, including *Hazel, Dennis The Menace, I Dream of Jeannie, Father Knows Best,* and *Bewitched.*

Peter is the son of *Bewitched* executive producer Harry Ackerman, who also served as the head of Screen Gems (and before that CBS) and actress Elinor Donahue, best known for her roles on *The Andy Griffith Show* and *Father Knows Best* (the latter during which she met and married Harry). So, like Lizzie, he's the offspring of noteworthy parents in the entertainment industry, parents who raised him with strong family values at the height of their Hollywood careers. Again, like Lizzie, Peter's interest couldn't help but be piqued by the industry that surrounded him. He recalls a rare show business party at the Ackerman home with all the trimmings—caterers, bartenders, servers, TV stars, athletes, and more:

> I remember waking up as a little kid, practically invisible to a discussion with a fellow who had just returned from Africa studying pigmies. I still remember where I was standing in the house when I said to myself, "This is what I want to be a part of when I grow up."

He was afforded the luxury of visiting the sets of Columbia's most classic shows, namely, the adventures of *Samantha* and *Darrin*, where he would meet and chat with Lizzie, Dick Sargent (the second *Darrin*), Agnes Moorehead ("She clearly liked kids"), and Paul Lynde (". . . did not like kids").

One day, Peter visited the *Bewitched* set when Lizzie was in her *Serena* guise. "I was probably the most gullible kid in those days," he recalls. "And it didn't help that outside my Dad's office were two autographed photos, one of and signed by Liz, and one of and signed by Liz as *Serena*."

When he finally did meet Lizzie as *Serena*, "she couldn't have been nicer," he says. But then someone, probably Bill Asher, yelled from the set, "Hey—where is Liz?!" At that point, Lizzie/ *Serena* turned to Peter and said, "I think she went to tinkle," politely excused herself and then left to see if they needed her on the set. "For years," Peter concludes, "I told my school friends that Liz and *Serena* were two different people, and I was convinced!"

Upon its debut, *Bewitched* had immediately established itself as a hit for ABC. So much so, rival network NBC and *Samantha* proprietor Columbia Studios sought to regurgitate the magic formula, at first requesting the assistance of *Sam*-scribe Sol Saks, who declined. "I had already created one show about a witch," he said in 1988. "I didn't want to do another."

Consequently, NBC approached producer Sidney Sheldon, who had befriended Bill Asher on *The Patty Duke Show*, which they had co-created. Sheldon agreed to do a new supernatural sitcom, and suggested to Columbia and NBC a concept that ultimately became *I Dream of Jeannie*, starring Barbara Eden as a female genie in love with her male master played by Larry Hagman. But Sheldon was concerned that Asher might object to *Jeannie's* similarities to *Bewitched*. "Sidney was very polite about the whole situation," Bill explains. "He came to me and said, 'How do you feel if I do a show about a genie?' And I told him I didn't care."

Lizzie, however, was irate. When she first got wind that Sheldon was developing *Jeannie*, she gave it little thought—until, that is, she and Bill met for a social chat with Sheldon in Beverly Hills.

As she recalled in 1989:

> Sidney was a friend of Bill's, and he invited us to lunch. The more Sidney talked about what he was going to do with his show, the more I sat back in my chair in awe. I thought to myself, "Elizabeth—are you hearing this right? Are you really listening to this conversation?" I was in such a funk. And when I heard Sidney say, "I must think of some way for her (Jeannie *blinked* her eyes) to motivate the magic just like *Samantha* does (with her nose twitch)," I just couldn't believe it. I had to prop my hand under my chin to keep my mouth from falling open. I was annoyed. That doesn't mean I was annoyed with Barbara Eden and Larry Hagman. I was annoyed

with Sidney. I was struck dumb. And I usually have something to say. But as I recall, it was a silent drive home.

Despite such a detour, Sheldon's show enjoyed a smooth ride with home viewers. Like *Bewitched* on ABC, *Jeannie* proved to be a ratings dream for NBC—from the moment it debuted in the fall of 1965. What's more, *Samantha's* training reels were not derailed, as *Bewitched* continued to inspire *Jeannie*. Lizzie offered her double-play of *Samantha* and her mischievous raven-haired look-alike cousin *Serena*. Eden later delivered a twin take as *Jeannie* and her brunette doppelganger sister, all of which further infuriated Lizzie. "People were even laughing about *that one*," she said in 1989, particularly because *Bewitched* and *Jeannie* were filmed at the same studio. "Had I been Barbara, I would have said, 'No, sorry. How can I do this? How can I play the dark-haired double to this character?'"

By this point, Lizzie was "flabbergasted," and thought, "Sidney Sheldon should have said, *Wait a minute. I've known Bill Asher for years, and I'm his friend.* ("At least I think they were," she added.) *I can't go in there and steal from this other show,* which is in essence what it was."

Although Lizzie was always cordial to Barbara during the *Bewitched-Jeannie* cross-over years, she was periodically annoyed with her, particularly in the Screen Gems makeup room that both women shared while working on their respective shows. For a time, actress Sally Field was there right beside them, during her time on *Gidget* and *The Flying Nun*, both of which, like *Bewitched* and *I Dream of Jeannie*, were produced by Screen Gems, and aired on ABC in the 1960s.

When Field appeared on *The Rosie O'Donnell Show* (May 10, 2001), she talked about having her makeup applied in that room, while she sat between Lizzie and Barbara. Apparently, Barbara liked to sing, which she happened to be doing a lot of this one particular morning, and it got on Lizzie's and Sally's nerves. According to what Field told O'Donnell, when Barbara left the makeup room one day, Lizzie turned to her in frustration and said, "Does she have to sing *all the time*?!"

In her memoir, *Jeannie Out of the Bottle* (Crown/Archetype, 2011), which she wrote with Wendy Leigh, Eden apologized to just Sally and not Elizabeth for the musical annoyance. Apparently, Eden used her *Jeannie* time in the makeup room to rehearse for a nightclub act she was performing in

Las Vegas. "Sorry, Sally! If only I'd known, I'd have practiced in the shower instead."

On September 21, 2005, a few years later, Eden appeared in the second episode of TV Land's *TV Land Confidential* series. She mentioned the morning makeup sessions, some baby talk, and ignored the singing sensationalism. In the *Confidential* segment "When Real Life and Screen Life Collide," Eden explained how she'd frequently see Lizzie in the makeup department. "In fact," she said, "we were pregnant together. She had many babies on that show [*Bewitched*]."

Still, those in the *Bewitched* circle tried to calm Lizzie's nerves regarding the general intermingling of their show and *I Dream of Jeannie*. David White thought Lizzie riled herself up for nothing. In 1989, he said:

> There was little noteworthy comparison between *Bewitched* and *I Dream of Jeannie*. *Samantha* and *Darrin* were trying to lead a normal life with their children. There was a great deal of love within the *Stephens'* household, and there wasn't that kind of love on *Jeannie*. And the humor on *Bewitched* was less impacted. It didn't hit you over the head with one-liners as much as it allowed the humor to develop from the situation.

Years after *Bewitched* and *I Dream of Jeannie* completed their original network runs, Lizzie still felt a measure of contempt for the witch-inspired genie series, particularly when in 1985, Bill Asher, from who she had long been divorced, signed on to direct the NBC TV reunion movie, *I Dream of Jeannie: 15 Years Later*. Produced by Sidney Sheldon, the film became one of the highest rated small screen flicks in history, surpassing Lizzie's 1974 NBC film, *A Case of Rape*. "You should have heard Liz," he recalled in 1988 when discussing his work on the film. "She said, 'You idiot!'"

She wasn't upset that the movie was a hit, or that it surpassed *A Case of Rape* in ratings, or any of that. Bill says she was just upset that he was involved with the movie at all.

However, in 1989, when she was reminded of his association with the film, Elizabeth remained loyal to her ex-husband (the father of her three children), saying, "I didn't care about that. That was his business. And they could not have picked a better person to do it."

After the *Jeannie* reunion aired, she was frequently approached about doing a TV reunion movie of *Bewitched*. Various networks offered her a substantial salary to reprise the role of *Samantha*. But as she explained in 1989, she never considered it even a slight possibility, despite the potential cash flow:

> Absolutely not; it's not about the money. That has nothing to do with it; for the networks and studios that might not be the case, but screw that. I'm approached about this all the time. And I know there are people out there who really want to do this . . . but there's not a shot in hell . . . forget it. I think once you've done something, you've done it . . . and that's fine. And I'm proud of it. But now, let's just, as my grandmother used to say, "Leave it lay where Jesus flung it!"

Or as she later and less passionately relayed to writer Ed Bark of *The Dallas Morning News* on March 26, 1994:

> I wouldn't want to do it again. It's still playing all over the place in reruns. It was a wonderful experience, and I had a blast doing it. But when you've done something like that, let it have its life and let it go where it's going.

Media steward Rob Ray offers his take on the *Sam-Jeannie* doubles debacle:

> The conceit of one actor portraying multiple roles is probably as old as the acting profession itself. Classic playwrights in their work as varied as William Shakespeare's *King Lear* to James M. Barrie's *Peter Pan* have created multiple parts designed to be played by the same actor. The idea that one actor could play two roles simultaneously was born near the dawn of film-making and achieved early renown in the films of Mary Pickford. Pickford, known as *America's Sweetheart* with her long curls and petite five-foot frame, could play children as easily as adults and often performed in movies requiring her to age from childhood into adulthood. In several films, such as *Stella Maris* and *Little Lord Fauntleroy*, surprisingly sophisticated split-screen effects were used to enable her to appear onscreen in two roles at the same time. In *Little Lord Fauntleroy*, the petite Miss Pickford portrays the title male role and his own mother and in one scene we actually see Miss Pickford as a

boy kiss the cheek of Miss Pickford as the mother using a split-screen technique as sophisticated as any used today. Later, in 1921, Buster Keaton played nearly every role in his two-reel short entitled *The Playhouse*. In the fifties, Alec Guinness played eight roles in *Kind Hearts and Coronets* and Peter Sellers played almost as many in 1964's *Dr. Strangelove*. Examples of one actor portraying twins are too numerous to mention, but *The Parent Trap* is one of the more famous examples. However, the idea of one actor playing identical *cousins* may go back to the first silent version of Anthony Hope's *The Prisoner of Zenda* in 1913, which has been remade countless times. In that story, the heir to the throne of a mythical European kingdom is abducted just before his coronation and his identical British cousin, a commoner, is drafted by the palace to pose as his royal relative until the kidnappers can be thwarted. To the baby boomer generation, the most famous identical cousins may be *Patty* and *Cathy Lane*, both portrayed by Patty Duke in *The Patty Duke Show* from 1963 to 1966, a series that Bill Asher and Sidney Sheldon co-produced. Imitation is the sincerest form of praise, one might say!

Maybe so; but it simply bothered Lizzie that *I Dream of Jeannie*, an already blatant replica of *Bewitched*, would go the next step and showcase the brunette and slightly-more lascivious relative look-alike scenario. It got to the point where *Bewitched* writers were ordered to stay away from *I Dream of Jeannie*. Unfortunately, one of *Samantha's* main scribes didn't adhere that ruling—and was subsequently fired as a result of writing a *Jeannie* segment behind Lizzie's back.

The *Bewitched/I Dream of Jeannie* scenario was never more evident as when, on July 16, 1994, *TV Guide* ignited *The Great Jeannie vs. Samantha Debate*. The magazine essentially invited its readers and Nick at Nite watchers to respond to this poll:

Which magical blonde is more powerful: *Samantha* the witch on *Bewitched* or *Jeannie* the genie from *I Dream of Jeannie*? Exactly 810,938 out of approximately one million Nick at Nite viewers voted *Samantha* the stronger supernaturalist. But editors of the *Guide's* popular "Cheers 'N'& Jeers" column were astounded by the results:

Are you crazy? *Sam* didn't even have enough wattage to keep the same *Darrin* for the run of her show. She also received frequent paranormal assists from *Endora* and her TV coven. Meanwhile, bottled *Jeannie* not only kept *Major Nelson* (Larry Hagman) in a trance for five seasons, she wed him, kept her evil sister in check, and did it all with nothing but her crossed arms. We think *Tabitha* was stuffing the ballot box.

Two weeks later, Lizzie fans were livid and fearless and continued with their *strong* opinions, which *TV Guide* had no choice but to publish. In the issue dated, July 27, 1994, the editors wrote:

What a fuss! When Nick at Nite sponsored a '60s sitcom showdown pitting *Samantha* against *Jeannie*, we weighed in with our opinion. We chided the 810,938 viewers who picked *Sam*, and boy, did we hear it. Since we couldn't make the letters go away by blinking, we decided to devote this page to your most(ly) bitter rebuttals.

Some of which were as follows:

Don't you realize that *Bewitched* all but put the ABC network on the map? Get a grip, *TV Guide.*—Mason Cargone, North Chili, New York

Put them in a sealed vault, which one do *you* think would get out?—Yancy Mitchell, Ardmore, Tennessee

Bewitched appeared a year before *Jeannie,* so there wouldn't have been a *Jeannie* if not for *Bewitched,* nor a blink if there hadn't first been a twitch.— Randolph Sloan, Greece, New York

Whoever wrote that Jeer, was male and prefers a pleasing-you-pleases-me-syndrome slave to a loving, equal partner in relationships.—Wendy Martin, Owosso, Michigan

Any woman who calls her husband "Master" is already a loser.—Jimmie Welt, Gunter, Texas

Of course *Samantha* had more power than *Jeannie*. She didn't have to rely on a skimpy costume to keep ratings high!—Mary Campbell-Droze, San Mateo, California

How many women are powerful enough to replace their husbands—unnoticed—with someone who not only goes by the same name but is a foot and a half taller?—John Moreland, Pasadena, California

Fourteen

Public Broadcasting

"I grew up in Hollywood, so I've seen what
kinds of damage loose talk can do."
—Elizabeth Montgomery, *The Advocate Magazine*, July 30, 1992

Lizzie could just as easily chat with the "go-fer" on any studio set as mingle at the most elegant Hollywood affair. But book her on a talk show? No way. Such appearances were "too personal" for her shy nature. As she explained to *Picture Life Magazine* in December 1971, "They terrify me."

It was an emotion she would mention time and again when addressing live TV performances, interviews, or personal appearances of any kind. On December 21, 1985, she went on *Entertainment Tonight* to promote her CBS TV-movie, *Amos.* Reporter Scott Osborne asked if she enjoyed doing interviews ". . . like this one."

"Not really," she replied. "In fact, you have no idea just how panic-stricken I am right now."

On February 6, 2012, *Time Magazine* published a fascinating cover story, "The Power of Shyness: The Upside of Being an Introvert (and Why Extroverts are Overrated)" by self-admitted introvert Bryan Walsh who wrote:

Shyness is a form of anxiety characterized by inhibited behavior. It also implies a fear of social judgment that can be crippling. Shy people actively seek to avoid social situations, even ones that may be inhibited by fear. Introverts shun social situations because, Greta Garbo–style, they simply want to be alone . . . Caution, inhibition, and even fearfulness may be healthy—and smart—adaptations for the overstimulated person, but they're still not characteristics many parents would want in their children, especially in a society that lionizes the bold. So it's common for moms and dads of introverted offspring to press their kids to be more outgoing, lest they end up overlooked in class and later in life. That, however, can be a mistake—and not just because our temperaments are difficult to change fundamentally.

Still, Lizzie did somehow manage to show up that day in 1992 with Scott Osborne on *Entertainment Tonight*, and she made four other rare appearances on TV talk shows with live audiences. She was by no means a frequent talk show guest, like Totie Fields, Burt Reynolds, or Zsa Zsa Gabor, but there she was on: *The Dennis Miller Show* (in 1992 with Robert Foxworth), *The Merv Griffin Show* (in December 1970 to promote her favorite *Bewitched* episode, "Sisters at Heart"), *The Joey Bishop Show* (in 1967 with Michele Lee, who would later appear with Elizabeth in the 1976 TV-movie *Dark Victory*), and *The Mike Douglas Show*, on November 4, 1966, an especially riveting segment in which she proved telling, honest, and protective, all at once.

Here are some highlights from the *Douglas* interview in particular, by far her most fascinating talk show appearance:

Douglas opened the show with his routine musical number, she emerged from behind the program's sliding stage doors with a strange companion: a small statue of a fox's head that Bill Asher had purchased for her at an antique shop. She brought it with her for good luck, and kept it on her lap when not in her hand.

The figurehead worked like a charm. She, Douglas, and his co-host Cesar Romero (then playing *The Joker* on ABC's camp classic *Batman*) played darts, and she won.

Later, Douglas turned to the studio audience (and the home viewer) and said, "I'm not sure if any of you know this, but Elizabeth is the daughter of Robert Montgomery." The studio audience applauded in recognition, while she smiled and said, "I like him, too."

When Douglas wondered if she felt her father played a role in her career, she went on to address several key aspects of the core relationship with her father:

"Probably—because it was in the family my interests peaked. I don't think you can be around something like that and either not love it or just give it up entirely. My brother (Skip) tried it for a while and just decided it really wasn't for him. And I think probably he's the only sane member of the family. But Dad helped. And people say it is a help or a hindrance to have a parent who is known. And it's definitely a help. I think it's silly to say it isn't, because I know it certainly helps open doors that [would] not necessarily open that easily or maybe never. Afterwards, I guess, it depends on ability. But certainly it helps and I've always been very proud of him."

Douglas asked her to talk about her father's former duties as the appointed television advisor to President Eisenhower (a topic which author Steven J. Ross had touched upon during his CPAN interview at the 2012 Los Angeles Festival of Books). She said that her dad helped the President with makeup, eye-glass selection, and the teleprompter. But she couldn't remember if Eisenhower wanted to use one of those "tricky things," because she certainly never saw their benefit. "I don't trust them," she said. "They make me very nervous." If she was forced to count on the electronic cue-card machine for important presidential-like speeches, she'd be a "nervous wreck" because even the thought of using one forced her to have visions of "kind of snarling into a hole or something."

Romero chimed in and wondered if her father helped the President with speeches and diction. "Yes," Lizzie replied. "I believe he did. And it was funny because he was getting teased, unmercifully, when he was doing make-up for the President."

At one point, she explained when her father called her up and said, "Meet me at the White House," which sounded strange to her.

"That's just crazy."

But she agreed, on one condition: If he'd meet her in the makeup department.

She was kidding, but he wasn't amused. "I think that's a terrible thing to say," he complained.

No matter. She enjoyed her meeting with President Eisenhower: "It was very exciting." She walked into the Oval Office, and he was sitting at that "marvelous desk in that beautiful room."

At some point, the President rose from his chair, and the first thing she noticed was his casual attire, specifically, that he wasn't wearing a tie, which she thought "seemed kind of strange . . . He had on like a golf shirt—with the three little buttons and things."

Sure enough, before she met the President, he had asked her father, "Do you think I should put on a tie?"

After Lizzie detailed her travels to Washington, Douglas asked her about the challenges of raising children with Bill Asher amidst their busy *Bewitched* schedule. She replied: "Oh, yes, well . . . it's a little rough and thank goodness they're young. You know, the oldest one (Billy, Jr.) is a little over two; and the youngest one (Robert, named for her father) is one year old October 5. So they're quite a handful. But the children's hours are so peculiar. But I don't think it matters as long as we have enough time to really be with them if they're kept up a little later at night as long as they get their sleep. We see them every night when we come home. We're up at 5:30 in the morning which is before they ever get up."

Later, Cesar Romero, who *Bewitched* producers once considered to play *Samantha's* father (a role rejected by Lizzie's father and later won by Shakespearean actor Maurice Evans), interjected how he and Asher had roomed together when they were starting out in the business, and how he had once worked for Asher's father, a producer, at Universal Studios.

The interlocking topics, though not known to all, continued when legendary theatre producer David Merrick, famous for *Hello Dolly*, later appeared with writer Abe Burrows to promote their new musical, *Holly Golightly*, based on *Breakfast at Tiffany's*, and starring Mary Tyler Moore and Richard Chamberlain.

At the onset of his interview with Merrick, Douglas ignited an odd conversation with the somewhat controversial and very opinionated Merrick which caught him and most probably everyone else off-guard. With Lizzie sitting opposite him, and with Merrick smack dab in the middle, Douglas said, "David, your image with actors is a father image."

Lizzie's reaction remained hidden from the camera, but she might not have displayed one at all. In those days, talk show guests handled themselves with decorum and were not as outlandish, abrasive, and brutally honest or as "shock-expressive" as they are in today's "anything goes" style of reality TV. It was monumental enough that Lizzie was appearing on a talk show, let alone partaking in a segment that might open a potential can of worms.

In either case, Douglas' father-figure reference and Merrick's subsequent reply most assuredly gave her pause, considering her relationship with her dad, not to mention her then-present marriage to Bill Asher, and her prior nuptials with Gig Young—both of whom were older than she.

In response to Douglas, Merrick said:

"Well, I think that's what a producer is, sort of a father image of the whole project (in this case, *Holly Golightly*). To get it launched and to get the entire creative team together. . . . and when it gets into trouble . . . the show I mean . . . and it surely does very quickly, they come looking to the producer to keep it together and also to be sort of a referee in the fights. And perhaps that's the reason for the father image."

As if to add insult to injury, Douglas then wondered if Merrick watched television. The producer responded forthrightly that he did not—again, while seated directly beside Lizzie, who was then at the peak of her popularity with *Bewitched*—the television show that all but put ABC on the map. Despite the fact that it was established in 1948, the "alphabet web" was still the youngest of the networks and it needed a hit like *Bewitched* to solidify its status.

Merrick was granted a chance to recover his dignity in Lizzie's company when Douglas asked him about beautiful women. At which point he turned to the beloved actress, glanced back at his host, and said, "Here's a beautiful woman—and a beautiful witch is best of all."

Shortly after that, Merrick's colleague, the flamboyant Burrows, joined the panel, and brought along with him a glimpse of that future shock-expressive mentality. Within seconds of taking the stage, he mimicked "zapping" Lizzie with his hands—right before asking if she'd like to take the lead in his next play.

Possibly intrigued by the suggestion, she responded with only a giggle (and what looked like almost a twitch), certainly aware that her *Bewitched* schedule might not allow for such outside demands. Also, appearing in Burrows' next production might not have been a wise career move.

Holly Golightly, which he and Merrick were on the *Douglas* show to promote, did not become the hit it was intended to be (which may have been one reason why Merrick appeared so testy). It starred Lizzie's TV contemporaries, Richard Chamberlain and Mary Tyler Moore, both of whom had just finished successful series runs (*Dr. Kildare* and *The Dick Van Dyke Show*, respectively). Unlike Lizzie, however, they could more easily forget *Golightly* and pursue other such assignments. But as it turned out *Holly* failed to pay off, which may have already been evident to the wise and perceptive Lizzie.

Another guest proved to be an even more intriguing addition to the panel: Reverend Rudolph W. Nemser, then the Pastor of a Unitarian church in the suburbs of Washington, D.C., and otherwise known as the "Divorce Pastor," was seated right next to Lizzie, who was most certainly reminded of her previously failed marriages to Gig Young and to her first husband, Fred Cammann.

Former *Douglas* associate producer Kenneth Johnson would later produce and direct sci-fi TV classics like *Alien Nation* (Fox, 1989–1990), the original *V* series (NBC, 1984–1985), the original *Bionic Woman* (ABC/NBC, 1976–1979), and *The Incredible Hulk* (CBS, 1978–1982), the latter of which was one of Lizzie's favorite shows ("I absolutely love it!").

Johnson remembers the week Lizzie appeared on the Douglas show with guest co-host Cesar Romero, "mostly because (fellow producer) Roger Ailes and I took Romero out to see Sammy Davis, Jr. in performance. And then we all spent three hours in Sammy's dressing room afterward."

As Johnson recalls producing the daily *Douglas* show, he was one of three producers who divided the guests amongst themselves. But as he explains:

> Elizabeth did not fall to me that day, so I didn't have that much communication with her. But the confluence of discussion on the show that day was truly happenstance and it's interesting in retrospect to see how it dovetailed with Elizabeth's own life. I do remember that we were delighted to have her on and that she was charming and the audience loved seeing her.

As it turns out, many fans of Lizzie and *Bewitched* are also fans of Johnson's original *Bionic Woman* series starring Lindsay Wagner (and not the NBC remake from 2007), and have for years compared the two shows and the characters of *Samantha Stephens* and Wagner's cybernetic *Jaime Sommers*. For one, performing and visual artist Ray Caspio:

> *Bewitched* is the first TV show I remember watching. It was on a small color television in the front room of my grandma's house when I was probably three years old, if that. The animated opening sequence combined with the music transfixed me, and when Elizabeth appeared on the screen, she did the same. There was something very accessible, yet private about her. Her

heart was open and something deep was going on within. Elizabeth, as *Samantha*, represented possibility to me. Anything I wanted, I could have if I worked for it. She had the magical abilities to obtain whatever she wanted whenever she wanted, but she wasn't satisfied with that. Her power was in herself: a theme that ran through many of her characters, and a theme that runs through characters I've been inspired by since childhood, such as Lynda Carter's portrayal of *Wonder Woman* and Lindsay Wagner's *Jaime Sommers*.

Johnson explains why Wagner was cast as *Sommers*:

She had a truly real, girl-next-door quality and brought a refreshing spontaneity to the scripted material. She had a facility for really making it sound like she was making it up as she went along. Part of that came from me listening carefully to her idiomatic speech patterns and writing the character of *Jaime Sommers* in a fashion that Lindsay could most easily embrace.

A similar strategy was utilized by Bill Asher and the other *Bewitched* powers that be with Lizzie's interpretation of *Samantha*, whether it was strategizing on how to transfer her real-life nose wriggle into *Samantha's* twitch, or with phrases like these from *Samantha* that stemmed from her real-life colloquialisms: "Well," "Oh my stars!" and "Good grief" (although Lizzie told me in 1989 that she lifted that last one from *Charlie Brown* and the animated *Peanuts* cartoon by Charles Schulz).

That said, Johnson never watched *Bewitched*, so he "can't accurately compare Elizabeth's acting style, but certainly both Lindsay and Elizabeth became America's darlings and deservedly so," he says.

As fate would have it, Johnson later served as the producer/director of *The Incredible Hulk* TV series starring Bill Bixby and Lou Ferrigno. As Lizzie expressed to *TV Guide* in 1979, *Hulk* was one of her favorite shows and she had at one time played opposite Bixby in a pre-*Incredible* segment of *Password* (April 5–9, 1971). Johnson's response:

It's very nice to hear that Elizabeth was a fan of *The Incredible Hulk*. High praise, indeed. We certainly labored to make each episode as meaningful and substantive as possible. Our largest audience was actually adults—with women as the largest single group. Working with Bill and Lou was always a treat. We all cared a lot. I'm glad it impacted on her so favorably.

As to the general adventures in working on *The Mike Douglas Show*, and the irony of those guests who appeared with Lizzie on her particular segment, Johnson concludes: "There is a wealth of stories from those years that range from the sublime to the ridiculous."

Lizzie's appearance on *The Merv Griffin Show* in December of 1970 was much less involved than *The Mike Douglas Show*, because her reason for doing the show outweighed her actual appearance. It was here she discussed her favorite *Bewitched* episode, "Sisters at Heart," a Christmas story that originally aired on December 24, 1970. Written by a multiracial tenth grade English class at Thomas Jefferson High School in Los Angeles, the episode condemned prejudice and rallied against injustice.

The idea for "Sisters at Heart" was generated after Lizzie and Bill Asher responded to a phone call from a twenty-three-year-old California teacher named Marcella Saunders. As documented for *TV Picture Life Magazine* in December 1971 (when ABC aired its second and final screening of the episode), Saunders had alarming news: only six students in each classroom were reading at the proper level. At Jefferson High School, less than 1 percent were reading at the ninth grade level; 44 percent read on the third grade level and the other approximately 65 percent were either down or slightly up from that figure. The problems didn't end there. Many of the students were not writing nor comprehending at the high school level. If able to read their textbooks, they often were unable to understand what they read.

Saunders had a solution, and her twenty-four African-American children went on to reap the benefits from what ultimately was Lizzie and Bill's compassion and concern. Upon first speaking with Saunders, the Ashers learned that *Bewitched* was her students' favorite show. Consequently, the class, all of whom did not have cars, and many of whom did not even have the money for bus fare to Hollywood, were invited to the show's set, with Bill and Lizzie making certain the students arrived safely by chartered bus. "They were so shy at first, withdrawn," she said at the time, "but so well behaved; so courteous and polite."

After a relaxing lunch with the Ashers at the studio commissary, the youngsters returned to the set, relaxed, and full of meaningful, intelligent questions. They had discovered something that held their interest. The apathy had vanished, as if by magic. They had been invigorated, and wanted to know as much about television production as possible. Suddenly, children who could never write before, were writing three pages. During rehearsals, kids who could not read were now doubling up on scripts and fighting over who would portray *Samantha* and *Darrin*.

Saunders asked the students to write compositions detailing the studio experience. The papers, the way she described them, "were fantastic," and the class returned to the *Bewitched* set on three different occasions; each time they were welcomed by Bill and Lizzie who said, "They seemed more interested, more eager to know about the technicalities of the production. What kids! Just marvelous. Outstanding!"

As to the actual script for "Sisters at Heart," the students knew it had to be unique. Beyond solid writing and good grammar, it had to say and mean something. So they worked together and eventually created this story:

> *Tabitha* (Erin Murphy), *Darrin* and *Samantha's* little sorceress, befriends *Lisa* (Venetta Rogers), the African-American daughter of one of *Darrin's* clients (Don Marshall) who stays with the *Stephens* while they're away on a business trip with *Larry*. After she and *Lisa* are bullied in the park for being of different colors but still wanting to be sisters, *Tabitha* employs *wishcraft*, and *wishes* they could become siblings. Consequently, white polka dots appear on *Lisa*; and brown polka dots appear on *Tabitha*, literally painting them as equals. In the most poignant scenes in the episode, *Samantha* tells *Tabitha* and her friend, "All men are brothers; even if they're girls."

When the script was completed, the students made a trek back to the studio to present their gift-wrapped present to the Ashers. "We were overwhelmed," Lizzie said at the time. Not only because of the magnitude of the gesture, but because the script was so impressive. "Really," she added. "We've had bad scripts submitted by professional writers that weren't as well written or creative."

"Sisters at Heart" became an official *Bewitched* episode, a secret the Ashers shared only upon being certain the script could be utilized. To move things along, Bill hired professional scribe Barbara Avedon, who had written for *Bewitched* (and other family shows like *The Donna Reed Show*). She helped to expand the story into the required length of a 30-minute teleplay.

In 1989, some eighteen years after "Sisters at Heart" debuted, Lizzie reflected on filming the episode and its core theme of prejudice, which she also view as the central theme of the entire series:

> Yeah . . . this is what *Bewitched* is all about . . . how people can sometimes get off track, and [get on] the outside trying to belong. It was also one of the few things that *Samantha* and *Endora* agreed on. . . . There were times when I certainly would have liked to have gotten a little bit more political (on *Bewitched*). But there were just certain parameters that we could not pass. Also, the underlined theme was the exaggerated promises-that-you-make-and-can't-quite-keep-sometimes. And the feeling that *Maybe if I do help, maybe getting caught doing something you promised you wouldn't do won't be so bad if the end result is okay.* I mean, people have that in everyday life. *Bewitched* was not about cleaning up the house, zapping up the toast . . . and flying around the room. It was about a very difficult relationship. (*Samantha* and *Darrin's* marriage) was a very tough match. I mean, who the hell would want to go through that kind of stuff? It wasn't the easiest of relationships. It had to be very difficult for *Darrin Stephens* to be married to this woman who could have anything that she wanted . . . and chose not [to] . . . except sometimes. It was a love story. But that's not all of what it was. That was a part of what it was.

In other words, the romantic notions of *Bewitched* were only part of its charm—and Elizabeth's. Despite her shy demeanor, she went on the *Griffin* and *Douglas* shows and her appearances were and remain riveting, if only for the fact that she was not one to grant such personal, non-scripted TV spots.

Conversely, *Bewitched* co-star Agnes Moorehead once served as co-host for an entire week on the *Douglas* show. Charles Tranberg, Moorehead's biographer, explains:

> For a private woman, Agnes was quite public. She did like appearing on talk shows, but she gave instructions about what she would and what she wouldn't discuss. She wouldn't discuss her marriages or her private life—except for social things she did. She loved, however, to discuss her career, she loved to discuss what she thought was the declining morals of the theatre and of younger people in general. She was very opinionated on the social issues of the day—usually from a more conservative point of view. Elizabeth was equally private. She had been married several times and didn't

want to discuss those marriages. She really didn't even want to discuss, openly, her upbringing and her father, Robert Montgomery—all that much. When she wasn't working she wanted to be there for her kids—and she was, by and large. By most accounts, Elizabeth was a wonderful mother. So being on talk shows or game shows (although she did enjoy guest-spots on *Password* and *Hollywood Squares*), wasn't a priority.

PART III

Disenchanted

"I'm likely to have my share of flops as well as successes . . .
as long as I don't have to wriggle my nose for eight years again."

—Elizabeth Montgomery, to journalist Steve Jacques,
during an interview to promote *A Case of Rape* (1974)

$\mathcal{F}$ifteen

$\sim$

To Twitch Or Not To Twitch

"She hated it when people asked her to twitch her nose."

—Liz Sheridan, chatting about Elizabeth's post-*Samantha* disdain on
Bewitched: The E! True Hollywood Story, 1999

By the mid-1960s, TV shows had switched from black and white to color, and *Bewitched* was not any different. In later seasons, Elizabeth would preface each episode with voice-over and visual promos, each of which she instilled with a vivacious energy that encouraged the viewer to watch with eager anticipation. "This is Elizabeth Montgomery," she'd say. "Stay tuned for *Bewitched*. . . . In color."

The show's first color episode was "Nobody's Perfect," which opened the third season, airing September 15, 1966. This episode also introduced *Samantha* and *Darrin's* daughter *Tabitha* as a full-fledged young supernatural. Consequently, *Samantha* was forced not only to curtail her own powers, but her daughter's as well, mostly instructing her with the phrase, "Mustn't twitch!"

Upon first hearing that, *Endora* pops in and says, "Oh, how charming. When every other mother in the world is telling her child, mustn't touch, you'll be saying, 'Mustn't twitch!'" Simultaneously, off-camera at home in Beverly Hills, Lizzie was parenting her real-life children.

In an in interview with *Photoplay Magazine* in 1968, she acknowledged the challenges facing a working mother. At the time, she and Bill Asher only had the two young boys, Billy, Jr. and Robert, but because of *Bewitched's* heavy workload, it was not always possible to give her sons a so-called *normal childhood.*

Still, she was determined to maintain as regular an environment as possible under the circumstances. She wanted her sons to feel the same way about her work. One day, she invited Billy, Jr. to visit her at the studio, but he wasn't all that impressed by the Hollywood glitter. It was just a place where his parents went to work. He liked to come to the studio, but only to play with Erin and Diane Murphy, the twins who played *Tabitha.* They were the same age, and Lizzie said they had "a perfectly fine time."

She tried to avoid the pitfalls that accompany being a working mother. At the time, the major concern was finding a nurse who could be firm-but-friendly to her sons. As she told *Photoplay,* "We have one now who is a gem. She knows just when to crack down on the boys and when to let them alone. That's important."

Lizzie had experienced nurse troubles before. They expected her to supply the discipline when she arrived home from *Bewitched.* "*That* would have been great!" she mused. "Here the mean old Mommy came home and whacked them for something they did at 10:00 o'clock that morning and had already forgotten about."

Then there was the day she came home and found Billy, Jr. pouring a glass of water on the living room carpet.

"Don't do that!" she told him.

"Nanny let me," Billy replied.

Lizzie turned to the nurse and asked, "Is that true?"

"Poor little thing, what harm can he do?" the nurse wondered.

Lizzie exploded: "What harm can he do? In the first place, he's playing with a glass and could cut himself if it broke. In the second place, he's ruining the rug." Needless to say, the nurse's services were no longer required.

She tried to "remain firm with the boys," she said, but it wasn't always easy. When she came home at night she had a tendency to indulge them, to compensate for her absence. "That's a mistake," she admitted.

When she wasn't working, she gave them as much time as she could. On the weekends she and Bill, Sr. were home most of the time, and on their off days during the week, they were with little Billy and Robert. One time, she and Bill, Sr. went to Palm Springs for a few weeks without the kids, if only because she felt it was easier than "uprooting the boys."

"They didn't mind," she told *Photoplay.* "They prefer being at home."

Years later, Lizzie still felt she could have done more as a mother to all of her children. As she expressed to John Tesh on *One on One* in 1992, "Parenting is probably the toughest job anyone could ever have. I haven't been very good at it. But I think I've gotten better."

However, after she passed away, Billy Asher, Jr. appeared on MSNBC's *Headliners & Legends* in 2001, and said she was a "great parent." And although she believed she wasn't maternally accessible because of her career, from Billy's perspective, she provided nothing but unconditional love.

Each of her children acknowledged how fortunate they were to have had Lizzie as their mom; just as the *Bewitched* cast and crew appreciated working with her on the set.

As the show's executive producer Harry Ackerman said in 1988: "We were the luckiest people in the world to have someone as warmhearted and appealing as Elizabeth Montgomery."

Echoing what her friend Sally Kemp said upon first seeing Elizabeth do the "bunny nose" when they were kids, Ackerman concluded, "No one could twitch her nose like she did. Believe me, we all tried."

Once Lizzie walked away from *Bewitched*, she walked away for good. She would not twitch again on screen, except for a series of Japanese TV commercials in the 1980s, and American public service announcements for the visually impaired in the early 1990s. Beyond that, her famous facial tic became a harness around her adenoids. Over the years too many negative nose encounters took their toll, ad nauseam, and she could not always wriggle her way free.

According to what her friend Liz Sheridan said on *Bewitched: The E! True Hollywood Story* in 1999, Lizzie was not at all pleased when people asked her to twitch her nose.

But what was she to do? She retained one of the most dedicated followings in TV history—and in turn felt obligated to her fans. "They have given me what I have, and I'm grateful," she told *Screen Stars* magazine in 1965.

She liked a "normal amount of privacy," but she wasn't the "dark-glasses type" who scurried behind hedges or ducked out back doors every time a fan approached her for an autograph. If they were "reasonably courteous," she intoned, "I felt I should be also."

Years later, in 1989, she said, "People are nice. They really are . . . most of the time." Other times, not so much, as when a random parent would force their child to say hello. "This inevitably happens at least once a year," she said, "and it's heartbreaking."

On one occasion, she was shopping and a somewhat abrasive woman, with her reluctant preteen daughter in tow, approached Lizzie and made a scene. "You come over here and say 'hi' to Miss Montgomery," the mother insisted to her offspring.

"No," the child responded. "I don't want to."

Yet the woman insisted how much her daughter wanted to meet *Samantha*.

"If that's true," Lizzie wondered, "why is she yelling to the contrary?"

"She's just shy," the mother replied, and then to threaten her child, she said she'd told her that if she refused to greet the *Bewitched* star, the actress would twitch her nose and "turn her into a toad."

Lizzie was livid: "You told her *what*?! How *dare* you say such a thing? No wonder she's scared to death!"

Upon hearing that, the mother grabbed her daughter by the hand, and scuffed away in a fit of anger.

Another time, early in *Bewitched's* run, Elizabeth was filming a promotional spot on the set of *Bonanza*, as both series had the same sponsor (Chevrolet). "Every time I did the twitch," Lizzie remembered in 1989, the director of the spot would yell, "Cut!'"

She thought, "What the hell is the matter? I'm getting bored with this. I thought I could do this in one take and then get out of here!"

No such luck. Suddenly, the director turned to someone on the set and said, "I don't know how she's ever going to do a series. She's got this terrible *twitch*!"

"Everybody was like, 'Oh, my God . . . he doesn't know,'" Lizzie laughed in recalling the awkward moment. "He saw the storyboards but just never made the connection. He must have been the most humiliated person. But I was hysterical."

A third uncomfortable public twitch encounter, this time, somewhat more intrusive, less comical, and downright insulting, occurred shortly after *Bewitched* debuted. As Elizabeth recalled in 1989, it happened one night in the ladies' room of Chasen's Restaurant in West Hollywood. "Of all the weird kinds of old fashioned places to be in," she said, "Right?"

"I was powdering my nose or whatever it was I was doing," she went on to explain, and this woman kept pacing back and forth in front of her. Lizzie was like, "What is going on here?"

She found out, when the woman approached her and said, "Pardon me, but I just have to ask you . . . *where did you get your nose job?*"

"Being the quick thinker that I am," she mused to herself, "Oh, God— what do I say? Don't say (anything like), 'My Mummy and Daddy gave it to me.'"

Instead she replied, "The Farmer's Market," which only further confounded the woman. But Lizzie continued taking delight in sending her inquisitor on a detour: "You know, there's a place called *The Coral Reef*, and right in back of that little kind of hut . . . there's a doctor's office . . . and it's absolutely amazing what they can do. I was only bruised for like a couple of days. They're fantastic."

"In California you can just find anything," the woman replied sincerely, if a little befuddled.

Lizzie recalled in 1989:

> To this day, I still think of that woman, because I knew she had to be a tourist. And then I thought, Why did I say "The Farmer's Market?" It just popped into my head . . . and I just had to make something up. But she was like, "Oh, wow! That's really great." And I just pictured this poor woman wandering around The Farmer's Market (looking for just the right plastic surgeon).

David White listened to Lizzie tell this story, and said the *nosy* woman should never have questioned his famous twitch-witching friend about such a delicate subject, not to mention, operation:

> She should have known that you didn't, if she looked at your nose, she would have realized that nose jobs sink after a while. A girl I knew in New York had one, and she was beautiful when she just had it done (but only for a few years afterwards). And then I saw her later, and it had sunk . . .

because they take the bone out . . . and they put gristle in there or something. So it isn't as sturdy a bone like the bridge of your nose . . . Your nose is just like your Dad's.

While filming *Bewitched*, he and Lizzie would meet in the makeup room every morning, "And there she'd be," he said, "without any makeup o, and her hair pushed back. I used to think, 'She could never say *Robert Montgomery isn't my dad.*'"

"People do say that I look like him," Lizzie interrupted.

"Yes, around the eyes," David said.

"My Mom and Dad both had these (arched) eyebrows."

Overall, Lizzie may have shielded many aspects of her personal life from the press, specifically with regard to her marriages and other personal issues that she may have had, but a fine balance of her trademark humor and decorum ever lurked behind the scenes. On occasion, if selectively so, she was refreshingly honest and self-deprecating, whether discussing, for example, her father or her appearance. She cheerfully addressed both topics during an interview with *TV Radio Mirror* magazine in January 1965, concluding:

> I myself believe there was some kind of hocus-pocus afoot in my getting to be a TV star. In spite of my being Robert Montgomery's daughter, the odds were against me. I'm no Hollywood glamour girl, and my so-called "beauty" calls out for a plastic surgeon. I feel sorry for the poor makeup man in the morning. I'm his greatest challenge.

At the start of *Bewitched's* third season, executive producer Harry Ackerman offered the position of story editor to then-twenty-six-year-old *Bewitched* writer Doug Tibbles, who penned a few segments of the show including the "Nobody's Perfect" episode that introduced the catch phrase, "Mustn't twitch." But Tibbles, now seventy-two, turned down the job. He explains:

> I just didn't want to do it. I felt like I was good at the dialogue, but I just didn't like the show. It just didn't hold my interest. I just didn't care about it. It didn't mean anything to me. And I had a string of money coming in, which dried up later. But at the time, it seemed like I could pick and choose.

Because Tibbles rejected the promotion, Ackerman offered the position to Bernard Slade, who later became famous on Broadway for writing *Same Time Next Year* and for creating *The Partridge Family* for ABC in 1970. "To be honest," Tibbles says, "Slade was 'more qualified' for the job. I was too young. I was good with the dialogue and that's what I was known for. My trick was to 'make 'em laugh out loud' twice on a page, even if they couldn't use it, or even if Standards and Practices threw it out for some reason."

But according to how Lizzie felt about Tibbles' talents, his words weren't going to land anywhere except in the mouths of the *Bewitched* actors. For example, there's a "perfect" moment between *Samantha* and *Tabitha* that is quite touching and eloquent, and representative of the core "acceptance" message of the entire series. When *Sam* catches her daughter using witchcraft for the first time she experiences a circle of emotion, but ultimately pride and joy. She says:

> Oh, I know . . . I know what it is like to be part of the magical life, to have so much at your finger tips. But we're living in a world that isn't quite used to people like us. And I'm afraid they never will be. So, I'm going to have to be very firm with you. You're going to have to learn when you can use your witchcraft and when you can't. Now, your wonderful daddy wants us to be just plain people. So you're going to have to stop wiggling your fingers whenever you want something.

Besides "Nobody's Perfect," Tibbles penned "I Don't Want to Be a Toad, I Want to Be a Butterfly" and "*Samantha* the Sculptress," all of which he wrote while only in his mid-twenties.

"*Samantha* the Sculptress," from the fifth year, 1968–1969, involved very odd special effects that featured talking-head clay busts of *Darrin* and *Larry*. It was a quirky entry, just this side of *The Twilight Zone*.

"Toad/Butterfly," also from the fifth season, turned out to deliver what Lizzie considered to be one of the funniest lines in the entire series. The episode aired on December 12, 1968, and featured Maudie Prickett as *Mrs. Burch*, *Tabitha's* mortal teacher who talks with *Ruth Taylor* (Lola Fisher) about her daughter (and *Tabitha's* fellow classmate) *Amy Taylor* (played by Maralee Foster, and named for Doug Tibbles' real-life daughter).

Ruth Taylor: I understand about playing in the forest, I understand why you wanted to make my Amy a toad instead of a butterfly. But the fact is that my child is still missing.

Mrs. Burch: But I have never lost a child in all my years as a teacher.

Ruth Taylor: And you start by losing mine.

Mrs. Burch: Look—somehow I'll make it up to you.

Ruth Taylor: I'm calling the Police.

It was that second last line, "Look—somehow I'll make it up to you," to a parent about the misplacement of their child to which Lizzie took a liking. "For whatever reason," Tibbles explains, "she loved that line." Whether or not her appreciation of that line had anything to do with the troubled kinship she experienced with her father Robert Montgomery is left to the imagination.

In the meantime, Elizabeth's other core relationship of the day, her marriage to Bill Asher, may have already been in trouble. According to what Tibbles can remember, the Montgomery-Asher-Richard Michaels triangle began long before the final season of *Bewitched*. He, like William Froug, saw signs of tension as early as season three, while working on "Nobody's Perfect."

But before discussing the details of what Tibbles recalls about that complicated relationship, it's pertinent to provide some background on his own fascinating life and career:

Doug is the son of the very successful writer George Tibbles, who penned the pilot for *My Three Sons* (which starred Fred MacMurray) and that sitcom's subsequent first season. He also wrote episodes of fantasy shows such as *The Munsters*; both to which Doug would also contribute scripts. Doug also wrote episodes for *Happy Days* and, just as with *Bewitched*, he was offered the story editor position on that show. This time, however, he accepted the job. For five hours. Then, as he recalls, "I said to myself, "That's it! I'm never doing it [writing a TV sitcom) again!"

"It was my father's business," he explains, "and I just jumped into it because I needed the dough. My dad was a piano player who always wanted to be a writer, and I was a drummer who never wanted to be a writer. But I didn't like writing, even though I was successful at it."

Because of his father's musical and subsequent writing success, from the time he was a child and on into his twenties, Doug found himself hobnobbing the Hollywood party circuit. His father played the piano in the 1940s and toured with the likes of the legendary Eddie Cantor. Doug accompanied him to the crossroads of the Los Angeles Union Station, where he would meet Cantor, as well as Charlie Chaplin, Ed Gwynn, and Lou Costello, all with whom George Tibbles had been associated. "And I was only seven years old!" Doug exclaims. "It was an amazing time. I mean, we used to go to places like [director] Walter Lang's house, just to play cards. I even remember playing cards with a twenty-year-old R. J. (Robert) Wagner, and Fred and June MacMurray before my Dad even really knew them or did *My Three Sons.*"

Others on the Tibbles party circuit included the iconic Elizabeth Taylor and Alan Ladd. It was Ladd who starred in the classic 1953 feature film, *Shane*, which as Bill Asher explained in *The Bewitched Book*, was the basis of the "*Shane* Theory":

Shane was a gunslinger who only used his weapons as a last resort; first he would address the issues at hand with his wit, his intelligence, even his humor. When all else failed, then he would bring out the big guns and save the day. That's how Bill explained the power of the twitch to Lizzie who was initially impatient with *Samantha* holding back her witchcraft. She should not overuse the twitch, Asher cautioned. "You're *Shane!*" he told her. "You don't twitch until the audience wants you to."

Doug Tibbles, meanwhile, was not holding anything back, and his perspective as a child and teenager growing up in Hollywood was always clear. Except occasionally . . . as when he'd confuse Lizzie's father Robert Montgomery with George Montgomery, both of whom frequently visited the home of early film idol Van Johnson, where Doug and his family attended parties.

Doug recalls one party in particular at the home and pool of Dean Martin, Lizzie's co-star from *Who's Been Sleeping in My Bed?* Standing by the pool at Martin's home, Tibbles was approached by none other than actress Janet Leigh. "Doug," she began to ask, "would you like a drink?"

"Want a drink?" he reiterates today. "I don't even know how she knew my *name*?!"

However, everyone at the party certainly knew Leigh's identity. She was a respected actress, who became best known for two creations, both of which are connected to Lizzie: Leigh's *shower-stealing* performance as *Marion Crane* in Alfred Hitchcock's classic 1960 film, *Psycho*, which starred Anthony Perkins, who was good friends with *Bewitched's* Dick York; and Jamie Lee Curtis, Leigh's daughter with actor Tony Curtis, who also fathered David and Greg Lawrence (though not with Leigh), the twins who played *Darrin* and *Samantha's* son *Adam* in the last three seasons of *Bewitched*.

Also, too, of course, Martin was a member of the Rat Pack, which included Sammy Davis, Jr., Peter Lawford, and Frank Sinatra, all of whom knew Lizzie. . . . and Doug Tibbles. He remembers visiting Sinatra's home:

> We knew his daughter Nancy, and Dean Martin's kids, too. We knew all of them. You see, to grow up in L.A. at that time, if you were our age, and went to our high school (Hollywood High), you would have gone to Sinatra's house, too.

At one point, Doug had also befriended Jim Mitchum, younger brother to classic screen idol Robert Mitchum. As he recalls:

> Bob Mitchum called my house and spoke to my Mother, as I was standing right next to her. He wanted to take me to Greece with the Mitchum family. But I didn't want to go, and I told my Mother that. I knew they just wanted me to keep Jim busy, and I didn't feel like playing babysitter to Jim Mitchum.

On yet another occasion, Doug had made contact with another legendary actor. He explains:

> Marlon Brando was having a meeting with director Walter Lang. But we didn't even look at him. It was no big deal to me and my friends. We grew up with movie stars' kids. By that time, we were teenagers, and all we cared about was looking at pretty girls. Other than that, we really didn't give a shit. I was numb and desensitized to the whole celebrity game.

Flash-forward a decade or so to *Bewitched*: From Tibbles' perspective, he had known and grown up with A-list movie stars. So when he arrived on the *Samantha* series, he explains, he still felt the glitter and glamour of the big screen, and television was a step down for him. But he was still impressed with the small screen charisma of the stars of *Bewitched*, namely, Lizzie and Dick York.

"Dick was a nice guy," he says, ". . . a gentleman," while he remembers Lizzie as "not the least bit arrogant." In fact, Doug continues, "she was one of the kindest people in the entire business, along with Andy Griffith and Dean Martin" (both with whom he had collaborated on various projects). "She was always lady-like, always polite and down to earth. And she was always very nice to me."

So nice, in fact, it used to rile Bill Asher, especially one day, when Lizzie approached Doug and said, "We think you're marvelous!" She was referring to herself and Asher, who was standing beside her. But according to Doug, "Bill didn't seem to take that too well. He just seemed like a jealous husband. It was seemingly a rough time in their marriage . . . he was very on edge."

Shortly after Lizzie complimented Doug, he met with Asher and Michaels to discuss one of his scripts. Bill asked Doug to rewrite a few pages of dialogue. Doug agreed, but apparently, not to Bill's immediate or complete satisfaction. "Okay, Bill," he said, "but I'm not going to fake it and pretend that I can come up with a few lines now; let me go home and think it over."

Asher went ballistic, and screamed, "You're a professional, Doug! And you should be able to come up with something on the spot!"

Taken aback by Asher's response, Doug thought, "What is *wrong* with him?" Upon hearing Asher's tantrum, Doug didn't know what to think and he had a knee-jerk reaction. But in time, he saw the big picture. He explains:

I got so mad, that I took the script—which was not bound, and threw it in the air; and it came fluttering down all over the floor, and I left. Young and impetuous, I was saying things like, "[Forget] this! I'm not doing this shit!" And I ran out the door and out onto the Screen Gems lot. It was Richard Michaels who then chased after me, running outside into that lot. I just remember him saying, "Doug, please come back." And I may be wrong about this, but I thought something was going on *then* between Richard and Elizabeth, and I don't know how well known it was. There was definite tension in the offices, not so much on the set. But you could feel it in the offices, especially with Asher. I mean, here I am a young guy, and Elizabeth was saying I was marvelous, and I'm not making myself out to be Rock

Hudson. All I'm saying is that when she paid the slightest bit of attention to someone else in any way, it seemed to bother him.

When asked why Asher didn't fire Michaels if he knew about the affair with Lizzie at this stage of the game, Doug replied:

> But that's just it. I don't think he knew. That's my guess. He might not have believed it. It's like after we all found out none of us could believe that she would do that. I'm not saying that she wouldn't have done it out of fear of Bill Asher, but that she didn't seem like the kind of "fooling-around" girl. I mean, the way she looked, she didn't seem like the kind that would go sneaking-around. That's just my perception today.

In further retrospect, Doug finds it ironic that it was Michaels who chased him down on the Columbia studio lot to reconcile with Asher after their confrontation. He explains further:

> Dick Michaels was a really nice guy and very level-headed no matter what happened. And to clarify, I had no idea what exactly was going on. I just noticed a jealous man in Bill Asher. And only later did I piece things together. But you wouldn't have pictured Dick Michaels in an affair with Elizabeth, and you wouldn't have pictured her in an affair with *anyone*. And I hate to say this, but either way, I really didn't give a shit. I was like, "Just get me out of here!"

Today, Tibbles is living his musical dream. With songwriter wife Barbara Keith and stepson John Tibbles, they headline the respected trio, *The Stone Coyotes*, based in Greenfield, Massachusetts. Barbara is on the electric guitar and vocals, John plays bass, and Doug plays drums.

In Tibbles' *Bewitched* episode "To Twitch Or Not To Twitch," which aired in the show's fourth season, *Samantha* and her ad-man husband *Darrin* bicker over the use of witchcraft. It's an especially dicey disagreement this time, because her not doing so ultimately causes him embarrassment at a client's dinner party.

Whether or not certain impediments had developed behind the scenes in previous seasons, by the show's eight and final year, 1971–1972, all hell broke loose. Lizzie was growing if not tired of *Bewitched*, at least slightly weary of the notoriety that came along with the "nose job." She was also hurt. Her marriage to Bill Asher was in trouble. As Asher told A&E's *Biography* in 1999, "The show itself was not as strong as it had been. And that bothered her, and so she said, 'I don't want to do it anymore.' "

Sixteen

~

Temperatures Rising

"We enjoy each other. Our interests are the same; I think our
temperaments go together."

—Elizabeth, describing her relationship with Bill Asher, two years
before they separated, *Modern Screen Magazine*, July 1970

According to *The Schenectady Gazette*, in the fall of 1971, Bill Asher had
noticed an attractive professional ice skater–turned–New York actress in a
toothpaste commercial. She was the perfect fit for the role of a female expert
skater he was seeking to cast for the *Bewitched* episode "*Samantha* on Thin
Ice." Upon his invitation, Nancy Fox flew to the West Coast, on her dime,
for an interview. Charming and talented, Fox could act and skate at the
same time, and she won the role, Asher's heart, and a regular spot on a new
series he was developing.

But he was on thin ice with Lizzie. Their days were numbered and by
the summer of 1972, they separated. Hollywood columnist Marilyn Beck
confirmed the news, August 4, 1972:

[While the] Elizabeth Montgomery–Bill Asher estrangement continues,
Asher is managing to snap out of the blues a bit with the help of actress
Nancy Fox. She is the young cutie who portrays the nervous student nurse
in Asher's new *Temperatures Rising* ABC series. His attentions on and off the
set are making her feel much less nervous about her first shot at stardom.

232

Temperatures Rising

And this from *The Los Angeles Times*, August 30, 1972:

Now Nancy Fox, who plays the nurse in *Temperatures Rising*, is said to be helping raise Asher's temperature lately.

He was working overtime on *Rising*, developing another sitcom, *The Paul Lynde Show*, and allowing his marriage to Lizzie to fizzle. Consequently, it was now clear that she had found at least a measure of comfort in the arms of Asher's *Bewitched* protégé Richard Michaels, who explained it all to *Entertainment Tonight* (E.T.) in 2006. By the eighth and final year of *Bewitched*, his and Lizzie's friendship had developed in a "deeper way," he said. It was something they both tried to "repress. But as the year went on, it became more and more compelling."

So they moved into a one-bedroom apartment in West Los Angeles and kept their affair hidden. Reports in the press suggested she had retired and moved to Europe. But Michaels said such was not the case. Lizzie simply did not want to be hounded by the tabloid media. So they kept their relationship a secret.

By 1986, Asher hired Michaels to direct an episode of his CBS drama series *Kay O'Brien*. According to what Michaels conveyed in 2006 on E.T., any animosity that may have existed between the two men had dissolved. "That was then," Asher told him. "This is now."

Michaels said he and Lizzie were friendly until the end. It proved challenging, but "anytime something like this happens, it's always tough on the principals," he said, as if they were actors performing in a play. "It was tough saying good-bye. But absolutely we were on good terms when it broke."

It's been nearly five decades since he and Lizzie were together, but as Michaels told E.T., he still thinks of her as *Samantha*, even though he knew her as Elizabeth all those years before. "I don't think any of us can forget the sweet lady who could twitch her nose and make everything okay in the world," he said.

Michaels, who retired from directing in 1994, lives in Maui, Hawaii. Ironically, his daughter, Meredith Michaels-Beerbaum, shared a love of horses with Elizabeth, as she was the first woman to be ranked Number One in the world in equestrian show jumping.

In time—if not *just* in time—Bill Asher realized his liaison with Fox was a mistake and blamed himself for his divorce from Lizzie. In 1999, he appeared on A&E's *Biography* and admitted that ". . . the whole thing was my fault. I was going to work every morning and she was doing nothing. And it got to her. And she finally took off. I was very angry that she left. So I left."

Apparently with Fox, and then Lizzie divorced him in 1974. But in 1976, Fox was out of the picture and Asher married actress Joyce Bulifant, who subsequently divorced him in 1993. Since 1998, he's been married to Meredith Asher.

Through it all, Lizzie had found a "fox" of her own—Robert Foxworth—whom she met on the set of *Mrs. Sundance* in 1973. He became the only other man in her life, the one she frequently referred to as the love of her life.

Nancy Fox, a childhood friend of *Charlie's Angels'* star Jaclyn Smith, would continue acting, at least through the 1980s, when she'd appear in films like, ironically enough, *Warlock*, released in 1989. It was in 1982 that she appeared in what is arguably her largest role: the lead for *The Sonja Henie Story*, a feature film based on the life of the Norwegian blonde Olympic star and ice-skating movie queen of the 1940s.

Beyond that, she was never heard from again, at least publicly. She now leads a quiet life in New York, which is how she always wanted it. In November 1977, she repeated to *The Youngstown Vindicator* almost exactly what Lizzie said to *Look* magazine in 1965: "I don't care about being a big star. I don't even think I'd like that. I just want to stay well-adjusted and happy."

While Lizzie and Nancy may have had more in common than either may have realized, *Bewitched* co-star Irene Vernon felt left out in the cold, pushed to the curb. She had played *Louise Tate* on the show before she was replaced by Kasey Rogers or, as Vernon said in 1988, "I was fired!"

Apparently, it was because of her friendship with Danny Arnold, the show's original producer. According to Vernon, Bill and Lizzie were not at all fond of Arnold. So, they let her go in the spring of 1966, the end of the second season. "Devastated," Vernon then left Hollywood, geographically and figuratively, and gravitated towards a more successful career, in real estate, in Beverly Hills.

In the big scheme of things, some actors are willing to do whatever it takes to make it in Hollywood. Others, like Fox and Vernon, vote against a *no-holds-barred* approach and leave show business behind, savoring their lives and their sanity in the process.

Performers like Elvis and Michael Jackson, for example, were not so lucky. They didn't know when to stop. They succumbed to the intoxicating environment the entertainment industry provides, almost like a drug; and in some cases, exactly like a drug. There's so much opportunity, so much potential to succeed, and when that success arrives, it simply becomes too much to handle.

Fortunately, in Lizzie's case, she was never forced to choose between a career and personal happiness. She was born into wealth and status that stabilized her life, at least financially. Although her father was demanding and she for many years lived in his shadow, Elizabeth would later carve out her own brand of stardom that allowed her the luxury to pick and choose to work as she pleased. In short, even with her various issues, she had her head on straight.

Entertainment curator Rob Ray explains it all:

One type of performer is the tenacious, career-is-all person with the determination to succeed at all costs. They will succeed at anything they strive hard enough to do because nothing else in their life matters. Most classic stars like Bette Davis, John Wayne, and Lucille Ball fall into this category . . . today, maybe even George Clooney, Tom Cruise, and Oprah Winfrey, certainly. Another type is the person who has the drive but can't cope with the pressures of the business. As a result, they crash and burn with their life ending in tragedy. Marilyn Monroe and Judy Garland and now, unfortunately, Whitney Houston, are classic examples of vulnerable souls who couldn't handle the pressures. But most people fall into a third category. They have the desire to make it, but whether they succeed or not, once they realize what sacrifices and struggles a career entails, they decide for their own personal happiness and survival to leave the table. Their survival instinct impels them to move on. Greta Garbo is the ultimate example from the classic film era, and I suspect Irene Vernon and Nancy Fox, and even Elizabeth herself, to a certain extent, fell into this third category, too. For most people, career isn't everything. Personal happiness and fulfillment is. For that group, life is too short to deal with the stress of show business day in and day out, and Elizabeth knew that.

Cliff Robertson was Lizzie's good friend in the early, pre-*Bewitched* portion of her career. Other than that, he didn't know much about, for one, her relationship with Bill Asher, because as he said, "I didn't know him. But I do know he was very possessive, and a rather domineering figure, although he was a little fellow. And maybe because he was so short a fellow, he had a complex?"

During the *Bewitched* years, Robertson didn't see much of Lizzie, whom he affectionately referred to as "Lizbel" (as if she needed yet another nickname!). "She went into an envelope," he says and the closest he came to her in those days was through mutual friends whom he'd periodically stop and ask, "Have you seen Lizbel?"

One day, however, at a restaurant in Santa Monica, he finally ran into her, walking out the door with Asher. By that time, Robertson was set to marry his second wife, Cynthia Stone, who was by his side. "I wanted to introduce Elizabeth to my new bride-to-be," he said. When his Lizbel caught sight of him, much to Asher's displeasure, she shrieked, "Oh, Cliff! It is so great to see you!"

"We hugged," Robertson recalled, "I guess, in what would be perceived as a typical Hollywood encounter. I don't think Bill was too pleased. He seemed a little bit impatient with her as if to say, 'Quit talking to this silly actor.' But I didn't give a damn, because I was just seeing an old friend." From this brief encounter, and from what he heard through the Hollywood grapevine, Robertson perceived that Asher was exerting a "certain control" over Lizzie. "He was very protective of her in that way. From a professional standpoint, at least from what I can gather, it proved beneficial for her. From a personal standpoint, I don't think he ever had it so good."

Bewitched actor David White agreed. In 1989, while in Lizzie's presence, White assessed the Montgomery-Asher marriage/business relationship in one sentence: "She was tremendously supportive of him almost to the point of sainthood."

Upon hearing that, Lizzie added: "Bill was such a good director and if it hadn't been for him, [*Bewitched*] wouldn't have happened anyway. But I tell you, there were times when I was frustrated, and I'm sure there were times when he was just as frustrated with me."

As if on cue, David then recalled when Bill directed a scene with him and Lizzie. He was proud of his performance that day, and assumed Bill was going to say "Print!" after the scene was completed. "But he didn't," David recalled.

Lizzie chimed in with each account of his memory of that day:

> David: One time Liz and I did a scene and it was just marvelous. She was so spontaneous and she was so great. And we didn't quite finish, and suddenly Bill says, "Cut! Now, quit horsing around, Liz!" Remember that?
>
> Lizzie: I sure do.
>
> David: And she looked at me like, *Who's crazy here?*
>
> Lizzie: I was like, "What is going on?"
>
> David: Well, I thought I'm gonna get him a book on directing. You're supposed to watch the actors.
>
> Lizzie: Boy, that was funny.
>
> David: It was so beautiful, you know.
>
> Lizzie: I remember that.
>
> David: You were in shock.
>
> Lizzie: I know. Asher always figured that I should know what he meant even when he didn't say anything, which wasn't true, necessarily.
>
> David: Not necessarily.
>
> Lizzie: He was wonderful with the guest actors and stuff. He could always think of nineteen different ways on how to tell them to open a door if that was absolutely necessary.
>
> David: And he did often.
>
> Lizzie: Yes, he did.

To David's surprise, Lizzie recalled a tense moment of her own with Bill on the *Bewitched* set, when they weren't exactly on the same page . . . of the script. The incident transpired while filming the fifth season segment, "*Samantha's* Power Failure," during which Lizzie happened to be pregnant with their last child, daughter Rebecca, while Bill was about to have a baby all on his own:

> We had a short day for some reason, and there was some party being given on the next stage. And I had been running back and forth between stages to check the lighting for a lengthy scene that Bill planned to direct on the following day.

However, he surprised her and said, "Well, as long as we're set up for it, let's do that speech where you appeal to the Witches Council." It was an intricate special effects–ridden scene that would also include Agnes Moorehead, who would be stationed at a lower level of the set, glancing up at Lizzie as *Samantha* chatted with the Council. But Lizzie was unprepared to shoot the scene and shocked at Bill's demands.

"*Holy shit!*" she thought. "*What does he mean? I haven't even looked at that scene!*"

So she told him, straight out:

"I don't know it."

"Well, why not?"

"Because I wasn't supposed to know it until tomorrow."

"You mean you don't look ahead?"

"Bill!! What do you mean, 'I don't look ahead?' Of course, I do. But this is a long scene."

"You can handle it. Just throw yourself into the witches' robes [the black frock or 'flying suit' that *Samantha* was prone to wear when she meant serious witch business], and let's get going. Let's not waste any more time. We've got another forty-five minutes."

Lizzie was furious, but as usual, she deferred to Bill's discretion, and did what he requested. She retreated to her dressing room to change and to give the script a quick study or, as she said, "To look at this damn thing, and try to memorize it, feverishly."

But there was more trouble ahead. Suddenly, there were visitors on the set and not just regular visitors, but crew members' wives. "And wives of the crew are never trustful of their husbands, anyway," Lizzie recalled. "They really aren't."

By this time, she's uncomfortable for several reasons. 1) She's frustrated with Bill's impatient demands for her to know lines she did not need to remember until the next day. 2) She's feeling the various physical discomforts of being pregnant. 3) Potentially jealous crew members' wives are now roaming the set. 4) The watchful eye of Agnes Moorehead is ever present.

When Bill finally said, "Okay—let's get through this once," Lizzie was out of sorts to say the least, but trudged on to face the music—or at least the conductor.

"Can we just go ahead and shoot it?" she asked.

"No!" Bill insisted. "I just wanna go ahead and *run it!*"

Lizzie caved, "Okay."

She then found her mark on the set, readied her lines, and with "Aggie standing right there in front" of her, she heard this woman say, "Jesus Christ! She's fat. I had no idea she was that fat!" A jealous crew member's wife had spoken—and Lizzie was her victim.

Oh, how nice, Lizzie thought upon hearing that hurtful phase, just as Bill was about to scream one very important word: "Action!" But instead, he yelled "Cut!"

Lizzie was trying to concentrate on her lines and they went through the scene twice. But after hearing that disturbing comment, as she recalled, "I just couldn't remember what the hell I was doing, and Bill blew up":

> You're not concentrating! This is ridiculous. There is no reason under the sun why you shouldn't be able to do this.

"Under any other circumstances I would have agreed with him," she mused in 1989.

But at least there was a break in the clouds and no one was more surprised than Lizzie at what transpired next:

> Do you know that Aggie turned to me and said, "Don't let him get you down. You can do it!" And that was the first time she ever said anything like that to me, because she knew it was beginning to get to me. So I took this big deep breath and said, "Okay—let's go then!"

The result? One of the most beloved scenes in the entire series:

> *Samantha*, in her elegant ebony and emerald robe, defending herself, *Cousin Serena* and *Uncle Arthur* before the high court of the Witches Council, which has stripped them of their powers. By this time, *Sam* had ignored the Council's demand that she end her mortal marriage, and her cousin and uncle stood firm in support of their favorite relative. Mouthing words that represented the core message of *Bewitched* as well as Lizzie's own philosophy, *Sam* said to her magical elders: "Remember the Witch burnings at Salem? Remember the innocent who were condemned simply for being different? Remember your rage at that injustice? Well, aren't you guilty of

the same injustice? Aren't you condemning me simply because I choose to be different? You can take away my powers but I'll always be a witch. It's you—the highest of all courts—who are taking the risk—[risking] your integrity—your right to sit in judgment."

Three years later, in what became *Bewitched's* swan season, 1971–1972, ABC had scheduled its once-supernatural powerhouse against CBS's new reality-based sitcom ratings' giant *All in the Family*, which though it began with a slow start in 1971, became the "eye" network's staple of newly crowned contemporary comedies. By this time, the network had rid itself of country-geared hits like *Mayberry R.F.D.* (1968–1971; a spin-off and continuation of *The Andy Griffith Show*, which had debuted in 1960), *The Beverly Hillbillies* (1962–1971), *Green Acres* (1965–1971), and *Petticoat Junction* (1963–1970); each perhaps more realistic than the fantasy fare presented by *Bewitched*, but nowhere near the edgy modern truths that would mark the scripts of producer Norman Lear's *All in the Family*, and his subsequent CBS spin-offs like *Maude* (1972–1978), *The Jeffersons* (1975–1985), and others of this ilk.

The issue-laden adventures of *Archie* and *Edith Bunker* (played by the Emmy-winning Carroll O'Connor and Jean Stapleton) on CBS' *All in the Family* were very different than the magic escapades of *Samantha* and *Darrin* on ABC's *Bewitched*. The television landscape had changed, right along with the times, and viewers were apparently ready for the alterations, although *Bewitched* executive producer Harry Ackerman once relayed how the networks were too quick to make such sweeping changes. "There was room for all kinds of programming," he said. Most assuredly, he was referring to *Bewitched*, which in fact, was renewed for three more seasons in the spring of 1970, the end of its seventh year.

But Lizzie had first resigned from the show in the spring of 1969, the close of its fifth season which just so happened to be Dick York's final semester as *Darrin*. At that point, certain terms were renegotiated in a new four-year deal that was put in place for seasons six and seven with a mutual option for seasons eight and nine. An additional *Bewitched* TV-movie would then follow in the tenth year, but only if both sides—Columbia, and Lizzie and Bill Asher—agreed upon all terms. If not, one party could not then force the other to undertake the optional year.

Before season seven commenced in the fall of 1970, that year would be designated as its final semester. Screen Gems and ABC then renegotiated another deal with Lizzie and Bill, granting them close to 80 percent of the show's ownership, along with complete creative control, which in effect they had always had, except that now it was official. It was also a way of sticking it to Jackie Cooper for the way he had treated them in 1963, when the show was first developed.

Consequently, in March of 1971, it was announced that *Bewitched* would be back for its eighth season, and *that* would become its last year in production. Somewhere in the midst of that final season (circa March 1972), Lizzie consented to a ninth year and then, after everyone else had agreed to move forward, she changed her mind. ABC once more met with their favorite star and offered her the farm, as it were. She politely listened, thanked all attending parties, but declined their generous offer, and that was that.

In the interim, Bill Asher admittedly made some personal and professional missteps. He spent too much time on the sets of ABC's *Temperatures Rising* and *The Paul Lynde Show*, both of which he and Lizzie bartered to produce in place of *Bewitched* through their Ashmont production company which was still in operation. At which point, Richard Michaels could have easily stepped in as *Samantha's* core producer/director, if not Lizzie's potential next husband.

Peter Ackerman remembers hearing a conversation between his parents, *Bewitched* executive producer Harry Ackerman and *Father Knows Best* actress Elinor Donahue, who were unaware of his close proximity. It had to do with Lizzie and another crew member, possibly Michaels, approaching his father about continuing *Bewitched*, "obviously pushing Bill Asher out."

He explains:

> My dad, as loyal a man as you could ever meet, determined not to stab Bill in the back like that, and kindly but firmly told Liz and the other fellow "no." I recall another part of that same conversation between my parents which, if true, is a bit salacious and would only be seen as gossip today. So I will keep that to myself. I do recall that on this very same day Bill Asher and his kids came over to the house, probably to commiserate with my dad. I was out playing with his and Liz's kids and I told Willie, their oldest son about what I overheard; both what I shared here and what I did not. And I

realize now that it probably got back innocently to one or both parents. Again, we were young and would not have had the filters to keep things to ourselves. I still believe to this day that I may be the reason that the Asher kids never came to play with us again. Years later Bill mentioned that right after that visit, Liz made it clear that their kids were no longer to go to our house. It could be that Willie shared what I said to him with his mom and dad and because of that, or perhaps only because Liz was disappointed that my dad did not continue the show with her and the other fellow, [that] made her decide to separate herself from the Ackerman family as much as possible, including not having her kids play [with us].

As time went on, Peter never sensed any hard feelings between the two families. "My parents would see Lizzie at events," he says, and in 1975, his father took to him visit her on the set of *The Legend of Lizzie Borden*, "and she could not have been nicer to me or my dad."

Harry Ackerman passed away in 1991 and Lizzie entertained the idea of attending the service, for which Bill Asher hosted the post-funeral gathering with his then-wife, actress Joyce Bulifant, *Marie Slaughter* on *The Mary Tyler Moore Show*, and mother of John Asher (former husband to Jenny McCarthy). "But ultimately," Peter says, "Liz decided not to attend."

In 1997, the Asher family organized a surprise seventy-fifth birthday party for Bill, who was by then divorced from Bulifant, and now married to Meredith Asher. Peter was invited to the bash, along with many of the *Bewitched* crew. Also in attendance were two of the Ashers' adult children, Billy, Jr. and Rebecca, both with whom, Peter says, he "happily, and most importantly, was able to reestablish contact." Unfortunately, he says, the Ashers' middle child, Robert, did not attend the gathering.

There was likely a large list of directors/producers who could have easily taken the *Bewitched* reigns in Bill Asher's absence, even with another actor besides Dick York or Dick Sargent potentially playing a *third Darrin*. But there was only one *Samantha*, and she was portrayed by the irreplaceable Elizabeth Montgomery—who was simply not interested in moving forward with the series.

Consequently, ABC developed and aired *The Paul Lynde Show* and what ultimately became *The New Temperatures Rising Show* with Lynde replacing James Whitmore from the old *Temperatures Rising* sitcom, all of which aired in place of *Bewitched's* nonexistent ninth season and subsequent TV-movie sequel (intended for the 1972–1974 seasons).

But when *Bewitched* switched to Saturday nights in the fall of 1971 to do battle against *All in the Family*, Lizzie had chosen not to continue with the series, even though ABC had opted to renew it. She was tired and viewing episodes from that eighth year, that became abundantly evident to the audience. Beyond the "liberated woman" braless look that she was sporting by that time (as was Marlo Thomas as *Ann Marie* in the final season of ABC's *That Girl*, 1966–1971), Lizzie looked as though she was dragging her feet in every scene. By this time, too, Dick Sargent was into his third season playing *Darrin,* and the show started reworking previous Dick York episodes. It remains puzzling as to why Bill Asher and company simply did not hire an entirely new batch of writers to create all new scripts. Instead, many of the show's episodes in that final year were mere retreads of previous segments.

Essentially, the rewriting of such scripts paved the way for the writing on the wall, and the end was near for *Bewitched.* Peter Ackerman remembers those final hours:

> Although I was young I had a sense then that it had run its course. I remember watching a "new" episode with my grandmother, in which *Darrin* was squawking through his living room dressed as a chicken or something and I recall thinking, "This show is starting to get too silly," although I never told my dad that.

In the eyes of Ackerman, the *Bewitched* cancellation "cancelled something else. With it or, more to the point, because of it, Bill and Liz ended their marriage."

By then, Screen Gems/Columbia was co-producing the series with Ashmont Productions, Lizzie and Bill's company that took its cue from Desilu Productions, presided over by Desi Arnaz and Lucille Ball. A pattern was beginning to take shape, for better and for worse, with female TV stars and their business partner/husbands, one that Jackie Cooper had first recognized with Donna Reed and her business partner/husband Tony Owen and their power struggle over *The Donna Reed Show.*

Yet, whereas Reed and Owen stayed together until after the *Donna* show's demise, the end of Ball's half-hour weekly series *I Love Lucy* in 1957 was followed by her real-life marriage dissolution from husband and show producer Arnaz. Twenty years later when *The Mary Tyler Moore Show* ended its CBS run in 1977, Moore called it quits with her show producer/husband Grant Tinker. After CBS gave the pink slip to *The Carol Burnett Show* in 1978, Carol gave walking papers to her husband and *Burnett* show producer Bob Hamilton. When Sonny & Cher ended their famous *CBS Comedy Hour* in 1974, so did they end their real-life once wedded bliss. Now *Bewitched* was closing its doors, and so soon would be the Montgomery/Asher love affair.

As writer K.V. Burroughs expressed in *Movieland and TV Time* magazine, September 1972:

If I were to repeat rumors of reasons the Ashers may have decided to call it a day, it would be talking about something I simply know nothing about and refuse to pass along. It really isn't important and is between Liz and Bill. It is sad and obviously must be painful to both of them. Divorces are very painful and create a sense of failure in both parties. There are always the questions, *Where did we go wrong? We were so much in love. How could it be gone? Was it my fault?* Sometimes there just are not good answers to any of these questions, but they still torture the two who are going through the death of their love. It is even worse if love is still strong in one of the parties and not in the other. At any rate, no divorce comes about overnight. It takes years of marriage erosion to cause two wonderful people like the Ashers to decide to call it a day. It takes a lot of intolerable living to be convinced that the children would be better off with two separate parents than one unhappy pair trying to hide their marital trouble from the eyes of their little children. If it is true that they have decided to divorce, it is a great tragedy for them and we are sorry to hear it. Liz would not be the first wife to deny trouble in her marriage right up to the last minute. There have been cases in Hollywood where stars denied splitting even on the day they filed for divorce. So far as we know, Elizabeth is resting after a long run in a very popular TV series. The Ashers should have no money problems because the series has made them wealthy. It is a time for resting and thinking and reviewing their lives. Perhaps in the more relaxed atmosphere they will decide to go on together. We'll all know soon enough. Meantime keep your fingers crossed. I am.

As an item from *The Daily Star* reported in 1974, Burroughs' noble words and heartfelt wish did not prove prescient.

Bewitched actress Elizabeth Montgomery has divorced her husband of 10 years, director William Asher. The reason for the divorce is unknown at present. In the divorce settlement, Liz was given the house and full sole custody of their three children, William, 10, Robert, 9, and Rebecca Elizabeth, 4. William Asher was given full unlimited access to their children. Elizabeth does not wish to discuss her divorce. All she will say is, "I had to divorce Bill. It was too painful to continue, and I think our children would be better off with two separate parents than one unhappy pair trying to hide their marital troubles from them. I do have my children to consider. They are so young, especially Rebecca. I have to think of what's best for them."

Lizzie was always thinking what was best for *everyone*. And whatever personal or professional relationships she established by way of *Bewitched*, whether with Bill Asher, Agnes Moorehead, Dick York, Dick Sargent, David White, Paul Lynde, Richard Michaels, or any number of the cast and crew, she made a lasting impression on each of them. As R. Robert Rosenbaum, one of the show's directors, explained in *The Bewitched Book*:

Elizabeth was a very caring person. She was one of the most loved actors in our business. It was fun working on *Bewitched*, and she helped make that happen. The whole crew adored her. She was sincerely interested in the welfare of everyone and their families.

In that same publication, Michaels added:

Liz was the darling of the *Bewitched* set. She was just as friendly with the gofer as she was with the director. She immediately disarmed people, and not everyone is like that, especially in the entertainment industry. She was a dream come true.

Actor Art Metrano (*Joanie Loves Chachi, Baretta*) was featured in several *Bewitched* episodes, initially, "*Samantha's* Wedding Present," which aired in the fifth season. In 1990, he summarized his years on the series, as well as the show's series of events:

Bewitched was the second show of my Hollywood career. Bill Asher became a big supporter of my career. He hired me in early 1970 to play a garbage man on my very first *Bewitched* show. I kiddingly said to him, "Please let me know when this will air so I can call my mom in Brooklyn." Bill did let me know when it would air and hired me for many other episodes of *Bewitched*. I would say it was Burt Metcalfe who cast the show, and Bill Asher who directed, got my career started in Hollywood. From that show at the Columbia lot, I was hired to do many other TV shows. Elizabeth was always nice to guests on the show and years later her daughter Rebecca and my daughter Roxanne became friends during their high school years. I remember Dick York as always being in pain and David White and Dick Sargent as being two terrific guys.

In the end, the rise and fall of *Bewitched*, as well as the Montgomery/ Asher marriage, was a learning experience for all, especially Lizzie. As she explained at length in 1989:

I learned a lot from being on *Bewitched* . . . People were so willing to let you in on their secrets or their not-so-secret likes and dislikes about what they were doing . . . from props to the gaffer . . . to lighting . . . to cinematography. It's not like it was this closed kind of shop where they didn't want to share their expertise. They enjoyed telling other people how good they were and what they did, and they had a damn good right to be proud of what they did because everybody did it so well. I have fond memories of these people and the reason is because we shared so much. It's not like we were isolated. You'd be hard-put to be isolated from anybody you'd worked with for eight years unless you're a total *do-do*.

I always thought it was like going to college. It really was like taking a course, and I learned an enormous amount on every level. And I don't think I ever missed a day. And the thing I found most amazing, was that any member of any crew at any given time is infinitely more important than the actors on the set, because they are so expert in what they're doing. If you ask them, 90 percent of them are more than willing to help, to tell you that this is that . . . and that is what that plug is . . . and that's what that light does.

It's a fascinating business, and what I found so rewarding is that I was never bored . . . never . . . for one minute. And a lot of people can sit around and be bored (on any set). I've noticed that. But there's never any reason to sit around and be bored because there's a whole lot of other stuff you can be doing. I think being bored is extremely boring and unproductive. There's just no excuse for it . . .

I learned about special effects. I learned a whole lot about a whole lot of stuff. I learned about things that I never even thought existed before. It's just a revelation to me. It's just so much more fun. And it makes you appreciate what everyone else is doing. And that the crew is the most important (group of) people on the set. They are what make it come together. It's everybody's production. The harder you work together and the closer you get—the better it's gonna be . . .

Nobody was afraid of making an ass of themselves, particularly me. I figured that's what I'm here for. And it's always nice to have people around who are that secure . . . who will trust. We had a company that really trusted each other . . . that worked that well together. You knew that nobody was out to get you . . . or how to hurt you. And that whatever happened happened because that was what the other person was really feeling should happen. And no one was out to upstage anybody, or snarl at anyone. It was amazing.

Seventeen

Post Serial

"The scenes were pretty much traumatic, and I would find myself
feeling depressed afterwards."

—Elizabeth Montgomery, expressing the emotional and
psychological strain that resulted from filming *A Case of Rape*
(*People Magazine*, March 1974)

When *Bewitched* debuted in the fall of 1964 its main commercial sponsors
were Chevrolet and Quaker Oats cereal. After Lizzie ended the series in the
spring of 1972, she would appear in various other television productions
with all new sponsors. Namely, her TV-movies, which she addressed in
summary in 1989:

> All of them have been different from each other, except perhaps *Act of
> Violence* and *A Case of Rape*. They've all had different kinds of "feels" to
> them, and that's one of the reasons that I've done them. I get letters from
> people saying, "The wonderful thing that we like about what [you do]
> since you left *Bewitched* is that we never know what you're going to do
> next." . . . [The movies] are all strange. (I'm) not being pigeonholed, which
> is good. And being afforded the luxury to do that is nice, to be able to pick
> and choose and only do what you want to do. Audiences really like that.

In 1993, she told journalist Bart Mills in short, "I can wait to do another
series. I'm happy doing movies for television."

As research has shown, Lizzie became the *Queen of TV-Movies . . .* by retaining a high *Television Quotient Rating*, or *TV-Q.* In fact, according to Ronny Cox, her friend and co-star in the small screen movies, *A Case of Rape* and *With Murder in Mind*, she had the "highest TV-Q of anybody."

TV-Q scores are a research product of New York–based business, *Marketing Evaluations. Qs*, as they are now known, were originally developed in the early 1960s for television programmers to calculate awareness of and favorability toward those public personalities on or associated with *The Ed Sullivan Show* and *The Tonight Show Starring Johnny Carson.* Over time, the panel survey was extended to include all broadcast and cable network shows and stars, sports celebrities, products and brands. In each case, the key factor was the likeability quotient, with collected data analyzed and summarized by the various perceptions accumulated on and by consumers into a single measurement.

For example, Tom Hanks topped the charts as the most likeable overall actor since 1995 and his TV-Q score has consistently been at least double the score for the average thespian in any medium. As another example, the CBS drama series, *NCIS* finished the 2010–2011 season as the top-rated scripted show on network television. When the latest TV-Q ratings of the most popular actors in prime time were released on August 4, 2011, it came as little surprise that a *NCIS* cast member or two ranked high on the list.

Pauley Perrette, who plays the "gothic" forensic scientist *Abby Sciuto*, earned the top spot on the survey; followed by Cote de Pablo, who came in second; Mark Harmon in fourth place; and David McCallum (originally known on TV from *The Man from U.N.C.L.E.*) in fifth place. The only non-*NCIS*-actor in TV-Q's top five for that season was Jim Parsons, who plays *Sheldon* on *The Big Bang Theory*, another CBS show (this one, a comedy).

While Marketing Evaluations believes the Q popularity measurement is a better indication of viewers' fondness for a show versus more traditional methods like TV ratings, networks are able to barter their compounded Qs to charge higher ad rates during their programs.

In short, TV-Qs, which are conducted twice annually, calculate how much the general public likes or dislikes a particular TV star. With specific regard to Lizzie's reign on television, author Michaels McWilliams stated it another way in his book *TV Sirens* (Perigee, 1987): "Montgomery is to the tube what [Greta] Garbo is to the cinema. She's as emblematic of *TV actress* as Garbo is of *movie actress.*"

Despite those small screen calculations which could have projected wide screen margins, post-*Samantha*, Lizzie shied away from feature film work beyond her narration of the controversial documentaries *Cover Up* (1988) and *The Panama Deception* (1922), and for many, this was a disappointment.

Bewitched writer John L. Green, who created *My Favorite Martian* (CBS, 1963–1966, a show that once included a "twitch" reference), once compared her special brand of TV quality to journalist Jane Pauley. "You can just see the intelligence in her eyes," he said.

And Lizzie stayed with television because she enjoyed it, she wasn't overly ambitious with regard to her career, and there were few big screen parts available for women.

In 1988, *Bewitched* writer Richard Baer said of Lizzie, "I think she wanted to be Jane Fonda. She sure looked like her, but it wasn't meant to be. *Bewitched* came along and, though she never admitted it, I think she was tired of doing the show after the first few years."

In 1978, Elizabeth went on a promotional tour for her NBC mini-series, *The Awakening Land*. While she believed the film-TV comparison was an odd thing, she never really thought in those terms. She left that up to network and studio executives. She continued working because she loved her job. And she was in a position to pick and choose projects at will. She was frequently granted first choice on various projects and many times rejected significant offers for both television and film. She went by her instincts and never regretted any decisions for TV or the big screen.

With regard to feature films in particular, she welcomed opportunities when they presented themselves, but she was never compelled to do one. In 1988, Columbia Pictures approached Sol Saks about doing a *Bewitched* feature film. The studio approached Elizabeth about the idea, and Saks said she was "intrigued." But as it turned out, Saks owned the TV rights, but not the motion picture rights. Consequently, thirteen years later, a very different *Bewitched* feature film hit theatres, a movie that got a lukewarm reception by critics, but which nonetheless paid loving tribute to Lizzie's memory.

Back on the small screen, between 1972 and 1993, Elizabeth was satisfied with the work at hand. For her, the quality of television movies was closing in on theatrical motion pictures. Her success from *Bewitched* had allowed her to work as she pleased, even on a limited basis, doing two TV-movies a year. For her, money was never a concern and she never felt underpaid.

Instead, all that mattered was the quality of the script and production. An astute judge of material, and a severe critic of what she managed to have and not have produced, Lizzie thought television executives never gave enough credit to the home audiences, whom she believed craved sophisticated programming like PBS' once-popular and somewhat suggestive British series, *I, Claudius*. But airing such risqué programming on any mainstream American network in 1977—and for a few years to come— wasn't going to happen, and she knew it.

Truth be told, Lizzie constructed a solid career in television because she was talented, charismatic, and female, and because audiences had separate perceptions of the small and big screens. At the time, TV projects were not usually given the green light unless there was significant indication of a solid female interest. In fact, many TV-movies of today, specifically for networks like The Hallmark Channel or Lifetime, are still geared specifically toward a female audience.

In Elizabeth's core TV-movie era, the mainstream target audience for feature films was, with few exceptions, young adults with limited female appeal. At the same time, television proved to be an extraordinary challenge because of its boundaries, and although she never felt too confined by the small screen's size, she particularly embraced daring subject matters, which she viewed as strategic career moves.

In 1961, she may have once dubbed TV a "mediocre medium," but by 1994, when she chatted with reporter Ed Bark and *The Dallas Morning News*, she had clearly changed her mind:

> I love television. I like the pressure. I like the lack of wasting time. I would love to do a feature, but that's a whole other animal. I'm lucky to be able to kind of hang in there and wait a bit for really good scripts. I like to try to pick something a little unlike anything I've done before.

Certainly, her first post-*Samantha* screen performance in the 1972 ABC TV-movie, *The Victim*, a nerve-wracking thriller, reflected that decision:

A wealthy *Kate Wainwright* is trapped on a rainy night at the home of her sister, *Susan Chappel* (Jess Walton), whom she soon discovers has been murdered and stuffed in the basement. And *Kate* may the next victim.

The Victim debuted in what would have been Lizzie's ninth year on *Bewitched* had she agreed to her extended contract with the series. Instead, twitch-fans were treated to her take on *Kate*, who looked like *Samantha Stephens* and dressed like *Samantha Stephens*, but who wasn't *Samantha Stephens*. Not by a long shot. Lizzie's hair as *Kate* was as it was styled in the final season of *Bewitched*, but the happy, chipper *Samantha* persona, although subdued in that last year, was nowhere to be seen when Lizzie played *The Victim*. Her break from *Bewitched* was loud and clear, and she wanted *Samantha* fans to hear her cry of freedom.

In 1977, Leonard Nimoy, star of the original *Star Trek*—one of Lizzie's favorite TV shows—authored *I Am Not Spock* which he hoped would send a message of independence to "Trekkers" the world over. With *The Victim* Lizzie followed suit, as if to say, "I Am Not *Samantha*"; it's considered one of her best movie portrayals since her big screen debut in 1955's *The Court-Martial of Billy Mitchell*.

But in playing *The Victim*, she may have frightened more than a few viewers in the Bible Belt, which certain studio and network executives thought she had already done with *Bewitched*.

Although the violent themes and scenes of *The Victim* are considered mild by today's standards, there are still some solid scares in the film, which offers a strong supporting cast. Besides Jess Walton as Lizzie's on-screen sister, George Maharis (*Route 66*) played her brother-in-law, *Ben Chappel*, and veteran actress Eileen Hackert was a slightly sinister housekeeper, *Mrs. Hawkes*.

Through it all, the entire cast and crew enjoyed near-perfect weather conditions, as the movie was shot on location on the Monterey Peninsula in California. But that didn't help the film's premise, which was centered around a treacherous rain storm. Lizzie explained to *The Florence Morning News* on March 2, 1974:

"The lack of rain meant that we had to create our own deluge. Over 100,000 gallons of water (was) used on the location and each time they set up the rain towers it was an expensive job. My major concern was the problems that would result if re-takes were necessary. My hair would have to be re-done, the wardrobe dried and the area re-dressed. I've always tried to be a one-take actress," she said, "but with this film that objective proved especially challenging. I felt easy coming back to drama after so many years, but there were special problems that made this the toughest story I have ever done. The technical work was the best I have ever seen, but it was so complex that the crew and I had to have absolute perfect timing to make everything work properly."

When it was all said and done, irony refused to take a holiday. Only seven days after *The Victim* completed production, near-monsoon-like rains flooded the area.

But rain or shine, working on the movie boosted Lizzie's performance stamina, while her career received a breath of fresh air. In 1964, she was playing *Samantha*; in 1974, she decided that television drama in particular was "as good or better than it was ten years ago. The advances in the technical areas are almost staggering. I saw some of them on *Bewitched*, but on this film I saw how new cameras and lenses can be a tool of both the director and the actor."

Between *Bewitched, The Victim,* and her other 1970s TV-movies, she was still approached about resurrecting *Samantha* in some way, even as a supporting character on a short-lived ABC spin-off called *Tabitha*, the pilot for which debuted on May 7, 1977. The show was about *Samantha* and *Darrin's* now grown-up magical daughter, and it featured future *Knots Landing* star and aspiring singer Lisa Hartman (today married to country crooner Clint Black). William Asher had directed a previous *Tabatha* (with an "a") pilot segment starring Liberty Williams, which aired on April 24, 1976. This edition was actually more mystical than *Bewitched*, but it didn't sell. However, a second pilot with Hartman caught ABC's fancy and it went to series. Asher set the stage, premise, and the theme of the spin-off, but was not hands-on involved following his work on the first pilot. He later directed a few episodes of the series (in which *Bewitched* originals Sandra Gould, George Tobias, and Bernard Fox reprised their *Gladys, Abner Kravitz,* and *Dr. Bombay* roles), but other than that, Asher only became an advisor on the show.

Lizzie's presence as *Samantha* was requested in both editions of the *Tabitha* series, but she declined, even in a guest-star capacity. The sequel faced many casting challenges.

On the later years of *Bewitched*, the child *Tabitha* was played by twins Erin and Diane Murphy until the show ended in 1972, when the character was only eight years old. By the time the *Tabitha* series debuted, she would have only been thirteen years old. A hallmark of the original series was that, despite its fantasy premise, whatever transpired within its fabricated world made sense. There was always "logic within the illogic."

As Elizabeth explained in 1989:

> Ease is facilitated only by construction. If it's not constructed well, you find yourself walking into blank walls, and tripping and falling down. And there's just no way to rescue anything unless something's been constructed [well]. And that's why with ease we could flip from one thing back to another [mortal to the witch world]. That was one of the great advantages of our kind of format. It opened itself up into many ideas, and we could really pretty much go in any direction, as long as we kept to the ground rules.

Needless to say, such ground rules were feet of clay on the *Tabitha* series, which didn't have a logical-within-the-illogical leg to stand on. Meanwhile, too, making the *Tabitha* character twenty-something in 1977 also went against the basic premise idea that witches are immortal and tend not to age swiftly.

As Elizabeth continued to explain in 1989, such confusing plot developments and other aspects of *Tabitha* were troubling for her as well as fans of the original series:

> First of all, I didn't see the show, but I heard that she didn't twitch as well as I did. I kept getting mail from people were who outraged, saying, "Where is Erin Murphy? What in the world (is going on)?! This woman is 25 . . . this doesn't make any sense." I was getting mail from people like it was my fault, although also saying, "Thank God you didn't have anything to do with this." I wrote every single person who sent me letters like that. They felt betrayed. I thought, "How can you be betrayed by a TV show?" But they were irate. I got almost as much mail about that as I get about

anything else. It was very funny . . . ranged from kids who hated it to grownups who said, "This is the stupidest thing I've ever seen."

Like it was all my fault. I'm saying (to myself), "Why are they blaming me for this? I had absolutely zero to do with this." People were getting pissed off at me. I remember walking into stores and having people say to me, "Did you know they were going to do this? How could you have allowed this?" All I said [was] "I didn't want anything to do with this." People were getting downright nasty to me . . . People were just annoyed.

Ten years after the *Tabitha* series failed, Bill Asher began to develop yet another *Bewitched* off-shoot, this one called *Bewitched Again*, about an entirely new witch and mortal love affair. Whereas *Darrin* on *Bewitched* prohibited *Samantha's* use of her special powers, the mortal on the new show would do nothing of the sort. Instead, he encouraged his supernatural love to practice her craft.

It was a fresh take on the original series and, to help jumpstart the program, Bill had convinced Elizabeth to make a cameo in the pilot. She was to reprise her role as *Samantha*, introduce the new witch/mortal couple, and then pop off forever. Her consent to become involved with *Bewitched Again* was monumental and enticing, and Asher placed a great deal of energy into the project. Unfortunately, the intended new series, which was to be produced in the U.K., lost its financing and the idea was shelved.

To help ease the stress that resulted from *Tabitha*, her divorce from Bill Asher, and the general anxiety that accompanies the life of a major television star, Lizzie made frequent appearances on game shows like *The Hollywood Squares* hosted by Peter Marshall and *Password* hosted by Allen Ludden. According to what *Bewitched* producer/director Richard Michaels said in 1988, "She loved that stuff!"

For many of the *Password* spots, which were videotaped live, she played opposite her good friend Carol Burnett whom she met on the set of 1963's *Who's Been Sleeping in My Bed*. In Burnett's wonderful book, *This Time Together* (Crown, 2010), the super-talented redhead recalled one particular *Password* game with Lizzie in the section "Viewer Discretion Advised." It had to do with Burnett's team-partner on the show, whom she referred to in the book as Louis, and his somewhat improper, although innocent, use of the word "twat."

Burnett delicately defined the word as an unflattering term that referenced a particular body part of the female anatomy. In either case, she, Lizzie, and *Password* host Allen Ludden (who was married to Betty White, then of *The Mary Tyler Moore Show,* later of *The Golden Girls,* and today of *Hot in Cleveland*) were in hysterics by the end of the segment.

In 1989, Lizzie remarked just how much she enjoyed her frequent *Password* game play-on-words with Burnett: "Oh, we were terrific, weren't we? In print I know that sounds terrible, but we were! Carol is just a super wonderful lady, and I really appreciated the fact that we did become friends."

However, post-*Password*, their bond somewhat loosened. Lizzie explained:

> It's a funny thing, because so many friendships are like that in this town and anywhere. You work together so closely and then you hardly ever see that person again. Well, it's true. Carol and I don't see each other very often— but when we do, it's always nice. And I think instinctively she knows that if she picked up the phone and called me at 3:00 in the morning and said, "Can you be here?" I think she knows that I would be there for her, which is odd, as I say, when you don't see somebody that often. But I wouldn't respond with [as if she were annoyed], "Oh, Carol, what is it?!" I'd say, "Ok, I'll be there as soon as I can." There's certain people you feel that way about.

Despite her close friendship with Carol, and extensive comedy experience, Lizzie continuously rejected invitations to guest-star on *The Carol Burnett Show* (CBS, 1967–1978). As she went on to say:

> It's one of the many regrets I have, though it's not really a regret because even today I wouldn't do it. I'm just too terrified of that kind of stuff. She asked me to do it, and I said, "I just can't." I would have been so panic-stricken. It's not as though I haven't done stuff like that. It's not like, "No—I don't like spinach." "But have you tried it?" "No, but I don't like it anyway." It's that I know how terrified I get on the live stage. And it's just not worth it to me.

While promoting her singing performance as *Serena* in the *Bewitched* episode, "*Serena* Stops the Show," Lizzie addressed her TV variety show conundrum with *The Los Angeles Herald Examiner* for the article, "Liz Montgomery Makes Night Club Debut, but on TV," published February 9, 1970. "I've always thought of some big Miami Beach or Vegas hotel for my singing engagement," she mused. "I'd have settled for Joe's Bistro in Toluca Lake."

At the time, she had been asked to create a nightclub act and was offered a TV special of her own in which she was to sing and dance, but ultimately nothing came of the idea. "To me," she said, "a nightclub appearance or a special would involve more rehearsal time than I can afford. And I wouldn't want to go out and fall flat on my face because I hadn't prepared sufficiently."

Instead, she decided to utilize her harmonic vocal chords in a more controlled atmosphere . . . on the set of *Bewitched*, in character as *Serena*, singing "Blow You a Kiss in the Wind," by 1960s pop stars Boyce and Hart (who were under contract to Columbia and made a guest appearance in the episode). Her performance was a one-shot segment in a half-hour sitcom as opposed to the hour-long continuous song-and-dance routine that would be required in a variety show format.

"Who could resist that? It was like having your cake, et cetera, et cetera," she joked about the *Serena* segment that ultimately became a choreographed production number with psychedelic lighting which transformed *Samantha* and *Darrin's* living room into a nightclub.

It all proved so puzzling, if consistent with her unpredictable spirit. She'd sing as *Serena* on short *Bewitched* segments, but was reticent about appearing on the *Burnett* show; and come March 19, 1966, things became more confusing.

That's when she hosted *The Hollywood Palace*, which featured frequent *Bewitched* guest-star Paul Lynde with whom she got along famously. She enjoyed Carol's company, too, but Lynde's presence on *Palace* may have proved more comfortable because: 1) He was hand-picked from Lizzie's *Bewitched* stable, and 2) *Palace* aired on ABC, *Samantha's* home network, whereas *Burnett* aired on rival CBS. Also, too, her *Palace* spotlight as host allowed for more creative control as opposed to only being a guest on *Burnett*.

After her early appearances with Carol on *Password*, Lizzie became less enthusiastic about the game after it changed formats. The original show debuted on CBS with host Allen Ludden in 1961 and ran until 1967. ABC brought it back with Ludden from 1971 to 1975, during which it briefly became the celebrity-drenched *Password All-Stars*. NBC did an update in 1979 with a new edition called *Password Plus*, which also ran with Ludden though only until 1982 when failing health (stomach cancer) forced him to relinquish his hosting duties. NBC tried once more in 1984 with *Super Password*, now hosted by Bert Convy, and this new format ran until 1989.

Lizzie's final *Password* appearance was with actor Wesley Eure (*Land of the Lost*, NBC/CBS, 1974–1987) within the *Plus* format, hosted by Ludden, airing August 3, 1979. But throughout each of the editions, as bonus rounds were added along with elaborate sets, the once simple and popular word game became overly puzzling or, as she said in 1989, "It all just got kind of convoluted. It was so pure the other way, when it was what it was."

During one of those pure *Password* games, specifically, the week of November 19–23, 1973, she appeared with Robert Foxworth, whom she met and fell in love with on the set of the ABC TV-movie *Mrs. Sundance* (which aired in 1974 but filmed in September 1973). Although they later played *Password* within the 1979 *Plus* format, it was their 1973 session that proved most advantageous. "When Bob and I did the show that year," she recalled in 1989, "we raised $11,000 for the L.A. Free Clinic, and no one would play with us anymore because we just got so good at it. I guess when you're together a lot you kind of think on the same level."

She and Foxworth were together a great deal. He contributed to her comfort zone when they appeared at charity events or on talk shows like John Tesh's *One on One*. It was to Tesh she explained her attraction to Foxworth (who most recently provided the voice of *Ratchet* in the *Transformer* feature films): "He's got one of the most wonderfully inquisitive minds . . . of anybody I've ever met. And he's compassionate. He cares about things. He also cares a great deal about his career. He's got a wonderful sense of humor."

☆

Before and after his best known role as *Chase Gioberti* on *Falcon Crest* (CBS, 1981–1990), Robert Foxworth had numerous screen and stage performances, including his television debut in the 1969 CBS *Playhouse* drama, *Sadbird*. After starring in *The Storefront Lawyers* (aka *Men at Law*), a 1970–1971 series for CBS, he appeared opposite Faye Dunaway in "Hogan's Goat" (NET Playhouse, 1971).

Besides his appearances with Lizzie, his TV films included but were not limited to: *The Devil's Daughter* (ABC, 1973); *The FBI versus Alvin Karpis* (CBS, 1974); *Act of Love* (CBS, 1980); *Peter and Paul* (CBS, 1981); *The Memory of Eva Ryker* (CBS, 1980); and *The Questor Tapes* (NBC, 1974). The latter project, also known as just *Questor*, was written by *Star Trek* legend and Lizzie-favorite Gene Roddenberry.

Intended as NBC's answer to ABC's super popular superhero series *The Six Million Dollar Man* (1974–1979), *Questor* was a slightly more imaginative tale than Lee Major's earthbound bionic cyborg *Col. Steve Austin*. Foxworth's *Questor* was an all-robotic philosophical character in search of his alien creator. He was *The Fugitive* meets *Kung Fu* on the way to Brent Spiner's *Data* from Roddenbery's *Star Trek: The Next Generation* (syndicated, 1987–1994). As it turned out, Bob later appeared in more shows from the Roddenberry/*Trek* sector, including *Star Trek: Deep Space Nine* in 1996 and *Star Trek: Enterprise* in 2004. In fact, Foxworth, like Lizzie, has become a legend in the sci-fi/fantasy world with additional guest-star spots on shows like: *The Sixth Sense* (ABC, 1972); "Frankenstein" (ABC's *Wide World Mystery*, 1973); *Tales of the Unexpected* (1977); *The Outer Limits* (syndicated, 1996); *Stargate: SG-1* (syndicated, 2003); and feature films such as *Beyond the Stars* (1989).

Besides lending his voice to *Ratchet* in all three *Transformer* movies (2007, 2009, 2011), he provided various vocal talents to animated TV shows like *Justice League*, as *Professor Neil Hamilton* (Cartoon Network, 2004–2005) and *The Real Adventures of Jonny Quest*, playing *Race Bannon* (Cartoon Network, 1996–1997). His countless live guest-star appearances date back to small screen classics like *Kung Fu* (ABC, 1974), *The Mod Squad* (ABC, 1971), *Mannix* (CBS, 1971), *Law & Order: SVU* (NBC, 2000–2005), and *The West Wing* (NBC, 2005), the latter in which he portrayed *Senator George Montgomery* (which was a nod to Lizzie's family name, as well as to the actor the public periodically misidentified as her father, George Montgomery, who was once married to Dinah Shore). Other of his theatrical film credits include *Airport '77* (1977), *Damien: Omen II* (1978), *Prophecy* (1979), and *The Black Marble* (1980), and more.

His stage performances include the role of *John Proctor* in *The Crucible* at Lincoln Center, for which he won a Theatre World Award; Off-Broadway productions of *Terra Nova, One Flew Over the Cuckoo's Nest*, and *Mary Stuart* in Los Angeles, and *Long Day's Journey into Night* at Atlanta's Alliance Theatre. In three seasons at the Arena Stage in Washington, D.C., he appeared in twenty productions ranging from *The Skin of Our Teeth* to *Room Service*. He made his name in *Henry V* following work at the American Shakespeare Festival in Stratford, Connecticut.

Unlike the older Gig Young and Bill Asher, and her first husband Fred Cammann (who was only four years her senior), Foxworth was the only younger man she married. Her penchant for all things *Trek* and sci-fi/fantasy may have contributed to her initial attraction to Foxworth, but the actor's diverse talents and varied charms assuredly contributed to his appeal.

In 1992, he expressed his attraction to Lizzie on *One on One with John Tesh*, and noted her ability to see the funny side of life as one of her most appealing traits (as did she of him on the same show): "I would describe her as perhaps the most intelligent woman I've ever met. And one of the things that makes that bearable is that she has a fabulous sense of humor, besides the fact that she's beautiful and sexy."

Lizzie and Bob Foxworth performed together live on stage in a short-lived production of *Cat on a Hot Tin Roof* at the Bell Theatre, Los Angeles, 1978. In the fall of 1989, they were together again on stage, in the play *Love Letters* at the Edison Theatre in Broadway. Only a few months before, *Bewitched* actor David White visited with Lizzie at her home in Beverly Hills, and suggested that she and Foxworth return to the stage.

"Why don't you and Bob do a play? You've done stage work before? Don't you like it?"

"Yeah."

"Here I am messing in her business."

"Oh, you could mess in my business. I don't mind."

"Well, then do one! I think that would be great!"

At which point, Lizzie explained how London's historic Globe Theatre had invited her and Foxworth to perform in Edward Albee's classic play, *Who's Afraid of Virginia Woolf?* In 1966, writer Ernest Lehman had adapted this monumentally depressing play, about a bitter, middle-aged couple who use alcohol as a pawn in and to fuel their already angry relationship, into a feature film directed by Mike Nichols, and starring Elizabeth Taylor and Richard Burton. But Lizzie thought that tackling such a play with Foxworth would have been "totally crazy":

> I'm not sure that two people who really care about each other should do
> that play. I think it would be better to rehearse it, do it, go home, and then
> get really kind of attracted to the person that you're working with, so that
> you're on an entirely different level than to having to live and rehearse with
> the person doing that play. And when the Burtons did the movie . . . that's
> different because they didn't have to all be on the same set at the same time.

Needless to say, they turned down Globe's invitation to do *Woolf,* but years before they were on the same set at the same time in *Mrs. Sundance,* the 1974 TV-movie in which she played *Etta Place* opposite his *Jack Maddox.* They met and fell in love while working on this film which ultimately served as a sequel to the 1969 big screen flick, *Butch Cassidy and the Sundance Kid* (in which Katharine Ross portrayed *Etta*).

A review of the film appears in the book, *The Great Western Pictures* (Scarecrow Press, 1976) by James Robert Parrish and Michael R. Pitts:

> It was a catchy gimmick to produce a semi-sequel to *Butch Cassidy and the*
> *Sundance Kid* (1969), with Elizabeth Montgomery, the queen of the telefea-
> tures, as the title figure. The intriguing premise had *Etta Place* (aka *Mrs.*
> *Sundance*) in a ticklish situation when she learns that the *Sundance Kid* did
> not die with *Butch Cassidy* but is waiting for her at their old hideout. What
> makes the set-up so dangerous is that bounty hunters are aware of the
> planned reunion of the famed outlaw and the schoolteacher of a small Colo-
> rado town. Elizabeth Montgomery, very much Robert's daughter, offered
> a strong performance in this flashy role, giving an enriched characterization
> in a genre far removed from her days as the star of the teleseries *Bewitched.*

Once more, Lizzie's on-screen performance mirrored her off-stage life, and this time, Foxworth successfully played into the scenario. Although his *Maddox* character was a cagey, weak-spined character who first viewed *Etta* as a way to get out of jail free, he was big-hearted and fell prey to her charms, just as had Foxworth with Lizzie. *Etta's* love may have made *Jack* heroic and strong, but they were always a team, partners for humanity, again, much like Lizzie and Foxworth would be for various charitable causes.

After *Mrs. Sundance*, Lizzie and Foxworth would co-star in two other TV films: *Face to Face* for CBS in 1990 and *With Murder in Mind* for in 1992.

Face to Face was their shining moment, debuting January 24, 1990 under the prestigious *Hallmark Hall of Fame* banner:

> *Diana Firestone* (Lizzie), a brilliant paleontologist, traveled to Africa with a team of assistants in search of the remains of a three-million-year-old man, a potential discovery that would rewrite the anthropological textbooks. *Tobias Williams* (Foxworth) was a rough and ready miner who explored the same territory for meerschaum (a special clay used for making smoking pipes). Sparks flew as they both claimed digging rights in Kenya's high country. She considered him the epitome of a Philistine, narrow-minded, devoid of culture, and indifferent to art. He patronized her "naïve" outlook on life and regarded her as better suited to an ivory-towered academic institution than the African bush. Compromise was out. Occasional attempts to be cordial took mutual turns for the worse. But despite their stubbornness and fiercely independent manner, their hostility gradually changed to reluctant respect and finally to unexpected romantic love.

Lizzie and Foxworth may have played themselves on *Password*, but *Face to Face* marked the first time since 1974's *Mrs. Sundance* that they performed together on screen in character. "It's not the usual kind of romance you see on television," he said of *Face* in a press release for the film in 1990. "It's a mature love story, with two very interesting and very independent characters whose relationship changes from mutual animosity to mutual respect."

The movie was filmed on location in remote Kenya, on the banks of the Engare Odare River. When additional laborers were needed on the set, ten Maasai warriors were hired. Interviewed around a campfire near her tent (her home for the three weeks of filming), Lizzie talked with CBS publicity about the African location shoot. "The innocence, the beauty, the harshness," she said. "It's all here. This is life of another dimension."

Certainly, it was a life that was foreign in terms of her teen years growing up in Patterson, New York, her young adult life in New York, and her later days in Beverly Hills. But she felt compelled by *Face* when, upon first reading the script, she said: "It was so good you couldn't bear to turn the page because you were afraid the next page would disappoint you . . . I kept thinking, 'I hope it stays this good.'" *Face* may have also jogged memories of her youth on the family farm—and even *Bewitched*.

Robert Halmi, Sr. served as the film's executive producer. Jim Chory was the co-producer and actor Lou Antonio directed and also cast himself in a small role. Antonio had first worked with Lizzie on *Bewitched* for an episode called "Going Ape," which debuted on February 27, 1969, in which he played, of all things, a monkey who was turned into a man (the show's slight acknowledgement of the first and most popular *Planet of the Apes* film that had premiered approximately one year before).

Around this same time, Antonio directed episodes of ABC's *The Flying Nun* and *The Partridge Family* (later, NBC's *McMillan & Wife* and *McCloud*, while more recently, *Dawson's Creek, Numbers,* and *Boston Legal*). In 1983, he even directed Lizzie's friends, Carol Burnett and Elizabeth Taylor, in their hit TV-movie, *Between Friends*.

In *With Murder in Mind*, which premiered on May 12, 1992, Lizzie and Bob Foxworth worked together for their third and final time on screen within a scripted format. *Mind* was a fact-based story in which Lizzie played a real-life realtor:

> Gayle Wolfer (Lizzie) was shot and nearly killed by a client (Howard Rollins, best known from the TV version of *In the Heat of the Night*, 1988-1994; NBC/CBS). Physically and emotionally scarred from the incident, Gayle remains determined to find her attacker, which she finally does at a county fair. But he's a part-time auxiliary policeman who's established his own security company. The case eventually goes to trial, but at first no one believes her because of his position in the community.

Through it all, Foxworth played *Bob Sprague*, Gayle's longtime live-in boyfriend, which is exactly what he was in Lizzie's real life. He was strong, calm, resilient, logical and practical; loving and family focused; supportive, independent with a strong sense of self even though he was living with his boss. He didn't put up with too much. But he was honest, a straight shooter, and not afraid to speak his own mind. Once again, all qualities which Foxworth also possessed.

In 1989, Lizzie expressed her theories on acting, addressing the more specific challenges of performing comedy as opposed to drama.

> Laughing on screen is more difficult than crying for a lot of actors. It's quite a challenge to laugh on cue in front of the camera. Both laughing and crying are hard for me. There must be something that's easy in the middle of that. Comedy is more difficult on many levels. If you have ten people come into a room and say "I just saw a dog hit by a car in the street." Those ten people are going to go, "Oh, my God." You're going to get the same reaction, presumably, from those ten people. But if someone comes into the room and tells those same ten people a joke, you may get ten different reactions. Some may think it's funny; some may not think it's funny. Some may think it's moderately funny. So you're not hitting the same emotional chord with everyone (compared) with something that might be a very sad kind of event.

Lizzie's friend and fellow-actor Ronny Cox co-starred with her in *With Murder in Mind,* and nearly twenty years before in *A Case of Rape.* He has an upbeat theory on acting that he believes they shared:

> The fun is in the work. The fun of acting is reacting . . . playing off of someone else. I'm not a proponent of rehearsing lines with certain voice inflections or physical gestures. That's distracting. The line can be, "I love you" and I can make it mean "I hate you," depending on how I say it. Therefore, it's presumptuous to decide ahead of time how you're going to say a line . . . until you know how (the other actor) is going to say their line. That becomes the be-all and end-all of acting. I have little patience for actors who over-strategize how they're going to say a line and how they're going to move while saying it. That's not acting. That's robotics. I hate to *see* "acting" and that's what always happens when you see that kind of

work. It's technically very proficient, but lacking in the conveyance of truth. I'm one of the few actors who will vociferously defend American actors over British actors in that respect. Brilliant actors are brilliant actors no matter whether they're British or American. But run-of-the-mill British actors are more technically proficient. They work out how they're going to say the lines. Technically they're way ahead of [American actors] but they don't "invest" in a scene as much as less technically proficient American actors. For my money, if you take the very best of the American actors and the very best of the British actors, the British actors will have far superior technique and American actors will have a far superior grasp of the character! I also don't have much patience with actors who improvise their lines. Acting is like a great piece of jazz. The key to it is listening. You listen to what's being said and allow that to manifest how you're going to reply to what's being said. And I think that's the thing that Lizzie and I were able to do quite well.

It's Cox's brand of passion and love for his craft that contributed to his solid bond with Lizzie while they filmed *A Case of Rape*. In fact, they became so close Cox says "some people on the crew thought we might be lovers." But such was not the case. His wife Mary died in 2006, and they met as children:

> Just so everyone knows. I'm a widower now; but I was the most married man you've ever seen in your life. I never had another date. She was, is, and will always be the love of my life! But having said that, Lizzie and I were very close; I was hanging out in her dressing room all the time . . . and I mean all the time. It paid off for us, I think, in the acting (department), because there was this familiarity where we could be at ease. And that ease translated into playing scenes with each other.

In 1979, five years after Lizzie starred with Ronny Cox in *A Case of Rape*, her friend Carol Burnett appeared in the ABC-TV movie, *Friendly Fire*. This acclaimed film was based on the real-life story of Peg Mullen—from rural Iowa who worked against government obstacles to uncover the truth about the death of her son Michael, a soldier killed by American "friendly fire" in 1970 during the Vietnam War.

All of sudden, it seemed, critics heralded Burnett's acting, as if she had never excelled in any worthy capacity for eleven years on *The Carol Burnett Show* (CBS, 1967–1978), on *The Garry Moore Show* (CBS, 1958–1966) before that, or in any of her countless prior stage, TV, or film appearances (including *Who's Been Sleeping in My Bed?* with Lizzie in 1963). This time, because she was performing drama as opposed to her trademark comedy, her talents were praised as if she were royalty. Her crowning as a *Queen of Comedy* was apparently not enough for the critics.

Lizzie received a similar response when she left *Bewitched* behind and ventured into *Rape* and other extremely shocking roles in ground-breaking TV-movies like *The Legend of Lizzie Borden* (ABC, 1975), and *The Black Widow Murders: The Blanche Taylor Moore Story* (1993), among others. Only rarely would she return to the comedic tones and timing that she honed on *Bewitched*, as she did with *When the Circus Came to Town* (CBS, 1981) and in *Face to Face* (CBS, 1990), the latter in which she starred with Robert Foxworth.

In fact, according to her friend Sally Kemp, it was Foxworth who urged Lizzie to delve deeper into these "meatier" roles. She discussed such performances for an interview in 1980 with writer Lewis George of *The Globe*, while promoting her part as yet another female bandit of the Old West in the CBS TV-movie *Belle Star*, which she was initially apprehensive about doing:

> I would rather be known as a serious . . . and good . . . actress now. I've always enjoyed playing real lady creatures like *The Legend of Lizzie Borden*, who was supposed to have axed her family. I also portrayed a lady who was raped in *A Case of Rape*, and a lady beaten up by toughs in my most recent film *Act of Violence*. What concerned me was that the script was stark with dramatic violence. It was such an unusual script. I was afraid executive producer Joe Barbara might have to alter it because of ears of network censorship. My fears were needless. Joe Barbara is just as much opposed to network and creative censorship as I am and agreed completely on the script. An actress can't be anything less than honest when she's working. And I am aware the *Belle Starr* story may be not for the entire family. But this woman had to survive by her own code of ethics in a very difficult environment. She's a fascinating person and very real. She made many drastic mistakes in her life, including murder. There's a certain ugliness about her, but there's also an inner beauty and strength.

In an interview with *The Minneapolis Star Tribune*, on March 30, 1980, she added:

> The real Belle Starr is so clouded by legend and fiction that you can come up with several versions of her life, depending on which history of the old west you study. One thing we do know for sure is that she was an exceptional and amazing woman, if not a good one, and an important figure in the history of the West.

Of all the legends of the west, Starr's was one of the most romanticized by the dime novelists of the day. To them, she was a daring and noble woman who fulfilled the role of a female *Robin Hood*. Her real name was Myra Belle Shirley; she was born in 1848 in a log cabin near Carthage, Missouri. Her family moved to Texas and Belle had not yet grown out of her teens when she began hobnobbing with Jesse James and his gang, and bore one of its members, Cole Younger, a daughter. She then married a horse thief named Jim Reed and bore him a son. After Reed was killed, Starr took up with another gang and moved into Indian Territory (now Oklahoma), where she met and married a handsome Cherokee bandit named Sam Starr. From their hideout on the Canadian River, Belle acted as organizer, planner, and fence for cattle rustlers, horse thieves, and traffickers in illegal whiskey to the Indians. When the law captured her friends, she spent her money generously to buy their freedom. When bribery failed, she would employ her powers of seduction.

After Sam Starr was killed in a shootout, Belle continued her amorous pursuits. To the sorrow of romantic readers from coast to coast, she was shot in ambush in 1889. Her daughter had a monument erected on her grave with a bell, a star, and a horse inscribed on it.

In an early scene in the *Belle Star* film, the lead character is seen encouraging her young daughter to practice the piano. Lizzie explained in *The Minneapolis Star Tribune*:

> She apparently loved music of all types, and had learned to play the piano at the age of eight. She actually was quite a genteel young lady until the Civil War caused her to strap on a gun and change her life, with a little help from her outlaw lover, Cole Younger. But she never gave up her love of music. She displayed her talent at every opportunity, even at church for

weddings and funerals. After the war Belle played the piano in Dallas gambling halls and mastered the guitar. Even after she had become a much-hunted woman, she managed to have a piano in her hideout.

As it was during the *Bewitched* years, Lizzie worked hard on *Belle Starr*, and she maintained a strong sense of priorities and family life for her children. By now, her sons Bill and Robert were in their mid-teens, while daughter Rebecca was only ten years old. She was five years divorced from Bill Asher, and Lizzie and the kids now shared their country-style Beverly Hills home in Laurel Canyon with a beagle named "Who," a cat named "Feather," and Bob Foxworth, who was then starring in *The Black Marble* feature film.

At the time, she and Foxworth were not married. But a decade or so later, and after a twenty-year courtship, that status changed. On January 28, 1993, the two wed at the home of Lizzie's manager Barry Krost, and they remained devoted to each other until the end.

Eighteen

Awakenings

"I've just reached another plateau in the type of work I want to do. It's like a man working all of his life as a gardener and suddenly waking up to the fact that he wants to be a landscape architect."

—Elizabeth Montgomery, as quoted by Ronald L. Smith in his book, *Sweethearts of '60s* (SPI Books, 1993)

In 2005, Sony Pictures released the *Bewitched* feature film, starring Nicole Kidman and Will Ferrell, produced by Doug Wick and Lucy Fisher, and directed by Nora Ephron, who also served as co-writer with her sister Delia. Penny Marshall (better known in classic TV sectors as the co-star of *Laverne & Shirley*) co-produced the movie for which she had originally hired good friend Ted Bessell (*Don Hollinger* from TV's *That Girl*) to direct. When Bessell unexpectedly died of an aneurysm in 1996, Marshall was overcome with grief and the production shut down. By 2003, she had moved on to other projects, but remained in force with the talented Wick/Fisher/Ephron team, which ultimately brought *Bewitched* to the big-screen.

Back in 1990, some fifteen years before she dabbled with the possibility of bringing *Samantha* and *Darrin* to theatres, Marshall directed a motion picture called *Awakenings*.

Based on the best-selling book by Oliver Sacks, and starring Robert De Niro, Robin Williams, and Julie Kavner, this film was about a new physician (Williams) who seeks to help a group of patients (including De Niro and Kavner) who have been comatose for decades, without any sign of a recovery. When he discovers a potential cure, he gains permission to experiment with a new chemical drug that may help his cause. The inspirational film then goes on to showcase the new perspectives that are awakened by each member of this extraordinary group of doctors and patients.

In 1985, Lizzie played a character named *Abigail Foster* in the similarly-themed TV-movie *Between the Darkness and the Dawn*.

Abigail Foster—a young woman who awakens from a 20-year coma only to discover a world that has moved on without her, especially the world she had so lovingly created with her high school boyfriend (David Goodwin) who's now married to her younger sister (Karen Grassle of *Little House on the Prairie* fame). In this new reality, *Abigail* must foster the pieces of her broken life, while coping with a devoted mother (Dorothy McGuire), who knows no other identity than to be her daughter's caregiver before and after she awakens.

In 1978, Lizzie appeared in the acclaimed three-part, seven-hour NBC mini-series, *The Awakening Land*, adapted from Conrad Richter's trilogy of a pioneer family in the Ohio Valley. It aired February 19, 20, and 21, and co-starred the esteemed Hal Holbrook as *Portius* (Holbrook, meanwhile had already chiseled new ground a few years before with the controversial 1972 TV-movie, *That Certain Summer*, in which his and Martin Sheen's characters introduced gay love to the American television mainstream).

Like *Mrs. Sundance* (1974) and *Belle Starr* (1980), *The Awakening Land* was also classified as a western, but far removed from the brightly-brushed Technicolor movie westerns of old. Whereas Lizzie's *Etta Place* from *Sundance* and *Belle* from *Starr* featured slightly more shady traits, her *Awakening* role of *Sayward Luckett Wheeler* was more clearly defined as a pioneer woman.

In 1978, Lizzie wasn't sure if *Sayward* sincerely loved Holbrook's *Portius*. According to Montgomery archivist Tom McCartney, Lizzie believed that *Sayward* needed *Portius*, because he was educated, and a provider for her children. In *Sayward's* day, such a bond was "typical," Lizzie said. It was considered more respectable to first be married, then have children.

Meanwhile, atypical filming for this movie began in September of 1977, and it was grueling. Lizzie, the cast and crew spent the two and a half months on location in the reconstructed post-colonial Village of New Salem, Illinois. Producers were convinced the movie should be made there once the State of Illinois film office persuaded them to peruse the village, and once the Springfield city fathers agreed to fill up a nearby lake so it would resemble the Ohio River.

A vacant Springfield gymnasium was then utilized to house an indoor log cabin for inside shots, as well as extensive prop and wardrobe departments. Other parts of the state got into the act when American Indians from Chicago's uptown were transported to the location to play their forefathers, while hounds, cougars, wolves, and one skunk from the Plainsman Zoo in Elgin were shipped to the location to help legitimize the setting.

As reporter Blecha explained, even the weather in New Salem complied with the production as warm, summer breezes and lush flora and fauna surfaced for the filming of Part 1: *The Trees*, while brisk autumn air and changing colors were there for Part 2: *The Fields*, and dark, dismal winter cold, even with a day of snow, showed up for Part 3: *The Town* (all of which were consecutively broadcast on Sunday, Monday, and Tuesday nights).

According to what Lizzie remembered in 1978, the country was "absolutely beautiful there, but whatever the territory offered, we got . . . viruses, poison oak, bees, mosquitoes, varmints, nettles. It gave us a vague idea of what it must have been like."

She herself contracted a bad case of poison ivy and the shoot overall was physically exhausting (especially on the days in the fields behind oxen and plow). But for Lizzie the most challenging part of portraying *Sayward* was the aging process, learning how to slow down, physically and psychologically.

Despite those challenges, Lizzie gave her usual 100 percent and had great respect for the character:

> *Sayward* wasn't stupid, just uneducated. Her instincts were extraordinary. She didn't say much, but when she did she made a lot of sense. She had a tremendous amount of fortitude. If it wasn't for people like her, you and I wouldn't be here today.

However, Lizzie admitted that the 1880s in the Ohio River held no personal appeal for her. And even though she was a pioneer woman in television, off screen, she had no desire claim the western frontier edition of that title. "No, I definitely would not have liked to have lived then. No one in their right mind would make that choice."

For a live online chat on December 12, 2002, Montgomery archivist Tom McCartney asked *Awakening* costar Jane Seymour, what it was like to work with Lizzie. She replied:

> Elizabeth Montgomery was a wonderful woman and very supportive to me. She was the first, indeed only, star to invite me into her trailer. I remember this as being a very special treat and vowed that if I ever had a trailer, I would share it with younger actresses. It set a precedent for me, one I follow to this day.

Etta Place from *Mrs. Sundance*, *Belle Starr*, and *The Awakening Land's* *Sayward* could be described as pioneering female roles for Lizzie (or any other actress) to portray. These were parts for her in particular that fueled ambition, expanded career opportunities, and strengthened artistic muscles. Each of these characters fit into what became her very strategic objective to work with daring projects. And if a network executive or producer objected to a particularly questionable script that may have held her interest, she was further ignited to bring the idea to fruition. "That's the kind of stuff I want to do," she told *Entertainment Tonight* in 1994.

"I think television has grown up," she said to *Tonight* reporter Scott Osborne in 1985, but she believed those "running it" were afraid of doing just that. "I don't know why." At this point, Lizzie was still open to performing in a comedy film, which she believed were "a lot harder [to do] than drama." And such properties were also "very hard to find," she said, partially because "on television there is so much censorship that it's tough to do really sophisticated comedy" that the Standards and Practices divisions at the networks will approve.

While network executives may not have met Lizzie's standards and practices, she dealt with her own challenges head-on, namely her shyness, which she overcame, at least on camera, whenever she assumed a dramatic role in one of her post-*Samantha* TV-movies.

By the time *The Awakening Land* premiered in 1978, *Bewitched* had been off the air six years and she was still mostly known as *Samantha*, the *Queen of the TV Witches.* Now, she had added a new twist to the title: "Lizzie—Queen of the TV-Movies," a crown that would later be bestowed on Valerie Bertinelli (then just exiting the sitcom *One Day at a Time*, today starring in TV Land's *Hot in Cleveland*) and on Jane Seymour (Lizzie's co-star in *Awakening*, who later starred in the family medical western, *Dr. Quinn, Medicine Woman*, a female TV pioneer in her own right).

Due to *Awakening's* success, Lizzie was in a position to command the highest price of any TV star and had her choice of roles. Her acquired wealth from *Bewitched* secured the already stable financial arsenal she amassed by way of her father's inheritance.

Through it all, she not only retained an unaffected demeanor, but remained devoted to her three children. She had it all, and she knew it. But she didn't flaunt it. She didn't have to because everyone else in the industry knew it, too. Long gone were the days when she butted heads with the likes of Screen Gems executive Jackie Cooper at the dawn of *Bewitched*. She was no longer demanding, but in demand. Her success commanded attention. No one could turn away from her, and no one could turn her away.

The Victim, her first TV-movie since leaving *Bewitched*, had attracted a large enough audience for ABC in 1972 that her services were requested for a second film with the network: *Mrs. Sundance*, which premiered in 1974. She was on a hot streak, and the groundwork for her royal TV-movie status was in place.

The free spirit was now a free agent, no longer tied down to one series, one character, or one network. When ratings for NBC's *A Case of Rape* went through the roof and delivered with it her first Emmy nomination since *Samantha*, there was no stopping Lizzie. She was a bona fide legend by the time she'd play yet another one: in ABC's 1975 film, *The Legend of Lizzie Borden*.

After that, came the remake of *Dark Victory* in 1976 on NBC, which also presented the indiscriminate *A Killing Affair* in 1977—all of which garnered upwards of 35 percent of the audience. Today, network suits and producers would kill for such ratings. In the era of *The Awakening Land*, those were the kind of stats they worshipped.

The grungy, gnarled locks, and weathered look of *Sayward Luckett* in *The Awakening Land* are light-years away from *Samantha* on *Bewitched*. Although her age was not yet an issue off-screen, in *Awakening* Lizzie was transformed from a young girl to an elderly woman. *Bewitched* makeup artist Rolf Miller was Emmy-nominated for gracefully aging her (and Dick Sargent) in the December 3, 1970 episode, *"Samantha's* Old Man," which was directed by her friend Richard Michaels.

But now it came time for a dramatic turn, under the insisting guidance of Boris Sagal, who helmed *Awakening* and who, according to Tom Mc-Cartney, she once called "an extraordinary man" and said she would not have done the film without him.

Lin Bolen Wendkos is the widow of director Paul Wendkos, a versatile talent who among other productions guided the Sandra Dee/Gidget films. According to *The Los Angeles Times*, he died November 12, 2009 of a lung infection. His career spanned fifty years and covered more than 100 films and television shows, including several episodes of *I Spy*, *The Untouchables*, and the acclaimed 1978 TV-movie, *A Woman Called Moses*, starring Cicely Tyson. He was one of Lizzie's choice directors dating back to the *Playhouse 90* segment "Bitter Heritage" from 1958 through to 1975's *The Legend of Lizzie Borden*, and *Act of Violence* in 1979. Bolen Wendkos has a theory as to why Lizzie took such a dramatic departure with her later work:

> I think she earned the opportunity to do so by playing a very commercial part as *Samantha* on *Bewitched*. In her mind, she may have wanted to give something more of the talent that she was holding back. For example, to play a strong female lead as she did in *Act of Violence*, in which her character (*Catherine McSweeney*) was forced to defend herself.

From 1971 to 1978, Lin served as the first female vice president of a television network when she worked for NBC's daytime operations, bringing the "peacock" network from number three to number one within a two-and-a-half year period when such positions were held mostly by men. Suffice it to say, she knows all too well of what she speaks. As with *Act of Violence*, Bolen Wendkos says Lizzie's 1974 NBC TV-movie, *A Case of Rape*, aired at a time when "women weren't being allowed to tell the truth, or to talk about their inner fears, or to challenge people who treated them in a way that was inappropriate. So Elizabeth was challenging the system and saying 'I am much more than you think and I have something to say, and these characters are going to say it for me.' "

Lin explains how her husband's perspective on *Borden* jibed with Lizzie's theatrical abilities:

My husband worked with a lot of interesting actresses and Elizabeth was definitely one of his favorites. She was a magnetic personality to look at. She captured that character in a way that I don't think anyone else could have. She *became* that person she was playing. If you look at her face in the movie, she had become that character. How many actresses on TV ever did that? Not many. She gave herself to that murderess spirit, and she did not stop until the end. He controlled the set of every movie he worked on. But what he didn't do was control the actress. If the cinematographer, the lighting director or the wardrobe assistant or anyone had something to offer, they would have to wait for Paul's word. But when it came to the actors, he always gave them the opportunity to go on set and do their thing first. Because he knew that's where the picture was. If the actor didn't feel secure in allowing their innermost ideas to surface in that first run-through . . . that first rehearsal . . . then it was a lost cause. He would say to each actor, "What is your character doing in this scene? Let's see it!" He wouldn't just stand there and stare at them. Instead, he'd ride the camera crane, or peer through the camera lens to allow the actor to retain *the privacy of their moment*. He absolutely believed that the photography was very important, and that [it] would need to be real. That's what it made a new creation . . . a real human outline, right there in front of you. He knew the camera had to capture that. So he gave the actors a chance to move around. He didn't just stage a scene and then instruct an actor to walk through it. He let the actor find their moment before he staged the scene and Elizabeth played into that very well.

Actress Bonnie Bartlett performed with Lizzie in the *Borden* film. Although they did not share any scenes together, Bartlett was a fan of her work:

She was an extraordinary actress. She was a major TV-movie star and she could have done almost anything. She was very serious about her work and an extraordinary professional. Every little detail was important to her. She was also a very cheerful person. She came to work with a good attitude, a really good attitude. She really enjoyed being an actress. And I do know that Paul [Wendkos] adored her, and loved working with her. He had that same kind of enthusiastic spirit that she had. The movie was one of his favorite things that he had ever done.

Lizzie's other film with Wendkos was 1979 CBS TV-movie, *Act of Violence*. Originally airing as part of the network's *Special Movie Presentation*, this Emmet G. Lavery production featured Lizzie's *Catherine McSweeney* as a television news writer whose liberal beliefs are challenged when she's brutally attacked by three young gang members, who happen to be Latino. Here's a closer look at the story:

> Divorced, Catherine lives with her young son in a lower-middle class neighborhood. She is assigned to a *crime in the streets* news series with *Tony Bonelli* (James Sloyan), a reporter with zero tolerance for her liberal perspective, so much so, he calls her "ignorant, soft-minded; sheltered." Then, upon returning from work by taxi, she's assaulted in the hallway of her apartment building. A short time later at the hospital, a detective looking into the incident is puzzled by her explanations. "I didn't ask to be mugged," she protests. "Didn't you?" he asks, suggesting that she, the victim, is responsible for the crime. In time, Catherine turns increasingly paranoid, flinching involuntarily at the sight of a minority's face. In effect, she becomes a different person, but not for the better. In the midst of this transformation, *Tony* convinces her to tell her story on TV. So, in a consequent interview, she bitterly condemns her attackers: "I am a bigot, a racist, a fascist, that's what they made me, that's why I hate them." By the movie's conclusion, Catherine regains a measure of her former self.

And Lizzie gains increasing respect as an actress.

Act of Violence aired on November 10, 1979, the same date *TV Guide* published the article, "From *Bewitched* to Besieged," writer Tabitha Chance deduced that Lizzie:

> had undergone more transformations than Henry the Eighth had wives. But unlike some of Henry's consorts, she has kept her charming head intact upon her charming neck—and used it to the dedicated, sensible furtherance

of her profession. Indeed, she is no longer *Somebody's Daughter*—Robert Montgomery's daughter. She is *Somebody*. Elizabeth Montgomery.

She had already proved that, of course, with her stardom from *Bewitched* (on which *Samantha*, ironically enough, had missed by a hair the tragic fate of marrying King Henry—in the two-part episode, "How Not to Lose Your Head to King Henry VIII"). It's safe to say that Lizzie always kept her head in the midst of a storm that frequently encircled the airing of post-*Samantha* films like *Act of Violence*.

Approximately five years before, she appeared in *A Case of Rape*, which Tabitha Chance described as "a fairly explicit examination of the subject, without a happy ending." But Lizzie resented any suggestion that there were (and are) obvious similarities between the two films.

"Comparisons are odious," she said, a trifle royally. "I can't worry about things being similar. As far as I'm concerned, they are two very separate kinds of violations and violence."

On December 21, 1985, Elizabeth talked about her creative choices with reporter Scott Osbourne for *Entertainment Tonight*. She found "fun" in "stretching" herself as an actress and "not feeling safe all the time." She didn't like to feel safe when she worked and believed that actors did their best work when they don't feel safe "because [otherwise] they don't set themselves up for any real challenge."

On May 12, 1992, she appeared on *CBS This Morning* to promote her TV-movie, *With Murder in Mind*, which in some ways was reminiscent of *Act of Violence*. She told *Morning* host Kathleen Sullivan that she liked the "kind of diversity" in each of her TV-movies. "I don't like doing the same thing over and over again. And I like being a little bit scared . . . a little teeny bit."

By "scared," Lizzie once again meant "challenged" with performing in what she felt were unique projects. She wasn't necessarily referring to the fear that some of her characters may have experienced within context of the movies she made or the fear that such films may have instilled in the viewers.

Either way, many of her TV-movies were and remain similar. When she first began making them, each film was diverse: *The Victim. Mrs. Sundance. A Case of Rape. The Legend of Lizzie Borden. The Awakening Land. Jennifer: A*

Woman's Story. Second Sight: A Love Story. The Rules of Marriage. When The Circus Came to Town. And even though it was a remake of her friend Bette Davis' 1939 classic, *Dark Victory* was also a unique addition on Lizzie's distinctive resume.

But the others, not so much: 1985's *Between the Darkness and the Dawn* was derivative of 1976's *Dark Victory* (albeit with a much happier ending). 1979's *Act of Violence* was reminiscent of 1974's *A Case of Rape*, 1980's *Belle Starr* echoed 1974's *Mrs. Sundance.* 1993's *The Black Widow Murders* hearkened back to 1975's *Lizzie Borden.* And again, 1992's *With Murder in Mind* was reminiscent of 1979's *Act of Violence* (not to mention the 1955 "Relative Stranger" episode of the CBS anthology series, *Appointment with Adventure,* in which Lizzie co-starred with William Windom).

Yet while Lizzie did repeat herself with certain performances, each of her post-*Bewitched* TV-movies proved to be ratings blockbusters. So Tabitha Chance wondered:

> Could it be that viewers, on some unconscious level, enjoy seeing an elegant, beautiful woman like Elizabeth Montgomery get mucked up and knocked about by deranged sociopaths? Perhaps her audience wants to see Elizabeth suffer in the roles she assumes on TV. That is one theory.

Psychotherapist Annette Baran shared another with *TV Guide:*

> [Elizabeth] presents a picture of a haughty, independent, prepossessing woman. One sees her as a woman able to take care of herself. Yet even she is helpless and vulnerable—just like anyone else. Women who might feel some awe of her see her as powerless as they would be in the same circumstances. Men, on the other hand, would have a chance to feel chivalrous and protective.

In September 1966, Lizzie explained to *TV Radio Mirror* magazine that she and her cousin Panda were "terribly close":

> I sometimes don't see her for a year but that has nothing to do with it. If I ever had a problem, I can't conceive of having one—I'd call her and there'd be no "why" and "where have you been," we're just close and I guess we always will be.

But according to Sally Kemp, "There was a darkness in Elizabeth's life," a shadow that she believes Panda sensed as well:

> She was as caught up in the mystery of Elizabeth as I am. She was never allowed to see Elizabeth's children. Panda would visit L.A. and they'd have dinner together, but Elizabeth wouldn't wake her children and let Panda visit with them. And Panda never understood why. It was like Elizabeth was two or three other people all mixed into one.

In order to play the darker, more textured roles, Lin Bolen Wendkos believes that most actors have "a hidden story":

> You have to have some kind of experience in your childhood or in your life that was so devastating that you could recall those kinds of feelings. Because, otherwise, how could you play it and how do you become that person. How do you give yourself to a character like that? You're giving yourself over to an audience in such a way that is so . . . inner destructive. That is why so many actors shun the public, and maybe why Elizabeth did, too; because they give so much of their inner selves to the world when they're working that there's not much left when they're not working.

Upon meeting Lizzie in 1979, *TV Guide's* Tabitha Chance said:

> [She had an] air of quiet command and cool amiability. She seemed infinitely unknowable; it is unimaginable to think she might ever be sloppy or have bad breath. At 46 [and marking her birth year as 1933] and easily looking a full sixteen years younger, Elizabeth is smooth of face and perfect of figure. Were one to come upon her suddenly in Saks Fifth Avenue [which she frequented], the conclusion would be that this woman had never done anything more than slice a catered chateaubriand . . . [She was] as carefully nurtured as any rich man's privileged daughter. And yet, breeding, private schooling, riches, looks, and derivative fame were not enough.

Robert Montgomery's shadowy presence still lingered, blurring Lizzie's own identity. But as Chance explained, Lizzie contributed to that stigma. She was no doubt grateful to her father for jump-starting her career. Although she enjoyed drawing and painting pictures, whenever Lizzie said things like, "My art belongs to Daddy," she was talking about her inherited theatrical craft . . . a lucrative craft, one that certainly materialized in a big way via *Samantha's* witchcraft, as well as other performances.

By 1979, Lizzie had negotiated an exclusive contract with CBS to craft two TV-movies a year for the following three years, for which she received more than 1.5 million dollars. That would buy a truckload of art supplies today, let alone over three decades ago.

Of the scripts offered to her in that period, she selected *Act of Violence*. From the minute she agreed to do the movie, Lizzie wanted it shot as written or, as Chance wrote in *TV Guide*, as "sexy, violent; rough in word and deed." While she may have looked like "a tea rose," Chance pointed out, Lizzie was ready to fight network executives, if need be, to keep that approach. "If somebody says no and it's important, you argue," Lizzie said. "But I prefer the word *negotiate*."

Such was the case with *Rape* in 1974, when NBC executives were nervous about a scene involving Lizzie's character, *Ellen Harrod*, and her examination in a doctor's office. "I didn't like doing that scene," she told Chance, "but we fought for it and it stayed in and we were right."

Chance then explained, "Well brought-up women usually don't discuss their private lives with anyone but their mothers, best friends, and hairdressers," and while Elizabeth was willing to bare her soul on camera, she was no exception to that rule, further confirming her intense need for privacy.

She was by this time living happily with Bob Foxworth and felt no need to share with anyone, the press or friends alike, the soap-operatic details of her failed marriages to Fred Cammann, Gig Young, and Bill Asher. But she did enjoy sharing with pals her hilarious, complicated plot recapitulations of daytime TV soap operas.

As she told *TV Guide*, she would indeed "forget" to return phone calls, but she also still wondered if her "Daddy" was proud of her. She remained down-to-earth, but drove a Mercedes, albeit a ten-year-old Mercedes (which was adorned with a "Lizzy" license plate, a misspelling of her favorite nickname). As during her days on *Bewitched*, Lizzie was never late to the set of any of her TV-movies and she was always professional. She readily convinced the crew to adore her by acting like what Chance called "a normal nice person, telling jokes and joining in with the four-letter word patois rampant in Hollywood sets."

"If that bawdiness may seem a strange paradox for the queenly Elizabeth," Chance concluded, "it isn't. A lady always puts everyone at ease . . ." as opposed to the heartless woman Lizzie portrayed in the 1991 CBS TV-movie, *Sins of the Mother.* Based on the book, *Son,* by Jack Olsen, *Sins* was written for television by Richard Fiedler, and directed by John D. Patterson:

> As a public figure, *Ruth Coe* (Lizzie) is a prestigious socialite. In private, she abuses her adult son, the charismatic Real Estate agent, *Kevin Coe* (Dale Midkiff). The consequences are devastating, when his most recent ladylove realizes he's the serial rapist that has decimated their community.

An especially harsh review of this film appeared in *The Hollywood Reporter,* February 19, 1991:

> Montgomery turns in a peculiarly mannered performance and appears not to have been directed to her best advantage. Though her lines seethe with vitriol and need, she seems disconnected from any emotional underpinning at all, as though she's reading the lines off the page . . . CBS' best shot may be to market it to fans of Elizabeth Montgomery who want to see her play a witch again.

In a strange twist of TV fate in 2001, Mary Tyler Moore, Lizzie's contemporary classic TV female star of the 1960s (via *The Dick Van Dyke Show*), took the lead in the similarly-themed and titled TV-movie, *Like Mother, Like Son: The Strange Story of Sante and Kenny Kimes.*

Just as some *Bewitched* fans may have been taken aback by Lizzie's portrayal in *Sins of the Mother,* Moore's admirers (by way of her happy character portrayals of *Laura Petrie* on *Van Dyke* and *Mary Richards* on *The Mary Tyler Moore Show*) may have been just as stunned when she played *Sante Kimes* in *Like Mother, Like Son.*

Sante's childhood abuse and exploitation leaves a legacy of amorality that she passes on to her son *Kenny* (with a "K" played by Gabriel Olds), just as Lizzie's *Ruth Coe's* sins were instilled in her son *Kevin* (also with a "K"; played by Dale Midkiff).

What may prove to be further compelling, and a little confusing, is that Lizzie later played a similar role in 1993 CBS TV-movie, *The Black Widow*

Murders: The Blanche Taylor Moore Story (the subtitle of which is similar to Mary Tyler Moore's real name).

To top it all off, Lizzie and Mary's hair styles are very similar (and the same color) in *Sins of the Mother* and *Like Mother, Like Son*, while all three films are, sadly, based on true stories.

While it may be fascinating how it all worked out, in 1993, journalist Bart Mills delineated the premise of *Black Widow Murders* in particular, and Lizzie's subsequent participation, taking the lead role of *Blanche Taylor Moore*:

> Life was placid in shabby-genteel central North Carolina, where *Blanche Taylor Moore* worked in a grocery store, lived in a trailer park, went faithfully to church, raised her daughters well, gossiped with her friends, and poisoned every man who went to bed with her. When the police finally confronted her with her crimes, she was flabbergasted. How dare they accuse an innocent woman, even though everyone close to her seemed to wind up in the cemetery, stuffed with arsenic? Elizabeth Montgomery is apt casting for this sly, chilling look at psychopathy. Elusive, elliptical, more likely to smile enigmatically than explain exhaustively, Montgomery gets behind the formality of *Moore's* way of speaking and offers convincing hints of the innocence of evil.

Today, Blanche Moore, who told authorities she was sexually abused as a child, has terminal cancer and is on North Carolina's Death Row, convicted of the murder of her long-time lover. Her first husband, her mother, and her father are others whose exhumed bodies revealed large concentrations of arsenic. Her second husband, a minister, who nearly died of arsenic poisoning, testified against her at her trial in 1990.

As Lizzie explained to Mills in 1993:

> Blanche was very lucky. Thirty or forty years ago, she would have sizzled by now. I don't believe they will wind up executing her. She's appealing at the moment. I think she doesn't feel she did anything terribly wrong. It was something she had to do, particularly to the second husband, who was an ordained minister . . . Blanche truly believes she is innocent. No, I mean, she truly believes she is an innocent. She didn't think what she did was wrong, because of the sexual abuse she said she suffered as a child. People

have different ways of dealing with their problems. Once she started on her way, there was no going back.

In 2012, classic TV curator and author, Ed Robertson, host of the popular radio show, *TV Confidential*, put it this way:

> Once *Bewitched* ended she was looking for projects that would allow her to grow as an actress, and further develop her dramatic skills, which she was not always able to do as *Samantha*, particularly in the last couple years of the show. I don't think she was necessarily trying to "shed" her image as *Samantha*, but I do believe she wanted to show audiences (and for that matter, casting directors and the like) that she could do much more than *Samantha*. That's why I think she did *A Case of Rape*, which had aired the year before in 1974, and I think that's what may have attracted her to doing *The Legend of Lizzie Borden*. That, plus the project itself had a strong pedigree. Paul Wendkos had already established himself as an excellent director, plus Fritz Weaver, through his work on such shows as *Twilight Zone*, was an accomplished, respected stage actor. I don't know whether Fritz worked with her father, but I imagine Elizabeth would have relished the opportunity to work with someone like him.

She also embraced the chance to work with screen legend Kirk Douglas in the 1985 CBS TV-movie, *Amos*, which also starred Pat Morita, best known as *Arnold* from TV's *Happy Days* and later as *Mr. Miyagi* in the original *Karate Kid* movies. This time, Lizzie not only played a heartless character, but a seemingly soulless one as well:

> *Daisy Daws* (Lizzie) is a psychopathic abusive nurse at a senior facility that houses *Amos Lasher* (Douglas), her main patient, and *Tommy Tanaka* (Morita), and other seniors who ultimately band against her in a battle for their very lives.

Shortly after this film was rerun in the summer of 1986, a Los Angeles viewer wrote in to the *Television Times* supplement of *The Los Angeles Times*, pining for Lizzie to return to her own "happier days" on screen and her most beloved role. Interestingly, the viewer also addressed what Lizzie later described in 1989 and during other interviews as her personal philosophy about acting. But more than anything, the writer expressed what had been on the minds of countless fans of Elizabeth's and *Bewitched*. In his letter dated August 9, 1986, home audience member Bob Thompson of Burbank, California composed his thoughts and said:

> *Amos* with Kirk Douglas and Elizabeth Montgomery had to be the most brilliant television movie I've seen this year. Montgomery displayed her true talent for portraying a *witch*. Her performance was incredible. However, with all the reunion movies on television lately, I would love to see a revival of *Bewitched*. All I've seen Montgomery do in the last decade is heavy drama. Enough already. Let's see some comedy. I believe it to be her forte. Isn't it harder to make people laugh than cry anyway? What I'm trying to say, I guess, is . . . "*Samantha*, where are you?"

SUGAR ... Elizabeth as she is best remembered, in this prime photo of her as the pleasant, sweet-natured witch-next-door *Samantha* ... from the fifth season of *Bewitched*, 1968–1969. ABC Photo Archives, courtesy of Getty Images

...AND SPICE: To shake things up a bit on *Bewitched*, Elizabeth periodically played *Samantha's* diametrically opposed (in every way), daring, look-a-like cousin *Serena*, seen here in a publicity shot from the episode, "*Cousin Serena* Strikes Again (Part Two)," which originally aired January 9, 1969. ABC Photo Archives, courtesy of Getty Images

LOVERS AND OTHER ANIMALS: Elizabeth's love for animals was never more evident than on *Bewitched*, during which she worked with, among other critters, dogs, mice, frogs, monkeys, and her favorite . . . horses. In this scene from the episode, "Daddy Does His Thing," which originally aired April 3, 1969, it's a mule into which Sam's father *Maurice* (Maurice Evans) transforms *Darrin*, played by Dick York. It was these kinds of plots that allowed for the absence of York, who had missed fourteen episodes of the series due to the ongoing struggles that accompanied a back injury he acquired while working on the 1959 movie, *They Came to Cordura* (which featured Gary Cooper, with whom Lizzie appeared in her first feature, 1955's *The Court-Martial of Billy Mitchell*). In fact, it was on the set of this *Bewitched* episode that York collapsed, which led to his resigning from the series and being replaced by Dick Sargent the following fall. ABC Photo Archives, courtesy of Getty Images

PEACE, LOVE, AND UNDERSTANDING: Elizabeth flashes the "peace sign" to adoring, if barricaded, young fans in 1969. It's a telling scene. First, in a nod to the times, the peace sign of sorts would show up (in reverse and around the nose) on *Bewitched* as the "witches' honor sign." Second, she appreciated her admirers, but only at a safe distance. And third, she protested the Vietnam War and frequently battled with her father over personal politics. Meanwhile, her political advocacy for various charitable and global causes was renowned. She narrated the controversial feature film documentaries, 1988's *Cover Up* and 1992's *The Panama Deception* (which won the Oscar for Best Documentary), and she was one of the first celebrities to advocate for those suffering with and because of AIDS. ABC Photo Archives, courtesy of Getty Images

PLAYING FAVORITES: Elizabeth with (from left) Janee Michelle, Venetta Rogers, Erin Murphy, David Lawrence, co-stars from her favorite *Bewitched* episode, "Sisters at Heart," which aired on December 24, 1970. The segment was co-written by the multicultural Jefferson High School Class of 1971, and won the Governor's Award that year at the Emmys. The story's premise centered around prejudice which, in May 1989, Elizabeth said was the central message of *Bewitched*. ABC Photo Archives, courtesy of Getty Images

MONUMENTAL MONTGOMERY MOMENT: Elizabeth with (from left) makeup man Rolf Miller, hairstylist Peanuts (with hand on glasses), and Robert Montgomery, during his one and only visit to the *Bewitched* set (with his second wife, Elizabeth "Buffy" Harkness, not pictured). Here, all take delight in the "pig mask" which was adorned by Dick Sargent (not pictured) for the episode, "This Little Piggy," which aired February 25, 1971. In the background: David White (*Larry Tate*) takes it all in from afar. He very much respected Elizabeth and her father, and was pleased to see them together. White was a father himself. But sadly, his son Jonathan (for whom Larry's on-screen son, *Jonathan Tate*, was named) was on board the Pan Am Flight 103 that went down over Lockerbie, Scotland, in 1988. No bodies were ever recovered, and David certainly never recovered from the loss of his son. Courtesy of Everett Collection

FOX IN THE FOLD: Robert Foxworth and charity played interconnecting roles in Elizabeth's life. Here, the two are seen at a charity event in 1974, about a year after they met on the set of *Mrs. Sundance* in 1973. They would ultimately marry . . . twenty years later. Unlike Lizzie's three other husbands, the much older Bill Asher or Gig Young, and even the slightly older Fred Cammann, Foxworth was Lizzie's junior in age. He also shared the same first name with her father and, upon their initial meeting, he had not seen one single episode of *Bewitched*. At the time, that was definitely in his favor as Lizzie was in the midst of divorcing Bill Asher and wanted nothing to do with any aspect of *Samantha* whatsoever. According to Lizzie's friend Sally Kemp, it was Foxworth who encouraged Lizzie to stretch her theatrical talents for "meatier" roles beyond *Bewitched*. Ralph Dominguez— Globe Photos

A SHATTERING PEFFORMANCE: Elizabeth received her first post-*Bewitched* Emmy nomination for her portrayal of the battered housewife *Ellen Harrod* in the groundbreaking television film, *A Case of Rape*, which became one of the highest rated TV-movies in history, and which paved the way for future issue-oriented small screen productions. Courtesy of Everett Collection

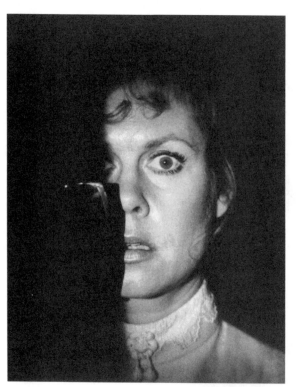

AN EYE-OPENING EXPERIENCE: Elizabeth's heralded performance as the real-life murderous Lizzie Borden in the 1975 TV-movie, *The Legend of Lizzie Borden*, earned her a second post-*Bewitched* Emmy nomination, but her father's disdain. Strangely, from the moment she played Borden, who was never convicted of the brutal killings of her father and stepmother, Elizabeth wanted to be referred to as "Lizzie." Courtesy of Everett Collection

THE MID-CAREER FRONTIER: Elizabeth received her third post-*Samantha* Emmy nomination for her portrayal *of Sayward Luckett Wheeler* in the elegantly filmed three-part TV mini-series, *The Awakening Land* in 1978. Her co-stars in the film included Hal Holbrook, a very young William H. Macy (in his first role), and Jane Seymour, who would go head to head with Elizabeth as the "Queen of TV-movies" in the 1980s and early 1990s, before she would take the lead in her own female pioneer TV role as *Dr. Quinn, Medicine Woman*. Courtesy of Everett Collection

A "STARR" IS BORN: Elizabeth once more appears in a strong female character of the West in the 1980 television film, *Belle Starr*, one of her better TV-movies from every perspective (writing, directing, cinematography, and performance). Courtesy of Everett Collection

LIFE IMITATES ART: Elizabeth as the visually-impaired *Alaxandra McKay* with her seeing-eye best friend *Emma* in a scene from *Second Sight: A Love Story*, which aired on March 13, 1984. The two bonded so closely off-screen that Elizabeth ended up adopting Emma in real life. Sadly, Emma died shortly thereafter. Courtesy of Everett Collection

MURDER, SHE WROTE IN MIAMI: Elizabeth is seen here in a publicity shot from her first appearance as real-life *Miami Herald* crime reporter *Edna Buchanan* in *The Corpse Had a Familiar Face*, which originally aired on CBS, March 27, 1994. Lizzie would later return to the role in 1995's *Deadline for Murder*, which became her final on-screen performance. She and CBS had intended to continue with a series of Buchanan films. Courtesy of Everett Collection

A STAR COME RAIN OR SHINE: Elizabeth finally received her much-deserved star, if posthumously, on the Hollywood Walk of Fame, January 4, 2008, during a thunderstorm that proved no match for the love and devotion of hundreds of her loyal fans who ignored the downpour and focused on honoring their favorite star. Lizzie's family and friends said she would have laughed at the fact that it was raining. Michael Germana— Globe Photos

PART IV

Reconciled

"My darling, charming Elizabeth . . . she has a touch of immortality. *Bewitched* is her light-hearted gift to the world, whatever shadows she battled."

—Sally Kemp, 2012

Nineteen

Spirits and Angels

"You almost got the feeling that she was
a little girl playing a grown-up."

—Doug Tibbles, *Bewitched* writer, assessing Elizabeth's personality

In character or in reality, Lizzie employed a carefree spirit and wit even in the most challenging of situations. Whether she was playing *Samantha* who frequently defended her mortal marriage before her mother *Endora,* or whether she was playing herself in real life fighting for independence from the troubled Gig Young as well as from her father Robert Montgomery. In each scenario, scripted or nonscripted, Lizzie was *playing*. She maintained a strong sense of decorum, while not losing her stable sense of humor. She was beloved by viewers at home who were bewitched by her charm on screen, and the people she met off camera were just as bedazzled by her presence in person.

In the early 1990s, former restaurant manager/hostess DD Howard used to work at the toney Le Dome restaurant on Sunset Boulevard in Beverly Hills. At the time, Le Dome (which has since closed its doors) was the hot spot for the Hollywood elite to meet, eat, and mingle. Celebrities as diverse as Goldie Hawn and Kurt Russell, the Kirk Douglases, even Ronald and Nancy Reagan among many others, walked through its fashionable doors.

As Howard recalls, Lizzie and Bob Foxworth were frequent patrons of the establishment, and both were cherished by Le Dome's staff for their unaffected and unassuming ways:

> After managing restaurants for over ten years, you really come to recognize personalities for who they are really when they come into a restaurant. You know who the nice people are and you know who the not-so-nice people are. You can see it right away. The essence of who they are is right there in front of you.
>
> Well, not only were Elizabeth and Bob two of the nicest people who ever came through our doors, but they were two of the nicest people I have ever met in my entire life. They definitely made my top ten list. They were a charming, sweet, beautiful couple. And she was always laughing and smiling.
>
> Many times she would come in with [her manager] Barry Krost, who she had a great banter with, or groups of friends. Whenever she arrived, you knew a party was gonna happen. The staff certainly always looked forward to seeing her. She was just always so interested in everyone, and who they were as a person, whether it was someone she and Bob were dining with, or whether it was one of the waiters or busboys. It was almost like she diverted attention from herself back to you.
>
> When she'd walk in the door, I would say, "You look so fabulous!" And then she'd turn it around and say, "And '*you*' look gorgeous!" We'd then go on to have a regular conversation about what *I* was doing that day, or what was going on in *my* life.
>
> She was just so sincerely interested in other people. She was curious and interested in everyone and everything. And that really represented just how endearing she was.
>
> She was simply a shining star if there ever was one. The place just lit up when she walked in the room. She was an angel.

According to Tom McCartney, Lizzie discussed her sunny side of life in 1993 with journalist Bart Mills, who interviewed her, strangely enough, about her quite unsunny performance in the TV-movie, *Black Widow Murders: The Blanche Taylor Moore Story*. Portraying Blanche was by far her darkest characterization since her appearance in 1975's *The Legend of Lizzie Borden* (both films were also based on true-life tales). But Lizzie read between the lines and found laughter between the tears. In speaking with

Mills, she recalled the day the *Widow Murders* cast met for its first pre-production read-through of the script. Many of writer/co-executive producer Judith Paige Mitchell's lines drew laughs, and Mitchell said to the cast, "But I didn't know this script was funny."

But as far as Elizabeth was concerned, and as she expressed to Mills, "Life is funny even when it's upsetting. The more human a story is, the more real and the more true it is, the more likely you are to find subconscious humor in it. You may not see it on the page, but when you say it out loud, you have to laugh."

Lizzie also "just had to laugh" about *I Dream of Jeannie's* attempts to duplicate *Bewitched's* success in the 1960s, as well as when the *Tabitha* series tried to do the same in the 1970s, and when TV audiences actually laughed, at least to some extent, at various magic-based, female-oriented shows or characters that tried to replicate the guffaws Lizzie created as *Samantha* on *Bewitched*. While the *Tabitha* series may not have fared so well, *Jeannie* certainly found a resounding success, as did other "re*sorce*ful" women on the small screen:

Sabrina, the Teenage Witch (with Melissa Hart, ABC, 1996–2003) sky-rocketed in the ratings, as did *Charmed* (1998, CW; Alyssa Milano, Shannon Doherty, Holly Marie Combs, Rose McGowan). Before those good-smitten witches came along, *Angelique/Cassandra Collins* (played by Lara Parker) did her best on the gothic daytime soap *Dark Shadows* (ABC, 1966–1971), right beside *Witchiepoo* (Billie Hayes, on ABC's Saturday morning's *H.R. Pufnstuf* from 1969–1970; who also played a storybook witch on *Bewitched*), and Juliet Mills was *Phoebe* on *Nanny and the Professor* (ABC, 1970–1971, which also starred a very young Kim Richards, before her quite different performances on today's *Real Housewives of Beverly Hills*). Even ABC Family's recent *Secret Circle* drama features a young band of sorceresses.

But in the fall of 1989, ABC's main network tried to more directly recapture the magic of *Bewitched* with a new "witch-uation comedy" called *Free Spirit*. It starred Corinne Bohrer (a kind of pre-*Friends* Lisa Kudrow) as *Winnie Goodwinn* who was reluctantly sent to Earth as a housekeeper/babysitter for the *Harper* family led by Franc Luz as *T. J. Harper*, the father. The children included *Jesse Harper*, as played by *How I Met Your Mother's* Alyson Hannigan (who would later portray the witch *Willow Rosenberg* in *Buffy*, *the Vampire Slayer*, not to mention a character named *Samantha* in the short-lived 1993 series *Almost Home*, created by a writer named Lynn Montgomery, no relation).

Free Spirit was a noble attempt, but it failed to appropriately reimagine the magic of *Bewitched* on several levels, not the least of which was the poorly funded cinematic quality. The show was videotaped in front of a live audience (allegedly), which meant it already had two strikes against it. Supernatural sitcoms should neither be videotaped nor presented in front of a live anything. The on-camera tricks and effects need to be properly executed and filmed. Imagine the tediousness of waiting in the studio seats while the crew sets up the magic for the home audience? Needless to say, *Free Spirit* was gone by the following January, with the ghost of *Bewitched's* stellar past lingering in its wake.

Meanwhile, "free spirit," the phrase, remains to this day the best way to describe Lizzie's personality. Throughout her life, good, bad, or indifferent, she took everything in stride, with an occasional grain of salt over old wounds. Her core relationships always proved challenging, but she dealt with them head-on, although at times moving on too fast. Not one to offer second chances, she subscribed to the old adage, "Fool me once, shame on you; fool me twice, shame on me." Lizzie tended not to let things fester, even when she learned that she had cancer. At first she was angry, but then came to immediate terms with her tragic reality in 1995.

According to her commentary from 1989, Elizabeth responded to less serious and complicated circumstances in simple terms, whether discussing the possibility of a *Bewitched* reunion ("Forget it!") or hearing about those who sought to do such a movie without her ("Anybody can do whatever they like. I don't care!"). Her amassed fortune from *Bewitched* coupled with her family's cache of cash allowed her the freedom to do as she pleased. She worked by choice, and from her work she gave choice performances, even if that work was only recognized with Emmy nominations and not a single victory.

Politically minded and theatrically gifted, she never ignored her ability to communicate, but always made certain to share a laugh amidst the probable pangs of losing Emmys to her peers, pangs she may have hidden with a Pagliacci smile. Whether engaged in a game of darts on *The Mike Douglas*

Show or a home tennis match with Bill Asher or Bob Foxworth, her true victory was never spoiled.

Whether riding colts on her family's sprawling properties stateside or in the English countryside, or rushing to play the mares at the Santa Anita or Hollywood Park Race Track, for Lizzie it was never about winning the horse race; it was about the human race to live, work, and play.

The essence of that playful spirit was thoughtfully reiterated by family members and friends on January 4, 2008 at the Hollywood Walk of Fame ceremony that cemented her star.

Liz "Dizzie" Sheridan approached the podium. She described the first day she met Lizzie through a mutual friend (writer William Blast, *The Legend of Lizzie Borden*), shortly after moving to Los Angeles, how they played croquet, and became fast friends.

The next day Lizzie called Dizzie and wondered what kind of shampoo she used and if she'd like to go the race track, all in the same breath. Lizzie also insisted that Dizzie stay in her guesthouse, which Sheridan proceeded to do until she found a place of her own. At which time Lizzie lent Dizzie the required down payment. A few weeks later Sheridan paid her back on their way to the race track . . . in Elizabeth's chauffeur-driven limousine. Upon seeing the cash, Lizzie screamed and playfully tossed the money all over the car, the chauffer, Sheridan, everything. From there, they journeyed on to the track and proceeded to spend the extra loot.

As it turned out, Dizzie was one of the few people who ever paid Lizzie back for her generosity, a true and loyal friend indeed. Elizabeth could not have cared less if Sheridan ever paid her back, but the fact that she did earned Dizzie high marks in Lizzie's highly selective realm of friendship.

Actor David Knell played Elizabeth's son, *Ed Reed*, when she took the lead in the 1980 TV-movie Western, *Belle Starr*. This film was the second professional acting job Knell had won upon moving to Los Angeles only a short time before. The first production he appeared in was for a segment of *Great Performances*, called "Life on the Mississippi" in which he played Mark Twain. Two weeks into the performance Knell broke his arm and his role had to be recast, all of which somehow later led to his being cast in the ground-breaking (and ironically titled) 1979 feature film *Breaking Away.*

At the time, Knell was only in his late teens, and because he was just starting out in the business, had little free cash to spread around. He didn't even own a car, only a bicycle, which he'd ride to various auditions, location shoots, and/or rehearsals.

One day, shortly before *Belle Starr* began filming, Lizzie hosted a first read-through of the script at her home in Beverly Hills, which Knell defined as "interesting." It had dialogue that he defines today as "very stylized and not modern at all." At any rate, those present at the reading were the film's entire main cast and crew, including the movie's director John Alonzo, as well as Robert Foxworth, who Knell remembers as "a nice guy."

Knell, who lived in Laurel Canyon at the time, says he took the "longest route possible" to Elizabeth's home. "It was very scenic and wonderful." But when he arrived at Lizzie's door, it was very comedic and hilarious, for it was at this point that he was introduced to her trademark sense of humor. "She was very playful!" he says.

Indeed, upon first seeing Knell at her door, alongside his bike, Lizzie mused, "What time *yesterday* did you leave?"

Knell laughed, and from that moment on, enjoyed working on *Starr* with Lizzie, whom he called "great," particularly when it came to mounting horses during filming. "She rode very well," he recalls. Little wonder, of course, because Lizzie had been riding since she was three.

The exterior scenes for *Starr* added to the movie's realism. It was filmed on location in Agoura Hills, California, which is now a modern, developed area. But in 1980, the cast was in awe of its then-wilderness. Having just completed filming for "Life on the Mississippi," another production filmed on location in a hinterland setting, Knell in particular was "very much into authenticity" when it came to acting. So much so that when he was cast to play Lizzie's son *Ed* of the Old West in *Starr,* he decided not to wash his hair because "nobody did back then, and it seemed like it would be weird if I did." Instead, while filming one *Starr* moment, it became "weird" for Lizzie that he did not.

The scene was in *Ed's* bedroom on the farm he shared with *Belle,* shortly before a great fire in the barn, which is ignited by vigilantes who seek to rid the county of *Belle* and her band. Knell as *Ed* is sitting on the bed and the script calls for Lizzie as *Belle* to run her hands through his hair. Upon noticing that his locks were somewhat hygienically challenged, Knell muses, "Lizzie let out a big '*Yick!*'" As to just how "authentic" Lizzie's hair was during the shoot, Knell sustains, "I think she probably washed hers and just made it look dirty."

In all, Knell says his time with Lizzie on *Starr* was well-spent. "It was just a joy working with her. I think the one particular scene that I remember the most [is the one] where I almost got to kiss her, which was great, but they changed the script and we never got to do it." Just as well the kissing scene never took place. Having such a moment between *Belle* and her son, no matter how troubled they were, would likely have been too ambiguous an endeavor for the network censors. However, as Knell concludes, "It definitely would have added an additional layer to [their] already complicated relationship."

While network officials continued to censor scenes from Lizzie's fictional films, she, of course, was no stranger to complicated relationships in real life. Yet, again, her playful nature, like a good portion of her very real character, was inspired by her grandmother Becca.

As Elizabeth expressed to *TV Radio Mirror* in April 1970, Becca . . .

> . . . made games of everything. You asked the meaning of a word, she'd say, "What do you think it means?" And, when you came up with your childish' explanation: "That's marvelous, Elizabeth; now let's look it up and see what the people say it means." In short, the dictionary. And often [after] we found out, she'd say, "But I like your definition much better."

As Bob Foxworth had expressed on A&E's *Biography*, it was Becca who had also inspired Elizabeth's obsession with the race track. In fact, one day in her dressing room while filming *Bewitched*, she was sprawled out on the floor with a copy of the racing form.

As was explained in *TV Radio Mirror*, November 1969, a publicist walked in on her and howled in protest. Lizzie looked up from her scratch-sheet, pencil-clenched in teeth, and wondered what was wrong. "If you ever want to ruin your image," said the publicist, "this sort of thing will do it."

Elizabeth didn't give it a thought and continued on in her carefree way. It was an effervescence that today might be described as "emotional intelligence." But she had developed that part of her being years before science came up with a name for it, particularly when she was a young lass playing on the Montgomery family compound in Patterson, New York, with her cousin Panda and friend Sally Kemp. "Of course we all enjoyed playing together as children," Kemp recalls, "and Panda had the same little exquisite face as Elizabeth. But Elizabeth had that *intellectual curiosity*; her intelligence, her interest in being alive in the moment. I don't think she had any aspirations about being a classical actress."

Whereas Sally, on the other hand, is still eager to act in, for example, a live stage production of *Trojan Women*, the Greek tragedy by playwright Euripides (that was once made into a 1971 feature film starring Katharine Hepburn). She wants to play *Hephzibah*, and she wants do it in an amphitheater "in Greece somewhere," and she doesn't care if "anyone ever sees it."

Conversely, she believes Elizabeth "never gave a hoot about any of that. Life was fun for her and she wanted it to be that way."

As reporter Rose Perlberg assessed in *TV Picture Life*, October 1965, "*Fun* was the word that cropped up most constantly in our conversation with Liz. To her, work is fun . . . the idea of having . . . babies is fun, and being married seems to be the most fun of all."

Lizzie herself admitted as much to *Modern Screen* magazine in May 1965. "I'm not riddled with ambition," she said. "Acting is something I've done because it's fun and hard work. I enjoy hard work. But a career with me is about as close to last as second can get. First is my life: love, children, and a home."

In January that year, she added in *TV Radio Mirror*:

When women choose a life of competition with men in the marketplace, it is usually due to circumstances beyond their control . . . like sickness in the family or some inner drive for success that's caused by a childhood frustration. Most women try to walk the tightrope between home and office, and some of them manage to do surprisingly well at it. In my case, the problem is much the same for both *Samantha* and me. For the sake of home and husband, she'd like to kick the witchcraft habit, but finds it too hard to do. I'd like to concentrate all my heart and soul on my private life, but I find it impossible to forsake acting. I grew up in the actor''s world of make-believe, and it's become part of my living tissue. My great hope is that, like *Samantha*, when I pursue my special brand of witchery, it will not offend my husband but make me more intriguing to him.

Of course, none of that was easy in 1965 when *Bewitched* was a massive hit and she was married to Bill Asher. It was difficult before she worked on the show, and remained a challenge after she ended the series. Lizzie may have pursed acting, but she never pined after economic success. She was born into that. However, she hungered for other forms of success, in romance, friendship, and family. She never gave up on love in any of its forms, even if she sometimes found too much of it, too soon.

At twenty, she married socialite Fred Cammann, and divorced him one year later. At twenty-three, she wed actor Gig Young and after six years, divorced him, too. Shortly after that, she fell in love with Bill Asher and their honeymoon lasted approximately eleven years. It was her twenty-year romance with Bob Foxworth, whom she finally married approximately eighteen months before she died, that was her lengthiest relationship.

Over the years, she endured personal disappointments throughout the long, grueling professional hours, beginning with *Robert Montgomery Presents*, and followed by numerous TV guest star appearances, feature films, *Bewitched,* and then later, her TV-movies. She survived the heartache of her personal life with the backbone she sustained by way of her strict upbringing. She viewed herself as a Hollywood product, and she was okay with that. She pegged the glamour and glitz for what it was worth, well-aware of the countless actresses who looked to their careers for happiness because they lacked inner peace within themselves. For Lizzie, acting was a normal, natural thing.

Her parents had talent and performing was something she did. It was "fun" to do. It was not something for which she compromised her life. And she knew that from the onset of *Bewitched's* popularity, and most probably before, as she relayed to *Modern Screen* in 1965:

It's wonderful and gratifying to know that people are enjoying the idea that you enjoy . . . bringing them something that gives pleasure. But if you're lucky enough to have success with a series, it's something that you really can't think of as being your own. You should be grateful, of course, and you have a responsibility to the people who are watching, but success itself is something just loaned to you. Once it's gone, if you felt you'd lost something then the other part of your life, your basic personal life, would not be completed. That's not right! I've always felt that way.

In 2004, New Path Press published *The Seesaw Girl and Me: A Memoir* by Dick York, who appreciated Lizzie's playful spirit. As is explained in this very honest book, there were moments in *Bewitched* when he and Lizzie:

> . . . really did develop a close personal relationship above and beyond the characters, but necessary to the characters (of *Darrin* and *Samantha*). I mean, we did play games. Liz was a game player and a crossword puzzle fan, and we invented all kinds of guessing games and word games . . .

Her TV-movie co-star, veteran actor Ronny Cox, agrees with that.

Cox is best known in classic TV history for his short-lived role as the father on *Apple's Way*, created by Earl Hamner as a contemporary take on his mega-hit family period piece, *The Waltons* (which was set in the Depression). The liberal-minded Cox is also known for iconic feature films like 1972's *Deliverance*, in which he co-starred with Burt Reynolds, Ned Beatty, and Jon Voight (father to Angelina Jolie).

Farrah Fawcett, in one of her first pre-*Charlie's Angels* TV roles, made a guest appearance on *Apple's Way*, and would later star in NBC's acclaimed 1985 TV-movie, *The Burning Bed*—a film that shared many similarities with the network's 1974 TV-movie, *A Case of Rape*, in which Cox had co-starred with Lizzie (both movies featured iconic blonde stars who played characters that were physically assaulted and mentally abused). Cox also worked with Lizzie in her 1992 TV-movie, *With Murder in Mind*. But it was on *Rape* where they met and bonded, mostly due to her approachable personality, their shared political ideals, and because they both enjoying playing games. Real games. Not head games. Cox explains:

> I grew up poor in New Mexico, really poor. All we had was a radio and a deck of cards and dominoes. So I knew every card game known to man

and I played those kinds of games my whole life. Plus, those were the kinds of things that you could do that didn't cost money.

Like Cox, Lizzie enjoyed such everyday games, he thinks, because she craved a certain amount of normalcy in her life. "She came from a world of acting and the theatre," he says, where there's such "vicious competition. And I don't discount for a second Lizzie's competitiveness."

But Lizzie's love for games, be it Gin, Scrabble, Charades, or Backgammon, the last which was all the rage when Lizzie and Cox met, were outlets for her "competitive nature," says Cox, who classifies himself as a "real competitor." So much so, he used to have a tennis court on his property and on every day that he didn't work (which was rare, because he's not stopped working since *A Case of Rape*), he enjoyed playing tennis. And if it came down to who wanted to win more, he or Lizzie, Cox says,

> . . . it would be me. Most people I know of who are as fiercely competitive are also not the best losers in the world. But whether I win or lose, I don't lord it over people. And I think that's a rare thing, and that was also Lizzie's quality. And the thing about Lizzie is that she was never a prima donna in any sense of the word. Working on [*A Case of Rape*] was one of the smoothest sets I've ever been on, and that was mostly because of her. We connected more on a personal level. It was not that I was knocked out by her stardom or [that] she was knocked out by me. We just immediately hit it off.

Time and again, Lizzie earned the veneration of her peers, at least in word, if not always in deed. According to Kasey Rogers, who replaced Irene Vernon as *Louise Tate* on *Bewitched*, she was "a very gifted actress. She excelled at whatever she did, be it drama or comedy. And when she appeared on *Bewitched*, she played *Samantha* with the same sensitivity and love that she possessed in real life."

Rarely, however, did such praise transfer to actual public acknowledgement in any formal award, at least when it came to television. For example, she was recognized on several occasions for her theatrical craft on the New York stage, as when she received the "Daniel Blum Theatre World Award for Most Promising Newcomer"—for *Late Love* in 1953–1954 (which was also Cliff Robertson's debut). Past recipients of the award included James Dean, Eva Marie Saint, and director Leo Penn (Sean's father).

The television world, however, was a whole other ballgame. Although she received a total of nine Emmy nominations, five of which were for *Bewitched*, Elizabeth never won. Her non-*Samantha* nominations were for non-*Samantha* performances: The self-centered *Rusty Heller* on *The Untouchables* ("The Rusty Heller Story," ABC, October 13, 1960); the abused housewife *Ellen Harrod* in *A Case of Rape* (NBC, February 20, 1974); the vile ax murderess in *The Legend of Lizzie Borden* (ABC, February 10, 1975); the pioneer woman *Sayward Luckett* in *The Awakening Land* (NBC, February 19, 20, 21, 1978).

Still, an Emmy victory eluded her—"a bridesmaid, but never a bride." Why?

According to what Richard Michaels said in 1988:

That's just the way this town is. They [the Academy of Television Arts and Sciences] just didn't want to give it to her. And I think she was a little hurt. But she was also an adult. Even though the Emmy is a major form of acknowledgement, it's not the only form of acknowledgement in the world. Audiences adore her today, just as much as they did in the 1960s. No one will ever forget her or the show. When people find out that I directed the show, especially little kids, who by the way, weren't even born when the show initially aired, the first question I hear is, "What is Elizabeth Montgomery really like?" or "How did she twitch her nose?" That, more than anything, proves her mainstay in television history . . . In the motion picture and television industries, personalities are involved in the awards, and you have to consider winners and losers in the context of their times. Elizabeth was a very private person, and she was never a socialite. She'd never go to a Hollywood party just to be seen. Maybe if she [had] rubbed more elbows, she would have won. But that wasn't her style.

Some years before Lizzie and *Bewitched* were Emmy contenders, the Television Academy had awarded another female TV icon the accolade, not once, but twice. Lucille Ball had won for her various *Lucy* personas over the years and embraced the attention. But when she returned to weekly TV in 1986 with ABC's short-lived *Life with Lucy*, she failed to win points with her peers, her fans, and the critics, and she was devastated by the lack of support on all fronts. But as Michaels also pointed out, shortly before Ball died in 1989 (of a heart ailment), droves of fans lined up around the hospital in which she spent her final days. "She couldn't believe it. She was amazed. And just thank God she found out [how much she was loved] before she died. But I'm not so sure Elizabeth was as lucky."

Before he won an Emmy for his work on *Bewitched*, Bill Asher, Michaels' mentor, received the coveted accolade for helming episodes of Ball's first comedy, *I Love Lucy*. When Ball later switched formats to *The Lucy Show*, during *Bewitched's* rein, Lizzie lost the Emmy twice to the red-headed phenomenon, and Asher was not at all pleased. At the press conference following the 1966 awards ceremony that included his own *Bewitched* victory as a director, he refused to speak with the press unless Lizzie's contributions to *Bewitched* were acknowledged.

Notwithstanding, Asher, like Michaels, thought Lizzie remained unfettered by failing to win over her peers with an Emmy. "It just didn't matter to her," he said in 1988. Yet consider this: Don Knotts was nominated and won the Emmy five times for his beloved interpretation of the shaky gun-shy *Deputy Barney Fife* on *The Andy Griffith Show* (CBS, 1961–1968). It is the stuff of Hollywood legends how much Knotts enjoyed his life off-screen, but one would not exactly define the actor as a heavy socialite. Lizzie, on the other hand, most probably never won an Emmy, at least for *Bewitched*, because her performance as twitch-witch *Samantha* was under-rated and natural. "It didn't seem like she was acting," says film scholar Rob Ray, "But it was actually great acting. She made it look too easy."

Fellow media archivist Tom McCartney adds:

From what I understand, apparently only a dozen people vote for the Emmys from the nominations cast by everyone in a category; unlike the Oscars where all actors vote for the Best Actor or Actress, etc.; and with all members of the Motion Picture Academy voting for Best Picture for example. With the Emmys, it's always been a small group of cronies who did the voting, and it's still controlled by a small group of people. Maybe (the animated) *Lucy* was right (in *A Charlie Brown Christmas*) . . . maybe it *is* also all controlled by a syndicate back East.

McCartney muses about something that may hold more than a measure of truth. According to *The Emmys* (Perigee, Third Edition, 2000), author Thomas O'Neil reveals what can only be classified as shocking information about how the awards are allegedly distributed, at least by that time. For example, one year, *The Mary Tyler Moore Show* garnered Emmy wins for nearly its entire cast, excluding the star herself. As a result, *Moore* co-star Ed Asner, who won that year (and other seasons) for playing *Lou Grant*, was none-too-pleased and gave it good to the Emmy board, claiming his lead actress (and off-screen boss, Moore's MTM Productions produced the series) was "robbed"; he called the voting process "thoroughly inconsistent." "Thankfully," Asner says, today, "Mary did win, and much deservedly so."

Apparently, the Emmy committee that voted on the nominees consisted of a very select group of business suits from Beverly Hills. For many years, the Emmys were nothing but a battleground between the West and East Coasts, with the East boasting the sophistication and style of New York and Washington, D.C., news programs and variety entertainment, and the West glorifying modern technology and celebrity appeal.

While this select and affluent sector would allegedly be some sort of avant-garde, they were also products of the confines of L.A.'s cloistered television industry, periodically falling victim to their own sequestered arrogance. Consequently, they may have dubbed *Bewitched* and its like as unworthy, most likely because they never objectively watched the programs in the first place, thus dispelling any potentially sincere winners or losers. However, none of that mattered to Lizzie. She failed to win the Emmy for female comedy series lead three more times, losing twice to Hope Lange for *The Ghost and Mrs. Muir* (NBC, 1968–1970) and once to Mary Tyler Moore for *The Mary Tyler Moore Show.*

"I think it's funny," she said in 1989 about her frequent losses. She then proceeded to compare herself to Susan Lucci, another legendary multi-nominated actress who never won, at least not until ten years later. Fortunately for the soap star, she finally garnered the amulet for playing the iconic *Erica Kane* on *All My Children* (ABC, 1970–2011). "Maybe the two of us should work together," Lizzie laughed, "do something really brilliant, and then both lose. That would be extremely comical."

But seriously, Lizzie "always knew" that she wouldn't win. "There are a lot of people voting," she said before going to praise the work of fellow Emmy-nominee Lange who won the Best Actress in a Comedy in 1968 for playing *Mrs. Muir* opposite Edward Mulhare as *The Ghost.* "I thought she was very good, actually. I liked that series," she said of the show that was spawned from the 1947 feature film starring Gene Tierney and Rex Harrison. "You know," she added, "I saw that movie for the first time about three months ago (approximately March 1989). What an amazing movie!"

As it turned out, Robert Montgomery was also never recognized with an award from his peers. As Elizabeth recalled to Ronald Haver in 1991:

"There are times when I think that perhaps he was a bit underrated. And that might be because of the fact that he never really fell into any kind of niche . . . But I just feel he was versatile. He'd try different things. I think that certainly he was appreciated for *Night Must Fall*, because he got an Academy Award nomination for that one."

Released in 1937, directed by Richard Thorpe, and co-starring Rosalind Russell and Dame May Whitty, *Night Must Fall* was based on the play by Emlyn Williams with a screenplay by John Van Druten:

> *Mrs. Bramson* (Whitty) is a wealthy but crotchety matriarch who rules over a sequestered estate for which [she] hires *Danny* (Montgomery) a proficient handyman, whom her niece/companion *Olivia Grayne* (Russell) does not thoroughly trust.

As Lizzie told Haver, her father was excited about the possibility of winning an Oscar for the role, and her mother had already picked out a dress for the event. But Robert Montgomery didn't stand a chance. "It was kind of sad," Lizzie intoned. Approximately two days before the dinner ceremony, an annual event that Elizabeth said was once tastefully presented (as opposed to today's "big hoopla stuff"), the Montgomery household received a call from MGM, the film's studio. "Don't even bother to show up. (Spencer) Tracy's going to get it."

On February 28, 2012, *The Hollywood Reporter* published the article, "The Artist's James Cromwell Slams Academy Awards, Proposes Solultion for Flawed Voting Process." Using one of Lizzie's words, Cromwell said the Oscars have become:

> . . . a lot [of] hoopla, which is not really what we do as actors and as artists. We like to do the work, and the work stands for itself, and then the industry takes over. The Academy Awards were basically created by the industry to

promote pictures. They weren't really to acknowledge the performances. Then it became sort of this great popularity contest and now, it's an incredible show and it's seen all over the world. But the strain on us to put ourselves up against other people to think that it's some sort of a contest, and it isn't a contest . . . we're all in this together.

Cromwell then recalled his own experience as a nominee and what then-Academy president Arthur Hiller told him in 1995: "Listen, the Academy Award is just a crapshoot. To be nominated, for your peers to tell you that your film or your performance is one of the five best, that's the Academy Award."

A random *Letter to the Editor* in *The Hollywood Reporter*, dated February 13, 1990, may have best defended Elizabeth's particular talent in the small to big picture scheme of things. In response to the trade magazine's unappreciative review January 24, 1990 of her performance in that year's premiere of her CBS TV-movie, *Face to Face*, Gary Bennett, of West Hollywood, wrote:

> I hope Elizabeth Montgomery didn't read your review of her telefilm *Face to Face*. While your reviewer's lazy critique was generally flattering, his comment that she made the Emmys "'look bad'" by garnering five nominations for her "'junky'" *Bewitched* work was downright insulting, not to mention inaccurate. In its prime, *Bewitched* was an enchanting show, and it is to Montgomery's credit that she was nominated so often. As for his statement that she *now* shows "considerable talent," she proved that fifteen years ago with the telefilm *A Case of Rape*.

In 1975, three years after Elizabeth decided to end *Bewitched*, Harry Ackerman, the show's executive producer, took his young son Peter to visit her on the set of *The Legend of Lizzie Borden*, which like *A Case of Rape* was a stark departure from her previous comedic work.

For Peter, *Borden*, *Rape* and other of Lizzie's non-*Bewitched* TV-movies, such as *The Victim* (ABC, 1972) and *Act of Violence* (NBC, 1979, which like *Borden* was directed by Paul Wendkos) were too jarring to watch. He explains:

> During the time she made those movies, I was not an actor, beyond school plays, anyway. So, the creative choices that she made did not reach me. I

was kind of grossed-out by the idea of the *Rape* movie, and to this day I have never watched it, or believe this or not, any of her other post-*Bewitched* work. I think I so loved the Liz I knew, which is just like *Samantha*, I just never wanted to watch her not being *her*. TV-movies like *A Case of Rape* were a new trend back in the day so it was hard for me as a pre-teen or young teen to grasp the subject matter, unlike [it is for] the youth of today.

It was, however, still riveting and "fun" for Peter to meet Lizzie on the *Borden* set:

My Dad was working at Paramount and took me to see her. I had not seen her since the end of *Bewitched* and in fact never saw her again after that. But she was the same *Liz* to me, and I do not recall any tension between her and my Dad who had remained loyal to Bill Asher after their divorce. In fact, upon hearing that I was taking tap lessons, Liz asked me to show her my steps. And I did!

Besides that challenging day when the wives of a few crew members visited the *Bewitched* set and called Lizzie "fat," she was usually cool when kids or adults visited a set. According to Montgomery curator Thomas McCartney, the cast and crew who worked with her from her 1985 CBS TV-movie *Amos* were impressed with her informal persona: "She was around the set a lot and liked to watch everyone work. She was always very sweet, and many specifically remembered her eyes and the way they smiled at whoever she was talking to. In fact, they sparkled and smiled. She was a little bashful, but kind, considerate, and very much a down-to-earth."

Apparently, there was one particular crew member on *Amos* who had more directly experienced Lizzie's kind heart. He had recently lost his wife and infant son in childbirth and fortunately had a honey-eyed four-year-old daughter to help soothe his grief. For a time, however, he was unable to find a regular babysitter and a few makeup girls from the set volunteered. But when shooting fell behind schedule, the makeup team was unable to pinch-hit, and the little girl's father went into panic mode. Who would babysit his daughter now? Of course, the answer was none other than Lizzie Montgomery.

According to McCartney, Lizzie actually volunteered for the job. "And the little girl's father was just astonished," McCartney declares. "He couldn't comprehend that Elizabeth Montgomery was actually babysitting his child. It was all pretty humorous."

Equally charming and surprising was how Lizzie responded to a reference to her age, a topic of which she was quite protective and sensitive. At one point during this adventure in babysitting, she and the little girl were playing a game. "And they looked really cute together," McCartney explains. So cute, that someone on the set turned to Lizzie and said, "Oh, how sweet. She looks like she could be your daughter."

To which Lizzie laughed and replied, with her acerbic humor intact, "You mean my *granddaughter*. I'm a little long in the tooth to have a four-year-old."

McCartney deciphers:

She was just an incredibly modest lady, and treated that little girl with such respect. Some mornings, the little girl would come in looking all disheveled and Elizabeth would just shake her head, and try to make the child presentable, but in a non-obstructive way. She'd laugh and say to the little girl, "Your father dressed you this morning, didn't he, kiddo?" But she would also tell everyone how polite she was, and how refreshing it was to encounter such a well-mannered child. She constantly complimented the girl, and her father, on her manners. She would play games with the child like hopscotch. She even got on the floor in her nurse's white (costume) to teach her how to play jacks, and apparently, that was quite a sight.

Lizzie even grew concerned whenever the little girl's father made not-so-wise moves. One day the child fell asleep on the set and curled up in a fetal ball. She immediately covered her with a blanket or towel of some sort, then approached the father and politely explained: "When children *curl up*, they're usually cold and too tired to do or say anything." According to McCartney, the father looked at Lizzie as if she was Moses giving a sermon from Mount Sinai. "I doubt he forgot whatever it is she told him that day."

Similarly, it's not likely that Sally Kemp and Rebecca Asher will ever forget what happened the day Kemp's little grandson apparently had an encounter with Elizabeth's playful, carefree spirit, literally. Elizabeth once professed to *TV Photo Story* magazine that she had seen a ghost in England. Billy Clift, her former hairstylist, talked extensively about his encounters with her spirit in his fascinating book, *Everything Is Going to Be Just Fine: The Ramblings of a Mad Hairdresser.* And now, Lizzie "transparently" materialized to Kemp's youngest relative. Sally explains:

> Elizabeth's daughter, Rebecca Asher, came to visit with friends of ours. And my grandson, I think he was three or four, asked Rebecca how her mother was, and [said] that she (Elizabeth) had *visited* him. Rebecca and all of us were surprised, but couldn't get any more out of him. He was busy playing with his trains. Small children can very often see spirits and accept them. I guess Elizabeth just decided to *pop in* to see us since Rebecca was visiting too. Good timing on Elizabeth's part since she had never met my grandson and my daughter, who I was staying with in L.A. when this happened. Pity it couldn't have happened in life. But it didn't surprise me. It's something Elizabeth *would* do.

Twenty

Humanities

"I hope to continue to live my life so that [my children] will be
proud of me. I don't mean as an actress, but as a mother, and as a
human being."

—Elizabeth Montgomery, *Screen Stars Magazine*, August 1967

In many of her post-*Samantha* interviews, Lizzie frequently related working
on *Bewitched* to taking an eight-year college course in the entertainment
industry.

However, as do many from all walks of life, she attempted to learn
something from *every* experience. She was an intelligent, open-minded individual, ever-willing to consider perspectives and opinions on any topic. She
was shy, but that just made her a good listener. She was a dedicated worker,
daughter, and wife, even when her father and a few of her husbands weren't
all that supportive or encouraging. She was a loyal friend to many in her
close circle who loved her dearly and, as far as her children were concerned,
Elizabeth was an outstanding parent who cared a great deal about not only
her immediate family, but the family of humanity. As Billy Asher, Jr. relayed
on MSNBC's *Headliners & Legends* in 2001, she was "a great influence and
. . . role model."

Despite being raised in the self-absorbed community of Hollywood,
West or East Coast divisions, Elizabeth always had a solid grasp on priorities.
She appreciated diversity and possessed integrity. Although reserved, she

would speak her mind when discussing the importance and power that accompanies ignoring differences among peoples and nations, and instead concentrating on what makes everyone the same. As she explained in 1989:

> I've never liked the exclusivity of other people because they are of another race, another religion, another whatever. If you don't like somebody, don't come to me and say, "I don't like that person because he's black"; that's not an excuse; or "I don't like that person because he's Italian"; that doesn't make any sense to me. But if you say, "I don't like that person because he's rude and kicks dogs," well, then, I'd say, "You're probably right."

Lizzie's common human charm contributed to an across-the-board allure that remains today. She appeals to a variety of people for different reasons in a multitude of roles, on screen and off. She was the kind of person you could approach at parties. And according to the June 1965 issue of *TV Radio Mirror*, that's exactly what happened at one festive first-season gathering on the set of *Bewitched*. A gentleman advanced toward her and said, "Miss Montgomery . . . you not only play the part of a witch to perfection, you *are* that witch."

Whereupon she responded, "Why, isn't everybody?"

Not really. Liz Sheridan believed the role of *Samantha* fit Lizzie like a glove. As Sheridan expressed to MSNBC's *Headliners & Legends*, "She *was* that person. She was so much like that lady that I guess it was not like acting to her. She [had the] chance to be herself."

Ironically, it was advice from Robert Montgomery that helped his daughter "be" *Samantha*. In doing so, she became more popular with this one character on TV than he ever was with several roles he portrayed in various mediums. As was explained in *Cosmopolitan Magazine*, July 1954, he once reminded Elizabeth that every time she walked onto to a stage, she must bring something of herself with her. She couldn't just depend on scenery and lines. He had instructed her to bring the audience some special essence of herself, no matter how small; something that wasn't there before she stepped out from behind the curtain. He didn't care whether it was sadness or "an air of being afraid of somebody or a feeling of slapstick comedy," just something that would make the audience "sit up and notice" her. "All good actors do that," he added, thinking Elizabeth had that quality.

"She enters a scene with an air of authority, making a strong, positive contribution."

As Lizzie told Ronald Haver in 1991, "It's every actor's dream to bring originality and part of what you are to every part you play, if you can, or else delve deeply into all sorts of research." In more directly connecting the dots between playing *Samantha*, the sensitive issue of age, and maintaining a balance of priorities between home and career, Elizabeth offered a unique perspective to *TV Radio Mirror* in June 1965:

"I'm very much like *Samantha* in some respects," she said, but in one particular way, "I can never be like her. *Samantha*, being a witch, can remain young, beautiful and charming, indefinitely. I'm only a woman and can hold on to my attractions for a limited period of time. Nothing is sadder to me than to see a woman who rolled along on her sex appeal when she was in her twenties suddenly wake up to the fact that she has reached forty. The beauty and cuteness that were once thought so attractive have gone, and it is a revolting sight to see a fortyish female trying to be a sex kitten. This is why I am trying to base my own life on more substantial and longer-lasting qualities; a home, a loving husband, fine children, longer-lasting things. A happy home is as valuable to you at fifty as it was in your twenties. And to be loved and admired by a husband and children, whom you love and admire in return, grows better as time wears on. It's a much better investment in happiness than playing the social butterfly . . ."

She didn't define herself as an ambitious career woman. She thoroughly enjoyed acting, but not to the degree where it became a compulsion that dominated her life. She didn't have to work to be content, but if she found a part that fascinated her, one that she perceived as entertaining or significant, then she was happy going to work. This was reportedly one of the reasons why she never signed a long-term contract before agreeing to do *Bewitched*; she envisioned playing *Samantha* as a challenge and signed on in a heartbeat.

She didn't always agree with her agents, who often urged her to take large roles that she classified in June 1965 as too "showy." Such parts were rejected if she sensed "something false to myself in them." At which point, she'd agree to take on more modest characterizations.

By the time she settled in as *Samantha*, Elizabeth sought to at least temporarily distance herself from nonconformist characters. "I'm not comfortable in such parts. But give me a normal young woman to do, and I'll play it for all I'm worth."

Strangely, the twitch-witch *Samantha* was one of her most "normal" roles. Others, like the prostitute *Rusty Heller* from *The Untouchables* or ax-murderess *Lizzie Borden* certainly cannot be classified as normal, at least not within the "likability" mode of America's mainstream. But somehow, as she did with *Samantha*, Lizzie's talent so captivated her audience that she allowed them to identify with even the most unlikable characters, mostly because her *performance* was likable.

When she played characters like the compassionate, but stubborn paleontologist *Dr. Diana Firestone* in 1990's *Face to Face*, as with *Samantha*, both the character and the performance were likable. In such instances, as with the plight of wildlife, Lizzie somehow utilized that combination for a good cause, off-screen, just as she had allowed *Samantha's* struggle for acceptance in the mortal world to represent the quest for equality among all people in the real world.

On January 24, 1990, Lizzie appeared on *CBS This Morning* to promote Hallmark Hall of Fame's *Face to Face* TV-movie. At first, *Morning* host Kathleen Kennedy asked her to talk about the movie, which was shot on location in Kenya, Africa. When Kennedy then wondered if Lizzie learned anything while working on the movie, Elizabeth went on to speak in support of wildlife conservation on the resplendent African continent. She had always wanted to travel to Africa performing in *Face to Face* provided the ideal opportunity for her to do so, and she was happy to get paid for it in the process. She also expressed how pleased she was to be working for Hallmark, how the entire journey to Africa was a "great wonderful" educational experience.

However, she added, "Not to be morbid, but we better get pretty interested very fast in the conditions there about the poaching. It has gotten so outrageously out of hand. And it's scary to think that if it keeps up, Africa just may not be there as we know it. It is Eden is what it is, and it should be left that way."

Or as she concluded in 1989, in general, "There are certainly a lot more important things to care about in the world besides acting."

According to Sally Kemp, her childhood friend and former classmate at the New York American Academy of Dramatic Arts, "Elizabeth really wasn't that driven to act. I may be wrong and she may have just played it cool, but she was more interested in living. She wanted to be alive. She cared about things."

As previously discussed, Lizzie's involvement with the 1984 CBS-TV movie, *Second Sight: A Love Story*, proved to be an emotionally draining experience for her, mostly because, in real life, she adopted the seeing-eye dog used in the film. A closer inspection of *Second* uncovers further insight into Lizzie own life-affirming perspective:

> The visually impaired *Alaxandra* (Lizzie) discovers life's boundless possibilities with the assistance of *Emma*, her seeing-eye dog. After she's assaulted by a burglar and realizes she can't rely just on herself anymore, *Alaxandra* reluctantly teams with *Emma* and, for the first time since being blinded as a teen, comes to trust another soul, this time, an animal; although in more time, she accepts the love of a good man (portrayed by Barry Newman).

For Lizzie, it was a happy ending to a project she had wrestled with for two years. "We went through three writers before getting it right," she told *TV Week* magazine at the time. What concerned her most was that *Alaxandra* needed to be authentic:

The tendency in movies was to make the visually impaired "so saintly and adorable that you could hardly stand it," Lizzie said. She objected to the way the character was initially written in the first few drafts of the script, but was later pleased when the writers gave *Alaxandra* flaws. "Now she has a real edge and is quite imperfect," Elizabeth decided.

By the time *Second Sight* aired, she was a veteran of countless stage and screen performances, but copped to the challenges of playing a visually impaired character. She couldn't work out the *non-focusing* since she had "a tendency to look at people a lot." Even when she was a child, her mom scolded her for staring at other people, which reconfirms her parents' sometimes stern insistence on proper social graces.

However, her research and preparation in playing *Alaxandra* was extraordinary. She blindfolded herself at home and conferred with sightless people and their instructors. When she was "in the dark," she became frustrated and disoriented even when certain of her territory. "To tell the truth," she admitted, "I had this enormous desire to peek out from the blindfolds."

Emily Wickham, a teacher of the blind, served as consultant on *Sight* and instructed Lizzie on the proper use of a cane. "You just don't tap anywhere and get by," Lizzie revealed at the time. "You always have to have a border. A person can't just go freewheeling down the street like in a swashbuckling movie."

In further research for the film, she discovered that the majority of those who are visually impaired desire more independence and less assistance from others. She found that many such individuals are self-sufficient and able to cope. They have everything laid out at home and labeled. They know where their clothing is; their colors are even categorized. They know what is in the refrigerator and in their closets, and the location of the furniture.

From her perspective, the visually impaired had already conquered their handicaps, but the moment someone with the best of intentions even offers assistance, they lose ground. "To a blind person," she said, "this is the most annoying thing possible. The last thing they want to feel is helpless."

According to Christian Beltram, a life-long fan of Lizzie's who is visually impaired, a decade or so after she completed work on *Sight*, she donated her time to the Recording for the Blind and Dyslexic Foundation or RFB&D, a nonprofit organization which records educational books on audio for the disabled. This association in particular "deeply mourned her passing," as she had volunteered throughout the last year of her life, recording a book of children's verse, *When We Were Very Young*, along with several radio and television public service announcements. One televised public service announcement even involved her reprisal of the famous nose wriggle, which she had not performed on camera since appearing in a series of Japanese TV commercials that were only broadcast in Japan, and certainly not since filming her final *Bewitched* episode in the spring of 1972.

Her efforts generated a great deal of excitement and national interest for the RFB&D, which led her to enthusiastically agree to be the honorary

chairperson for the organization's third annual *Record-A-Thon*, which transpired on June 3, 1995 in Los Angeles. "She generously lent her name to all
of our letters of appeal for the event and was planning to be one of our
celebrity readers for the days," said Don Haderlein, who then served as
studio director and media coordinator for RFB&D's Los Angeles branch.
"Tragically, a month later she was diagnosed with the cancer that took her
life."

With the modern-day onset of the Internet and social networking, and
as with many retro pop culture icons, Lizzie's online fan base has increased
significantly, documenting just how popular she remains.

New Yorker Kathy Perillo has been blind since birth. She has also been a
huge fan of Lizzie's and *Bewitched* since the show's debut. She was just ten
years old when she first heard Elizabeth in 1964. "I just loved her voice and
her acting ability," Perillo says, ". . . the way she spoke to *Darrin* and in
different scenes with her mother (*Endora*)."

Perillo's mother and relatives read her magazine articles about Elizabeth.
"And I got to find out more about her life," she recalls. "I just loved her
personality and the way she would talk and say, "*Well!*" I [had] never heard
such a beautiful voice. Then I came to understand that she was so beautiful
and attractive. She also had a great personality. Very charming."

And Perillo should know. She met Elizabeth a few times in person over
the years. She explains the events leading up to what became very special
moments in her life:

> My family and I were planning a trip to California, around 1969. And I said
> to my Mom, "You know, I'd really love to meet Elizabeth Montgomery, if
> it's possible." So we found out that her father was then the President of
> Lincoln Center, here in New York. So we said, "Let's start locally." So we
> called Lincoln Center. We got to speak to his secretary and we told her the
> situation, that I was a blind fan of his daughter and we were planning a trip
> and could we possibly meet her in July. She said, "Okay, I'll send a letter
> off to her secretary's office and we'll see if we could arrange it."
>
> On May 12, we then received a letter from Elizabeth Montgomery's
> secretary saying it wouldn't be possible [to meet her] because she was having

a baby, and that she'd be away somewhere resting. So I was disappointed. Anyway, we [arrived in California] in July, and me being the persistent person that I was, I said to my Dad, "C'mon, can't we please rent a car and go there? We have her address and just drive up and see if anyone's there? If anyone can give us any information?"

So we arrived there, went right up to her house, and rang her bell. They didn't have any security or anything. She had like twenty steps, I believe. And her governess came out, with Elizabeth's two little sons and said, "She's not home, but let me get Mr. Asher for you."

So, shortly thereafter, the governess returned to the door with Bill Asher alongside her. He said it was so nice to meet us, and that he would try and arrange a meeting for us the next day if we would tell him our hotel and he would call us that evening.

So we were staying at the Ambassador Hotel at the time on Wilshire Blvd. And he said, "I'll call you around 6:30 tonight and tell you what time to call tomorrow." It got to be after 6:30. It was like 7:15 and I said, "Oh, no . . . maybe he didn't want to make us feel bad. Maybe she wasn't able to meet us!"

All of a sudden, the phone rang. I almost died. And I remember all of this, every detail like it was yesterday, when in fact it was over forty years ago.

Anyway, my Mom answered and spoke to him and he said for us to come by, 1:30 the next day, and we did.

We finally met her, on July 16, 1969, the day the astronauts took off for the moon. She talked about how she had gotten up early that morning to see the take-off and she was so cordial and friendly. And Bill was there again, too. He was on his way to a meeting, and they allowed us to take pictures of them and us together. Liz gave me a straw handbag, which had a three-dimensional horse on the front of it that I could feel. It's something I'll always treasure. She then went on to talk about how she loved horses and how she always went to the race track; how she enjoyed horseback riding. She talked about her dogs and cats.

I had also given her a scrapbook of some articles that I put together, and she appreciated that. But she said they always got her age wrong, that she was born in 1936 and not 1933.

Right before we left she gave us her phone number and I did call her that year to wish her a Merry Christmas. Bill Asher answered the phone, and then put her on the line. She was very sweet and wished me and my parents a happy holiday.

Then later in 1989, when Lizzie did *Love Letters* on Broadway with Robert Foxworth in New York, my parents went backstage to meet her and she hugged us all, me, and my friends Linda and Paulette.

Paulette had a guide dog and Elizabeth bent down and hugged the dog and said that she had the dog from *Second Sight*. She raised it after the movie, and kept it as her own.

I said, "Remember me? I met you when I was fourteen!"

"Oh, yes! I wish we were 'all' fourteen!" she said. She had beautiful perfume on. I remember that and when she hugged me and everything, but he [Foxworth] didn't come to the door. I don't think he would have been as gracious. We really never met him. But Mr. Asher certainly was gracious.

I met him again in 2008, when I attended the *Bewitched* Fan Club at one of the conventions in Burbank. They had a tribute to Bill Asher and they asked me to speak and pose [for photographs] and then I got to sit next to him, and he had his arm around me and he kissed my hand. He was still gracious then, you know, even though he was in a wheelchair and everything.

I thanked him and said, "You made my dream come true. If it wasn't for you, I never would have been able to meet Elizabeth!

Vince Staskel, born with cerebral palsy, is another of Lizzie's fans. Today, he is the principal and executive producer of VPS MediAbility Productions in Poughkeepsie, New York, which is currently producing radio shows for Able Pathways (formally Disabled Radio). He is also promoting a stable of six authors with disabilities and assisting in the development of the "This Is Life" radio show on KFWB in Los Angeles.

Vince also serves on the board of directors for The Classic TV Preservation Society, a nonprofit organization that seeks to close the gap between popular culture and education.

A television fan his entire life, Vince grew up in Shenandoah, Pennsylvania, during the 1950s and 1960s, when the small screen was his companion and playmate. He walked with crutches as a child and found it difficult to participate in many outdoor activities due to limited mobility. Classic TV shows granted him not only the opportunity to watch but actually participate in the on-screen action.

As he recalls, "Television was a big part of my life. I would dance [with] *American Bandstand*, wear my coonskin cap during *Davy Crockett*, fire my toy rifle with *The Rifleman*, and clown around with *The Three Stooges*. These shows became my friends and playmates."

Bewitched, in particular, was also one of his favorite programs, and Lizzie one of the TV stars who most inspired him, both as a human being and to work in the entertainment industry. As a youngster, he followed her career and was "thrilled to see her starring in her own sitcom. Of course her beauty is only one of the first things that caught your eye. But in addition to that, it was her acting versatility. I loved watching her. She had such a wonderful way to draw you into her character. You knew right from the start that she was a good witch who only wanted to do positive things for people. *Samantha* has a great deal of power but only used it sparingly for only good purposes."

"To me, spiritually," he concludes, "it showed the existence of true love in the world. I followed her career and saw the full range of her acting ability. Yes, Ms. Montgomery could also play bad, excellently. As her fan base grew, so did she as an actor. I was captivated by her. *Bewitched* was and still is a major part of my life experience."

Lizzie clearly hit a chord with the disabled community, the down-trodden, the under-privileged, the put-upon, the physically, mentally, visually, and vocally impaired, and minorities of every kind. The late gifted author Lauri E. Klobas was a loyal advocate of the challenged community, she was also as a big fan of Lizzie's. In her book, *Disability Drama in Television and Film* (McFarland, 1988), Klobas included a review and analysis of Lizzie's renown TV-film, *Second Sight: A Love Story*, about a blind woman's relationship with her seeing-eye dog and the new man in her life. The year her book was published, Klobas offered an explanation of Lizzie's diverse popularity, touching on closed captioning for television programming, which is widely available now (and which Lizzie had unsuccessfully once rallied for on *Bewitched*):

> Before closed captioning was available on TV, people who were deaf tuned into action shows where the story line could be followed without dialogue. I remember asking deaf friends in the pre-captioning days what they liked

to watch and *Bewitched* was at the top of their list. It was Montgomery's expressive face and "speech-readable" mouth that attracted them. Of course, the graphic manifestations of magic needed no dialogue to be enjoyed by any member of the audience.

Emmy-winning TV producer Dan Weaver has worked on acclaimed talk shows such as *The Phil Donahue Show* and *Hour Magazine*. In 1996, Weaver, who is hearing-impaired, was the guiding creative force behind a tribute to Elizabeth on *Entertainment Tonight*. He had the wonderful fortune of meeting Elizabeth twice. First, in 1986, when he produced a special for *Donahue* called "AIDS: Face to Face." Weaver recalls:

> Phil had wanted to do a show on people battling AIDS in their final stages. It was a powerful experience, and the program was nominated for two Emmys, and received an Alliance for Gay and Lesbian Artists (AGLA) Award. These awards predated the Gay and Lesbian Alliance Against Defamation, (GLAAD) Awards, which also celebrate the most outstanding images of the LGBT community in the media.

On behalf of the show, Weaver, who is gay, proudly accepted the award. "It was a magical night," he says, including a surprise meeting before the program with Lizzie and Robert Foxworth. Before showtime, Weaver couldn't resist the chance to introduce himself and his life partner, Lee. "Thinking back," Weaver intones, "Elizabeth and Robert were early allies in the LGBT equality movement in Hollywood. That was during the time when many people believed that you could *catch* AIDS and that it was *God's punishment of gays*. Yet there they were, and she was as gracious and beautiful as I'd imagined."

During their brief conversation, Weaver said he also "felt her incredible sensitivity." In a nervous attempt to make small talk, he mentioned that a friend of his was being considered to do some publicity work for her. Upon hearing this, Lizzie's expression changed and she became "defensive," Weaver recalls, "saying that [it] wasn't true," and proceeded to ask Weaver if that's the line his friend was telling everyone. "I felt the panic in her voice."

In hindsight, Weaver believes his innocent remark was probably inappropriate, since he was a stranger to her. Also, too, his friend may have been exaggerating his prospective employment as her publicist. "I regretted that I had said anything," Weaver goes on to explain, "yet it made me drawn to her even more . . . her feelings, her vulnerability, and her fragility. I think these qualities motivated her to help the underdogs, others that may have those feelings sometimes, too, like [those in] the LGBT community and the disabled."

One of Weaver's favorite autographs is a beautiful note he received from Lizzie, thanks to a mutual producer friend who met her at a PBS fundraiser. Weaver's friend told Elizabeth of his incredible fascination with her which, Weaver admits, "I have gotten teased about over the years."

No matter. Both he and Lizzie kept a sense of humor about it all. Her note to Weaver said, "You may be demented, but you obviously have impeccable taste."

"I loved her humor," Weaver adds.

His other meeting with Elizabeth transpired at a "looping session," where an audio track is recorded after either a movie or TV show is filmed. As a surprise, Weaver's partner Lee had arranged this "second chance" for me. Weaver explains:

> I walked in and there she was in the sound booth, speaking Swahili for her TV movie, *Face to Face*. When she came out for a break, I practically pounced on her. Luckily she hadn't remembered our first encounter, but this one became equally uncomfortable for me. This was finally a chance to connect with her. But I overwhelmed her on what amounted to a short work break. I did what many fans do. I couldn't stop talking and did a soliloquy on why she was important to me. Ugh! She was flattered at first and then became uncomfortable. Thinking back, if I were in her shoes, I would have felt the same way.

Years later, in 1996, he was producing the tribute to Elizabeth for *Entertainment Tonight*, where he met "her wonderful daughter Rebecca," who smiled upon hearing how he met her mother. I am sorry I never got to convey this in the right way to Elizabeth, but it meant a lot to be able to share my thoughts with Rebecca. I'm just someone who truly felt a connection with Elizabeth, someone who sensed her shyness and her goodness. I felt her compassion even as a child. There was a universal appeal of *Bewitched* that made people from many diverse groups feel welcomed each Thursday night at 8:00 PM [when the show originally aired on ABC]. Echoing Lauri Klobas' thoughts, Weaver recalls:

> I remember it being one of the first shows I watched with special effects, and for a hearing-impaired person where there weren't subtitles back then, I am sure it was a fun show to watch. Her real-life passion for social causes, witnessed in some *Bewitched* episodes, came through.
>
> The show found innovative ways to work in messages (with episodes like "*Samantha* Twitches for UNICEF," and "Sisters at Heart," the latter of which dealt with bigotry). In those days, dealing with such a real issue like racism was rare on TV; and for a supernatural sitcom to take it on was very courageous and creative. Elizabeth and Bill Asher were pioneers in social cause storytelling.
>
> I learn best through storytelling and visualization, perhaps another reason I was drawn to this series that was so visually interesting
>
> As a video storyteller some four decades later, the show had a huge impact on my career, and using TV as a creative tool in educating others on social issues that impact us all. . . . Elizabeth's beauty both externally and internally, had a truly magical ability to take such a supernatural and *out-there* concept and give it so much grounding and reality
>
> I always sensed a bit of insecurity with her, one that I have known well throughout my own life. When I would watch her on the screen I had strong feelings about what Elizabeth, the actress, was going through personally. I've learned over time that she so wanted to please her dad; and I felt that. She was a tremendously gifted woman, but I imagine a very sensitive person who, like all of us, had her demons. But I totally also got that she was a very loving person who cared deeply about people, and never saw herself as a celebrity.
>
> I think she struggled with being a celebrity. In a way, she was probably similar to *Samantha*, just wanting to live the simple life, one where people didn't see her any differently than themselves. I think she accomplished this by never forgetting the underserved in this world, and the power in changing lives by taking on personal actions, like doing narration of audio books for the blind. She was a terrific actress and funny. But there was a depth in her that showed much sensitivity and vulnerability. She played *Samantha* as simply someone who was trying to fit in, to have her family accept her husband's world. There was always love for both sides, but it was a challenge. And *Samantha* always had respect for everyone's point of view. It was

not easy for her to be in a minority in a mortal world, but she so wanted to embrace it and share those simple and universal family values.

That one word answer she gave (prejudice, in defining *Bewitched's* central theme) really crystallized why the show was so real to me and why I have loved it on one level; I could sit and be entertained yet on another level really consider a much heavier philosophical perspective.

Today, Weaver is a partner and Senior Vice President of Talent Development for Diversity Works LLC (www.diversityworksllc.com), a marketing and communications agency whose clients include lesbian, gay, bisexual, and transgender (LGBT) certified businesses, nonprofit organizations, and corporate allies. Their tagline is: Turning Pride into Profit.

"We work with companies to help build their strategic relationships in the LGBT Marketplace," he explains, "which is an $800 billion dollar industry. As a minority group, the LGBT market is third only to the African-American and Hispanic populations, and actually exceeds the Asian-American buying power."

What's more, Diversity Works supports all groups, but has particular interests in LGBT seniors, LGBT people with disabilities, and the transgender community. "We believe these groups have some of the most significant unmet needs and face the most discrimination."

According to Weaver, one quarter of all gay seniors fear revealing their sexuality even to their own doctors, while an estimated 40 to 60 percent of the transgendered population is unemployed due to workplace discrimination. So for him, "It's been interesting finding out about Elizabeth's compassion for diversity and disability groups. She was a special soul put here, who used her time well, and is on to her next mission. Her work, whether on screen, at home, or with her charitable causes, lives on like a beautiful tale in a storybook."

Twenty-one

Political Science

> "My parents never tried to force their opinions on me, politically, religiously, or any other way."
>
> —Elizabeth Montgomery, *Modern Screen Magazine* (July 1970)

Lizzie frequently employed her widespread image for the benefit of others, remaining civic-minded throughout her life and career, in spite or despite conservative views expressed by her mother and father. As she explained to Ronald Haver in 1991, broaching politics with her father was like talking to a brick wall.

For one, her stand on Vietnam was not a popular topic with him. As she put it, "He just figured, 'Well, there's no sense of even getting into this with someone like that!'" She felt it was more productive that they were on different coasts; she on the West (*the left*); he on the East (*the right*). "And it was just as well that we weren't in each other's company a lot because it would have been unpleasant . . . for a whole mess of people."

Despite such political friction with her father, Lizzie went on to protest the Vietnam war, and lent her name, along with a great deal of personal time, money, and energy to a wide variety of charitable and political causes, including supporting human equality and the Peace movement; helping to further AIDS research, and reaching out to the disabled community. However, she modestly defined her social involvement as adequate. "There are times when I know I could still be doing more," she said in 1989.

According to Ronny Cox, Lizzie's liberal-minded co-star from the issue-driven TV-movies *A Case of Rape* and *With Murder in Mind*, their shared political views were at the core of their friendship:

> Elizabeth was very left-wing, not as left-wing as me, but very left-wing. And it was refreshing for each of us to run into someone whose politics were sort of as vociferous as the other person's . . . someone who we could each blow off steam with, especially at that time.

While *Bewitched* was on the air through the 1960s and early 1970s, Ronny was "there in '68 . . . working in the streets with the kids" during the upheaval surrounding Martin Luther King, Jr.'s assassination and the subsequent riots.

At the time, the Civil Rights Movement was in full swing. There was massive resistance to, among other things, desegregation of public restrooms, buses, restaurants, and schools. The anti–Vietnam war movement was commencing. Michael Harrington's book, *The Other America* (Scribner, 1997) would later document the gaps between America's rich and the poor; the haves and the have-nots. Cesar Chavez was challenging America in the Grape Boycott; music was alive with revolution, from the likes (and dislikes) of The Beatles to The Smothers Brothers. It was the day of *The March on Washington* (from the Washington Monument to the Lincoln Memorial) for jobs, to halt discrimination against African-Americans, and equality for all. *Everyday people* of every race, creed, and color were there, in numbers 250,000 or more, walking arm-in-arm down Constitution Avenue, alongside celebrities such as sports legend Jackie Robinson (who had shattered the color barrier in Major League Baseball).

By the time *A Case of Rape* aired in 1974, Ronny says influential people like the Harvard educated poet Robert Lowell refused to visit the White House due to the U.S. involvement in the Vietnam war. In Ronny's view, Lowell (born in 1917) in particular, played an important role in the revolution of the 1960s.

But from any perspective, Lowell's writings are significant, especially his early works, including *Land of Unlikeness* (1944) and *Lord Weary's Castle*, the latter for which he received the Pulitzer Prize for Poetry in 1947 at the age of thirty. Both books were influenced by his conversion from Episcopalian-ism to Catholicism, and explored the dark side of America's Puritan legacy. Before Vietnam, he also actively objected to World War II, became a con-scientious objector, and was subsequently imprisoned.

According to Cox, it was only after Lowell began questioning main-stream artistic choices that issue-oriented films like *Rape* (which helped to push forward nationwide landmark legislation that changed the rights of rape victims) could be produced and introduced to TV home viewers. Before then, Cox says:

> It was either frothy comedy or some sort of made-up drama. We were a nation still going through the throes of the Southerners disagreeing with the Civil Rights Act and us coming out of Vietnam. Everyone was vilifying the hippie movement. People were still having trouble voting. We were not that far removed from '65–66. And just look around at the world today! We still have inequalities!

Back in 1974, Cox had serious arguments with those in the artistic com-munity who questioned the association between politics and the arts. "Because in those days," he says, "there was this total segregated idea, that entertainment was *here* and the real world was *there*. So I think in some ways (*A Case of Rape*) probably made some people squirm a little bit."

The same could also be said for his 1972 big screen film *Deliverance*, which hit theatres slightly before *Rape* premiered on TV. This movie also made an integral artistic contribution to the era, for it too dealt with the issue of sexual assault, but this time a man was violated. Cox shares his memories of working on the film in his new book, *Dueling Banjos: The Deliverance of Drew* (Decent Hill, 2012). He says *Deliverance* was ground-breaking if only for the healthy social dialogue it created:

> This was the first time men had had to deal with the whole concept of rape. For the first time people were realizing that rape isn't [just] a sexual crime. It's violent and out of control. I'm not even sure there's hardly any sexual component to it. It's an act of humiliation . . . the *me-dominating-you* aspect.

In comparative analysis of *Case* and *Deliverance*, he believes both films "changed a lot of people's psyches. Because now for the first time, men had to deal with the kind of thing that women had to deal with for years." Before *Case* in particular, he says, once a woman was raped, her sex life was open to extreme scrutiny. "If she just dated someone, the deck was stacked against her. And you couldn't say anything if a man had prior arrests. He was completely off limits."

Yet it was Lizzie's caring and compelling drive to serve others that made her so accessible to Cox on the set of *Case*. He was impressed with her unaffected demeanor, considering her father's conservative stance and her prestigious upbringing, as well as with her obvious decision to shun arrogance, and retain an open-minded and keen understanding of priorities:

> You have to admire Lizzie. She could very easily have just been one of the *haves*. And that's what sets her apart; that sensibility of saying, "No! I don't agree with the right wing paradigm." To them, it's the *zero sum game* . . . getting a lot of money or getting a lot of power or getting [a] lot of stuff doesn't mean anything (unless the *Left* loses). They want this trickle-down-stuff, and if they would just be historians and realize that when the least of us—especially the middle class—does the best that's when everybody else does the best. The paradigm for this country is to make sure that [the] vast middle is doing well and then you'll pull the poor up from the bottom and the rich still do well. And Elizabeth realized that.

Although he's enjoyed his share of stardom, Cox admits to not experiencing Lizzie's level of success. He did not know her father, nor did they have discussions about her father. "I can only talk from my own sense of it," he says, "but I think she looked around and saw those right wing guys, the soullessness of them, not caring for the other people," and decided from there.

However, he remains particularly puzzled as to how Lizzie became part of an artistic community like Hollywood, filled with celebrities of all shapes, sizes, and success levels, some of who may be defined as arrogant and self-centered:

> Who knows? In some ways it sounds paradoxical. In some ways it's as though our religions almost mitigate against us ever getting together . . . in lots of ways. If you take what I call *the right-wing extreme religions of the world* . . . *the right wing elements of the religions of the world* . . . *right wing Christian*

fundamentalists, right wing Muslims, right wing Jewish, right wing Buddhists . . . those ultra-right wings . . . they always mitigate. . . . they always propagate an *us-against-them* mentality. But that's the way of these guys having their power! I grew up in a small town of fundamentalist right-wing religion bigots of the worst order. I was overwhelmed with what I observed as deep hypocrisy and disregard for humanity. So, I vowed at a very early age to choose a more productive path. In some ways, I'm sort of prejudiced against organized religion because of that. Because I saw such hatred, such bigotry coming from those kinds of places, no caring for humanity at large, no caring for our fellow man. That turned me off.

Ronny Cox doesn't know for certain, but he'd "like to think that Lizzie saw the same things from the *excessives* . . . the same lack of caring from *her* side of the tracks."

If Lizzie was the most down-to-earth actress in Hollywood, then her male counterpart, beyond Robert Foxworth in that community, would have to be none other than Emmy-winning actor Ed Asner. Asner is best known for playing the tough-as-nails-but-gentle-of-heart *Lou Grant* on *The Mary Tyler Moore Show,* and its sequel *Lou Grant.* The *Grant* role, a supporting role on a half-hour situation comedy, was the first in TV history to be spun-off into a one-hour dramatic series. He made TV history again when he recently reprised his role as wealthy art collector and smuggler *August March* on updated edition of *Hawaii Five-O.* He first played *March* on the original *Five-O,* starring Jack Lord, a frequent co-star of Lizzie's. According to the article, "Ed Asner Visits Hawaii," published in *The Los Angeles Times,* on March 19, 2012, the day the new *Five-O* segment aired, it was the first time a guest performer played the same character on separate versions of the same series.

But Asner is also well-known for heralded performances in countless other television programs and feature films, everything from programs in which Lizzie also appeared (*Armstrong Circle Theatre, Alfred Hitchcock Presents, The Untouchables*), to mini-series like *Roots* and *Rich Man, Poor Man,* TV-movies like *The Gathering,* to big screen family films like *Elf* and *Up!*

Like Lizzie, Asner's success never went to his head, even at the super height of his popularity during the *Mary Tyler Moore Show* days. Although he could well have afforded a Mercedes or BMW like many of his Holly-wood peers, Asner pulled into various studio parking lots of the day in a 1977 Oldsmobile Cutlass. He explains how and why that happened, and more:

I came from a middle class Jewish Orthodox family. My Father couldn't read or write English. He had morals and standards. I was afraid of him because the four older kids made me afraid of him. And yet he never laid a glove on me. I was a mama's boy. Up until the beginning of second grade we lived in a railroad apartment which we owned, which was above my father's junkyard. My classmates were Mexican. The junkyard was across from a farmer's packing house. So I certainly had humble beginnings in terms of ostentation.

We moved to what I regarded as a white bread village. So I made friends in the class. I went through public school and high school and being the youngest, I was more sheltered than the rest of my siblings, who before long were all away and I was on my own. I encountered whatever I had to encounter on my own.

I became a success in high school but in my sophomore year, all my friends were invited into fraternities and I wasn't. And I saw which way the wind blew for me. I said, "Okay, I had been the class clown up to that point. I can't look to friendship to be surrounding me, I've got to excel, so I started excelling and achieved."

My greatest regret was joining a fraternity in my senior year! It was totally unnecessary, but my buddies were in it, so I thought I'd join and I betrayed my standards by doing so. I went to college, the University of Chicago. I was there a year and a half. I got involved in acting, which was extracurricular, became open to acting, dropping out of college.

I then took on a series of jobs, all of them blue collar and I suppose the fact that I held onto the Cutlass signifies two things: That I was tight and that I identified and I'd always be identified as a common middle class working stiff!

Both of my sisters were social workers in their post-college years. Maybe some of that rubbed off on me. I know in certain cases it did. They certainly had their liberal ideals.

And [World War II] was on at the time. And we were Jews. We had some idea of what befell Jews, not only in Europe but the anti-Semitism that was certainly rife in America at that time!

I was willing to join a fraternity that my friends were in at one time and after I went to three meetings they voted on you. And I found out that two people blackballed me: A guy from the next block and a football player I knew and was friendly with. But my friend who was in the fraternity told me about it and I said, "Was it because I was Jewish?" He said, "Yeah." I was greatly relieved! "Oh," I thought, "it wasn't because it was me!" How goddamned stupid can you get?!

Anyway, I went on and joined the other fraternity to my regret.

So, being a Jew in Kansas City, Kansas, discrimination was of that mild a nature, but it was enough to make me realize I was one of the *others* but being an *other* I think makes you tend to identify with the character of others who are *others*.

I think that primarily dictated, having been a working stiff and a union man, [that] finally it was natural that I should pursue whatever causes I spoke for, because I was always a loudmouth, a clown. How do you say it? *A loudmouth goon clown.*

Asner later combined his voice, refreshing self-deprecating humor, compassion for his fellow man, and keen sense of priorities to do good work. And although he and Lizzie clearly came from very different backgrounds, they attained an equally successful footing in Hollywood, while retaining the same strong sense of integrity, if not always aware that they were on the same side.

Asner, a liberal and political advocate like Lizzie, had appeared alongside her at many charity functions, while also playing opposite her on game shows like *Password*. Oddly enough, Asner had no idea that Elizabeth was a liberal; he thought she may have followed in the footsteps of her conservative-minded father. He explains:

The fact that she was the daughter of *Mr. Republican* was intimidating to me. He was the tuxedo-and-top-hat-and-tie type. I was never offended by anything he said or did that I can recall, but in those days he represented the *other side*. I never approached politics with her. I never got familiar with her other than as Bob Foxworth's wife. The fact that she was married to Bob had to indicate something. He certainly was a liberal, but we never really exchanged familiarities. I certainly enjoyed her (performances) and was terribly depressed at her demise. Heartbreaking! And I thought she was a fine upstanding woman. But I did not identify the liberal (in her), although she certainly didn't get in the way of her liberal husband. From what I've now learned about her, I deeply regret not having been able to exchange some warmth with her, now knowing exactly who she was (as a human being). But she was not forthcoming.

Lizzie's shy behavior struck again, but her heart, as usual, was in the right place. Knowing Lizzie, she may have been just as intimidated by Asner as he was of her. But certainly she must have respected his integrity and the sacrifices he made in his life and career due to his liberal beliefs, specifically when his political views once cost him his job. Asner explains further:

There were times when I spoke up for causes. I was lucky that some of those times I hadn't done sufficient background (research) but I was still correct in my positions. When I came to New York, being a member of both SAG and AFTRA, I had signed the Stockholm Peace Pledge. And I wondered . . . I had heard of people being denied because of signing.

When I had to fill out my Loyalty Oath for clearance with the networks and I only filled out one, evidently that applied across the board. I wondered if they'd catch me up on signing this Stockholm Peace Pledge. That's how fearful I was. It didn't reflect on me. Most of those years until I came out to speak up on Central America, El Salvador, I kept my mouth shut, not willing to be identified, not willing to be tagged.

And when I spoke out on El Salvador—speaking out on what I consider to be a humanist position, not liberal, it produced a maelstrom of opposition that led to the cancellation of *Lou Grant*. And when I did speak out, we went to Washington to announce the initial contribution of aid to El Salvador. There was a large press conference and the second questioner at the table, and he said, "Are you for free elections in El Salvador? What if those elections turn out a Communist Government?" It's like a freight train hit me in the face. And I gave some wimpy answer and I went on to the third questioner, but I was troubled with what I had answered. I gave some cockamamie answer and I went back to the second questioner.

In my mind, I'm saying, "I've come all this way for this, all this distance? And I'm gonna waffle?" Not here! And I said I wasn't satisfied with my initial answers: "All I can say to you is if it's the Government the people of El Salvador choose . . . then let them have it!" And with that, I felt I was signing the end of my career. I felt that it would rebound. There was rebounding but it wasn't over that specific answer, but I'm sure it was the provocation that led to all the attacks. I was labeled a *commie* and this and that and the *Lou Grant* series got cancelled!

Although it's been nearly three decades since Grant's cancellation, Asner has never stopped working or fighting the good fight. Lizzie would have been proud.

Had it not been for the loyal original following of Trekkers and Trekkies, the original *Star Trek* series, broadcast on NBC from 1966 to 1969 (and one of Lizzie's favorite shows), may not have made it past its first season. One particular episode, "Plato's Stepchildren," involved the virile *Captain Kirk*, as played by Caucasian William Shatner, under alien mind control, forced to kiss *Lt. Uhura*, portrayed by African-American Nichelle Nichols. It was the first time a scripted TV series presented an interracial intimate moment between characters, however contrived within a sci-fi/fantasy storyline. Even more significant was that the segment was broadcast November 22, 1968—the fifth anniversary of President Kennedy's assassination, which was also the anniversary of the day rehearsals began for the *Bewitched* pilot.

In 1977, Lizzie starred in *A Killing Affair*, a CBS TV-movie co-starring African-American athlete turned actor turned controversial public figure O. J. Simpson. They were big city detectives who were partners on the street and at home, locked in a heated romance that included one water-downed bedroom scene with Simpson stationed just above her, to one side.

According to the article, "TV Breaks Old Taboos with New Morality," published in *Jet Magazine*, a progressively mainstream African-American publication, December 1, 1977, Lizzie rallied for additional scenes in the bedroom, but CBS censors rejected her suggestions. So, she had to settle for what she could get or the scenes, and potentially the entire film, would have been shelved. But even the subtle sequence that did manage to make the cut was considered cutting edge television. As *Jet* worded it, "Black skin lovingly pressed against white skin on television screens is a delicacy rarely seen."

It took *A Killing Affair* to pull back the covers on this sensitive and usually avoided interracial material, which was then one of TV's most inflexible taboos. But the audience was not repelled. Instead, the film was embraced by its viewers. Broadcast on Wednesday, September 21, 1977 it garnered a 29 percent Nielson rating share. Although it ranked behind the popular and quite tame *Charlie's Angels* on ABC, *Killing* toppled *The Oregon Trail* on NBC by four points.

David Gerber, the movie's producer, explained to *Jet*: "The story started off with a white couple, but we wanted to do something different with the script and turned it around to an interracial couple. CBS had the guts to show it and I think they handled it right."

Considering the uneasy nature of *Killing's* racially mixed romance, reaction to the movie was generally mild. Neither Lizzie nor Simpson received any significant letters of protest. However, as *Jet* perceived it, America didn't completely sit on its anger. A Chicago television station and newspaper received a few crank calls and letters, and far more seriously, one southern station received a bomb threat convincing enough that the building was momentarily evacuated.

"We all expected such response as an inevitable result," CBS censor Van Gordon Sauter told the magazine. "The movie featured the kind of relationship many viewers feel uncomfortable with. If there were a proliferation of such programs (depicting interracial relationships) there would probably be a considerable degree of indignation expressed."

According to a September 1977 edition of *The Abilene Reporter-News* in Texas, Lizzie was at the time visiting a Renaissance Faire in the San Fernando Valley in California when a middle-aged female *Bewitched* fan approached her and asked what she was working on. "I'm doing a television movie with O. J. Simpson," she replied. "It's a love story between two police detectives."

The woman's face went blank and she said, "You. O. J. Simpson. A love story? Well!" She then went back into the crowd.

"Oh, I'm sure I'll be getting hate mail and I don't care," Lizzie told *The Abilene*. Both O. J. and I realized we would get a strong reaction from the show, but we went ahead and did it. I think it's a good show, though I hate the title."

According to further reports in *Jet*, and just as *A Killing Affair* aired, a flood of hate mail was credited with destroying the then on-screen love affair between white actor Richard Guthrie's character and his on-screen African-American girlfriend played by Tina Andrews on NBC's daytime serial *Days of Our Lives*. Guthrie had argued that the show's producers "got cold feet on the budding romance" because the story line was unpopular. "The studio had been getting a lot of hate mail from people threatening to stop watching the show," huffed Andrews at the time, "when they get enough of those letters they respond. One letter said, 'I hope you're not going to let that (n-word) marry that white boy.' Apparently they are not. I was canned."

Why would an America that for the most part tacitly accepted the O. J./ Lizzie flame turn against the fledgling Guthrie-Andrews lovelight?

Harvard psychiatrist Dr. Alvin Poussaint took his analysis a bit further. "During the day television is watched mostly by white women," he observed, who might have then have viewed Tina Andrews' performance as a threat. Whereas in the 9:00 or 10:00 PM time slot of that era you may find a significantly different audience that might observe this: an African-American (like O. J. Simpson who was not at that time the controversial figure he would later become in 1994) having an affair with a white woman, which would fit the stereotype that successful black men desire white women, via what Poussaint called the "guess who's coming to dinner" scenario (in reference to the 1967 Sidney Poitier film of the same name that was remade in 2005 with Will Smith).

Poussaint added:

> Plus *A Killing Affair* was a one-shot thing. We don't know what protests might have come if the movie were a continuing series. Soap operas are ongoing and they reflect a slice of real life. The viewer usually lives a fantasy through the characters, which is why Tina Andrews' character may have run into trouble. Then too, TV is still uncomfortable with interracial romances. For *A Killing Affair* they picked a superstar like O. J. Simpson and that may have been why there weren't more protests. Simpson represents a big, virile, handsome cat who seems gentle and non-threatening.

At least that was the perception at the time. Today, the film is almost unwatchable. Not because of the interracial romance between Lizzie's and Simpson's characters, but because of the questions and incriminating circumstances that have since surrounded and assassinated Simpson's real life character (the murder trial after the death of his wife Nicole Simpson, attractive and fair-haired like Lizzie; while the movie's ironic title doesn't much help its case).

Beyond the racial, political, and particular controversies that surrounded the lives of certain performers, Lizzie's involvement with *A Killing Affair* further proved her attempts to push the creative envelope and ultimately allowed television—by way of her career choices—to become an educational platform for narrative mainstream entertainment outside the realm of PBS.

Unlike *Samantha's* singular marriage to two *Darrins* on *Bewitched*, Lizzie was married four times to different men, ultimately to Bob Foxworth. When Lizzie and Foxworth appeared on *The Dennis Miller Show* in 1992, Miller looked at Foxworth and asked, "Which *Darrin* are *you?*"

Foxworth played along with the gag, and replied, "The third one!"

Six years later, and thirty-six months after Lizzie died, Foxworth wed Stacy Thomas, and they remain married today. Before he met Lizzie on the set of *Mrs. Sundance* in 1973, he was with Marilyn McCormick, whom he was married to from 1964 to 1974—nearly the same time Lizzie was married to Bill Asher. Lizzie and Bill divorced in 1974. So did Bob and Marilyn, though not before they had two children, Bo and Kristyn Foxworth (both actors), who later became step-siblings to Lizzie's three children (with Bill Asher), Rebecca, Robert, and Billy Asher, Jr.

When Lizzie and Bob moved in together, it was like *The Brady Bunch*, combining families from two different marriages, and that kind of fit. Lizzie had attended the New York Academy of Dramatic Arts with *Brady* star Florence Henderson, while Foxworth's curly brown locks and piercing blue eyes resembled *Mr. Brady* actor Robert Reed.

All five children were lights in Lizzie's life, although she was never satisfied with her maternal performance. As she expressed in 1992 to John Tesh on *One on One*, "I will never win any Mother of the Year awards," but she also believed "parents and kids have to grow up together."

When asked if it was tough being Robert Montgomery's liberal daughter, she replied:

Yeah, absolutely . . . There were people who didn't like him and, as a result, they were people who decided they didn't like me. And those are things you just kinda have to cope with and that's a little tough, but you get used to it. I guess.

She never got used to it. Her father's political views were not always welcome in Hollywood which, in 1989, she described as "a town that claims to be so damned liberal all the time, but isn't." It was outspoken opinions like that which probably didn't help her case in winning the majority Emmy vote amongst her peers.

Fortunately, she was adored by millions of fans, while her political advocacy and love and respect for Foxworth quenched her slight desire to pontificate. They were a glamorous humanitarian team, superheroes of the Hollywood set, battling for world peace, the disadvantaged, the downtrodden, and those suffering from the pain and discrimination of AIDS, and for the rights of those in the lesbian, gay, bisexual, and transgender (LGBT) community.

Although it was Foxworth who usually voiced their collective concerns in the court of public opinion, at various forums Lizzie would stand beside him, firmly, silently, with that famous closed-lipped smile which became one of her many facial trademarks. While that periodically perky smirk may have represented her apprehension to speak, she believed in exactly whatever Foxworth professed which, according to *The Los Angeles Times* in 1986 was the following:

> Before I am an actor and a famous face, I am a human being and a (parent) and a citizen of this nation and of the world. I think I have a right, as well as a responsibility, to speak to the [nuclear arms] issue as well as any other issue.

It was a speech he gave at a rally for The Great Peace March for Global Nuclear Disarmament of 1986, which was undermanned, plagued by insurance problems, heckled by protesters, and attacked by bureaucrats. Nevertheless, Lizzie and Foxworth, along with numerous other celebrities, showed their support as approximately 1,400 marchers struck out across 3,235 miles of American desert, mountains, plains, and cities, bent on mass persuasion against the perceived evils of nuclear arms.

The march was the brainchild of David Mixner, then twenty-nine years old and a longtime activist in several liberal causes, specifically in regard to LGBT issues. His credentials include the 1968 presidential campaign of Senator Eugene McCarthy, directing Los Angeles Mayor Tom Bradley's 1977 mayoral campaign, co-chairing Senator Gary Hart's 1984 presidential quest, and the Vietnam Moratorium. Mixner was also one of the prominent LGBT fundraisers for Bill Clinton during his 1992 campaign but famously broke with the President over the "don't ask, don't tell" policy implemented in 1993, and was ultimately arrested at a protest in front of the White House. At such events, Lizzie was usually a figurative if not oratorical voice.

Mixner says today:

> Elizabeth was one of the first Hollywood celebrities to step forward to fight for LGBT rights. At the time, everyone in Hollywood was keeping a respectful distance from the issue, but not Elizabeth. She attended events, helped raise money and often dined at Mark's, a famous gay restaurant in West Hollywood. Never wanting to receive accolades for her work, since in conversation with me she just kept saying, "It is the right thing to do." She was a person who made us feel we had value by her presence in those dark and difficult years.

Lizzie's presence certainly gave value to Dick Sargent's life.

In 1991, her former *Bewitched* co-star announced his homosexuality, and requested her presence as Co-Grand Marshall for the 1992 Gay Rights Parade in Los Angeles. "You wouldn't see her at parties," Sargent's former publicist Howard Bragman told *People Magazine* in 1995, "but you would always see her at benefits."

Shortly before Sargent died in 1994 of prostate cancer (and *not* AIDS, which has been falsely reported over the years), he gave an interview to writer Owen Keehnen for *Chicago Outlines* magazine, "the voice of the gay and lesbian community," which was later published in Keehnen's book, *We're Here, We're Queer* (Prairie Avenue Productions, 2011), during which he commented on Lizzie's support. She knew of his sexuality, Sargent said, because his "lover was alive when we did *Bewitched*." He and his partner, Albert Williams, a screenwriter, would attend parties and play tennis with Lizzie and Bill Asher. "She really loved my lover very much," Sargent said of the man who in 1979 dropped dead of a cerebral hemorrhage at the home they shared in the Hollywood Hills. He said Lizzie respected "the hell out of me for doing this [coming out]. She thinks it's marvelous and has nothing but encouraging words."

In 1991, *The Star* magazine decided to out Sargent and as he told Keehnen, "they quoted everyone like they talked to them." Sargent called Lizzie and read what the tabloid had quoted her as saying: "Well, if that's his lifestyle, I just hope it makes him happy."

"Oh, shit," Lizzie mused to Sargent over the fabricated line. "They gave me the only cliché in the article."

"I love her," Sargent concluded. "She's a very bright and caring lady."

In 1992, Elizabeth touched on the subject of Sargent's once-secret sexuality for an interview with *The Advocate*, a national gay magazine. In Robert Pela's article, "The Legend of Lizzie," she said the topic never came up. She simply decided his sexuality was none of her business and that such discretion at times was the very definition of friendship.

In the same article, she also addressed the long-circulated gay rumors surrounding another *Bewitched* co-star: Agnes Moorehead, who died of cancer at sixty-seven in 1974, ten years after the show debuted and two years after it was cancelled. Again, the topic of sexuality, this time with Moorehead, as before with Sargent's, was just not something that arose.

Elizabeth then further explained how some members of the *Bewitched* cast and crew considered the series a metaphor for the social and cultural issues confronting those individuals outside the mainstream. *Samantha* was forced to conceal her supernatural heritage, and pretended to be mortal ("normal?"), like some gay men and women were forced to pretend they were straight. As far as Elizabeth was concerned, *Bewitched* was about repression and the subsequent frustrations that follow. She felt it was a positive message to relay in a clandestine manner, while she admitted that being raised in Hollywood exposed her to alternate lifestyles since her youth.

The Advocate then made note of her support of Sargent and the LGBT community in general and wondered if she felt she might be perceived as gay herself. But none of that phased Elizabeth; she had more important things with which to concern herself. For one, she appeared in the Gay Pride Parade in support of Sargent.

But she was considering playing a lesbian in a TV-movie that never went into production. It wasn't anything specific, but she thought portraying such a role might have proved intriguing.

Then again, she had already, years before, played a similarly-repressed character . . . in the guise of *Samantha Stephens* on *Bewitched*.

On April 15, 1989, Lizzie's fifty-ninth birthday, she and Bob Foxworth served as honorary co-chairs and hosts of the National Gay Rights Advocates Eleventh Anniversary Celebration, which was held at the Museum of Contemporary Art in Los Angeles, and whose honorees included Lizzie's devoted manager Barry Krost.

More than anything, the caring couple was heavily involved with amfAR, the American Foundation for AIDS Research, and APLA, AIDS Project Los Angeles.

In 1989, they attended "The Magic of Bob Mackie," a fashion presentation celebrating the designer's countless years in the business. Known for his work with Elizabeth's good friend Carol Burnett on *The Carol Burnett Show*, Mackie's event was held at the Century Plaza Hotel in Los Angeles, and also attended by Burnett, Cher, Jackie Collins, Joan Rivers, and Cheryl Ladd, all proceeds for which supported APLA's service to people with AIDS and AIDS-related complex (including mental health counseling, dental care, and in-home health care).

In 1987, Lizzie and Foxworth helped to raise more than $15,000 at a benefit performance of the stage play, *Tamara*, in honor of the Twenty-seventh Anniversary of Amnesty International.

She also joined him at the preview party of the eight-part PBS miniseries *Television*, which was given at the KCET-TV headquarters in L.A. According to a press packet for the program, this series documented the "evolution and the astonishing global power and impact of the world's most powerful communication medium."

The Los Angeles Times called Lizzie radiant in a gown bedazzled by her grandmother Rebecca Allen's diamond and emerald brooch. Foxworth wore Western accessories including a unique bolo tie, trimmed with silver feathers, and a diamond stud in his left ear. The latter, a gift from Lizzie, who once more worked that celebrated silent smile, as Foxworth explained how the stud symbolized his "freedom from *Falcon Crest.*"

Shortly before he left the series, however, Lizzie was invited to join the show for an arc of episodes, but she declined. Instead, another media sorceress, Kim Novak, who played a witch in the 1958 feature film, *Bell, Book, and Candle,* stepped into the part.

Lizzie had more important fish to fry, as when the opportunity to express and expand her political arena arrived in 1988. It was then she narrated *Cover Up: Behind the Iran-Contra Affair*, the feature film documentary that was critical of Reagan-Bush policies in Central America. She would later lend her voice to the follow-up film, *The Panama Deception*, which won the Oscar in 1992 for Best Feature Length Documentary.

Lizzie was dedicated to both films, but her work ethic was always sound. As she said in 1989: "Work takes a certain amount of concentration and energy, even though it always looks like I'm having fun (for example) when I'm looping. Luckily, I'm pretty good at it" (as Dan Weaver experienced in 1990 during Lizzie's looping session for *Face to Face*).

One day, Barbara Trent, director of both *Cover Up* and *The Panama Deception*, had asked Lizzie to loop a few lines of narration under slightly challenging working conditions. As Trent later told *People* magazine in 1995 after Lizzie's death: "We were too embarrassed to [ever] ask her to come back into our little Santa Monica studio, where the temperatures sometimes went up to 80 degrees."

But none of that mattered to Lizzie. She was hot for the topic. The message she was sending was in direct opposition to the Reagan administration and the man himself, who had long been a friend to her parents. But when it came time to vote for Reagan (in 1980 and again in 1984), her mother Elizabeth Allen refused to debate the issue. As Lizzie recalled in 1989, the conversation went something like this:

"Well, you and Daddy knew him."

"But your father must have talked about him to you, didn't he?"

"Are you kidding?" (Lizzie knew her father was wise enough not to debate such topics with her, but that didn't stop her from telling her mother exactly what she thought of Reagan.)

"If you asked him what time it was, he would tell you how to take a watch apart and put it back together again, but you'd never find out the time; never. Nothing's changed, except he's probably not smart enough to take apart a watch and put it back together."

"Oh, Elizabeth!" her mother protested (in much the same way Agnes Moorehead would at times object to Lizzie's forthright opinions on the set of *Bewitched*).

336

"Okay, sorry," Lizzie concluded to her Mom. "No more politics. Promise. Never mind."

"I just wouldn't get into it with her," she said in 1989. "But the man is loathsome." David White listened to Lizzie's Reagan rant and agreed.

He had worked with the former president on an episode of TV's *G. E. True Theatre* (aka *General Electric True Theatre*)—an anthology series Reagan hosted from 1953 to 1962. As David recalled, Marc Daniels (Bill Asher's precursor on *I Love Lucy*) directed the episode and, at one point between filming, various conversations transpired, periodically turning to the subject of politics, a hot topic between Reagan and White in particular:

"You know, David, what's good for General Electric is good for America."

"No, no, Ronny boy . . . *what's good for General Electric* is what's good for *Ronny Reagan* . . . and the stockholders. And besides . . . we always have Westinghouse."

Upon hearing David relay this interchange in 1989, Lizzie laughed and said, "I never met (Reagan), and I probably would have hated him . . . I *hope* I would have hated him."

"He's just shallow and incompetent," continued White, who was angry with Reagan and the first George Bush on an entirely different level. His son, Jonathan White, after whom *Larry Tate's* son was named on *Bewitched*, died in the Pan Am Flight 103 incident over Lockerbie, Scotland in December 1988. It was Pan American World Airways' third daily scheduled transatlantic flight from London Heathrow Airport to New York's John F. Kennedy International Airport. On Wednesday, December 21, 1988, the aircraft flying this route—a Boeing 747-121 registered N739PA and named "Clipper Maid of the Seas"—was destroyed by a bomb, killing all 243 passengers and sixteen crew members. Eleven people in Lockerbie were also killed as large sections of the plane fell in the town and destroyed several houses, bringing total fatalities to 270. As a result, the event is also known as the "Lockerbie Bombing." During the 2011 Libyan civil war a former government official claimed that Muammar Gaddafi had personally ordered the attack. (According to *The Los Angeles Times*, Abdel Bassett Ali Megrahi, the Libyan intelligence officer convicted in the bombing, who denied any role in the plot, died in Tripoli, Libya, May 20, 2012.)

For David, it was a personal attack of another nature and a tragedy from which he never recovered. As he told Lizzie in 1989, only a short time after the incident, he received a letter of sympathy from the White House, specifically, from Reagan's successor, George H. W. Bush:

> It arrived on my birthday, about four or five days after the parents of the victims of Pan Am 103 went down and met him. And by then I'm sure he thought *I better get my ass in gear. "A kinder gentler nation" is what I said we were going to have repeatedly.*

But when David opened letter, he was unimpressed. In fact, he laughed. Or as he put it, "I cracked up." He was indignantly amused by the cardboard backing that was placed behind the letter in order for it not to wrinkle. "So I can hang it up in my den," David assumed. "They thought I should think it's a big deal. And I don't think it's a big deal."

"That's incredible," added Lizzie who expressed her own fury about the Pan Am incident. "I was angry when it happened. And when I realized that Jonathan was on the plane, I just couldn't believe it. When I called *Mouse* (*Bewitched* producer Marvin Miller), I said, 'Are you sure?' He said, 'Yeah . . . I talked to David at the gym.' "

But now David was right in front of her, in near tears. As he went on to assess, "In October of 1988, they [international officials] knew there were bombs (on the plane) that they put in cassettes. I have an article from *Newsweek* [that states this]. They were warned a couple of times, not just for Helsinki."

According to the Report of the President's Commission on Aviation Security and Terrorism, on December 5, 1988 (sixteen days prior to the Pan Am attack), the Federal Aviation Administration (FAA) issued a security bulletin saying that on that day a man with an Arabic accent had telephoned the U.S. Embassy in Helsinki, Finland, and had told them that a Pan Am flight from Frankfurt to the United States would be blown up within the next two weeks by someone associated with the Abu Nidal Organization. He said a Finnish woman would carry the bomb on board as an unwitting courier.

David concluded with a heavy heart and even heavier words, that he missed his son immensely, and was clearly not pleased with those he thought were responsible for his death:

Bless his heart. I wanted him to be his own person. [But] I say you don't need an enemy when you have a government like ours. I have no faith in this country at all. Individual people, I like, but [not the] people who run the government.

Then, in a swift shift to help lighten the mood, David turned to Elizabeth and asked:

"So how many children do you have now?"

"The same three," she replied. "Bob [Foxworth] and I finally went, '*Uh, no, I don't think so*' [with regard to the possibility of them having more children when they first got together in 1974]. He has two, and I have three, and they're all grown. They're wonderful. We've got five between us, and that's more than enough."

"You don't want to raise children any more, do you?" White continued in jest.

"Every time we get tempted," Lizzie answered, "this friend of mine, who's a costume designer, Frances Hays, one of my best friends, says, 'Call B.A.' And I said, 'What's that?' And she said, 'Babies Anonymous.'"

While Lizzie was working on *Bewitched* in 1960s, Ronald Reagan hosted another anthology series, this one a western syndicated show called *Death Valley Days*. She was more than familiar with his work and his persona, and subsequently reveled in performing one particular scene from her 1985 NBC TV-movie, *Between the Darkness and the Dawn* when her character *Abigail Foster* made sarcastic reference to Reagan in a dinner-table scene. *Abigail* had been in an epileptic coma for twenty years. Upon awakening in 1985, she learned of America's new leader, and was shocked. "Ronald Reagan is president?!" she said incredulously, in response to the election of a former actor as the world's most powerful decision-maker.

Twenty-two

~

Final Exams

"I keep thinking about how I might have cancer."

—*Blanche Taylor Moore*, as played by Elizabeth in *Black Widow Murders: The Blanche Taylor Moore Story* (1993)

One of Lizzie's favorite *Bewitched* guest stars was Christopher George, who played the lead in the first season episode, "George the Warlock":

Endora seizes an opportunity to dissolve *Samantha's* mortal marriage by enlisting the assistance of the supernaturally suave warlock named *George* (Christopher) to romance her daughter.

Like many of the show's guests in its first two years—Adam West (*Batman*), James Doohan (*Star Trek*), Billy Mumy (*Lost in Space*), and Bill Daily (*I Dream of Jeannie*), Christopher George went on to star in a weekly series of his own: *The Immortal*, a fanciful, if short-lived (only sixteen episodes) take on *The Fugitive*, a wanted-man story with a positive twist:

Ben Richards (George) is a test-car driver whose blood contains certain miraculous antibodies that allow him to live forever. In the interim, *Ben* searches for his long lost brother *Jason* (never seen), in the hope that he too may contain the same rare form of blood-type; while the wealthy senior *Arthur Maitland* (David Brian) who once rejected a blood transfusion from *Ben*, is now in hot pursuit to track him down.

Ben, like *George*, the warlock, was immortal, as were the entire band of charmers on *Bewitched*. None the least of which was *Samantha*, as played by Lizzie who leaves her own immortal legacy with a body of work that echoed and foreshadowed portions of her reality that warrants further examination.

In 1976, she appeared in the TV-movie *Dark Victory*, a remake of the classic 1939 feature film starring her friend Bette Davis.

TV producer *Katherine Merrill* (Lizzie) is stricken with a brain tumor. Consumed with work, *Katherine* ignores her personal life and the symptoms of an impending physical disorder until finally collapsing at a cocktail party and tumbling down a flight of stairs. Once hospitalized, she falls in love with the attending physician, *Dr. Michael Grant* (Anthony Hopkins).

Here, Lizzie takes the viewer through the varied emotions connected with a devastating illness (surprise, frustration, anger), and the challenges of maintaining an intimate relationship through that period. In the end, and just as in the original Bette Davis movie, *Katherine* dies. But in the last few moments of Lizzie's edition, *Katherine* turns to *Dr. Grant*, smiles, and the camera freeze-frames on the love light in her eyes. It's a bittersweet ending to one of Lizzie's better post-*Bewitched* films.

Nine years later, in 1985, she starred in another TV-movie, *Between the Darkness and the Dawn*:

Abigail Foster (Lizzie) awakens from a decades-long viral-induced epileptic coma. She finds her sister (Karen Grassle) has married her boyfriend (Michael Goodwin), and her mother (Dorothy McGuire) has become obsessed with being her caregiver. Fortunately, in time, *Abigail* manages to foster an alternate happiness with the new man in her life (James Naughton).

The ending for *Between the Darkness and the Dawn* is less bitter and more sweet than it is with *Dark Victory*, but a glaring discrepancy detracts from this movie's credibility beyond its far-reaching premise (although similar events have transpired). The story opens in 1965, when actress Lori Birdsong portrays a seventeen-year-old *Abigail* who is soon stricken into her catatonic state. The setting then swiftly shifts forward twenty years, and Lizzie is seen playing *Abigail*, who is now apparently thirty-seven years old.

Although Lizzie blurred the age of her documented birth, April 15, 1933, by the time this film aired, December 23, 1985, she was in reality fifty-two years old. Actors sometimes play younger characters. It's an unwritten Hollywood rule. But it's a bit of a stretch for Lizzie to have played a thirty-seven-year-old in the later period suggested in *Between the Darkness and the Dawn*.

However, she embraced the opportunity to change the face of time; as she had in 1992, when according to Tom McCartney, she registered as forty-nine years old for a medical examination during filming of the TV movie *The Black Widow Murders*. That meant she would have been born in 1943, and fifty-two years old when she died in 1995. But that didn't measure up either.

When Elizabeth died in 1995, writer Lynn Elber reported in *The Associated Press* that Lizzie was fifty-seven years old. That meant she would have been born in 1938 which, as previously documented, is simply not true.

Lizzie and younger brother Skip were in England in 1939 while their father Robert Montgomery worked on *The Earl of Chicago*. They were then shipped back to the States when he was called to service for World War II. They traveled on the S.S. Arandora Star, sailed from Southampton, England for New York on September 1, 1939 and arrived in New York City on September 12, 1939. According to the passenger list chart lines that were posted on www.harpiesbizzare.com, one of the top *Bewitched* websites, Lizzie was then six years old, and born in 1933, which was also her documented birth year in early studio biographies. All of which means that, in reality, she had just turned sixty-two on April 15, 1995 three days short of a month before she passed away on May 18.

In August of 1975, Elizabeth broached the birthday subject with an interview for *TV-Movies Today* magazine, claiming she always told the truth about her age because of her third most influential relative: Rebecca Allen. As Lizzie explained it, when her grandmother was sixty, Becca told everyone she was sixty-five. "People always think you're older anyway," she said. "They therefore think I'm really seventy and are impressed with how youthful I appear.'"

When asked her age, Lizzie replied, "I was born on April 15, 1936, which has since become Income Tax Day and therefore is easy to remember." So that would mean she was fifty-nine when she died in 1995 which, again, is untrue.

More age-old tales were spun on the set of her 1985 CBS TV-movie *Amos* the premise for which dealt with, appropriately enough, the elderly residents at a nursing home. According to Montgomery archivist Thomas McCartney, Lizzie took a particular liking to Pat Morita, who co-starred in this film as one of the senior residents that was abused by Lizzie's maniacal nurse *Daisy Daws*. Morita had found fame late in life, first as *Arnold* on *Happy Days* (ABC, 1974–1984) and then with *The Karate Kid* movies of the 1980s. On the *Amos* set, Morita, who was born in 1932 and died in 2005, realized he and Lizzie were approximately the same age, and while he portrayed the elderly *Tanaka*, she played a middle-aged *Daisy*.

Morita laughed off the same-age reference, claiming it must have been the water in Japan that helped him retain his youth. Lizzie blushed and made every attempt to downplay the somewhat awkward assumption. "She'd get real embarrassed about the age comparison," McCartney explains, claiming that makeup had contributed to her youthful appearance and Morita's older look. "But no one was buying it. She had a naturally young, blithe spirit," he says.

She also had a way with numbers. Upon further early influence from her beloved grandmother Becca, Lizzie frequented the race track and loved to gamble, which is really what her life became. And although *Dark Victory* and *Between the Darkness and the Dawn* had comparatively uneven endings, both films foreshadowed what would later become Lizzie's darkest hours.

In the final analysis, it was never Lizzie's performance as *Samantha* or any of her characterizations or unique talents that were in question. It was her *choices* for certain roles, before and particularly beyond *Bewitched* that proved to be intriguing, if not downright mind-boggling. But her friend and TV-movie co-star Ronny Cox wouldn't have had it any other way. She was "an actress, and the fun is in playing the roles that stretch you," he says. In the decades since Cox was the affable dad on TV's *Apple's Way*, (CBS, 1974–1975), he's mostly played "bad guys," similar to Lizzie's choices in films like *The Legend of Lizzie Borden* and *The Black Widow Murders*. And although not evil in nature, her character in *A Case of Rape* was eons away from *Samantha* on *Bewitched*. "Hell!" Cox proclaims, such roles are "*twenty*

times more fun to play," because films like *Rape,* he says, give actors a chance to showcase and expand their talents.

Case in point: When former *Charlie's Angels* star Farrah Fawcett appeared in NBC's shocking TV-movie, *The Burning Bed,* directed by Robert Greenwald, this film was based on the book by Faith McNulty, with a teleplay by Rose Leiman Goldemberg:

> *Francine Hughes* (Fawcett) is the loving mother of three children. But she is also the battered wife of *Mickey Hughes* (Paul Le Mat), who is both verbally and physically abusive. However, whenever *Francine* reaches out for help, she's turned away, and ultimately becomes incapable of bringing *Mickey* to justice. So, one terrifying night, after he rapes her, she sets their bed on fire with him still in it, asleep. As a result, *Francine* goes on trial for her life.

Just as in Lizzie's *Case,* Fawcett (who worked with Cox on *Apple's Way*) played an abused woman who is forced to defend herself within a closed-minded judicial system. Both actresses were allowed the opportunity to utilize what Cox calls their theatrical "muscles" for what became physically demanding and emotionally draining performances.

For some *Bewitched* fans, watching Lizzie—their once-cheerful witch-with-a-twitch—get raped in *Case* may have been a traumatic experience. But Cox believes that was the "essence of why she desperately needed" to do such roles—so fans would "realize that this person on the screen" is only a character played by an actor. Often times, actors are mostly identified with one particular character, as it was and remains with Lizzie and *Samantha.* But according to Cox, too many fans of actors mistake "brilliant acting for the person."

In further defense of Lizzie's post-comedic *Bewitched* performances, Cox poses:

> You can't play *Lizzie Borden?* You can't play an ax murderer? You can't play *King Lear* who goes crazy? I mean, that's what acting is! Lizzie didn't want to walk around for the rest of her life being *Samantha!* It's asking way too much to say, "No, no, no . . . don't be anything else! Just be *Samantha* for the rest of your life! I can't stand it if you do anything but being *Samantha!*"

"God, that's prison!" Cox bellows, figuratively, adding, "Slit your wrists!"

How would Cox compare Lizzie's childhood "play-acting" performance as *Snow White* (for her grandmother Becca) to her portrayal of the *Wolf* in her Westlake School's French language production of *Little Red Riding Hood*?

"In playing *Snow White*," Cox deduces, "you still have all these people that love you and care for you and you're dealing with morality and things like that. At the end of the day you're still dealing with dwarfs and the wicked [queen], so you're dealing in fantasy."

Yet, he loves "the lightweight stuff, too," especially his friend's much later and more professional fanciful role as *Samantha*:

> Lizzie was brilliant on *Bewitched*, but that tapped like this much (gestures small space between index finger and thumb) of her talent. And I talked with her about this, too. She could play that character and phone it in. One of the things that Lizzie knew about acting [were] the tricks of the craft. She had that special spark . . . her personality sort of shone through in roles like *Samantha*. And in lots of ways she could just get by on that persona . . . that personality. But that wasn't all of her talent, only a measure of it.

Post-*Bewitched*, Elizabeth certainly leaned toward those edgier roles, more times than not, playing people with malevolent traits. Her manager Barry Krost explained in 2001 on MSNBC's *Headliners & Legends*: "If there was a wicked gene in a character, odds are, Lizzie would do it."

On A&E's *Biography* in 1999, Robert Foxworth said Lizzie was "thrilled" with the idea that she surprised her fans and detractors with Emmy-nominated performances as in *The Legend of Lizzie Borden*. To have viewers accept her in such a non-*Samantha* role and subsequently respect the theatrical diversity that she would bring to such a role as an accomplished actress was "probably one of her great victories in life."

The Legend of Lizzie Borden was helmed by Paul Wendkos, a favorite director of Lizzie's, who also guided her in the 1958 "Bitter Heritage" episode of *Playhouse 90*, and the 1979 TV-movie, *Act of Violence*.

Director Boris Sagal was another of her favorite directors, guiding her and Ronny Cox through *A Case of Rape* in 1974. Before that, he directed her in the 1960 TV *Kraft Theatre* production of *The Spiral Staircase*, in 1978's

The Awakening Land, and in 1981's *When the Circus Came to Town*, the last which stood out from the rest, if only due to lighter content.

The actual driving force behind *Circus* was legendary producer Robert Halmi, who conceived of the story idea and was responsible for casting not only Lizzie, but acting legend Christopher Plummer, best known for his performance in the 1965 classic feature, *The Sound of Music*. By then, Halmi had produced more than 140 feature and TV films (and went on to produce countless more), and was considered one of the industry's busiest and most respected producers. As he revealed to *The Toronto Star* in 1981, Halmi viewed working with the former-*Bewitched* star as "a wonderful opportunity for Liz to do what she does best. She's fantastic. She makes you laugh, she makes you cry. She's physical. She's sexy."

While Halmi's words could have just as easily described what Lizzie brought to playing *Samantha* on a weekly basis, her *Circus* co-star Christopher Plummer would never as willingly embrace a regular TV role. "It's bad news, I think, for someone like me," he told *The Toronto Star*. "You get so terribly identified with one role you can't be taken serious as an actor."

For years, Plummer was identified with the role of *Captain von Trapp* in *The Sound of Music*, just as Lizzie had been identified for so long with *Bewitched*. In 2011, he won the Academy Award for Best Supporting Actor for *Beginners*, in which he portrayed *Hal Fields*, a dying gay senior who comes out of the closet.

Four decades ago, both actors should have been pleased with the critical praise showered upon *When the Circus Came to Town*, which proved to be a nice addition to their already impressive resumes. In his 1981 review in *The Toronto Star*, critic Bill Kaufman said the film "convincingly manages to develop *Mary's* character and how she becomes involved with the raggle-taggle touring circus. Plummer plays *Duke Royal*, owner and ringmaster of the shabby big top, a flamboyant man who ultimately changes *Mary's* life with boy love and a guiding hand. The progression of *Mary's* involvement with circus life is skillfully fleshed out under the guidance of veteran director Boris Sagal."

In 1989, Lizzie said her performance in *Circus* was "tough work, physically, but so much fun to do." For many scenes, she was outfitted in a heavy headdress, and she wore fishnet stockings with runs and holes, in order to better authenticate the slight seediness of that particular circus portrayed in the movie. Prior to filming, she spent several weeks training with legendary stuntman Bob Yerkes and his son, Mark, who had trained actors, singers, etc. to participate in TV shows like *Circus of the Stars* (the era's answer to today's *Dancing with the Stars*). He's also worked on feature films like *Back to the Future*, *Star Wars: Return of the Jedi*, and *Hook* (and he currently hosts stunt training, on invitation only, at his Los Angeles home).

She always knew that certain productions would prove challenging. Actors are never sure of what lies ahead until the day of the shoot. Certainly, timing is imperative and performers must trust their colleagues on the set, behind and in front of the camera. In Lizzie's case, she was pleased that she would be allowed to do some of the stunts they had planned for her stand-in.

For example, she had donned a clown's garb for a few *Circus* scenes, but according to Thomas McCartney, she confessed at the time: "I have never been a clown person. Maybe I was scared badly by a clown when I was a child."

The "fear-factor" in that last sentence may have been some subconscious allusion to the intimating presence her father pervaded over her young life. It was a character flaw that Robert Montgomery may have developed by way of the tragic loss of his daughter, Martha Bryant, Lizzie's infant sister. Into this mix there were the other tragic losses in the early Montgomery lineage, namely with regard to Henry Montgomery, Lizzie's grandfather.

Author and genealogist James Pylant concludes:

[Henry's] suicide clearly had an impact on Robert Montgomery's life, and it would have extended into the relationship with his own children. Perhaps what is seen as his jealousy of Elizabeth's success as an actress was his resenting of her achieving fame too easily because she was Robert Montgomery's daughter. His father's early demise led Robert to toil as a railroad mechanic and an oil tanker deckhand before his big break in Hollywood, and maybe he felt Elizabeth hadn't earned her dues. And the death of his first child, Martha, may have made him more emotionally distant to Elizabeth.

Consequently, she may have attempted to earn those dues and her father's approval, while also igniting his fury by later fanning a bigger star than his via *Bewitched*, the lighter fare of which she then replaced with roles like *Lizzie Borden*.

Classic TV author, curator, and radio show host Ed Robertson offers these thoughts:

Once *Bewitched* ended she was looking for projects that would allow her to grow as an actress, and further develop her dramatic skills, which she was not always able to do as *Samantha*, particularly in the last couple years of the show. I don't think she was necessarily trying to "shed" her image as *Samantha*, but I do believe she wanted to show audiences (and for that matter, casting directors and the like) that she could do much more than *Samantha*. That's why I think she did *A Case of Rape*, which had aired in the year 1974, and I think that's what may have attracted her to doing *The Legend of Lizzie Borden*. That, plus the project itself had a strong pedigree. Paul Wendkos had already established himself as an excellent director, plus Fritz Weaver (who played Borden's father), through his work on such shows as *The Twilight Zone*, was an accomplished, respected stage actor. I don't know whether Fritz worked with her father, but I imagine Elizabeth would have relished the opportunity to work with someone like him . . . The Lizzie Borden trial was, for its time, considered the *trial of the century*, as was the O. J. Simpson case more than a century later. Like Lizzie Borden, O. J. Simpson became a pariah, even though he was acquitted. And of course, a few years after doing Lizzie Borden, and about fifteen years before the Simpson murder trial, Elizabeth did a TV-movie with O. J. for CBS [*A Killing Affair*, 1977].

As to how all of this to relates to Elizabeth's performance on *Bewitched*, Robertson believes it's

kind of an *apples and oranges* comparison. The subject matter of Lizzie Borden is much darker and more disturbing than anything she'd done on *Bewitched*. Which goes back to my earlier point: It appears she was looking for projects that would challenge her as an actress, as *The Legend of Lizzie Borden* certainly did. Given that the movie portrays Borden as having committed the murders [the case, though closer to closures, remains unsolved, even after all these years], it was Elizabeth's job to somehow make this cold, calculating, mercurial woman evoke sympathy from the viewers, even though she committed these heinous acts. To her credit, I think she did.

I'm sure some (of her fans) were shocked, especially those who may have been clinging to her wholesome image as *Samantha*. But I'm just as sure that those who loved her as an actress, taking into her account her body of work prior to and after *Bewitched*, were pleased and mesmerized by her performance.

When the Circus Came to Town at least offered a glimmer of the comedic sparkle Lizzie presented on *Bewitched*. The 1981 movie was made in association with her production company, Entheos Unlimited Productions. According to Roland L. Smith's book, *Sweethearts of the '60s* (S.P.I. Books, 1993), Lizzie had signed a deal with CBS in 1979 that paid her $275,000 per film, an amount that would increase over the years. Add to that the shrewd investments and stellar profits from *Bewitched* (of which she and Bill Asher were part owners) and her annual income became substantial.

However, as Smith observed, retaining her integrity and remaining visible in pertinent television films wasn't always easy, "sometimes even the most determined efforts were in vain."

Plainly stated, it was challenging for Lizzie to find a good script. By 1981, she had one more movie left in the CBS deal, and she was considering several ideas, one of which was a comedy, but nothing was a lock. But then the *Circus Came to Town* which, as Tom McCartney says, Lizzie viewed as "a romantic comedy," the first such lighter concept she would consider since *Bewitched*.

The idea for *Circus* was generated by one sentence from Doug Chapin, who produced her previous film, *Belle Starr*. She was ready to drop the project altogether until writer Larry Grusin impressed her with his script, which McCartney says CBS executive William Self was initially apprehensive about sending her way. It was then her manager Barry Krost, Chapin's business partner, who then suggested she read it.

She did so, and subsequently hired director Boris Sagal, who besides guiding her through *A Case of Rape* and *The Awakening Land*, had also directed the 1980 TV-movie edition of *The Diary of Anne Frank* with Melissa Gilbert (of *Little House on the Prairie* fame), and would soon helm 1981's *Masada* mini-series (with Peter O'Toole and Peter Strauss, of *Rich Man, Poor Man*).

Krost had played an interconnecting role in Lizzie's post-*Bewitched* life and career, protecting and guiding both her personal and professional deci-sions. She trusted him implicitly (it was in his apartment where Lizzie and Bob Foxworth secretly tied the knot on January 28, 1993), and Krost had enormous respect for her as a client and as a human being.

In 1999, author Michael Anketell published, *Heavenly Bodies: Remember-ing Hollywood and Fashion's Favorite AIDS Benefit* (Taylor, 1999). In the book, producer Doug Chapin, Krost's business partner, explains how in 1986 Liz-zie and actor Roddy McDowall (who died of lung cancer in 1998) were the first two celebrities to lend their support to the initial Los Angeles fashion-show (displaying the 1930s Hollywood designes of Adrian) to benefits HIV/ AIDS awareness. According to what Chapin told Anketell, Elizabeth attended every one of their events up until the time of her death.

Other celebrities who attended the Adrian function, included Carol Kane, Brenda Vaccaro, Bess Armstrong, JoBeth Williams, and Jackie Col-lins. Anketell writes:

> Had it not been for the valiant efforts of a few of Hollywood's favorite stars and their managers, Barry Krost and Doug Chapin, who encouraged them, neither Hollywood nor the fashion world would have taken any but passing notice of our efforts. Without stars, there would have been little press cov-erage and our message would not get out. But on the night of the Adrian show, the stars did come.

Anketell went on to explain how Lizzie was a stand-out participant:

> Possibly our most popular star that evening was Elizabeth Montgomery, the beloved *Samantha* of *Bewitched*. Elizabeth was the daughter of film star Rob-ert Montgomery and the wife of actors Gig Young and Robert Foxworth. She had starred in a couple of dozen TV movies in which she was often a victimized woman who would find her personal strength, though she also portrayed Western bandit Belle Starr and parent-hacker Lizzie Borden.

Krost then talked about Lizzie's personal involvement in bringing awareness to AIDS and other causes:

> Elizabeth became very political and very caring and yet, at the same time, always was strangely shy for a lady who had all her life been around press and Hollywood. She protected her private life and she found the spotlight, at times, very uncomfortable, unless it was about a specific project—a

movie or a cause she believed in. She was one of the first public people to get involved in the very early days of the fight against HIV.

I think Elizabeth was on the side of anybody, any group of people that she thought was being treated inappropriately. But she was still shy. I remember when we arrived that first year at the Adrian event. There was a press line outside and she suggested we stop the car, get out and go in the side entrance. I said, "It sort of defeats the point of your being here." And she said, "Oh, yes, you're right," and she went in the front way, through the press.

In 1999, on *Bewitched: The E! True Hollywood Story*, Krost said: "If she was your friend she was there, good times, bad times. She was there. And if she was in your life, somehow you went to bed at night and the world was just a little bit safer. And very few people have that effect on you."

In 2001, on MSNBC's *Headliners & Legends*, he added: "When HIV came along, not only in a charitable sense, raising money and awareness . . . but also one-on-one with people; she spent an awful lot of time that way." She cherished her private life with, for example, her children of whom, as Krost explained, she cared a great deal. "It's a very delicate balance between being a star and what happened in the house. And I think she really protected that and felt very vulnerable."

Lizzie's son Billy Asher, Jr. relayed on the same show: "She felt a responsibility with her life and her career as being a celebrity . . . to use that at times to make other people aware of issues that she felt were important."

In all, there are those who are critical of celebrities, specifically, actors, intermingling their public personas with politics, believing that the twain should never meet. But during his appearance at the Los Angeles Festival of Books on April 22, 2012, Steven J. Ross, the author of *Hollywood Left and Right*, explained it this way:

I would say yes, you can have celebrities divorced from politics if you have business leaders divorced from politics, if you have all the CEOs in America divorced and if you have every other American divorced. They are citizens first. They are actors second. Why should we single out actors? And the reason why most people don't like it is nobody wants their dream factory burst. We all have our celebrity images. We all have our belief of who they are, and as early as 1918 you had people like Sid Grauman, who founded the famous Grauman's Chinese Theatre where we have all the handprints and the footprints, telling actors to keep your mouths shut when it comes to politics, because the moment you open your mouth you alienate half your audience.

Certainly, there was little sign of audience alienation when Lizzie's fans turned out by the droves when she, if posthumously, received her star at the Hollywood Walk of Fame ceremony, January 4, 2008. Her fans, co-workers, and family, including her three beloved children, were there to partake in the honor.

Today, Billy Asher, Jr. is the proprietor of a highly successful and respected music business (Asher Guitars). Rebecca Asher is a renowned TV script supervisor (*Raising Hope, Mad Men, Samantha Who?*), and Robert Asher is an artisan of many talents and crafts who at times works with his brother Billy (as does Bob Foxworth's son Bo). In one way or another, they each have followed in their parents' professional footsteps.

In looking back at the development of Lizzie's character, she evidently believed in at least some form of positive higher-consciousness that somehow guided her decision-making process with her life and career. It may not have always been a consistent belief, but it was a belief nonetheless. And although she may have enjoyed pulling Agnes Moorehead's religious leg during their *Bewitched* era, it was clear she was no slouch in the spiritual department, even in the most basic or sporadic way.

When she and her brother Skip were children, their grandmother Becca instructed them to pray when their parents were away. It was a solid, traditional way to handle a child's temporary, if intensely emotional feelings. But as Lizzie explained in the February 1970 edition of *TV Radio Mirror* magazine, she and Skip never said nightly prayers, nor did they attend church on a regular basis. "I suppose we believed in God," she acknowledged, but ". . . in our own way." She and Skip apparently did at least attend Sunday school and looked forward to going. But to her the Bible stories were more like fairytales. She didn't really take them seriously.

And by 1970, that seemed to fit. She was no longer a child of a star, but a star herself, many times over. She was also a mature adult, on her third marriage, with three children of her own. Her childhood days with Skip were long gone, and even though her child-like manner remained, she now faced adult decisions, and was responsible for leading the way for three little people who would one day become adults themselves.

By this time, she had become disillusioned with the way many parents of the day instilled the mortal fear of a condemning God who took pleasure in punishing bad children. "Using fright to teach religion seems to me to be very unhealthy," she said. "After all, if we can't base our beliefs in a Supreme Being on love, that how can any of us truly believe?" Lizzie also believed that many people turned to religion out of a deep need, and thought it was productive that they employed their faith to help deal with the turmoil of Vietnam and the race riots. Her three children, including Rebecca, just born in 1969, were then too young to ask about God. If they had wondered, Lizzie hadn't a clue as to how she would have replied. But she did want her kids to attend Sunday school like she and Skip had when they were young. "I feel that it is a good foundation for any child," she said. "After all, even as a piece of literature alone, there is so much that is fine and wonderful in the Bible."

"I think of God as the beauty in life," she concluded, ". . . it's loving and being loved. It's feeling good inside because you are living the life of a good person. Maybe it's a good idea to try new ways of looking at the subject."

It was a fresh perspective that helped to close an age-old generation gap between her and her conservative-minded parents. Years before, when she was only twenty, they had been pleased with her decision to at least be baptized if only shortly before her marriage to Fred Cammann, and even though that union ended in divorce.

In May of 1970, she addressed it all with reporter Nancy Winelander of *TV Picture Life* magazine. The conversation mixed religion, her marriages to Asher as well as Gig Young, and again, raising her children. The article described Lizzie as Episcopalian. Young was a Protestant; Asher, Jewish. As she intoned, both she and Asher "love our religion. Bill isn't the most religious man in the world. He doesn't go for a lot of the ritual, but he believes deeply in his Jewish religion and cultural heritage. I really haven't been a practicing anything for years. Still, I don't want to divorce myself from my heritage either."

Yet, she was surprised at how "meddlesome people can be," when it came to raising a family under one particular faith or the other. "After all," she added, "whose business is it how our children are raised?" But at the time, it was an issue, one that she had not confronted before. As Winelander explained, Lizzie had no children by the much older Young. If they had had kids, apparently, there would not have been any religious quandary with the Protestant Young. [Note: All Episcopalians are Protestants but not all Protestants are Episcopalians. Protestants include virtually all Christian sects outside of Roman Catholicism: Episcopalians, Baptists, Presbyterians, Methodists, Lutherans, etc.] Lizzie told Winelander:

> Gig wouldn't have cared anyway. He was very easy-going on matters like that. He had kind of a live-and-let-live philosophy. I think he would have left it pretty much up to me, no matter what he had been. Besides, our marital problems became so overwhelming the question of christening children just never had a chance to arise.

Former TV actor and present day Episcopalian priest Peter Ackerman is a happy anomaly with a unique perspective on Lizzie's persona, spiritual and otherwise. As the son of Screen Gems head and *Bewitched* executive producer Harry Ackerman and *Father Knows Best* actress, Elinor Donahue, Peter started acting on shows like *The New Gidget*, the 1980s syndicated reboot of his father's 1960s ABC/Sally Field sitcom (a few episodes of which were directed by Bill Asher). After a time, however, he became disinterested with acting on-screen (as did Lizzie, at least for a while), mostly because he found it more challenging to create and sustain a character on the stage. So after Peter married in the late 1980s, he began working in production for TV commercials, music videos, and in various other such capacities. This new career path culminated with him serving as a producer's assistant on the second and third seasons of TV's mega-hit, *Friends* (NBC, 1994–2005).

With *Friends*, Peter was happy at home (with his wife and now two children), but his vocational life was lacking. He subsequently embarked on a spiritual journey that lead him back to the Episcopal Church he grew up in, "where priests can be married and women." After an especially difficult day on the set of *Friends*, he made a dramatic and desperate plea to God: "I know I will like whatever You have in store. I am ready to do it. Just show me what YOU want. I am tired of trying to figure it out on my own."

So, today, he's not only an Episcopalian priest, but a married Episcopalian priest with a family; while in the 1960s, for him:

> *Bewitched* felt like family and was. After all, Bill Asher and Liz came over to the house a lot with their kids, Willie, Robert, and Rebecca, and they became the godparents to my youngest brother, Chris. There was really no difference that I saw growing up with *Samantha* on TV and Liz who came over our house. She was friendly, had a sense of humor and definitely had that fun/wicked 'pixie' sense about her.

Quite young at the time, Peter did not have a sense of Lizzie's eminent heritage, but he was always impressed by her unaffected disposition. It was a trait he says she shared with her brother Skip, with whom one day, Peter, his father, Lizzie and others had shared a limo, "probably all going to a Ram's game," he says. As Peter recalls, Skip "was a relatively quiet, thoughtful, and serious man, but not aloof or anything. To me, a kid, he was just a guy."

Peter has a theory as to how the Montgomery siblings absorbed the same approachable demeanor:

> Social scientists will one day figure this all out, but remember back in those days there were no paparazzi hunters. My mom (Elinor Donahue) and I would go grocery shopping or to get an ice cream and people would ask her, "Aren't you . . . ?" and sometimes ask for an autograph. But it was no big deal. As people began playing the *game* of Hollywood, and making themselves less accessible, that's when the mess happened that we have today with celebrity. Suffice it to say, I assume Liz, like my parents, never played "the game."

Former child star and *Bewitched* guest actor Eric Scott has a contrasting take on Lizzie's affability. Best known as *Ben Walton* on *The Waltons* (CBS's long-running and critically acclaimed family series; 1972–1979), Eric appeared on the *Samantha* episode, "Out of the Mouths of Babes," which aired in 1971. This was right around the same time he was cast in the CBS

TV-movie *The Homecoming,* which ultimately was the backdoor *Waltons* pilot that led to his weekly stint as *Ben.* In "Babe," on *Bewitched,* he played *Herbie,* a basketball-loving neighborhood boy who befriends a shrunken and pre-teen *Darrin* who is made so by one of *Endora's* manipulative spells. Eric had several scenes with Lizzie in this episode, and remembers her fine balance of humility and sophistication on the set:

> I thought she was one of the most beautiful ladies I had ever seen. I had worked with people like Elke Sommer and other actresses that were just gorgeous. But there was something about Elizabeth that was just *wow.* And at the end of the production, when I asked everyone for their autograph, she wrote hers like a movie star. And she carried herself so very regally.

Like Lizzie, Eric retained a strong sense of normalcy amidst the glitter of Hollywood. After *The Waltons* ended its original CBS run in 1979 (only to return as various CBS and NBC TV reunion movies until 1997), acting roles were few and far between. Forced to explore alternative sources of income, he began work for Chase Messenger Service in Los Angeles. Today, some forty years after his first scenes as *Ben Walton* and *Herbie* on *Bewitched,* he is now the proprietor of Chase, and acts periodically. He found TV stardom as a child and business success as an adult, while remaining cordial and unassuming in every decade—a demeanor he credits to his parents, who raised him within a solid moral structure. His family was not wealthy like the Montgomerys, and his mother (who served as his manager) and father (a hairstylist) struggled to make ends meet. But ultimately, the Scott brood triumphed, most assuredly because they worked as a team. He knows why he survived Hollywood unscathed, but is amazed as to how Lizzie managed so well to retain her firm grip on priorities.

> I don't know how she did it. I really don't. Someone was looking out for her. And hopefully it was her parents. I know that's what did it for me. As a parent of three children myself, I've realized it's the environment that we create for our kids that dictates how they're going to end up. If you give them a lot of love and give them a lot of structure, they thrive. If you have them vacillating and trying to figure out too much, they falter. My eldest is in college. My middle one is in grade school. And my youngest Jeremy is just seven, the same age I was when I started acting. In fact, he's a mini-me.

He reminds me so much of myself. He's a Cub Scout and I'm a Cub Scout leader. He plays guitar, is taking up drums, and will soon start to play the keyboard.

Jeremy also plays baseball and basketball, just like Eric's character *Herbie* did on *Bewitched*. "It's funny," Eric goes on to say, "Jeremy has been in baseball for the last two years, and our family became close friends with the coach's family. And I had recently attended a *Waltons* reunion in Virginia, so my wife Cindy explained to the coach's wife that we'd be out of town for a while for the reunion. And they were like, 'Why?' "

"Because," Mrs. Scott replied, "Eric was on the show," a fact about which the coach's wife had not a clue. Since that time, and upon learning of Eric's childhood fame, other parents of kids on the team have approached him in awe and said, "I just heard."

"I live in a small town and the word got out," he says with a laugh. "And the recognition is actually very sweet, but I would never want my kids to live in that shadow. So, I don't know how Elizabeth's parents did it . . . how she grew up so well . . . without being in *that* shadow . . . or even if that shadow was attainable."

Twenty-three

~

Graduation

"I remember telling everybody that I was her best friend.
But then I realized that everybody in the theatre, and there were
hundreds of people there, could probably say the same thing.
She made you feel important."

—Liz Sheridan, reflecting on Elizabeth's memorial service,
MSNBC's *Headliners & Legends* (2001)

From the moment she graduated from the American Academy of Dramatic Arts, at only twenty-one, Lizzie was working, non-stop, so much so she lost her diploma at an NBC rehearsal hall the day after she received it. Such a loss, however, did not diminish her ambition or her career. As detailed elsewhere within these pages, Elizabeth went on to make over 200 guest-appearances on various TV shows of the era, and then came *Samantha*.

Beyond *Bewitched*, Lizzie never again played a regular character in a weekly series. She had *been there, done that* with the twitch-witch for eight years, which she viewed as a college extension course in entertainment and adult education. She was tired of the grind, plain and simple. She wanted to have a life, to live the scripts of life, rather than star in one every week.

After she stayed the course as *Sam*, she wanted to spend more time with her children, and still be able work periodically, which she did with her various TV-movies. Today, actors can star on weekly shows, make TV-movies, feature films, even appear in live stage plays. In Lizzie's day, there were contract confinements and it wasn't as easy to cross over and/or in between different media. Today, with the blur of television, features, DVD, movies on demand, streaming videos, YouTube, new online networks, it's a different world.

Upon completing *Bewitched*, Lizzie was many times approached about starring in a new weekly series. But she kept rejecting them, along with a few TV-movies she felt were not the right fit.

In 1976, George Schaefer directed the television film, *Amelia Earhart*, about the famed female pilot. Lizzie was offered the lead, but turned it down, and the part went to Susan Clark.

In 1979, CBS wanted to transform Lizzie's hit TV-movie, *Jennifer: A Woman's Story*, about a wealthy widow who takes over her husband's company, into a series. But she declined the offer.

In 1981, ABC approached her about playing *Krystle Carrington* on *Dynasty*. She said no, and the role went to Linda Evans, whose career was rejuvenated because she said yes. Evans had not been seen on TV in any regular capacity since her *Big Valley* days (1965–1969) on ABC. Before that, she appeared in *Beach Blanket Bingo*, directed by William Asher. Two decades later, she ended up playing *Krystle* until 1989. That could have been Lizzie, but for her, a nighttime soap was unappealing.

And as previously mentioned, in 1986, Elizabeth even deflected a chance to work alongside Bob Foxworth in CBS' *Falcon Crest*. Instead, the part went to Kim Novak (who years before had also played a witch, in *Bell, Book and Candle*, the 1958 feature that was said to have inspired *Bewitched*).

In 1987, Lizzie was asked to portray *Poker Alice* in the CBS TV-movie ·of the same name. *Alice* had an incurable penchant for gambling, and Lizzie loved to gamble. But maybe that plot hit too close to home, or maybe she declined because this movie was a back-door pilot for a weekly series. Either way, it was no dice. The part went to another Elizabeth . . . Elizabeth Taylor, who at one point called Lizzie and asked, "Are you *sure* you don't want to do this role?" For whatever reason, Lizzie was sure.

Then, in 1994, she agreed to star in the CBS TV-movie *The Corpse Had a Familiar Face*, based on the career of murder mystery investigative journalist Edna Buchanan. Lizzie loved doing the movie. According to what Liz Sheridan told MSNBC's *Headliners & Legends* in 2001, she was fascinated with Edna's courage, and subsequently wanted to appear in an entire series of Buchanan films. When the *Familiar* ratings proved substantial, CBS complied with Lizzie's wishes.

The following year, she starred in a sequel: *Deadline for Murder: From the Files of Edna Buchanan*, for which *Variety's* Adam Sandler gave a scathing review, May 8, 1995:

> The explanation in the opening credits of the telefilm *suggested by the life and career of Edna Buchanan* should warn viewers that the two-hour spec is likely to have little resemblance to the Pulitzer Prize-winning Miami Herald crime reporter's novels or life, both of which make for far more interesting fare than this dubious offering.
>
> The first confirmation comes with show's use of Santa Monica to double for Fort Lauderdale, and MacArthur Park as downtown Miami, serving as the backdrop for the travails of *Buchanan* (Elizabeth Montgomery).
>
> Her days are spent responding to the call of the wild, writing about the town's gruesome murders and shady characters, while solving crimes the cops seem incapable of closing.
>
> In Buchanan's Miami, drug lords rule and the town is populated by mafia kingpins, ponytailed bodyguards, and marble-floored estates.
>
> When a local mobster is murdered along with his mistress and a tow truck driver who came to the couple's aid on a dark, rainy night, ace reporter Buchanan and a local tabloid show reporter, *Joe Flanigan* (Scott Cameron), race to discover the identity of the killer and a motive.
>
> In the process, story's subtext has Buchanan solving a pair of crimes unrelated to the main murder, resulting in the clearing of one man and the conviction of another.
>
> But writers Les Carter and Susan Sisko create a script that lacks the staccato tempo or vivid articulations of the real-life Buchanan's novels, such as *Suitable for Framing*, which chronicles the exploits of her fictional alter-ego, police beat reporter *Britt Montero*.
>
> Show's dialogue frequently is lame, lacking any punch even in the most crucial of circumstances and delivered by cardboard characters who fail to connect with viewers or each other.
>
> Montgomery's *Buchanan* is a rumpled but efficient sort, who sleeps with a gun under her pillow and argues frequently with her mom (Audra Lindley), who is temporarily sharing *Buchanan's* home while the exterminator is debugging mom's pad.
>
> A relationship with police detective *Marty Talbot* (Yaphet Kotto) is

equally strained, as they frequently butt heads on investigations led by *Talbot* and written about, and ultimately solved, by *Buchanan*.

But *Buchanan* presumably can relate only to the town's new coroner, *Aaron Bliss* (Dean Stockwell), and the pair strike up an instant friendship.

Though attempts to advance the relationship often are interrupted by the call to service—hers a ringing cellular phone; his a pager—the pair try in earnest nonetheless.

The movie suffers from a lack of credibility on other fronts: Viewers may have difficulty believing Montgomery as the hard-bitten scribe, toiling endlessly without regard for the clock. Her acting style makes its hard to tell whether a joke or a dramatic line meant for serious cogitation was just delivered.

The only bright spot in this laborious offering is the tow truck driver's widow *Rosinha*, played convincingly by Saundra Santiago, who viewers may recall as *Gina*, a detective in the popular *Miami Vice* series.

Santiago delivers show's best dramatic perf, rising above the din of her co-stars. But it comes too late.

Joyce Chopra's direction is perfunctory at best, and takes no risks in telling this mostly vapid tale.

However dismissive that review may have been for *Murder*, like *The Corpse Had a Familiar Face* before it, was a ratings bonanza. In fact, it became the highest-rated TV-movie of 1995. Consequently, Elizabeth had intended to play *Buchanan* in two or three movies a year, as Peter Falk had reprised his *Columbo* character for new ABC-TV movies in the 1990s based on his popular *NBC Mystery Movie* series of the 1970s. (At one point, Lizzie had even been interested in playing *Mrs. Columbo* in a semi-sequel to Falk's seminal show. But the lead for that series, which failed, went to Kate Mulgrew, who later starred as *Captain Janeway* on *Star Trek: Voyager*.)

Meanwhile, *Deadline* co-star Saundra Santiago's memories of working with Lizzie are "nothing but pleasant":

She was a gem of person to work with . . . very giving in her scenes with actors, particularly with my scenes. My character [*Rosinha*] had a lot of emotional moments and she was very attentive to those moments. She was one of the most gracious women I've ever worked with, and I really had a lot of fun with her. She was very open and forthcoming in our conversations. I remember clearly how she was so completely available to me as an actress at all times. She was not one of those actors who stayed in their trailers and only came out when they had their scenes. That was not her at all. She talked about her children. She loved them very much. It was clear that she had a loving relationship with them, and she was proud of the job she did with them as a mother.

Mirroring Cliff Robertson's recollections of Lizzie in their youth, Santiago goes on to say how "grounded" Lizzie was as a person. "She knew how to keep herself *real* [in Hollywood]. She was the most unassuming actor I've ever worked with . . . very humble and very sweet. She was a real pro . . . a very lovely woman."

A fan of *Bewitched*, Santiago was initially apprehensive about talking with Lizzie about her most famous role:

> I didn't want to mention *Bewitched* when we first started working together, because I figured everyone did that with her, and I wanted to keep things on a professional level. And I certainly didn't want to ask her if she would wiggle her nose. But after a while, I felt safe enough to at least bring up the show. I expressed to her what an iconic role I thought *Samantha* was . . . how I loved all the characters on the show, and how I used to run home from school just so I could watch it [in reruns]. And she seemed proud of that. She looked at *Samantha* as a fond memory. She spoke of *Bewitched* very well . . . almost . . . wistfully.
>
> But, you know, when you're sick, you start to appreciate *everything*. I couldn't imagine that she didn't know she was sick. She might not have wanted to say anything because of the insurance. They [the studios, networks] make actors get physicals. I remember Kathy Bates [who battled cancer] once talking about how she hid her [chemotherapy] treatments because she was afraid of not getting any work. And Elizabeth very much wanted to work. She enjoyed [doing the Buchanan films], and *Edna* was a good role for her.

And since *Murder, She Wrote* was on its way out at CBS, the network was looking to fill that older-female-mystery demographic. But fate had other plans.

"No one ever knew she had cancer," Santiago says of Lizzie. "And then when she died, it was shocking to me . . . to work so closely with someone like that . . . and then only to have them pass away such a short time afterward. It was just so sad."

Upon working with Lizzie, Saundra was not aware that her father was Robert Montgomery, who in 1981 had succumbed to cancer, which, as it turns out, had also taken the life of Saundra's father. "It's not a discriminating disease," she says. "It'll grab onto whoever it can."

And as much as she wants to remember the happy experience of working with Elizabeth, Saundra can't help but recall a few other developments that transpired on the *Deadline* set that she calls "eerie and kind of weird." She explains:

> At one point during filming, Elizabeth's appearance was very *ashy*, and someone on the set said, "Give her some color." But she didn't make a big deal of it. The makeup man just came over and touched her up a little bit. She took it all in stride. I also noticed that she was very thin, but everybody in L.A. is thin, and you just don't think anything of it. She still looked beautiful, and she never complained about anything . . . or being tired or any of that.
>
> And then after we completed the movie, I wanted to get a picture with her. But I didn't have my camera. So I asked one of the crew to take our picture, and these were the days before digital cameras, and all he had was a Polaroid [instant camera with film that immediately develops]. So he took the picture, and we had to wait for it to dry. But it didn't come out clear. It was all blurry. And I remember thinking to myself, "Geez . . . why didn't that picture come out?"

Santiago had become apprehensive of taking pictures ever since a trip to Santorini Island in Greece, which she calls "a very superstitious place. It's a volcanic island, with all kinds of 'spirits.' And I took a few pictures there, and they all came out like the Polaroid picture that crew member took of me and Elizabeth. There were a lot of ghost-like images all over the place. It came out very strange."

Away from the set of *Deadline for Murder*, Lizzie was busy nursing Robert Foxworth, who had recently undergone hip-replacement surgery. As the actor told *People* magazine on June 5, 1995, Lizzie was strong and confident, whereas he was apprehensive. "She was there for me when I first tried getting up on crutches."

Foxworth "was quite devoted to her," says actress Bonnie Bartlett, who had known Lizzie from New York in the 1950s and when they both appeared in 1975's *The Legend of Lizzie Borden*. Like Saundra Santiago had lost her father to cancer, Bartlett lost her father, mother, and brother to colon cancer, the same form of the disease that did not spare Lizzie's life. "If my father would have had the proper exam, he would have pulled through," Bartlett says. Just like Lizzie, "he didn't have to die. And as I recall, she was never tested for colon cancer, and neither was my Dad."

According to *People* magazine, Foxworth, Bill Asher, and Lizzie's children each tried to get Lizzie to see a doctor. But she refused, even after her daughter Rebecca noticed how thin she had become on the set of *Murder*. Still, Lizzie disregarded the notion, and ultimately ignored what were in effect warning signs that something was wrong . . . deadly wrong.

But as Saundra Santiago has revealed, and as Liz Sheridan once explained on A&E's *Biography* in 1999, that's how Lizzie was; she kept things to herself. There was "no dwelling." She was secretive and preferred that people didn't know if she was upset or worried or in pain, in anguish of any kind; she toughed things out. As Sheridan later expressed to MSNBC's *Headliners & Legends* in 2001, Lizzie never really wanted to face anything that was "bad or ugly." She was in a "huge state of denial."

Such denial, however, still did not betray her loyalty. Lizzie instructed the powers-that-be to cast Sheridan in *Deadline for Murder* so the two could visit. As Sheridan later revealed at Lizzie's Hollywood Walk of Fame ceremony, January 4, 2008, "She was getting ill and I didn't know it. She didn't let on."

Then, in mid May 1995, the phone rang at Sheridan's home. She picked up the receiver, and heard Lizzie's voice with a simple, "Hi."

In attempt to break through the tears with a smile, Sheridan asked, "So, what's new?"

"Oh, a little of this and a little of that," Lizzie replied, bravely. Then she giggled, Sheridan followed suit, and in between those little laughs were the last words they spoke.

By then, Lizzie had finally checked into Cedars-Sinai Medical Center in Los Angeles. As *People* magazine reported, exploratory surgery had brought the tragic diagnosis: colon cancer. Bill Asher said Lizzie's mood was upbeat but nervous. First she was shocked. Then she was angry.

By the time her doctors performed additional surgery to remove the cancer's growth, she was too weak for radiation therapy, and the disease had progressed. At that point, and as Bob Foxworth explained in 2006 on *Entertainment Tonight*, she wanted "to go home." He knew then, he said, that *she* knew she was going to die. And that she wanted to die at home.

As Billy Clift, Lizzie's hairdresser and good friend, relayed in his compelling book *Everything Is Going to Be Just Fine: Ramblings of a Mad Hairdresser* (Everything Is Going to Be Just Fine Society, 1998), Bob Foxworth had explained to him the events of Lizzie's last night of life. She had experienced a great deal of pain, made dire sounds, and her breathing was highly erratic. They were Foxworth's most challenging hours at her side. He made every valiant effort to remain awake, but by 6 AM, he needed some sleep. Then, two hours later, Elizabeth's nurse awakened him. There were new developments. Lizzie had become restful, tranquil, and then she passed away . . . at approximately 8:23 AM, May 18, 1995.

In the end, at least Lizzie was surrounded by the family she loved and held dear: Foxworth, Bill Asher and her three children with Asher, Billy Jr., Robert, and Rebecca in particular, who was most often at her mother's bedside, soothing her throughout interrupted bouts of sleep.

Foxworth told *People* those last days with Lizzie were "loving and intense," a fitting description for one who lived a life filled with many contradictions, some delightful, others confounding. One moment, she joked about wanting pina coladas poured into her IV. At another, she felt energetic enough to cheer on the New York Knicks during a televised basketball game—one of the simple pleasures which she embraced. But as Asher also told *People*, Lizzie knew she was "losing the battle."

It was a fight for her life that ended in the early morning hours of May 18, 1995, when she was alone in her bedroom at home, taking her last breaths, with her loved ones waiting quietly in the living room, as she had requested. "She didn't want anyone to see her that way," Asher said. Then she slipped away.

According to what Billy Asher, Jr. relayed to MSNBC's *Headliners & Legends*, his mother's physicians were surprised that she was still hanging on in those final days. She wasn't going to take-off during the dark of night, young Asher told them. When she's ready to go, he thought, it'll be in the morning with the light and the sun, "and that's kind of what happened."

As it had been for Lucille Ball—shortly before she died of a ruptured aorta on April 26, 1989 at Cedar-Sinai Hospital—countless cards, letters, gifts, and calls arrived at Lizzie's room at the same hospital and at her home in Beverly Hills before she passed away in 1995.

Lizzie, like Lucy, felt an overwhelming outpouring of adoration. Most of the senders were viewers who considered themselves family members and friends, people whom she had only met through the magic of television, and then others with whom she actually worked in television, like her friends Cliff Robertson and Sally Kemp.

But unlike Liz Sheridan, who at least had a chance to speak with Lizzie on the phone before she died, Cliff and Sally would not be granted that opportunity. Shortly before his "Lizbel" passed away, Robertson shared a random in-studio TV interview with Robert Foxworth after which he said, "Bob invited me to drop by the house . . . for a visit."

"I'm sure Elizabeth would love to see you," Foxworth said.

"I was looking forward to it," Robertson recalled in 2011, "because I had not seen her in a long time."

So, that spring day, sometime in mid-May 1995, Robertson followed Foxworth to the home he shared with Lizzie in Beverly Hills. Upon arrival, they parked their separate cars and Foxworth went inside to tell Lizzie that her friend was waiting outside. Only a few moments later, he emerged to tell Robertson that she was too ill for visitors. "And she died shortly thereafter," Robertson lamented. "I never got to see her. She just didn't want to see anyone, and I didn't blame her. But to this day, I miss her . . . because we had such a rollicking good-pal relationship."

"I loved her dearly," says Sally Kemp. "You know . . . some people are a source of light in your life, and she was just a source of light in mine." And Sally was "deeply saddened" when she heard of Lizzie's passing because, like so many of her friends, Sally "hadn't known that she had been sick."

On June 18, 1995, a memorial service for Lizzie was held at the Canon Theatre in Beverly Hills. Herbie Hancock provided the music, and Dominick Dunne spoke about their days together in New York when they were both starting out in the business. Other speakers including Robert Foxworth, who read out loud sympathy cards from fans, her nurse, her brother, daughter, and stepson. Amanda McBroom sang, and the entire service ended with the lights going down. A beautiful shot of Lizzie on a video screen, flickered in the dark, and those in attendance rose and applauded. Lizzie had asked that any donations in her memory should be made to the William Holden Wildlife Association in Kenya or the Los Angeles Zoo.

Kemp, in New York at the time, was unable to attend the service, but a mutual acquaintance who was there said most of those present were "not old friends. They were people who were kind of new friends."

At the service, Sally and Lizzie's mutual acquaintance was approached by yet a third party, who asked, "Are you an old friend of Elizabeth's?"

To which the second party replied, "Yes—but I hadn't seen her for years and years. Are *you* an old friend?"

"Well," the third party responded in return, "I had only known her for about five years. But I think I was on my way out."

Says Kemp:

> So, that was like Elizabeth and not like Elizabeth, because she wouldn't make you feel like you were on your way out. You just were out. And I just wonder where that influence came from. I do know that her relationship with Bob Foxworth was a very challenging relationship. So, maybe it stemmed from that. She did seem to be attracted to troubled guys, and felt maybe that she could fix them, or that she felt comfortable with them.

In 1999, Liz Sheridan told A&E's *Biography* that Lizzie and Foxworth "became dear friends and lovers," and after that, it was difficult to keep them apart. They were two strong-willed people who "argued," but enjoyed reconciling, "making love and being happy and giggling."

Then, one day in 1993, Lizzie and Bob were sitting at their kitchen table, discussing some particularly important matter and he said, "You know—this situation would be so much easier if we were married."

Lizzie looked at him and asked, "Is that a proposal?"

He thought about that a half-a-second and said, "Okay."

To which she then added, "Yes."

So on January 28, 1993, they got married in a private ceremony in her manager Barry Krost's apartment in Los Angeles. About fifteen minutes later, Lizzie called her friend Sheridan to tell her the news. Sheridan said Lizzie was so "child-like and sweet."

According to Sally Kemp, Elizabeth was also "a multi-layered mystery, and I would love to one day know some of the answers, while I would also prefer to remember the young woman I knew."

Elizabeth had left an equally puzzling imprint on her friend author and investigative journalist Dominick Dunne. As he observed in his book *The Way We Lived Then*, after *Bewitched* made her a star, he and his wife Lenny never saw her again "for reasons unknown." She disconnected from her friends and those she knew between divorcing Gig Young and just before marrying Bill Asher and subsequently playing *Samantha*. In fact, as Dunne explained, he and Lenny once passed Elizabeth on a sidewalk in Beverly Hills, but she refused to acknowledge them, a slight that cut deep, particularly for Lenny. But it would hurt Lizzie even more later on.

In 1991, she was interested in playing the lead role of *Pauline Mendelson* in the TV-movie, *An Inconvenient Woman*, based on Dunne's novel of the same name. But as explained in *The Way We Lived Then*, in a wrath of anger, he blackballed her, and the part went to Jill Eikenberry (*L.A. Law*). However, Dunne made allowances for Elaine Stritch who, like Lizzie, was also once married to Gig Young, to have a small role in the film.

Come 1995, however, things changed. Dunne had been covering the trial of O. J. Simpson, who had co-starred with Lizzie in the 1977 TV-movie, *A Killing Affair*. Upon learning of her cancerous death sentence, Dunne decided it was time for reconciliation. Whatever had divided their friendship now "faded into unimportance," he said. He could now only recall the happier times they once shared.

So, while she was still at Cedar-Sinai Hospital, and only two days before she passed away, Lizzie received a note from Dunne expressing just how wonderful it was to have been her friend. Bob Foxworth had read her the message, and she was happy to have heard it. Foxworth subsequently invited Dunne, who had known Lizzie from their early days of television—when he was a mere stage manager on *Robert Montgomery Presents* and on which she was a budding starlet—to deliver a eulogy at her funeral.

"You're the only one who knew her from that part of her life," Foxworth told him, which was not entirely true. Sally Kemp and Cliff Robertson both knew and worked with Lizzie on *Robert Montgomery Presents* and would have welcomed the chance to bid their dear friend a loving public farewell.

But Robertson never saw much of Lizzie after her divorce from Fred Cammann. Kemp never saw much of Lizzie after her marriage to Gig Young. And Robertson, Kemp, and Dunne never saw much of Lizzie after she married Bill Asher and *Bewitched* made her a star. But Dunne's ability to write paved the way, and cleared the air . . . for at least one final transmission that reconnected what turned out to be an unbroken if unspoken bond.

But she had that kind of effect on everyone in her life, certainly Foxworth who told *Entertainment Tonight* in 2006, "To some extent, a part of her lives in me. And it's not so much about a thought. That's just the way it is."

On MSNBC's *Headliners & Legends* he added, she was "completely gracious and giving and kind, and easy-going and unaffected and unpretentious. And as we hung out together and played together and had dinner together I was more and more seduced and . . . bewitched . . . if you will, by this wonderful woman."

On that same show, Billy Asher, Jr. explained how his mom "lives in a lot of people's homes and in their hearts," and that her "greatest legacy is her ability to give young girls growing up the idea of how strong a woman could be."

One of those young women is assuredly Billy's sister, Rebecca Asher, who in also appearing on *Headliners & Legends*, said she more than anything misses hearing her mother's lyrical sounds. "She had a beautiful voice."

Today, Rebecca, who is just as private as mother was, went on to describe her mom as "almost child-like . . . She loved surprises, and art, and being creative at Christmas . . . she loved all of that. . . . She just had this kind of magical persona."

Billy, Jr. delivered a near identical description of his mother on *Legends*: "She had this mystical child-like quality about her."

Throughout Lizzie's life, however, her child-like ways played both in her favor and at times against her better judgment. It was productive when she transferred that real-life charming aspect of herself onto the screen as *Samantha Stephens*, which became one of the most popular and likable characters in TV history. It played against her in the immature way she established and then disavowed friendships.

As Sally Kemp and Dominick Dunne discovered, if Elizabeth felt affronted by or uncomfortable with something a friend said or did, intentional or not, even in the slightest way, that was it: the friendship was over. There were no second chances. However, like so much of her true-to-life character development, this character flaw can be traced back to her childhood relationship with Robert Montgomery. As she explained to Ronald Haver in 1991:

> It took me awhile to understand maybe why people either at school or other friends kids that I knew didn't pay any attention to me and then all of a sudden they did . . . It's like I'd get all tickled about, "Oh, somebody wants to come to my birthday." And then they'd come to my birthday, and I'd be hoping to see them again, and then I'd never see them again until like my next birthday . . . It didn't occur to me right away that there were some people who really only wanted to come to see (my father) . . . That was kind of hard sometimes . . . to think that you'd found a new friend and then realize that that wasn't it at all.

On New Year's Eve, 1967, in the prime of Lizzie's magical turn as *Samantha* on *Bewitched*, she had a friend in famed sportscaster Vince Scully, with whom she co-hosted ABC's *Tournament of Roses Parade*. In 2011, Yahoo! Sports reporter Dave Brown interviewed Scully for a segment he called *Answer Man*. Brown mentioned having screened Lizzie's promo for that classic *Tournament* broadcast and asked Scully what it was like to work with her during what was the peak of *Bewitched's* success. Scully replied:

> All I can tell you is that she was a sweet, unaffected superstar. In those days, forty years ago, she was queen of television. I was in awe of her presence. After being with her for a little while, I realized she was so down-to-earth. She was a mother, she was a wife; she was not theatrically inclined at all. I didn't realize until the day of the parade, but we had to go up a tower. It wasn't literally a tower, it was a platform of six or seven steps. And she couldn't go up it. She was scared to death. She had a phobia about heights. She put her face in my back and put her arms around me and I took her up the six steps and got her seated and she was fine. The most important thing for me about that is to tell anyone, including you, that she was the nicest girl. It was really an honor.

A *witch's honor* . . . as when on *Bewitched*, with either her left or right hand, but preferably her left, Lizzie's *Samantha* occasionally made a particular gesture to (either) *Darrin* that signified that she was revealing the absolute truth about a given situation, much like the Boy Scout's Honor, but not. Here's how it worked: she'd place the index and middle fingers of her hand on either side of her nose with her fingertips pointing toward her eyes. While giving the sign, she'd intone, "Witches' honor," which in many ways was an omen of things to come.

At the close of 2011, actress Donna Douglas, who played *Elly May Clampett* on *The Beverly Hillbillies* in the 1960s, settled a lawsuit over a Barbie doll that used her character's name and likeness. According to *The Associated Press*, Douglas had originally sought $75,000, but the details of her actual settlement were confidential.

On September 22, 1994, *The Toronto Star* reported a similar suit, although on a much larger scale in which Lizzie claimed Sony (by way of Screen Gems/Columbia) owed her $5 million in *Bewitched* licensing dues. A short time before she passed away in May of 1995, the suit was settled and, as with the Douglas case, the amount was confidential. But Lizzie was clearly looking out for her fortune, and ultimately did not want to have her children go through that legal battle without her.

On September 10, 1995, six months after she died, television's top executives, producers, agents and actors turned out to honor her at the *Women in Film's Second Annual Lucy Awards*. The award, named for Lucille Ball, had also been bestowed upon *Bewitched* guest star Imogene Coca (*Your Show of Shows*), Brianne Murphy, Fred Silverman and Tracey Ullman, and it is given for innovation in television. During the three-hour ceremony, which was held at the Beverly Hills Hotel, Robert Foxworth delivered a touching tribute to Lizzie, while afterward her daughter Rebecca Asher accepted the award.

On April 19, 1998, the Duet Nightclub in Los Angeles hosted a birthday celebration/wardrobe sale/auction in Lizzie's name. Donations of her belongings collected by her children and Robert Foxworth were auctioned to benefit the AIDS Healthcare Foundation (which was established in 1987). According to www.bewitched.net, the benefit raised approximately $15,000 to $20,000.

On June 12 and 13, 1999, Lizzie's family—led by daughter Rebecca—

held an estate sale of her belongings at her Benedict Canyon Drive home in Beverly Hills. As documented by www.bewitched.net, some of the items sold included her 1977 Bentley (with the license plate, BENTLIZ), which fetched $15,000; a 1970 Oldsmobile Cutless in sound condition (which sold for $4000.00); and some African jewelry that Lizzie and Bob Foxworth had brought back from their on-location-in-Kenya shoot for their 1990 Hallmark Hall of Fame TV-movie, *Face to Face.*

Approximately six years later, on June 15, 2005, the network executives at TV Land announced plans to erect a nine-foot bronze statue of her likeness as *Samantha* in Salem, Massachusetts, which *TV Guide* had years before labeled "America's Number 1 witch city."

While *Bewitched* was still in production and at the onset of its seventh season (1970–1971), Lizzie and the cast and crew traveled to Salem for what became the show's only main on-location shooting for an arc-storyline involving *Samantha's* trip to a witches' convention. As Lizzie said in 1989, "The crowds were crazy in Salem. It was really spooky. I mean it was terrific because it meant they felt (we) were terrific." Lizzie's co-star Dick Sargent also said in 1989, "It was the first time I felt like one of The Beatles."

Decades later, the scene was not all that different in Salem at the induction of Lizzie's *Samantha* statue. According to *The Boston Globe,* the *Bewitched* minions were still present in droves, as nearly 2,000 people gravitated toward the city's Lappin Park at the corner of Washington and Essex Streets to unveil Lizzie's larger-than-life likeness:

She sits on a broom. In the background, a crescent moon rests atop a cloud on a pedestal. She's dressed as she mostly appeared on *Bewitched*: as an average housewife of the 1960s in a typical housedress. She's smiling, with her left arm turned up at the elbow, and legs crossed at the ankles; the perfect lady; the perfect woman . . . at least of the era.

On stage partaking in the commemoration: Bill Asher, *Bewitched* performers Bernard Fox (*Dr. Bombay*), Erin Murphy (*Tabitha*), and Kasey Rogers (*Louise Tate*, 1966–1972), Salem's Mayor Stanley J. Usovicz, Jr., and Larry W. Jones, President of TV Land and Nick at Nite, who explained:

> *Bewitched* was and still remains a magical and beloved series. The series has been enchanting audiences for over forty years, and it is filled with heart

and humor. Because several episodes were filmed in Salem, it is truly fitting that we would celebrate it with a statue here.

Added Mayor Usovicz:

> We are pleased to welcome the statue of Elizabeth Montgomery as *Samantha Stephens*, to Salem. Our connection to this beautiful piece of contemporary art goes beyond the episodes filmed here. *Samantha* saw the magic in everyday life, and so do we.

The sculpture represented the network's fifth effort to honor people, places, and moments from America's small screen heritage by recognizing the *Sam* site as a "TV Land Landmark." The network's first salute—a bronze statue of *Ralph Kramden* of *The Honeymooners*—was unveiled in 2000 and now adorns the entrance to New York City's Port Authority Bus Terminal. In May 2002, a bronze statue of Mary Tyler Moore from *The Mary Tyler Moore Show* was uncovered and now stands on Nicollet Mall in downtown Minneapolis, MN. An *Andy Griffith Show* statue, which depicts Griffith and a young Ron Howard as *Sheriff Andy Taylor* and his son *Opie* walking, hand-in-hand (as in the opening credit sequence of that classic series), is located in Raleigh's Pullen Park and was unveiled in October, 2003. In July of 2004, TV Land honored yet another of television's most enduring icons, Bob Newhart, with a life-sized bronze sculpture commemorating his role as *Dr. Robert Hartley* on *The Bob Newhart Show* in Chicago.

Thomas Hill, Vice President and Creative Director for TV Land, explains how Lizzie's *Samantha* likeness joined their statuesque legacy:

> One of the very first statues we did was Mary Tyler Moore—and the original concept was to find some way to have her tossed-hat be floating forever above her outstretched hand (as in the opening credits sequence of *The Mary Tyler Moore Show*). But the laws of physics and the limitations of forced air/magnets/tricks with mirrors forced us to capture the moment just before her hat actually left her hand. In those same conversations, we quickly generated other ideas for dozens of beloved TV characters—and we wanted *Samantha* to fly! Since *The Flying Nun* didn't have quite the pop culture staying power of *Bewitched*.

Creating a TV Land Landmark required extensive preparation and conversation between the various stakeholders. "Finding just the right location was never easy," Hill acknowledges. He once even suggested placing Dick Van Dyke's *Rob Petrie* on an endless commute between his *Alan Brady Show's* writer office in New York City and the New Rochelle home he shared with Moore's *Laura Petrie* and Larry Mathew's little *Richie*, "but train seats are hard to book permanently."

As to Lizzie's potential *Samantha* statue landing, Connecticut was once considered as an option, but as Hill recalls, "the civic leaders in Salem seemed more open to embracing the connection."

Into this mix, Studio EIS, a three-dimensional design and sculpture studio in New York founded by brothers Ivan and Elliot Schwartz, created Lizzie's life-sized bronze sculpture, as well as the Griffith and Newhart sculptures. The Schwartz brothers also created statutes of the Founding Fathers—which are located in the National Constitution Center in Philadelphia, and commemorative objects for museums, including the Smithsonian. The week Lizzie's statue was erected, Studio EIS was filled with more than a dozen life-like military figures, part of a project for the Marines.

All EIS's statues were initially received without pause or controversy, that is, except for Lizzie's *Samantha*, due to its placement in the middle of Salem, a town best known for its historic hanging of nineteen citizens accused of witchcraft. It all transpired in 1692 but remained a hot topic centuries later in 2005. As was discussed in the article, "*Bewitched* Statue Bothers Some in Salem," by David Segal, and published in *The Washington Post* (May 10, 2005), capitalizing on that history with a statue of a broom-gliding media witch rubbed a few locals the wrong way. "It's like TV Land going to Auschwitz and proposing to erect a statue of Colonel Klink," said John Carr, a former member of the Salem Historic District Commission. "Putting this statue in the park near the church where this all happened, it trivializes the execution of nineteen people."

But that night on June 15, 2005, the statue's mold and fate had already been cast, shaped, and determined by a vote of the Salem Redevelopment Authority, which owns Lappin Park, where Lizzie's likeness was placed. Mayor Usovicz liked Carr's odds. No disrespect intended, he said. The town takes its dark past seriously and deals with it reverently in museums, but that doesn't mean it should have declined to showcase a pop culture icon.

"Will this statue redefine Salem? Absolutely not," he explained. "Will it add to the experience of coming here? Definitely."

On *Bewitched*, *Samantha* and company may have lived in Westport, Connecticut. (In fact, as Screen Gems executive Harry Ackerman explained in *The Bewitched Book* [and elsewhere], he had drafted an original "eight- or nine-page treatment" for a show he called *The Witch of Westport*.) But as to those few seventh year episodes shot in Salem for the witches' convention, it made the city a logical place for TV Land to erect its statue, especially when they visited the town during Halloween and found that thousands of revelers had descended upon the area.

"What we saw was a huge Halloween party," said Robert Pellizzi, a TV Land senior vice president. "So we thought, it certainly makes sense to ask." They sought advice about where to place the statue and they made a generous offer. Not only would the town get the bronze for free, but TV Land also offered to renovate Lappin Park and to pay for upkeep of the statue, too. In return, of course, TV Land hoped for public relations points, including some good photo opportunities when the statue was unveiled.

"If I were one of the people who had a house on the beautiful common there, would I hate it?" asked Ivan Schwartz, partaking in a conference from June 15, 2005 that addressed the issue. "Yes, probably. But it seems like [Salem] was going down that path long before this TV Land thing ever surfaced."

"That path" was the path of cashing in on Salem's witch backstory, something the town has been doing for a while (that is, police officers have a witch and broom stitched into their uniform emblems; at Halloween, various costume shops and haunted-houses open, etc.). Yet, for residents such as John Carr, the camp was getting a little out of hand. "God bless the mayor, but he thinks that statue is contemporary art," Carr said at the time. "The whole idea is bad taste beyond belief." Either way all these years later, the controversy has subsided, and Lizzie's stilted bronzed presence remains.

"Unfortunately," Thomas Hill was unable to attend the statue's dedication, so he has "little recollection of the imbroglio," but he's sympathetic with the historians who "didn't want this dark chapter in Early American history to be treated frivolously. But, naturally, I see America's pop culture history as a valid inspiration for public art."

However, Hill does recall TV Land's President Larry Jones partaking in a TV news discussion program during which he defended the statue against someone representing the historically minded. "But the show had also booked a third guest, representing the modern day *Wicca* perspective—pro-witch, I suppose?"

Hill concludes, this particular Wiccan's presence "made the entire debate appear rather absurd." Consequently, despite even her physical absence, Lizzie's name—and likeness—remained infused with political conflict and social issues—and she would have loved it.

On January 4, 2008, at yet another ceremony, this time presided over by honorary mayor Johnny Grant in Hollywood, California Lizzie, finally received her star on the Hollywood Walk of Fame. In attendance at the rain-drenched ceremony were a multitude of her fans, including radio host and journalist Jone Devlin, who recounts her experience of that day:

> It was a cold, blustery, day, very rainy. Yet in spite of the awful weather, there was a good sized crowd there—and most of us arrived literally hours early just to be ensured of a *good spot*. Everyone in the group was happy and excited, sharing their memories of *Bewitched* and Elizabeth Montgomery and happily greeting people that they'd only ever *met* on *Bewitched* websites. The presentation was wonderful, touching and heartfelt, but what I remember the most is how everyone stayed for the entire thing . . . even when it was pouring down icy rain, even when people's umbrellas gave out, drenching them and everyone around them, even when a small brook began to form beneath our feet as the drainage system lost its race with the driving downpour. To me that, above everything else was a testimony to how much Elizabeth Montgomery meant to her fans and friends; and it is a moment I'll never forget.

Devlin and her fellow *Bewitched* fans then heard special memories shared from Lizzie's children Rebecca and Billy Asher, friend Liz Sheridan and Robert Foxworth. Each of those who spoke mentioned how delighted Lizzie would have been with the ceremony. The downpour of rain, which all speakers believed she would have found amusing, could not compete with the outpour[ing] of respect from the loved ones and fans who attended the event despite the cloudburst. "It is *so* awesome that it is raining," Rebecca said at the ceremony. "I can't even really express it. She [Lizzie] is so happy right now."

According to Devlin, Rebecca went on to explain how there are not many things more gratifying than seeing "someone you care about" being recognized for their work, especially if that individual happens to be a parent. Rebecca then described her mother as "an incredible human being . . . full of grace and wit and beauty and brilliance." How every day, Lizzie brought a sense of wonder to everything she did, and gave a unique perspective to everything she rested her eyes upon. In short, Rebecca enthused, "She was incredible!"

Rebecca then expressed how she and her brothers Billy, Jr. and Robert appreciated how they directly experienced their mother's influence on the lives of others. They saw it that day at the ceremony, and continue to see it every day in the eyes of those who find out that they're Lizzie's children. Rebecca said her mother worked hard and always challenged herself and her audience with the characters she chose to play. Rebecca expressed how much she and her brothers always loved their mom and still do; how proud they remain of her; how honored they were to have been present at the ceremony on their mother's behalf. Rebecca then thanked the crowd for their loyalty to Lizzie, and left the podium.

At which point, Bob Foxworth approached the podium, and delivered an equally heart-felt and revealing sentiment. He began by defining Lizzie as shy, a quality of her character and personality that he said benefitted her life and career. He said her shy demeanor added a special sparkle to every character she portrayed because in the process of discovering who the character was she would "dig into herself and reveal someone that maybe she didn't even know she was."

Consequently, to each of her roles Lizzie brought a special quality, whether it's with what Foxworth called "women of the west," as in TV films like *Belle Star* or *The Awakening Land*, the latter of which he described as a "beautiful and historical film," or *The Legend of Lizzie Borden*, which he called "a classic for television." Each time, he said, she revealed more of herself—"it was like the peeling of an onion."

Foxworth was certain that the crowd was well aware of her comedic talents by way of *Bewitched*. But what they might not have known, he said, was that Lizzie was "hysterically funny" in her private life as well. He explained how she was not "terribly enamored with the glitz and glitter of Hollywood," how she would much rather dirty her fingers in the garden than get "all gussied up" and attend some "fancy function," and even though she loved doing that, too, it wasn't her favorite thing in the world.

Foxworth then concluded his speech as he had started it, saying, "She was a very private person and that sense of privacy came from her shyness."

But when it came to advocating for young minds or human rights, the ill or disadvantaged, Lizzie's personal objectives took a backseat to compassion and concern for others . . . for better or for worse. More times than not, "she had a lot of problems with her self-confidence," Bill Asher said in 2001 on *Headliners & Legends*. So, she stayed home a great deal. She could at times be considered a Hollywood recluse. Other times, not so much, because she enjoyed parties, especially if they were charity events.

In keeping with her indeterminate style, she kept everyone guessing, while one thing was certain: Elizabeth had little desire to age.

Ginger Blymer is a retired movie hairdresser whose famous clientele included the likes of Natalie Wood, Sean Connery, Tom Cruise, Tom Hanks, Meg Ryan, and more. She worked with Lizzie on *The Awakening Land* and *Belle Starr*, both of which Foxworth had defined as classic films about "women of the west."

In 2002, Blymer authored *Hairdresser to the Stars: A Hollywood Memoir* (Infinity Publishing), in which she remembers how much Lizzie loved horses, the racetrack, games, and any sort of mental competition; how Elizabeth's home was filled with "wonderful things," like a merry-go-round-horse in the bar, and a hundred pillows on her bed. At Christmas, Blymer wrote, there were amazing decorations throughout Lizzie's home. "The staircase with pine wound up the bannister. It smelled great."

Blymer also recalled how Lizzie once called Foxworth "the love of her life"; how Blymer talked with him shortly after Elizabeth passed away; how he told her that Lizzie never wanted to get old.

"So, she didn't."

☆

Award-winning actress, comedienne, talk show host, writer, political blog-ger, social advocate, and comedienne Lydia Cornell is a loyal fan of both Elizabeth's and *Bewitched*.

Best known as *Sara Rush*, the "virginal blonde bombshell" on the classic sitcom, *Too Close for Comfort*, Cornell became one of the most popular blonde female sex symbols of the 1980s, as was Elizabeth in the 1960s. On *Comfort*, Cornell was the happy-go-lucky TV daughter of the Emmy-winning Ted Knight, who had found fame playing the egotistical anchor-man *Ted Baxter* on *The Mary Tyler Moore Show* in the 1970s. Off *Comfort*, Cornell was struggling with an addiction to alcohol and drugs.

Beginning with the discovery of her young brother's body after he died of a drug overdose, Cornell has endured one shattering personal tragedy after the other. At one point, she says, "I had three boys and two dogs, including my husband, and they were all going through puberty at the same time." Her stepson, whom she raised since the age of four, suffers from brittle bone disease. "He's amazing," she adds.

Cornell's pretty amazing, too. In 1994, she halted her substance abuse during a "catastrophic spiritual awakening." Today, she is a grateful recover-ing alcoholic, who mentors teens and is a motivational speaker for recovery groups across the country. "Every bad thing I've ever been through has turned out to be something good or something hilarious. I have turned it all into comedy, somehow. I am grateful for every 'wrong turn.'"

Lydia's poignant stories of transformation are laced with an innate sense of humor and comic timing, some of which was inspired by Lizzie. She explains:

> *Bewitched* was my favorite show growing up. What a beautiful, wonderful soul Elizabeth Montgomery was! I looked up to her as a role model. She had this mysterious secret intelligence behind the eyes, which gave me hope as a woman in a man's world in Hollywood. There was nothing vacuous, shallow or *bimbo* about her.

As to any personal struggles that Elizabeth may or may not have had with substance abuse, Cornell says:

My heart goes out to her. As an artist who struggled with alcoholism, I know full-well the darkness that clouds the joys. At seventeen years sober, I have found that nothing in the material world, no drink, drug, marriage, lover or career success can fill that hole in our heart with a permanent peace until we seek a spiritual solution. I only wish she could have found the peace she was seeking while she was alive. Like Steve Jobs, I believe our secret lives and the resentments or bad thoughts we harbor about ourselves and others often fuel our *diseases* which show up as a reflection of our deeply engrained mindset.

A mindset Ed Asner (who co-starred with Cornell's TV dad Ted Knight on *The Mary Tyler Moore Show*) believes may have been instilled into Elizabeth by her father Robert Montgomery. "Maybe that's where the cancer came from?" Asner suggests. Or maybe it stemmed from a combination of a number of sources?

Whether an actor, singer, dancer, writer, or director, be it for the big screen, TV, or the stage, there are many prevalent and destructive patterns that develop for those within every section of the entertainment industry. The fame, the money, the perks: it all becomes intoxicating and self-destructive, in more ways than one.

For one, Whitney Houston's tragic death from a toxic mix of drugs, drowning, and alcohol on the eve of the Grammy Awards in 2012 shocked the world. Consequently, on March 8, 2012, *The Los Angeles Times* published an informative article about the rampant substance abuse issue pervading the music industry in particular. *The Day the Music Died* was written by Randy Lewis, who wondered, "If celebrities who have access to every resource available can't get help, what hope is there for the majority of people who haven't even experienced the smallest fraction of their success?"

Or as Harold Owens, senior vice president of MusiCares/Musicians Assistance Program (MAP) Fund told the *Los Angeles Times*, "You can't reach an addict when he's not ready." Owens should know. He's been counseling others in substance abuse since he became sober approximately twenty-five years ago. "I've been through the struggle," he said. "To an alcoholic, I like to think it's a self-diagnosed disease: Nobody can tell you you're an alcoholic until you tell yourself."

Suffice it to say, Lizzie may have joked about drinking in interviews with John Tesh and Ronald Haver, and may have even joked about wanting pina coladas poured into her IV on her deathbed (as was explained in *People Magazine*, June 5, 1995). She may have inherited a drinking problem from her mother and her fraternal grandfather Henry Montgomery, Sr. Her father Robert Montgomery may have driven her to drink. Her relationship with the father-figure alcoholic Gig Young may have increased that drinking. The social drinking era of the 1960s may have camouflaged her drinking issues. Her drinking issues may even have compromised her relationships with her peers, thus cutting her chances for any Emmy victories, and on and on.

Either way, if she had any real issues with alcohol, Lizzie never acknowledged them, at least not publically. She may have admitted it to herself, or to her family and maybe a few close friends. but not to the world, and no medical documentation or statement was ever made to suggest it.

Maybe that's all because, as Liz Sheridan had expressed on MSNBC's *Headliners & Legends* in 2001, Elizabeth never wanted to face anything that was "bad or ugly." Upon learning that Lizzie had cancer, or even when she was started to lose weight, Sheridan believed her friend was in that "huge state of denial."

In essence, Lizzie may have been inadvertently "protected" from the truth, because admitting the truth in such instances of substance abuse or even potential substance abuse, usually hurts. However, nothing hurts more than death.

Studies have shown that alcoholism contributes to and exacerbates colon cancer, which is what killed Lizzie. Her weight also seemed to fluctuate over the years, if ever so subtly. And research has proven that weight fluctuation also contributes to colon cancer.

The bottom line is this: Whatever adversities Lizzie may have failed to conquer, that doesn't tarnish her memory, or make her a *bad* person. Her losses, just as much as her victories, merely make her a human person. She was someone who cared for others, but somehow neglected her own well-being. She may have needed help in certain areas, but didn't know how to seek it, and then ultimately never received it, for whatever reason. Either way, she's not any less wondrous a being who brought countless hours of magic to the world. And her death may not have been in vain.

As Harold Owens went on to tell the *Los Angeles Times*, "There's a harsh saying, 'Some must die so that others can live.' I think the impact that the deaths of Freddie Mercury and Rock Hudson had on the public perception of AIDS are a good analogy to the situation we have now."

Randy Lewis of the *Times* also interviewed Recording Academy President Neil Portnow, who has worked in the music industry since the 1970s as a record producer, music supervisor, and record company executive. Portnow said:

> We need to have a clear-cut understanding of (substance abuse) as a disease, the things that lie behind it and the things that are necessary to treat it. Given the breadth and scope of who this affects in our culture, a more healthy perspective would be very welcome.

Or as Lewis himself deduced, "If (Whitney) Houston's death contributes to a broader understanding of addiction and substance abuse, her legacy might include more than the million-selling recordings she left behind."

In like manner, if Lizzie's demise contributes to the same, on supposition alone, her legacy might include so much more than *Bewitched*, her TV-movies, and even her charitable work while she was alive.

AFTERWORD

Elizabeth Montgomery may have placed too much emphasis on age, and she may or may not have made the best choices with regard to her health, consciously or subconsciously. Either way, she died much too young and long before her time.

Instead of expiring at a ripe old age, following the climactic incidents of what, by most accounts (wealth, fame, good looks) was a happy (public and private) life, Elizabeth swiftly withered away, taking with her extraordinary occurrences, circumstances, and situation comedies and dramas. Instead of her death momentously culminating with a massive celebrity funeral that could have easily been monitored by a widespread audience as a spectacular turn of events, she protected with great dignity a personal agony from becoming a three-ring circus (that she would never have invited *to town*).

She gave herself little credit for artistic accomplishments that also failed to win the formal acceptance of her peers. Her life had been full, exciting, difficult, short, and then she died, without the usual large-scale Hollywood horns and whistles services that have become popular in recent years.

Sometime before or after that, Lizzie's body was cremated, and she departed into a timeless realm, a world of the ageless.

Beyond the unbreakable bond with her devoted children, Lizzie's most intimate relationships with husbands and friends were not always the lengthiest. Her link with her parents, particularly her father, wasn't always the healthiest. Although she never won the coveted TV Emmy amulet and once deemed herself unworthy of any "Mother-of-the-Year" award, the lives of everyone she touched—be they family members, co-workers, peers, recipients of her altruism, once-close friends, or all-too-distant fans—were indelibly changed forever, and for the better.

For the ever-shy Lizzie, such illumination, by way of her celebrated birth in the limelight to later carving out her own celebrity status, came with a lofty price. The public perception of the fanciful *Samantha*, coupled with the high expectations of her father and her lack of confidence, was overwhelming, even for someone who was used to the glimmer and clutter of Hollywood. Robert Montgomery, her most influential relative, may have been her severest critic. Rebecca Allen, her most beloved grandmother, may have been her most loving influence. But Lizzie herself was her own worst enemy.

She lacked certain career ambitions, but still pushed herself too hard. She was raised in a chic environment, but her surroundings were underpinned with a weak foundation. She craved the *average* life, clamored for it away from what often becomes the false glitter of Hollywood. As an adult, she rejoiced in the simplest of pleasures, whether seeing a movie or sharing a pizza (as she would sometimes do with the crew on any one of her TV sets). Such everyday experiences were foreign and nonexistent in her protected and privileged youth.

But as she matured, she retained a youthful spirit. She abhorred haughtiness, but at times could be perceived as much too proud. She welcomed routine conversation, but entertained power-lunch types. She reveled in the spectacle of everyday living, but like most TV and film personalities, felt the periodic anguish that was magnified by celebrity status—a status that was placed upon her extremely likable persona. As Bill Asher said on 1999's *Bewitched: The E! True Hollywood Story*, it was "hard not to" like Elizabeth.

Asher met the criteria of the father-figure type that frequently caught her eye, an appeal also evident in her second marriage to Gig Young, whom she wed after divorcing her first husband Fred Cammann, who was her contemporary in age (she was twenty-one, he was twenty-four).

Her fourth husband Bob Foxworth was ten years her junior and fell outside the confines of the father-figure scenario, although his first name matched that of her dad's. They had met on the set of *Mrs. Sundance* in 1974, two years after the original network demise of *Bewitched*, not one episode of which Foxworth had ever seen and a creative staple that Lizzie wanted to leave behind. She was immediately enchanted with Foxworth who in turn fell expediently under her still potent spell.

Had she and Cammann met at a later time and place, their marriage may have stood the test of time. Instead they wed too young amidst the sophomoric pretense of high society that left them ill-prepared to meet the responsibilities required to make a mature marriage work.

Lizzie was a sophisticated and cultured descendent of American royalty, a royalty that may have had a skeleton or two in its closets, but royalty nonetheless. Throughout it all, she was still imbued with a delightful candor and near naiveté that some in even the most economically challenged families may never grasp. Although not metaphysical like *Samantha*, she was just as heavenly in her appeal. She may have lacked the magical capabilities of her most celebrated role, but that only meant she was a mere mortal like the rest of us, flaws and all. We're all human. We all make mistakes. To quote the title of Doug Tibbles' third-season opening *Bewitched* episode— the show's first color episode, and one in which we learn that *Sam* and *Darrin's* little daughter *Tabitha* has supernatural powers just like her mom— "Nobody's Perfect."

Although Lizzie lived a colorful life, textured with various hues, she did not have super powers like *Samantha* or even *Tabitha,* but she retained a super spirit. Even in her darkest hour, she shined her bright light, and we all basked in her glow.

With or without conscious clarity of her mission, she accomplished extraordinary levels of charitable work, via the fame by which she felt sometimes burdened. For her it was the worst of times, the best of times. The fun, enchanting woman that bewitched us all was periodically bothered and bewildered by an era that she helped create. She seemed much too ready and only strong enough to "pop out" one last time, possessing until the end a complex inner glow and beauty that was coupled with an insecurity that at times was publicly perceived as unassuming poise, and yet a legitimate poise, refined in the finishing school of life.

Overwrought by an underlining thread of sorrow that seeped into, was expressed by, and heralded in her later dramatic TV films, her psyche may have been drained. Pummeled by colorectal cancer, her body had no chance of recovery. Overpowered and racked with emotion, she may not have lost the will to live, but merely succumbed to the difficult decision to die.

Yet before it was too late, prior to the unbearable pain, there was a break in the black cloud of her turmoil. Knowing Lizzie, she realized it was okay to be remembered and so dearly loved by so many people so many years after she turned the world on with her twitch. She realized that, in the eyes of those who love truly, in the *big picture*, flaws and blemishes, physical or otherwise, are endearing, identifiable, and ultimately acceptable, leading to growth of the soul.

From this perspective, and in the eyes of millions, she remains a *supernatural* presence in the fondest way. Her physical being is no longer here, but her metaphysical spirit remains with countless performances: recorded on television, in film, online, in audio, in print, in word, and in deed.

Although not especially religious, she was a spiritual person. For as she once said, rather profoundly, in reflecting on the true priorities of her life and career, "I think of God as the beauty of life. It's loving and being loved."

For family members, friends, colleagues, and countless fans, she was and remains both loving and loved. Elizabeth Montgomery may be gone from this world, but Lizzie is nowhere near forgotten by this world. She lives on in her work and in the cherished memories of those who knew her personally and in what has come to be known in certain esoteric circles as the collective unconscious.

Along this mystical, magical stream of thought, some believe our journey is mostly a spiritual one, with our final destination likened to a rocket soaring into space. The pieces of us that we don't need, namely, all the negative stuff, melt away as we move closer to what some call the "Light," until all that is left is the little capsule that holds our soul.

If true, and why not believe it so, then Lizzie's capsule is missing her father's critical voice, her own self-doubt, the failed relationships, the dark performances, the Emmy losses, the political divide, her missteps, and any and all disease.

All that's left are the positive, productive thoughts—the happy horseback rides, the victories, all of the hugs and kisses she gave and received, her carefree spirit, the countless hours of laughter she instilled by way of her more joyful performances, the generous acts of loving-kindness that she displayed and experienced, and the indelible spark of intelligence that gleamed in her pretty green eyes—all bundled together, magnified, and multiplied somewhere *above*. It is her good deeds, fine work, and noble heart, mind, and soul which have become her immeasurable, priceless, and immortal legacy on Earth.

As her friend Bud Baker wrote nearly fifty years ago, using one of her favorite words, "Bad tomorrows don't exist for her," from here on in, "they're all going to be good for her. That's the great rudder in the turbulent waters of show business, this sense of balance. There is always going to be a dawn and green grass and sun, kids to play with and footballs to kick. . . . She's having *fun*."

In this sense, Elizabeth's . . . Lizzie's . . . Lizbel's ethereal essence is somewhere beautiful, nose-wriggling the light fantastic, leaving Hollywood to wonder if it will ever again emanate a more luminary . . . twitch upon a star.

"We are quicksilver, a fleeting shadow, a distant sound.
Our home has no boundaries beyond which we cannot pass.
We live in music, a flash of color.
We live on the wind and in the sparkle of a star."

—The *Bewitched* witches' anthem

APPENDIX

LIVE ON STAGE

Brigadoon (summer stock, circa 1952)

Biography (summer stock, Luise Rainer Company, circa 1952)

Late Love (National Theatre and the Booth Theatre, Broadway, 1953)
Opened: 10-13-53 Closed: 1-2-54 Performances: 95

The Loud Red Patrick (Ambassador Theatre, Broadway, 1956)
Opened: 10-3-56 Closed: 12-22-56 Performances: 93

Romanoff and Juliet (summer stock, Plymouth Theatre, 1956)
Opened: 10-10-56 Closed: unknown Performances: 389

Cat on a Hot Tin Roof (Bell Theatre, Los Angeles, 1978)
Opened: 3-5-78 Closed: 3-11-78 Performances: approximately 9

Love Letters (1989, The Promenade, Off-Broadway/Edison Theatre on Broadway)
Opened: 10-31-89 Closed: 1-21-90 Performances: 96

TV GUEST STAR ROLES

Robert Montgomery Presents (NBC, 1950–57, 60 minutes, twenty-eight episodes):
"Top Secret" (12-3-51), "The Half-Millioniare a.k.a. The Vise" (7-6-53), "Two of
a Kind" (7-13-53), "A Summer Love" (7-20-53), "Anne's Story" (7-27-53),
"Duet for Two Hands" (8-3-53), "Red Robin Rides Again" (8-10-53), "Pierce
3098" a.k.a. "Whom Death Has Joined Together" (8-27-53), "Grass Roots"
(8-24-53), "Our Hearts Were Young and Gay" (2-15-54), "Once Upon a
Time" (5-31-54), "In His Hands" (6-28-54), "The Expert" a.k.a. "The Mar-
riage Expert" (7-5-54), "Story on Eleventh Street" (7-12-54), "It Happened in
Paris" (7-19-54), "Patricia" (7-26-54), "Home Town" (8-2-54), "About Sara
Caine" (8-9-54), "Personal Story" (8-23-54), "A Matter of Luck" (8-30-54),

"The People You Meet" (9-6-54), "Ten Minute Alibi" (9-13-54), "The Bao-
bab Tree" (4-23-56), "Dream No More" (7-21-56), "Catch a Falling Star" (7-
23-56), "Southern Exposure" (7-30-56), "The Company Wife" (8-27-56),
"Mr. Parker's Rhubarb" (9-3-56)

Armstrong Circle Theatre (NBC/CBS, 1950–63, 30/60 minutes, two episodes):
"The Right Approach" (6-2-53), "The Millstone" (1-19-54)

Kraft Television Theatre (NBC, 1947–58, 60 minutes, six episodes):
"The Light is Cold" (9-22-54), "Patterns" (1-12-55, 2-9-55), "The Diamond as Big
as the Ritz" (9-28-55), "The Last Showdown" (4-11-56), "The Long Arm" (7-
11-56), "The Duel" (3-6-57)

Studio One in Hollywood (CBS, 1948–58, 60 minutes, three episodes):
"Summer Pavilion" (5-2-55), "The Drop of A Hat" (5-7-56), "A Dead Ringer"
(3-10-58)

Appointment with Adventure (CBS, 1955–56, 60 minutes, two episodes):
"Relative Stranger" (11-20-55), "All Through the Night" (2-5-56)

Warner Brothers Presents (ABC, 1955–56, 60 minutes): "Siege (2-14-56)

Climax! (CBS, 1954–58, 60 minutes): "The Shadow of Evil" (5-24-56)

Playhouse 90 (CBS, 1956–60, 90 minutes): "Bitter Heritage" (8-7-58)

Suspicion (NBC, 1957–59, 60 minutes): "The Velvet Vault" (5-19-58)

The DuPont Show of the Month (CBS, 1957–61, 90 minutes): "Harvey" (9-22-58)

Cimarron City (NBC, 1958–60, 60 minutes): "Hired Hand" (11-15-58)

Alfred Hitchcock Presents (CBS, 1955–62, 30 minutes): "Man with a Problem" (11-
16-58)

The Loretta Young Show (NBC, 1953–61, 30 minutes): "Marriage Crisis" (2-15-59)

The Third Man (BBC, syndicated in U.S., 1959–65, 30 minutes): "A Man Takes a
Trip" (4-15-59)

Riverboat (NBC, 1959–61, 60 minutes): "The Barrier" (9-20-59)

Johnny Staccato (NBC/ABC, 1959–60, 60 minutes): *Tempted* (11-19-59)

Wagon Train (NBC, 1957–65, 60 minutes): "The Vittorio Bottecelli Story" (12-
16-59)

The Tab Hunter Show (NBC, 1960–61, 30 minutes): "For Money or Love" (9-
25-60)

Alcoa Presents: One Step Beyond (ABC, 1959–61, 30 minutes): "The Death Waltz"
(10-4-60).

The Untouchables (ABC, 1959–63, 60 minutes): "The Rusty Heller Story" (10-
13-60)

The Twilight Zone (CBS, 1959–64, 30/60 minutes): "Two" (9-15-61)

Thriller (NBC, 1960–62, 60 minutes): "Masquerade" (10-30-61)

Frontier Circus (CBS, 1961–62, 60 minutes): "Karina" (11-9-61)

Checkmate (CBS, 1960–62, 60 minutes): "The Star System" (1-10-62)

Alcoa Premiere (ABC, 1961–63, 60/30 minutes): "Mr. Lucifer" (11-1-62)

Saints and Sinners (NBC, 1962–63, 60 minutes): "The Home-Coming Bit" (1-7-63)

Boston Terrier (6-11-63, 30 minutes, ABC): "Salem Witch Hunt"

Burke's Law (ABC, 1963–66, 60 minutes, two episodes): "Who Killed Mr. X?" (9-27-63), "Who Killed His Royal Highness?" (2-21-64)

Rawhide (CBS, 1959–66, 60 minutes): "Incident at El Crucero" (10-10-63)

77 Sunset Strip (ABC, 1958–64, 60 minutes): "White Lie" (10-25-63)

The Eleventh Hour (NBC, 1962–64, 60 minutes): "The Bronze Locust" (11-6-63)

Bewitched (ABC, 1964–72)

Season One (1964–65)

1) "I *Darrin*, Take This Witch, *Samantha*"; 2) "Be It Ever So Mortgaged"; 3) "Mother, Meet What's His Name?"; 4) "It Shouldn't Happen to a Dog"; 5) "Help, Help, Don't Save Me"; 6) "Little Pitchers Have Big Fears"; 7) "The Witches Are Out"; 8) "The Girl Reporter"; 9) "Witch or Wife"; 10) "Just One Happy Family"; 11) "It Takes One to Know One"; 12) ". . . And Something Makes Three"; 13) "Love is Blind"; 14) "*Samantha* Meets the Folks"; 15) "A Vision of Sugar Plums"; 16) "It's Magic"; 17) "A is for Aardvark"; 18) "The Cat's Meow"; 19) "A Nice Little Dinner Party"; 20) "Your Witch is Showing"; 21) "Ling Ling"; 22) "Eye of the Beholder"; 23) "Red Light, Green Light"; 24) "Which Witch is Which?"; 25) "Pleasure O'Riley"; 26) "Driving is the Only Way to Fly"; 27) "There's No Witch Like an Old Witch"; 28) "Open the Door, Witchcraft"; 29) "Abner Kadabra"; 30) "George the Warlock"; 31) "That Was My Wife"; 32) "Illegal Separation"; 33) "A Change of Face"; 34) "Remember the Main"; 35) "Eat at Mario's"; 36) "*Cousin Edgar*"

Season Two (1965–66)

37) "Alias *Darrin Stephens*"; 38) "A Very Special Delivery"; 39) "We're in for a Bad Spell"; 40) "My Grandson, the Warlock"; 41) "The Joker is a Card"; 42) "Take Two Aspirins and Half a Pint of Porpoise Milk"; 43) "Trick or Treat"; 44) "The Very Informal Dress"; 45) "And Then I Wrote"; 46) "Junior Executive"; 47) "*Aunt Clara's* Old Flame"; 48) "A Strange Little Visitor"; 49) "My Boss the Teddy Bear"; 50) "Speak the Truth"; 51) "A Vision of Sugarplums"; 52) "The Magic Cabin"; 53) "Maid to Order"; 54) "And Then There Were Three"; 55)

"My Baby the Tycoon"; 56) "*Samantha* Meets the Folks"; 57) "Fastest Gun on Madison Avenue"; 58) "The Dancing Bear"; 59) "Double Tate"; 60) "*Samantha* the Dressmaker"; 61) "The Horse's Mouth"; 62) "Baby's First Paragraph"; 63) "The Leprechaun"; 64) "Double Split"; 65) "Disappearing *Samantha*"; 66) "Follow that Witch (Part One)"; 67) "Follow that Witch (Part Two)"; 68) "A Bum Raps"; 69) "Divided He Falls"; 70) "Man's Best Friend"; 71) "The Catnapper"; 72) "What Every Young Man Should Know"; 73) "The Girl with the Golden Nose"; 74) "Prodigy"

Season Three (1966–67)

75) "Nobody's Perfect"; 76) "The Moment of Truth"; 77) "Witches and Warlocks Are My Favorite Things"; 78) "Accidental Twins"; 79) "A Most Unusual Wood Nymph"; 80) "*Endora* Moves in for a Spell"; 81) "Twitch or Treat"; 82) "Dangerous Diaper Dan"; 83) "The Short Happy Circuit of *Aunt Clara*"; 84) "I'd Rather Twitch Than Fight"; 85) "Oedipus Hex"; 86) "*Sam's* Spooky Chair"; 87) "My Friend Ben (Part One)"; 88) "*Samantha* for the Defense (Part Two)"; 89) "A Gazebo Never Forgets"; 90) "Soap Box Derby"; 91) "*Sam* in the Moon"; 92) "Ho Ho the Clown"; 93) "Super Car"; 94) "The Corn is as High as a Guernsey's Eye"; 95) "The Trial and Error of *Aunt Clara*"; 96) "Three Wishes"; 97) "I Remember You . . . Sometimes"; 98) "Art for *Sam's* Sake"; 99) "Charlie Harper, Winner"; 100) "*Aunt Clara's* Victoria Victory"; 101) "The Crone of Cawdor"; 102) "No More Mr. Nice Guy"; 103) "It's Wishcraft"; 104) "How to Fail in Business with All Kinds of Help"; 105) "Bewitched, Bothered and Infuriated"; 106) "Nobody But a Frog Knows How to Live"; 107) "There's Gold in Them There Pills"

Season Four (1967–68)

108) "Long Live the Queen"; 109) "Toys in Babeland"; 110) "Business, Italian Style"; 111) "Double, Double Toil and Trouble"; 112) "Cheap, Cheap"; 113) "No Zip in My Zap"; 114) "Birdies, Bogeys and Baxter"; 115) "The Safe and Sane Halloween"; 116) "Out of Synch, Out of Mind"; 117) "That Was No Chick, That Was My Wife"; 118) "Allergic to Macedonian Dodo Birds"; 119) "*Samantha's* Thanksgiving to Remember"; 120) "Solid Gold Mother-in-Law"; 121) "My, What Big Ears You Have"; 122) "I Get Your Nanny, You Get My Goat"; 123) "Humbug Not Spoken Here"; 124) "*Samantha's* Da Vinci Dilemma"; 125) "Once in a Vial"; 126) "Snob in the Grass"; 127)" If They Never Met"; 128) "Hippie, Hippie, Hooray"; 129) "A Prince of a Guy"; 130)

"McTavish"; 131) "How Green Was My Grass"; 132) "To Twitch Or Not To Twitch"; 133) "Playmates"; 134) "*Tabitha's* Cranky Spell"; 135) "I Confess"; 136) "A Majority of Two"; 137) "*Samantha's* Secret Saucer"; 138) "The No-Harm Charm"; 139) "Man of the Year"; 140) "Splitsville"

Season Five (1968–69)

141) "*Samantha's* Wedding Present"; 142) "*Samantha* Goes South for a Spell"; 143) "*Samantha* on the Keyboard"; 144) "*Darrin* Gone and Forgotten"; 145) "It's So Nice to Have a Spouse Around the House"; 146) "Mirror, Mirror on the Wall"; 147) "*Samantha's* French Pastry"; 148) "Is it Magic or Imagination?"; 149) "*Samantha* Fights City Hall"; 150) "*Samantha* Loses Her Voice"; 151) "I Don't Want to Be a Toad"; 152) "Weep No More, My Willow"; 153) "Instant Courtesy"; 154) "*Samantha's* Super Maid"; 155) "*Cousin Serena* Strikes Again (Part One)"; 156) "*Cousin Serena* Strikes Again (Part Two)"; 157) One Touch of Midas; 158): Samantha the Bard; 159) Samantha the Sculptress; 160) "*Mrs. Stephens*, Where Are You?"; 161) "Marriage, Witches' Style; 162) "Going Ape"; 163) "*Tabitha's* Weekend"; 164) "The Battle of Burning Oak"; 165) "*Samantha's* Power Failure"; 166) "*Samantha* Twitches for UNICEF"; 167) "Daddy Does His Thing"; 168) "*Samantha's* Good News"; 169) "*Samantha's* Shopping Spree"; 170) "*Samantha and Darrin* in Mexico City"

Season Six (1969–70)

171) "*Samantha* and the Beanstalk"; 172) "*Samantha's* Yoo-Hoo Maid"; 173) "*Samantha's* Caesar Salad"; 174) "*Samantha's* Curious Cravings"; 175) "And Something Makes Four"; 176) "Naming *Samantha's* New Baby"; 177) "To Trick or Treat or Not to Trick or Treat"; 178) "A Bunny for *Tabitha*"; 179) "*Samantha's* Secret Spell"; 180) "Daddy Comes for a Visit (Part One)"; 181) "*Darrin* the Warlock (Part Two)", 182) "*Samantha's* Double Mother Trouble"; 183) "You're So Agreeable"; 184) "Santa Comes to Visit and Stays and Stays"; 185) "*Samantha's* Better Halves"; 186) "*Samantha's* Lost Weekend"; 187) "The Phrase Is Familiar"; 188) "*Samantha's* Secret Is Discovered"; 189) "*Tabitha's* Very Own *Samantha*"; 190) "Super Arthur"; 191) "What Makes *Darrin* Run"; 192) "*Serena* Stops the Show"; 193) "Just a Kid Again"; 194) "The Generation Zap"; 195) "Okay, Who's the Wise Witch?"; 196) "A Chance on Love"; 197) "If the Shoe Pinches"; 198) "Mona *Sammy*"; 199) "Turn on the Old Charm"; 200) "Make Love, Not Hate"

Season Seven (1970–71)

201) "To Go or Not to Go, That is the Question (Part One)"; 202): "Salem, Here We Come (Part Two)"; 203) "The Salem Saga (Part One)"; 204) "*Samantha's* Hot Bed Warmer (Part Two)"; 205) "*Darrin* on a Pedestal"; 206) "Paul Revere Rides Again"; 207) "*Samantha's* Bad Day in Salem"; 208) "*Samantha's* Old Salem Trip"; 209): "*Samantha's* Pet Warlock"; 210) "*Samantha's* Old Man"; 211) "The Corsican Cousins"; 212) "*Samantha's* Magic Potion"; 213) "Sisters at Heart"; 214) "Mother-in-Law of the Year"; 215) "Mary, the Good Fairy (Part One)"; 216) "The Good Fairy Strikes Again (Part Two)"; 217) "Return of *Darrin* the Bold"; 218): "The House That *Uncle Arthur* Built"; 219) "*Samantha* and the Troll"; 220) "This Little Piggie"; 221) "Mixed Doubles"; 222) "*Darrin* Goes Ape"; 223) "Money Happy Returns"; 224) "Out of the Mouths of Babes"; 225) "*Sam's* Psychic Slip"; 226) "*Samantha's* Magic Mirror"; 227) "Laugh, Clown, Laugh"; 228) "*Samantha* and the Antique Doll"

Season Eight (1971–72)

229) "How Not to Lose Your Head to King Henry VIII (Part One)"; 230) "How Not to Lose Your Head to King Henry VIII (Part Two)"; 231) "*Samantha* and the Loch Ness Monster"; 232) "*Samantha's* Not-So-Leaning Tower of Pisa"; 233) "Bewitched, Bothered, and Baldoni"; 234) "Paris, Witches' Style"; 235) "The Ghost Who Made a Spectre of Himself"; 236) "TV or Not TV"; 237) "A Plague on Maurice and *Samantha*"; 238) "Hansel and Gretel in *Samantha*-land"; 239) "The Warlock in the Gray Flannel Suit"; 240) "The Eight-Year Witch"; 241) "Three Men and a Witch on a Horse"; 242) "Adam, Warlock or Washout"; 243) "*Samantha's* Magic Sitter"; 244) "*Samantha* is Earthbound"; 245) "*Serena's* Richcraft"; 246) "*Samantha* on Thin Ice"; 247) "*Serena's* Youth Pill"; 248) "*Tabitha's* First Day at School"; 249) "George Washington Zapped Here (Part One)"; 250) "George Washington Zapped Here (Part Two)"; 251) "School Days, School Daze"; 252) "A Good Turn Never Goes Unpunished"; 253) "*Sam's* Witchcraft Blows a Fuse"; 254) "The Truth, Nothing But the Truth, So Help Me, *Sam*"

BEWITCHED-RELATED PERSONAL APPEARANCES

"Chevrolet's *Bewitched* Bonanza Commercial" (9-27-64)
"Lux Beauty Soap Commercial" (broadcast in Canada, 1965)

"ABC Fall Preview Special" (August 1965)
"Jan & Dean" (unsold series pilot, 1966)

General Personal Appearances

Igor Cassini "Movie Revival Ball" (1953–54) Segment: 11-1-53
Here's Hollywood (NBC, 1960–62, 30 minutes) Segment: 6-15-61
The Mike Douglas Show (syndicated, 1963–82, 90/60 minutes) Segment: 11-4-66
The Hollywood Palace (ABC, 1964–70, 60 minutes) Segment: 10-1-66
The Tournament of Roses Parade (1-2-67, ABC)
The Joey Bishop Show (ABC, 1967–69, 90 minutes) Segment 12-22-67
Password (CBS, 1961– 67/ABC, 1971–75, 30 minutes) Segments: December 12–16, 1966; May 15–19, 1967; May 5–9, 1971; September 13–17, 1971; November 29–December 3, 1971; February 7–11, 1972; July 17–21/1972; October 2–6, 1972; December 4–8, 1972; April 9–13, 1973; June 11–15, 1973; November 19–23, 1973; January 7–11, 1974; April 22–26, 1974; July 15–19, 1974; July 29–August 2, 1974; March 24–28, 1975
Password Plus (NBC, 1979–82, 30 minutes) Segments: January 8–12, 1979; February 26–March 2, 1979; July 30–August 3,1979
The Hollywood Squares (NBC, 1966–81, 30 minutes) Segments: November 9–13, 1970; May 1–5, 1972; June 19–23, 1972; November 10–14, 1975; January 19–23, 1976
The Merv Griffin Show (syndicated, 1962–86, 90/60 minutes) Segment: 12-21-70
The 28th Annual Tony Awards (NBC, 4- 21-74, 120 minutes)
"Japanese Cook" commercials (eight in total, 1980–83)
Entertainment Tonight (syndicated, 1981– present, 30 minutes/60 minutes) Segments: 12-21-85, 2-18-91, 3-25-94
CBS Morning Show (1987–99, 120 minutes) Segments: 1–24-90, 5-12-92
KCBS News (Los Angeles CBS affiliate) Segment: 2-19-91
One on One with John Tesh (NBC, 1991–92, 30 minutes) Segment: 5-12-92
The Dennis Miller Show (syndicated, 1992–2004, 60 minutes) Segment: 5-8-92
The Los Angeles Gay and Lesbian Pride Parade (6-28-92)

TV-Movies

The Spiral Staircase (NBC, 10-4-61, 60 minutes)
The Victim (ABC/Universal, 11-14-72, 90 minutes)
Mrs. Sundance (ABC/20th Century Fox Television, 1-15-74, 90 minutes)

A Case of Rape (NBC/Universal, 2-20-74, 100 minutes)
The Legend of Lizzie Borden (ABC/Paramount Television, 2-10-75, 100 minutes)
Dark Victory (NBC/Universal, 2-5-76, 150 minutes)
A Killing Affair (CBS/Columbia, 9-21-77, 100 minutes)
The Awakening Land (NBC/Warner Bros., 420 minutes, three-part mini-series): "The Trees" (2-19-78), "The Fields" (2-20-78), "The Town" (2-21-78)
Jennifer: A Woman's Story (NBC/Marble Arch, 3-5-79, 120 minutes)
Act of Violence (CBS/Paramount Studios, 4-10-79, 100 minutes)
Belle Starr (CBS/Hanna-Barbera, 4-20-80, 97 minutes)
When the Circus Came to Town (CBS/Entheos Prods/Meteor Films, 1-20-81, 90 minutes)
The Rules of Marriage (CBS, 5-10/5-11-82, two-part film, 240 minutes)
Missing Pieces (CBS/Entheos Unlimited, 5-14-83, 96 minutes)
Second Sight: A Love Story (CBS, 3-15-84, 100 minutes)
Amos (CBS, 9-25-85, 100 minutes)
Betweeen the Darkness and the Dawn (NBC, 12-23-85, 100 minutes)
Hallmark Hall of Fame: Face to Face (CBS, 1-24-90, 93 minutes)
Sins of the Mother (CBS, 2-19-91, 93 minutes)
With Murder in Mind (CBS/Bob Banner Associates, 5-12-92, 100 minutes)
The Black Widow Murders: The Blanche Moore Story (CBS, 5-3-93, 92 minutes)
The Corpse Had a Familiar Face (CBS, 3-27-94, 120 minutes)
Deadline for Murder: From the Files of Edna Buchanan (CBS, 5-9-95, 92 minutes)

FEATURE FILMS

Your Witness (a.k.a. *Eyewitness*) (U.K./released in U.S. 8-26-50)
The Court-Martial of Billy Mitchell (Warner Bros., 12-31-55, 100 minutes)
Bells are Ringing (MGM, 6-23-60, 126 minutes)
Johnny Cool (United Artists/Chrislaw Productions, 10-2-63, 103 minutes)
Who's Been Sleeping in My Bed? (Paramount/Amro-Claude-Mea, 12-26-63, 103 minutes)
How to Stuff a Wild Bikini (MGM, 7-14-65, 93 minutes)
Bewitched (Sony/Columbia, 2005, 90 minutes)

VOICEOVERS

On the Radio

Craven Street (five-part radio play, 1993)

Appendix

For Audio Books

Beauty's Punishment and *Beauty's Release* (Publisher, 1994, each 180 minutes)
When We Were Very Young (Penguin Audio, 5-12-1995)

In Movies

Bikini Beach (American International Pictures, release date: 7-22-64, 99 minutes)
Cover Up: Behind the Iran Contra Affair (Empowerment Project Studios, 7-13-88, 72 minutes)
The Panama Deception (Empowerment Project Studios, 7-31-92, 91 minutes)

On Laserdisc

Here Comes Mr. Jordan *(Columbia, 1991, Laser Disc Audio Track, 88 minutes)*

On Televison

The Flintstones (ABC, 1960–66, 30 minutes): episode: "*Samantha*" (10-22-65)
Batman: The Animated Series (Warner Bros., syndicated, 1992–95, 22 minutes): episode: "Showdown" (9-12-95)

AWARDS AND ACCOLADES

The Daniel Blum Theater World Award

1953: Most Promising Newcomer (*Late Love*)

Emmy Nominations

1961: Outstanding Single Performance by an Actress in a Leading Role (*The Untouchables*)
1966: Outstanding Lead Actress, Comedy Series (*Bewitched*)
1967: Outstanding Lead Actress, Comedy Series (*Bewitched*)
1968: Outstanding Lead Actress, Comedy Series (*Bewitched*)
1969: Outstanding Lead Actress, Comedy Series (*Bewitched*)
1970: Outstanding Lead Actress, Comedy Series (*Bewitched*)
1974: Outstanding Lead Actress, Drama Series (*A Case of Rape*)
1975: Outstanding Lead Actress in a Special Program, Drama/Comedy (*The Legend of Lizzie Borden*)
1978: Outstanding Lead Actress in a Limited Series (*The Awakening Land*)

397

Golden Globe Nominations

1965: Golden Globe Award Best TV Star, Female (*Bewitched*)
1966: Golden Globe Award Best TV Star, Female (*Bewitched*)
1969: Golden Globe Award Best TV Star, Female (*Bewitched*)
1971: Golden Globe Best TV Actress, Musical/Comedy (*Bewitched*)

Other Awards

Laurel Awards Nomination
1964: Golden Laurel Top Female, New Face (Fourth Place)

The Women in Film Crystal + Lucy Awards
In recognition of excellence and innovation in creative works that have enhanced the perception of women through the medium of television.
In 1995, The Lucy Award went to Elizabeth Montgomery, accepted by Rebecca Asher

TV Land
Superlatively Supernatural Series
2004: Winner: *Bewitched*

Favorite Dual-Role Character
2003: Nominated: *Samantha/Serena, Bewitched*

2005: Honorary Statue
Elizabeth Montgomery as *Samantha Stephens*, Salem, MA

Star on Hollywood Walk of Fame
2008: Hollywood, CA
Accepted by Rebecca Asher and William Asher, Jr.

"Elizabeth Montgomery was an inspired choice to play a witch, because her natural affect was such a perfect counterpoise to the traditional Halloween witch. Fit and beautiful, with a bright and sunny disposition, she was one of those rare beauties who somehow remain accessible, oblivious to their own powerful allure."

—Thomas Hill, Vice President, TV Land (2012)

"Elizabeth Montgomery was TV's version of Grace Kelly . . . a legend . . . so wonderful at playing comedy, drama, and romance. She was one of a kind and is sorely missed."

—Monika Cottrill, television historian (2012)

"Thank you."

—Elizabeth Montgomery, on *The Dennis Miller Show*, responding to enthusiastic audience members voicing their adoration: "I love you" and "We all do"! (May 12, 1992)

SOURCES

Many organizations, publishers, books and publications, documents, and online sources proved invaluable to the writing of this book, beginning with:

Jon Mulvaney of The Criterion Collection, who granted generous permission to quote excerpts from Ronald Haver's interviews with Elizabeth Montgomery that are heard on the 1991 audio commentary from the fiftieth anniversary laserdisc release of the Robert Montgomery film, *Here Comes Mr. Jordan*; Eileen Spangler of *TV Guide* magazine; Steve R. Biller at *Palm Springs Life* magazine; Gwen Feldman from Silman-James Press; Claudia Kuehl and Joan "Joey" York for the excerpts from *The Seesaw Girl and Me: A Memoir* by Dick York; James Pylant and his online article, "The Bewitching Family Tree of Elizabeth Montgomery," from www.genealogymagazine.com; Rene Reyes, Martin Gostanian, and Gary Browning at The Paley Center for Media in Beverly Hills, California, where, on February 27, 2012, and March 2, 2012, I was graciously allowed access via Console 11 in the Scholars' Room to view the following programs: *Appointment with Adventure*: "Relative Stranger" (original airdate: CBS, 11-20-55), *The Spiral Staircase* (original airdate: NBC,10-4-61); *Kraft Television Theatre*: *Patterns* (original airdate: NBC, 1-12-55), *Mr. Lucifer* (original airdate: NBC, 11-1-62), *Kraft Television Theatre*: *The Diamond as Big as the Ritz* (original airdate: NBC, 9-28-55); Jim Pollock at MSNBC; and Kevin Burns at Prometheus Entertainment.

Additional sources that were referenced for this book include *The Complete Directory to Prime Time Network and Cable TV Shows* by Tim Brooks and Earle Marsh, *Total Television* by Alex McNeil; www.bobsbewitching daughter.com; www.earlofhollywood.com; www.harpiesbizarre.com; www.bewitched.net; and www.imdb.com.

Portions of chapter 8, "Spirits and Demons," were drawn from *Final Gig: The Man Behind the Murder* by George Eells (Houghton Mifflin, 1991). Portions of chapter 10, "Lizmet," were drawn from *Please Don't Shoot My Dog: The Autobiography of Jackie Cooper* (William Morrow, 1981).

Additional book sources include: *Heavenly Bodies: Remembering Hollywood and Fashion's Favorite AIDS Benefit* by Michael Anketell (Taylor Publishing Company, 1999); *Sweethearts of the '60s TV: The Women of Action, Dream Wives, Girls Next Door, Comic Cuties, and Fantasy Figures from Your Favorite Shows* by Ronald L. Smith (S.P.I. Books, 1993); *Straight Shooting* by Robert Stack (Berkley Books, 1981); *Everything Is Going to Be Just Fine: The Ramblings of a Mad Hairdresser* by Billy Clift (Everything Is Going To Be Just Fine Society, 1998), among others.

Various commentary and references from articles from *TV Guide* appear throughout this book, and all such commentary and references appear courtesy of *TV Guide Magazine*, LLC. (See full list on in Periodicals section of Bibliography.)

In all, new quotes and commentaries that appear in this book were culled from exclusive interviews with Elizabeth Montgomery and selected individuals; conversations that took place directly with the author in person, via telephone in 1988 and 1989, or in person or via telephone in 2011 and 2012. Additional quotes and commentaries were resourced from various magazine, newspaper, or TV interviews and/or documentaries relating to or about Elizabeth Montgomery, and dated from 1933 to 1995. TV and movie character quotes were culled from various fictional TV show or films associated with the roles performed by Elizabeth Montgomery and her co-stars in scripted performances from 1953 to 1995.

The television program and film character quotations and actor commentaries from the various nonfiction and fiction TV shows or movies are reproduced within this book for educational purposes and/or in the spirit of publicity for those particular productions, be they scripted or unscripted in nature.

In each case, every effort was made to acknowledge specific credits whenever and wherever possible, and we apologize in advance for any omissions, and will undertake every effort to make any appropriate changes in future editions of this book if necessary.

BIBLIOGRAPHY

BOOKS

Anketell, Michael. *Heavenly Bodies: Remembering Hollywood and Fashion's Favorite AIDS Benefit.* Dallas. Taylor Publishing Company. 1999.

Arce, Hector. *Gary Cooper: An Intimate Biography.* New York. Bantam Books. 1980.

Barney, William Clifford. Preston, Eugene Dimon. Editors. *Genealogy of the Barney Family in America* (Springfield, Virginia: Barney Family Historical Association, reprinted 1990), entry 3251.

Blymyer, Ginger. *Hairdresser to the Stars: A Hollywood Memoir.* Infinity Publishing. PA. 2002.

Brooks, Tim. Marsh, Earle. *The Complete Directory to Prime Time Network and Cable TV Shows (1946–Present).* Ninth Edition. New York. Ballantine Books. 2007.

Boyer, G. Bruce. Cooper Janis, Maria. Lauren, Ralph. Ansel, Ruth. *Gary Cooper: Enduring Style.* PowerHouse Books. 2011.

Burnett, Carol. *This Time Together: Laughter and Reflection.* New York. Harmony Books. 2010.

Carpozi, George. *The Gary Cooper Story.* New Rochelle, New York. Arlington House. 1970.

Clift, Billy. *Everything Is Going to Be Just Fine: Ramblings of a Mad Hairdresser.* Everything Is Going to Be Just Fine Society. 1998.

Cooper, Jackie. *Please Don't Shoot My Dog: The Autobiography of Jackie Cooper.* New York. William Morrow & Company. 1981.

Cooper Janis, Maria. Hanks, Tom. *Gary Cooper Off Camera: A Daughter Remembers.* Harry N. Abrams. 1999.

Dunne, Dominick. *The Way We Lived Then: Recollections of a Well-Known Name Dropper.* Crown. September 1999.

Eells, George. *Final Gig: The Man Behind the Murder.* Harcourt Brace Jovanovich. 1991.

Esposito, Joe. *Remember Elvis.* TCB JOE Enterprises. 2006.

Grams, Jr., Martin. *The Twilight Zone: Unlocking the Door to a Television Classic.* OTR Publishing. Maryland. 2008.

Jordan, Rene. *Gary Cooper.* Utica, New York. Pyramid. 1974.

Karol, Michael. *The ABC Movie of the Week Companion.* September 1977. (*The Abilene Reporter-News*; Texas).

Lamparski, Richard. *Whatever Became Of . . . ?* Volume III. New York. Ace Books. 1970.

McClure, Rhonda R. *Finding Your Famous (& Infamous) Ancestors.* Cincinnati. Betterway Books. 2003.

McNeil, Alex. *Total Television: A Comprehensive Guide to Programming from 1948 to the Present.* New York. Penguin. 1991.

Parrish, James Robert. Pitts, Michael R. *The Great Western Pictures.* Scarecrow Press. 1976.

Pilato, Herbie J *Bewitched Forever.* Texas. Tapestry Press. 2004.

Pilato, Herbie J *The Bewitched Book.* New York. Dell. 1992.

Podell, Janet. Editor. *The Annual Obituary.* St. Martin's Press. 1982.

Russo, J. Anthony. *Creativity or Madness: The Passion of a Hollywood Bit Player.* BookSurge Publishing. 2005.

Wayne, Jane Ellen. *Cooper's Women.* Prentice Hall Press. 1988.

Smith, Ronald L. *Sweethearts of '60s TV.* S.P.I. Books. March 1993.

Stack, Robert (with Mark Evans). *Straight Shooting.* New York. Macmillan. 1980.

Stetler, Susan L. *Biography Almanac. Volume 1.* Detroit. Gale Research Company. 1987.

Thompson, Gary. *Gary Cooper (Great Stars).* Faber & Faber. 2010.

Wayne, Jane Ellen. *Cooper's Women.* New York. Prentice Hall Press. 1988.

Wright, John W. (a passage from). *History of Switzerland County, Indiana. From their Earliest Settlement.* Chicago. Weakley, Harriman & Co. Publishers. 1885.

York, Dick. *The Seesaw Girl and Me: A Memoir.* New Jersey. New Path Press. 2004.

Zicree, Mark Scott. *The Twilight Zone Companion.* Second Edition. Los Angeles. Silman James Press. 1992.

PERIODICALS

Anderson, Nancy. "Liz Montgomery's Mother Role." Online. *Ladies' Circle.* July 1970. Downloaded January 7, 2012.

Ardmore, Jane. "An Old Beau Tells All about Liz Montgomery's Past." Online. *TV Radio Mirror.* September 1967. Downloaded January 7, 2012.

Ardmore, Jane. "Elizabeth Montgomery: My Two Husbands Are Expecting." Online. *Silver Screen*. September 1965. Downloaded January 7, 2012.

Ardmore, Jane. "How Would You Like to Try My Sourdough Bread?" Online. *TV Radio Mirror*. September 1966. Downloaded January 7, 2012.

Armstrong, Lois. Cortina, Betty. Gliatto, Tom. "That Magic Feeling." *People*. June 5, 1995. pp. 42–47.

Asher, William. "The Love Letter that Made Liz Montgomery Weep." Online. *TV Radio Mirror. July 1967*. Downloaded January 7, 2012.

Barbee, Pat. "Featuring Elizabeth Montgomery and Robert Foxworth at Home." *Beverly Hills 213*. February 5, 1992.

Bell, Joseph N. Bell. "TV's Witch to Watch." Online. *Pageant*. April 1965. Downloaded March 7, 2012.

Bostick, Jim. "Salem's *Bewitched* Statue." *Gather Entertainment*. June 19, 2006. Online. December 12, 2006. Downloaded March 26, 2012.

Brandt, Lily. "Liz Montgomery Says: I Hope This Spell Lasts." Online. *Inside Movie*. October 1966. Downloaded January 7, 2012.

Braxton, Greg. "Ed Asner Revisits Hawaii." *Los Angeles Times*. March 19, 2012.

Burroughs, K.V. "Elizabeth Montgomery Divorcing." Online. *Movieland and TV Time*. September 1972. Downloaded January 7, 2012.

Butterfield, Alan. "*Bewitched* Star's Brave Last Days." *National Enquirer*. May 30, 1995.

Chance, Tabitha. "From *Bewitched* to Besieged." *TV Guide*. November 10, 1979. pp. 14–16.

Cook, B.W. "William Asher: The Man Who Invented the Sitcom." *Palm Springs Life*. December 1999.

Deane, Ellen. "Liz Montgomery Says: Too Much Happiness is a Bad Thing." Online. *TV Circle*. August 1970. Downloaded January 7, 2012.

Del Valle, David. "Getting Lizzie with It." Camp David. May 18, 2010.

Dozier, William. "The Man Who Helped Deliver a $9000 Baby Tells How It Happened." *TV Guide*. January 27, 1968. pp. 15–18.

Efron, Edith. "He's Almost Invisible in the Glare of Success." *TV Guide*. May 29, 1965.

Elber, Lynn. "*Bewitched* Star Dies from Cancer." *Fort Worth Star-Telegram*. May 19, 1995.

Fischer, Paul. "Interview: Nicole Kidman." Online. www.darkhorizons.com. Downloaded June 6, 2005.

Fleishman, Jeffrey, and Johnson, Glen. "Pan Am 103 Bomber Dies in Tripoli." *The Los Angeles Times*. May 21, 2012.

Francis, Terry. "One of These Babies is a Witch: Only Samantha Knows Its Real Life Secret." Online. *TV Radio Mirror.* 1966. Downloaded January 7, 2012.

George, Lewis. "Now Liz is a Shooting Star!" *Globe.* 1980.

Hano, Arnold. "Rough, Tough and Delightful: The Ashers Agree on What They Want, Including Who's the Boss." *TV Guide.* May 13, 1967. pp. 19–22.

Hesse, Earle. "Liz Montgomery Confesses: Those TV Ratings Give Me the Willies (Yes, Even When I'm on Top of Them)." Online. www.harpiesbizarre.com. *Screen Stars.* August 1965. Downloaded March 22, 2012.

Holland, Jack. "What Makes Samantha Run?" Online. *TV Mirror.* March 1968. Downloaded January 7, 2012.

Hubbard, Ben. "Lockerbie Bomber in Coma, Near Death, Brother Says." Online. *Associated Press.* Downloaded August 29, 2011.

Jacques, Steve. "A Case of Rape: Liz and the Secret Fear All Women Face." 1974.

Jason, Jackie. "Elizabeth Montgomery's Baby Book." Online. *TV Photo Story.* April 1966. Downloaded January 7, 2012.

Kaufman, Bill. "Plummer Joins the Circus to Romance Former Witch." *The Toronto Star.* January 20, 1981 (Newsday).

Kessner, Jane. "*Bewitched's* Liz Montgomery: My Husband Pushes Me Around (And I Love It!)." Online. *Motion Picture.* September 1966. Downloaded January 7, 2012.

Kessner, Jane. "Her Past Catches Up with Liz Montgomery." Online. *TV Radio Mirror.* April 1970. Downloaded January 7, 2012.

Landy, Jane. "Liz Montgomery's Real-Life Miracle." Online. *Modern Screen.* July 1970. Downloaded January 7, 2012.

Lewis, Richard Warren. "Double, Double, Toil and Trouble." *TV Guide.* November 28, 1964. pp. 20–23.

Lim, Dennis. "That Special Cassavetes Touch." *The Los Angeles Times.* May 27, 2012.

Massarella, Linda. "*Bewitched* Star Dies of Cancer." *The New York Post.* May 19, 1995

Mayher, Jane. "Sisters at Heart: A Very Special *Bewitched*." Online. *TV Picture Life.* December 1971. Downloaded January 7, 2012.

McCabe, Kathy. "*Bewitched* Statue Charms Salem Fans." Online. *The Boston Globe.* June 16, 2005. Downloaded January 7, 2012.

McCartney, Anthony. "Drowning Killed Houston but Drugs Took High Toll." Online. *Associated Press.* Downloaded March 23, 2012.

McConnaughey, Janet. "Settlement in Elly Mae Clampett Barbie Doll Suit." Online. *Associated Press.* Downloaded December 12, 2011.

Perlberg, Rose. "Natural Childbirth: What Liz Montgomery Says." Online. *TV Picture Life*. October 1965. Downloaded January 7, 2012.

Post, Kathleen. "A Second Baby, A Special Problem." Online. *TV Radio Mirror*. November 1966. Downloaded January 7, 2012.

Post, Kathleen. "To Hex With Sex: How Liz Montgomery Found Something Even Better." Online. *TV Radio Mirror*. June 1965. Downloaded January 7, 2012.

Pylant, James. "The Bewitching Family Tree of Elizabeth Montgomery." Online. www.genealogymagazine.com. Downloaded. February 8, 2012.

Rand, Flora. "Pregnant Liz Montgomery Tells Why: My Next Baby Will Be Born on TV!" Online. *TV Radio Mirror*. August 1965. Downloaded January 7, 2012.

Resnick, Sylvia. "The Day Liz Montgomery Drew Closer to God." Online. *TV Radio Mirror*. February 1970. Downloaded January 7, 2012.

Sanders, Lynn. "Elizabeth Montgomery Sounds Off on Parents, Protesters and the Problems of the Generation Gap." Online. *Silver Screen*. October 1970. Downloaded January 7, 2012.

Searle, Ronald. "Wherein a Dastardly Plot is Uncovered by Our Artist, Ronald Searle." *TV Guide*. June 18, 1966. pp. 15–18.

Segal, David. "*Bewitched* Statue Bothers Some in Salem." Online. *Washington Post*. May 10, 2005. Downloaded January 7, 2012.

Stang, Joanne. "The Bewitching Miss Montgomery Hollywood." Online. *New York Times*. November 22, 1964. Downloaded January 7, 2012.

Starr, Jacqueline. "Liz Montgomery Worries: Are My Babies in Danger?" Online. *Screen Stars*. August 1967. Downloaded January 7, 2012.

Wilkie, Jane. "Two Babies in One Year: 11 Babies in Five Years." Online. *TV Radio Mirror*. November 1969. Downloaded January 7, 2012.

Windeler, Robert. "TV's Top Series Add Ingredients." Special to *New York Times*. Hollywood. July 20, 1967.

Winelander, Nancy. "Liz Montgomery Tells: How Her New Baby Made Her More of a Mother." Online. *TV Picture Life*. May 1970. Downloaded January 7, 2012.

Winelander, Nancy. "This is the Baby Liz Montgomery Thought She Could Never Love!" Online. *TV Picture Life*. October, 1969. Downloaded March 17, 2012.

"Cheers 'N'Jeers." *TV Guide*. July 16, 1994. p. 6.

"Dressing Up for Parties." *TV Guide*. October 30, 1953. p. 22.

"Like Dad, Like Daughter." *TV Guide*. July 24, 1953. pp. 8–9.

"More Montgomery Magic." Online. *TV-Movies Today*. August 1975. Downloaded January 7, 2012.

"Salem's Samantha Statue." *New England Travels*. Online. October 30, 2007. Downloaded March 26, 2012.

"Samantha Goes Home." *TV Guide*. September 5, 1970. pp. 6–7.

"Samantha/Jeannie: The Debate Continues." *TV Guide*. August 27, 1994. p. 29.

"10 Actresses Pick Hollywood's Greatest Lovers." Online. *Photoplay*. February 1965. Downloaded January 7, 2012.

"The Tide Has Turned for Elizabeth Montgomery." *TV Guide*. August 19, 1961. pp. 8–10 (also titled on p. 8 as "Along Came the Untouchables").

"TV Breaks Old Taboos with New Morality." *Jet*. December 1, 1977.

"TV Land Landmark Immortalizes Samantha Stephens of *Bewitched* in Salem." Online. *PR Newswire*. June 15, 2005. Downloaded March 27, 2012.

ADDITIONAL SOURCES

Bewitched: The E! True Hollywood Story. August 22, 1999. Recorded on videotape.

Biography. A&E. February 15, 1999.

CBS This Morning. January 24, 1990. Recorded on videotape.

CBS This Morning. May 12, 1992. Recorded on videotape.

Cheers 'N' Jeers. *TV Guide*. July 16, 1994. p. 6.

The Earl of Hollywood: The Life and Career of Robert Montgomery (www.earl ofhollywood.com).

"Elizabeth Makes Bell Ring." *Minneapolis Star-Tribune*. March 30, 1980.

"Elizabeth Montgomery Reveals Surprising Truth Behind Squeaky-Clean '60s Sitcom." *National Enquirer*. August 4, 1992.

Internet Movie Database (www.imdb.com).

Lawrence Witte Static. *Denton Journal*. Denton, Maryland. November 20, 1964.

The Mike Douglas Show. November 4, 1966.

"More Montgomery Magic." Online. *TV-Movies Today*. August 1975. Downloaded January 7, 2012.

MSNBC's *Headliners & Legends*. August 1, 2001. Recorded on videotape.

One on One with John Tesh. May 12, 1992. Recorded on videotape.

Salem's Samantha Statue. New England Travels. Online. October 30, 2007. Downloaded March 26, 2012.

Samantha Goes Home. *TV Guide*. September 5, 1970. pp. 6–7.

Samantha/Jeannie: The Debate Continues. *TV Guide*. August 27, 1994. p. 29.

Social Security Death Index, Online.

10 Actresses Pick Hollywood's Greatest Lovers. Online. Photoplay Magazine. February 1965. Downloaded January 7, 2012.

Bibliography

Thomas Crane Library. "Lee Remick, Quincy Star of TV and Movies Bride of William A. Colleran in New York City." St. Vincent Ferrer Church. August 3, 1957.

The Tide Has Turned for Elizabeth Montgomery. TV Guide. August 19, 1961. pps. 8-10 (Also titled on p. 8 as *Along Came the Untouchables.*)

"TV Breaks Old Taboos with New Morality." *Jet.* December 1, 1977.

William Asher's 2003 interview with Terry and Tiffany DuFoe, today of www.cult radioagogo.com.

TV Land Landmarks Immortalizes Samantha Stephens of Bewitched in Salem. Online. PR Newswire. June 15, 2005. Downloaded March 27, 2012.

www.emmytvlegends.org/interviews/people/william-froug

www.hw.com

www.spenceschool.org

1870 U.S. Census U.S. Census of Kings County, New York, population schedule, Brooklyn, 6th ward. Dwelling 643, family 1017; National Archives microfilm M593-948.

1900 U.S. Census of Dutchess County, New York, population schedule, town of Fishkill, ED 8, SD 3, sheet 15, p. 148A, dwelling 271, family 331; National Archives microfilm T623-1022.

1900 U.S. Census of Kings County, New York, population schedule, Brooklyn, ED 356, SD 2, sheet 7. National Archives microfilm T623-1022.

1920 U.S. Census of Dutchess County, New York, population schedule, Beacon, enumeration district (ED) 6, supervisor's district (SD) 7, sheet 11B, p. 216, dwelling 217, family 217, National Archives microfilm T625-0197.

1930 U.S. Census of Los Angeles County, California, Los Angeles. ED 19-68. 2815-24-25.

ACKNOWLEDGMENTS

Twitch Upon a Star is a result of the support, talent, diligence, and general enthusiastic assistance from several individuals, not the least of which was Elizabeth Montgomery. Who could have known that the unpublished excess of our original *Bewitched* interviews would later be incorporated into this new biography on her entire life and career? She generously offered her time, memories, and boundless energy, and this book simply and clearly would not have been possible without the unique imprint of her remarkable personality, wit, words, and wisdom.

I appreciate everyone who granted interviews for this book, each of whom delivered intimate recollections, professional perspective, and insight into Elizabeth's illustrious life and career in either, 2009, 2011, and 2012 via telephone, email, or in-person: Peter Ackerman, Ed Asner, Bonnie Bartlett, Christian Beltram, Ray Caspio, Lydia Cornell, Ronny Cox, William Daniels, Jone Devlin, Kenneth Gehrig, Florence Henderson, Thomas Hill, DD Howard, Kenneth Johnson, Sally Kemp, David Knell, June Lockhart, David Mixner, Kathy Perillo, David Pierce, James Pylant, Rob Ray, Cliff Robertson, Ed Robertson, Saundra Santiago, Eric Scott, Randy Skretvedt, Doug Tibbles, Charles Tranberg, Lin Bolin Wendkos, Dan Weaver, David White, and Vince Staskel.

Into this mix, entertainment historian Thomas McCartney and his unending efforts, knowledge, and extensive research into the archives of Elizabeth Montgomery and all media proved to be an invaluable resource. Tom is worth his weight in gold and is the best in the business. There is no way this book would have become what it is without him.

I would also like to thank the professional and courteous team at Taylor Trade Publishing, including although not limited to editorial director Rick

Reinhart, acquisitions editor Flannery Scott, senior production editor Alden Perkins, copyeditor Jocquan Mooney, and Kalen Landow, director of marketing and publicity, all of whom trusted, believed in, and supported my vision for this book. They are a testament to integrity and patience in the world of publishing.

An especially grateful acknowledgement is extended to my representative Roger J. Kaplan who worked exhaustively in seeing this project through long before we had a publisher.

Although the following individuals did not grant interviews directly for his book, they provided substantial memories from my previous interviews (from 1988 through 1990) and/or conversations (from 2001 to 2006) that were incorporated into this book: Harry Ackerman, Billy Asher, Jr., Rebecca Asher, Richard Bare, Frederick G. Cammann, John L. Greene, Art Metrano, Richard Michaels, Kasey Rogers, Sol Saks, Dick Sargent, Dick York, Irene Vernon, and especially William Asher, Sr. If it hadn't been for Bill (who passed away shortly before this book went to print), I would never have met Elizabeth. No matter how many times he was married before or after he was with Elizabeth, it was always abundantly clear that she remained the love of his life. And now they're together again . . . forever.

Further appreciation to the following for inspiration in a variety of ways that contributed to this book in one way or the other over a twenty-year span: Meredith Asher, Robert Asher, Abigail Borwick, Carol Burnett, Elinor Donahue, Michael Dambers, Dominick Dunne, Brian Feinblum, Bernard Fox, Robert Foxworth, William Froug, Alice Ghostley, Sandra Gould, Michael Greenwald, Angie Horejsi, David Lawrence, Greg Lawrence, Dewey Mee, Diane Murphy, Erin Murphy, Ben Ohmart, Wendy Ogren, Melanie Parker, Alice Pearce, Scott Penney, Steve Randisi, Brendan Slattery, Ed Spielman, John Scheinfeld, Charles Sherman, Tom Stevenson, Steve Thompson, Fredrick Tucker, Dan Wingate, and Karen L. Herman, Director, Archive of American Television, Academy of Television Arts and Sciences Foundation.

Additional gratitude is expressed to many dear friends for their unfailing support in countless ways: Chris Alberghini, Sam Amato, Rudy Anderson, Matt Asner, George Barrett III, Lex Blaackman, Thomas Centron, Matthew

Cook, Jim Cutaia, Giovanna Curatalo, Danny Gold, Kathe Finucane, Lawrence Finucane, Tamara A. Fowler, Cindy Heiden, Jim Heil, Martha Hinds, Ann Hodges, Roger Hyman, David Keil, Mark Langlois, Jeff Lindgren, Monica Lindgren, Andrea (Whitcomb) May, Marty McClintock, Gwen Patrick, Marypat Pena, John Perevich, Rene Piacentini, Louis Tomassetti, Peter Tomassetti, Frank Torchio, Thomas Warfield, Lele Winkley, and Carol Zazzaro.

The stamina required to complete this book could not have been sustained without the unconditional love and guidance provided by my sister Pamela R. Mastrosimone, brother-in-law Sam Mastrosimone; nephew Sammy Mastrosimone; my cousins Marie Burgos, Nicolas Burgos, Noreen D'Agostino, Eva Easton-Leaf, David Leaf, Mary Sue Wiengard, Susie Arioli, Gerald Maranca, my aunt Susan Borelli, and my uncle Vincent Tacci.

A special note of thanks to the kind and encouraging loved ones and friends who are no longer here, but who offered a great deal of support through the years: Mary Turri, Elva and Carl Easton, Tony and Anna Fort, Rita (Turri) Tacci, Rita Valerie, Val and Amelia Valerie, Angelo and Alice Schiano, Jerry and Fay Maranca, Frank and Alice Arioli, Anthony Pilato, Ludwig Pilato, Sonny Turri, Pat Borrelli, Donny Arioli, Linda and Mario Bosio, Doris Prince, and my beautiful dog, Boo Boo.

Continued gratitude to Love-Is-God who I believe not only lives in the *Light,* but *is* the Light—an awe-inspiring source that constantly offers instructions as to how we are to best lead our lives for the highest good of all those concerned. All we have to do is listen . . . the instructions are sometimes delivered through whispers and dreams; other messages are loud and clear (Thank God!).

A particularly personal note of deep appreciation to my parents who have passed into spirit: Herbert Pompeii and Frances Turri Pilato or, as they are now known in the Light, *Saint Pompeii* and *Saint Frances of Turri.* When I think of them, I think of life itself, and a great spiritual instruction that directly contributed to this book:

Honor Thy Mother and Father not only commands us to respect our parents while they are alive, but directs us to live fully the life we've been granted by way of them after they're gone.

Elizabeth Montgomery did that. She lived fully the life she was given via her mother Elizabeth Allen and father Robert Montgomery, as well as through her maternal grandmother Rebecca Allen, all of whom, for better or worse, were core figures in the development of her refined character.

By completing this story of Elizabeth's life and career, which is a reflection on the past, I have finished a chapter in my own journal, and will continue to embrace my life and vocation to the best of my ability.

In doing so, I honor my mother and father . . . as well as the great mother and father of us all.

SUGGESTED READING

BOOKS

Bewitched Forever: The Immortal Companion to Television's Most Magical Supernatural Situation Comedy (Special 40th Anniversary Edition) by Herbie J Pilato (Tapestry, 2004)

The Bewitched Book: The Cosmic Companion to TV's Most Magical Supernatural Situation Comedy by Herbie J Pilato (Dell, 1992)

I Love the Illusion: The Life and Career of Agnes Moorehead (BearManor Media, 2009)

The Bewitched History Book: The Omni-Directional Three-Dimensional Vectoring Paper Printed Omnibus for Bewitched Analysis by David Pierce (BearManor Media, 2012)

Everything Is Going to Be Just Fine: The Ramblings of a Mad Hairdresser by Billy Clift (Everything Is Going to Be Just Fine Society, 1998)

Dizzie and Jimmy: My Life with James Dean: A Love Story by Liz Sheridan (Regan Books, 2000)

Hollywood Left and Right: How Movie Stars Shaped American Politics by Steven J. Ross (Oxford University Press, 2011)

WEBSITES

www.harpiesbizarre.com
www.bewitched.net
www.bobsbewitchingdaughter.com
http://earlofhollywood.com/
http://montgomeryin-moviesondvd.blogspot.com/
http://bewitchedcollector.tripod.com/
http://vicmas.tripod.com/sight.html/
www.mischahof.com/bewitched
www.1164.com

www.asherguitars.com
www.elvispresleynews.com
www.emmytvlegends.org
www.jeanniebottles.com
www.tvconfidential.net
http://stusshow.com/
www.queervoices.org
www.stonecoyotes.com
www.classictvps.blogspot.com

INDEX

Page numbers in *italic* indicate illustrations. Numbers preceded by *C* indicate color inserts; numbers followed by lower-case letters indicate black-and-white inserts following those respective pages.

ABOUT THE AUTHOR

As the author of *Bewitched Forever* (Tapestry, 2004) and *The Bewitched Book* (Dell, 1992) writer/actor/producer **Herbie J Pilato** has researched, studied, and chronicled the life and career of Elizabeth Montgomery, and the history of *Bewitched*, its content, and development, for countless TV shows, magazines, newspapers, and websites. He has appeared on hundreds of radio shows around the world and has served as a consultant and commentator for A&E's *Biography* of Elizabeth Montgomery; *Bewitched: The E! True Hollywood Story, Entertainment Tonight's* tribute to Elizabeth Montgomery; *Entertainment Tonight's* weekend special on *Bewitched;* Nora Ephron's *Bewitched* feature film of 2005; Sony's DVD release of the original *Bewitched* series; and Sony Signature's licensing of *Bewitched* merchandise.

Pilato is also the author of *NBC & ME: My Life As A Page In A Book* (BearManor Media, 2010); *Life Story: The Book of Life Goes On* (BearManor Media, 2008); *The Bionic Book* (BearManor Media, 2007); *The Kung Fu Book of Wisdom* (Tuttle, 1995); and *The Kung Fu Book of Caine* (Tuttle, 1993). He has worked as a producer, consultant, and commentator for the TV Guide Channel's five-part series, *TV's 100 Most Memorable Moments;* TLC's *Behind the Fame* specials on *The Mary Tyler Moore Show, The Bob Newhart Show, L.A. Law,* and *Hill Street Blues;* Bravo's five-part series, *The 100 Greatest TV Characters;* as well as for the DVD releases of *Kung Fu* and *CHiPs.*

Pilato has also been published in magazines such as *Sci-Fi Entertainment, Sci-Fi Universe, Starlog, Classic TV, Cinema Retro, Retro Vision,* and *Electronic House.*

As an actor, Pilato has appeared on daytime serials *General Hospital* and *The Bold and the Beautiful,* and classic TV shows like *Highway to Heaven* and *The Golden Girls.* As a public relations representative for NBC in the 1980s,

Pilato worked on *The Tonight Show* starring Johnny Carson, the Bob Hope Specials, *An All-Star Salute to President Ronald "Dutch" Reagan*, and the *1984 Democratic Debates*, among countless other TV shows and specials.

Pilato presently writes the heralded *Classic TV Corner* blog for Jack Myers' renowned mediabizbloggers.com, and is the president and creative director for Pop-Culture Consultants, an entertainment consulting firm. He lives in Cerritos, California, where he founded *The Classic TV Preservation Society*, a nonprofit organization that seeks to close the gap between popular culture and education.

STRANGE
FLESH

MICHAEL OLSON

SIMON & SCHUSTER

New York London Toronto Sydney New Delhi

Simon & Schuster
1230 Avenue of the Americas
New York, NY 10020

First Simon & Schuster hardcover edition April 2012

SIMON & SCHUSTER and colophon are registered
trademarks of Simon & Schuster, Inc.

For information about special discounts for bulk purchases,
please contact Simon & Schuster Special Sales at
1-866-506-1949 or business@simonandschuster.com.

The Simon & Schuster Speakers Bureau can bring authors
to your live event. For more information or to book an event,
contact the Simon & Schuster Speakers Bureau at 1-866-248-3049 or
visit our website at www.simonspeakers.com.

Designed by Renata Di Biase

Manufactured in the United States of America

10 9 8 7 6 5 4 3 2 1

Library of Congress Cataloging-in-Publication Data
 Olson, Michael.
  Strange flesh / Michael Olson.—1st Simon & Schuster hardcover ed.
    p. cm.
  1. Computer hackers—Fiction. 2. Cyberterrorism—Fiction. 3. Sex toys—
  Fiction. I. Title.
PS3615.L75256S77   2012
813'.6   dc22   2011016615

ISBN 978-1-4516-2757-2
ISBN 978-1-4516-2759-6 (ebook)

for my parents

Even as Sodom and Gomorrah . . . giving themselves over to fornication, and going after strange flesh, are set forth for an example, suffering the vengeance of eternal fire.

—JUDE 1:7

STRANGE
FLESH

PROLOGUE

The human mind is prone to infection.

I don't mean the scorching fevers of meningitis or the insidious tunneling of parasites from unclean food. These days we tend to use the language of disease to discuss ideas: viral memes, contagious media. Vectors and payloads.

We've all seen things that take root and keep us up nights. Many of us harbor thoughts that gradually poison our souls. In my case, a single vision has plagued my dreams for the past year or more, and I'm sure it will haunt me for life:

The body of a pretty, pixieish brunette with spiky hair and huge brown eyes rests on a primitive wooden seat made of a few raw boards. Behind her is bolted the upper part of a large drill press tipped on its side. Its spindle extends into the back of the chair. From there, the bit plunges through her skull.

Blood has drenched the front of her white silk robe.

The entry point is right below the hairline of her neck. Her chin is pressed all the way down on her collarbone by the restraints. The drill bit thus protrudes from her mouth: a two-inch ring of high-speed steel with a row of razor teeth around the outside.

Her bonds are subtle, appearing almost innocent. A slender white nylon line at her chin, and one low on her neck.

But they're part of the mechanism.

The cords run up through a series of pulleys set along the heavy oak ceiling supports and finally down again to a large rusty-brown rock hanging in space. Below it are the charred remains of a thick cardboard tube. A trail of burnt flooring extends back to an orange disposable lighter lying inches below her left hand.

These remnants tell a brief, violent tale. The orange Bic lit a liquid fuse of accelerant. A line of flames began licking at the cardboard support holding up the rock. When the cardboard collapsed, the rock fell, jerking her head back into the whirring drill bit.

Clearly the product of a sick imagination.

I was first exposed by watching a short video. A record of the actual event, but only a narrow view. Just a tight head shot in which all you can see is the poor girl crying while she recites a cryptic verse. There's a brief flicker of light . . .

And then carnage.

Finally, you're left with the gore-stained drill spinning relentlessly where her mouth once was. Spraying blood until the camera runs out of memory.

That picture lodged itself in some dark part of my mind and began feeding on the information I placed next to it: police photographs, the forensics report, stories I heard from those close to her. It grew into a nightmarish scene, like one of those rare cysts surgeons sometimes find filled with hair, fingernails, unseeing eyes, and, of course, teeth. The image grew until that clip stood far above all the other things I wish I'd never seen.

But you can't unsee something. There's no cure for an experience.

Learning the story behind the video would radically alter the course of my life. Like an avalanche blocking the only viable pass through a forbidding mountain range.

Looking back, I see how swiftly the illness spread. How she infected me. How her story took over mine. And the strangest thing about the fever this otherworldly woman ignited in me?

I never even met her.

I

THE JACK OF HEARTS

One Year Earlier

1

The Norn seeks you.

Eeyore, one of my friends at work, has marked the message "Urgent."

What could she want?

The project I've toiled on for the past month remains far from finished. It should be weeks before I'm due an accounting with her.

I stumble into the bathroom to get functional, trying to avoid looking in the mirror. Not yet anyway. I take a deep breath and turn the shower on hot.

The Norn is my boss, Susan Mercer, one of the managing partners of Red Rook, a global network security company based in DC. She's called the Norn—after the Norse pantheon's Weavers of Fate—due to the degree of her control over the destinies of the firm's employees. The name is made especially fitting by her habit of embroidering circuit schematics for signals intelligence equipment from the NSA's Cold War glory days. She is not someone you keep waiting.

The elevator opens onto Mercer's dimly lit corner suite at our New York office. She sits at an antique desk in her Shaker rocking chair. A bright lamp casts a circle of light on her hands, which move with preternatural authority over an ivory hoop. Her eyes are focused on me.

"James, good of you to come," she says in a Brahmin drawl.

"No problem." I take a small glass box out of my bag and set it on her desk. It contains a rare "Bohemian Garnet" Venus flytrap for her terrarium. Mercer adores carnivorous plants, and she tolerates my gifts as sincere expressions of filial devotion. I know little about her domestic situation, but it's hard to imagine a husband, and I like the idea that at least somebody gives her something. "I hope you don't kill this one *quite* so quickly," I say.

"This plant's predecessor was a decadent vegetarian. No aptitude for hunting."

"You probably froze it."

"My office isn't a South Carolina swamp. If a thing can't adapt—"

Her look of delight fades into one of concern as she sees the scrapes on my wrist and then clocks my totally uncharacteristic turtleneck. The morning's cleanup had required some improvisation. I was robbed last night. That's how I've chosen to characterize it. Just the innocent victim of a simple theft. Happens every day.

"James . . . ?"

She lets the question hang there, but I just smile at her. Mercer is way too old-school to pry into an employee's personal life, in conversation at least. She watches me for a while but only asks, "Can I offer you some tea?"

"No thanks." I perch on one of the unstable chairs in front of her desk.

She sets down her project, the blueprint for some ancient mechanical encoding machine; pours herself a cup; and spends a moment regarding the steam as it spirals up into the shadows.

I notice her tea service rests on a set of black lace doilies that have Red Rook's logo stitched into them. A logo that says a lot about our operation. Its black circle holds a little red symbol in the center that, while decorated with simple battlements and a drawbridge, conforms to the shape of an hourglass more than the outline of our eponymous chess piece. Close observers will see the image for a rendering of the underside of a black widow spider.

Unusual that a legitimate consultancy would use the color black in its trade dress, given that the hacker term "black hat" means "outlaw." But we are by no means a normal company. Our clients are Fortune 1000 corporations and any American security-related acronym you care to name: FBI, DEA, ATF, CIA, NSA. While we ply our trade only against criminals, the means we use are often of questionable legality. In fact, we maintain a vast array of unlawful botnets, undisclosed "zero day" software exploits, salaried moles in various black hat syndicates, and even a couple agents in foreign cyber-intel organizations. So the felt of our hat is a tasteful gray.

Just as her silence begins to make me nervous, Mercer asks, "The LinkDjinn affair?"

"Looks pretty standard, and I think we already have hooks into the network the attackers used."

"One of our Ukrainian honeypots?"

"Exactly."

"I suppose we have Phissure to thank for all this mischief?" This was a group of Vietnamese net scam artists with whom we occasionally did business.

"That's what my new friends are telling me. The Brains are trying to confirm it."

Functional roles at Red Rook are classified according to retro high school social stereotypes. The Brains practice traditional hacking like network recon and searching for useful software flaws. Our Greasers run groups of informants. Jocks do "physical" penetrations.

I'm a "Soshe," a social engineer, one of the lazy reptiles who use the time-honored techniques of the confidence man to compromise our opponents. After all, why spend weeks snooping around trying to capture a password when almost anyone will just tell it to you if you ask the right way? We Socials believe that a bug in your firewall program, once discovered, can be patched in minutes, but the software running the human brain will stay broken forever.

Mercer says, "Well, that may get awkward. But I'm afraid the matter will no longer concern you."

"Okay . . ." Surely wearing a turtleneck to the office isn't grounds for a mental-health suspension.

"Tell me, James, what do you know about the Randall family?"

That gets my attention. While quieting the mental turmoil their name causes me, I stall. "The ones who own most of IMP?"

She nods slowly.

"Well, Integrated Media Properties controls enough of the mediascape to be considered, by some, a threat to American democracy. The Randalls have almost all the voting shares."

"Correct. Anything else?"

"They've got newspapers, cable, film studios . . . I understand they're picking up web start-ups like it's '99."

She arches an eyebrow. "And?"

"And I went to school with them. The twins. At Harvard. They were two years older than me. I can't say I really know them anymore, but we were in a club together."

"Phi Beta Kappa, I presume?"

"Ah, no, ma'am." Mercer is well aware of all of my affiliations, starting with the League City, Texas, Cub Scout pack number 678. The club in question was the Hasty Pudding Society, an ancient order of alcoholism.

A predatory smile. "Hmm . . . Though you claim only a passing acquaintance, apparently the Randalls remember you quite well. And have tracked you to our humble enterprise here. It's very unusual, but you've been requested for a meeting with them by name. Or by a diminutive at least. Please tell me you don't answer to 'Jimmy Jacks' anymore."

That means it must have been Blake who called her.

No one ever calls me by my real name: James John Pryce. I've been called Slim for my build, Tex for my place of origin, JJ for brevity, and Thump for reasons that were never quite clear. That's to say nothing of the brigades of online aliases marching around cyberspace on my behalf. In college what stuck were any of several variants of "Jack," which is more or less appropriate given my middle name.

J-Jacks, Jackie, Jackalope, Jackamole, Sir Jax-a-Lot. "Jimmy Jacks" was the one in general use. I received that nickname the same night I met Blake Randall.

2

For a school perceived to host a driven and introverted population, the number of social clubs one can join at Harvard is surprising. They run the gamut from coed cocktail societies like the Hasty Pudding to artistic clans such as the Signet and the Lampoon.

In the fall of 2000, I'd accepted membership to the Bat, one of the college's Final Clubs, our slightly refined version of fraternities. After the holidays, I began my pre-initiation "neophyte" period, wherein you serve as a party Sherpa to the senior members. On a bitter Tuesday evening, I was ordered to report to the club for my mandatory shift in the Texas Hold 'Em game we'd run continuously during the entire two-week reading period before exams.

Late that night, I found myself seated in our book-lined card room drinking neat bourbon and inhaling an atmosphere saturated with exotic smoke. I watched with wonder the massive pile of chips growing in front of me.

The state of my finances had been much on my mind. Like many of my classmates, my father had a blue-chip doctorate; in his case, aeronautical engineering from Stanford. I grew up within miles of the Johnson Space Center in Houston. Unfortunately, his commitment to the nation's space program was supplanted just after my mother's death, when I was too young to have formed memories of her, by a far more zealous embrace of Jim Beam. By the time I received my heavy envelope from Harvard, he was going to work in a begrimed jumpsuit, and I was left with a complex financial aid package, now proving itself hopelessly inadequate. Despite a grueling work-study job in my house's cafeteria and moonlighting at Rav-elin, a nearby network security start-up, I would likely be forced to take the next semester off to work full-time in order to pay off swelling credit card balances. As I turned over a Big Slick, I contemplated the fact that while poker may contribute to my academic undoing, it would provide a respite from the debt collectors, at least until next month.

The only other player at the table with any kind of stack was a senior named William Baldwin Coles III. The son of a notorious currency trader, he was the club's vice president (in the Bat, this is the highest office) and had been playing in the game for almost four days without cease. Just as I began the theatrics to set up a devious double bluff, he looked down at his cell and grinned.

"Gentlemen, things are about to get a lot more interesting."

A couple minutes later, three new players arrived, led by the Bat's reign-ing carnal Achilles, Raffi Consuelo. The second was Matt Weeks, the president of the Spee Club, who spent more time at his family's Las Vegas casino than he did on campus. And finally, Blake Randall stepped inside.

Blake resembled one of the better-looking busts of a young Julius Cae-sar. He had the same strong nose and penetrating eyes, and his pale skin was the white of new marble. He stood a couple inches taller than my six-two and had a full head of blond hair. His chiseled physique came from hours logged on the Charles River as captain of our heavyweight crew.

Though he was a notable presence in his own right, when I looked at Blake, all I could see was his twin sister, Blythe, the legendary beauty of her class. She was also intimidatingly tall and had the same snowy complexion as her brother, which prompted her inevitable female detractors to call her "that starving vampire bitch." Of course, her rich-girl celebrity status and willowy elegance ensured all sorts of male admirers flocking to her banner.

I was utterly bewitched the first time I laid eyes on her.

The twins' glamour alone would have been enough to stimulate gos-sip at school, but combined with their alien mirrored beauty, we really couldn't keep ourselves from trotting out sensational fantasies, often mak-ing use of the delicious term "twincest." Further inflaming such rumors were their matching crooked ring fingers. A congenital abnormality? Had a ten-year-old Blake broken his while skiing, causing Blythe to snap her own in sympathy? Or maybe it was ritual mutilation: no wedding ring would ever pass over either finger to vitiate their perfect love.

As if to demonstrate contempt for our trifling opinions, Blythe and Blake did nothing to discourage such chatter. In a cocktail circle, her hand would seek his arm. They would clutch and whisper when they met. On formal occasions, they danced together splendidly.

Seeing these three arrive, a couple of the current players began packing up their chips. I followed suit, but Coles put his hand on my shoulder and said, "A little early for the money leader to cash in, don't you think?"

The newcomers sat down as the others hustled out like the roof was on fire. I started counting out chips.

Blake smiled benignly at me. "Evening, James. What do you say we raise the stakes?"

I found it strange that Blake would want to disrupt the game right away— and even stranger that he knew my name. I looked to Coles for guidance.

My stomach turned over when the group agreed to increase the blinds by an order of magnitude. There was simply no way I could come up with a four-figure buy-in. But the words "I can't play" wouldn't quite come out of my mouth. I stacked plastic slowly as I imagined how I might get myself out of this situation.

Coles leaned over to grab the Wild Turkey bottle and whispered, "Just deal, man. I'll cover you."

A wispy rumor tickled my bourbon-fogged brain. Coles was dating Blythe Randall. Blake supposedly didn't care for the match and did a poor job of concealing his feelings. I wanted to explain that there was no way I'd be able to pay him back. That I'd never played for that much. That it was impossible, because I'd have to drop out of school and live on the streets if I lost. But I didn't say any of that.

I dealt.

I dealt myself seven hours' worth of pocket pairs, flopped sets, and nut flush rivers. I was playing like a field mouse surrounded by hawks, and yet a mountain of valuable chips steadily accumulated under my chin.

But Blake held the chip lead all night with his unfailing instinct for the

jugular. Having folded a huge pot, Raffi got up in disgust after watching
him flip over a garbage hand of two-seven unsuited. Matt passed out after
writing his third five-digit chit to the bank.

"And then there were three," said Coles.

My next cards were a pair of jacks, spades and clubs. I almost had to fold
them in the maelstrom of pre-flop raising that went on between Blake and
Coles. But with only three players, my jacks couldn't be that bad.

True to form, I flopped myself a set. The center cards were:

The pot rocketed over two grand before it got to me. It was weak, but I
just called.

Coles said, "Shit!" and folded his cards. That worried me. Something
about the hand scared him off. I glanced over at Blake for any sign of
what Coles had seen, but he was a mannequin. He made a courteous gesture for me to deal another card.

I did, and up turned the jack of hearts. Giving me four of a kind for the
first time in my life.

Silently screaming at myself to stay cool, I kept staring at the card until
I had it together and then slowly raised my head to meet Blake's eye.

He betrayed nothing. "Thirty-five hundred." His bet said a full house,
probably kings.

"Up five," I said, trying to lure him in.

Blake smiled cruelly. "Table," he said, indicating that he bet everything
I had in front of me. At the bottom of my innocent columns of colored
discs, I had three obsidian placards. These were ten-thousand-dollar
markers. He raised me confidently enough that I took a second to reexamine the board and realized he could be holding cards that already beat

even my fantastic hand. The ace of diamonds and queen of diamonds made a straight flush that would impoverish me utterly. I studied him, trying to evaluate whether the universe could be so unjust.

Blake had politely averted his gaze from someone wrestling with base monetary calculations. I started figuring odds but was interrupted by a voice inside me.

If you let this rich bastard muscle you off four of a kind, you might as well cash in your chips and prepare for a life of absolute mediocrity.

The black rectangles emerged. "It's thirty-seven thousand five hundred. And I call."

If Blake was surprised by the amount, he didn't show it. Maybe he became slightly more still, but my hand was the one shaking as I flipped over the last card, cultivating nightmare visions of him pulling a miracle winner.

The last card was the Queen of Hearts.

He turned over his *caballeros* and shrugged. Fortune is a cruel mistress.

I had to give him credit, though. He didn't bat an eyelash when he saw my jacks. He just took them in for a second and then murmured something I almost didn't catch.

"Knaves. How apt."

My brain was about to start leaking out my eyes as Blake casually counted off four black placards from his stack and tossed them over to me, making me wealthier than I'd ever been. Allowing me to quit my humiliating job in the cafeteria. Changing everything about my time in college. I was expecting him to insist that we keep playing for another two days, and I planned for a protracted period of trench warfare to protect my newfound riches.

But Blake said, "Well, I doubt we'll do better than that this morning. What do you say we wrap it up?"

Ten minutes later, he slipped out the door into the cold Cambridge dawn. Coles gave my shoulder a painfully hard squeeze and said, with a certain lilt of passion in his voice, "Thank you."

I lifted my glass and began an epic bender that still makes my toes curl to think of.

At the time, I was too beside myself with joy to think much about Blake's parting shot. It was only later, while researching a paper about the iconography of playing cards, that I realized what he meant. I always believed that the jack was the prince of the deck, the heir to the king and queen. But he's not. He's the servant. Another word for which is "knave." My jacks beating his kings was "apt" because the ranks of our cards matched the players. Blake the aristocrat was defeated by the scullery boy.

Once I understood this, I told myself that I'd gladly suffer far greater insult for that much money. That I would try to remember him only with gratitude.

By and large Harvard is a resolute meritocracy, free of the old overt classism. But I guess among any group of relentlessly ambitious people, weird hierarchies and castes develop. When we spoke of our aspirations, you'd occasionally hear someone disparage those choosing even such lucrative professions as the law or investment banking as "mere wage slaves," the unspoken idea being that the real elite operated on the "principal side." In business, this meant you owned the enterprise; if you didn't have one to inherit, you started one. In other fields, you'd hear similar language about acting "on your own portfolio." Being an artist, not a gallerist. Being a politician, not a consultant. Being the talent, not the handler. The subtext was that there were two classes of people: masters and servants.

Blake had called me a knave. I didn't let it bother me at the time.

But I'd be lying if I said it doesn't bother me now.

The prospect of seeing his sister is more bothersome still. I find it eerie, now that I'm once again drowning in emotional quicksand—and courting the consequent physical danger—that I'm receiving this visitation from Blythe, my original will-o'-the-wisp.

I'm supposed to go and drink their fine whiskey, pretending to be old friends, while the Randall twins interview me for a job. Though it may well demand my brand of skills, there are others they could have called.

At the end of our meeting Mercer says, "Dear boy, you *know* who these people are. I'm sure I needn't emphasize that you're to do everything in your power to accommodate their wishes."

I say, "Of course."

But I think, *Why me? Why now?*

3

_____

Blake's assistant, a tall Caribbean beauty in a black Chanel suit, opens the door to what looks like a salon, in the eighteenth-century sense of the word. The walls are graced with finely framed paintings that I feel like I should recognize. Ritual masks from obscure religions watch from the bookshelves. She seats me in a leather armchair with brass studs along the seams.

"Mr. Randall will be with you shortly."

Once she departs, a side door opens, and out slides Blake. As he extends his hand, he flashes me a mock anxiety smile, like we're old conspirators dealing with something unpleasant, but by no means unexpected.

"Pryce, good to see you."

"You as well, Blake."

As we shake, I notice a small tattoo emerging past the cuff of his shirt, unmistakable as the head of the King of Hearts playing card.

A bit more solemnity in his eyes. "I heard about your recent, ah, troubles. But you seem to be bearing up all right. Please join us."

He ushers me into an equally opulent office. Seated at his desk, looking up at the ceiling, is Blake's twin.

"James, I'm sure you remember my sister."

Blake knows that nobody forgets Blythe Randall, least of all me.

She stands languorously. Like a cat who's had just enough time in the sun. She cocks her head and fixes me with her lambent green eyes. "James Pryce. So nice to see an old friend."

My vision twitches.

Is she toying with me? Is that an ironic twinkle in her eye?

Luckily fatigue diminishes my need to obsess over her diction. So I fall back on blank courtesy.

"It's been entirely too long . . ." I find I can't say her name yet. "I hope you're both doing well."

Blythe flicks her eyes toward Blake. She lets out a long breath, almost a sigh, and mashes a cigarette that had been burning in the ashtray next to her. Which is interesting. Blythe only ever smoked when she was drinking. Or when she was nervous.

She says, "Of course you've heard about . . . our brother."

"Well . . . I can't say I know the details," I manage, willing myself to stop gaping at her like a moonstruck toddler. "I take it he's in some kind of trouble?"

Blake frowns. "Half brother actually. Our father took it upon himself to impregnate and then marry our au pair when we were eight. Our mother never really recovered and, after we enrolled at Exeter, has been in and out—well. . ." He shrugs. "Needless to say, we were not close. He fancies himself an avant-garde artist, so some time ago he changed his name. It's now 'Coit S. D. Files.' You're meant to say it 'coitus defiles.' But nobody does."

"Everyone still calls him Billy, even when they don't know who he really is. The name followed him despite his efforts to reinvent himself," says Blythe.

Blake asks, "We assume you adhere to some principle of client confidentiality in your . . . line of work?"

"With Red Rook it's more like omertà."

Blythe nods. "So after the divorce, our father tried very hard to create a functional stepfamily. But it wasn't to be. Billy's mother Lucia was very beautiful and naturally fifteen years younger than our mother. But she was also . . . emotionally unstable. After a huge fight, they separated—this was in 2000 when we were at college."

"She was found dead at our old beach house a month later," Blake says. "Overindulgence in her twin passions for Stoli and Seconal."

Blythe pats her brother and leaves her hand on his shoulder as if trying to physically restrain him from further interruption. "Billy was the one who found her. He was only thirteen . . . Our father was devastated as well."

"And as you know, he was killed in a car accident a year later." On saying this, Blake unconsciously shoots his cuff, covering up his King of Hearts tattoo. His gesture makes me curious about its significance. That card is named the "Suicide King" for the sword he appears to be stabbing into the back of his head. The twins' father, Robert Randall, had driven his Bugatti off a cliff on Mulholland Drive. His death had been ruled an accident, but there was talk about a lack of skid marks on a dry road. I assume the tattoo is some kind of tribute. Or maybe a reminder of whatever tragic epiphany his father's death inspired.

Blythe continues. "Billy wanted nothing to do with us and went to live with his godfather, Gerhard Loring, who was our father's best friend and now chairs IMP's board. Eventually, Ger got him into the Rhode Island School of Design, and he seemed to be doing okay there. The problem with art, though, is that what it craves more than anything is attention. Despite the level of media interest our father's business has always attracted, we dislike publicity. I'm not sure what changed, but Billy began producing these . . . I don't even know what to call them. Installations? Happenings? Art games?"

Blake says, "I would call them frivolous garbage, were it not for the lawsuit."

"*Colton et al. v. Randall.* A delightful piece of civil litigation—settled out of court of course. For his thesis, Billy designed a sort of live role-playing game called *NeoRazi.* He wanted to create an oppressive celebrity culture on campus, so he set up a tabloid website that recruited participants to take photos of various attractive coeds. The more tasteless and degrading the image, the more money they got. His classmates, most of them being quick with a camera to begin with, promptly generated a litany of police complaints: invasion of privacy, stalking, assault charges against irate boyfriends. One of the girls even had some kind of breakdown." Blythe lights another cigarette. "The horrible thing was that, due to the abuse these poor women suffered, they became *actual* local celebrities, and some real paparazzi materialized to continue tormenting them after Billy's 'game' had officially ended."

"I take it his work was not well received?"

"The members of the Rhode Island State Bar were big fans. The girls suing the Razis for harassment; Razis suing them for battery; everybody suing Billy for setting the whole thing up."

"I guess one must suffer for his art."

Blake adds, "The story was nasty enough that the regional media ran with it for a cycle or two. Including some of our own stations, God damn them. And even they weren't above asking whether this was the sort of novel content we could expect as the new generation of Randalls takes the reins at IMP."

Blythe blows smoke. "But the inquiries that really worried us came from our board."

"So we made some changes in Billy's trust to take the issue off the table. He was not pleased." Blake smiles like a pride leader who has just gutted an annoying rival.

His sister examines him, something flickering in her eyes. "The *issue* could have been handled better. But there's nothing to be done about it now."

He breaks eye contact. "You could say that. But either way, we still didn't . . . solve the problem. Amazingly, our brother found a warm critical reception for this kind of stuff. Reviews complimented his refined understanding of how the internet's anonymity promotes gender oppression. So he thinks maybe there's a future in this racket, and after a couple years drifting through the far reaches of Brooklyn 'fauxhemia,' he goes to grad school to hone his 'insight.' His work gets even worse."

"Worse?"

Blake picks a glossy magazine off the coffee table and tosses it into my lap. It's a recent number of *Art Whore* with a feature set off by tape flags. Inside I find a two-page photo spread: a shot from the rear of five people standing arm in arm in front of a giant video screen. The back of each neck bears a tattoo. The title reads:

Jackanapes
Five downtown interactivists hacking your reality

The tattoos from left to right are: an Ethernet jack, a USB hub, a standard quarter-inch amplifier input jack, a drawing of an eye screw with a string running up the neck, and finally, on the only woman in the photo, a small image of the Jack of Hearts from the standard English deck of playing cards.

This last one makes me smile. I'd been spared a far less tasteful display of cards across my shoulder blades on the day after my great poker victory by Cambridge's uptight ordinance that you actually have to remain conscious in order to have ink done.

I skim quickly through the article, which describes in maddening postmodern jargon the recent work of this loose confederation of artists broadly dealing with "issues of identity malleability in digitally constructed narrative spaces." According to the caption, their brother is the one with the string running up his neck. The text covering Billy says that he's worked with LARPs (Live-Action Role Playing), BUGs (Big Urban Games), and ARGs (Alternate Reality Games). The last of these explains his tattoo.

ARGs are new-media hybrids using the whole communications spectrum—phone, email, web, forums, video—to allow a group of players to discover a hidden narrative that plays out over the course of the game. The people who organize them are called the "puppet masters." So Billy's screw-and-string tattoo favors the ARG paradigm by making him a giant living marionette. I guess *NeoRazi* could be seen as an early experiment in the genre.

I want to read the article more thoroughly, but I look up at the twins and say, "So . . . ?"

Blythe inclines her head at the magazine. "Two of the people in that picture are now dead. Second from the left, an ambiguous drug overdose a couple months ago. Then the last one, the girl, almost decapitated herself three weeks later. Billy used her as an actress in this repulsive video he made. I'm sure you can find it online somewhere."

Blake says, "Which leads us to another video . . ."

Blythe steps over to an end table on which stands a ceramic statue holding a long remote as though it's a scepter. She plucks it from his grasp, and while she thumbs a sequence of buttons, I take a moment to study the thing. It's an ugly-but-cute blue-scaled creature with spindly appendages, small pointed pig's ears, and a large head filled almost entirely with a single massive eye. I decide he must be an imp, his peculiar anatomy a mordant representation of IMP's customers: giant eyeballs dedicated to consuming company product. A private jest.

The lights dim and a white screen descends from the far wall. A projector opposite whirs quietly to life.

Blythe selects a file called Jacking-Out. "This video was sent to Blake from a dummy email account two days ago."

Darkness. Then a shot displaying a naked man of maybe twenty-seven seated in front of a bank of monitors. He presents a striking contrast to his siblings. His head is covered with a tufted anti-haircut, a few jet-black locks hanging limply over his face. His eyes are so dark that pupil and iris seem to merge into inhuman anime dots. He shares the twins' pallor, but where on them you'd describe it as luminous, on him the word that leaps to mind is "sickly." The periodic beeping of a heart monitor on one of the screens behind him enhances that impression.

Billy's sense of physical malaise is deepened by a painful-looking Prince Albert piercing through his penis. Hung from which he's got a large golden crocodile pendant that closely replicates the world-famous logo for Lacoste sportswear, the touchstone of preppy culture until Ralph Lauren's polo ponies nearly trampled it to death in the eighties.

The chair he's sitting on is made of rough planks. Affixed to its back is a rusty metal band that's fastened around his forehead. Thick wires descend from the band and attach to a bank of car batteries at his feet. While it's impossible to follow exactly, a large throw-switch next to his right hand appears to control the circuit.

An improvised electric chair. I tense in anticipation.

Billy declaims in a slow rasp:

As a final farewell, Blake, I thought to indulge your greatest fantasy. I know you've often wished that I'd just jack out like she did. But be careful what you wish for. My ghost may come back to haunt you. And lead you down your own path of torment. For I will rain down brimstone and fire upon your festering Sodom. And when you look, lo, the smoke from your life will rise up like the smoke from a furnace.

He then throws the switch, sending his body into violent convulsions. His eyes bulge, and his hands form unnatural claws. Blood trickles down his chin after he bites his tongue. It goes on for an excruciating ten seconds or so, his skin blackening around the metal head restraint. The heart monitor becomes a frenetic screech of trauma. Then the beeping abruptly stops. At this point, the juice must have cut off, since Billy's body relaxes. Foamy mucus drips from his nose and mixes with the blood now freely coursing from his mouth.

The camera lingers on his still form and then cuts to black.

Blake brings up the lights, and the three of us sit looking at one another. I'm not altogether sure what I've been shown, so I just say, "I'm sorry."

He sniffs. "Don't be. It's a fake. Our brother is extremely disturbed, and—"

"He needs help." Blythe's words are soft and almost without affect. I can see Blake framing a sarcastic reply, but some subtle detail of her posture must alert him to the fact that she's holding back a reservoir of pain. His initially dismissive gesture blends into one of apology. He stares at her expectantly. I'm no longer in the room.

I clear my throat and ask, "Why do you say it's fake?"

Blake looks away from his sister. He pulls up the video again. "It's just his typical plug-head drivel." He stands up and points to one of the monitors behind Billy.

It shows a 3D scene set in the courtyard of a ruined castle.

Blake says, "Watch this space when the heart monitor stops." He plays the video, and sure enough, as Billy's body slumps, an avatar modeled to resemble him slowly fades into the game world with a ghostly particle effect.

"He's not dying. He's just virtualizing himself. Which, at least for the moment, is science fiction. Ergo, this video is bullshit."

"It certainly looks convincing."

"He may have used real electricity. Maybe even harmed himself for the sake of realism. But we don't believe Billy has the good grace to actually . . . Well, anyway, this is just another stupid shock-art project." Blake grimaces at the rogue pun. "So to speak."

"You know it's more than that, Blake," says Blythe.

"What do you mean?" I ask her.

"We can't find him. It's like he really has dematerialized."

Blake adds, "His apartment is cleared out. None of his . . . associates have seen him in weeks. He hasn't been at work. No financial transactions, cell phone calls. Nothing."

"But you think he's alive. He's just"—I'm reaching here—"faked his own death? Why?"

"Why does someone like him do anything? He's totally bug-fuck. I'm sorry, Blythe, but it's true."

"I understand that his work is, ah, on the dark side, but what makes you believe he's actually crazy?"

"Oh, I don't know." Blake starts ticking things off his fingers. "In the years since our differences over that first lawsuit, he's sent me a ream of threatening emails. His work has become even more depraved. Recently he's taken to getting himself arrested for petty outbursts."

"But this feels like . . . a more significant departure. Like he's planning to target Blake in some way," Blythe continues. "That online world you see Billy enter is the ever-popular NOD. The only clue we have to his whereabouts is this place that doesn't really exist."

"I see."

Blake says, "Ms. Mercer assures us your technical skills are top-notch. She also says you've had a number of assignments involving . . . undercover work."

Blythe says, "We want you to find our brother. Before he really does harm himself. Or someone else."

4

Standing under the imploring gaze of the woman who, it could be argued, ruined my life, you'd think I might exercise some caution. Obviously this assignment will place me in a mental landscape so perilous that I should refuse it point-blank. All I'd ever wanted was to be there for Blythe when she needed me. In the end, she declined. Back then, I was devastated, and turned my sorrow inward. I told myself that I'd manufactured an epochal love story purely in my imagination. Blythe never made me any promises.

Why then, after all these years, do you feel the need to make promises to her?

The answer of course comes from my abraded wrists and the scabby bruise around my neck. Wherever this work takes me can't possibly be worse than where I am now.

Those were my thoughts after the meeting. In that moment, though, accepting Blythe's charge had the feel of a spinal reflex.

"I'll find your brother," I said.

Blythe smiled at me, and that was all it took.

Pathetic, sure. But my pride has deserted me these days.

To say that I have a weakness for women is like saying Ernest Hemingway enjoyed the occasional cocktail.

After my mother's death, my father made the disastrous decision to enroll me at an all-boys former military academy in an effort to curtail some of the tantrums brought on by her absence. The education, dispensed by a staff of retired air force officers, was exceptional, but by age eight, I was spying on my friends' mothers. One of them caught me observing her step out of the shower. She was really kind and understanding about it, and even hugged me once she got her clothes on. But I was never invited back.

The advent of my interest in computers can be precisely fixed at the instant a low-res image of a nude Victoria Principal rolled off Rory Cullenden's dot matrix printer when we were in the fourth grade. My hacking skills went critical after I discovered those underground bulletin boards for swapping naughty files. I spent high school knowing that I'd do the computer science course at Stanford.

So, how did I end up at Harvard? Sonali Mehta. I followed my rival high school's gorgeous Intel Talent Search winner there. Though she declined all my advances, my grief didn't last long, since there were any number of distinguished young ladies for me to spend my freshman year mooning over.

Then I met Blythe Randall.

I've always known that the idea of perfect, all-consuming love is a myth invented by ancient writers in order to move units. And yet acknowledging that left me without an explanation for the unprecedented feelings she aroused in me. After Coles introduced us at the Pudding one night, I felt like I'd discovered an alien species, awe and fear wrangling for control of my brain.

What was it about her?

Blythe's beauty was somehow original. She had a refinement of face and figure that you hadn't seen a million times on magazine covers. And she used that peerless vessel to radiate goodwill. Not a common sort of gushy niceness, nor the protective shell of polite reserve often found in the insanely rich. She seemed to instantly hold the conviction that you were an interesting person, and even if that wasn't true, she had the confidence and alchemical grace to make you so. In her presence, people, at least those not prone to jealousy, would just beam with pleasure.

A month after that monumental poker game, her relationship with Coles ended in a pyrotechnic argument in front of the Bat. I'd heard that the subject was her brother.

For a dismal couple of weeks I didn't see her at all. Then one night just after winter break, Rex Ainsley and Raffi Consuelo burst into the card room to demand that at least three of us make ourselves presentable for some ladies coming over from Pine Manor, a local women's college, for a round of Circle of Death. This was a drinking game expected to segue into strip poker and hopefully some kind of orgy-type activity. We were skeptical since these often-promised orgies never really seemed to materialize.

Ainsley said, "And Coles is coming by for this, so whichever one of you cum dumpsters let in Blythe Randall, you need to get her out of here. Now."

"She's here? Where?" asked Tim Fielding, the dealer.

"Upstairs, bombed out of her skull, and looking to make trouble. We are her friends, so clearly we're not going to deal with her. It has to be one of you lot."

"You want us to throw her out?" This from a fellow sophomore.

Ainsley snorted. "I'd like to see you try. That woman could crush your testicles with her *mind*. No, one of you must use his feminine wiles to lure her nicely out of here, so she doesn't suspect that her ex-boyfriend is coming over to molest wet-brained goo poodles before a decent mourning period elapses. We Batsmen are classier than that."

There were blank looks all around.

"Jesus, what a bunch of worthless—"

I was astonished to hear myself say, "I'll do it." I flipped over the pair of queens I was betting, drawing a sigh from the nut flush.

Blythe was sprawled in a wingback chair in the upstairs members-only lounge. Eyes closed, ashing into a full tumbler of scotch. Around her neck hung her trademark pearls, a stunning string that glowed with an extraordinary scarlet luster.

To me such unique jewelry spoke to the ethereal nature of its owner, but I'd heard a sour-pussed Grotonian complain that they were just "tacky dye-cultured fakes." Spiteful, yes, but I later found out she was right in a sense. They *were* a replica of a strand that had been assembled over centuries, but only because to wear the originals demanded a massive security detail. Anyway, those were on loan to a museum in Kyoto because a small war had been fought over them during the Tokugawa shogunate.

According to legend, the pearls were collected by a bloodthirsty witch-queen who had a special hidden grotto over which she liked to hang her victims after they'd submitted to her twisted pleasures. Eventually their bodies would fall and be consumed by the local sharks, their blood seeping into the oyster beds below. After each victim, the queen then sent a virgin village girl to harvest a single pearl. Blythe's strand grew to over a hundred stones before the peasants revolted, and a minor warlord, sensing opportunity, invaded the prefecture. Though the evil queen was eventually fed to her rather ungrateful familiars, members of her cult retrieved the pearls, and the strand continued to grow. How Blythe ended up with them is a saga unto itself.

I stood there for a minute thinking desperately of what to say. An attitude of servility seemed best.

"Would the lady care for a fresh adult beverage?"

She smiled but didn't open her eyes. "They've made poor little Jimmy the hatchet man, huh?"

"Not at all. *Nous casa, vous casa.* I think you'd make a fine member here."

One eye opened. "What a revolting idea."

"That's not likely to be the most revolting idea you hear tonight if you stay with us."

"Pryce, go away. I'm looking for someone to fight with."

"Try me. I can be very irritating when called upon."

"I don't know who put you up to this, but I'm not leaving."

"'Course not. Why would you? You'll be thrilled to know we have a lively round of COD on tap, followed by strip poker. We may even have an orgy, at which you'd be more than welcome."

"Oh, barf. Wellesley?"

"No, I believe our guests tonight hail from Brookline High School."

"Liar. You're not going to have any orgy."

I cut my eyes over to the giant stuffed fruit bat perched over the bar and winced. "I think Fulgencio may beg to differ." The club mascot's head came off to reveal a secret compartment intended for Cuban cigars but in practice used as our ceremonial stash locker. It was generally filled with at least ten hits of Ecstasy.

"You are all vermin . . . Fine, you can walk me home."

"And miss my first orgy?"

"If you think *you're* in line for an orgy, you're probably too stupid to help me find my way. Enjoy yourself with your boyfriends." She got up, a trace of sway in her step. I offered her my arm.

Despite having devoted long hours to speculating about what I might do to please Blythe Randall, all I could come up with was a plan so ridiculous, I suppose it had a certain childish charm. "Why don't we go to the vault at Herrell's and tell each other secrets? They have milk shakes there." Herrell's was an ice cream parlor housed in an old bank.

She gave me a long appraising look and finally pointed to our bar. "Might I suggest you liberate that scotch?"

Out on the street, Blythe was less stable. She whispered into my neck, "You know, you're very sweet, but all this really isn't necessary."

"Well, I'm getting a milk shake, and it's going to seem a little strange if I'm sitting there by myself mumbling about how I used to jerk off to *Murder, She Wrote* in junior high."

Blythe allowed a ripple of laughter and slapped me on the chest. She turned to face me and said, "Milk shakes, then. But I must warn you, I have a lot of secrets." She wobbled, and I caught her in a half embrace.

Behind me I heard a soft male voice say, "Blythe."

At first I thought it was Coles, in which case I'd have retreated and let her have the fight she was looking for. On turning, however, I saw that it was Blake, headed toward the Bat. Blythe stiffened, her buzz draining right out of her.

I said, "Hey, Blake."

"How are you doing tonight, Blythe?"

"I guess I'm getting by. James was just taking me for a milk shake to cheer me up."

"Well . . . What a gentleman you are, James. Listen, I need to have a word with my sister. Would you mind having your milk shake another time?"

I shrugged and gestured to her.

Blythe closed her eyes briefly and said, "Fine. What do you want?"

He put his arm around her, saying, "Let's talk on the way back to your room."

I watched them cross Mt. Auburn Street, Blake speaking into his sister's ear. She began rubbing a temple. After another moment of his rebuke, Blythe stopped in the middle of the still, snow-covered street and said, "Blake, I can do whatever *the fuck* I want."

Blake raised his voice too, but he was turned away from me, so I couldn't hear him.

Whatever he said, the last bit of his speech caused Blythe's face to freeze. She slowly straightened, and then unleashed a wicked backhand that connected with Blake's cheek so hard he stumbled sideways. He grabbed her and shook as if building up to further violence.

I had enough Texan chivalry in me that I wasn't going to stand by while a woman was assaulted in the street. I started walking over to where the Randall twins were locked in their vehement pas de deux.

Blythe saw me move, and she went rigid. Blake, always attuned to her, let go instantly and turned. Doing so snapped him out of his rage, and his face displayed plummeting grief as it dawned on him what had almost happened. A desperate urge to make amends flowed into his eyes, and he reached out to his sister.

But Blythe was having none of it. Looking back to ensure he was still watching, she marched up to me, took a deep breath, and then, incredibly, kissed me gently on the mouth.

Even at the time, I was well aware of my role as a mere prop in their family drama, but nonetheless, the touch of her lips was clearly the greatest thing that had ever happened to me. All my thousand versions of this dream uniting in one surpassing moment of consummation.

I might have felt differently had I known that when she kissed me, that surge of divine electricity she sent through my mind would prove overpowering. So strong that it melted the delicate reset circuitry that would allow me to ever really love anyone else.

5

After Blythe, I, like my father, transferred my passion for women to one for men: Jim Beam, Jack Daniel, and Basil Hayden.

Memories of my sophomore summer are pretty blurred around the edges. By the end of it, a vast misunderstanding with the Cambridge police had landed me in a tense meeting with my house master, an old Bat alum. He suggested that I could avoid a dire encounter with the Administrative Board—famously eager to make disciplinary examples at the beginning of a term—by voluntarily taking a year off in order to "better reach my full maturity." The date was September 8, 2001.

A week later, I got a message that a grad was looking for me at the Bat. He was a fairly young but professorial guy, and without so much as an introduction, he asked me, "So how'd you like to help us rat-fuck Osama?"

Seeking vengeance quickly cured my depression, and I developed a reputation as a technical asset who also enjoyed the "operational" side of our work. This led to training across a wide spectrum of the clandestine arts, and I discovered a certain bloodlust and an aptitude for duplicity, both of which served me well during several pretty hairy undercover assignments.

All told, I guess we know that bin Laden's life wasn't much affected by my efforts in the Global War on Terror. But there are several Saudi financiers who are right now wondering how the hand of Allah guided them to Kazakhstani prison camps.

I never went back to school, and five years of such quiet victories garnered me Susan Mercer's contact information. Which proved to be worth a quadrupling of my salary upon joining Red Rook Security.

I found myself well suited to my new job and advanced rapidly. But my pleasant routine was again swamped by romance. I managed to meet and hang on to a lovely girl named Erica, a whip-smart redhead brimming with levity. Though a member of the class two years below mine at school, she'd already made vice president at a stylish record label. We spent long nights at outer-borough rock clubs and abused the flexibility of our work schedules with endless mornings of canoodling sloth. Last winter I tendered a big diamond on a Balinese beach under an almost unrealistic canopy of stars. We'd been very happy.

Six weeks before our wedding, I walked into my study to find Erica leaning over a series of pictures spread out on my desk. I prepared a guilty cringe, thinking of the palliative measures my friends had recommended for when the fiancée discovers your porn stash. But as she turned, I noticed that the photos had been scattered with wet blotches.

She regarded me red-eyed, evaluating. And I realized how bad this was. Which pictures she'd found. I stayed silent for a moment, thinking, *I'm not that awful. It's not as terrible as it seems.*

"You know there's really nothing you can say."

She was right.

I'd often marveled at the way my peers tended to date bad women. Bossy drunks and fashion monsters. But the peril of living with a brilliant and marvelous lady is that she's hard to fool, and the guilt is crushing when you disappoint her.

The images would look almost innocuous to most people. The surprisingly tasteful artifacts of an intimate photo session between two young lovers. But the model was a slender collegiate woman with long blond hair. You'd have to call her willowy. Her only adornment in the last of them: a string of pale scarlet pearls. I was always amazed that Blythe had let me photograph her, and I savored those demonstrations of her trust.

"James, I just can't ever be her. I'm sorry."

I wanted to explain. Not to defend myself; I'd have gladly swallowed a puffer fish if I thought it could magically draw away her pain. I wanted her to know that I'd kept those pictures not as fetishes to creep in and venerate late at night, but rather as proof that I could bear thinking about Blythe. That it was safe to revisit those moments. In the same sense that former smokers always say, "You haven't really quit until you can walk around for a month with a pack in your pocket." The fact that I hadn't pulled them out in years proved that I was cured.

But the last stage of beating cigarettes is when you tire of carrying around that stupid box and finally discard it. Erica had said to me at the beginning, "Creature, I know what she meant to you back then. I know how intense young love can be. So I *need* to know, once and for all: you're not still holding on to any of that, are you?"

And now she'd run the numbers and come up with the only logical answer. Weaselly quant that I am, I fought to suppress the protest that numbers are just symbols and thus are infinitely malleable. Two and two *doesn't always* equal four. But normal people view those who make such arguments with even greater contempt than the ones who can't do the arithmetic to begin with.

The undeniable fact of the matter remained: when I bought the ring, those pictures had to go into the fire.

Classy to the end, Erica departed without hysteria. She left me alone with the images I had kept to help master the moment when the fissure in my heart had first formed. But the spell had backfired, and now my protective wards were streaked with tears from the wonderful woman whose heart they broke in turn.

Harvard's tragedy telegraph operates with shameful efficiency. Though six months have passed since our broken engagement, I'm sure I have that episode to thank for Blythe's reappearance in my life. Blake hears of my "troubles" and then thinks of me when he has some trouble of his own.

Of course, mine have gotten even worse in the interim. Women, naturally, remain the problem.

Men invariably prescribe a single remedy for a serious breakup: get as many bodies as possible between you and her. The underlying theory being that your anatomy will convince your pining mind that there isn't really any "one" woman. There is only all women. And that by screwing a diverse cast of these lovelies, you're reminded of all the scintillating possibilities life has to offer.

Though I've fully adopted that course of treatment in recent months, the difficulty has been recruiting willing therapists. I don't know what does it; maybe my eyes skitter away from theirs, maybe my manufactured smile betrays the flux of pain within. But most women can sense that there's something a little broken with me. And the ones who can't, well, there's usually something very broken with them.

This state of affairs leaves me, like the majority of my demographic, to content myself with the fire hydrant of pornography that is my cable modem. I can't imagine what people did before the internet arrived with its grand smorgasbord of pictures, video, chat, and webcam girls. But too much netporn turns one's mind into a Superfund site of frustrated lust. I find myself wearing out into the world the subtle but alienating caul of shame one gets from constantly wallowing in commodified filth. Another thing women can sense. Which makes me a more and more permanent citizen of this virtual Gomorrah we've built, the gateway to which sits innocently on our desks, pretending it's for work.

But on occasion, the ache of solitude simply demands real human warmth. So I've recently been driven to the teeming swamp of no-strings dating sites, erotic social networks, and "casual encounters" ads on Craigslist. In that arena, "real" becomes a somewhat loaded term.

One thing the internet reveals is that the world contains multitudes of people *just like you*. We've always known that there's this vast nation of lonely, isolated people out there, but now we're not just watching TV anymore. We've started coming up with ways to reach out. Some people are looking to share their thoughts, others are looking to share . . . other things.

Usually one finds a fellow forsaken soul who just wants a dose of companionship or a specific act performed and isn't very particular about the details. But often enough, you'll open the door on a lunatic or a criminal. The varieties of each are astounding.

On the crazy side, I've found everything from garden-variety weepies to scary "Miss Andreas"—women trying to work out profound man-hatred through anonymous sexual episodes. They want to hurt you, or at least scare you.

For example, Penny_S_Evers delivers a very hot oral experience with perhaps a little too much biting. In the morning, you wake to find "AIDS" scrawled on your mirror in lipstick. Of course, we've all already heard that story, but it's still enough to make you upchuck your Cheerios. I took the time to scope her medical records. She doesn't have AIDS, just a whopper of a borderline personality disorder. There are freelance voodoo surgeons and ladies possessed by dead celebrities. I'm still not able to parse the treatment I suffered at the hands, or rather other body parts, of Ms_Ophelia.

It all makes me curious what kind of ghastly characters the W4M dredge up.

The criminal side is occupied mostly by those aspiring to blackmail straying husbands. Rumors of organ harvesters abound, but I've never uncovered a credible case. Though as illustrated by my most recent debacle, I have run across plenty of more traditional thieves.

Last night, I'd found someone calling herself 1Ton_1—which I read as "wanton one" rather than "one-ton Juan"—posting about her desire to "party with an open-minded stud." A possible sneeze hooker, but since she didn't actually demand "skiing" (cocaine), I thought I'd take a chance with the pic4pic exchange. She emailed me an authentic-looking shot from her phone that showed a slender Mediterranean girl who could well have been the nursing student she claimed to be. I traced her IP and ran the name and address on her account through the NICS and KnowX crime databases just to make sure. She came up clean, so I invited her over.

In my foyer, she seemed a little nervous, but that's not unusual. Some guys like to play up the erotic tension of walking into a complete stranger's home for sex with dangerous looks and chilly silence, but I try to put people at ease with church-social friendliness.

I made drinks while she took off her shoes and got cozy on the couch. She savored the first sip of her rum and Coke and then asked slyly if perhaps I might have a lime. Something breathy in her voice implied she had perverse intentions toward the fruit, so I eagerly brought her drink back to the kitchen and sliced up a garnish.

A rookie mistake.

When I got back, she'd shed a layer of clothing and had draped herself with a blanket, which helped prevent me from thinking clearly. We clinked glasses, and she downed her entire cocktail, a gesture meant to impatiently dispense with the preliminaries. I slammed mine too, liking this girl more by the moment.

I registered the faintest hint of an acrid taste to my bourbon, like an evil spirit had crawled into the barrel while it aged. But she started kissing me with an ardor that emptied my head of petty cares. My last impressions were that her mouth didn't feel quite right, and for that matter, neither did mine. And why was I drooling down my chin?

I woke up bound, choking on an inexpertly applied gag. 1Ton_1 was a honey trap after all. I assume her boyfriend had been waiting in a car downstairs.

The appalling thing is that this has happened before. I've been prowling the no-strings world relentlessly in the past months. The incessant probing of my day job now leeching into my nightlife. Always searching, always trying to connect. In the past six months, I've been left tied up three times, robbed four times, and assaulted twice. Yet none of it has been enough to make me stop. The compulsion is strong, the risk outweighed by what I'm seeking.

But what exactly am I looking for? Solace? Pleasure? Action?

This last incident makes me fear the real answer is a darker word.

In penance for my behavior, I make it a point to flag or otherwise warn the community about the more egregious scams, blackmailers, and crooks I happen upon, alerting the police when it feels warranted. As though I fancy myself some kind of prurient superhero. Of course, the lonely and lustful are ever willing to make themselves victims. The police are correspondingly unsympathetic.

Despite this, my nighttime search goes on. And it had appeared I'd keep collecting rope burns until one day, not unlike this morning, the devil would take his due, and I'd miss my next meeting with Mercer.

But now I've felt the earth shift, and a new passageway has opened. This morning, Blythe's delicate smile made me remember a time when I felt almost normal. And she's asking me to take on an undercover assignment that offers a brand-new artificial world to inhabit. Just the thing for someone who insists on making a shambles of his real one.

6

E ven if I wanted to ponder the merits of their cause, the Randall twins don't allow me the leisure. Judging from the welcome message I get from the director of Billy's most recent "place of business," my assignment has already begun.

They want me to infiltrate GAME, the Gnostic Atelier for Machined Experience. Founded as a colony for artists working in tech-heavy media, it's become the forward operating base for the Jackanapes movement.

The abuse of the term "Gnostic" by so many New Age sects has drained it of precise meaning. I gather from reading their online manifesto that GAME uses its original definition: that certain esoteric knowledge allows one to transcend the corrupt material universe into the realm of mystical Truth. This idea has been repurposed by hard-core transhumanists who believe that as mankind merges with machines, we'll be able to remake reality into a Platonic wonder of pure data. Thus liberating ourselves from the scarcity, ugliness, and strife of physical existence. Unsurprisingly, obsessive gamers make up the bulk of adherents to that theory.

The twins have secured a position for me at GAME based on a large donation that eliminated whatever red tape might otherwise complicate the process of adding a new fellow. My cover is that I'm a "conceptual video artist" with a manufactured portfolio who wants to make a documentary about Coit S. D. Files and his cohort of avant-gamers.

My real objective is to integrate myself into the community by joining whatever backgammon tournaments or tantra workshops they might hold to keep themselves occupied while awaiting the digital rapture, with an eye toward finding out whether anyone might know where Billy is. There's likely to be only some trivial hacking and casual surveillance. Best of all, GAME is reputed to throw fantastic parties. If you're into strip Twister and prescription bingo.

Since I'm officially undercover as of now, I'm banned from the Red Rook offices. So I go home to my apartment, a spacious loft at Lafayette and Bond near NYU, to change out of my suit, pour myself a Kentucky coffee, and get up to speed on this online world called NOD. The Randalls hadn't really touched on why their brother might want to symbolically electrocute himself into it, but I suppose that's a question I'll ask when I speak with IMP's security chief about Billy's recent corporeal whereabouts.

One of the biggest cultural trends of this century's first decade was the rise of the Massively Multiplayer Online (MMO) world as a truly widespread phenomenon, consuming an ever-growing share of the public's spare time. NOD is one of these digital environments that range from Tolkienian role playing like World of Warcraft to kiddie-crack mini-gaming like Club Penguin.

Akin to Second Life and IMVU, NOD appears on-screen as a 3D game, though there's no actual objective other than to amuse yourself if you can. This pursuit of virtual happiness can inspire people to do curious things. They quit their real-life jobs to become pretend haberdashers and legally marry people whom they first met as lime-green panda bears. Once in NOD, you quickly find yourself reducing the whole concept of "real life" to mere initials: RL. And untold millions of people worldwide have taken on new identities in one of these microtopias.

To start, you sign up and create a character called an avatar, which could be anything from a busty milkmaid to a ham sandwich. I already have one: Jacques_Ynne (pronounced "Jack In"). NODlings harbor a passion for double entendres equaled only by professionals in the adult film industry. Sadly, I never really bonded with my av. Poor Jacques has been even more lonely than I have in the past weeks.

After I log in to my account, the default location resolves from wireframe to lushly shaded volumes like a skeletal mummy coming back to life.

NOD Zero (NOD0), the center of the world, is a cross between an interplanetary Epcot Center and Bangkok's Patpong red-light district. Giant garishly colored buildings loom around the Tiananmen-sized central square. Like a NASCAR driver's uniform, every square inch of real estate is drafted to serve commerce, which is denominated in "Noodles" (NOD dollars). Blinking animated advertisements offer to satisfy unbelievably specialized fetishes:

```
Victorian Firefighters for your discreet pleasure.


Fraggle Bed-wetter?


Cum 2 Hershel's Hate Hotel. U WILL Regret It.
```

Throngs of ersatz Wookies, zombies, and anatomically enhanced Pokémon stand around chatting.

Immediately I'm besieged by avs teleporting to my location to make lewd pitches in Viagra-spam patois. The first in line are a woolly mammoth, a female Napoleon, and a little Oliver Twist clone.

```
DeeDee_Pea:              Caveman Enema??? Don't wait!

Jessica_A_Belle:         Hottt Machinima Man-Sluts ONLY
                         N$399.99 / min. Yes!!! HAVE
                         SOME!

Raymond_Richard_Euliss:  Hello, fine sir! Might I be of
                         some assistance?
```

Their appeals are unsurprising. I'd first rezzed into NOD a couple months ago, in an attempt to add some variety to my diet of online smut. "Cybering," slang for in-game sexual activity, is a favorite MMO pastime, and NOD is notorious among the major social worlds for having the best cybering tools by a long shot. NODlings like to flaunt this fact by making huge libraries of 3D animation, called machinima, that document their skills in the v-rotic arts. Recently, an anonymous developer produced LibIA (Library of Intercourse Applications), an extremely swanky tool set for neterosexuals that has the population of NOD acting like bonobos on crystal meth.

I dispel the first two avs as obvious NoBots (NOD robots are avatars controlled by programs rather than people). Raymond might be worth talking to. Right-clicking him shows me his profile data:

```
Name:            Jonathan Gurwicsz
RL Location:     Boca Raton, FL, USA
Rez Date:        03/16/2008
Interests:          . . .
```

Only the elderly and fraudulent chat-bot operators trying to make their automata more convincing use actual information in their profiles. I decide to give little Raymond a Turing test—queries meant to determine whether a fellow av is an actual person.

```
Jacques_Ynne:              What does NOD stand for?
```

A trick question. The world's denizens love debating what its name signifies. The obvious answer comes from the Bible. The Land of Nod is the place to which Cain fled after killing Abel. Scholars observed that the Hebrew root of the word means "wandering," so the verse could refer less to an actual place than to the act of fleeing. Nod later came to be known as the "land of dreams," primarily through the popular children's poem by Robert Louis Stevenson. So most people see the name as derived from the idea of "wandering through a dreamscape."

```
Raymond_Richard_Euliss:    Nerds Only Dungeon
                           Network Often Down
                           No Obscenity Denied
                           Take your pick. I've got
                           others.


Jacques_Ynne:              Thanks.
```

Raymond_Richard_Euliss: You're welcome . . .

                            So does the noob want to spank
                            me, or what?

Before I can evaluate his proposal, my screen goes black. Eventually I determine that some asshole griefer has affixed a giant black starfish to my
face, and I can't see any obvious way to remove it.

Such is life in NOD.

Which raises the question of why Billy would choose this world as the
place to receive his final reward. It's only to be expected that a game-
focused artist would take an interest in MMOs. Though taking an interest in one and faking your death to send some kind of message to your
brother are very different things. Not to mention the meaning conveyed
by flipping the switch wearing nothing but a gilded lizard dangling from
your urethra.

And if Billy's motivations are opaque, I'm also uneasy about the twins'.
Why are they so concerned about his virtualization video? If there's so
little love lost with their obnoxious sibling, why do they want to find him
so badly?

What is it they're afraid of?

7

That evening I start getting some answers.

I'm at my desk, still starfish encumbered, when I feel a sudden twinge of apprehension. I turn off my music and listen. A soft ticking sound comes from my entryway. It stops for a second, and I'm halfway to convincing myself I'm imagining things, but then I hear my door's dead bolt slide against its strike plate. Someone is breaking into my apartment.

Given my professional propensity for making enemies within the criminal element, I try to keep two pistols around for ready access. From my file cabinet I grab the one that wasn't stolen by my recent house-guests. I flick the gun's custom-installed external safety and ease past the corner to take a bead on the intruder.

There's a man in my entryway with his back to me quietly shutting the door. He wears a plain gray suit and stands about five foot ten with a triathlete's build. He hears me come around the corner and turns fluidly.

The man actually smiles and says, "Nice Glock, bud."

Embarrassingly, I yell, "Freeze!"

He takes no notice of the "nice Glock" aimed at him and starts pulling open his jacket with his left hand. I can't believe he's doing this and can only come up with, "Hands up, motherfucker. I will fucking—"

"Let's just take it easy, killer."

Before I can track what's happening, he's retrieved a black object from his coat pocket, like he's performing a magic trick. I almost fire but am just able to restrain myself. He simply doesn't seem overtly threatening.

The object in his hand is a leather tri-fold he flips open and holds out for my inspection. He says, "John McClaren. IMP security. I thought you'd be expecting me."

I let out the breath I've been holding. "I wasn't expecting you to break into my apartment."

"Oh, I didn't break anything. But if you want to work with the Imp, we got to talk about hardening your perimeter."

He snickers, reviving my urge to pull the trigger. I just shake my head and lower the pistol.

He looks around brightly and says, "Got any scotch?"

I decide to just relax and go to the kitchen for some ice. He makes himself comfortable on my couch while I pour us each a slug.

Still a little suspicious, I use my phone to pull up his online bio. West Point class of '89. Fought with Special Forces in the first Gulf War. He spent the next decade with KBR and DynCorp. Then there's a dead space in his CV starting right around our invasion of Afghanistan. In '04 he set up his own modest security firm, McClaren Partners, which an IMP acquisition vehicle purchased four years ago. His picture matches the guy lounging in my living room.

I hand him his lowball and say, "Now that we've got whiskey, I guess the laws of hospitality say I can't shoot you."

"Well, I'm glad that's settled." McClaren speaks with a sunny Georgia twang. He doesn't use it to apologize. "I been looking forward to meeting you. Did some recon, and I must say I'm impressed." He rattles the ice in his glass. "I've got some former spooks sitting on Billy's last knowns. A couple ex-Bureau agents doing the normal shoe-leather inquiries. We've got plenty of tech people, but none with your shop's particular, ah, *o-ffensive* posture. And you, an honest-to-God covert operative too. Just the guy to help us find our Billy." He shakes his head in disbelief. "Boy's been nothing but trouble since I joined the enterprise. Nothing *too* serious. Has a fiery temperament, you know? But now he's got his loving family real worried. Haven't seen head nor tail of him in over a month."

"So I hear."

"But you're on the case now, so I'm sure we'll find him in no time. 'Course his safety is our top priority. We just want to take care of him. And plus, he's one of the Imp's biggest shareholders." He nods thoughtfully at his drink.

"What makes you think his safety's at risk?"

"Ah, well, I'd say he's exhibiting what his brother calls 'a crescendo of aberrant behavior.' Let me run you through the timeline." McClaren settles deeper into my sofa. "So after his dust-up with Blake over his trust, Billy moves to New York and a few years later enrolls himself in this techy art program called PiMP. NYU's Pervasive Media Program. He gets sued again over some project he did there, but with his new name, none of it bothers the twins all that much. After that stuff in college, he doesn't want to advertise who he is. Distracts from the work, I guess. Anyway, he graduates last spring and gets himself a fellowship at this GAME place, where you're going to be. Right?"

McClaren pulls from his jacket a folded set of eight-by-ten photos. He places one on the table between us. It shows Billy walking into an indistinct building.

"Wait a minute, you had Billy under surveillance?"

"Yeah, the twins just wanted to check up on him when that first Jackanapes guy kicked off—they showed you that article?"

I nod.

"Right, so Trevor Rothstein injects an unhealthy amount of herowine. There's this video of him shooting up and going on about how much everything sucks. Which the cops take as a suicide note."

"Was Billy close with him?"

"We don't think so. If anything, they didn't care for each other. But the next one to go *was* a big deal. Gina Delaney. A good friend of Billy's from grad school. She offed herself two months ago. Videotaped it, too. And what a mess that was."

"Blythe said she almost decapitated herself?"

McClaren winces. "Yeah, best you hear about that from the horse's mouth. I'll hook you up with the detective who investigated, and he'll give you all the gory details. We don't think they had an actual romantic relationship, but suffice it to say, Billy's a little more broken up about this one. After the funeral, he gets arrested for disorderly conduct outside some bar in Boston."

"What did he do?"

"From what the officers say, he got in a fight. By the time they arrived, the other party had taken off, and they ended up letting him go. Said he looked like he got the worst of it. A couple weeks later, he gets arrested again. Another disorderly-conduct citation from the NYPD. Late night, up around Forty-sixth and the West Side Highway."

"What was that about?"

"We don't really know. We got hold of the ticket, but it doesn't say much beyond the charge. Talked to the guy who busted him, but he was uncooperative."

"So all this is acting out because his friend killed herself. And you're worried that the end point is him following her? That these suicides are contagious?"

"You don't watch out, you wind up with an epidemic. Recent rash in Wales finally petered out at twenty-five corpses. So yeah, that kind of stuff worries us. Just on its face. But with Billy it gets worse."

"Worse than him dying?"

He smiles. "No, our worry gets worse. When he disappeared, some of these extreme-gaming blogs wondered if he'd gone the way of his friends. The curse of the Jackanapes, they called it. So we took the liberty of checking his apartment and found this." He hands me a series of photos taken in a sparsely furnished luxury apartment. The element that jumps out is that all the appliances have been disassembled. "So that just don't seem right. Like maybe he's gone paranoid. Hearing voices from the TV and all that. We get ahold of his bank and credit card statements."

McClaren places some papers in front of me. The statement for Billy's private bank, which begins with a seven-figure cash balance, shows normal activity and then a large wire transfer to another bank in Lichtenstein.

"So from this we concluded Billy was planning to go incognito. Probably had lawyers set up an offshore corporation to get new accounts and credit cards through. We're afraid he's trying to put himself beyond help. Then the twins get that electrocution video. All in all, not the behavior of a sane person, is it?"

"I don't know. Maybe he spotted your surveillance. That could explain the disassembled electronics. Could be the main thing he's doing is hiding from his siblings. The video is just an artistic 'fuck you.'" I shrug. "Maybe he's protecting himself."

"Protecting himself?"

"Yeah. I know I'm the new guy here. But I wouldn't call him crazy for believing his big brother is trying to put him in a place where the people with electrodes strapped to their heads aren't performance artists."

McClaren takes a moment to ponder this. A little of the cornball friendliness departs from his voice. "It's always good to try to think like your quarry, bud. I just hope you remember that your job is to help find him. What happens after that ain't your concern."

He knocks back his drink and stands, glancing at his watch. "Well, no rest for the wicked, right?"

On his way out, he's kind enough to lock the door behind him.

Curious now about the gears grinding in Billy's head, I find online a copy of the video he created with his friend Gina Delaney. Blythe had mentioned it with sincere distaste, and its title indicates why: the clip opens with the words "Getting Wet."

A profile shot of a delicate girl seated in a high-backed wooden chair. Attached to its central post is a wide band of rusted iron that encircles the girl's neck. She struggles against the leather restraining straps and whimpers. I recognize the contraption from a James Bond film. It's a vile garrote, beloved as an execution device by the Spanish up to the end of General Franco's reign. These machines employed a dowel, or if the executioner was merciful, a spike that was screwed into the back of one's neck, creating the pressure necessary for strangulation. In this case, Billy has replaced the spike with an oversized male Ethernet plug pressing insistently against the nape of her neck. Her breathing is labored, and as the thing presses harder, she starts to moan with progressively more erotic energy. Her body arches forward against the metal collar, throwing her small breasts into relief against the white silk of her robe. This goes on for a few beats until the network cable rears back like a snake and drives itself into her spine with a small spurt of blood. A close-up of her face as she inhales sharply in a sudden apex of ecstasy. The camera zooms in on her left eye, where, via some nifty special effects work, the spiderweb of broken veins slowly morphs into hexadecimal code.

The screen cuts to black.

Getting Wet isn't the first video I've seen that sexualizes the now classic sci-fi concept of the "wet interface." To create a direct connection between one's nervous system and a computer, you must penetrate the skin. So the idea really doesn't need a lot more sexualizing. Billy's video takes a dim view of the prospect in suggesting that Gina is actually being strangled in her moment of networked transcendence. Making such a video might well get a woman interested in sexual asphyxia. And certainly there are a lot of both suicides and accidental deaths that stem from this sort of fantasy.

But I'd like to know how this girl went from risqué playacting to almost decapitating herself.

8

Suffocating images from Gina's video invade my dreams, and I wake the next morning with a drained and uneasy feeling, like a family of affectionate pythons has shared my bed. But better rest will have to wait. I have an early orientation meeting with a woman named Alexandra Xiao.

The GAME facility stands just on the edge of New York's Lower East Side nightlife mecca. The building is a seven-story neo-Gothic that takes up half the block. Ringed by intricate iron railings, fronted with mullioned windows, and embellished with irate gargoyles, it looks more like a place to house impenitent nuns than a modern interactive arts facility.

I find Ms. Xiao in the large front hall that serves as one of their public event spaces. Her online bio says that she's an '11 alumna of PiMP and already an adjunct professor there as well as a senior GAME fellow. An accomplished 3D artist, she's best known for a series of female characters from a hit martial arts title whose images now decorate the walls of fanboys the world over.

She's supervising the installation of a large aquarium, pointing with one hand and holding an iPhone in the other. "And you're absolutely sure we don't need any kind of permits for transgenic piranhas?" She sees me and says, "Look, I have to call you back."

While the exquisite planes of her face speak of northern China, her musical English accent indicates a Hong Kong childhood. She's wearing a navy pinstripe pantsuit over an *Urotsukidoji* T-shirt. The film is an

X-rated anime about a shy young student who grows a three-headed prehensile penis that ends up destroying Tokyo. My kind of woman.

"You must be our new resident. I'm Xan, your welcome committee as it were. Come to my office, and let's chat."

She leads me down a long hallway into a room whose every available surface is occupied by screens. There are banks of monitors connected to expensive workstations, multiple game consoles, and a group of wifi picture frames cycling through landscapes from popular shooters. I sit across from her desk, and she surveys me intently.

"Are you a gamer, Mr. Pryce?"

"James, please. And no, I'm more of a spectator by nature."

Her mouth forms an evil smile. "I'm not sure your fellow residents will allow that. Passive engagement is considered *quite* last-century here. Abstinence is not an option. In this place if you're not playing the game, the game plays you."

"You're obviously quite the ambassador."

"Well, we have you in our clutches now, so better you understand right away that GAME is no fun if you don't know the rules. Fancy a bit of background on the place?"

I nod.

"We humans have played games since the very dawn of time. But as we digitize them, it's got to where, for some of us, that's *all* we do. Our generation grew up playing video games, but those were just dollhouses: tidy wee worlds that live in your monitor. Today we're capable of far more immersion. Not just modeling reality anymore. Now we want to manipulate it. To 'machine' it, if you will. Maybe even *replace* it."

"I can think of a few improvements."

Xan smiles. "Quite so. But a bit of caution's in order. Something about treading the line between the virtual and real makes GAME's little monsters hopelessly transgressive. If there's an observable border of decency or prudence, the hateful players we breed here want to cross it like fighting cocks."

She adopts a long-suffering expression. "Just this year we've seen the premiere of *Kewpie*, a game intended as a profound comment on the casual misogyny you find with internet culture. But in playing it, you'd be forgiven for mistaking it for the real thing. Then there was the staging of a piece called *Flash Mob*, which resulted in several residents getting nicked for indecent exposure. If we GAMErs hold the keys to the future, I'm not sure I want to live there."

"What about Coit Files?"

"Coit? Ah, you mean *Billy*." Apparently Xan disapproves of people inventing absurd handles for themselves in RL.

"How would you characterize his art?"

Xan weighs my question. "I can say this: it ain't pretty."

I raise my eyebrows, looking for more. But she stands and takes my arm. "Why don't I show you?"

As we walk back to GAME's main entrance hall, Xan says, "Your Billy's idée fixe is something he calls 'The Bleed.'"

She treats me to a disquisition about how throughout history we've tended to surround ourselves with ever more sophisticated imaginary environments. It used to be books and plays, then film, but now we have these giant online spaces. Part of their allure is how they grant us the ability to act as someone else, through the use of these ornate masks we call avatars.

Xan tells me that Billy liked to explore how our enthrallment to lavish fantasy worlds can have a pronounced impact on the real one. He sought to inspire moments when your biological self *bleeds* into your avatar, and vice versa.

She leads me to a small alcove set up as a public gallery space. While most of the "work" produced at GAME is intangible, they've filled the room with posters and exhibits illustrating demos, play-tests, and events. A corner of the space is dedicated to one of Billy's previous offerings.

On a glass pedestal poses a hideous sculpture of Satan. Spiraling ram horns, cloven feet, barbed tail. Oddly, he appears as though he's been burned by his own hellfire. His crimson skin shows large black and brown spots. The latex has bubbled in some places, melted all the way through in others. I look closer and find not a statue, but rather a devil costume arrayed on a neutral mannequin. He's reaching forward with one of his clawed hands holding a charred wooden frame that houses a fifteen-inch video screen. A small brass nameplate reads HELL IS OTHER PEOPLE. The screen cycles shots of human faces contorted in horror.

Xan explains, "So one advantage of having this scary old building is that it makes a jolly good venue for our annual haunted house fund-raiser. We often invite visiting artists to do special 'installations' exploring fear."

"That sounds scary."

"No, they're generally quite good. We only select those who don't place themselves above delivering cheap thrills. Many of our residents hail from PiMP, and so in 2012 a couple of the new ones had met Billy. Just starting the program, wasn't he? They knew he had a yen for high-concept nastiness, so why not see what he could do with a room?"

"I suppose you're about to tell me."

"On the contrary, many thought it a smashing success. At the debut, we were disappointed to find a cheesy mockery of those evangelist hell houses that dress some oaf in a Satan costume"—she gestures to the thing in front of us—"to frighten teens into preserving their virtue. We asked, 'Is this really the best he can do?' But just watch."

She touches the screen a few times, and a video starts rolling.

In a dark room packed with people, the actor dressed as Satan stands on a slightly elevated stage. He makes a showy gesture to summon his dark powers. Behind him erupts a shower of sparks. Flames jet toward the ceiling. The devil turns and throws up his hands with malign ecstasy. But in doing so, his tail drags through one of the gas jets. His costume catches fire like rayon pajamas. Spasming with terror, he trips into the room's painted backdrop, which ignites in a blazing sheet. The devil starts screaming. After an agonizing moment of indecision, so does the crowd. Two GAME staffers run from offstage to extinguish the actor, but by now the flames have ascended to the heavy curtains draped around the room, and the fire is clearly out of control.

The crowd surges to flee, and you can make out the accordion impact as they hit the exits. Then the cascading frenzy of panic when they realize: *the doors are locked.*

But those nearer the fire keep pressing forward. A petite woman goes down calling for help. This is obviously the moment at which Billy's portraits of horror were taken. Someone being pulverized against the doors screams, "I can't breathe!"

The video cuts to black.

— — —

"Ouch," I say.

"Yeah. Anyone who's been near the stage at a big music festival can tell you it's not a pleasant feeling. But with an inferno at your back . . ."

Xan pauses, remembering the experience. "Billy had rigged that wall with sensors that tripped when a certain 'safe' amount of pressure was applied. At the critical moment, it just fell down like a drawbridge, and people got out without any serious injuries. The fire was all just special effects. He'd hired some guys from the Madagascar Institute to teach him how to rig them." Madagascar is a Brooklyn-based collective known for staging wild bashes involving flamethrowers, pyrotechnics, and rocket-powered carnival rides. "But needless to say, that was the one and only performance of Billy's hell house."

"Not afraid to set fire to a crowded theater."

"Yeah, he has a pretty aggressive attitude toward your First Amendment. Toward his audiences too. The guy goes around saying, 'Art, like games, must have something at stake.' You can see why, even here, people find him hard to take. But I have to credit the little blighter. He set himself the task of creating real fear in the most contrived setting. People come to a haunted house *knowing* that you're going to try to scare them. It's easy to get a yelp when you have someone in a funny wig jump out at them. But then they're laughing about it the next second."

"But no one was laughing after this."

"More like hyperventilating. Billy was really able to jar us out of our role as 'fake' victims. The way he'd built the context helped. Prominent fire code warnings posted at the building's entrance. He search-optimized a news story to appear just under the links to our ticketing website so almost everyone would read the headline 'Ninety-six die in Rhode Island concert blaze,' before they came to the show." She shakes her head in admiration.

"With all that in our subconscious, his artificial fire shattered our superficial suspension of *disbelief* and made us actually *believe* we were about to die. That, for him, is the Bleed, the moment when the imaginary becomes shockingly real. When you and your persona fuse."

"People must have gone crazy."

"Across the board. One critic wrote that it was the most transformative artistic experience he's had in years. Another coined the term 'terrartist.'

An audience member filed a suit asking ten million in damages for giving her PTSD."

"Do all of his projects end in lawsuits?"

"I think he'd be disappointed otherwise. He believes litigation is America's only authentic form of public discourse. If no one is suing you, you're obviously not very interesting. He indemnified GAME against that little stunt, and we actually saw a marked increase in donations when news broke about the legal action. Seems supporting the arts is tedious, but defending them stirs the blood."

Xan smiles at me and then steps back toward the hall. "Come along then. I'll show you around."

I'm impressed by the building's size and scope. Along with the main gallery on the first floor is a performance space fit for an audience of over two hundred. The next three levels house studios, increasingly industrial in nature. There's a state-of-the-art computer lab and a full-service metal shop bedecked with warning signs emphasizing the dangers of welding while under the influence of controlled substances. The fifth floor is divided into "collaborative spaces" that all seem to be padlocked, and the last two floors, Xan informs me, consist of garrets for those residents who need "accommodations suitable for alternative lifestyles."

She adds, "But I'll spare you the zoo tour. I'm sure the beasts are still asleep."

Xan then takes me to find an office. Given the sort of work I need to do, I ask for one that's fairly out of the way.

She says, "A cave dweller, are you? Well, we can give you one of the PODs, but—"

"PODs?"

"The work spaces in the Pit of Despair. Here, follow me." We walk toward a small antique elevator. It descends creakily after Xan hits the button for the basement.

"I have to warn you," she says, "your associates down here are a different breed. POD people, we call them. Not the most gregarious."

We step out into an area that looks like the set of a grindhouse feature. It's a rat's nest of narrow brick corridors with rusty pipes overhead and industrial doors spaced at irregular intervals. To enhance the atmosphere, residents have covered the walls with prison graffiti, and at one intersection, a realistic skeleton hangs from shackles.

Xan stops at an office and appears surprised at the oversized Master Lock hanging from its latch. She consults a sheet in her portfolio and mumbles, "Bollocks. This is supposed to be open."

I drift halfway down the hall to where a rickety door stands ajar. A naked overhead bulb reveals the room to be a tiny dank cell with a slouching brick wall running along one side and a set of water-stained drywall planes composing the other three. In the back, an ancient desk stands devoid of contents.

"This looks okay," I call out.

Xan seems hesitant to abandon the room listed on her clipboard, but she walks slowly over and checks out the one I've selected. She darts a glance across the hall at a sturdy steel door.

Finally, she says, "Right. Well, I hope you're very happy here. I should say that we're having a bit of a fete tonight. If you meet me outside at eleven, I'll hand you around to your new colleagues."

"Sounds great."

"Welcome to the GAME, James. You know where I am. If you need anything, don't hesitate to ask."

"Well, there is one thing. I understand Billy has disappeared. You haven't seen him recently, have you?"

Xan chuckles softly. "Billy? I don't believe I've laid eyes on him for quite a while. But that's not so unusual."

"Seems like there's some reason to worry. What with the Jackanapes suicide epidemic."

"Now James, I like lurid drama as much as the next girl, but two separate tragedies hardly make an epidemic."

I nod amenably but silently reply, *Yeah, but who says it's over?*

9

Approaching the GAME building that night, I'm surprised to see a scene resembling the sidewalk of a hot nightclub. There's a brace of enormous black bouncers accompanied by a transvestite in an astro-Krishna getup holding a clipboard. Beyond the perimeter, a group of the unnamed angrily thumb their phones. Xan, ravishing in leather pants and black cashmere, leads me smoothly past the doorgoyles.

Inside is a labyrinth of giant screens, each providing a window into some strange universe of grave jeopardy and eternal resurrection. Projectors mounted in any available corner make surfaces crawl with a chaos of ill-defined images. Smoke from DIY holographic displays pervades the place with a sense of spectral menace. Condensing mist drips onto the cables crisscrossing the floor. Having considered the topic recently, I assess the possibility of electrocution.

The crowd is a pan-tribal confab representing suits, geeks, and the new-media media. Omnipresent black lights impart a *Tron*-ish computer glow even to those guests not dressed like gaudy NOD avatars. A series of statuesque women, faces hidden by Boschian beaked-creature masks, are dancing up on platforms.

A DJ I dimly recognize is working through a dissonant eight-bit set, occasionally manipulating a panel of raw circuitry.

Though it seems like typical art-rave eclecticism, eventually I notice that the unifying undercurrent here is *play*. Scanning the room I see a group of what I'm forced to characterize as upscale punk intelligentsia running around trying to assassinate each other with their cell phones. There are several home-brewed *Magic: The Gathering*–style card games going, hard-core LARPers fencing with prop-quality light sabers, and a techno-hippie drum circle gathered around an iPhone collaborative music app. They're wearing headphones, so the group's synchronized nodding comes off eerie in its silence. The aquarium I saw Xan working on earlier now allows players to fight phosphorescent piranhas with a remote-control submarine.

My host sees a passing waiter, all of whom are dressed as snow ninjas, and liberates two magenta drinks. She hands one to me.

"*Gan bei*, James." We clink glasses. "So here you have GAME in all its degenerate glory."

She gestures to a group way out on the thrash end of the spectrum who have imported a bottle of Everclear and some powdery substance and are lighting their sneezes on fire.

Xan downs the better part of her drink and then grabs the elbow of someone behind her. "Looks like I'll need another cocktail. Be right back, but in the meantime, meet Andrew Garriott."

Garriott is a diminutive Brit with short hair and dancing eyes that give him a sprightly quality. He shows the well-wrought smile of someone groomed to be a child star. After a warm handshake and some preliminaries, he asks me what I do.

"Video, mostly. What's your game of choice?"

"Game? Oh, I'm complete crap at games. More of a gearhead, really. I was making robots at Cambridge . . . I suffer to think how I ended up here. Good parties though. I guess you could say I—"

Garriott is nearly carried off his feet by the ardent embrace of a strikingly tall blonde. Her back to me, she puts him into a precarious dip while whispering into his ear. Garriott's initial frown at being mauled smooths into an expression approaching bliss. She sets him back on balance, grabs his hair, and gives him a violent kiss on the forehead. I begin to turn away, as it seems clear they have something important to discuss, but Xan reappears by my side and taps her shoulder, saying, "Olya, how beastly! You're alienating our new man here."

She turns, and I have to strain to keep my mouth closed and my eyes from wandering along uncivil trajectories. Olya puts one in mind of mythology. With cascades of nearly white hair, eyes a color of blue Icelandic geneticists are no doubt struggling to patent, and a radiant complexion, she has all the unnatural perfection of the Valkyrie one might find painted on the side of a van at Comic-Con. This impression is not hindered by her wearing a metallic corset that, while possibly providing some protection in battle, seems more contrived to bring confusion to her enemies by what it does for her tremendous décolletage. Her voice is the low Slavic purr of a Bond villain:

"Ah. Hello. I am Olya Zhavinskaya."

I start to offer my hand, but she envelops me in a Russian triple kiss. The last one lingering enough to make me fumble my own name. Olya seems to ignore it anyway and says, "Now, *zaichik,* we welcome you here, and I'm sure we'll be great friends. It is very rude of me, but I must take away the little ones. We have business."

She puts her arms around the shoulders of Garriott and Xan and marches them off toward a dimly lit corner by the DJ booth. Xan puts up a mollifying finger for me, but something Olya says makes her head snap around as they disappear into the crowd.

After some time spent making small talk with other GAMErs, I notice, across the crowded main gallery, Olya stepping up onto the DJ's stage.

"Shitfire," observes a guy standing nearby.

The DJ shakes his head at whatever she's asking. But with her lips at his ear, he finally nods reluctantly, earning a brisk pat on the ass. The DJ abandons his abstract composition of low-fi bleeps and segues into an up-tempo version of the Smiths' "Girlfriend in a Coma," but with Morrissey's bleak baritone artfully mixed with a James Brown classic:

Girlfriend in a coma I know I know it's serious—Get up! Get on up!

Olya then steps back to Xan and Garriott, who are wrestling with a bottle of champagne. There's a barely audible squeal of delight as the cork goes and foam explodes all over them.

I feel a strong impulse to slip over and play cabana boy with my cocktail napkin. But I make it only a few steps in their direction when I'm thwarted by a girl turning away in disgust from losing at some handheld game. This hefty cyber-goth with Muppet hair and a pincushion face slams into me, and my drink spills all over the most incongruous part of her outfit: a pastel pink polo shirt she's wearing along with plaid vinyl pants. I apologize and offer her the napkin meant for Olya.

She says, "Ha. Forget it, dude. That won't be the worst thing I'll have—well, anyway, don't worry about it."

Then she's distracted by one of her friends hollering at her. I check out the mess I've made. Curiously, her soiled shirt bears a crocodile logo over her left breast. But this one isn't the usual preppy embroidery. It looks more like it's been embossed into the fabric. I guess she notices me staring at her chest. When I glance up, she smiles and flicks the crocodile with a black fingernail, making a soft click.

"See anything you like?" she asks.

I realize that the logo is actually a metal pendant affixed to her nipple. Having recently seen its twin dangling from Billy's pecker, I know I have to overcome my mortification to ask her about it. But she's already wheeled away from me back into the crowd.

I push forward to follow her but can't see where she's gone. As I scope the nearby guests, however, I discover that several of them are also wearing gold croc insignia through a wide variety of piercings.

In the bar line I find a bored-looking man with the pendant hanging from a bull ring through his nose. "I've seen a bunch of people wearing that crocodile tonight. What does it mean?"

"Just swag, man. This stupid guerilla marketing thing. We thought we might win something."

"Can I see it?"

He takes it out, and I examine it, feeling like he's handed me the key to a treasure vault.

"Where'd you get it?"

"It came in the mail a couple days ago. I've been wearing it this whole time, but nothing's happened. Which is bullshit if you ask me."

"Did it say who sent it?"

"No. No return address or anything. It was clipped to a card with this fucking poem. I brought it in case we needed it to get our prize."

He pulls out a small ivory square of heavy-gauge card stock. Printed in a medieval script are the words:

𝔉or reward look to me,
𝔜our divine 𝔏ouis 𝔐arkey,
𝔄nd so yoke your breath
𝔗o the 𝔑arration 𝔒f 𝔇eath.
𝔏et my word be your bond,
𝔈t voilà: my beau monde.

Underneath the last line are the two holes from the pendant's pin.

The guy sees my quizzical expression and says, "People here think it's from a new game someone's starting. But I bet it's just some corporate hipster anti-fashion irony thing."

New York is rife with dernier cri marketing agencies that promote brands through in-crowd secrets rather than the traditional media blare. Some of these PR judo techniques were actually developed as launch strategies for various bleeding-edge games like *The Beast* and *I Love Bees*. The "inscrutable mailed item" being a favorite device.

The guy refuses my offer to buy the pendant, saying I can just keep it.

I go outside for a cigarette and contemplate my good fortune.

My fortune gets even better a few minutes later when Olya emerges from GAME heading toward me. She glides smoothly down the steps despite her rapier heels. The giant martini glass she's carrying contains enough alcohol to sicken a hippo.

"Ah, my new friend. Maybe you have a cigarette for a poor babushka?"

I offer her one, and she demonstrates her contempt for my choice of Camel Lights by removing the filter with a flick of her thumbnail. She deftly tends the ragged end with her tongue and leans into me for a light. Then a long French inhale.

"Xan tells me you are making a film about Billy. I very much wonder why you want to glorify this person with documentary."

"I take it you're not a fan? Do you mind telling me why?"

Olya makes a staccato teeth-sucking sound. "I don't think so. I know him for long while now. From graduate school. And he is not a good topic for conversation, I think." She finishes her drink and tosses the glass into a nearby tree planter. With a sleepy smile, she slaps me lightly on the cheek, saying, "Maybe I see you tomorrow."

This woman's every departure must be closely observed by frustrated men. My lizard brain is certainly screaming furiously as she recedes down the block. She turns right at the corner, and I notice that a fellow admirer, smoking on the opposite side of the street, is taking in her progress as well. As he steps off the curb in her direction, I think, *moths to the flame,* and wish that the cloak of anonymity permitted me a few more minutes witnessing the glorious pendulum of her hips.

But what sets me in motion isn't the natural jealousy of a rival. It's when our casual peeper affects tossing away a half-smoked butt and glances up the street. The hours of surveillance I've clocked at Red Rook have imparted a keen appreciation of body language, and this subtle action was clearly taken *to check if anyone is watching.* Suddenly the guy flashes from just another devotee of the female form to a potentially dangerous creep. And now I've found a reason to follow Olya after all.

I hustle after them down Delancey and check myself as I turn left onto Allen. The street is crowded with late-night revelers. Olya crosses an intersection about a block ahead of me. She ignores some appreciative whoops from a pack of men coming the other way. I start thinking that maybe my mind's reptile regions are making me overreact. Then I see the guy speed up to make the light and slide in behind a group heading in the same direction. He's definitely following her, and trying not to be seen.

A lucky gap in traffic allows me to keep her in sight. She turns right at Grand, and the guy stops to light another cigarette before pacing her down the block. I merge into a line formed at the ropes in front of an unmarked bar. From here I can see that he's a short but thick man, with stringy hair and a mean, acne-scarred face. He's wearing a bulky black jacket and baggy jeans. Thick glasses disrupt his otherwise thuggish look.

He waits a beat and then proceeds after her, and I hurry to the corner. I start to cross the street, thinking I'll watch from the opposite side, but Olya extracts her keys at the door of an old tenement building, no doubt converted into resplendent lofts. The guy has picked up speed. He's turning into the doorway. I go into a dead run.

Fifty yards ahead of me, Olya startles as she notices someone behind her. Too late. He's already on her. He grabs her shoulder with one hand, his other reaching toward her chest. His face is close to her ear, and he seems to be giving her some kind of order. Her gaze drops down to his hand for a split second.

Then Olya fights. She twists in his grasp and aims her keys at his eyes. He takes the blow on the side of his head, but it knocks off his glasses. When he grabs her hair, something small and shiny drops to the ground.

That's when I hit him full tilt. My shoulder nails him at the base of his neck, rocketing his face into the glass door and leaving an impressive splatter of blood from a long gash that opens over his eye. He slumps, dragging Olya down. I take his wrist, twisting it backward to break his grip. Olya jerks upright, strands of her hair tearing free. I grab the guy under his jaw and hurl him out of the entryway. He collapses on the sidewalk stunned, blood running down his face.

I start dialing 911, but Olya puts her hand over my cell.

"No! . . . James. I—I'm sorry. Thank you, but—"

"Are you out of your mind? This guy just attacked you. We need to call the police."

Olya takes a long trembling breath. "No, please. Do not call police." She looks away, and I see a sad expression steal across her face. She lowers her voice. "James, I don't want to say this . . . But my papers. My, ah, immigration status. Maybe it is not quite current. I'm fixing, but you see . . ."

So that's it. She's overstaying a student visa. And GAME is probably quite lax about its payroll. I let the phone fall to my side. "Olya—"

But she can tell she's prevailed and follows up with a deep embrace. She kisses my neck and ear, whispering, "Thank you so much. My guarding angel."

"Well, are you okay?" I can't help adding, "Do you need some company?"

Her eyes slide away from mine. "Oh . . . James, I appreciate—"

"I didn't mean it like that."

Olya's smile blooms at my discomfort. "Of course not, you silly man. But no, I am fine. I have a hot bath and some tea. Everything's okay." She brushes my cheek with her hand. "Again, thank you." She reaches down for her keys.

Not quite ready to let it go, I ask, "What about him?"

Offhandedly, she grabs the neck of a wine bottle poking out of the adjacent recycling bin and hurls it at him, shouting, *"Poshol ty na khuy!"*

It shatters next to his head, which seems to revive him somewhat, and he slowly crawls to his knees. When he sees me advance, it prompts him to lurch to his feet and hasten away, cradling his injured wrist. Olya and I watch him limp down the street, but he turns and, pointing at her with his good hand, yells something that sounds like "Don't pretend you didn't want it, you fucking bitch."

I glance back at Olya, but she's sliding through her door. She turns at the stairs and blows me a kiss.

As I stand there in the entryway trying to understand what just happened, a sparkle catches my eye. In a clump of dirty snow next to the trash cans, there's a necklace. I pick it up.

A simple platinum chain suspends a large deep-purple stone carved into an icosahedron. Tiny integers are engraved into each of its faces. The necklace isn't Olya's. I would have noticed her wearing it, and I have trouble believing that she'd adorn herself with a universal emblem of the über game-geek: the twenty-sided die from Dungeons and Dragons.

But if it's not Olya's, where did it come from?

I know I saw it hit the ground earlier, which brings me to a strange conclusion. Rather than trying to steal from her (or worse), could the guy have been attempting to give her a present? If so, he received poor thanks for it.

But that doesn't feel right. There was something off about that encounter and Olya's reaction to it. Something else is going on.

That brilliant insight's confirmed when I suddenly realize that I'm not alone on the street. Almost obscured between two parked SUVs, there's a short guy with a shaggy beard pointing a small black object at me. I flinch, thinking, *Gun.* He sees this and smirks before he backs into the shadows. I hear him jogging up the street.

What was that? Not a gun. He was looking at it, not me. So . . . a camera, I guess.

I start running, but he's got too much of a lead for me to catch him. I pull up at the corner and check in every direction. Nothing.

My familiar cityscape now vibes weird and hostile. A cold fog is sweeping in, giving the street a disquieting, dreamlike feel.

Who were those guys? Why would they record themselves giving Olya a neck-lace?

It can't be a coincidence that in one night I've come across two myste-rious pieces of jewelry that seem like cryptic symbols. Separately they'd rate as minor oddities. But together they feel like, what?

Game pieces.

I think about Billy and his "Bleed" and suspect that maybe I've been cut.

10

At breakfast I reexamine the ornaments I acquired last night, puzzling over their significance. I figure I'll just ask Olya about the die. But the crocodile pendants trouble me since their prevalence means others far more familiar with Billy's games must be working on the riddle. I can't see McClaren's team of spooks being much help, so I settle in and resolve to crack it myself.

> For reward look to me,
> Your divine Louis Markey,
> And so yoke your breath
> To the Narration Of Death.
> Let my word be your bond,
> Et voilà: my beau monde.

At first, the verse reads like nonsensical doggerel, though I catch another reference to NOD in the capitalization of "Narration Of Death."

What is this project Billy's asking people to undertake for some reward? Who is Louis Markey? Where is this beau monde *he wants us to find?*

I suspect the GAMErs will have a much easier time with these questions. I hold one advantage over them, however: I've seen the video he sent his siblings, which gives me a set of clues no one else has. So maybe I should begin with that speech.

He starts with:

As a final farewell, Blake, I thought to indulge your greatest fantasy. I know you've often wished that I'd just jack out like she did.

I assume "she" is his mother. Billy's implying here that Blake celebrated the loss of the au pair home wrecker and hoped her unloved spawn would follow her example, thus cleansing the Randall family history of that unfortunate chapter.

Then Billy threatens this occult revenge:

But be careful what you wish for. My ghost may come
back to haunt you. And lead you down your own path of torment.

After which he invokes the Old Testament story of Sodom and Gomorrah, promising some end-times punishment for Blake's sins against him.

For I will rain down brimstone and fire upon your festering Sodom. And
when you look, lo, the smoke from your life will rise up like the smoke from
a furnace.

My biblical knowledge is weak, so I have to review an online summary of the story from Genesis.

God sends two angels to ascertain the level of evil shit going on in Sodom. They meet Abraham's nephew Lot at the city gate, and he offers them hospitality for the night. Lamentably, the other Sodomites notice the strangers and gather outside Lot's house, demanding access to his guests. My summary quotes the King James version:

```
And they called unto Lot, and said unto him, Where are the
men which came in to thee this night? Bring them out unto
us, that we may know them.
```

Does that "know" refer to knowledge in the *biblical* sense? Are the people saying, "Lot has two houseguests. Let's go over there and anally rape them," or are they just looking for an introduction, and who knows what might happen after a couple glasses of date palm brandy?

In light of his obligations to his visitors, and knowing the propensities of his neighbors, Lot feels that he can't allow this. So the gracious host offers the mob his two virgin daughters instead. Which doesn't speak well of the family feeling in the Lot household. I'm not sure that angels possess the anatomical equipment in which the Sodomites were interested, but regardless, they obviate Lot's proposition by striking the villagers with a spell. The summary is vague on the details.

Was it blindness? Impotence?

I can't remember. At any rate, because of their churlishness, the fate of the Sodomites is sealed. For reasons that aren't made clear, the Gomorreans are lumped in with them to share their punishment.

The angels offer Lot the chance to escape with his family, provided they don't look back once the show starts. They make it out just as the fire and brimstone start to fall. Of course, Lot's wife looks back, and, in a rather arbitrary twist, she becomes a pillar of salt. But Lot escapes with the rest of his family. This is where the summary ends, but if I recall correctly, their descendants become some important tribe until the Assyrians come in and kill everyone.

What I can't figure out from Billy's speech is how NOD plays into all this. His electrocution video implies that this online world is somehow going to be the medium of his revenge. Maybe the location his ghost rezzed into would tell me more. The riddle he sent to his fellow GAM-Ers solicits them to find or do something in NOD as well, a mystery to which the croc pendant seems the most important clue.

I fire up NOD and send Jacques_Ynne searching for crocodile-related content. I visit a simulated crocodile farm. Then an overwrought Steve Irwin memorial. I try an actual Lacoste sportswear store for virtual clothes. Finally, I exhaust Jacques searching locations tangentially related to the company's namesake, tennis great René Lacoste.

At none of these builds do I find anything resembling Billy's fingerprints. No answers. No further puzzles. And no suspicious characters lurking around to interrogate. Though in a place where representing as a psychedelic amoeba is considered de rigueur, "suspicious" can be a hard quality to pin down.

Despite all of NOD's vastness, I end up nowhere.

At a loss, I try placing the pendant in its original context by reattaching it to the card. Now I notice the last line above it, "*Et voilà:* my *beau monde.*"

The French word "voilà" means "there" or "there it is." "Beau monde" is a term for "fashionable society," but taken more literally from the French it means "beautiful world." So the line would read, "There it is: my beautiful world." And then we have this crocodile pendant. Maybe it refers to a place rather than a person or company.

I search for Lacoste on Wikipedia. I'm confronted with a disambiguation page that mentions several other prominent people, including Carlos Lacoste, the former president of Argentina; and Jean-Yves Lacoste, a "postmodern theologian," whatever that might be. But also listed are a few specific places. The Bordeaux winery Grand-Puy-Lacoste and also Lacoste, Vaucluse, an ancient town in Provence.

Something about this last one resonates ever so slightly.

There's nothing like the endorphin bath you get in reward for making a successful guess. My mind wallows in pleasure upon reading the first sentence of the history section that appears when I click through:

```
Lacoste is best known for its most notorious resident,
Donatien Alphonse Francois comte de Sade, the Marquis
de Sade, who in the 18th century lived in the castle
overlooking the village.
```

The identity of the town's favorite son fits with enough contrived perfection that I know I've solved my riddle. The Louis Markey of Billy's verse isn't a real person, it's his NODName. Via "Lou Markey," you arrive at "Le Marquis." Sade enthusiasts often style him the Divine Marquis. A curious title for one of history's most infamous villains.

To find out where Billy's going with all this, I guess I need to take a trip.

NOD's geography is based on our real-life Global Positioning System, so I just type the coordinates of Lacoste into the teleport box. Before hitting return, I make sure to mask my IP address so it looks like any session I start with Jacques comes from GAME's open wifi network.

Jacques materializes on top of one of the few remaining walls ringing the ruins of the Château de Sade. The little town of Lacoste, with its cobbled streets and ancient buildings sagging under red tile roofs, nestles into the forested Provençal hill below. A roman bridge spans a small stream as it meanders through the village.

Billy's castle, which I see matches his virtual destination at the end of *Jacking Out,* is a limestone husk with a crumbling curtain wall rising to the east. A maze of walled ditches and open cellars surrounds the empty courtyard, and only a two-story side building attached to a stubby tower remains intact. I walk in there and see that Billy has created a modest presentation of biographical artifacts commemorating Sade's exploits.

His biography disappoints at first blush. Sade was really more of a persecuted writer than anything else and spent much of his life in prison at the behest of his formidable mother-in-law. The crimes for which he was actually convicted consisted primarily of some minor assaults on prostitutes. Poor behavior, of course, but hardly the stuff of enduring infamy.

The tour begins with a display of the bloody shirt taken off the Prince of Conde after the ferocious beating Sade gave him when they were childhood playmates, an incident that would prefigure a lifetime of conflict with authority. We then move to the box of anisette candies he used to allegedly poison three prostitutes with Spanish Fly in the Marseilles affair, which resulted in one of his many stays in prison. The associated info card points out that Sade most likely had them eat the candy solely intending to make them copiously flatulent. Which was apparently how he liked his courtesans.

There's a collection of props from the plays he staged at Lacoste once he escaped prison for the first time. Then the dreaded *lettres du cachet* his mother-in-law obtained that condemned him to the Bastille.

Next up are the giant glass dildos he had his poor wife Renée procure for him while he was imprisoned. These "engines," or "prestiges," as he called them, used in his superhuman jailhouse masturbatory regime, were the source of considerable marital strife.

The last exhibit is a straitjacket of massive proportions that conveys how grossly fat he had become after the revolution, when he was jailed again for obscenity and confined to the lunatic asylum at Charenton. Thus did Donatien Alphonse François, *comte* de Sade, die: fat, impoverished, and officially insane.

But he left an immortal legacy due to the body of written work he created in life. The château's exhibits end in a library up a narrow spiral staircase into the castle's lone remaining tower. There I find volumes that, when selected, offer to download PDFs of all Sade's major works: his plays, essays, and novels. These writings explore the pleasures to be found in cruelty at such length that the word "sadism" was coined in his honor. Furthermore, his books serve as the foundational documents for the genre of sex practices known as "bondage." The line in Billy's rhyme "Let my word be your bond" could refer to no one else. Indeed, all the submissives right now tied up in dungeons across the city surely have him to thank for their restraints.

I download all of them and point my av out of the room. But right at the exit there's a tasteful placard written with a calligraphic font that says:

I hope you enjoyed my small exhibition,
And that you're inflamed past all thoughts of contrition.
If now there is more that you desire to know,
Then find and explore my eternal château.

—Louis_Markey

If the Château de Sade isn't his eternal château, then what is?

For that matter, why would Billy want to send his players to this place? Judging by some of his work, I can see that he might harbor an affinity for Sade, but the renowned rake doesn't seem to have much to do with either GAME or the Randall family. Still, the card suggests an obvious next move, alleviating any doubt that I've discovered a space on Billy's game board.

I feel a rare tingle of excitement as I start sorting possibilities. Though I haven't so much as stood up in hours, finding this place in virtual France makes me feel like I'm getting somewhere.

Minutes later, an even more exciting aspect of my investigation demands cycles. I get an email from Olya expressing with the charming formality of a non-native writer her gratitude for my help last night. A quick look at the header tells me she sent it from GAME's internal network.

Rather than reply, I jog downtown in the hopes of catching her. Of course I'd like to question her about the incident and her relationship with Billy, but my overriding motivation is that I want to accept her thanks in person.

And to see what more I can do for her.

11

But she's not there. I must have just missed her.

Irritated, I start scouting locations for the hidden cameras I'll install to better monitor the GAMErs' movements, on the off chance that Billy decides to drop in on his old friends.

As my eyes trace the moldings above the main elevator, I'm surprised to find a small video camera on a gimbal mount already focused straight at me. This must be the detritus of a surveillance game called *Gotcha* someone last night told me took over the building during the previous spring like some form of voyeuristic kudzu. I'm amazed the other residents tolerated it, but for me the remaining network is a blessing from above.

It's only a few minutes' work to track a couple cables to a file server dumped in an otherwise abandoned rack room. I glom its address and network ID and head back to my office to probe the box.

Whoever set up the project lacked any notion of network security. I find their server riddled with yawning orifices, and I have root-level control over it within the hour. The box contains about a terabyte of compressed video streams captured at irregular intervals over the past several months.

The last image recorded in many of these is Olya's stunning countenance, squinting angrily. Then static. She represents a *Ringu*-like supernatural force for them: the last thing the cameras see before they die. Why would such a broadcast-quality woman be so protective of her privacy?

I don't have time to wade through all this video. Luckily Red Rook has availed itself of a Defense Department development grant to explore robust facial recognition. The software is called ProSoap, from a combination of "*prosopon,*" Greek for "face," and its ability to "scrub" non-useful frames from a video file. I train the engine with photos from the GAME website's profile pages. The goal here is to see if the cameras can tell me the last time Billy was at GAME, and with whom he spent time before he disappeared.

While I'm waiting for results, I get up in search of a bathroom. As I'm passing by the steel door across the hall from me, Andrew Garriott peeks his head out. He offers a disappointed, "Hey, mate," before ducking back in.

It takes quite a while, but ProSoap picks out some interesting action.

As I click through videos starring Billy, they paint a pretty clear portrait of a guy not well liked. He sets down a plate of takeout in the upstairs dining area, and his neighbors promptly get up. He joins a conversation at a bank of vending machines, and the group disperses until he's left staring at a girl who's too stoned to acknowledge his presence. He leans over the shoulder of a fellow resident working at a computer, making what seems like a well-intentioned comment. But the guy gives him the bird without even looking at him.

This ostracism feels strange to me. Normally any number of people would be willing to make nice with someone like Billy simply due to the gravitational pull of his bank account. Although his name-change indicates that he was tired of that sort of attention and wanted to be taken on his (apparently dubious) merits. After about a month, almost all of Billy's appearances consist of his entering at the front, going down to his workspace in the POD for a few hours, and leaving without speaking to a soul.

One of the most recent feeds shows him carrying a stepladder down the hallway outside my office. He stops right in front of my door. His other hand holds a tiny piece of electronics, which he carefully places on top of the doorjamb. Then he checks his iPhone's screen and makes a twisting motion with his finger on the gear he's setting up. Finally satisfied, he departs.

Looks like the surveillance gamers aren't the only ones installing hardware around the building. And if a wireless camera was sitting on my doorjamb, then it must have been pointed at the door behind which Garriott is currently working. The one Xan seemed slightly nervous about when I chose my office.

So Billy was eavesdropping on Garriott? Now, why would that be?

I gathered from their group champagne bath at the party that Olya, Garriott, and Xan are working on some joint endeavor. And if Billy's paying them special attention, so should I.

Hours pass as I sift through more results. I linger on a selection that shows a cocktail party for the summer's new residents, at which there is a lot of handshaking and convivial chatter. I see Olya has already made friends with Xan and Garriott, and the three stand in a circle conversing. Billy steps into the frame, causing them to stop talking. Olya glares at him like an angry wildebeest, while the other two look away in discomfort.

As Billy shuffles off, shoulders slumped, a small brunette puts her hand on his arm. She says something in his ear and then kisses him on the cheek before skipping away. Billy's gaze follows her, abject devotion in his eyes, his face growing a fragile smile.

I rewind and zoom in on the girl: Gina Delaney.

So Billy had at least one friend, though evidently there's some bad blood pulsing in from PiMP between Billy and Olya. Yet in the clip it seemed like he was trying to edge closer to his former classmate. That's not surprising given her gale-force sexuality. But she despises him. So maybe it's something else between them.

Which brings me back to that guy who accosted her. He said, "Don't pretend you didn't want it." And tried to give her that necklace. The street asylum of New York is replete with Delphic utterances and aberrant behavior, but the guy following her just as Billy starts his new game? And sidewalk crazies don't normally employ cameramen. Is it possible that Billy would have recruited someone to attack one of his colleagues as an opening move? For a guy willing to create a dangerous stampede in a haunted house, I'd have to say, "Sure." But if so, why?

Then I realize I'm looking right at the answer. I zoom in again on the shot of Gina kissing Billy and sharpen the area around her neck. Hanging there is a purple twenty-sided die. So the necklace I found was either Gina's or a replica of one she used to wear.

What's the implication? That the necklace was some kind of trophy? Maybe "Don't pretend you didn't want it" was an accusation. But of what?

It's clear I'm going to have to crawl inside Billy Randall's head to get through his game. Digging into what goes on in this building will help. But where he made mostly enemies, I want to make friends.

I get my first opportunity half an hour later when I hear an outburst of plummy cursing through the door of Garriott's work space. After a brief interval of quiet, there's some keyboard banging accompanied by "Bloody arseing swine-fucker!" The bump of his chair being kicked against the wall. I go to his door, which opens slightly at my knock.

"Everything okay?"

As I step into the room, I see it's a raw but spacious studio dominated by five large worktables arranged in a U shape. Garriott is bent over in front of his computer clawing his head. Hearing me, he jerks upright. "Oh, yeah. You know these damn retromingent machines."

I have no idea what that means, but I ask, "Anything I can help with?"

Garriott resumes his seat, and I notice one of his windows minimizing without him touching the keyboard. He's got a series of foot pedals below his desk. These are used by very serious programmers to replicate the CTRL, ALT, SHIFT, and TAB keys.

"Oh, I'm okay, it's just—" He examines me with a sense of desperation. I can see him mentally dismiss my offer as coming from an ineffectual "video artist."

He says, "That's all right, mate. I think only God can help me at this point."

I nod slowly, reading the code remaining on his screen. On a hunch, I say, "Okay. But you know our God is a jealous God and responds to the recursion of fathers by dealing buffer overflows unto the third and fourth generations."

He looks from me to his monitor. "Wait, what? How do you know that?"

"I don't. But it's often a problem when you're starting from scratch."

"I'm a bot jock. This networking shit . . . How is it you know so much about—"

"I wasn't always a video drone. Mind if I sit?"

Garriott pulls over another chair, and I start scrolling through his code. For someone who's spent the better part of thirty years getting reluctant or even hostile systems to follow orders from a distance, it's pretty elementary. I haven't done much real programming in a while, but I'm sure I can assist him.

"What's all this for, anyway?"

"Sorry, mate. Can't really say. I mean, *I'd* tell you, but my team is sensitive to—"

"You're working on this with Xan and Olya?"

"Yeah," he says with a slight wince at the disclosure.

"Right on. Well, I respect that. Sometimes things need to gestate until they can spring upon the world fully formed."

"This brat is like to kill her mother in the process."

"Anyway, all this stuff is pretty abstracted. I'd be happy to help you with it."

He's clearly torn, but I guess the late hour and his frustrating lack of progress combine to force his assent.

A little after two AM, Garriott hits the compile button and says, "It better work this time."

We've scrapped most of his original code, and I put him onto an open-source library that rigorously implements the bulk of what he's trying to do.

We see our test data start whizzing through various monitoring programs. After about a minute, we cut it off and get a readout of "exceptions: 0." This elicits more keyboard banging, but now in unrestrained joy. These are the occasions engineers live for: when hours of tedious effort result in a lone number that means success. Seeing that simple flag come up is better than all the slot machine cherries in Vegas. Because you know your baby has taken its first step. Garriott slaps my back.

"Thanks, mate. That could have taken me weeks."

"No problem. It's nice to stay sharp on this stuff."

He checks his watch. "Well, I'm not going right to sleep after this; why don't you let me stand you a—I mean several—pints?"

So here's the perfect chance to establish trust with someone using the most time-honored of methods: get drunk with him.

"Done."

We walk over to Foo Bar, an underground cocktail fetishist's joint south of Delancey. Garriott texts for part of the walk, perhaps extolling his recent triumph. As we enter, it's clear that he spends enough time in this place to have achieved a Vulcan mind-meld with the staff. A waitress delivers three Guinnesses just after we sit down.

A minute later, Xan slips into our booth. She says, "My fierce warriors retire to the mead hall to sing of their great victory."

Garriott raises his glass. "I propose a bumper to it!"

Guinness isn't my normal choice for high-volume drinking, but I follow the other two in draining my glass. These children of the Commonwealth were probably fed stout in their baby bottles. I prepare myself for a long evening.

Shots of Jameson and more beer appear unordered. Garriott and Xan grin at each other and then make a series of hand gestures: first a V-sign, then they point at themselves, and finally, a pinkies-extended pantomime of sipping from a cup. Then they drop their shots into the beers and chug them. They look at me, and I do the same, finishing with a contented gasp as the ethanol and oxygen deprivation set about working their sweet magic.

"I take it y'all served in some kind of alcoholic militia together."

Xan says to Garriott, "I'm sure we're not supposed to tell him."

"Luv, tonight he earned the juice, and it has to be consecrated. So, he might as well do it properly."

"What does it mean?" I ask.

Xan repeats the gestures, saying, "Two, I, tea. That's the toast."

"I like Information Technology as much as anyone—"

"No, no. Not the acronym. The neuter pronoun: 'it.'"

"I've never lifted my glass to grammar. Why do we do that?"

Xan says, "We mean 'it' in the sense of 'the thing of the moment,' like an it-girl. Or the sui generis, if you will. As in, 'That is *it!*'"

I shake my head. Their toast lacks the gravity of "God save the king" or "*Viva la revolución.*"

Garriott explains, "Mate, you know Dean Kamen, right?"

"Yeah, the famous inventor; he made one of the first insulin pumps."

"So remember back in 2002, there was all this buzz coming out of his shop in New Hampshire that they were about to unleash a new device— something that would totally change the world. Which they code-named 'IT.' And the net went nuts theorizing about what 'IT' was."

"Yeah. IT was the Segway. Big deal."

"Exactly. A *scooter.* I mean, where's my fucking *jet pack*?"

Xan adds, "Now, granted, it was the greatest scooter ever made, and they had all these bollocks theories about how such a thing might change urban transportation, yea, even the very fabric of our cities—"

"But it was all just hype," I say.

"An *Attack of the Clones*–level disappointment." Garriott winks at the waitress, calling for more whiskey.

Xan continues. "So GAME is this rare place where you get paid to do whatever you want. And yet somehow we end up with all this derivative metagame crap. So we'd sit around bitching and ask ourselves why we weren't working on something really amazing. *Game changing,* if you will. Something that would be worthy of the name 'IT.'"

Garriott says, "Xan and I spend my first months there arguing about what might fit the bill. Eventually Olya comes to us with this idea—"

"Cold fusion?" I ask.

Xan giggles. "No."

"A laser death ray?"

"Nope."

"Total enlightenment delivered in a convenient suppository?"

She and Garriott stare at each other, obviously contemplating whether or not to tell me.

Suddenly there's a bang on the table that makes our glasses jump. We look up to behold Olya wrapped in the type of leather trench coat favored by Hollywood SS officers. Her eyes blaze with fury.

"So, I must find you drunk and gossiping like peasants? What is this?"

Garriott closes his eyes in sorrow. Xan hits a button on her phone and groans, saying, "My Foursquare. I left it on auto check in. Sorry."

"Oh, so you think you must hide from me? Why is this, little ones? What is it that you are doing?"

Garriott musters himself. "We are celebrating the birth of our primary network interface."

"And this tiny bit of code is such heroic feat that you need a videographer?" she asks, eyeballing me.

Garriott breaks the tense silence. "Our man James here is the finest net-coding documentarian GAME has ever seen. We're buying him a couple rounds in thanks. So stop glowering and join us."

I try to soothe things. "Hey, guys, I'm going to go ahead and take off. Let y'all have a meeting or whatever."

Olya puts a firm hand on my shoulder. She gives me an almost warm smile. "No, no. Please stay. We are very grateful for . . . all of your assistance." She motions to the waitress, who's already on the way over with a round. A glass of neat vodka for Olya. She makes an impatient sketch of their toast, murmurs, "*Na zdorovye,*" and downs it at a smooth draw. The other two look askance at their fourth round but bear up and get it down. I just sip mine.

Olya raises her empty glass. "Mr. Pryce, thank you . . . But I think now you must not do the work of the little ones. In English you say something about lazy people and Satan?"

"Idle hands make the devil's work."

"Just so." She slaps a crisp C-note on the table and glares at her teammates. "So now we have nice party. Tomorrow, I think we meet at seven in the morning, yes?"

With that, Olya marches off. Xan and Garriott make comic faces at each other.

I ask, "Why do you put up with that? Not like you're Spetsnaz troops trying to kill Chechens."

Garriott laughs. "Olya's like a Soviet supercollider. You're not sure the wiring's all straight, but she does generate strong impulses in a man."

Xan adds in a low voice, "Women too." Garriott glances at her inquiringly but then looks down and sighs.

Xan grabs his arm. "Come on, let's share a cab. You okay, James?"

Without waiting for my reply she takes my cheek and lightly kisses me good night. The tingle left from her lips takes me well past okay.

Since losing Erica, I would normally let myself obsess over even a casual kiss from a woman like Xan. Which might lead to a risky online search for a surrogate. But tonight, my mind wants only to hammer away at this vein of secrets I've discovered at GAME. I hurry home so I can start delving into today's most pressing lead:

Billy was in love with a dead girl. And he doesn't seem inclined to let her rest in peace.

12

People with elite tech degrees usually maintain pretty extensive online identities. But Gina has left only a void. Old links to her pages on various social networking sites now come up empty. Her blog returns "404—page not found." While she appears in the alumni list at the PiMP website, her profile has been removed. After dredging up the name of her main NODSkin, Joanne_Dark, I see that she's been "transcended," NOD's euphemism for having terminated the underlying account. She seems to have taken pains before her death to wipe out any online evidence of her life.

A lot of recent websites are totally dynamic and therefore hard to record. But leave it to the creaking IT systems of a university to save the day. The Wayback Machine crawls of the PiMP site from September of '12 give me a hit on Gina that includes a fairly recent résumé.

She describes her academic specialties as "Interface Design and Social Computing." Her picture shows an old City of Heroes avatar in place of herself. She did her undergrad at MIT: a Course Six (electrical engineering) degree awarded in 2003 with a minor in mech-E. Right out of college she racked up some pretty impressive publication credits for work she did at Monotreme Research on novel collaboration environments. Then a stint at her lab's spin-off, Ichidna Interface, which made prototypes of new training gear for the military market. In 2012, she headed to PiMP for another degree. Her skills section is a dense block of trendy acronyms. For personal interests, she simply lists "pwning." Gamer slang for "owning" or dominating other players.

Her death on October 29 of last year didn't elicit a whole lot of media interest. Mentions in the major papers rate only a brief unembellished blurb, as if the reporters were quickly frustrated by a lack of forthcoming information. A weepy *Washington Square News* article quotes friends evincing shock, one going so far as to say, "She's the nicest, most talented person I know." Her parents didn't have any comment for the student reporter.

In contrast, the write-up on the other recent GAME suicide, Trevor Rothstein, diplomatically refers to his "struggles with substance abuse," and his mother's requiem strikes a weirdly positive tone: "We're just happy he's finally at peace."

Gina's death leaves one with nothing but questions.

Why does an attractive, brilliant, successful young woman commit suicide? And why do people grimace whenever they mention her death?

I send an email to McClaren reminding him of his offer to hook me up with the officer who handled Gina's case.

With disturbing promptness he replies:

```
Go see Detective Paul Nash tomorrow at the Union St.
Station House. He'll be expecting you. Nash is a friend,
but for op-sec keep your current cover. He's been told
the twins are "privately supporting" your work.
```

13

The staff sergeant at the precinct office sends me to a small conference room on the second floor. Standing up to shake my hand is Detective Paul Nash, a tall man in his early forties. I expected an overweight mustached guy, so it's interesting to find this clean-cut, soft-spoken person who looks like a business retreat leader and whose tan indicates a lot of time spent on the links. As we sit, he asks what he can do for me.

"Well, I'm mostly here to talk about Gina Delaney, but before we get to that, can you tell me anything about Trevor Rothstein?"

He cocks his head. "Not my body. But since he was sort of connected to Gina, I heard about it. What do you want to know?"

"Was there anything unusual about the case?"

Nash shrugs. "Nothing unusual about a dead junkie. These are people who poison themselves daily."

"His was like any other overdose? Nothing noteworthy?"

"Just that he wasn't already dead, the amount of smack that guy was doing."

Trevor seems like a blind alley, so I switch gears. "Okay. So you caught the call for Gina Delaney."

He slides me a file containing her casework.

"Of course that can't leave the room," he says.

"I see. I'm just trying to understand what happened."

"The pictures make that pretty clear."

I open the envelope and pull out a report that is several pages of forms stapled together and a set of glossy eight-by-ten photographs of the scene. The first is the worst: a wide shot of Gina slumped against a horrible contraption, impaled through the mouth by a large circular cutting bit. Called a hole saw, I think.

The close-ups of her corpse are bad enough, but the Byzantine sickness of her machine makes my fingers shrink from touching the photos that follow. Restraining cords, pulleys, burnt cardboard tube, blood puddle on the floor. I'm struck by the lethal similarities to Billy's *Getting Wet* video, which now seems tame in comparison.

When planning their end, most people don't look to Rube Goldberg for inspiration. Or maybe it's surprising that the many artist suicides over the years are so unbelievably pedestrian.

I say, "Bizarre way to go."

Nash nods grimly. "I think all suicides are bizarre. But this . . ." He whistles.

"You get any idea what led her to this particular method?"

"I suppose you've seen that *Getting Wet* video she made? Normally I'd say it's this gasper obsession people have, but the drill makes that seem wrong. 'Course, she *was* an engineer. She had all the tools at hand. But to be honest, we don't really know."

"It didn't seem like there was much press interest in the story."

"True. We suppressed the details, for the family's sake."

I flip through a series of pictures, presumably taken by the medical examiner, depicting the extent of her injuries. The coverage of her back shows that the drill bit went in smoothly, creating a surgically precise two-inch hole. The facial photos reveal the horrendous mess of her mouth. A full-length shot shows some scratches on her torso, as well as jagged stripes of scar tissue on either wrist.

Nash sees my finger hover over this detail. He says, "This wasn't the first attempt. Maybe the machine was meant to take it out of her hands."

"They do follow orders," I mumble. Paging through the paperwork, I pause at the ME's death certificate. "No autopsy? I thought they're required for suicides."

"Generally, yes. But in this case the family requested a religious exemption. They're an offshoot of some Pentecostal denomination. Can't have organs missing come Judgment Day." Nash frowns. "There might have been a hearing, but at the time, the ME was dealing with a bad meth package hitting East New York and a shipment of contaminated beef getting served through a food bank for the elderly. There wasn't any doubt about the cause of death, so I guess they just let it go."

"What did her family have to say about all this?"

Nash pinches his temples and lets out a long breath. "Not a whole lot. Dad was ready to explode. Barely keeping it together. Her mother looked like she was planning to join her daughter any minute. I got the impression that the Delaney home was not a happy one."

I lift an eyebrow. But he just shrugs.

I return to the shot of her back. Another image I've seen of Gina flickers through my mind.

"Huh. The entry wound here. It's right over her tattoo."

"Tattoo?"

"She had a little Jack of Hearts playing card inked there on the back of her neck. The wound obliterates it."

"There are easier ways to remove a tattoo."

"Yeah. But she was part of this group of artists into virtual reality, so it's interesting she'd want to destroy that symbol. Her brand of membership. If that was a big part of her identity, maybe this reads as a repudiation. Like she's saying she wanted out of the Jack—"

Those words suddenly click for me. "Jacking out" was exactly what Gina was doing. Taking out her jack. Decoupling from life. The same act Billy was simulating with his video to Blake. But he also used the term explicitly. What was the line? *I know you've often wished that I'd just jack out like she did.* I'd thought he meant his mother, but having seen Gina's fatal wound, I'm now certain he was talking about her.

But why refer to her *death in his message to Blake?*

Nash seems disinterested in my theories but politely prompts me: "What's that?"

"Ah, never mind . . . She leave a note?"

"No. This one was all electronic. Almost no paper in the entire apartment. Except these framed pictures. Like most people have shots of their friends at parties? She's got a bunch too, but they're all video game characters. No books, just one of those tablet things. We fired up her computer to see if she might have left a statement, but she'd wiped it."

He sees me starting to interrupt and puts up his hand. "We checked the hard disk: it was overwritten up and down. Completely destroyed her phone too. Really just erasing everything about herself that she could."

"So you have a dead girl, this ugly mechanism, some previous attempts, but if you don't mind my asking, how did you establish for sure that this was a suicide? I don't mean to be ridiculous, but couldn't—"

"Yeah, I thought the same thing at first. But she taped it."

"She taped it?"

He nods.

"Can I see it?"

Nash twists his face into a portrait of unease. Thinks for a moment, but then says, "The thing's in total lockdown. We had problems a while back with people leaking shit to snuff sites, creeps, even the straight press. This, well, this is bad enough that if her mother ever saw it, I don't think she'd last the day. Other kids see it, maybe it sparks their imaginations. I can't have anything like that on my conscience. I'm sorry."

"Okay. Maybe I don't need a copy. Can you just show it to me?"

"Look, I've been real cooperative here, per my understanding with your friend. But I'm afraid I just can't do that. Why do you need to see it anyway?"

I sense he's not going to budge. Because we may need him later, I decide not to push it. "I guess I don't. I understand your position. Can you tell me, though, did she make any kind of statement? Say anything to the camera?"

"Yeah. She said, 'You must have thought / I'd play the daughter of Lot / but I will not.'"

"The daughter of Lot?"

Maybe that explains the Genesis reference in the video Billy sent to his brother. How does Billy know Gina's last words? Has he seen the video?

"That's what she said."

"What did you make of that?"

"A lot of people cite the Bible in their final words."

"Yeah, right . . . But that's not quoted in this report here. Did you tell anyone else about it?"

"No." A waver in his intonation makes me think there's more to it.

"But maybe someone else did?" I ask.

Nash frowns. "We had an incident a couple days after we found her. One of the crime scene techs was trying to access the video in our evidence repository. Something he wasn't authorized to do since the case had been closed. I asked him about it, and he said he was 'doing follow-up.'"

"And you think he was going to leak it to someone interested in the case?"

"Seemed that way. But people do things for all kinds of crazy reasons."

Maybe this tech's reason came from Billy seeking answers about his friend's death.

"So this tech didn't have access to the video. What information might he have turned over?"

"He'd have his own crime scene photos, and he was the guy who found the video, so he'd be able to tell someone what was on it."

"Can I talk to him?"

"I'd rather you didn't. Guy's mad enough at me already. They put him on leave pending an inquiry."

"Really? That seems pretty severe."

"Yeah. Well, when pressed on his 'follow-up,' rather than come up with some exculpatory bullshit, he calls a fancy lawyer. Which is an extreme reaction to a minor disciplinary matter."

"Strange."

Though not so strange if money had already changed hands.

"Yeah. Strange that you'd be asking that. You know something about this that I don't?"

"I seriously doubt it."

"You want to tell me exactly why you're interested in this girl?"

"She was a friend of my subject. They were part of the same art group as Trevor Rothstein too."

"Well I'd keep an eye on him then."

"I'm trying to."

14

I zip over to GAME on my way back from the police station, trying again to catch up with Olya.

I can hear her as soon as the elevator door opens. There's a high-volume stream of Russian cursing coming from outside the room belonging to her group. Which I've mentally named the "iTeam."

As I turn the corner, I see Olya snatch a disposable video camera from one of a pair of GAMErs and smash it on the floor.

The guy steps back from her and says, "Take it easy, bitch. It's just a game."

"Gina is dead," she says, her voice climbing registers of distress, "and you want to make a game of this? What kind of sick fucking perverts are you?"

The other guy puts his hands up. "Look, we're sorry, Olya. We thought that you were part of it."

Olya takes a deep breath and says with a thick voice, "Dixon, you have seen what I think about this *dolboeb* Billy and his games. Maybe you tell your little friends what happen to them if I hear any more of this."

She pushes past them and stomps the opposite way down the hall without seeing me. I decide it's not the right time to interrogate her. Dixon and his buddy follow her at a respectful distance.

That scene certainly confirms that Billy's recruiting GAMErs to harass Olya. At first I'd thought Blake would be his primary target, but maybe he harbors a whole list of enemies he plans to sic his players on. Given what the twins told me about *NeoRazi*, I'm not surprised. Game designers will often co-opt early participants into an elite cadre they use to help advance the narrative.

Olya however clearly has no intention of cooperating, though Billy seems bent on forcing her to play along. Maybe he sees her as the white queen he's beset with pawns from GAME.

I spot Garriott standing just inside their workroom.

"Trouble in paradise?" I ask.

He peeks out to make sure she's departed. "What, that? That's nothing. You should see what happens when she gets stroppy. I think your man Billy disappeared to prevent her from killing him."

"They fought a lot?"

"Hammer and tongs, mate. You didn't hear about the funeral?"

"You mean Gina Delaney's?" McClaren had mentioned that Billy's first arrest happened at her funeral.

Garriott tilts his head with an anxious grin, like he's considering something that he's supposed to abhor but secretly loves. "You *must* see this."

He brings his laptop over to my office and pulls up a video.

Someone's cell captures a group somberly toasting the departed. The person leading the toast addresses the camera. Maybe they're streaming the recording to friends who couldn't make it to Boston.

In the far left of the shot, there's a violent motion. Garriott stops it, expands that part of the clip, and starts a frame-by-frame. He's got it focused on the back of a tall blonde in a black dress, clearly Olya. Then Billy enters the frame and leans over to say something to her. Olya doesn't look at him, but almost lazily, she pulls her right hand across her body and then rams her elbow hard into Billy's face. He goes down, lights out, and the camera now pans over to the commotion.

Olya steps forward to continue her assault, but someone grabs her and wrestles her away. The camera stays on Billy, but you can see her in the background breaking free and striding coolly out of the frame. We do not see Billy get up.

The feed ends.

— — —

I blink at Garriott. "I guess y'all won't be putting that in your team re-cruiting videos."

Garriott grins. "Isn't that just *fucked* though?"

"What happened to him?"

"Oh, nothing life-threatening. Badly split lip, a bit of a bump on his head. I don't think his nose was broken. But all in all, a rather poor show-ing. Especially given all his aggro theatrics from earlier."

"What was he doing?"

"So the service was closed casket, and when Billy walks by, he tries to lift the bloody lid. He wants to place something in the coffin with her. Her dad sees this and is having none of it, and he confiscates whatever it was. Makes it known that poor Billy isn't welcome. Fine. But then the barmy bastard comes back for the actual burial, and he's taking photos. And again, her dad, who is a bit off it himself, goes over, grabs his camera, and tosses the kid out on his ear. Sasha, one of their PiMP friends, goes off to try to console him, and that's the last we expect to hear of him."

"But he came back again."

"There wasn't a reception, so her friends gathered at that bar for a post-funeral piss-up. Imagine our consternation when he shows up there. The family wasn't around, and we knew he was close to Genes, so we don't say anything, just avoid him like the plague, right? And everything's aces for a bit while he's downing Bombay and sort of talking to himself. Then he fancies having a chat with our savage Siberian, and . . . well, you saw how that interaction turned out."

"Scary."

"After all that shite, I suppose he deserved it."

"What did he say to her?"

"I didn't hear it, but our mate Dix was standing right there. Told me he said, 'Are you happy now?'"

15

Later that night, as I return from GAME, I see three orange-vested municipal workers standing around a steaming manhole. They peer into it as if one of their number just disappeared down there and they're about to draw straws to see who has to go after him and wrestle the albino alligators. The scene reminds me that I've yet to discover an entry point to Billy's latest rabbit hole from the clues he's offered. So by the time I flop down on my bed, my mind is spinning up on the problem, and I know I won't be able to sleep.

I send Jacques back to Sade's castle to stare at its crumbled crenellations. This can't possibly be a dead end. The placard inside speaks of an "eternal château," so must I now canvass all the period theme communities in NOD for another stupid castle? In the Nerds Only Dungeon every other build is a fortress, and the place's swarming immensity would swallow any direct search. So where in the world should I start looking?

Well, how did I find my way here?

I followed a reference from the poem that came with the croc pendants. Maybe it has yet to yield all its instructions.

The verse invokes NOD with the phrase "Narration Of Death." Focusing on those words again, I decide that an "eternal" castle wouldn't be one subject to the entropy of the real world. But such a building could be preserved forever through art, like the castle in a painting. Or a book.

All of Sade's work deals liberally with death and the suffering that precedes it, but "Narration Of Death" would apply to one title above all the others. One that also happens to feature a castle infamous in the history of literature.

I scan through the first several pages of the book, and then start typing coordinates into Jacques's teleport box.

My av winds up staring into a thousand-foot ravine. I take a second to pull up the sim's property page and confirm that it's owned by an av named Louis_Markey. The ruined castle at Lacoste was just a set of virtual objects on one of NOD's public servers—the equivalent of an inert brochure. But now I've discovered a complete, privately hosted NOD build, which is more like someone's personal website.

Panning my view, I see a mountain landscape with jagged peaks looming all around me. Just to the side is a stout wooden bridge that leads across the chasm toward an ominous gothic castle. The kind of place a monster would take his kidnapped princess in one of the darker fairy tales. One that revolves around revenge rather than escape.

Chiseled below the ramparts of the gatehouse I see the name of the fortress: the Château de Silling.

This castle is the setting of Sade's epic of filth *Les cent vingt journées de Sodome, ou l'Ecole du libertinage,* known in English as *The 120 Days of Sodom.* I'd first flipped through it in college, where it was somebody's bright idea that the Bat call our big winter party "120 Minutes of Sodom."

Unfortunately the book is more of a catalog of heinous atrocities than a novel. The entries run along the lines of:

```
31. He fucks a goat from behind while being flogged; the
goat conceives and gives birth to a monster. Monster
though it be, he embuggers it.
```

While such a spectacle would certainly be entertaining, we didn't have the special effects budget to bring it about. Given that even the very first, ostensibly mild, crimes mentioned involve priests, children, and urophilia, we quickly realized that this wasn't going to work as a party template.

The self-described "most impure tale ever told" concerns four wealthy libertines: a bishop, the banker Durcet, a judge named Curval, and their leader, the Duc de Blangis, who serves as a sort of Sadean superhero.

He's an aristocrat blessed with the ability to ejaculate at will, an attribute as important as any to the basic plotline.

These four hit on the idea of sequestering themselves for the winter in an impregnable fortress where they'll aspire toward an eternal pinnacle of debauchery. Perhaps an honorable goal, except that these characters' tastes run to pedophilia, coprophilia, torture (not the slap-and-tickle variety), and murder. To aid them in their endeavors, they kidnap sixteen of the most noble and beautiful children from across the country. Four wizened whores (Madames Duclos, Champville, Martaine, and Desgranges) come along to stimulate the goings-on by telling stories from their lifetimes spent in carnal riot.

The book consists of descriptions of the six hundred tortures inflicted upon the castle's inmates over the course of the winter. Sade wrote this monstrosity in thirty-seven days while in prison. Due to his incarceration, he had to write the book on a twelve-meter toilet paper–like scroll that he could easily hide from his jailers. He claimed to have "wept tears of blood" when his manuscript was lost during the storming of the Bastille.

But after the rioters looted his former cell, someone found the scroll and kept it in his family for over a hundred years before a German psychologist discovered it and had the nerve to publish it in 1905. Of course, it was immediately banned, but by the midfifties Sade was receiving a radical rethink among certain intellectuals, and they started printing it again.

One can now easily find Sadean ideas and aesthetics throughout popular culture. Indeed, NOD already has several builds that pay homage to his work. It seems Billy's decided we need another one, which means I have to search the place until I find out why.

Just to the side of the portcullis is a small iron door over which is engraved a double-headed eagle, the Sade family crest. Beside this entrance I find the Château de Silling's guest registry. I have to fill in a bunch of personal information, including email address and phone number, in order to unlock the postern gate. For these I use new Gmail and Google Voice accounts forwarded to a brand-new work cell. Upon doing so, I get a message telling me that I have to install this NOD build's special plug-ins for "enhanced features." I shudder to think what those might be, but I agree.

Through the courtyard is a spooky gallery lit with torches standing in bronze sconces. The seeping stone walls are hung with obscene tapestries. After wandering through several hallways admiring the period detail, I enter a room I remember well from the text: the amphitheater.

This is the chamber in which much of the book is set, the place where the Libertines gather every evening to hear the whores' stories. There's a small stage in front that supports an extravagant gilded throne. Madame Duclos, the first of Sade's courtesan raconteurs, sits there. Cut into the curved back wall of the room is a series of five alcoves, each containing a comfortable couch. Four of them seat avatars representing each of the Libertines.

The fifth one, in the center, is empty. I presume it is meant for me.

I trip a hidden switch somewhere that causes the Duke to rise and say, "Welcome to Château de Silling. Our redoubt was built for those who wish to walk in the shadow of the Divine Marquis. Enjoy yourself. We'll be watching."

I walk over to the center niche and sit on the chaise. As my av relaxes into it, Madame Duclos begins her narration in a deep French-inflected voice:

```
Although I had not yet attained my fifth year, one day,
returning from my holy occupations in the monastery, my
sister asked me whether I had yet encountered Father
Laurent.
```

I get impatient quickly. I've always thought audiobooks proceed at an insufferably slow pace, and with Sade you know generally what's about to happen anyway (here, a golden shower). So I drop a "listener" object to keep streaming her stories aloud and then begin a tour of the rest of the castle.

The door on the other side of the great hall leads to the chapel. Sade was rabidly anticlerical throughout his life, so this room is tricked out as a voyeur's privy with an abundance of peculiar glass furniture, containers, and tools. I carefully search the chamber and finally settle on the stone step in front of the altar. It opens to reveal a staircase spiraling into the floor.

The entrance to the dungeon.

Silling's dungeon is the site of the worst crimes that take place at the climax of the book. It's supposed to contain all the specialized torture mechanisms needed to mount a successful Inquisition. However, Billy's rendition has only a dark stone hallway that passes a long row of wooden doors. I randomly try the fourth one, which opens onto the av of a frail girl around seven years old. Next to her is a small table with some cups and a glass tube with a rubber bulb at its end.

The waif sniffles. Then she turns to me, and a text bubble says:

```
Zelmire:                    You wanted to see me?
```

I stare at the odd configuration of objects and the little girl, and it dawns on me that this is an exact staging of the story Duclos is telling now: a bracing episode involving the ingestion of a child's snot. I hit F6 to bring up NOD's machinima interface. Sure enough, Billy has helpfully placed a series of pose balls, sound effect notes, and camera tracks around the room. Handy props for making some virtual kiddie porn. That is, if the act in question can be considered pornographic. By any reckoning, it isn't *Sesame Street*.

I shut the door.

What is this place?

I doubt it's just a celebration of one of literature's more demented imaginations. Billy's recent behavior points to a larger agenda. Also, his Château de Silling appears to make demands on its guests. He's constructed a factory for twisted animation that will probably make the stuff currently coming out of NOD look downright quaint.

But why?

In the threatening video he sent Blake, Billy alludes to his friend Gina's death. Here I find the word "Sodom" connecting the most loathsome book ever written to Lot's story in the Bible, which Gina mentioned in her last words.

This elaborate NOD build suggests a major investment of time and resources, so Billy must have been planning it for quite a while. And yet, Gina died only two months ago. So maybe he decided to transform a project already in progress into a kind of eulogy. But though Gina may have loved NOD, this virtual porn studio is a strange form of tribute.

Billy's creation will demand a detailed exploration, but I have a feeling it's not going anywhere, and I'm well overdue a trip to the real Land of Nod. Before signing off, I fire up a sniffer program to trace the details of my connection. I'm talking to a box hosted at a server farm here in New York owned by a company called Scream Communications.

So now I've got a fixed internet address Billy must use to run his game. I briefly indulge myself by picturing Blythe's smile when I bring this to her. Our first real line on her brother. One I'm sure we can use to start reeling him in.

16

Early the next morning I shift my attention from Billy's virtual fortress to the iTeam's dungeon laboratory. Learning more about their endeavor might help me worm my way into their confidence. I hope someone in the group will then illuminate why Billy's so fixated on Olya.

As befits a secret project, the iTeam likes to be alone during the wee hours. Excepting Olya's occasional morning punishment meetings, they have yet to arrive in time for breakfast, so now is a good time for some light recon.

Unlike most of the workrooms, the iTeam's studio outside my office has a new Yale dead bolt securing its door to a steel frame. I have some primitive lock-picking skills, but this imposing matron would take a far surer hand than mine. I'll need to find an alternative.

The basement's center hallway runs from the elevator to the back bulkhead doors that lead to a thin, grimy alleyway at the south side of the building. The iTeam workroom's door opens off this hall, so I'll see if there's another way in from the back.

A simple lock bump gets me into the office of David Cross, GAME's resident puppeteer, who has permanent tenure as the person most essential to mounting the haunted house. The back wall of his office is penetrated by a huge air-handler duct running along the low ceiling. Cross has rigged a decorative curtain that pulls back to expose a large piece of plywood roughly cut to cover the much larger hole in the wall created during the duct's installation. Only a couple screws connect it to the surrounding drywall, and removing it opens a space I can just wriggle through.

The beam from my Maglite cuts through the dark, illuminating a three-sided storage niche adjoining the main work area. Some strenuous contortions get me through the gap, and I roll onto the floor below.

In the center of the room I now find two odd pieces of equipment that look like lawn chairs from the future. They're made of nested aluminum tubes, and each has three mesh surfaces that permit a wide range of orientations. One is set up as a straight-backed chair, the other is configured to resemble a camp bed. Draped over these things is an array of exotic devices including a pair of late-model eMagin head-mounted displays (HMDs) and matching CyberGloves that allow one to control a computer with finger gestures. There's a pile of black fabric decorated with shiny polka dots. Off to the side of the chairs are six high-resolution video cameras with tiny infrared lights clustered around their lenses. While not really my technical bailiwick, I can identify this stuff as mocap—motion capture—gear used to track the movement of one's body. Toward the front of the room, a bank of new PCs rounds out the setup.

So the iTeam is working on a virtual reality project.

Not at all what I would have predicted. While online worlds have seen amazing growth recently, we still interact with them using mostly the same interface technology as we did in 1983. The hardware side of VR has long been a graveyard of broken dreams for its visionaries.

I'm disappointed. The idea that some gamer-artists are going to revolutionize anything with the outdated technical notions of the late eighties strains credulity. And yet the iTeam members are far from stupid, and they seem genuinely consumed with their secret project.

What could it be?

Next to the bank of computers are two large metal cabinets, each fastened with a rugged padlock. Maybe this is where the real treasure is stored. I unroll my picks and am just starting to fiddle with the first when I hear steps coming down the hall.

Could be nothing, but it wouldn't do to get caught in here, so I grab my tools and retreat to the storage nook. A wedge of light breaks the darkness, and I hear something dropping onto one of the tables. The room's fluorescent lights flicker to life.

Damn.

Xan and Garriott enter. They're in the midst of a dispute about the quality of data passing between two elements of their project. There are some brief clicking sounds, and then I hear the squeak of one of the cabinets' doors swinging open. I'm dying to take a look but decide I can't risk it.

They argue for another minute until I hear the sound of someone relocking the cabinet. The lights go out, and the second they throw the dead bolt, I scamper back through the hole in the wall and drop into Cross's office. I run out the door and around to the main hallway.

Xan is saying, "—never going to work unless you can clean the stream—"

I almost slam into Garriott as I turn the corner.

Xan yelps. Her hand snaps to her mouth. Andrew jumps back, bumping into her. He drops the handle of the large aluminum case he's rolling behind him. It hits the ground with a loud crack.

I try to mollify them, saying, "I didn't mean to—"

"Christ's tits, mate, I think my testicles have undescended," he says.

Xan is cross. "James, what are you doing racing about in the dark?"

I can see hackles rising, so I temporize. "I, ah, was getting a drink, and I heard y'all come in. So I just wanted to catch you before you left again."

They both squint at me.

"I'm crawling the walls with boredom. Capturing hours of video. I thought maybe I could help y'all if you want."

Xan starts to say, "Thank you, but no, we'll—"

Garriott interrupts her. "Xan . . . Let him have at it. You know we don't have time for arsing around. Give him the simulated stuff and see what's what. He sorted me the other night." Garriott suppresses a yawn and consults his watch. With a shriek, he grabs his case and scurries toward his office.

Xan gives me a long appraising look and says, "Really, I can handle it myself. I've no need to impose on your rather suspicious generosity."

"It's not suspicious at all. Maybe I need a favor from you."

"All right, what?"

"I'd like to interview you. But we'll get to that later. For now, show me this dastardly data."

Nine hours pass. Xan and I are cloistered in her office, sitting close, staring at her monitors. I stretch my wrist and solemnly tap F7 to test the latest version of her program. "This is it. We got it this time."

Xan drops her head, her fingers digging at pressure points around her face.

The problem we've been working on is a thorny one. Xan is trying to use a stream of sensor values to determine the position of a number of points linked together like the joints of a robot arm. That would be straightforward, but the underlying points' ability to shift of their own accord makes them jump around crazily. We need them to move smoothly, but it's like we're trying to deduce the exact postures of two fencers only knowing the forces on their foils.

I run the program. The graphed output of the data looks different than it has all night.

I say cautiously, "I think we may have a win—"

"Wait."

None of our debug breakpoints trip, and the program runs to completion for the first time. This triggers a burst of graphic fireworks we rigged on the end line.

Xan wraps me in such an exuberant hug that the ball chair I'm sitting on tips over backward, and we thump onto the floor. She screams comically, levers herself off my chest, and then gives me a hand up. She's concerned that I hit my head and starts inspecting it for a bump. I should say that I'm fine, but the feel of her fingers running through my hair has dissolved my capacity for speech. I want to turn to face her, but my spine has locked itself in place.

Perhaps she picks up on this, because seconds later my head is pronounced "quite sound," and I'm dismissed with effusive thanks and a sisterly peck on the cheek.

Sisterly, but this is the second time she's kissed me.

17

Billy's virtual Silling remains the province of a select few until some-one posts this thread to the NOD forums on Saturday night:

Thread: New Game Trailhead?

Cal_Iglooa	So here's something:
Joined:9/17/11 Posts: 357 Location: your business	Check out this NOD shard we found at: http://nod.com/ule_find/grid:334.118.797 Screen Grabs: [http://www.flickr.com/photos/Cal_ Iglooa/737027084/] Those among us who actually still read might recognize that castle. We've now got a sim based on *120 Days of Sodom.* The stakes? Foul lucre it seems. And any of you who have read *120* will know that I mean *foul*. For those that haven't, *educate* yourselves: A summary The full text

We've only explored a little, but here's how it works:

Every day one of the whores tells a story involving 5 "passions."

Once she starts telling each, you can go into the dungeon and there are rooms set up corresponding to each situation. You reenact the stories with the provided NoBots, sounds, and cameras. Then post your videos back in the amphitheater.

Good ones play up on the wall above the whore's head. After a submission, the Duke puts out his hand with a Louis d'Or. When you take this, your NOD account is credited with 7,500 Noodles [about $5 per video].

Not even minimum wage, you complain? Wait, it gets better. After we tipped him off, Hal_LaCoste took his time and made a couple quality nut nuggets, like the ones already playing in the rotation. We rezzed in today, and when we entered the theater, the Duke got up and said to him, "Your work has pleased us. It is now part of the Telling." He holds out his hand, and in it there's a purse: 75,000 Noodles! That's $50 per video. For all 600 tortures, that == serious spaghetti.

So much pasta raises questions:

1) I can haz?

2) If not, why would someone want to spend so much to crowdsource a machinima version of *120 Days*?

```
                    | 3) Is this new game related to the recent
                    | bubble in NOD cybering tools like our
                    | much-loved LibIA?
                    |
                    | Those of you up for finding out the
                    | answers, hit us up at our new forum:
                    |
                    | Savant
```

I gather from browsing around in the forum that "Savant" is the nick-name for this new place that emerged during chats between early ex-plorers. It's a corruption of *"cent vingt,"* the French word for 120. There are already a number of replies to the post, most expressing "OMF-GROFJUADBBQ" enthusiasm.

But there are also some comments like this one from Anne_Sasha_Ball:

```
Is it just me, or does ANYONE maybe have a problem with
this? I cyber every day, but I have to draw the line at
making virtual kiddie porn. I mean is this even legal?
```

Her question ignites a firestorm of responses, and the discussion degen-erates into First Amendment bickering that then wades off into tendrils about whether George W. Bush was a "genocibal rapist" and the extent to which communist Jews control the media.

I check Cal_Iglooa's initial *Savant* forum posts in which he outlines essentially the same path I took to find Château de Silling. I'll bet the guy is one of the original GAMErs who received a pendant. What both-ers me is that the number of active participants has reached three hun-dred in the few hours since he posted to the NOD forums. So Billy's game has now infected a broad population of bored net people looking for something to do.

Savant is spreading.

18

The New York Harvard Club's two buildings neatly embody the dual nature of the university itself. The original neo-Georgian edifice features an old-boy décor of polished wood and animal heads, reputed to be the spoils of Teddy Roosevelt's shooting expeditions. The resolutely modern addition next door resembles the headquarters of an EU agency, more in the spirit of the school's current inclination toward international technocracy.

Blythe had texted me asking if I'd meet her for a drink after she finished with a speaking engagement here.

I can't think why she would have agreed to debate Mark Cooper '96, a communications professor at Hunter College, on the subject of media consolidation. Perhaps she considered it a practice bout to hone her message in advance of her imminent congressional hearings.

The big news at IMP is that they've agreed to buy TelAmerica, one of their East Coast rivals, in a twenty-six-billion-dollar combination that will make them the largest cable provider in the country. As VP for cable operations, the deal is very much Blythe's baby. Congress loves to make a circus out of major media mergers, so she's been called to Washington early this spring.

The press quickly jumped on the atavistic nature of the deal. Blythe's father first put himself on the map with a daring bid for CalCast, a much larger rival, in 1974, well before the leveraged buyout boom really caught fire. While analysts complained that Randall's balance sheet couldn't justify the debt required, interest soon shifted to larger deals elsewhere. Randall digested his prey and proceeded to ever-greater conquests. In taking a swing at TelAmerica, Blythe is paying tribute to her father's legacy.

I step in just as Blythe is winding up her closing argument. Judging by the way the crowd is nodding at her every sally, poor Dr. Cooper was badly overmatched.

She spends a long time chatting with the attendees afterward. Her performance has compelled even some of the audience's avowed socialists to try slipping her their résumés. Eventually she catches my eye and, covertly rattling a notional lowball, sends me to the bar to secure refreshment.

The words "double Laphroaig neat" come out a little husky and get me a double take from the bartender. I'm repulsed by my sentimentality, but the drink is ingrained in my mind as the enchanted love potion in my secret history with Blythe.

After the night she kissed me by the snowdrifts of Mt. Auburn Street, I took on the lone goal of wooing her. The project seemed futile to the heartsick adolescent in me, which left my autistic engineer side to take control by asking, "Isn't courting someone really just the oldest and most fundamental form of social engineering? Well, isn't it?"

A woman like Blythe, with legions of men falling all over her, looked like an exceedingly hard target. But I had a few advantages. I was already a more-or-less trusted party, I had ample resources harvested from her twin brother, and I had the determination fostered by my sincere belief in the hacker's creed:

There's always a way in.

One begins such an operation with detailed reconnaissance. I admit some pretty stalkerish gambits leapt to mind, but I decided that reading her email would be dishonorable. However, I did hack the registrar's systems to get her class schedule.

That prompted my rising early twice a week to stake out a cozy table at the always packed café at the Science Center so I could turn it over to her and her friends when they came out of Stats 139. After a couple weeks of this, she finally showed up alone, and I blew off my imaginary class to keep her company.

I was "delighted" by the coincidence of finding her in charge of the math/science tutoring program for Roxbury kids that I'd just joined to indulge my previously unexpressed need to serve the community.

I wandered Cambridge scanning for the minutest signal of her presence. Like a drug-sniffing dog let off his leash and free to pursue his fixations.

Finally, a breakthrough: I saw her coming out of the Harvard Provision Company carrying a box of liquor. In my first experience with dumpster diving, I fished her receipt out of the trash bin and found that she'd just purchased half a case of Laphroaig twenty-year. This fact evoked a memory of the slight tug of displeasure at her lips when the Hasty Pudding staff informed her that they only served Johnnie Walker.

The next Thursday, I stood in the Pudding rehearsing the details of my admittedly thin plan to start a conversation about scotch. Isn't it funny we're both Laphroaig fanciers? Perhaps she'd like to sample some rare Quarter Cask I have stashed back at my room?

As it happened, my contrived place at the bar simply allowed me an ideal vantage from which to observe our leading hockey stud, Pete Novak, asking Blythe to the next evening's Mather House formal.

Novak was one of those rare athletes who wanted at least part of a fancy degree before exploring his prospects in the NHL. He had a testosterone-soaked pulchritude, and I guess he represented a passable antithesis of William Coles. But I was still mortified when I heard her say yes.

Seething with jealousy the next morning, I couldn't help torturing myself with online pictures of him celebrating the winning goal in the Junior National Championship. But Novak was an academic all-star as well, so my rival had more substance than a mere well-marbled boy toy. He grew up in a tony suburb near Princeton, mother a professor, father a prominent local sportscaster. *Probably worked for her dad,* I thought bitterly.

Digging deeper, I learned that Robert Randall *had* in fact acquired Joe Novak's station ten years ago, but had fired him in the first round of automatic layoffs. Novak's parents divorced early the next year. Shortly after, Joe Novak killed two people in a DWI accident and was still in jail. So any relationship between Pete and Blythe would have heavier baggage than the First Armored Division.

Though I'd hesitated to invade Blythe's privacy, I had no compunctions about Novak's. He wasn't a heavy emailer, but his browsing history yielded an undue amount of research on powerful sedatives and queries about local doctors with liberal views on their use.

That seemed pretty dark, so I Photoshopped myself an invite to the Mather formal and started trying to figure out how I was going to warn Blythe.

But she didn't even show. I stood there nervously sipping club soda for two hours until I heard a couple of her friends talking about how after pre-gaming with them, she'd "stumbled off" for some "steak and cheese."

Where?

To get to Novak's dorm they'd have to walk right by the party. Not another bar. The Pudding was closed. If Blythe was still conscious, she'd probably balk at a hotel room. So a plausibly innocent place he could take her that would nonetheless offer plenty of opportunity to get her alone?

I called Blake and then ran all the way to the Zeta house.

The front door of the frat's dingy clapboard lair was propped open, and I could hear members bellowing out back. I sprinted up the stairs and wound through the dim hallway leading toward their den. Adjoining which I knew they had two former bedrooms pressed into duty as the "bong room" and the dismal "mattress room," where I thought I might find Blythe.

But the mattress room's door hung ajar, revealing only darkness. I turned back, trying to think where else she could be. Then, a bright light flashed from the alcove next to their most remote bathroom. Deep voices accompanied another flash.

"—society whore's not so pretty now, are you?"

"Daddy Randall's going to *love* this."

I crept around the corner and saw Novak standing in the doorway taking pictures with a digital camera. He was flanked by two of his team-mates, one of whom was struggling with his fly. I had to sneak right up behind them before I finally saw her.

Blythe hunched over the toilet, her lips resting on its soiled rim. Vomit covered the floor. Her backless dress had fallen to expose her breasts. I supposed she'd felt something wrong and tried to make herself sick but was too late. As the flash went off again, she looked up in mute appeal and reached for the plunger in the corner. To use as a weapon? The effort destroyed the remnants of her balance, and her face made a splashy thump as it hit the floor.

I shouldered my way in and reached for her. "Jesus Christ, guys, what kind of shit—"

Novak checked me with his forearm so hard that the back of my head bounced off the wall, and if he hadn't been holding me in place, I'd have joined Blythe on the floor.

"Who the fuck are you?"

As I closed my eyes against the next blow, I saw a pair of pale hands reach from the dark, fasten onto Novak's neck, and rip him back out of the doorway. His minions turned to confront the better part of our heavyweight crew's first boat. Several more hockey players followed just behind them. Seeing Blake and Novak wrestling viciously on the floor, they threw themselves at the rowers. Though the hockey team were surely the better fighters, the rowers had an average of twenty pounds on them, so the brawl escalated fast as more people kept coming up the stairs.

After wiping Blythe's face, I hauled her out of the bathroom and pushed my way along the left-hand wall to a short, dark hallway that led to the back stairwell.

I set her down on the sidewalk outside and tried to revive her. Seconds later Blake loomed behind me, bloody and breathing hard. Without a word, he tenderly picked up his sister and stalked out into the night.

The wee hours passed while I hacked the Mather House key card security system to give myself access to Novak's suite. At six in the morning, he and his roommates were passed out, presumably from celebrating their coup against the "society whore." I found Novak in an almost adorable state of helplessness: snoring loudly on his futon mattress, still in his shirt and tie, but sans pants. One hand remained inside his dingy white briefs, the other cradled his camera.

I grabbed the camera, my primary objective, but couldn't resist a little more payback. A quick sweep of their common room delivered the obligatory gay porn mag, always useful for infantile japery, which I opened on his chest. Then I tightened his tie and placed the tensioning end in his free hand. The dawn lent enough light for several pictures without the flash.

But it still wasn't enough. He'd gone after *Blythe*.

Inspiration struck, and I used Novak's phone to send a quick message.

The Bat's preferred Fulgencio-filler was eager to make a house call and supply me with the powdered methamphetamine that I slipped into the giant Gatorade bottle next to Novak's bed. Not so much that he'd go to the infirmary, but enough that he'd have an invigorating morning. And difficulty passing a drug test. And a sharp end to his hockey season. And a big problem with his scholarship.

At midnight the next evening Blythe knocked on my door. She looked the opposite of how she did the last time I'd seen her, crisp jeans and an immaculate white blouse covering her pearls. Heavier makeup than she usually wore.

Rooted in place on my doormat, she started a stilted speech. "James, I thought I should stop by to express to you my deepest gratitude . . ."

This was not at all what I wanted. She obviously loathed that I'd seen her in such a state.

I interrupted. "Hey, come on in. I have something for you."

She hesitated but stepped inside. As I closed the door behind her, I handed over Novak's camera, cued to my early-morning photo shoot.

She flipped back to the pictures of her and asked the question with her eyes.

"I checked the log. He hadn't downloaded them yet. I think everything will turn out fine. But you should be more careful."

Her silence stretched on, so I asked, "Are you going to be okay?"

She stared at me for another moment, visibly reassessing. Finally she said, "Yeah . . . I'll just need . . ." She glanced around abstractly, as though searching some alternate dimension for what could possibly redeem that awful experience. But then her gaze settled on my mantelpiece bar prominently stocked with exotic bottlings of her favorite alcoholic balm.

I guess its presence served as a celestial confirmation of my virtue, because her voice relaxed when she said, "I'll just need a drink."

She then drifted to my window and stared into the night. I couldn't believe she'd turn her back to me as I poured.

Blythe arrives down at the club bar minutes later and inhales deeply from the lowball I ordered for her.

I raise my drink and say, "To victory."

We tap glasses. "Kind of you. But one can't really declare victory in a training exercise."

"You can if you learn something. And you learned that you need a better class of opponent."

"I think my opponents are talented enough these days. If I—" She stops herself and takes a sip of her drink.

I wait for her to resume, but when she doesn't, I ask, "To what do I owe the honor?"

"Business, sadly. Though I hope that soon we can drink for pleasure."

Lightning surges down my spine. But it dissipates as I realize she probably means that I need to move my ass on locating Billy. She's also not necessarily implying that we'll be drinking *together* at the end of it.

She continues. "How are you finding the new you?"

"Liberating. I'm thinking of installing some new holes in myself. Turns out your brother isn't the only GAMEr with a soft spot for retro prep."

I show her the croc pendant I got at the party. Blythe stares at it. "I won't ask how you came by this."

I laugh. "Nothing like that. He mailed them out to some of his colleagues. An advertisement for this place he's set up in NOD."

She says, "So another game . . . Just a little harmless fun?"

"Well, I wouldn't—"

"Pardon my sarcasm. I know he's always taken them quite seriously." She thinks for a moment. Then changes the subject. "James, I also need to clarify a few things from our last meeting."

"Okay."

"Because of our past, ah, relationship, Blake thought it would be best if you worked mostly with him on this to prevent any . . . awkwardness."

"I see."

"I told him that was ludicrous, but he's obsessively protective of me, and once he gets an idea in his head—"

"I understand."

"But I just wanted to make sure you don't have any difficulty—"

"Blythe, I'm here to help you. Not create new problems."

She smiles. "Ah, good. The one we have is bad enough."

"I get the impression this isn't just an everyday sibling rivalry."

"It's beginning to display the hallmarks of a war of succession."

I nod as she takes a long sip.

"My father badly wanted the enterprise he built to last for generations. He set up the estate so we'd retain voting shares and, therefore, control of the company. Dad was acutely aware that family disputes can lead to dreadful headlines, lawsuits, and sometimes fire sales."

"And you see yourselves heading in that direction?"

"We'd have been there long ago, but my father took steps to prevent that. In his will, he divided financial ownership of IMP equally among the three of us, but not the supervotes. Coherence of control came before equal treatment."

Though it's forbidden throughout the club, she lights a cigarette. "So Dad gave each of us enough voting shares to guarantee a seat, but the full board decides which child will be placed in charge. A sort of meritocratic primogeniture. There wasn't a set deadline, but Ger Loring has started flouncing around in Hawaiian shirts, so everyone thinks the decision will be made soon."

"Sounds like a recipe for a strong company, but a broken family."

A sad smile emerges from the lip of her glass. "Of course Blake and I have stayed quite close. We are twins after all."

She tells me how they carved out separate spheres of influence in the company. Blake on the business development side, and Blythe in cable ops.

She continues. "Billy, on the other hand—"

"Is he even interested in IMP? I thought he dreamed of being a sort of Caravaggio two-point-oh."

"Maybe so. But he never got to make a choice. Blake was so enraged at the publicity from Billy's early legal troubles that he seized on a minor provision in the trust that allowed the board to delay giving Billy his seat when he turned twenty-one. He got the money from his regular equity but no real voice in the company."

"Your father gave the board the power to disenfranchise one of his children?"

"My father trusted Ger more than us, I suppose. He was sensitive to the fact that later generations often take an axe to the family tree. So he put in this 'against the interests' clause. I'm sure it was aimed at situations where the black sheep turns pinko, but Blake deployed it against Billy's freedom of expression. My family has an unfortunate belief that scorched earth is good ground for negotiation."

"I don't suppose he took it well."

"No. We had dinner to try to reach an understanding. To keep our dissension out of the press and maybe make peace." She closes her eyes. "Billy accused Blake of hypocrisy, idiocy, philistinism. Blake . . . There was an altercation. Quite undignified."

She sighs. "Blake thought he was doing it for the good of IMP, but sometimes I think the imp to which my brother seems most attuned is Poe's, not our father's."

She's referring to Edgar Allan Poe's short story in which he lays out a theory about the irresistible allure of self-destructive actions. The Imp of the Perverse, a creature with whom I'm all too familiar.

"Blake thinks I'm too soft on Billy. And maybe he's right. I won't pretend we ever had a warm relationship. But my father loved him, and I try to honor that. I constantly come back to this image I have of him when we picked him up at the airport after his mother died. The way he stood there with his little backpack and seemed so grief-stricken. So vulnerable. Even Blake felt sorry for him. And the look on my father's face was almost worse. I had this idea then that I could try to help them both with that pain . . . As it turned out, there wasn't much I could do. But now, I—I just know my father would want me to help Billy if I can. Blake too. Try to end all this senseless conflict."

"And your concern is—"

"I'm concerned that my two brothers are intent on harming each other. And that they're getting to the point where they don't care about the consequences. That's the message I see in Billy's video. So . . . though you'll be working mostly with Blake, please keep me informed. There may come a point where I'll have to ask you to help protect my brothers from themselves."

Saying this seems to cost Blythe something. She turns away from me. I lift my hand behind her, thinking to comfort her with a gentle pat. But it just hangs there, and I can't bring myself to touch her. I withdraw it and clear my throat.

"Don't worry. Everything will turn out fine."

Her eyes search for something in mine. "I'm sure we both remember what happened the last time you said that to me."

Then, with a subtle arch of her eyebrow, she knocks back her drink.

19

That arched eyebrow ignited a mental wildfire that consumed any thought I might've had beyond ransacking cyberspace for traces of her brother.

At midnight, several hours into my minute forensic probe of Billy's Château de Silling build, I receive the kind of jackpot break you forbid yourself from hoping for. A ProSoap alert from the elevator camera at GAME with recognition results on Olya, Xan, and Garriott.

After rewinding the stream to ten seconds ago, I see the trio troop into the frame, Olya and Garriott dragging large aluminum cases behind them.

I run the eleven blocks over to GAME, sure that seeing the contents of those cases will tell me what their techno-coven is all about. Since coming down the main elevator would probably alert them, I sneak around back to the metal cellar doors that lead to the basement. The doors are secured with a key card system, which only makes a slight click when the lock disengages. I haul one open as quietly as I can.

I tiptoe back to my office and see that the door to their workroom across the hall is closed tight with only a thin ribbon of light running underneath. Olya's sharp tones ring out behind it.

"No. We said we run trial tonight, so we must do this. We don't just slip and slip and slip every time."

"It's *supposed* to slip." This is Garriott's voice. "If it doesn't, it's going to break, and then where will we be? If we just take—"

"If it breaks, it breaks. Then maybe we build it better. They cannot be so fragile."

"But—"

"And we need to know *how* it breaks, yes?"

"Olya, we're not even done with all the component tests. Xan just got her last one fixed today."

Olya's heels click briskly as she walks across the room. She adopts a sugary, mollifying tone. "Little one. Don't you want to know how it feels? Not just the surface, but the connection?"

Andrew sighs. "I just—"

There's a smacking sound. "For luck. Now, let's go. You know it must be tonight."

A moment of silence. Then Olya again: "What is wrong? We work on this all these months, don't tell me now you are timid?"

"Olya, I just don't—"

"I won't laugh, I promise."

Xan intervenes. "Olya, take it easy."

"Andrew! It must be you. Why must I explain this?"

Garriott takes a deep breath and says, "Olya, I don't know what's gotten into you tonight, but I'm going to get some coffee, and we can discuss it after."

Their door cracks open a few inches.

Olya yells, "Get back here, you little—"

I figure this will be my best shot, so I push the door open hard and barge into the room with my BlackBerry in front of me like I'm finishing a text. I say, "Hey, Garriott, I had a new idea on that network problem we were working on that I want to run by—"

I stop about eight feet into the now completely silent room. I look up as though just realizing where I am.

"Oh . . . shit. Sorry, guys. I didn't mean to interrupt."

Eyes closed, Garriott massages his temples like he's trying to keep his skull from fragmenting. Olya has gone apoplectic and alternately stares at him and me as if trying to decide on whom to release the brewing tempest of her rage.

I take the opportunity to glance at the middle of the room, where I am finally confronted by IT.

Or make that THEM, since the top-secret project is composed of a pair of robots linked through a tangle of cables to matched high-end PCs. They resemble oversized swans in form, albeit with ungracefully large heads. Each has a rounded bulk of motors, electronics, and a small air compressor mounted on a wide stationary platform. From there a thinner neck of four motorized segments rises about three feet to culminate in an oblong cylindrical head of maybe nine inches in length and four in diameter. Two arms rise from points corresponding to where the wings would attach. They end in round pads supported by an array of small pistons set up so that the surfaces can quickly change shape. A vasculature of narrow tubes snakes up the neck into the head. At the head's other end, a circular opening is padded with bright red silicone rubber. The heads point downward, as if the machines are bowing in prayer, so I can't tell what's inside the holes. But having seen the rest of the devices, I can guess.

"So this is IT," I say.

My words snap Olya out of her shock. She walks toward me, her arm extended to the exit. "Out, goddamn you!"

She reaches as though intending to bodily throw me through the steel door. But I pivot around her and put up my hands soothingly. "Come on. I've already seen them. At least show me what they do. I'll be your lab rat, and you can kill me afterward if you have to."

Olya looks around for a weapon. "I think we kill you now."

Garriott lifts his head and says with resignation, or maybe relief, "Just let him do it, Olya. We're going to have to test it on other people soon anyway."

Xan is staring at me with a blank expression. Not hostile, more like evaluating. She doesn't speak for a second but then whispers something into Olya's ear.

Olya gives me a gimlet-eyed once-over. Her eyes flick disdainfully at Garriott, and then she says softly, "Well, Mr. Pryce, you want to be the first victim? Come and try our little project."

She edges past me to sit on one of the configurable chairs, where she reaches down and hikes up her skirt. She then leans back and whips off her panties with a lissome flourish of her legs.

This prods everyone into motion. Xan starts plugging more cables from the robots into the workstations, while Garriott tosses a motion-capture rig to Olya.

Olya places her hands on the nearest robot, and I hear a series of mechanical clicks and whirrs and what might be the sound of a fan coming up to speed.

Garriott then steps over to me and points at my belt buckle. A smile forms as he sees me hesitate. The implications of what is required here hit me suddenly, and I feel my whole body start to blush. I have disrobed in the presence of relative strangers before, but this situation represents a new level of weird. But if my duty to Blythe demands that I sacrifice my sense of propriety, so be it.

Besides, how bad can it be?

I drop my pants.

"So put these on. But first, I'm going to need the boxers as well, mate."

I expected this but am paralyzed by the sight of Olya shrugging out of her shirt, revealing a lace-encased bosom that could make Shakespeare's desiccated skeleton compose a 155th sonnet. She quickly pulls over her mocap rig. But for a net nerd like myself, that only makes my erection totally unavoidable.

Andrew glances down and smirks. "I see stage fright won't be a problem."

I snatch the mocap tights he's proffering and wriggle into them as quickly as I can. Naturally, I find they're crotchless and only serve to emphasize my rapid swelling. Along with the standard IR patches at the joints, there are reflective bits lining the seams along the tights' inner thighs, like rhinestones for a glammy fetish act. Xan tugs my shirt over my head and then drapes me with the mocap tunic as though I'm a futuristic knight about to sally forth. She does not resist lightly goosing me for good measure, which marks the end of my battle with modesty. I'm forced to brazen it out with my engorged tool waving in the chilly air.

The next article is my head-mounted display, so at least I don't have to look anyone in the eye. Garriott takes my hand, and with Xan guiding my hips, they recline me on the other chair and position one of the robots between my legs with its head in very intimate proximity.

As I settle in, I ask, "What do I do now?"

Xan, her lips alluringly close to my ear, says, "Now we let nature take its course."

The screens in my visor fade into a 3D rendering of a dungeon scene. I swivel my head and decide that it must be Hell due to the river of molten lava at my left. I'm sitting on a pagan altar in the center of a rock outcropping. A cavern opens to my right, out of which smoke billows lazily.

From the haze emerges a raven-haired succubus character, naked but for some beguiling cuneiform tattoos. Her barbed tail sways seductively as she walks toward me. She grins, and I hear a deepened version of Olya's voice intone, "So, Zhimbo, are you ready to play with me?"

"Mmm-hmm," is all I can manage.

"Well, I am yours to command. What do you want to do?" She's slowly moving closer.

"Uh . . . What *can* we do?"

"Why don't I show you?" she says as she's almost within range of an embrace. But instead she drops to her knees and motions with her hands for me to spread my knees apart. She moves in between, teasingly making sure not to touch me yet. Though I know this gorgeous demon is only a binary figment, my cock jumps at the proximity of her crimson lips. SuccubOlya's right hand darts out and she catches it with two fingers right at the base. The miraculous thing is that I actually feel this. I know it's just the robot. Just a lifeless mechanism. But it doesn't hurt to have Olya's sultry whisper in my ear, and the visuals are marvelous. Indeed, my game-cock, with its full Brazilian wax, lack of unsightly veins, and extra virtual inch or so, looks much better than in real life. But I'm not allowed much time to admire it.

What follows, as SuccubOlya's mouth descends, is without a doubt the most amazing thing I've ever experienced.

A feeling like warm wet flesh pours all the way down my length, but it's unusually hot and soft. I gasp as a glissando of small squeezes runs from stem to stern, and I almost lift my visor to see who's gotten hold of me, so convinced am I that the iTeam is pulling a bait and switch. But as the velvet wave pulls back by slow, agonizing increments, I observe that really it doesn't feel anything like an actual woman.

It feels *better*.

Olya's sex devil seems sprung from a lubricious reverie, but it's the thought of the real person behind her av that lends the scenario its blistering power. Far from the sterile repetition of porn, and yet still maintaining a pleasant buffer of fantasy, she's an ideal balance between the virtual and the real. While my brain indulges itself, my skin just believes.

But I quickly lose this train of thought as she plunges into a rapid full-stroke deep throat. No frightening snags on her hard palate. Super-human muscle control, like she's somehow able to use her very vocal cords to pleasure me. As she comes back up, I wiggle and notice the lack of teeth. She squeezes hard at the base, bares her fangs, and murmurs, "Hold still, *dorogoi*."

She speeds up the rhythm, and my jaw drops. I suppress the urge to place my hands on her head.

Well, what would happen if I did?

I send out an exploratory finger. Incredibly, something's there. Not exactly the silky black tresses I'm seeing, but there's a soft surface exactly where her cranium should be.

As sometimes happens in real life, SuccubOlya stops, but she leers at me, saying, "You like that?"

"Yeah."

"Why don't you stand up and really fuck my mouth?"

That's sufficient invitation for me. It's not like I'm going to stimulate any unfortunate reflexes in a robot. Being able to put my hips into it re-ally adds a dimension to the feeling. SuccubOlya even offers a few dirty words of encouragement that she couldn't possibly say under the circum-stances. Her av throws in some pornographic visual grace notes, but it feels so good that I actually close my eyes.

She allows me a few joyous moments of that before pressing me lightly back against the altar and then straddling me in a reverse cowgirl. The sensation is totally different, but I don't have time to analyze the variation, since seconds later, I realize this episode is about to come to its unnatural conclusion. Olya must sense this, because right then she dials up the heat and pressure. I don't want it to end, and I wonder if I can prolong things, or if I should just surrender to the inevitable. As usual, my genitals reach their own decision, and I'm helpless in the face of an all-consuming orgasm that feels like it's never going to stop.

Then suddenly—pain. It shoots into me like a bear trap just snapped shut on my package. The vids go out, so I'm drowned in blackness. Total agony throbs up into my groin, and I try to slap this horrible thing off my cock. It seems dead now, but there's still suction remaining. And *fuck!* It's completely unbearable!

Finally I wrench it off, and the pain starts to abate. A burnt, ozone-ish smell fills the air. I tear away my HMD to see what happened to James Jr.

This British twit is yelling, "Oh my God, what's he done?"

I still can't see my injury because the lights are inexplicably out, and Garriott is in my face with a flashlight.

I shout at him, "You people fried my dick!"

"You were supposed pull out!"

"You didn't tell me that!"

"It's a prototype. What did you think was going to happen?"

Xan comes over giggling. She grabs Garriott's light, places a steadying hand on my shoulder, and bends low to inspect me.

"Your penis is intact, Mr. Pryce, I assure you. There may be a small blister here at the end, but a little unguent will have you back at it in no time."

I take stock. The pain has lessened, and the stress hormones are slowly falling off. I get embarrassed about the spooge dripping down my tights. Garriott examines his gently smoking apparatus.

The overhead lights twinkle to life, and we see Olya over by the fuse box. She's out of her mocap gear, in a demure bathrobe, but I can see a rosy flush creeping up around the hollow of her throat.

"So, Zhimbo, how was I?"

I pause for a second, assessing what I've just experienced. The word forces itself out of my mouth:

"Electrifying."

20

W e're gathered around their usual table at Foo Bar. Xan twists the key to a magnum of Veuve Clicquot and says, "James will not be the only one popping a cork tonight." She thumbs off the foil while caressing the bottle's neck suggestively. Garriott begins moaning in falsetto. Xan is not afraid to hose down the table, and I become damp for the second time that evening.

When what's left is poured, Olya raises her glass and says solemnly, "Team . . . To a great fucking day at the office."

We all make the "2-I-T" sign, but Xan puts up a hand to stop the toast. "I guess we can tell James what 'IT' really stands for."

"What?"

"Imminent Teledildonics, mate," says Garriott.

"Teledildonics" is the fancy word for virtual sex coined by Theodor Nelson of "hypertext" fame. The term gained currency due to its fine blend of nerdy and naughty, though I think we'll need a new one to describe what I just went through.

After a boisterous clink that leaves much of the remaining champagne on the table, a waitress appears with an armful of Guinness and Jameson.

Garriott takes his shot glass and says, "To Fred!"

Xan follows, holding up her stout: "To Ginger. May she rest in peace." We drop our whiskey into the beer. Garriott is steeling himself for the race and says to me, "I can't believe you killed my girlfriend."

This causes a choking fit on Xan's part. Olya finishes smoothly and slams down her pint. She immediately waves to the waitress. I'm just behind her, and after a deep breath, I ask, "Why do y'all call the bots Fred and Ginger?"

Olya says, "This stupid obsession with scooters."

Garriott finishes quickly to defend himself. "Right. Remember how we were talking about that infuriating Segway hype? So the first prototypes were named Fred and Ginger, because they glided around so gracefully. And yet . . . there's something asexual about a scooter. So we took the names for our little darlings. Who *really* aspire to glide gracefully. They seem to move together well enough for you?"

"I guess the proof was in the pudding."

Olya, ever the heavy, says, "Of course, like any good demo, maybe eighty percent of it was faked."

"I'd say that's about par for the course."

Olya frowns. Xan clarifies. "He's talking about real women, and has betrayed the fact that he's never met one."

Olya rolls her eyes, as if the idea of women faking orgasms were a childish fairy tale. "Maybe now you can fuck penguins if you don't like women."

I want to change the subject from my bedtime preferences, so I try, "What do you mean it was faked? If it's virtual—"

Xan says, "No, she means the machines' capabilities. They can't really do everything you might think from your experience tonight. We preloaded most of that. It wasn't all real-time."

"You could have fooled me."

"Yeah, we're counting on the natural phenomenon that men don't tend to ask a lot of questions when they're getting blown," Garriott says. "Which is why certain transsexual prostitutes—"

"The point is we have very much work still to do," says Olya.

Xan and Garriott put on pouty faces. Olya throws her hands up. "But not tonight, not tonight. Now we celebrate the coming of Zhimbo."

"Well then," says Xan, "with apologies to Richard Powers and his beautiful, if rather chaste, book about our vocation, let me propose: to plowing the dark."

Our glasses clink again. Xan winks at me over the rim of her whiskey, and I feel like I'm finally inside.

− − −

Hours later, we're at an unlicensed club in a big loft in Greenpoint. Olya insisted we go due to the presence of some Polish DJ she knows, and she and Xan are out on the dance floor causing tension to flare between the male patrons and their dates. Garriott tries to train me in some of the simpler rituals of the iTeam, such as learning all the words (and grunts) to James Brown's "Get Up (I Feel Like Being a) Sex Machine."

After quite a while of failing to meet his rigorous but rapidly deteriorating standards, Xan comes over to take her leave. Olya leans over to finish Garriott's drink and bite him on the ear, which I suppose is what passes for affection with her.

She pours me a shot and says, "The little one always leaves early. She is delicate. Not like Andy here. But he is small too. He stays, but he can barely talk."

Garriott primly downs a shot in silence. Olya continues. "Speaking of talking. James, you are a smart man. And not afraid of sex. We have to complete this very fast. Maybe you want to help us. It's good work I think."

"I think I'd like that."

"Da. Good. Well, before you are officially on the team, you and I, we sit down. Have what they call the 'Come into Jesus' talk. Maybe eight AM?"

Only three hours from now. But I can't keep myself from saying yes.

21

All the champagne and stardust has fled from Olya's demeanor when I roll into GAME very near the appointed hour. I meet Garriott in the hall, and he mumbles that he's going to Bellevue to see about getting his stomach pumped, if not replaced. Olya seems completely fine. She's wearing a conservative charcoal pantsuit, albeit with a see-through blouse and patent leather demi bra. Her head starts shaking before I can even sit down.

"Zhimbo, this is no condition for serious talk—"

"Olya, trust me. You have my undivided attention."

A frustrated exhalation and pursed lips. Not much of a welcome, but what would someone raised under communism know about how to conduct a "Come to Jesus" meeting?

"So for background, you know I was at this Pervasive Media Program—where Xan teaches. A place for people who *love* computers. Webcams, online dating, social networking, all these things. So of course we *talk* of having sex with them all the time. But no one ever *thinks* about it. I have degree in materials engineering, so my knowledge of *surfaces* is very deep. But I spend my summers at boring design firm. Eventually I think, *Enough of this!*" A bona fide fist-thump on the desk. "Why not try to do this thing we all want? So at GAME I find the little ones—they are very bright, you know—and we start work. Now maybe we have you too."

"You had *me* at 'fuck my mouth.'" Olya squints quizzically. I realize that paraphrasing *Jerry Maguire* to a recent Russian immigrant is silly. "But do you really think normal people are going to want this?"

"Who is normal? No, it's not whether people want to do virtual sex. The question is, once you give it to them, will they want to do anything else?"

I chuckle and concede the point.

She continues. "Everybody in the world wants real VR. We know what it looks like, but we don't know how to get there. In the science fiction it is always these jacks you plug into network with. Jacks in the neck, chips in the head. Like Billy, this foolish *artiste* you are so interested in." She waves dismissively. "I think nature already has given us the right sort of jack." She places a hand over the juncture of her legs. "And this is the channel that will give birth to the technology. VR will arrive when it *comes*."

Her head tilts thoughtfully for a moment. "Now, are we the first ones to think of this? Of course not. People have always made love to objects. Sailors used dolls made of wood, burlap, and hair of horse. They called them 'sea wives.' Now we can do a little better."

She goes on to detail the more recent history of teledildonics. The subtleties of Allen Stein's "Thrillhammer," an internet-enabled dildo chair that, while something to behold, provides only a visual experience for hetero males. Many device enthusiasts swear by their Venus 2000 / Sybian setups; these are a powerful pair of his-and-hers sex machines, but they're operated only by simple remotes and cannot actually communicate. At the other end of the technological continuum, one finds the purely mechanical charms of a contraption called the Monkey Rocker.

If one artificial coupling strategy has been to sexually enable furniture, another is to simulate actual humans. In response to a crackdown on prostitutes, the Koreans created Robot Hotels, populated with anatomically equipped mannequins. The U.S. has seen the debut of the gorgeous but inert Real Dolls and their more cerebral cousin Roxxxy, who actually runs some pretty respectable AI.

But Olya scorns such literal substitutes. "All these robo-whores give new meaning to the term 'uncanny valley.'" She means the hypothesis that *almost*-lifelike human facsimiles produce feelings of revulsion in their living counterparts.

"Maybe one day, perhaps they will be very sexy, but now I think our way is better. We want the machine, the interface, to disappear, and leave you with two *real people* making love."

Other companies have taken the iTeam's approach as well. Currently on the market is the RealTouch, which is a belt-driven device for men that produces friction in concert with specially produced porn loops. For the ladies, there's the Sinulator, a vibrator control module that they've hooked up to Second Life. Olya sniffs, "A broken metaphor. I do not need someone else to run my Rabbit. If you're fucking, there must be thrust. We are trying to simulate, not just interact. The problem, it is much harder."

I'd like to explore Olya's ideas at length, but she abruptly stands up and moves over to the room's giant whiteboard. She wipes out a small colony of Garriott's intricate drawings and with precise strokes sketches a block diagram of the system. As she's doing this, she describes the team members' respective roles.

She handles what they call the "skinterface," literally where the machines touch the users. This includes much of the sensing package, which is currently being upgraded. The anatomical rendering is a series of air muscles operated by tiny valves controlling pressure from a small, but powerful, air compressor. Miniature heating elements provide an approximation of body temperature, and then finally there's the "lubrication management" system.

Garriott's responsibilities cover the gross mechanical engineering, including head and neck positions, the hand-tracking wings, and almost all the programming for the bots' internal computers. He also built the configurable seats they call "MetaChairs." Olya notes that while all these components seem to be working well, when run in real time, sometimes erratic, "maybe painful" behavior can result. Thus the software running in the devices' embedded brains is called the ErrOS, supposedly for "ERotic Operating System," but really a dig at the reliability of Garriott's code.

In fairness, his challenge is the most difficult. It's hard enough for two live humans to coordinate all the urgent motions of love, and the issues are multiplied exponentially when you insert two dumb robots into the mix. Olya explains that the team has found that people are very forgiving of sensory infidelity as long as *some* kind of rhythm is maintained. The dreaded "pop-out" in real sex must be avoided at all costs.

The iTeam combats this problem by having the large heads try to always maintain contact with the reflectors on their user's crotch. Internal to the heads one finds the appropriate sex organ, a mechanized vagina for Ginger and an adjustable dildo for Fred. As the male user enters into Ginger, she feels this and sends a message asking Fred to thrust out accordingly. Since the woman moves too, much of Garriott's massive code base is dedicated to hashing through data about who is doing what and determining the proper response for the robots.

Physically, Fred and Ginger are almost exclusively focused on points of genital contact. The exception is the "wings." These armatures provide a very rough sense of the rest of your partner's anatomy. They track the motion of your hands along the surface of your bedmate's virtual body, making no attempt to render subtleties like earlobes or nipples. They mainly just stand in for places you might be prone to hang on to: breast, torso, ass cheeks, and back of the head. The arms cover a large volume of space, but they also fold into a compact form that allows a single robot to be stored in a good-sized suitcase. The team planned for two more arms to allow v-lovers to feel the glide of each other's fingertips, but they've decided that the intricacies of that feature will have to wait for a future release.

Xan joined to create characters and animation, and she ended up with all of the demo's programming as well. But the iTeam's objectives have recently become more ambitious. They want a system that lets users all over the world come together using any skin they choose and start building their own scenes from day one. This is where I come in.

"James, the little ones tell me you are very good with networks."

"I've played around a little. I can't say I'm a 3D wizard though."

"I think this is okay. Maybe you have heard of NOD?"

I should have seen this coming. The whole reason I'm involved with these mecha-molesters is because a billionaire game maven seems unnaturally interested in them. Why should it surprise me that they'd use the same tech platform to pursue their deviant agendas?

Now that I think about it, NOD is perfect for the iTeam too. Being a feckless user-driven environment, it largely falls to the players to entertain themselves. The principal activity they've discovered is to copulate with all the frenetic energy and staggering variety one finds on earth.

More, probably. In NOD, you'll find everything from white weddings to gilded *scheisse* palaces. Bondage, age play, garment fixation, deformity adoration, and forbidden Orc-Ewok liaisons. But while this might seem exciting and new, it really boils down to spicy chat and some ribald but low-fi animation. Behind it is old-fashioned jerking off. Which, while amusing and effective, is perhaps in need of an update. This is the iTeam's mission.

"Absolutely. Nutting Over Data. I try to have all my sex there. It's cheap, hygienic, and nobody knows I'm a dog."

"A dog? Ah, you are kidding. But what you say is correct. Even more important, they are the only major world with the truly open-source software, so we can modify it to our, ah . . . specific needs. This is what you must now do: hook us up."

"That will not be trivial."

"Ya. So we give you four weeks."

The traditional absurd deadline. "What's the hurry?"

"We want to leak video then. So we can get TODD invite for formal launch."

TODD is a rapidly growing tech conference held annually in New York. The name stands for Totally Obsessed with Digital Depravity, and its founders conceived it as an antidote to the earnest nerdiness of the establishment's Technology Entertainment Design seminar, "TED." The target participants are dissolute digerati from all over the world, and the occasion tends to punch above its weight in terms of media coverage. Given their daily ration of boring cell phones and laptops, the tech press is notoriously receptive to stories with a little flesh tone.

"Formal launch. That implies you have a business plan."

"An artist is concerned about the filthy money?"

"They say it's the root of all evil. So if your filthy robots are going to enslave humanity, I suppose we'll need some pretty soon."

"But our robots will be very clean. Dishwasher safe, and they won't give you gonorrhea. The Dancers, we call them. The name is important. We want them to be elegant, classy. Like Fred and Ginger. Like iPhone. Expensive to make, but we get by so far."

"But eventually . . ."

"Eventually we need servants to peel our grapes, so yes, I have been talking to some people. You do not need to worry with this now. You worry about your work. We made the decision to start with a ready prototype, so we keep more equity."

"Speaking of equity . . ."

"Ya, ya. What is your 'end,' yes?"

"A girl's gotta eat."

"Right. We must all sign the papers soon. When we get corporate structure set up. A business, it must be capitalized. So, with all that, we determine correct shares very soon. But I guarantee"—she leans over and caresses the back of my neck—"we make you happy."

We both know that signing up for a venture without having the business elements on paper at the outset is totally moronic. Is Olya just reflexively trying to manipulate a number-dumb video geek, or does she really think that brandishing her cleavage at me like it's a mind-control ray will make me do what she says? Excellent breasts have elicited from me a long list of ill-advised actions, but their allure tends to wear off after a few hours of coding.

"Well, I guess we're working for love, not money."

Of course, in the workplace, money is the only thing that actually counts. That's true often enough in the bedroom as well. People say that sex drives technology, but they're skipping a step. Money drives technology. Sex is just one of the few things people are reliably willing to pay for.

But I'm getting paid in any case. What she doesn't know is that I might get fired from my real job if I queer this relationship by digging in my heels over a fantasy fortune.

Olya flashes a feral smile. "That is the correct attitude. Welcome to our team, Mr. Pryce." She takes my hand in both of hers. "We'll enjoy having you."

II

THE KING OF HEARTS

22

After the meeting, I'd planned to spend the next twelve hours in bed, but the lure of Olya's challenge proves too strong to ignore. So instead, I go to my office to start downloading the NOD software developer's kit, the files one uses to create customized NOD worlds.

A text from Blake asking me to breakfast disrupts this plan. He's chosen Demeter, a painfully recherché cafe near his apartment that's advanced the recent farm-to-table obsession to the possibly satirical point of allowing diners to inspect online the genealogy of the chickens supplying their eggs. Hoping a $34 thoroughbred omelet can at least do something for my hungover stomach, I head toward SoHo.

Blake's idea of breakfast varies widely from mine. As I walk into the haute-country dining room, I see him already surrounded by food, conducting a meeting. A tall, svelte gentleman in an ostentatiously well-tailored black cashmere suit is delivering a heated lecture, jabbing his finger twice over the remains of his French toast. Blake gives me a "one sec" gesture and turns his blank business face back to his companion. I go in search of some coffee.

Who in the world gets to talk to Blake Randall that way?

When I return, the guy has vanished, and Blake waves me over. I sit, noticing the absence of a menu.

"So I'm not your first breakfast." I tilt my eyes toward the door.

Blake isn't fielding inquiries about the argument. He just says, "Fourth, actually."

"You must be a hell of a morning person."

"The empire of trade tends to swift decay."

"Right. I assume your sister told you that I think Billy has started another one of his experimental games?"

Blake nods.

I continue. "So if you follow the clues in the riddle he sent out, they take you to a private NOD sim that's a replica of the castle from Sade's *120 Days of Sodom*."

"What's the point?"

"I don't know yet. Do you have any idea why your brother would be particularly interested in the Marquis de Sade?"

"No. Though he seems to delight in torturing me. Whatever this is, that'll be his ultimate objective." Blake goes pensive. Then he asks, "Can you, given your skills, ah, make this thing go away?"

"There are steps we could take to obstruct him. But someone with Billy's resources, if he wants to put something on the web, it would be very hard to stop him. Also, I don't know why you'd want to do that. Right now, it's our only line on him. My advice would be to tread very lightly until we know more. If we start attacking his boxes, he might go to ground again."

"Understood. What else?"

"I've found a group of people at GAME that your brother's been spying on."

A neutral nod from Blake.

I ask, "It doesn't surprise you to hear that?"

"Nothing you could tell me about my brother's behavior would surprise me. Spying is not unusual for him. As a child, he had a mania for it. He'd gotten ahold of a video camera by his sixth birthday. The same impulse led him to become a hacker. He's always been obsessed with snooping around in other people's affairs. Trying to learn their secrets." Blake stops for a moment, recalling something unpleasant. He blinks and then asks me, "So you've found files he kept on these colleagues?"

"Not yet. But his arrest in Boston was due to a conflict with someone in the group, and Billy clearly had an abnormal interest in these people. I'm insinuating myself among them to find out why. They've picked me up for this thing they're working on."

"Thing?"

I'm not sure why, but I can't bring myself to tell him. The Dancers just seem like something I need to keep to myself for the time being. Beyond the trouble I have getting my tongue around the word "teledildonics," I just don't know how he would react.

"Yeah. They're working on force feedback gadgets for these virtual worlds. So you can see the connection to your brother's pursuits."

Blake looks up at the ceiling. "So I'm paying your firm three hundred dollars an hour for you to play video games and tinker with vibrating joysticks?"

I have to suppress a smile at how close he comes to the mark. "You're paying us because we're adept at finding hackers in hiding. If your brother were into bird-watching, you'd have people out in a swamp somewhere."

He screws up his face like his salmon cake has gone off, shaking his head minutely. Then he exhales and closes his eyes. I'm disturbed at my jolt of anxiety that he might not approve this iTeam infiltration, and I'll have to resign my new post. The Dancers have excited me well beyond their possible relevance to my assignment. Odd that last night's virtual tryst has inspired the first real passion I've felt in months.

A waiter arrives to interrupt Blake's consideration. Skinny and unkempt, the guy's wearing chunky fashion-nerd glasses and sports a very thick, slightly off-color handlebar mustache, a parody of the kind seen on jazz age French waiters.

His accent is equally preposterous. As he sets a silver-domed plate in front of Blake and says, "Dessert, *compliments de le maître!*" it occurs to me that both are fake. He whips off the cover. Too slowly I recall that this is not a French restaurant.

Then the smell hits.

Lying on that field of pristine china like a bloating mackerel is a prodigious turd. A garnish of parsley and lemon serves to emphasize the thing's foul menace.

Blake leaps out of his seat. But the horror only hits his eyes. By the time he's standing, the veneer of control has locked back into place. He opts for that ubiquitous word of disdainful reproach: "Really?"

The waiter appears nonplussed by this, as though his duet partner has wandered from the score. He lifts the plate toward Blake's face, offering it again.

Trying to forestall anything too disgusting, I lunge across the table, but I'm only able to get the tips of my fingers on the upper edge of the plate. The turd tumbles back onto the table and then falls to the floor, leaving most of its reeking mush on the linen. Other patrons catch the scent and gasp in outraged revulsion.

The waiter frowns at me. "*Merde,*" he says. Then he takes off running. When I move to follow, Blake places a staying hand at my ribs. I gather he wants to avoid any further spectacle.

Across the room, another scruffy dude pockets a small video camera as he slips out the exit. Blake nods at a concerned diner to indicate he's okay. Seeing several financial luminaries on their feet, I realize he probably knows half the people in here.

He smiles broadly, delivering a fine rendition of the pie-in-the-face-at-Davos good humor charade. He says to the room, "Please forgive the disturbance, everyone. Another one of our adoring fans, I'm afraid." This gets a few knowing chuckles, but much of the crowd is still murmuring with opprobrium. I see a tiny muscle under Blake's eye start to twitch.

Demeter's owner bursts out of the kitchen looking like she actually *has* eaten something repellent. A crack team of gloved busboys follow her and attack the table like a trained hazmat squad.

Before Blake steps off with the owner, he says, "James, find my brother. Do whatever you need to do."

23

The weekend is filled with all-night work sessions for the iTeam. That means I spend sleep-deprived days making gross animation in NOD to establish Jacques as an avid player of Billy's game. Having to choreograph such vile puppet shows while barely clinging to consciousness proves to be a form of torture that would warm Sade's heart. However, the positive effect of all this virtual vice is that I haven't once indulged my compulsion toward dangerous RL depravity since I met with the twins.

As I delve into the lecherous minutiae of Billy's hybrid world, I find his ultimate purpose has become even less clear to me. While Sade's book is pretty good material on which to base yet another piece of virulent agitprop, we've assumed from the beginning that he's working to seriously attack his older brother. The stunt at Demeter, though unnerving, seemed juvenile and used a fairly limiting medium. I'm sure he has a more harmful message for Blake, but for now, I don't see the stiletto in his garter belt.

Maybe what we need is a strip search. Perhaps Billy has concealed his real agenda under all these layers of virtual-world frippery. His game timeframe is unlikely to accord with mine, which puts me in the position of wanting to know the outcome of a game without having to play it. So there's really only one thing to do:

Cheat.

Today I will spend the morning compromising the virtue of an innocent server.

Doing so is the skill I have the longest practice in. Fittingly, given my new job with the Dancers, the first thing I ever penetrated for sexual reasons was a computer. Even for a twelve-year-old, hacking has in it something of the same thrill of a successful seduction.

As with a real seduction, there are many ways to tempt a system. Unfortunately, given the male-dominated ranks of practicing hackers, penetration lingo tends toward distastefully sexualized terminology. At Red Rook we call script kiddies necrophiliacs, since they are looking for zombie systems with brain-dead security. "Physical" attackers, who actually break into a facility, are rapists. The most common type of system compromise is the inside job. These people are onanists: they represent the organization fucking itself. Normal hackers are Rohypnotists, always trying to slip something dangerous inside you. I prefer the more civilized approach of convincing someone that they actually want to sleep with me. I like to be gentle about it too.

The host of Billy's *Savant* box, Scream Comm, isn't such a roundheels as to use social-plus-mom's-maiden for verification, but she does allow users to reset their passwords by answering security questions. The internet is refreshingly promiscuous in its development methods. When working on a site, you check what other people are doing and just take the code or procedure you need. This practice makes it easy and fast to get things up and running, but it allows bad ideas to spread like mayonnaise. In this case, the problem is the queries used to establish a user's identity: parents' middle names, city of birth, first car, first pet, high school mascot, favorite movie. I don't know where these questions came from, but almost everyone uses them. And they're not very good.

I have answers to all of them for Billy except favorite movie, and for that one, I have a strong feeling about *The Game*. In the end, his high school mascot, the lion rampant, gets me in. I quickly create a stealth admin account and reset his password back to the old one. A lightweight process copies an image of the hard drive to a secure Red Rook server. When that comes back complete, I start drilling into it.

But what I find is a dry hole.

Billy's been quite careful in making sure that nothing in this public-facing server points to his current location. The whole NOD install that constitutes *Savant* was uploaded two weeks before the GAME party from an open proxy in Taiwan. The disk contains no documents that might give a read on Billy's plans. All I have from him is the source code, which is spread out over thousands of objects and will take days or even weeks to untangle. And in all likelihood that process will be futile anyway.

His players, on the other hand, have left loads of material to sift through. There are thousands of nefarious cartoons, of course, but I also see several offerings containing live action. Some of these are from mainstream porn, including a stimulating clip from *Marquis de Sade* starring Rocco Siffredi's monster cock. The nastier vignettes degenerate into low-rent amateur stuff barely related to the source material.

However, some of the most recent submissions come from groups of people making original pornography explicitly for the game. Today there's a new video holding top billing for the "Dog's Breakfast" story. It stars two Great Danes, both naturals in front of the camera.

The segment has high production values: good video quality, nice candlelight, and even a gesture at period costumes. At first, I resist the notion that someone in the eighteenth century would adorn his animals in feathered tricorne hats. But the most cursory research convinces me that the urge to costume one's pet is fundamental to mankind.

These homemade videos, irrespective of their quality, share one thing in common: they've all been declared winners for their vignette.

Maybe Billy's sending a simple message by elevating those clips: in this contest, images of real people are preferred. He didn't set up this sprawling virtual infrastructure to compile a scrapbook of odious little films, he wants to see the stories *enacted*. So his players' formerly virtual activities leach into the real world. The Bleed in action.

Curious though that when Billy rewards his more creative players for their accomplishments, they tend to stop playing. Or at least they stop posting new videos and go silent in the forums.

Now, why would that be?

I think he must be graduating them into an otherwise locked part of his game. And I suspect Blake's breakfast is an example of how these secret levels play out. They're still enacting elements from Sade's despicable script, but out in the real world, and sometimes with unwilling costars.

Olya's disrupted necklace delivery is probably another example. Though the reference behind it eludes me at first. There are a couple of possibly relevant scenes, but I'll bet it derives from the way Sade's villains mark their victims for specific tortures by decorating their necks with different ornaments. A promise from Billy of future persecution.

What strikes me about that idea is that if you read ahead in the book, you quickly get into some horrible behavior. Right now we're still in the first month, and already the stories gleefully violate a number of state and federal laws, to say nothing of the dictates of hygiene. Once into the month of February, we're talking about mutilations and murder. And so the question becomes:

Where does it stop?

Maybe that's exactly what Billy wants to find out.

24

That afternoon, I remind Xan of the interview she owes me, and we end up in the back corner of a busy French bistro in Alphabet City.

"So for this documentary I'm working on," I say, "I wanted to get a better sense of Gina Delaney. You were already teaching when she enrolled at PiMP. But weren't you two both '03 at MIT also?"

"That's right."

"Were you friends?"

Xan stirs the martini she's drinking and sets aside the olives before tasting it. "Yeah, we were friends. Especially our freshman year."

"Did you have a falling out?"

"Not really. That spring she withdrew from school near the end of the semester."

"She was depressed?"

"Quite."

"Something specific bring it on?"

Xan nods vacantly. Then she recovers herself and looks at me sharply. "James, I'll tell you this if I must, but you can't go putting it in your docudrama."

"Okay. Deep background helps."

She takes a slow breath. "So Gina was raised as some kind of religious nutter. This hellfire church her parents belonged to. Not just strict . . . weird. There are more of them in Boston than you might think. But she claws her way out of their local slum and goes to MIT. She's a brilliant engineer. Not just smart, but someone even we Beavers think is a *freak*. But college isn't all work. Anyone who's raised that way is going to experiment a bit once they're at liberty. She doesn't take it *too* far, so things are just ducky." Xan takes an olive off her cocktail spear. "That is, until she meets the *boy of her dreams*."

"And who was that?"

"One of your lot actually. Maybe you know Blake Randall?"

I pride myself on my poker face, but I guess Xan is able to read the word "holyfuckingshit" in my eyes.

"You do know him," she says.

I put on a thoughtful expression. "Yeah. Two years above me. I saw him at parties."

"Hmm . . . ," she says, still observing me.

"So, ah, I take it something happened between him and Gina?"

"Right, so we get hauled over to one of those inane Porcellian parties—everyone wearing rep ties and talking shite about sailing and hunting." This makes me wince inwardly since I'd enjoyed many such occasions. The Beavers always have been barbarians.

She continues. "So Blake is there, and someone introduces him to Gina. She was a very pretty girl as you might know, and so they're quite taken with each other. Maybe he thinks he's going to score, but Gina doesn't really play that way. Fine. So this bloke starts to woo her. Boat rides up the Charles. Picnics at his country house, if you can imagine such bollocks. Treating her like they're in a Jane Austen novel. But that's just how she believes it's supposed to be. He's hot and rich, and probably has a whole line of girls, but he's putting in time with Gina."

"Doesn't sound so bad."

"No, it doesn't. Not until he gets impatient." She leans back, quiet now.

"Did she press charges?"

Xan waves away the idea. "It wasn't like that. She comes back to the dorm in a party dress and tears. One of those big black-tie dinners you all seem to insist upon. So she has a little too much champagne. Then a lot too much cognac. And then a fat cosmo for dessert. Wakes up without her knickers next to a Somewhat Distant Boyfriend."

Hearing this as an indictment of my gender, I try frowning to convey that I would never, ever even think of being involved in such an episode. Xan tsks at my display.

"Anyway, it's pretty typical. Gina is exactly the type of girl to get buyer's remorse. Little sophisticates that we are, her friends try to convince her that it's not a big deal. But she's different. For her it *is* a big deal. She doesn't blame him or anything, probably never told him she was a virgin. Anyway, he should have known. But what do you expect?"

I can only shake my head at the predatory nature of my brethren. I don't pull this off well, and Xan kicks me under the table.

"Oh, I know you're a pig just like the rest of them."

"So this messed her up enough to make her drop?"

"I don't think so. The problem was that her friends didn't understand. So she got the bright idea to talk things over with her mother."

"Yikes."

"Yeah. Her father showed up at the dorm that day, and she didn't come back. I guess some real fire and brimstone shite went down in the Delaney house that spring."

"And then she was back the next fall?"

"Yeah. Commuting from home. But I was in Barcelona my sophomore year. So we basically lost touch. I guess she lost touch with most of her friends. She went virtual."

"It sounds like she had some success with it."

"Oh yeah. Gina was troubled, but still a complete genius. That first start-up she joined, Ichidna Interface, was a one-woman show, wasn't it? But I'd have thought her greatest success would be getting out of that awful house and coming here."

"So she seemed better at PiMP?"

"Not at first. When I saw her at the welcome party, she was like a totally different person. Shaky, nervous . . . like she'd been too long in a space station and wasn't used to people."

Xan tells me how she reintroduced herself, and while Gina had remained as sweet as ever, she couldn't really look her in the eye. Xan asked about some of her well-known professional triumphs, but Gina seemed like she was yearning to escape her former work, or at least the isolation she self-imposed while doing it.

Gina said to her, "I looked up my new classmates, and they all seem so creative and interesting. I'm—I'm just excited to be here where I can maybe make some new . . . things. Ah, you know, work on my own ideas."

Recalling that pitiful sentence makes Xan stop her narration and squeeze her eyes shut for a second.

Xan stayed with her a bit more, but eventually she got pulled away to welcome other new students. But she kept an eye on Gina.

"The poor girl just stood there, fairly shaking with terror. She kept checking her phone like she had a preemie in the neonatal ward. I could tell she was mortified by her awkwardness. One of our friendlier lads tried to chat her up, but he didn't get past one-word answers. I could see Gina's eyes start to well up. Obviously she'd made some kind of death pact with herself to resist her shyness. So she just stood there rooted in place. Alone and miserable."

Xan tells me she couldn't bear watching it anymore and moved to rescue her old friend. But before she got there, she saw Billy stomp his way over to Gina's side. He put his fist up in her face and said something in a hostile tone. Xan couldn't make it out at first and rushed toward them to stop any kind of trauma this little kook might inflict. But she pulled up short when she saw Gina smile for the first time that night. Later she figured out what Billy said to her:

"Best of seven. Bet I crush you in four. I'm throwing rock."

As Xan tells it, Gina's eyes lit up, and she said, "Bring it."

Rock Paper Scissors. The child's amusement that obsesses geeks the world over, since it forms the conceptual underpinning for certain types of video games. Contests can become mental duels requiring Jedi-like powers of perception and dissimulation.

Billy came with scissors. Gina threw rock. Xan was relieved to hear her giggle. She decided to leave her in the hands of her unlikely savior.

A while later, Xan witnessed Gina actually drinking a beer and laughing with a group of her new classmates who had started a mini Rochambeau tournament. She noticed her exchange a secret smile of thanks with Billy. For his part, he seemed utterly in awe that fortune had blessed him with such a moment.

"So playing a kid's game isn't exactly the kind of brilliant wit that's going to get you invited to meet the queen. But any game is a sort of conversation. And I mean, the lingua franca of PiMP is Klingon, for Christ's sake. Anyway, because of Billy, Gina's suddenly no longer this schizoid loser on the verge of tears. She's *winning*. Both of them love games, and because of that, along with some luck, I think they won a little love for each other too. In Billy's case, a lot. Things got better for Genes after that. She seemed more comfortable eventually . . . When you could catch her offline."

"Offline?"

"Yeah, she was working a lot with NOD. Playing there too, I guess. That's where she and Billy would hang out." I flash to Nash's description of the pictures in her apartment. The family photos of avatars.

"Sounds like the makings of quite a romance."

"Yeah, we all thought so. But it seems Gina's mind was elsewhere."

"Really? Where?"

"Well, nowhere at first. But then, after a while . . ."

"What?"

"She started fucking Olya."

"You mean . . . ?"

"Yes, James. Hot girl-on-girl action. Close your mouth, dear, you look retarded."

"So—"

"Yeah, software aside, the main thing Gina developed upon graduating was Sapphic tendencies. It's not that unusual. The women here in New York are amazing."

"And Olya?"

"Her sexual persuasion? I'd say it's carnivorous."

"Like Catherine the Great?"

"More like a praying mantis."

"I guess an aggressive interest in sex is only appropriate considering our project."

"That's not really what I mean. But forget it. We can't be gossiping about our partners in crime, can we?"

"Were they, ah, *dating* when . . ."

"I don't really know much about it. I was in Hong Kong when it happened. Before I left, I heard they'd had a couple fairly public blowups. The rumor was that the relationship was flaming out. Gina was devastated. Olya can be cold as winter in Moscow—"

"And Russian campaigns don't end in parades."

"Exactly. Anyway, I came back early for the funeral."

"So did people blame Olya for pushing her over the edge?"

"No. We all knew Gina was a bit of a head case. There was talk, but you can't really blame a person for someone else's suicide, can you?"

"I'm sure it happens."

"Yeah, now that you mention it, I guess that's what started her famous row with Billy. But then he was a head case as well."

"Does Olya blame herself?"

"I wouldn't mention it to her."

25

Back at GAME, things do not go smoothly.

Xan pulls me into the iTeam's workroom, affectionately known as the Orifice. She needs a new data loop for debugging the sex avs, which are still twisting into positions not seen outside of particularly violent *Road Runner* cartoons. The session runs well until Ginger drops into a catatonic loop and begins humping my kneecap. Not for the first time, I ask myself whether we're doing the devil's work by making sex subject to technical difficulties. Or maybe God is as prudish as they say, and through us he's working a subtle sort of revenge against the unchaste.

Even outside of mundane moral categories, I have to confess that after my initial fascination abated, I began feeling some unease with the larger aims of our project. IT is a technology meant to address the eternal problem that you can't have unlimited sex with whoever you want. But as such, it introduces its own set of limitations.

For me, sex represents the zenith of human experience, and much of my mental energy has always been dedicated to endlessly rehearsing the act and scheming about how to achieve it. Nature has given us this profound ability to really *connect* with one another in a way that feels nothing short of divine when done right.

As technology marches ever onward, we immerse ourselves in more and more connection but accept compromises that reduce its finer qualities. A hurried cell phone conversation is, and will always be, a far cry from words spoken while gazing into your lover's eyes. The rise of email, chat, and SMS has robbed us of even the emotive color of our voices. And so, with our current venture, do we risk allowing some of the ineffable beauty of Eros to leak out along the phone lines?

Sex had seemed pristine in this regard. But now we're making inroads. Excavating the mysterious and secret shrine. As a lifelong technophile, I can't turn back any more than an archaeologist on the precipice of a tomb, but I have felt the occasional shiver of dread that we're setting out to defile something sacred.

In counterpoint to my uneasy reflections, Olya and Garriott start a round of gleeful sparring over the spec. This culminates in Olya throwing the 150-page document at him. The impact knocks his hand loose from its hold on one of Fred's retaining rings. With the air pressure on high, Fred's plastic member rockets into the wall and shatters just over Xan's head.

We're expecting a well-deserved freak-out, but Xan just sighs and says, "We're not building the bloody Panama Canal here, are we? I should like to live to feel the fruits of this grand endeavor. So let's be more careful with our private parts, shall we?"

Later that day, I check in with *Savant*. Already the number of players has jumped by a factor of ten since that first post about it in the NOD forums. The formerly rather idle Château de Silling now hosts a continuous stream of NODlings, from cyber-swingers looking to meet like-minded avs to machinima drones obsessively working their way through the available scenes.

Billy's conjured all these people to help him build something, but despite their labor, I can't make out the structure. I'm sure his game holds a story beyond the retelling of Sade's malignant fairy tale, but so far he's left me in suspense. Though if he's aiming to honor *120 Days,* then we need to shut him up long before he gets to the climax.

26

Though much of my life is lived online in domains defined by data, long experience has shown me that the human antennae, quirky though they are, can pick up signals invisible to any machine. To the extent that Gina's death is a significant flash point for Billy's hostility, I want to see where it happened.

So the next morning finds me standing in front of 301 Conover Street in Red Hook: Gina Delaney's last apartment. My secondary reason for coming here is that since I'm supposed to be working on this documentary, I should be able to produce a bunch of relevant raw footage if called upon. This is a pretty obvious choice for coverage, and so I'm trying to achieve arty framings of the semiconverted warehouse against the bright January sky. A small sign in front indicates that unit 4B is for rent and that interested parties should inquire with the landlord in 1A.

From the police report, I remember Gina lived in apartment 4B. Given the newspaper jammed in the building's entrance and the cloud of marijuana smoke coming from a ground-floor window, I'm guessing that the landlord won't mind if I just let myself in. At the top of a groaning spiral of stairs, I find the apartment door ajar as well.

The place has been redone. The walls painted, the floors reconditioned. The raw wood columns to which she attached those fatal pulleys have been sanded and covered with thick white acrylic.

After taking a couple photos, I start a shot that I hope will evoke spectral wandering. Midway through, I jump at a loud creak coming from the front door. A small black lady stands there, making no effort to conceal the joint she's holding.

"What are you doing, son?"

"Oh, sorry, I was just looking at the apartment."

"You want to rent it?"

"Maybe."

"But you taking pictures like one of them sickos?"

"Sickos?"

"People come because of the girl that died here."

I flash her a photo of Billy and a portrait of Benjamin Franklin. "This guy come here?"

"Oh yeah. He's a strange one."

"How so?"

"He came three days after. Took lots of pictures. Then he just stood there for a long time. It got late, so I come up to ask him what he's doing. He said he's 'conducting a séance.' But I seen a real séance in Flatbush, and that boy, he was just standing there."

After I thank her for the information, she lingers to watch me for a while but then departs.

I walk to the large bank of windows along the front of the apartment to take in what would, in a better neighborhood, be a million-dollar prospect of the Manhattan skyline. In the background is the mercantile majesty of the financial district, with a gorgeous front view of the Statue of Liberty standing off to the side, her arm outstretched as though she's hailing a cab on her way to some important meeting. In the foreground is the ruined beauty of Red Hook, presenting a stark contrast to the spider-eyed gleam of Wall Street. The decayed industrial port now bears clear signs of financial miscegenation. A tony coffee shop inhabiting a former loading dock here, a shiny BMW zipping past rusted hulks there. It's like a bleached coral reef spontaneously regenerating. And yet still dominating the area are giant loading cranes standing as though sentinels for long-forgotten gods of industry.

My camera feels drawn to them, and I reflect on the way that the once-packed shores of Red Hook, which sat quiet for so long as blue-collar activity fled, are slowly growing new factories filled with artisans creating things that exist somewhere on a continuum between idea and object. Figments fixed in our electrical web that you can see and hear, and maybe soon feel, but that would disappear if you tried to remove them. Gina spent her life in this fiber-optic dream catcher.

Beyond the windows, the crystalline winter day has lured people outside to enjoy the unaccountable warmth of the sun. Kids joyously traverse a huge piece of playground equipment. I wonder what Gina saw when she looked out onto this world. What was it that made her first retreat from it, and then finally decide to abandon it forever?

I know the answer is usually just malfunctioning brain chemistry. But I can't picture how all those misfiring neurons twisted her eyes. How could her filter have been so dark as to compel her to set her grisly machine in motion and make the last thing she saw her own blood spraying the wall?

27

Today Olya demands a "Stakhanovite" effort from the team, and we do our best to emulate the Soviet earth-moving hero, though as latte-sipping developers, the results are weak. But we beaver with a will late into the night.

Xan is the first to break. I notice a long period of silence from her fancy Dvorak keyboard and turn to find her asleep. The weight of my gaze wakes her, and without a word, she rises from the table and walks out of the room. Garriott's eyes follow her longingly.

A few minutes later, she bursts back into the Orifice, flushed and breathless, vibrations of panic projecting ahead of her. She drops a neck-lace-sized felt jewel case on the worktable.

Garriott asks, "Good lord. What's the matter?"

Xan takes a second to steady herself and then says, "I . . . these men outside—ah . . . grabbed me."

I jump out of my seat. "Are you okay? What happened?"

She wraps her arms around herself. "Yeah. I'm fine. I—I was just leaving, and there was this car parked on Suffolk with two creepy guys with cameras leaning against it. I walk past, and one of them snatches my arm and says, 'You need to give this to your friend Olya.'" She points at the case. "I ran back here and locked the back door. I think they might have been following me."

Olya steps over to the case. Before I can object, she flips open the lid, which blocks my view of its contents. Whatever it is makes her teeth grind together. She spins toward the door, and I have to move fast to get in front of her. She tries to push through me.

"Olya, no! Stop. Let me. I'll take care of it."

"Fuck off—" She keeps struggling.

"Garriott, get over here and hold her."

With that laughable suggestion, I race down the hall toward the stairs to the alley. I can hear what sounds like someone trying to yank the door open. There's a short burst of muffled swearing. I pause until they're really pulling hard, then slam the latch forward, and the door wrenches outward. The person on the other side is caught off balance, and a jerk on his ankle sends him toppling to the ground.

I vault up the seven steps, scanning for the partner, but it seems he's alone. I'm about to jump on him, but then I recognize the steel bone through his nose. He's just Goat, an authorized PODling.

He says, "What the fuck?"

"Did you run into two guys coming in here?"

"Wha . . . Uh, yeah. Going through the gate. They were—"

I'm already running to the alley's entrance. Looking right and left, at first I don't see anything. But then a black Dodge Charger peels out, heading the wrong way up Suffolk. The parked cars obstruct my line of sight, and I can't get past them quickly enough to see the plate as the car makes a screeching left on Rivington, swiping out the brake light of an innocent Audi.

They're bombing up Essex before I can make the turn. The Audi's alarm wails as I entertain the bleak thought that dealing with a single determined stalker is challenge enough. And Billy's called up a whole battalion of them to torment Olya.

Back down in the POD, Garriott brews Earl Grey while Olya rolls out the third degree on Xan, who has recovered enough to get irritated.

"I said I didn't turn around to watch them. I, being a meek little Asian girl, as you're quite fond of pointing out, was fleeing!"

"But you must have seen—" Olya notices me come in and inquires, "So?"

"They took off before I could get there. I scared the shit out of Goat, however. Maybe they bailed when they saw him coming in."

Olya lets out a long exhausted breath and cracks her neck. She gives Xan a tender kiss on the cheek. "We're glad our Sashinka is okay," she says. "Maybe late at night we have this strong man escort you home." Then she leaves.

Garriott and Xan seem to be repressing a desire to look at each other. I step over and pick up the case. Glued to the velvet backing is a horrific mess of blood, bone, and metal. My mind takes a second to identify the mutilated remnants of a human jaw with a large hole saw stuck through it. Tooth fragments decorate the deep blue fabric like the pearls the case was made to hold. The circumference of the bit is filled with some kind of bloody meat. A reference to Gina of course, but within Billy's game world, perhaps also to the *120 Days* vignette wherein a deranged libertine uses a hollow drill to extract cylinders of flesh from his victims.

Attached to the sharp center point of the bit is a little sheet of paper bearing a calligraphic scrawl:

I demand tooth for tooth still
So forever you will
Hear the sound of a drill

Though Olya rallied quickly, for a moment there, I think Billy's present found its mark. I assume the bone is artificial, and the rest comes from a local butcher. The display is gruesome enough without considering the alternatives.

Garriott seems like he's about to say something but doesn't.

"Tomorrow we're going to have to talk about revving our security here," I say.

They both just nod.

"I'll go check on her."

I slip into her office and shut the door behind me. Olya is gazing out her window. She doesn't turn around.

"Why does Billy think you're to blame for Gina Delaney's death? What does he want from you?" I ask.

"I don't think about what crazy little men want. He is not significant. Like a mosquito."

"But we need to take certain measures. Aren't you concerned that he might come after the Dancers to get your attention? Or"—I think about Garriott's video of their fight—"do something violent?"

She gives me a long considering stare and then rolls her eyes. "Let's be real. Billy is an artsy *sooka* fuckwit, not a dangerous psychotic. And we make a slippery robot. Not a nuclear bomb."

"But, Olya, if I'm to believe the numbers you used to lure me onto this project, every time you walk through those doors with your silver cases, you're dragging millions of dollars behind you. What if he figures out he could use them to fuck with you?"

She turns down her mouth, acknowledging the point. "Ya. Zhimbo, you are correct. So maybe we get a safe."

But I think back to the look on Billy's face when Gina kissed him and then the photos of Gina's corpse. The message of revenge in this latest gift of jewelry to Olya tells me that Billy's rage is escalating. I don't think we have long before his next move.

And is it a safe the iTeam needs, or bodyguards?

28

Since the internet serves as high-test fertilizer for conspiracy theories, any game that harnesses the collective brain of an online community will have members who want to talk about what's *really* going on. With Alternate Reality Games in particular this tendency is overt. Solving the riddle of who's sponsoring it (and to what corporate end) takes on an importance that can supersede the game's actual story line. Given the obscurity in which Billy's cloaked his contest, I'm not surprised to find posts like this one:

Anna_Lynne_Goss	Let me put to rest all this nattering about what you have to do to "win" a vignette and get "promoted." Here's a list of current winners that haven't yet seen custom submissions:
Joined:01/09/15 Posts:047	
Location: In Deep	Day 3, Scene 3 -- Romeo in Juliet [1971]
	Day 4, Scene 5 -- Strapped [2009]
	Day 7, Scene 2 -- Paradise Lust [1973]
	Day 7, Scene 4 -- No Mercy [2000]
	Day 8, Scene 1 -- Marquis de Sade [1994]
	Day 11, Scene 3 -- The Whorestia [1972]
	Day 15, Scene 2 -- Dante's in Fern's Hole [1974]

> . . .
>
> And so it goes. Anyone see the pattern here?
>
> Like it's a coincidence that X-rated literary adaptations from the early seventies occupy half the top spots. Yes, Ronnie seemed more interested in Sade than his source texts. But please!
>
> These rumors about the Pyros are total bullshit. *Savant* is not an enlistment site for an insane cult. It is not an FBI sting operation. You don't have to do anything violent or illegal to win. Just pick the "right" porno and cash in.
>
> This "game" is just a stupid marketing gimmick to manufacture interest in Exotica's back catalog. Let's not give them the satisfaction. We're in NOD to satisfy *ourselves*.
>
> _Anna

For the most part, I have no idea what she's talking about. But one detail makes my hair stand on end: her line about "the Pyros." I should have known they'd come into this.

The Pyrexians are an urban legend, the demonic bogeymen of hardcore file-sharing rings. I first encountered references to them while assisting the FBI in penetrating a kiddie porn distribution network based out of Reno. The kind of low-rent psychos pushing that stuff often lead shifty, precarious lives. Any time someone in their circle disappeared, or an inexplicable tragedy struck, some credulous dolt would always name this shadowy group as the agent of fate.

Fans of torture porn, bestiality vids, and snuff films tend to obsess over their passions. Often, avid collectors call their compulsion "the Fever," another name for which is "pyrexia." Because supply is always severely limited, they constantly fantasize about abundant sources of new material. Seductive, then, to believe in the existence of this organization that possesses a massive reservoir of "the good stuff." That traffics in helpless victims while constantly turning out new ones, thereby controlling a global empire of sadistic violence. Of course, they're also very jealous of their treasure, and so you have to beware that certain material coming into your possession hasn't been stolen from them. If they catch you distributing it, you're marked for death. At once feared and revered, the Pyrexians represent a sort of Bilderberg group of kiddie porn.

At first, I thought the whole thing was a joke, one of many black fables from a marginal subculture. But in the crushed-anthill days following the Feds' first arrests, I discovered some genuinely worried conversations about them. Just as thieves fear each other more than the police, the same is apparently true of perverts.

From browsing the posts of early Château de Silling explorers, I can see wild theories cropping up that the place was a secret recruiting device for the Pyros.

But since the group is just a chimera from the folklore of the depraved, I decide to look into Anna's idea that someone made Château de Silling as a marketing stunt. While Billy's aims surely aren't commercial, if he's promoting players as a reward for such submissions, I should try to find out why. Which will require some diverting research.

I consult an online video service I belong to called Nutflux that specializes in soigné interface glosses on the Internet Adult Film Database. They also classify industry personnel according to everything from declared religion to "ejaculatory accuracy."

Four of the films she lists were all directed by the same individual, one Ronald Farber, a celebrated pioneer of modern erotica and I suppose the "Ronnie" that Anna tagged in her post. His detailed bio describes how in 1971, this lowly camera technician at a TV news station in Irvine, California, came out of nowhere to found Freyja Films, named after the Norse goddess of love. He created lush pornographic salutes to literary classics shot with the newly emerging video technology. His efforts, beginning with *Romeo in Juliet,* were well received. Freyja began minting money as the seventies porn explosion got under way.

Then in 1973, despite his obvious success, Farber took a large investment from the exploitation house Big Stick, run by "Big" Ben Mondano, a notorious industry asshole with reputed connections to organized crime. His product ran more to efforts like *Taste It, Don't Waste It,* parts 1–144, and so this merger of love and lust was a curious one to porn aficionados. The combined company was renamed Exotica Entertainment Enterprises, a.k.a. "Triple E."

Both Farber and Mondano died more than ten years ago, but Exotica has certainly thrived since then. The company is currently led by "Benito" Mondano Jr. and has become a diversified porn colossus. They're a huge blue-movie studio with a significant presence in the cable, pay-per-view, online, and mobile markets. They've got an adult novelty operation that sells everything from performance-enhancing herbal supplements to performance-obviating penile substitutes. They run the Amazone chain of high-end strip clubs, a sex education outfit, and even a political action committee.

Maybe I've let a specious forum post lead me off course here. I have trouble imagining why Billy might be interested in this specific porn company. Then I see at the bottom of their website that Exotica's headquarters are in New York above their Amazone flagship. Its location at Forty-sixth Street and the West Side Highway rings a bell. I check my notes and see that this is the address McClaren mentioned for the most recent of Billy's disorderly conduct charges. So maybe someone there was the last person to see Billy in the flesh.

29

At Amazone, Benito Mondano sits by himself in an aerie of leather couches commanding good views of the club's first floor. He's absorbed in a conversation on his cell phone, and a bouncer reads the paper on a stool next to the velvet barrier cutting off access to him.

I order a bottle of Michter's 25 from the bar and freak out the bartender when I take it from him as he's starting the tea ceremony prescribed for opening precious liquor.

Offering the bottle, I ask the bouncer, "Would Mr. Mondano like a drink?"

Without looking at me, the guy says, "He's got one, sir."

Mondano's eyes narrow at the label when I motion to him that I want a word. He gives a put-upon shrug to his security and hangs up his call. I walk up the short flight of stairs and introduce myself.

He looks like a sketch comedy cast member midway through a wardrobe change. Attired in the ugly suit and thick, too-short tie one expects from movie mobsters, he's adorned himself with bling-y D&G blue-tinted aviator shades and big diamond studs in both ears. Just the thing for schmoozing at Long Island nightclubs, but the kind of fashion choices that would provoke a capo of the old school to violence.

He lets me marinate in a decent Brando soul-stare for a while. Then he smacks his lips and in a much less accurate gravelly whisper says, "So . . . tell me, what can I do for you?"

A curious performance for someone not yet forty. I almost accord him a facetious "Don," but manage to resist. "Mr. Mondano, I'm working on a documentary—"

With a world-weary glance at the heavens, he says, "Please, my friend, let me stop you right there. You can't shoot in the club. Distracts the ladies and—"

"No, no. I just want to ask you a couple questions." I pull out Billy's photo. "This is my subject. He's an artist who designs these controversial games. Anyway, kind of an elusive guy. Right now I'm trying to track him down." He pretends to ignore the picture. "I heard he was tossed out of here a couple weeks ago. Maybe he was taking some unauthorized video himself?"

"Some douchebag comes in here with a camera, and we find him somewhere he's not supposed to be, he'll be lucky if he just gets tossed out. Very lucky."

Well, aren't you the tough guy?

In my research on the family business, I'd found out that when his parents divorced, Benito's mother raised him in Newport Beach, California, about as far away from Ozone Park as you can get. After his father died, the porn elements of the Mondano empire had been carefully extricated from his other shady pursuits and given over to non-Syndicate professionals. I'll bet anyone with pungent connections had been warned to stay clear. Thus, Exotica was preserved until Benito was ready to take the helm.

So despite his affectations, this guy has about the same level of authentic Mafia upbringing that I do.

"You mean he might get arrested?"

He squints, testing my words for sarcasm, but then just shrugs it off. "We handle our own business here. If he's still making a scene once he's off my property, maybe the cops show up."

"What was he shooting?"

Mondano's eyes sweep across the three sirens pole-humping on different stages and then settle on me to inquire whether I'm actually blind or just stupid.

"So he wasn't trying to plant a hidden camera to record, say . . . you?"

Mondano sneers. "*Paisan* . . ." I want to tell him what this word actually means. "That's real flattering. Maybe the kid, your friend, was a fruit. But if so, there are many better places for him in this city."

"But maybe he was interested in you for other reasons."

He shakes his head as though I've suggested the schools chancellor is going to mandate Stripperobics for P.E. classes.

I point at the picture. "Billy is working on a game that may have some connection to Triple E." I wait for a response, but he just stares at me. I try, "So you're not involved in any kind of game that he's producing?"

"The only game I play is the simplest one there is: You give me money, I show you naked girls. You crank it until you get off. Game over. Everybody wins. Why would I want to play a different one?"

"Maybe you wouldn't. But you're in the media business. A lot of companies use 3D worlds for promotions that—"

"You know, you remind me a lot of this fucking guy." He points at Billy's photo.

"How's that?"

"You both talk like you're broadcasting from Neptune."

I smile. "Fair enough. Do you remember what he said to make you think that?"

"Yeah. He said something like, the fruits from my plains would dissolve into smoke and ashes. As I said, we don't really serve fruits here. And because of that pussy Bloomberg, there's no smoking either." He smiles at me, fishing for acknowledgment of his wit.

"Huh. What do you think that meant?"

"It meant that he was a fucking lunatic."

"Have you seen him since then?"

"If I had, he'd be real easy to find now."

"How's that?"

"He'd be in the ICU over at Roosevelt."

He accompanies this statement with a practiced glower, implying that question time is over, unless I'm looking to warm up the hospital bed reserved for Billy. I want to laugh, but taking in the guys he's recruited as bouncers makes me think that maybe Benito's resurrected his father's violent business culture. One's sense of legacy can burn hot.

I thank him for his time and leave the bottle.

30

A mobbed-up pornographer represents perfectly the twin obsessions of humanity: sex and violence. But while certainly of a piece with the Sadean content of *Savant*, Mondano's precise role is unclear. Maybe he's supposed to serve as inspiration for Billy's players.

Though they don't seem to need much prompting. The next morning I find this blog post from Blue_Bella, a doyenne of cyber-kink chroniclers:

My deviant darlings:

Blue_Bella watches with delight the recent exxxplosion in concupiscent creativity sparked by *Savant*. So kudos to all you carnal cartoonists and video voluptuaries.

However, your sapphire seductress views with some concern recent reports of material mayhem attributed to our new hobby:

Item 1: We all heard about the house fire in Henderson, NV, caused by an amateur video troupe (filming day 13, scene 2) shorting out a battery pack when the barrel tipped over. Our thoughts are with the lead actor as he recovers from his "extremely unusual penile trauma."

Item 2: One Dr. Hans Vleiben, assistant professor of French literature at Portland State University, was arrested yesterday on charges of harassment and public indecency. Our hero followed a fetching young femme into the bathroom of a local church. There he unveiled for her appreciation no fewer than five full enema bags he'd sequestered in his waistband. A scene ensued.

Vleiben's lawyer maintains that the incident was a case of "mistaken identity" and that "discussions pertaining to colon health" are protected by the First Amendment.

Item the third: Miami's Lee_Cherry now seeks legal advice regarding the revolting rendezvous she had with a fellow Savant who proposed they reprise day 29, scene 2 (simulated necrophilia, natch). Something she takes pains to emphasize she's "very into." Once at his studio, however, he proposed certain measures to make the encounter "as realistic as possible." Was he actually aiming for a scene much later in the book? We'll never know, since our heroine clocked him with a handy shovel and fled. Poor etiquette, you say? Lee defends herself: "I'm not into *real* necro at all. Especially if I have to be the dead one."

Where are we headed with all this virtu-real xXx-pollination? No one knows. But your periwinkle paramour's sources high in the *Savant* hierarchy cryptically hint that this *February* will be the hottest on record.

Blue_Bella is not amused. She's all in favor of a little spanky-panky, but she thinks *violence* is vile, and the Fever is a *sickness*. A real Savant keeps her mind open, but also her eyes.

As with *NeoRazi*, Billy's courting a blitzkrieg of lawsuits. And if Blue_Bella's *Savant* source is right, even worse is yet to come. But her sniffy reaction to his February comment felt like a non sequitur. Maybe there's more to it. Something that makes her relate his words to the Fever.

The case during which I first heard rumors of the Pyrexians featured a lot of obscure code names and references to sinister groups. Some of these shared a particularly dire profile, and we thought they might all be aliases for the same imaginary entity. The Burning Lads, the Wetmen, the Febrillians.

Something about that last one seems related. "Febrile" is another word for "feverish," but it also shares a linguistic connection with the month February. I look it up: the Latin word for fever, "*febris,*" refers to the purging of the body through sweat. Our second month's name derives from an ancient Roman purification festival called Februa.

Flipping back through my Reno case files, I find correspondence among some wealthy collectors of rare etchings depicting brutal child murders. They discuss an apocryphal club of Victorian eroticists called the Februarian Society of Ring and Rod. This was the oldest extant allusion to such a group we found in our investigations. The association's name was mysterious though. The best my team could come up with was that it derived from various pagan religions' propensity to sacrifice children on leap days.

Blue_Bella's post implies that Billy wants to exploit his players' interest in evil cabals by convincing them that the Pyrexians are somehow involved with Château de Silling after all. I guess my target has done his research on traffic in black-market media, and in his game world, this group's aliases don't refer to an abstract state of erotic fever, but rather to Sade's *120 Days*. February, of course, being the month in which the most horrific atrocities are perpetrated in Silling's dungeon.

Whatever Billy's ultimate aims are, he must know that he doesn't really have any control over what his players do. We're already seeing them turn from naughty exhibitionism toward real violence.

What's the point of all this? Why convene this dangerous game?

It seems unlikely I'll learn the answer by passively watching it unfold. I'm going to have to really start playing along with him.

When I called my friend Adrian Paulson, he suggested we get together at one of these secret through-the-phone-booth bars. Why New Yorkers, otherwise inviolable in their self-regard, submit to jumping through such hoops for a cocktail, I'll never understand. In this case, his choice is made even more eccentric by demanding I meet him there at noon, when the place is certainly closed.

And yet the trick door opens at my push. He's sitting alone at a booth cut into the amber-lit cellar. Seeing my arrival, he stomps forward and lifts me into a fearsome bear hug that makes my spine crackle. He follows that with a kiss on the mouth before I'm able to extract myself from his grasp. Adrian is a big, blond Minnesotan who took up highly decadent ways after fleeing a stark Lutheran upbringing. The most apt description of him I remember from school was "the Viking drag queen." Not so much for his fashion sense but for the fact that he oozed this quality of pansexual theater. Also a certain amount of violence. He was the only person I knew in college who both wore ascots and got into brawls. Now he's the closest thing to a porn baron I know.

He found himself at loose ends after Boom 1.0 collapsed and decided to turn his web skills toward documenting the thing he cared most about: sex. His site could have ended up a worthless pornado trap, but he brought an edgy intellectual style to Compleat-jerk.com and somehow developed a loyal readership.

Since the last time I saw him, he's shaved his head, grown a blond devil's beard, and has a runic tattoo spiraling up his neck. He sports a black Armani suit, so I guess business isn't too terrible. Adrian grins and waggles his eyebrows under purple-tinted wraparounds.

He gives me a three-syllable "Dude" and then asks, "How's the cocklodoccus?"

"Nearing extinction. Thanks for meeting me."

"Been way too long." Adrian reels off a string of what sounds like Creole French to the guy waxing the floor. He stops pressing on his buffing machine and hustles to the bar, returning moments later with a gigantic tropical drink decked with a Calder mobile of fruit for Adrian and a double bourbon for me. Adrian tongues a cherry.

"So, Ade, how's business?"

"Business? This is art, brah. If it were business, I'd jab this skewer into my brain and then set myself on fire."

"Why's that?"

"The pirates, man. We spend all day thinking of interesting substances to rub on our 'photo interns' and ten seconds after they're posted to our premium section, I find torrents of them all over creation. Our customers are good loyal hand jockeys, but it's getting to be a lot to ask . . . The personals section, now, that's booming. Even though those Craigslist fuckers are cutting into it. 'Course we do a good job of finding some real freaks that make the network valuable. Ooh, and we've started flavors."

"Flavors?"

"The one we just put in beta is Rednekkid.com. If I see another shot of a girl in a hayloft pouring buttermilk on herself I swear I'll—well, I'll probably call her like the last one. But I'm getting close to being tired of it."

"But you're still making videos?"

"Everyone and their stepchildren are making videos. That's another problem."

"Ever do anything on commission?"

He grins. "Pryyyycie! I hadn't figured you for someone with such refined requirements. You having trouble explaining something complicated to your honey?"

"Nope. It's for work."

"Work? You change jobs on me? What's it for?"

"Confidential. Of course."

"I'm just playing. Seriously, what did you have in mind?"

"A scene from Sade, *120 Days*."

"Ahh, a Sadistic Savant, are we?" He smiles like he's pleased to hear this, but then quickly runs through the implications and frowns. "Wait a minute, this wouldn't be on assignment for one of those crypto-fascist law enforcement organizations you consort with, would it?"

"No. Nothing like that. I promise. I need three to five minutes of high-quality video. Live actors, good lighting. I was thinking maybe—"

"King of the Hill."

"What?"

"Day twenty-three, scene four. In which a man can only get off from being savagely beaten with canes in front of witnesses in the second-floor parlor of a brothel. Just before he nuts, he makes them *defenestrate* him into a pile of dung sitting in the courtyard below. Only then can he climax. The Sadisticats love that kind of shit. I even know a stunt man with, shall we say, liberal attitudes toward personal hygiene."

"Um, okay. You, ah, seem to know the book well."

"True. By nature I'm a lover not a biter, but in this business, it pays to be conversant in the ways of the world. That filthy little Frenchman carved out a whole dark continent we've spent the past two centuries exploring."

"So . . ."

In a strange display of delicacy, Adrian writes a number on a cocktail napkin and slides it toward me. Then he says, "Cash, preferably. I'll have it for you this weekend. Assuming I can find some non-union livestock for the prop work."

31

Blake speaks out of the haze. "So has my brother gone with the dead girl or the live boy?" He's quoting a Louisiana governor's boast about who he'd have to be caught in bed with to lose an upcoming election. But Billy's preoccupation with Gina's death makes the joke ring off-key.

We're sitting in the steam room of the Racquet and Tennis Club, an illegal martini slowly warming in my hand. Blake prefers live meetings away from his office, as if we're old mates who just happen to be doing a series of work-related favors for each other. Since we're also not Ukrainian gangsters, this location seems particularly odd, but, as Mercer pointed out to me weeks ago, I can't quibble with our billionaire client over appropriate meeting attire.

"I don't exactly know yet. Given his literary inspiration, I'd have to say both. At any rate, we're looking at some ugly developments."

"How so?"

"Well, he's been trying to drag you into his world with these pranks, but we should prepare ourselves that another strategy of his might be explicitly breaking his silence on the topic of your family—"

"Has he sent something to the media?" This is the first time I've heard a quaver of stress find its way into Blake's voice.

"No. But I bet he'll invoke your name in this game of his."

"What's the point? If the little bastard wants to slime us, why doesn't he just bawl it out to Oprah? Or run an ad in the *Journal,* God forbid."

"Well, would you agree that at his core your brother is an artist?"

"At his core, he's a perverted baby."

I smile but realize Blake can't see me through the steam.

He continues. "But he does adopt the pose."

"So I suspect the instigation of all this was the death of his friend Gina. For whom he probably had romantic feelings. Can you think why he might connect her with you?"

"That's ridiculous. And anyway, Billy likes games, not girls. He may have been sad about his friend, but he didn't need her death as an excuse to fuck with me."

I'm annoyed Blake isn't more forthcoming about having dated Gina in college, but clients are often dissembling about something. Confrontation just makes them more defensive. So I change the subject.

"Do you think he might be jealous of you and your sister?"

"Of what? He's got the money to do whatever he wants."

"Yes, but he's not famous. He doesn't have your celebrity. A couple write-ups in abstruse art rags. But no one really remembers you two have a brother."

"He changed his name."

"Maybe because he felt cheated. Like his inheritance had been stripped."

"Bullshit. He—"

"It may be. But we're talking about how he feels. Perhaps he wants to amp up his profile enough to put his status on par with yours, and he's willing to trade on the most valuable thing he has in order to do that. His identity as a Randall. If he just dishes scandal to the *Post,* then he's the tabloid freak of the week, but if he's able to parlay the public's interest in your family into a groundbreaking work of art, then that's more like a career."

"And he thinks harassing me is going to help him achieve this?"

"That's an element. But I get the feeling he's trying to make an argument. The medium he's chosen is designed to get people participating, not just passively receiving a message. They can be very powerful experiences and are fashionable right now in gamer and media circles. But they're still mostly seen as trivial entertainments. Imagine someone putting together a game that revealed important secrets about the *real* world. One in which the efforts of the players had a significant impact on actual events. Maybe that's what he's aiming for."

"What kind of impact? What are these secrets, James?"

I don't know where Billy's going with his mishmash of Sade, cybering, and salacious cinema. But to Blake's question:

What do his arrest near Exotica and his indirect references to the company in Savant have to do with the Randalls?

Given that the haute porn director Farber and his gonzo partner Mondano Sr. both died while Blake was still in college, I'd be willing to wager that any connection Billy makes will be with Robert Randall. The obvious similarity is geographic, all three men having lived near Los Angeles.

An insight slowly takes form. The article on Ronald Farber said he "came from nothing" to produce an immortal classic of blue movies. But no one comes from *nothing*. He was a camera technician at an Irvine TV station. Right around the time Blake's father was starting to build his SoCal broadcasting empire.

Making my voice as neutral as possible, I say, "I'm not sure yet, but I think where this is heading is that your brother will try to link IMP and your family to the pornography industry."

I wish I could see Blake's reaction to this. There's a short pause followed by a snort that sends pretty Mandelbrots of vapor toward me. "That's it? That's his raw meat for the gossip sheets? That IMP benefits from pornography? Everybody knows that. Anyone with a cable box can see that pay-per-view is mostly porn. We provide internet access to two million people in this city alone. Do you have any idea what proportion of all the bits sucked into their apartments is porn? At least a quarter. Maybe a third. Regardless of the real number, everyone knows it's high, and nobody gives a shit."

"I think he's getting at something more specific."

"What?"

"Have you ever heard the name Ronald Farber?"

"Ronald Farber?"

"A dead pornographer. I think Billy will disclose he had some sort of relationship with your dad."

More steam whorls. "It's possible . . . my father was democratic in the company he kept."

"Blake, I'm going to have to play Billy's game if you want to know what's out there, never mind finding him. To do that, I may need to know these things. Maybe go pretty deep into your family history."

Blake grunts skeptically. "Okay. We'll get you whatever you need. But, James . . ."

"Yeah?"

"I'm sure you're aware that an enterprise like IMP doesn't get created without taking a certain number of . . . liberties."

"Naturally."

"So I don't need to explain that if we're to show you where all the bodies are buried, as it were, you'll need to exercise pretty flawless discretion, if . . ."

"If I don't want to end up buried with them?"

Blake's face emerges from the mist disconcertingly close to mine. He chuckles and slaps me heartily on the back. "Now, why would I say such a thing? You don't believe I make *idle* threats, do you?" He stands up and grabs a towel, then turns to me and says in a faux lockjaw, "Let's repair to the bar. This drink tastes like piss."

32

With three of the R & T's colossal martinis under my belt, I'm buzzed enough to convince myself that productive work might be possible, so I catch a cab downtown to GAME. I'd been hoping to slip into my office without a lot of commotion, but Garriott appears at my door saying, "Mate, you have to help me." Then over his shoulder, "I will not submit to it, you deranged Cossack!"

Olya barges in, reaching for his ear. She stops when she sees me. "Ah . . . Maybe now we have a real man."

The way she assesses me as though I were a hound of questionable pedigree sets me on edge. "What's going on?"

"Olya needs a dick."

"Yes, and better now I do not have to chase around this . . . this child."

"I was going to finish up—"

Olya shakes her head. "Mmm, but today we need to do the casting. We have new skin materials, new sensors. We need molds for anatomy. The pussy, it's a bottleneck right now. And the cock—"

"We've been using off-the-rack components," says Garriott. "There's no reason—"

"Andrushka, we are spending all this time like hospital surgeons cutting up Cyber Cocks and Pocket Pets. And it still feels like you're fucking the Cuisinart. If we have the molds, we cast silky silicone around your machines in twenty minutes. And the seams we have now—" She snarls with loathing.

I say, "I have to agree with her, bud. Ginger gave me quite a blister in the last test."

"You were too vigorous! Plunging away at her like she's a defective toilet!"

Olya and I share a look.

Garriott recovers. "Well, I won't do it. Your blister is nothing compared to what happened the last time she tried this on me."

Olya has had enough. "Listen to me, infant—"

"Okay, I'll do it," I say. "But what the hell are we talking about?"

Ten minutes later I'm sobering up and regretting my bravado, as I'm strapped pantsless into one of the MetaChairs with Olya standing above me wielding what look like electric sheep shears.

From behind me, Garriott whispers, "Don't let her do it. Back in November she wanted a specimen off me. Five days later, it was like I had the worst case of genital herpes in the history of primate intercourse." He pats my shoulder but shivers with abhorrence. "Ingrown hairs, mate. Thousands."

Olya shakes her head. "Maybe I was a bit rough with the razor. But you wiggle like hamster." She kneels in front of me and places a cool hand on the inside of my thigh, pushing it gently to the side. "But for you, I am very gentle."

And she is. Maybe it's her sly smile as she says this, or maybe it's the heavy buzzing of the clipper as she drags it slowly down my groin, but an awkward turgidity takes root. Oddly, the thing that goes through my head is that this is somehow unprofessional.

Olya picks up on my thoughts as though she's an alien empath. She softly brushes my tumescence away from her line of attack with the back of her left hand but looks up directly into my eyes. "Zhimbotchka, this is very good. Necessary for casting. But it is maybe a little early." She says this quietly, but I still get a glance from Xan, who's at the main table mixing up tubs of exotic pastel-hued polymers. Garriott turns away with a stagy sigh. He busies himself with the electronics to be cast into the "anatomy."

I get through the initial clipping, but as Olya leisurely spreads fragrant shaving soap around my nether regions, I have to resort to small talk to keep myself together.

"I take it you'll be representing the better half of our species? So I can have my revenge if you butcher me."

Olya picks up a safety razor and playfully brandishes it at me. "Ah, you want a chance at me, do you? I am sorry to say it, Zhimbo, but already I have the laser."

"You mean . . . ?"

"Yes. It's permanent. Very convenient."

Xan snorts. "Convenient for gratifying closet pedophiles."

Garriott adds, "Mate, she tried to make me do it too. But there's no way I'm letting a technician—they don't even have medical training, you know. No way I'm letting anyone near the wedding tackle with a high-powered laser."

Olya begins a long, careful downstroke, causing me to clench my teeth with pleasure. She says, "Little one, you seem very concerned about this body part that on you I think it's, ah, ves—" She starts reaching for the word while making a frightening circular gesture with the razor. "Mmm . . . like the appendix?"

"You mean it's small and filled with poisonous bacteria?"

Xan says, "She means 'vestigial.'"

"Ah, yes. You're so careful with this thing, yet you do nothing with it. Maybe this is why you want virtual girl?"

Garriott mumbles under his breath about the pounding he'd give any vodka-slurping whore mad enough to try him. I have to stifle a laugh at the image of the pair of them together. Like the mouse and the elephant.

Olya takes her sweet time with the shaving. Eventually Xan asks, "So we about done there? We're getting close with this silicone."

After a quick inspection, Olya's satisfied with her handiwork. "Ya. You want me to put it on?"

Xan bustles over, carrying a large vat of blue liquid rubber. She nudges Olya with her hip and says, "I suggest you get your knickers off. We don't want Fred getting lonely."

Olya looks disappointed, but she shrugs and reaches into a shirt pocket and extracts a yellow ovoid pill. "James, I would never question your manhood, but . . . it's very important that you, ah, maintain while the mold sets. Maybe twenty minutes."

I open my mouth and dry-swallow the tablet. Olya steps over to the

other MetaChair and starts tugging off her suede pants. This sight combined with Xan slathering me with Vaseline is more than I can bear. But
she expertly stops before anything disastrous occurs.

Next she presses home a cardboard box, one end of which is cut to
conform to my crotch. She then begins to pour, and I feel a refreshing
bath of cold liquid. I close my eyes and give in to the moment, reflecting
that a replica of my member may well end up in the Smithsonian. Or
more likely somewhere in Amsterdam's Rossebuurt.

This reverie ends when I hear Xan say, "Andrew, I'm going to need
your hands here. I've got to do Olya now." I'm no kind of homophobe,
but there's something about this bait and switch that makes me uneasy.

He winks at me, saying, "Believe me, mate, I don't like it any better
than you do."

I try to distract myself by observing the two ladies. Xan reaches for
the jumbo-sized tub of Vaseline, but Olya waves her off and makes an
adjustment between her legs. Xan then carefully positions a much more
complicated casting apparatus than mine. She asks, "That angle seem
about right?"

Olya squirms slightly and giggles. "Ya, but this feels like I am exam-
ined by the space people."

Garriott asks, "So when we decide Fred is going to need an arsehole,
will your rig serve for that as well?"

Xan frowns. Garriott turns back to me. "I'm sure you'll make a lovely
model for that part too." He blows me a kiss.

Suddenly my body seems to realize the following: that Xan and Olya's
interest in each other is purely professional; that I'm not likely to receive
any more Vaseline-related attention in the near future; and that I am in
too intimate contact with a fey Englishman who probably attended years
of public school and is making vague proctologic threats against my person. Aided by all the gin sloshing around my brain pan, my libido checks
out completely.

I guess Garriott can feel a drop in the upward pressure on the box. He
says, "Guys, we've got a problem here."

Xan looks over and says in what I regard to be an overly severe tone,
"James, dear, we need about fifteen more minutes."

Garriott says, "Xan, maybe . . ."

"I can't. We'll lose Olya's cast if I move."

The urgency of this exchange adds to my anxiety. Also making things worse is Garriott giving the box a tentative wiggle. I shake my head.

But Olya saves the situation.

With a luxuriant yawn, she says, "Aieee . . . little ones. Don't worry. The Cialis kicks in soon. But maybe it would be better if it weren't so hot in here."

The basement is almost freezing, but in homage to the time-honored stag film device, she slowly begins to unbutton her blouse.

She's got a diaphanous slip underneath, which exposes to remarkable effect her nipples' response to the chilly air. As though trained to the elegant absurdities of glamour poses from birth, Olya fans herself and lets a fingertip trail against her breast. Xan's eyes could not be rolled back farther in her head. Garriott has averted his gaze, embarrassed by the transparency of this display. I, happily, feel a twinge. Perhaps things are turning around.

Olya purrs with satisfaction. "That is better I think . . . You know, having the pussy cast is a very unusual experience. Pleasant, but, you know, maybe strange. It reminds me very much of . . ."

"What?"

"Mmm . . . Of the first time I ever come. Have orgasm."

Olya closes her eyes and a faraway smile passes over her lips. What follows is a scorching set piece, told in her dark molasses voice. It concerns her uncle's farm outside of Yekaterinburg, two albino lambs she saved from Easter dinner, a pail of spilled milk, and a subsequent vigorous spanking. During this I see Garriott miming a broad thumbs-up at Xan. I close my eyes to blot out his antics and focus on the alluring images flitting around in my head. Her story sounds like something out of *120 Days,* but gloriously free of blood or defecation.

As her account winds down, I'm brought back by Xan asking, "Garriott, can you throw me the paper towels?" I open my eyes, and she's squinting at me. "You people are quite ridiculous, really."

Olya's eyes are still closed. She stretches her arms slowly above her head, giving me a crowning view, before collapsing and starting to button up. She looks at Xan and says, "But the casts, they will be perfect, so what do you say? 'The ends satisfy the means.' James, you will be okay now, I am sure."

The Cialis has kicked in. My cock is painfully hard, and it feels unconnected to my normal arousal mechanisms, like it's no longer really part of my body. I suppose, soon enough, it won't be.

"Um, how long is this going to last?"

Olya grins. "The drug last for a couple days. It's too bad our robot children are not ready; what are you going to do with yourself?"

33

Around midnight the next evening, I'm sitting with Adrian in a werewolf-themed bar in the West Village. He's just screened on his laptop the final cut of his Sade short *King of the Hill*. I have to admit I'm impressed, and, despite the outré behavior being depicted, a little turned on. Something about his ivory-skinned princesses swanning about in giant Marie Antoinette wigs, but then gathering to viciously belabor the poor stuntman with knotted switches, tickles a previously unrevealed part of me. Its discovery is unsettling.

He can tell I'm pleased. "The ladies are panting to do a sequel. They like the wigs. Maybe we'll find a small role for the executive producer. Up for it?"

"Tempting, but I'm pretty busy with something else. You guys ever do anything with 'adult novelties'?"

Adrian studies me. I'm just full of surprises these days. "Do we ever. Oh, but you mean *selling* them. Why? You getting into indecent inventions?"

"You could say that."

"So spill it. I ain't a cheap date. You might as well take off the trench coat."

"Let's say I'm involved in a project that, ah, ups the ante in the sex toy business, well, pretty much all the way."

"The full teledildonic enchilada?"

"Let's say."

"The real virtual deal?"

"Uh-huh."

"No way."

"Just humor me."

"Okay, but this better not be true, because you know I would have to murder you and toss your apartment. You realize you're talking about the Holy Grail?"

"Indeed."

"Seriously. Men have been wanting this since boners were invented. I mean, it's mythic: from Eve to *Weird Science,* for Christ's sake! We'd be able to start getting rid of those infernal females." Adrian frowns. "To be honest, I thought the Japanese would get there first."

"But let's say you had this thing, and it, you know, *worked*. What would you do?"

"You mean besides making calluses on my dick? Hmmm." He plucks the straw out of his cocktail and sucks daiquiri from the bottom. "I guess I'd get insanely rich."

"How exactly? That's my question."

"Right, so who, other than everybody, would want something like this?"

"Yeah. So maybe we start upscale? An expensive, luxury personal-satisfaction appliance. Design it like an iPod. So it doesn't have that adult bookstore stigma—"

Adrian shakes his head. "Nope. First you make it as cheap as possible. Your early adopters are going to be 'sexual progressives,' otherwise known as perverts—like us, buddy! And we like that nasty aesthetic. Eventually, yeah, the crystal-and-lace crowd. But without a doubt, you will have knockoffs immediately. Since this thing is physical and maybe a bit of an investment, you've got a shot at locking people in. Then creating network effects. My advice would be to lose money on the machine early on. Maximize your user base. Which will be expensive."

"Yeah. That's another—"

"And don't forget you'll need a tongue farm in place on day one."

"Tongue farm?"

"Yeah, a customer service center. You don't want a new user to take his toy out of the package and have there be no one on the other end, right?"

"I was thinking a social network."

"At some point, sure. But short-term you need to seed the clouds with a bunch of people who know how the thing works. And you'll make an assload of dough. Charging by the minute. I mean, in this day and age, *phone* sex is still making billions every year."

"It just seems messy."

"Well the sex business ain't a church picnic. That's for sure. We can make all the Baudrillard references we want in our videos, but that doesn't change the fact that we need an army of hot nonsense to sell our product. You have to be okay with that, or you'll flub the money shot, and I'm telling you, someone else will be there to get it right."

"Yeah. I just didn't really see myself as the Madam of the Metaverse."

"If you had one of these things, would you use it to fuck your wife? That's ludicrous. Your customers will be lonely people sick of balancing a magazine on their lap. And now that I think about it, let's not underestimate the lovely ladies."

"Right. They're generally more comfortable with devices. My teammate was telling me that one of the first uses of steam power was a vibrating massager for the treatment of 'feminine hysteria.'"

"It goes back way further than that. One of the many failings of our gender is that when man learned to brew"—he looks sternly at his cocktail—"woman learned to whittle." He shrugs and downs the rest. "So what are you thinking about in terms of front end?"

"Ah, we've got a simulated penis—"

"No, idiot. I mean—"

"Oh . . . Right. I'm working with NOD right now."

He evaluates this. "Good choice. That LibIA cybering software's coming in handy, isn't it? And free too! Now you've got a small country's worth of Cy' Ber-geracs honing their skills."

"The stars are aligning. Who would you go to for the money?"

Adrian assumes a martyred expression. "Any time you hook up with a player in this racket, someone's going to get fucked. The Industry doesn't attract Boy Scouts and choir girls. But you can both get your nut if you keep at it. So you really need to make sure your partner doesn't have the Bug. Because it will kill your business."

"What's the Bug?"

"AIDS. But in the porn world it's mostly fraud—well, and AIDS too. You just need to worry about someone running games on you. Organized

crime connections are also bad. Not because they're not lovely, upstanding people. Some of my closest friends and all that. But they'll be laun-
dering money, whether you know it or not, and that will bring down
heat. Even if you're innocent, heat is bad, because remember there are all
these anti-porn laws still on the books, and the Man can shut you down
pretty easy if you annoy him."

"What do you know about a company called Exotica?"

"Perfect example. On the face of it, they might seem good. Big, diversified porn conglomerate. They've got a novelties division, so they know
how to make and retail that stuff. But people think that the Mondanos
are mobbed up. Now, maybe that's bullshit. We get romantic about
the old days, and an Italian last name is probably enough to set tongues
wagging. But what's not bullshit is that Exotica is practically insolvent
because the IRS put a huge lien on all their accounts. God knows I hate
the IRS worse than rubbers, but as a businessman, I can tell you that it's
pretty easy to keep them out of your hair. So what's going on over there?
One thing you do know is that you won't have a fun time if you get in
bed with someone whose testicles have been nailed to the headboard by
Uncle Sam."

"Let's say you created this great system, but you want to make sure
your potential partners don't have the Bug. What would you do?"

"What would I do? Well, Jimmy, I guess I'd talk to me."

34

I made sure to upload my submission from a computer at GAME that belongs to Don Lanier, an ARG enthusiast who doesn't already appear to be playing *Savant*. If Billy's watching to see who his serious players are, I don't want him associating Jacques with James Pryce just yet.

By the next morning, my offering is posted as the winner for that day in the Telling, and I have a message asking me to seek out Madame Desgranges.

In *120 Days,* Desgranges is the most senior of the storytelling whores, and by far the most bloodthirsty. Her avatar is, true to her description in the book, an ugly hag who is "vice and lust personified." As I approach her, she doesn't register my presence, so I assume she's another NoBot. I right-click to get her "touch" menu.

Just as my finger releases the mouse button, my cover cell starts ringing, causing me to catch my breath. I remember having surrendered a forwarding number when signing up, but I'm still amazed by the feeling of disjunctive anxiety produced by a game suddenly reaching into the real world.

The low, rumbling cackle that boils into my ear when I pick up does nothing to soothe my nerves.

She says, "Have we found one who seeks to burn?"

I say, "Yes."

"And can you keep the Secrets of our Order on pain of death?"

"Yes."

She continues. "You have studied the Book. Now write your own chapter. Innoculytes must withstand the full Course of their Fever over the Month of Purging. You must commit five crimes for each Degree until you're *consumed*. You will begin with a confession in the chapel. Do you accept this charge?"

Rushing to jot down what I just heard, I mutter, "Yes, I accept the charge."

The line goes dead.

That exchange removes any doubt that Billy's set up Château de Silling as a virtual recruiting post for the Pyrexians. I guess the "Course of Fever" Madame Desgranges mentioned is a series of trials one must undertake to gain membership. Our puppet master probably planted the rumors about the Pyros to begin with. So is he trying to import this legend into reality, using his game to actually *create* a lodge of risqué Rotarians to do his bidding?

Seeing that the first step toward initiation is ready to roll, I suppose I'll find out soon enough. Silling's chapel now boasts a series of previously hidden confessionals. Once inside, my voice-chat indicator lights up, and the Duke's voice says, "We're listening."

I sit there for a moment hesitating about what exactly I'm supposed to confess. Finally, I load a voice-processing program and improvise an overwrought tale about an unusually solicitous assistant football coach and a secret place underneath the bleachers.

A sickly giggle sound effect plays. Then the Duke says, "We are pleased. You are getting warmer."

Well, that was simple . . . if somewhat horrifying.

As I leave the booth, I notice that now a key is hung over the handle of the opposite side, where the priest would normally sit to hear his parishioners. I take it into inventory and then see that it opens all the doors on the row. I step into one of the other booths and immediately hear someone else reciting his census of sins. This one is about the speaker's recent tryst with his brother-in-law, and unlike most confessions, there's no note of repentance in his tone.

So recording my first "crime" gives me access to the submissions of my fellow players.

I have root on Billy's server, so I dig around until I find a few videos that look like they might represent more advanced crimes. The associated note cards tell me that the game's next step requires a live video of one-self engaging in a "solitary passion." The third demands a video of you perpetrating an "outrage" upon someone else. The first entry I find in this category is a video of a Japanese string bondage enthusiast delivering a lecture about the virtues of the Kikkou style over the Hishi while he ties an intricate pattern of cords over his "victim." I suspect he'll have to try again.

But others have done better.

The next one I check, entitled *Embroidering Celadon,* queues up a pi-quer fetish video: an adolescent boy having a wide variety of needles and other sharp objects jabbed into his buttocks. Mild examples of this genre resemble a naughty version of acupuncture. But given the array of instruments laid out on the table beside the kid, I doubt his vital energy is about to be rebalanced. More like the opposite.

I shut it off.

So Billy's warped hazing program has appropriated the "storytelling" mechanism of *120 Days.* It also shares elements of most pornographic file-swapping rings. You show me yours, I'll show you mine. The quality of the content you submit determines your privileges within the group.

But that's the first video I've seen in Silling that seems like it might end on the far side of the law. Of course, fetish filmmakers master the craft of making adult actors appear underage. And much can be done to maximize the apparent savagery of the action. Have these videos been constructed to seem worse than they are? Does Billy even care?

He can't be too worried. The Degrees feel designed to channel players along the Sadean progression of ever-greater horrors, like future serial killers mutilating their first cats. As Sade says:

The more pleasure you seek in the depths of crime, the more frightful the crime must be.

35

Given the violence endemic to imaginary worlds, having placed myself on a giant game board with an army of demented Sade obsessives leaves me feeling unsettled. I'm not sure what the rest of the iTeam knows about Billy's game, but they've clearly learned enough from their GAME colleagues to make them uneasy as well. We're sequestered in our usual booth at Foo Bar, supposedly for a meeting, but in light of three quickly slugged rounds, it seems we've opted for pickling our anxieties over trying to work through them.

Even Olya, normally our productivity zealot, seems withdrawn. Watchful.

I join her in scanning the oddly boisterous Sunday night crowd. A cluster of progs from a social gaming start-up are downing shots in series and high-fiving each other. The spectacle screams "Series B round just came through." The organic-looking couple in the booth next to ours is alternately chugging beer and making out, like high school lovers who've ditched their chaperones.

At the bar, I notice three men sipping tequila who seem to be trying particularly hard to conceal their interest in our table. Two of them could be brothers, both with five o'clock shadow and similar spiky black hair. One wears a tight gray ski sweater with a red scarf, and the other a navy blazer and pink Thomas Pink button-down. With them stands a swarthy giant with unruly curls hanging down to the collar of a loud glen-plaid suit. I see that the bartender is watching us too. And the DJ.

Stop it. They're just admiring Olya's generous neckline.

Garriott's expounding on the thespian qualities of his favorite Fuck-ingmachines.com starlets, but I'm distracted when Xan gets up to refresh her drink. She reaches over the bar to signal our waitress, and that's when Pinky puts his hand on her shoulder.

I pop up instantly.

Xan starts at the contact and spins to face him. He leans in to say something, a sly smile on his face. Then the scarf-swaddled guy pulls a small digital camera out of his pants pocket.

I surge forward, pushing roughly through a knot of people, and grab Pinky by his lapels.

"Whatever the fuck you think you're doing, you better stop right now."

"Hey!" He jerks back awkwardly against the bar. Scarf grabs my wrist, trying to remove my hold on his friend. Plaid Suit steps around behind us to wrestle me away.

Olya's shoulder slams into Plaid Suit. She shoves her forearm across the neck of the guy holding me. "Get away from her!"

At first, her victims seem disposed to resist, but Olya's dazzling figure produces a severe primal confusion.

Pinky sputters, "What—what's your problem, man?"

"Whatever you sick bitches are planning, why don't you try it on me?"

"What are you talking about?"

I lean forward, renewing my grip. "Don't—" Xan's hand touches my arm.

Pinky says, "Look, psycho, I was just asking if she'd take a picture of us. It's my goddamn birthday."

I glance back at Xan. She nods.

"Guys, I guess I made a mistake. I'm sorry. Hey, ah, next round's on—"

They're not to be soothed. Plaid Suit shifts his bulk toward me and says, "Fuck you. Who the fuck do you think—"

Olya presses against him. "Eh, eh, eh. Maybe you let *me* buy you the drink. We don't mean—"

I don't hear the rest of her glamouring them because I'm thrown off by a movement in my peripheral vision. Back at our table, the guy that was sitting in the adjacent booth now stands in front of Garriott, shaking his hand. He puts his other hand on Garriott's shoulder and gestures at his date, who reaches over the back of the booth to greet him as well. The guy doesn't let go of his shoulder and bends down to say something else. I take a step toward them, not knowing exactly why.

Pinky grabs my elbow, evidently not done with our confrontation.

The woman next to Garriott raises her right hand. I'm horrified to see that her fist holds a steak knife. I try to yank my arm free, but Pinky's grip is tight. I call Garriott's name.

He can't hear me over the loud music. The woman cocks her hand, and anticipating the blow to follow, I set myself and twist my arm forward, breaking Pinky's grasp.

Too late, I think.

But then something strange happens. Instead of plunging the knife into Garriott, the woman pulls it back toward her own face.

And sticks the blunt handle all the way down her throat.

The resulting reflex delivers in one gushing eruption all four pints of beer she had consumed earlier, along with a full plate of macerated nachos and what might be a Greek salad. Garriott reels back in disgust as her partner lets go.

Another guy videos the incident from across the room. Rather than thoughts of vengeance, what enters my head is this simple observation:

Day 6, scene 3.

Olya gets there before me, and retribution *is* foremost in her mind. She stiff-arms the girl's head into the wall and then bashes the meat of her palm onto her nose.

In a low growl she says, "You stupid—"

I reach out to restrain her, thinking that nobody's really gotten hurt—yet. We can't have Olya getting arrested in a bar brawl. Unfortunately, the boyfriend also decides to wade in. I elbow him in the gut and jack him back away from the booth. Garriott composes himself by wiping his face with the corner of our tablecloth. He bears an oddly philosophical expression, like he's more disappointed than aghast.

I try to drag Olya off the girl, though she's literally spitting with rage. Just as I finally get them separated, I feel a hard jerk across my windpipe and am neatly ripped off my feet by someone with the physique of a bulldozer.

He says, "Not cool, James."

That would be Ray the bouncer, a former heavyweight wrestler. He hauls me fast through the door and hurls me, without undue rancor, into the gutter. As I lie there catching my breath, I see another bouncer politely but firmly escorting Olya out by her elbow. Garriott and Xan follow, upbraiding the bar manager on the way.

When I finally sit up, the Foo Bar staff has gone back in to deal with the other parties, though I imagine they've slunk out the back.

Xan kneels at my side and asks, "Are you quite all right, James?"

"Yeah, nothing a few more drinks won't cure."

Olya fumes, muttering to herself in Russian, no doubt detailing the hideous fate she has in mind for Billy. I could direct her to a few choice passages in Sade.

I edge upwind of Garriott. "You, ah, okay? That was pretty . . ."

Garriott musters the proper devil-may-care affect. "That? A little Roman shower? That's nothing, mate. I was a Wyvern at Cambridge, for God's sake. Not to say that'll stop me from pounding Billy's face into marmalade, if he ever has the stones to show it."

I'm glad Garriott can laugh it off, but Olya may well have broken that girl's nose.

And the Innoculytes are just warming up.

36

The next day I walk back from the corner deli through the icy morning sipping a cup of burnt, acidic coffee. It's not helping my tender head, which was already throbbing when I awoke. From my hard landing in the gutter last night? Or the unreasonable amount of Garriott's favorite Bordeaux we drank after escorting him home to change? I guess the group wasn't keen on traveling back to our respective apartments alone, because we tacitly decided to make a slumber party of it.

So this morning I'm exhausted and yet still anxious to get back to GAME and power through the bugs we left for today.

This intense impulse to resume work is alien to me. Am I feeling the first twinges of severe Stockholm syndrome? Maybe I need to take measures to get my personal shit together. Tamp down the Byronic passions I'm starting to feel for this tarted-up vacuum cleaner. Not to mention my paternal pride at seeing Fred make Xan or Olya go breathless.

On the other hand, the life I led before was tending toward the untenable. I was engaged in my work without being inspired. And my personal life after Erica resembled a speeding car in heavy fog.

At GAME, I've stumbled onto a project uniquely suited to my abilities and desires. Regardless of my qualms about the enterprise, in the past week or so, I've gone to work every day with a hard-on. Why? It's the difference between doing something and *building* something. While they're hard-won and all too rare, those flashes of triumphant creation satisfy like nothing else.

In combining them with the primordial lust I feel toward Olya—despite her obvious entanglement with the very target of my investigation—I've found myself creating a false identity I like better than the original.

Billy would be proud. Though when my job is done, I'm sure he'll want to see me bleeding in the more literal sense.

37

If Blake's SoHo spread seeks to frame its occupant with a discerning luxury, then Blythe's is much more of the "tremble now, all ye who come before me" variety. The very existence of a suite consisting of the top four stories of a seventies–and–Central Park West monolith testifies to an owner who controls things the rest of us don't even know about. I assume that's the message intended by this gym-sized foyer with carved-marble wing staircases sweeping upward toward an actual ballroom. The décor betrays an interior designer who recently visited Versailles and takes too much Xanax with her kir royales.

Not at all what I'd pictured for Blythe, something she acknowledges as she leads me into a cozy library for our meeting.

"Sorry about the place. I know it's gauche, but my stepmother forced it on my poor father when he was in no position to resist. She made him move to get away from his 'old life' in L.A., and all his stuff is still here. I know he was supposedly a corporate Antichrist, but a girl can still love her father, right?"

"No shame in loving a prewar penthouse either."

"I promise myself that one day I'll fill it with African war orphans to even the karma."

"I'm sure the co-op board will be thrilled."

Blythe had called me to ask if I could "swing by her place for a quick chat." It was eleven PM then, now almost midnight, and something in her voice made me believe she might be a little drunk. An exciting prospect.

The last time I'd seen Blythe get truly hammered was the night after I took her out of the Zeta house. The night she came by my apartment for a drink. The night, it is sad to say, that still stands as the clear apex of my life.

We'd powered through most of a bottle sitting close on my couch. Though at first she wasn't inclined to discuss it, after her third double, I brought the conversation around to the events of the previous night. I detailed my thoughts about exacting revenge on Novak, but she barely seemed interested, as though she'd already dismissed him from her mind.

"You're not angry?" I asked.

"Of course. But mostly at myself."

"Blythe, you can't blame—"

She puts up her hands. "James, I knew."

"What?"

"I knew all about Pete Novak. I knew his interest in me was . . . *profane.* It sounds so crazy, but I guess I wanted to see . . . Well anyway I never suspected he'd resort to such a cowardly cliché. I mean, a roofie? It makes no sense. The way he looked at me . . ."

She trailed off and stared contemplatively into space. I tried to survey the void with her while she collected her thoughts. But when I glanced back, I found myself transfixed by those unearthly green eyes.

"Was nothing like the way *you* look at me, James."

I racked my brain for something to say, but it had thrown a rod and juddered to a halt.

Blythe rose. I feared she was leaving, but she merely bent to pick up Novak's camera from my coffee table. She sat back down and regarded it thoughtfully.

I cleared my throat, but before I could speak, she said, "I want you to take my picture, James. I want to see what you see."

She offered me the camera. Her hand lingered on it before she let it go, the gesture saying to me, "I know I can trust you. That you'd never try to hurt me."

The images I made that night became for a long time the holy icons of my private cult, the same ones that years later drove away my fiancée:

A close-up of her glimmering eyes seeking mine through the lens.

A slightly tilted shot, from my shiver of excitement when she touched the first button of her blouse.

A profile of her lithe frame as she undid the front clasp of her bra.

A dark silhouette of her matchless figure as she leaned over me and undid my fly.

An extreme close-up of the appreciative quirk of her lips as she drew me out.

An unfocused picture of the ceiling that corresponds to my burst hydrant of a climax.

The curves at the small of her back as she rubbed her naked chest wetly against me.

A lascivious grin over her shoulder as she led me by the hand into my bedroom. Her body bare, but for those red pearls.

That was when I dropped the camera. It would never take another picture. But the memory survived.

Once inside her, my eyes snapped shut as I tried to parse the symphony of sensation played by her gently rocking hips. She smelled like the final dish of a twelve-course tasting menu. Some concentrated essence of citrus and vanilla cream that the chef had to consult a battery of chemists to concoct.

She grabbed my chin and said, "No. Keep looking at me, James."

I'd fantasized about sleeping with Blythe for more man-hours than they were wasting on the Big Dig. But I'd never imagined that the actual act could be better than all my fervid scenarios. Blythe was so in tune with herself, she was even able to make something of my amateur fumbling. She moved like she was a secret weapon the palace eunuchs trot out when the sexually ambivalent young sultan must produce an heir. Being a realist, I'm suspicious of over-the-top carrying on, but when Blythe subsided onto my chest with a self-conscious giggle and then bit my shoulder, I was so besotted I had to fight back tears.

But even then I knew the tears would come.

Only six weeks later, I was tracing her collarbone with my fingertips on a Tuesday afternoon. We'd both ditched class in favor of the coziness of her mammoth Chinese canopy bed, and we were listening to the ticking of snow starting to melt in the bright sunshine of late March. I couldn't imagine anything more perfect.

Yet true happiness had proven maddeningly elusive. I was unable to bask in the moment since it took all my energy to prevent myself from saying to her, "I love you." The words battered around my head like a thrush flown indoors, going frantic to escape.

This had been a problem for the past weeks, my finest hour made insufferable by my need to utter those three absurd words. I'd spent the better part of the previous four days creating a prop to help set the stage.

"I have something for you," I said as I reached for its hiding place under the bed.

A bouquet. Roses, yes, but not the hackneyed floral default.

They were heavy, hand-dyed stationery that I'd twisted into exquisite origami flowers. On each page I'd inscribed a love poem. Naturally, I spent dismal nights trying to compose my own, but the failure of that enterprise demanded that I let the masters speak for me.

The obligatory Shakespeare, of course, and Yeats. Her favorite, Byron, and mine, Dante. Lastly, Marvell's "To His Coy Mistress," to add a touch of plaintive irony, given the events of our first "date."

As I tendered them, Blythe's eyes flashed, instantly decoding their meaning. She studied my gift for a moment, then me.

Finally she said, "They're beautiful, but you know I'd rather hear it from you."

That sounded an awful lot like the invitation I needed. But the dare in her voice and some hint of amusement in her eyes frightened me. I was left speechless and miserable.

With her usual grace, Blythe rescued me by plucking out one of the roses. She took my right hand and wrapped its paper stem around my wrist. Then she tied the stem's other end around the carved framework of the bed.

"I have ways of making you talk."

Just as she started on my other hand, her phone shrilled us out of the moment. I tried to stop her from answering it but as always was no match for her. I'm not sure who had called, but he was certainly direct. After "Hello," she fell silent for a few seconds. Then she said, "No." And that single word bore the weight of a crushing loss.

When she hung up, she closed her eyes and said, "My father."

I have to admit feeling excited at this chance to show my empathetic mettle. I shook my hands free and gathered her gently in my arms, murmuring my consolations.

I said, "I'm here, Blythe. Anything you need."

She was stiff and disassociated, and I realized with dawning dismay that she was suffering this embrace for *my* benefit, not her own.

She said, "I need my father." I heard the "not you" loud and clear.

Of course, she called Blake. He'd already booked tickets home.

In her library I realize Blythe isn't at all tipsy and is itching to talk business. My hopes dashed, I say, "So you wanted to see me?"

"Yes . . ." She gives me a tight smile. "After I spoke with Blake about your most recent conversation, I just couldn't help thinking there were some issues I could, ah, elaborate on."

Interesting.

She turns and leads me to a small, book-lined reading room adjoining the library. There's an inlaid table upon which rests a stack of thick black binders. Blythe picks up a silver-framed picture lying on top. She hands it to me.

The shot shows the Randall family seated around a long dinner table. My eyes settle on Blythe in the full glory of her college years, her fingers brushing the shoulder of William Coles, her ex-boyfriend from the Bat. Billy slouches to her left. Robert Randall is beaming, with evident determination, at the head of the table. Blake sits across from Billy, and to his left appears Gina Delaney, smiling shyly a few degrees askew from the photographer, who I conclude must be Lucia Randall.

"My brother can be slow to trust, James. When you started asking about his connection to Gina, I think it surprised him. And when in doubt, his instinct is to withhold. I will try to get him to be less reticent. I certainly don't want these kinds of misunderstandings to impede your work."

"It's fine, Blythe. I already knew."

She cocks an eyebrow but doesn't ask me how. Instead, she seems to lose herself in the photo. "My father always tried to get his stepfamily together for Easter. Lucia, not unjustly, believed that our mother had poisoned us against her. And she didn't handle tension well. Billy of course absorbed tidal waves of stress from her. With my father insisting that everything was fine, well, let's say these were less-than-joyous reunions. Being the youngest, Billy was particularly affected."

She tells me how in that year, the twins decided that the emotional strain might dissipate somewhat under the view of outsiders, so they decided to invite their current significant others. Their idea turned out poorly. Lucia Randall took the innovation as a serious affront and was correspondingly rude to the twins, which precipitated a blowup with her husband. Billy, always terrorized by their fighting, suffered even more acutely in the presence of strangers.

Coles, "never a subtle creature," in Blythe's words, tried to take him aside and distract the poor kid with questions about sports, girls, and "partying." When Blythe checked on them, she found Coles looking at Billy like he was a three-headed porcupine, as her brother ignored him and played chess with himself. She could tell he'd focused on the game to keep from crying in front of a guest.

"I'd never seen Billy so dejected. I wanted to go to him and somehow comfort him. I don't know why, but he'd always flinch away from me like I was on fire. And my failed efforts just made things even more awkward between us. So, by that point, I'd almost decided that we should all just leave, whether my father liked it or not.

"But then Gina breezed into the room and took the seat opposite Billy. She cleared his chess pieces and started resetting the board. Without trying to meet his eye, she said, 'Best of seven. I'll bet I sweep you. Ten-minute games. I always open with the Latvian Gambit.'

"Billy was surprised, but ecstatic that he wouldn't have to keep talking to Coles. I believe what he said was, 'Bring it.'"

Blythe goes on. "She saved the whole weekend right there. Slowly got him talking about his alpha-gamer interests, and he was even laughing by the end of it. Gina was smart. She didn't let him win, which Billy would have hated."

She describes how he followed her around the next two days, obviously nurturing a Typhoon-class crush.

I smile and say, "In the right hands, I'm told the Latvian Gambit is irresistible." From what I've heard of the Delaney household, I can well imagine how it might move Gina to see a kid suffering from a poisonous family situation.

Blythe resumes. "It didn't stop there. Blake and I were blown away later that spring when Billy asked if he could come visit us at Harvard. A totally unprecedented request. Of course my father was thrilled to pieces. He hoped that his quarrelsome children were finally thawing toward each other. I had a feeling about Billy's real reasons for visiting. But we agreed anyway."

Blythe's eyes close in sorrow. "Imagine the catastrophe when he showed up at South Station to find that Blake and Gina had broken up. Blake snapped at him when he asked about her. Billy just marched back to the ticket counter and bought the next return without saying another word to either of us."

"Cherchez la femme." I hand the family photo back to her. "He must have been delighted to come across her again at PiMP."

She checks me for signs of irony to make sure I'm not a complete imbecile. Apparently satisfied, she props the picture on a nearby shelf and says, "Billy is like some kind of Terminator pit bull. Once he gets hung up on something, he doesn't let go easily. He needed that grad school like he needed an amateur lobotomy. But he is patient in pursuit."

Her phone rings. Glancing down at it, she says, "I have to take this. Those binders contain IMP's payroll records from before things were computerized. Feel free to flip through them. You'll find Ronald Farber in the earliest ones."

With that little daisy cutter, she leaves me alone in Robert Randall's archives.

Blythe has flagged the most important item: a human resources file on one Ronald A. Farber, an IMP employee for the three years prior to his founding Freyja Films.

So how does a lowly camera technician get the money to fund a high-end production company?

I'll check his tax returns for a rich uncle kicking off in '71, but I already know who Billy pegged as the silent partner.

From a chart of major IMP acquisitions that Blythe has helpfully included, I can see that the date of Robert Randall's bid for CalCast lines up almost perfectly with Mondano's investment in Freyja. So when he needed capital to take his shot, Randall had Farber take the investment from Mondano in order to buy him out.

If the CalCast deal represented Randall coming out of his chrysalis, then IMP was built squarely on a foundation of porn and mob money. Presumably, Billy thinks this tidbit might be of more interest to the general public than the fact that people jerk off in hotel rooms.

It wouldn't take much of a leap to suppose that some laws were broken or taxes evaded in one of these deals. If IMP expanded via financial fraud, that would be far worse than having grown from the fertile earth of heaving breasts and unimaginative dialogue.

That said, an allegation is one thing, proof another. I consider the disheartening prospect of having to gather evidence to support my theory. Melting the ice around transactions presumably handled by private banks is a pretty monumental task, like taking a blow dryer to an Antarctic glacier.

Then again, nobody asked me to prove anything. It doesn't really matter whether Robert Randall made shady deals with pornographers. What matters is that if Billy came to believe this, what is he planning to do with the information? Unlike his father, who tried to conceal his past, Billy wants to tell us the whole story.

Of course, people tell stories for many different reasons. Usually they entertain or enlighten, but some stories are meant to deceive or do damage. Others to scare or torment. And I think we know which kind Billy has in mind.

38

Wait, James, there's more."

I'm back in the Orifice working with Xan. After the incident at Foo Bar, I'd proposed we set up an alternate site. But Olya's warlike nature doesn't admit such concessions, and she wouldn't hear of it.

I flip up my visor and back my MetaChair away from Ginger's insistent maw. "Sugar, any more will mean an hour cleaning our girl here with Q-tips. Garriott needs to figure out the wash cycle before I go insane."

"I thought you might like that."

"I do. But Xan, you know, you're way off spec here."

She frowns. Xan has been crafting demos to show off the capabilities of our wanton WALL-Es. We've just been through a scene involving a Puritan tutor and his comely but recalcitrant charge. I'm honestly stunned by what she's done. Xan has a deep understanding of the machines' attributes and how they can pander to all our manifold lusts. Like any virtuoso, she can be prickly with criticism, so I hesitate over how to put this.

"I mean, it's genius. You're the Orson Welles of the feelies." The "feelies" are a VR-like entertainment medium that appears in Aldous Huxley's *Brave New World*. Simulated sex is naturally a favorite activity in futuristic dystopias.

"Patronizing bastard."

"You won't think I'm patronizing when I electrocute myself again. The good thing about this medium is that appreciation cannot be faked."

"You really liked it?"

"Yes, but I'm hurt you're not using my new program." I'm talking about my software called e-Jax that we're supposed to be testing. It gives users an easy way to control the Dancers in order to set up their own sex scenes. But Xan likes to write custom code directly to the machines.

She gives me a guilty smile. "I know, I know. I just . . . It's a bit limiting."

"Right . . . We designed it that way. You know, simple, streamlined. Straight to the fucking. Not everyone who uses these things is going to have a computer science degree from MIT."

"But I think we can assume that someone screwing a robot will be a bit *technically inclined,* yeah?"

"That's the whole point. They don't want to screw robots. Look . . ." I step back to my laptop and pull up a site. "Here is a whole community devoted to 'aquatic erotica.' It started as people swapping stories about disporting with dolphins, but now they're in Second Life, Red Light Center, and of course NOD. And they've diversified into walruses and, hmm . . . anemones."

She leans over and points to a picture of an otter. "Ooh. I wouldn't mind taking a dip with that little guy."

Olya picks this moment to breeze in with Garriott in tow. "Why do you speak of animals? This is not in the spec. Always wasting time, you two—"

"And you're always interrupting conversations you know nothing about."

She laughs. "Zhimbo, you are so fiery today. XanXan, I think you are torturing him with your naughty schoolgirl?"

Olya's project-management style falls somewhere between the Dog Whisperer and Pol Pot, so her graciousness is quite a surprise.

"You're in a suspiciously good mood."

"Yes. I have very good meeting with a large potential partner, a company with very much experience in the sex business."

"Who is it?"

"Ah, Zhimbo, be patient. I tell you all about it when things firm up."

"Olya, come on, this is ridiculous."

She has the gall to actually ruffle my hair. "Zhimbo, just give me a couple days. Then you'll thank me. I promise."

I look imploringly at the other two, but they both shrug as if they've become accustomed to life on a Soviet mushroom farm. Olya grabs one of our test laptops and walks out.

Garriott clears his throat and says solemnly, "Working on this with you has been the greatest experience of my life. But I want you both to know that all the money"—he nods his head, coming to a momentous conclusion—"the money absolutely *will* change me." He closes his eyes and takes a deep, cleansing breath.

Then he says, "I'm going to become a vampire."

Frustrated, I step outside for a cigarette. The team seems quite lackadaisical about the legal basis of our partnership. Garriott, who has the very distant relationship with money found in real droid-druids, I can understand. But for someone as meticulous as Xan, this attitude doesn't make sense.

As I light up, I see Olya had the same idea. She's at the front of the alley talking softly into her cell but adding spiky emphasis with her freshly rolled cigarette. She observes my arrival and rings off.

From playing Billy's game, perhaps I've absorbed an "everything is connected" paranoid perspective that makes me stroll up beside her and ask, "So is it Exotica?"

Olya doesn't look at me. But from my oblique angle I notice her eyes flare slightly and her lips compress by a fraction. What am I seeing? The chagrin of learning that someone has guessed your closely held secrets? Or is she betraying some actual anxiety about the state of her enterprise? Maybe she's entertaining second thoughts about hooking up with a shady pornographer while Billy's stalking her over the death of her lover.

I can't decide in the bare instant before she's again mastered her apex predator insouciance. She takes a long drag and exhales leisurely. "So maybe you think you have ESP now?"

"Is it?"

"Zhimbo, I know the, ah, 'tenacity' is a very good quality for programmer. But, *milyi,* do not act like badger with me."

"Just how much do you know about the company, Olya? Are you sure they're the right people to be getting in bed with?"

"You think I'm not careful? You think I am a promiscuous woman, Zhames?"

"Well I have to question that, if you're proposing that we deal with this company. I understand that they know how to market. I understand they have distribution channels. I'm sure *you* understand how expensive it's going to be to tool up Chinese factories to make such a complex device. But did you know that your hot date is getting sued by the IRS? That their working capital has been frozen by a court order?"

She grabs my belt buckle and drags me close to her. "Eh, you listen to me now. I have not proposed *anything*. You are making bullshit assumption about what goes on here. How is it you know so much about this Exotica company? Are you a fan, Zhimbo? This is strange, that with all their interesting material, you take the financials to bed. Why is that, James? Why are you researching this company, when we've never discussed it?"

"Look—"

"No, you look. I know you want to find out what's happening. But this is my party. You come late but want to start telling the tune. You think I will sell our daughter to the first man who wiggle his dick at her? When I find Ginger a husband, he will be rich, respectable, and *committed*. He will put a kingdom at her feet."

"First of all, she doesn't have feet. And you think Bill Gates and Nelson Mandela are going to serve on the board?"

"Don't be stupid."

"Well, why don't you clue us in? Why all this secrecy? This isn't espionage."

"Ah, but our Dancers will be very famous when they are ready for the main stage. So it must be very secret now. Someone else copies our design and beats us into production? I will not allow this. With my first company the thieving bankers take it all. Russia, those days, there's not so much you can do. But that will not happen again."

"But we're on your team. You have to trust us."

"No, James, you trust me. Maybe I have trusted you too far already."

"What do you mean?"

"Let us be honest. You are too good a programmer for a video artist. You are too good a fighter for a Harvard pussy. So, you see, we all have our secrets."

"Wait, you think—"

"I think if you want to be private about your history, fine. I don't tell everyone my whole life either. But that means we take things a step at a time here. You keep doing such good work, and our team becomes very . . . intimate." She slaps me gently on the cheek. I almost think she's going to kiss me. But instead she flips open her phone. "I enjoy our little talk, but please excuse me. I have to call."

Dismissed, I head back into the POD. Olya's little wince of uncertainty when I brought up Exotica indicates a sore spot. I need to probe further to see if that was just a reflexive twitch, or if our otherwise thriving team has been infected by the Bug.

39

Late Tuesday night, Amazone is crowded with hard-core patrons, mostly financial players eager to take on the proverbial losing proposition. I actually have to wait for a minute to pay my cover. In the main room, I see Ben Mondano standing by the bar speaking with one of his bouncers, an older gentleman built like a septic tank.

Olya wouldn't expressly admit that Mondano is her secret partner, but I'm betting a little pretense can extract an official confirmation from him. And maybe some more information about their plans. In light of Adrian's warnings, I can't resist letting him know there's someone new on the team who will be watching him closely.

As I approach, his eyes pass over me without recognition. I sidle up next to him and say, "Hey, can we have a 'sit-down'?"

The bouncer stares at me and says, "I'll be with you in a moment, sir." He turns back to Mondano.

"I'd like to talk to you, Mr. Mondano."

He turns. "With me?" A slight slur tells me he's pretty much in the bag.

"Yeah. In private."

"Do I know you?"

The bouncer puts his hand gently on my shoulder. "Listen, guy, I'm sure I can help you with whatever you need here."

I ignore him and focus on Mondano. "We met last week. I was working on a documentary."

"Oh, yeah. How's all that going?" He hits 'that' with derisive empha-sis, the booze having spared me from the solemn mafioso routine.

"It's over. I'm working with Olya now."

Mondano looks at me for a second, deciding whether to admit that he knows what I'm talking about. Finally, he sends his guy off with a side-ways flick of his head.

I continue. "I wanted to ask you about a disturbing rumor I heard about—"

"Disturbing . . . you know, I find it *disturbing* to be seeing you here again."

"Why's that?"

"Well, you show up out of the blue asking me these questions about a missing fruit. And then I find out you've inserted yourself into Olya's project. That a coincidence?"

"Not at all. We work together."

"Yeah? Well I work with Olya too. She's handling any arrangement we might make. So if you have questions, you need to just talk to her."

"I could do that. But I don't think she'd be real happy to hear that you're not in any position to be throwing money around."

"I'm not, huh?"

"Exotica Enterprises? I hear the most exotic thing about your enter-prise is its tax return. So maybe you can explain to me how you're plan-ning to fund our space-age cybrator factory when you don't have the capital to back a hot dog stand."

Mondano stretches his jaw like a boxer preparing for the bell. "You're beginning to piss me off."

"Really? 'Cause I'm just getting started. Why don't you tell me—"

Mondano goes volcanic with rage. He yanks my shirt so our faces are inches apart. "I'll tell you this, motherfucker. Olya knows the money is not in doubt. I don't have to justify shit to you." He jerks me again. Out of the corner of my eye, I can see two bouncers walking toward us. He continues. "You're fucking with things you don't understand. This shit will get taken care of at a level way over your head. We are dealing with Olya. Only. You keep dicking around, she'll have your nuts. And that's not even close to what I'll do if you come back here. You understand me?" He jabs his index finger at my face.

Though I'm suspicious that I've just been subject to his best Joe Pesci impression, I set my feet, preparing to make him wish he'd kept his hands to himself should this run to actual rather than affected violence. I say, "What I understand is that you're not the only two-bit pornographer on the block. So I suggest you behave yourself."

The bouncers arrive and look at him expectantly. But he just stares at me.

"I think I can find my way out."

I wheel away from Mondano and brush past his security. He watches me go. His expression is now pensive but saturated with menace. Like he's sorting through a list of ways to dispose of my body.

Both of the bouncers follow me out to the street.

40

A stinging sleet falls as I search for a cab on Eleventh Avenue. The ice feels as though it's negotiating with the frigid wind to unite and form a full-blown fusillade of hail. Since precipitation instantly melts all available taxis, I resign myself to trudging the seven blocks to the Port Authority subway.

At home, I find that Red Rook Research has turned around my inquiries into the companies relevant to my investigation. The page on links between IMP and Exotica Entertainment contains only a rehash of the extent to which mainstream media companies benefit from adult content. They do. A lot. Who cares?

The next section deals with NOD. It lists a day-old post from a free-culture blog whose headline is "Four (w)Horsemen Fly." Underneath this is a series of progressively closer photos of four casually dressed young men boarding a G5. The post reads:

```
Repent, cynners! The signs of the coming infocalypse are
manifest!
    How else to interpret these photos we get by way
of Planespotting.org? Oh yes, the flying fetishists
caught the founders of the righteously anti-corporate
NOD Collective boarding that classic conveyance of
capitalists: the G5.
    And not just any G5. See that tail number N071MT?
```

Fellow cynners, that serial registers as the number of
the IMP! The plane is the dread flying chariot of the
devil himself: Blake Randall. Expect news of NOD getting
its 30 pieces of silver presently. Shall the faithful
NODlings be thrown into the fiery pit of "special premium
access accounts"? Judged for the cyns of gambling and
obscynity?

One thing is clear: the end is near!

In the closest shot, one of the NOD founders has spotted the photographer and attempts to hide his face with the leather portfolio he's holding. On that folder are printed the words GOBLIN CAPITAL, underneath which is a nicely embroidered logo of a toothy goblin. The creature was clearly drawn by the same artist who designed the IMP cyclops statue in Blake's apartment. Instead of a giant eye, the goblin has an enormous open mouth, tiny beady eyes, and a wild thatch of electrified blue hair. A beast geared toward consumption. Gobbling, I suppose, enterprises.

So Goblin Capital must be the acquisition arm of Blake's business development efforts. I've been trying to figure out why Billy's unearthed his father's relationship with the sex industry in the seventies. But now I see that all the ancient history is but a prelude to his main point, which I'm starting to think will be some form of:

Like father, like son.

A substantial portion of NOD's user base has sex on their mind when they're logging in, but you can say the same thing about the internet in general. Billy's indictment remains weak. There must be something else.

His other major endeavor has been antagonizing Olya. It can't be a coincidence that she's dealing with this guy whose father used to do business with Robert Randall. So how does IT relate to Billy's family morality play?

Let's try the skeleton key for unlocking someone's motivations: money.

Mondano said, "Olya knows the money is not in doubt."

Olya said, "When I find Ginger a husband, he will be rich, respectable, and *committed*. He will put a kingdom at her feet." That does not describe Exotica. So if Mondano's involved, he's either a junior partner or a front.

Where then is the money coming from?

I hear Blythe say: "I think the imp to which my brother seems most attuned is Poe's, not our father's."

Mondano said, "This shit will get taken care of at a level way over your head."

They've all been hinting at the same thing, and until now it *was* going over my head.

Over my head: like at the rarefied level of billionaires. Billionaires with grand visions who can assemble portfolios of companies in order to implement them. To lay a kingdom at Ginger's feet. Blythe isn't referring to her brother's self-destructive propensities. She's talking about his corporate strategy.

As obvious as it is in retrospect, I wish I could say I knew it all along. Maybe the idea was simmering in my subconscious, but it took this NOD acquisition to shove it into my forebrain.

Blake is the real backer behind IT.

I can see it: Olya decides she's going to reinvent sex. She initially contacts Mondano for help, and he pulls in Blake to provide the funding. They grew up within miles of each other and have been acquainted for years due to their fathers' business relationship. I make a note to check for common schools or peewee football teams.

So Blake hears about the IT project and likes the idea. He's aware of the conjugal genesis of IMP and sees an interesting parallel between his father and himself.

But the nature of the opportunity and the coming hearings on his sister's big merger prevent him from grabbing it with both hands. If he starts ordering industrial quantities of K-Y jelly from his corner office, it will not go unnoticed. So the operational aspect has to be delegated to Mondano, a man with a familial tradition of successful transactions with the Randalls.

But Blake *could* invest in the *idea* through clandestine subsidiaries like Goblin. So he starts buying up companies like NOD that will help create this vast new virtual playground.

I'll bet some digging will place Blake behind the LibIA cybering suite. The goal being to put sex on the brain of every avatar in NOD. A whole population just waiting for IT to be unveiled. Waiting for a product that finally lets them really jack into their fantasy world with the long-awaited *wet interface*. After all, why jerk off at your desk when for the price of a cheap dishwasher, someone else can reach across the country and do it for you?

Like his father helping fund the transition from stag films to adult video, Blake wants to midwife a new era of sexual commerce. While the knave tinkers with bits and bolts, the king builds an empire of Eros.

Thinking about Blake's schemes causes me to consider Billy's as well. I call Adrian, wanting to bring his netporn savvy to bear.

"De-Jim-erate! I knew you'd be back for more. Dirty pictures can be habit-forming, buddy."

"I'm well aware of that, but right now I've got another question for you. What do you think *Savant* is all about?"

"You mean besides child abuse and poop?"

"I'm just thinking that no one does all that work without an agenda, right?"

"Segmented marketing," he says.

"What?"

"Seriously. Learning someone's kink is more valuable than gold. I'll bet whoever's responsible is using Sade's carnal catalog to slice up the NOD user base by their fetishes. Extremely valuable information if you're trying to move product. Think about selling your sex robots. Wouldn't you like to know whether to show someone an ad featuring a man, a woman, or a donkey?"

Adrian's idea seems to fit. Billy must have found out what his brother and Olya are up to and decided to interfere. To "rain down fire" on his "festering Sodom." If he seeks to disrupt his brother's plans for the Dancers, maybe he wants to do more than just expose them prematurely. Maybe he's offering an alternative story line as well, one his players will discover as they tease out the purpose behind his game. Given Savant's initial video preferences, Billy's implying that Exotica is at some level sponsoring the game. So perhaps we're to conclude that Blake and Mondano are members of the Pyros, and that this Satanic Elks Lodge is developing the Dancers as part of a worldwide Sadean conspiracy to debase our culture. To that end, they've set up this monstrous game to cultivate and then harvest the secret desires of their future customer base. A fantasy, of course, but might it be compelling enough to color the way other people view our machines?

If Billy discloses Blake's investment through his game, then he's setting the terms for the controversy the Dancers will inevitably stir up. He'd be dragging his brother into his jaundiced fantasy world in a less literal but more significant way than his fecal effrontery.

Sadly, I can't test that theory on Adrian, so I say, "And I guess I could be confident that someone who's spent a lot of time with *Savant* is going to consider a sex robot about as scandalous as a StairMaster."

"That's for sure. The whole point of *120 Days* is that in matters of vice, you must always escalate. Same thing with technology. The eternal question: 'What comes next?'"

"And the two often come together."

"Since cave painting, dude. Any time we think up a new way to communicate, we use it for smut. Writing, photos, film, phone. Maybe even smoke signals. You, my friend, are walking a well-trod path."

"But teledildonics won't just be an incremental step. More like a giant leap. I fear for the children."

"Well, if everyone's fucking robots, maybe there won't be any more. But don't worry about the kids we've got. They're already irredeemably warped: the first generation who have all seen bestiality vids before their first kiss. With all their 'sexting,' they're used to making their own porn. Online they simulate all kinds of sex long before they get down to the real thing."

"Yeah, but I don't want to drain *all* the mystery from the real thing. I mean, what's it going to be like to lose your virginity to a machine?"

"Better than the town goat, Jimmy. Don't be going soft on us now."

When his cell goes right to voicemail, I say, "Blake, we need to talk."

41

But it was Blythe who got back to me.

I'm steeling myself for another meeting with her two hours from now when she texts me to reschedule. We'd planned to meet in Tribeca after a cocktail reception for the Women in Media roundtable she had to attend. That engagement has been canceled due to a carbon monoxide leak at the venue, so she asks me if I can head up to her apartment.

This is my second invitation in a week from a woman with whom I'm not supposed to be working. I wonder if her place has a steam room.

I'm just turning under her building's awning when a Mercedes Maybach with reinforced windows pulls up. Blythe slips out, riveting as ever in a pale blue cocktail dress. She tells me to stay with the car. She's just going up to change, after which we can go somewhere else to chat. Then she disappears into her building. A bell guy makes way smartly, darting a glance at her legs as she passes.

Disappointed, I follow orders and crawl into the car, giving a mopey salute to her bodyguard/driver Brooks, who's calling in a status update. He turns around to look at me and is about to say something when the left side of his face goes orange from a bright flash of light.

The sound hits with a breathy roar. We both duck instinctively.

"The fuck was that?" I yell.

Brooks lifts his head for a peek out the driver's-side window, squinting at the light. I conclude it's safe to look.

Across the street from us, high flames lick the frame of a car, spewing smoke thick enough that you can see it even in the dark. For an instant, Brooks and I are captivated. Then we hear a woman scream.

Both of us jump out of the car and careen across the street. Oncoming traffic has already stopped, and people are getting out of their cars to bear witness. Brooks runs right up to the burning vehicle to check for passengers. I hesitate, thinking about how bomb makers love to plant a small preamble charge to draw a crowd before the big one hits. Then I hear the scream again and see that it's coming from a large Hispanic woman lying on the sidewalk a couple feet away. Dropping my cowardly calculations, I run over to her, where I'm quickly joined by two bellmen and the security guard from Blythe's building. We're all yelling questions about where she's hurt in what must be a confusing clamor.

It turns out she was screaming mostly with terror. Also that she'd dropped her leash, and her dachshund, Tupac, had elected to get the hell out of there. One of the bell guys rushes off to search for him. While she's bleeding from a couple scrapes she suffered in hitting the deck, I can't see any major injuries. I'm relieved at the sound of approaching sirens.

Brooks comes over to render assistance, having found no one in the car. The flames are dying, and really there wasn't much of an explosion at all. The frame is intact, and I notice that it's an eighties-vintage subcompact, an unusual specimen in this neighborhood. While flames are still billowing out the open windows, there's not even any glass spread around.

The glass.

If that was a real car bomb, this lady would have been peppered with glass from the exploding windows. But she's not. Implying what? That the windows were rolled down and the windshields . . . removed? Which means someone took care that this car fire wouldn't hurt anyone. Which means—

Blythe.

I sprint back across the street, dodging an oncoming phalanx of firefighters. I'm expecting a hassle from her building people, but they're all out watching the commotion. An elevator stands open, and I hammer the button for her floor until my finger jams.

As the numbers tick by, I bounce with tension, furious at myself for being taken in by one of Billy's spectacles. My fury turns to fear when the door opens on Blythe's apartment. Her alarm rings loud. It must have sounded in the lobby, but I didn't pick it out from all the sirens outside. Even above the grating blare, I can hear a rough voice straight ahead of me. I bless the low-level persecution complex I've absorbed from *Savant*, since it's prompted me to start carrying a pistol around.

"—that behind every great fortune is a great crime, dear sister. Maybe both of you will find your fortunes turning because of his crimes."

Holy shit. This isn't one of his game slaves. Billy's finally come calling in person.

"What are you doing here? This is our life, not some cruel game. Don't—"

"Cruel? That's fucking rich. You know you can't keep his secrets locked away anymore."

"Please calm down. You're scaring me, sweetie."

"You should be scared, Blythe. You keep this picture up like nothing ever happened. Like you don't know what he put her through."

I come around the corner and see Blythe standing in the doorway to the reading room where she showed me her father's old records. Directly in front of her, Billy holds a full messenger bag on his hip and a short but nasty-looking crowbar in his left hand. Behind him, a carved wall panel hangs ajar off a set of bent hinges. There's a hidden space behind it, now empty. His other hand thrusts at her the silver-framed picture Blythe showed me the last time I was here.

I draw my gun and advance quietly.

Blythe takes the picture in both hands. "Billy, you can't blame Blake for—"

"The pieces are coming together, Blythe. One more and Blake will face the consequences of what he's done. He calls *me* sick? We'll let the world judge that. Soon enough, everyone will know him for exactly what he is. Maybe then he'll suffer like she did."

I can't get a clean view of him through Blythe. Close now, I step to the side to try for a better angle. They're both looking at the picture.

Blythe sighs and says, "Can't we just try to work this out? For me?"

"Fuck you!" Billy lifts the crowbar.

I jump forward, angling my gun over Blythe's shoulder for a shot, but she throws herself backward, knocking my arm into the doorway. The crowbar slams hard into the picture she's holding, shattering the glass and mangling the frame. I hook one arm around Blythe to drag her away. But Billy lunges at us. He's tiny, and his bull-rush should be in vain, but my legs tangle with Blythe's, and even his slight impact is enough to send us down to the floor. My gun fires into the opposite wall. I brace for the blow from Billy's crowbar, trying to cover Blythe's face, but it never comes.

Billy dashes down the hall toward the exit.

Blythe rolls off me and jumps back to her feet. As I stagger up, I fight the urge to just collapse on the floor. But this is Blythe standing in front of me, her hand covering her mouth from the shock of what just happened.

"Are you okay?" I ask.

She nods wordlessly. I take off after Billy.

I rip open the door to the stairway and hear nothing, so he must have caught the elevator. It's a slow old-fashioned one, but it's also twenty stories to the lobby. I don't see any alternative, so I start rumbling down the stairs at ankle-breaking speed. On the way, I call McClaren and tell him to get his people to cover the exits.

"We're already there," he says.

A couple flights down, the building's fire alarm adds its staccato screeching to Blythe's system. Billy must be trying to engineer a crowd to help cover his escape.

A heart-pounding eternity later, I bang out of the stairwell to find a wide variety of firearms pointed at me. Through its open door, I see the elevator stands empty.

McClaren waves them down. "Well?"

"You guys don't have him?"

"He wasn't in the elevator."

"Well he wasn't on the stairs."

McClaren squints at me. "Please tell me you did not leave Blythe alone in that apartment."

The elevator ride back up is one of the longer minutes of my life, my head throbbing in time with the sounding klaxon.

But Blythe is fine, quietly crying to herself. When she sees us come in, she takes a deep breath and says, "Please, just give me a minute." Then she walks down the hall to her bedroom and shuts the door behind her.

McClaren grips my shoulder. "So where the fuck is our boy?"

"I guess he got down before y'all arrived."

"Impossible. My guys were there when you called. So—wait a sec." He presses a finger to his earpiece and mumbles something into the mic. "They just checked the security tape. The elevator didn't stop at any of the floors. And none of the stairwell doors have been opened in the past half hour, except floor three, which was some old guy leaving his apartment."

"So—"

We both hear a sound at the same time. The low thrum of helicopter blades nearby. Out the two-story window above the ballroom, we see a news chopper flying by, presumably to get footage of the car fire, or maybe some more important eruption of civic disorder.

McClaren gets it just before I do. He knows the building has a decommissioned helipad. "*Up* the stairs, James. He just went a couple flights up."

"You've got to be kidding me. I didn't even think you could fly a helicopter in the city."

"Kid's a crazy billionaire; he ain't going to rob his sister and then figure on escaping by bus. Got to hand it to the little bastard . . ."

McClaren turns on his heel, barking into his radio. I assume he's trying to get a trace on Billy's escape vehicle. Probably a waste of time.

I jog up the stairs and inspect the door to the roof. Its latch is alarmed and locks automatically from the inside. So not a viable way in. But once Billy got inside Blythe's place, it would make an ideal exit provided you could fly off the roof. How did he get a helicopter to land there? A licensed charter claiming temporary mechanical difficulties, maybe. The pickup quick enough to escape the notice of air traffic control.

I admire the elegance of the way his route flows in one direction through the building. Like the work of a good level designer making sure his player never has to retrace his steps.

— — —

I knock on Blythe's door and step into her room without giving her a chance to rebuff me. She's slouched on her grand canopy bed, and as I enter, her hand snaps up to wipe at her eyes. She realizes the futility of the gesture and relaxes with an uneven breath and a forced smile. I set a double Laphroaig on the nightstand and sit down beside her.

"Just thought I'd check on you."

She hesitates, but then grabs the drink and takes a hard swallow. "Thank you."

I notice she has a bloody towel wrapped around her other hand. She sees me look at it and puts it in her lap. "It's fine. Just a cut from the glass."

"Blythe, I'm sorry."

"You're sorry? What are you sorry about?"

"He shouldn't have gotten so close. We should have been . . ." She's frowning at me. "I think I've executed a very nice clock in your library."

Blythe laughs, though it's a sad little thing. "We'll inter it with full honors. I . . . I'm just glad you didn't . . ."

"What did he want?"

"I don't believe he meant me any harm. He . . . well, I think he took some, ah, family things."

"Family things?"

She looks away.

"Blythe. Come on."

She's crying again. Trying to pull herself together. After a moment, she says, "Some home movies. Private. That's why they were kept in that cabinet. Most of them were his anyway. Confiscated by my dad over the years. He could have just—well, I don't . . ."

"Home movies?"

"Yeah. We . . . Why don't I just show you?" She slips into her room-sized closet. I can hear her opening a safe. She emerges with a tiny black memory stick and slides it into her laptop. "Before he died, my father had all his records digitized. These were a few things I had pulled from the archive. Billy just took the originals." Sitting back on the bed, she turns the screen toward me.

— — —

The shot starts on the face of a maybe seven-year-old Billy, who has just turned on the camera, which rests on a bureau above his bed. He drapes a piece of clothing over it so that an edge of plaid fabric obscures the top of the frame. Billy then scampers down and secures himself under his blankets. He feigns sleep.

A few seconds later, his mother sits on the edge of his bed next to him. You can see the resemblance between the two. Dark coyote eyes. A sort of smoldering energy. She's wearing a sheer, light green negligee. She rubs his cheek gently and says, "Billy. I need to speak with you for a sec."

Billy slowly opens his eyes. He yawns, overplaying it.

"Sweetie, I heard you come into our room. You know you're supposed to knock first."

"I know, Mom. I'm sorry."

"Now, Billy, if you saw anything that maybe frightened you . . . I need you to know that everything is okay. You don't need to worry."

"But . . . was he hurting you?"

"No, honey. It's like a game Mommy and Daddy play. You'll understand when you're older. But what's important is that you know that your mommy and daddy love each other very much, and he would never really hurt me. Okay, cowboy?"

"Yes, Mommy."

She reaches to hug him. The motion twists her torso so that her back moves into the cone of light from Billy's bedside lamp. On the pale plane of her nightgown, stripes of blood have seeped through the fabric.

Uh-huh . . . Just another quiet evening in the Randall household. Jesus.

Blythe was never disposed toward confession, so her showing me that video is surprising. Is it supposed to *mean* something to me? Maybe she's trying to illustrate the emotional stakes involved in this confrontation between her brothers. Far from a mere fraternal tiff over corporate politics, Billy's looking to exorcise some very real violence he absorbed growing up in his father's household. A secret dark enough that I suppose Blake might resort to equally harsh means to suppress it.

My question from the beginning had been: what are the Randall twins so afraid of?

In showing me this video, Blythe is starting to make that plain.

I reach for something to say. Sadly I arrive at a brittle joke. "So I guess we know where his interest in Sade comes from."

Her eyes fill with tears again. "My father . . . My father wasn't . . ." But she just shrugs helplessly and dissolves into a racking sob.

She presses her face against my shoulder, and I hold on tightly. I'm ashamed to admit that even now, the touch of her skin suffuses my body with a warm narcotic feeling.

"It's okay," I whisper. "It'll be all right."

But some kind of dam has broken in Blythe and she starts speaking desperately. "But my father's not the reason. It's Gina. She's behind all of it. He blames Blake for her death. He only knew her in college, but Billy thinks that he did something to her. He won't tell me anything more. You know how he talks in these ridiculous riddles. But I know it's all about her. They say in her last words, she's talking about Sodom or something, and that's where all this shit comes from."

I can feel her tears melting into my shoulder. I say, "He was in love with her."

"But it's more than that with Billy . . ." She pauses to regain her voice. "He's only loved two women in his life. His mother and Gina. And they both killed themselves. Can you imagine?"

Leaving aside the grisly details, can I imagine losing my mother and the only woman I'll ever love? Yeah, I can.

"Blythe," I ask, "is it always going to take a crowbar to get you to open up?"

She shakes her head. "I should have told you all this . . . I'm sorry. I know our secrecy makes it hard for you. But it's just that . . . there's so much pain in our family. We've learned to bury it deep. And now poor Billy is digging and digging. You know what that's like? My brother, he's going . . ."

"But Blythe, you know that I . . . that of all people, I'd never do anything to hurt you."

"I know," she says, squeezing harder now. She lifts her head slightly so her cheek brushes mine. "I know that, James. That's why we called you."

Suddenly, I feel her pull away from me. I don't need to turn to know who I'll find rushing through the door.

"James, I need a moment alone with my sister," he says.

42

I had no desire to linger as Blake took in the sight of his wounded twin. Their voices were just audible through the door. Quiet but edged with fury.

Blythe's apartment has filled with serious men conducting themselves as if at a crime scene. Someone is checking the door for tampering, someone else photographs the damage to the reading room cabinet. None of these people are police. I doubt if anyone not directly accountable to the Randalls will ever see the inside of her home.

I look at the shattered remnants of the picture lying on the ground and think back to what Billy said to Blythe: "The pieces are coming together."

What "pieces" is he talking about?

Well, he stole videos from Robert Randall's hidden cache, and *Savant* is a game wherein the primary currency is video clips. Recordings of one's crimes and outrages. It stands to reason that Billy's planning to deploy his morbid home movies in some way. But he said he needed "one more" before his brother would be held to account.

Does he mean one more video?

Blythe said Gina Delaney's death is driving Billy's actions. Detective Nash told me that she videotaped her suicide. Which Billy blames on Olya, though according to Blythe, perhaps he's implicated Blake somehow as well.

So is Billy planning to use Gina's death video in his game?

Publishing an actual snuff film seems extreme, though he hasn't shown any tendency to flinch from strong content. He'll want his players to see Gina's sickening final moments and, by following his slowly unwinding narrative, come to blame his enemies for them as he does. I already assumed it was Billy who tried to buy the video from Nash's bent crime scene tech. And that implies a crucial detail about his agenda:

He doesn't have the video yet. And that means I can get a step ahead of him.

I start typing an email to Detective Nash.

I'm too charged up from my encounter with Blythe to sleep, so I decide to console myself in the immaterial arms of my digital dalliance.

Around one in the morning, I head back to the Orifice and find the place abandoned.

After spending some time to synch up to Xan's latest updates, I'm bending over to plug in our Ginger simulator when I get that shivery feeling that someone's watching me from behind. I turn around to see Olya silhouetted in the dim light of the doorway. She looks like she's just rushed away from an awards show after-party, wearing the kind of dress you have to use industrial adhesives to keep on. She glares at me with such rage that a ripple of fear runs through my guts. Like I'm a small child who has done something unmentionable and is about to receive the full wrath of my evil stepmother.

"Olya, hey . . . what's going—"

Two long strides bring her near. I can see her wind up from over her left shoulder, but I just watch, fascinated, as she unloads on me with a vicious backhand that hammers into my face. Her rings dig long welts in my cheek. My hand flies up to cover the damage and feels the slickness of blood.

"What the fuck?"

She's not listening. I barely get my arm up to deflect her forehand follow-up. She takes this in stride, grabbing a handful of my shirt at the shoulder. She steps in close, her foot just behind mine, and then uses all her weight to shove me backward over my chair. I sprawl disgracefully on the floor.

Olya seems ready to bolster this treatment with a good kicking. Maybe it's her heels, or maybe my abject state, but she decides against it and just looms over me.

"Who the fuck do you think you are?" Her voice is a fearsome hiss.

Trying to lever myself up against the wall, I say, "Look, I don't know what—"

This infuriates her enough that she bends down, plants a knee in my crotch, and grabs me by the hair. "Don't fucking lie to me!"

This time I'm better prepared. I take her hand and twist it back so she has to let go. Then I snatch her other hand and force it across her chest, so she can't hit me again. She fights it all the way, and I'm dismayed at how strong she is.

"Olya, you need to stop this shit now!"

She writhes violently, and I push her off me. I get up slowly, examining my torn cheek again. "What is your problem?"

She stands, and I check my guard since it doesn't look like she's finished. But she straightens her posture, composing herself. She says, "You think you can take this over? You think this, Zhames?"

"Would you calm down?"

"I spoke with Benito. You go and start making threats to our partner? How stupid a man—"

"Olya, relax. Let's talk about this."

"You want to talk? You don't talk to anyone but me. You're nothing. How could you think to do this?"

"Listen, I understand why you're upset. I'm sorry. It was a mistake."

"Oh, you make mistake?"

"Well, did you ever think maybe you were making a mistake?"

She closes her eyes. A long susurrant exhale is followed by, "I know what I am doing, James."

"Are you really sure about that? I know about Blake as well."

Her expression darkens again. She's about to deny it but then shrugs irritably. "So what? We will need lots of money. He has it. And he owns half the media in this shitty country."

"Well, let's leave the good old USA out of it. But Blake Randall is the leader of a public company, and so if he has to invest through this shady porno proxy—"

"Exotica knows the industry. Their experience is essential."

"Exotica is a mobbed-up filth factory that sells giant black dildos called 'the Negro Problem.' You want your brilliant invention competing for shelf space with that?"

"Ugh. Zhames, you think you're not working on a sex toy? What is this stupid saying? Ah . . . 'It is what it is.' Now you are getting romantic about a cow-milking machine." She steps over and grabs Ginger by her neck and drags her toward me. "So this is going to be your lovely new girlfriend? No. You will hide her under the bed."

"I thought we were going to challenge that impulse by injecting some class. Like Fred and Ginger, remember?"

"You are naïve. We could spend years making fine design. Nice packaging, but this is still a sex toy. The only thing you inject is *spermu*."

She moves closer, pulling Ginger with her. I put my hands up. "Olya—"

She bats them away irritably but without her former violence. "I show you."

Lots of things about Olya have amazed me to this point, but the new pinnacle is the dexterity with which she has my fly down and my dick out before I can react. She stretches across me and dips her fingers into one of the tubs of Ginger's special lubricant. It's sharply cold as she applies it. Exciting. Then Olya jams Ginger's mouth over me. Without the heating elements and wiggling air bladders, it feels plastic and alien.

"Eh, Zhimbo? It's like fucking a Barbie, no? You will not make love with this. You will never use it with a lover. It will be strange bitches who talk dirty and disappear, and charge you for the arm and leg. Exotica knows how to do this. Make you play with this plastic toy."

"You, ah, have to turn it on."

"No, Zhames, you cannot turn this on. It is a machine. It does what we tell it. And not very much at that. Just this." She jerks Ginger's head back and forth roughly. "*Da,* you like that?"

"It feels fucking great. That's why we're doing it. I don't know why you want to let them make it cheap and tawdry. Ugly, like all that other shit."

"Oh, do I insult your girlfriend? Please. You must know that this"— she raps Ginger's head with her rings—"is not at all like this."

She takes my hand and places it under her dress.

Had I been asked, I would have bet that Olya doesn't wear underwear with formal attire, but it's nonetheless shocking to feel bare flesh under my fingers.

"She will never be like a real woman, Zhames." She's close to me now, whispering in my ear. "You forget what one feels like?"

My head is still pounding from our earlier altercation, and I'm not entirely sure when this changed from an interrogation to a seduction. But it makes sense to me that Olya would operate this way. My blood was up before I got here, and I don't need to be asked twice.

Ginger goes hard over sideways as I lunge at her. Olya steps back and I get a twitch of panic that she's retreating. But the heavens open and hurl a bolt of sweet elation into my brain when she props herself on the table and seizes me with her legs. I go instantly inside, like our bodies are precision-milled parts finally snapping together.

It doesn't take long. She makes very little noise, just an occasional quick intake of breath. But as we recline, she's pushing against me with an urgency that I take to be a challenge.

For a few luscious moments I know nothing but the animal imperative to thrust for all I'm worth. Olya shakes so violently that my grip on her shoulder slips, and my knuckles thump painfully against the table. She convulses in a way that's borderline distressing. Like she really can't breathe, and it goes on for longer than I thought possible. Maybe I'm discomfited and hesitate, because she gasps, "Don't stop." I'm shaking right along with her moments later.

The end comes as suddenly as it started. She covers her face with one hand for a second. I take my weight off her and start to straighten up while remaining inside, because I can't bring myself to leave just yet. As I shift, her right leg flashes by my face. But she's not attacking me again, just stretching with her usual flamboyant aggression. Her lips twist slightly at my flinch, and she puts her foot on my chest and slowly pushes me out.

I gaze down at her breathtaking chest and see what looks at first like some horrible attack of hives spreading all the way up to her neck. But then I realize it's just an uncommonly intense sex flush. I reach out to trace the boundary of her inflamed skin, marveling at the depth of sensation that it must take to cause this. Her body feels like cooling lava.

When I glance up at her face, her eyes have turned dark, and she says softly, "We have so much to do."

43

We're at it again the next day. By unspoken agreement, Olya and I both show up at the unheard-of hour of six AM. I don't get so much as a "good morning." She just steps into my office, hikes her skirt, and beckons with a peremptory flick of her fingers. I start to say something, but she presses her hand over my mouth and unzips my fly. Olya's rule number one is no talking. Rather suspicious that our relationship flowered just as I started asking her uncomfortable questions. But for the moment, I'm more than happy to keep my mouth shut.

She's pretty indifferent to foreplay as well. I start trotting out what few lovemaking niceties I possess, but before I've even made a single circuit around her earlobe with my tongue, she's got me inside her and is hammering on my ass with her heels.

I've never been confronted with such naked physical need. Her eyes clamp shut, and I'm certain they won't open until she's done. Right now, my identity as a fellow human is of zero consequence to Olya. She's totally consumed with her own body, and all she needs from me is a strong rhythm and mammalian heat. In this, she's the opposite of Blythe, my only other experience with a goddess-level bedmate. For Blythe, ecstasy was a hollow thing if it wasn't shared and mutually reveled in.

I might feel depersonalized by Olya's sexual trance, but instead I find it incredibly liberating. There's no trace of anxiety about timing, performance, or emotional synchronicity. I'm left with the sheer joy of drowning myself in her incomparable flesh.

She comes hard, fast, and, as near as I can tell, automatically. During our second attempt she completely clears my desk. But a broken monitor is a small price to pay for the memory of this woman panting and writhing in my arms.

Last night she'd unsettled me with her dismissive talk about the robots she normally refers to as her children. Previously, I entertained certain doubts about our project. But finally having real sex after all this time has freed me of any ambivalence.

What I'm feeling with Olya now is a living dream.

This particular dream we've been chasing together for weeks now through a digital fantasyland. Far from being an alienating, sterile technology, the Dancers have fostered a sense of erotic ease among the iTeam. They've been a safe sandbox in which we've gradually gotten comfortable with each other. Not only Olya, but I'm beginning to see stirrings with Xan as well. Our dream world may even be working on Garriott's congenital shyness.

I wonder what Olya's like with other, normal lovers. Does she whisper endearments, stare longingly into their eyes? In a sense, she's already *had* sex with me any number of times, and she feels totally entitled to treat me like I'm a machine. Which may sound unfortunate, but in practice brings pure bliss.

People tend to be at their best when they feel empowered. And there's nothing like the malleable magic of virtuality for inciting that sense of possibility. Liberated from our corporeal prisons we feel superhuman, not ghostly. You can try anything, since mistakes can be wiped out with the click of a button. And that lets you do things, explore emotions you would never consider in the squalid permanence of meatspace. In NOD there's no conversation that can't be had. No activity too risky. No thing you cannot do.

Is it perfect? No, far from it. But the Dancers are powerful in this way, and I want other people to feel it. Not to adopt them as any kind of replacement, but to use them to explore. This sense of adventurous communion they can encourage seems to diffuse into reality. As evidenced by the glory of the current moment.

— — —

Just as I'm starting to worry about my endurance, Olya emerges from a decisive series of shudders and pushes me away. She steps back quickly and looks at me like she's awakened to find a stranger in her bedroom. Her eyes close as she takes a deep breath and cracks her neck. I get a veiled smile and an ambiguous, "Hmm . . ."

Then she walks out.

At nine fifteen AM, I get a message that the RAT embedded in the email I sent Nash last night has been activated. The text had simply requested that he download a voice sample of Billy and ask around if anyone had fielded inquiries from this guy about Gina's death. As hacks go, this one hardly deserves the name, but infecting someone when you've established a trusted relationship is always pretty easy.

Nash emailed me back, tersely saying he'd look into it, but by then, using a brand-new flaw Red Rook found in Microsoft's Media Player software, my file had already released its toxins, and I'm now busy dumping his hard drive and installing keystroke loggers. He doesn't have a copy of Gina's video, so I'll have to wait until he logs into the NYPD's digital evidence vault to get it.

44

Back in *Savant*, I find a message from the Duke congratulating me on reaching the Third Degree. To do so I've had to satisfy an ever-more-egregious series of commands. Sourcing abominable porn has been fairly easy due to my contacts in law enforcement, but four of the "crimes" have required that I personally appear in the videos. Though I seem to have no problem with robot sodomy, when it comes to Sadean levels of pain, perversion, and paraphilia, I'm simply not varsity material. Fortunately, the genre permitted me to wear a mask in each of these cases.

My most recent chore required that Adrian hook me up with a local role-play specialist to spend a couple hours reenacting a weird armpit frotteurism episode from *120 Days*. While probably not fulfilling the stipulated quotas of bodily fluids, we put enough vigor into it that I thought it might suffice. And it saved me from having to violate any health codes.

Normally, a new quest is transmitted right after completing the previous one, and today is no different. Though the tasks usually come as messages from one of the Friends, here I'm confronted by a NoBot called Madame Champville, who was another one of the storytellers from the book.

She hands me an envelope that contains a note written in flowing cursive with little pictograms substituting for certain words:

Gather the 🌹 *from the* ⵟ *in time*

Leave at the ▮*, and please know that I'm*

Observing your courage or noting its lack

So make sure in this case that you never look back.

So far, the orders I've received from Silling's inmates have been quite explicit. But this one is in code. As my tasks tread the line of legality, a criminal organization like the Pyrexians *would* start encoding their commands. I suppose anyone seeking to join them lusts after forbidden images and is therefore familiar with the methods one uses to conceal them.

This particular code seems fairly simple. The image files standing in for the words "rose," "table," and "grave" are unusually grainy. I could spend hours scouring them for information, but Red Rook has a whole department dedicated to this kind of image analysis work. So I zip them up and forward them to our Stegosauri.

Half an hour later, I get a response:

```
From:  denigma@redrook.com
Sent:  Saturday, January 23, 2015 0:45 am
To:  prycesryght@redrook.com
Subject:  Re: Lost my decoder ring
```

```
Mr. Pryce,
```

```
Please note that you sent these images to Red Rook's
Steganography department. Steganography means "hidden
message," not "message advertised by preposterously
sloppy enciphering." In this case, an insultingly
trivial high-density LSB encoding on the carrier files.
Your payloads are enclosed, but in the future, please
```

send such work to Red Rook's "dallying with dimwitted
dilettantes" division.

-DeNigma.

Though wanting in professional courtesy, I can't argue with our Cryp-
tiles' results. Attached to the note are three new, even-lower-resolution
files.

The rose holds a portrait of a skinny girl who looks about seventeen.
She has caramel skin and green eyes set off with too much eyeliner.
She's wearing a tight pink baby tee with the name "Rosita" spelled out
in gangster-Gothic script. The pattern I've seen with the Degrees is that
for any names that come up, Billy always picks some variation on a child
victim from the book. In this case, Rosita is a Spanish version of little
Rosette, the general's daughter kidnapped from her mother's house in
the countryside.

Needless to say, she does not fare well.

The wooden table's image shows a different kind of table: here the
schedule board at a train station. Given that it lists Metroliner departures
to both Boston and Washington, DC, I assume that it's Penn Station.
Only an Acela from DC currently occupies a gate. One of those red time
stamps, the kind nobody uses anymore, sits in the lower right corner of
the photo. The date reads "01.24.15 12:47 AM," which would mean that
the picture was taken tomorrow night, a revolutionary advance in digital
photography.

Finally, the headstone file contains an image of a graveyard, though the
flowering riot of tulips and overhanging redbud tree give this one a dis-
tinctly cheerful cast. I'm further cheered by the ease with which this particular graveyard can be identified. The building filling the background
has a granite façade inscribed with the words AMERICAN STOCK EXCHANGE.
That would place the shot at Trinity Church, which lies just at the foot of
Wall Street. The time stamp on this one shows two AM, about twenty-five
hours from now.

Substituting these new images into my original orders reveals pretty
clear instructions: pick up this Rosita woman from Penn Station at the
specified time. Leave her at the Trinity Church graveyard an hour later.

For Jacques, Billy's game so far has been purely virtual. It's located in NOD and deals with digital objects: avatars and video images. But now I've finally caught up with the elite players, and *Savant* seems primed to start hemorrhaging into real life.

45

The train is right on time. I see her step off the escalator and start scanning the station.

"Rosita?"

She examines me, a little startled, as though she hadn't expected to be met. In case someone is monitoring this exchange, I've disguised myself in a woolen cap with tinted glasses. A real human-hair mustache rounds out my "I drive at night until the art world evolves enough to understand my work" look.

Rosita's dressed in a dissonant combination of a nice suit, a casual blouse, and fuck-me heels. She seems young and nervous underneath it. Like she's going to a business meeting, but no one's ever told her how to dress. The way she squints at her surroundings tells me that she hasn't been to Penn Station before. But she marshals an edgy smile and puts out her hand.

"Rosa de la Cruz," she says. She's carrying a beat-up duffel bag, which I move to take, but she shifts away and says, "I got it," her accent second-generation Hispanic. We assess each other for a moment. She says, "You're with Sweetest Taboo?"

Her question resolves in my head too late to prevent me from saying, "What?"

"The Sweetest Taboo" was a hit single from the British-Nigerian singer Sade Adu. Her name is pronounced Shah-day, but the connection is clear. Rosa rocks back on her heels, reconsidering me.

I try to recover. "Oh, right. Yeah. I'm just the driver."

She thinks about this for a second and then hands me her bag. "So where are we going?"

Her second query also throws me. Unless Rosa's the consummate actress, she honestly doesn't know the answer. I can't bring myself to say that I'm taking her to a graveyard in the middle of the night, so I go with, "Downtown."

She relaxes somewhat in the front seat of my rented Lincoln Town Car. As I drive her down the West Side Highway, I wonder what happens once we get to our destination.

I start with small talk about her trip. Whether she's ever been to New York before. She gazes avidly at the bright skyline. I ask what brings her to the city.

"Business."

"You look a little young to be doing business. How old are you?"

"Twenty-one." She doesn't hesitate, but she paints her answer with an emphatically blasé shade that destroys the realism. "I'm a fashion designer. Your company wants me to do a line for them. That's why they invited me up here."

"A whole clothing line?" I take in her tone-deaf outfit. "For real?"

"No, man, it's virtual clothing. I design for NOD avatars."

"Oh, like one of those video games?"

"It's not a game. I get paid real money. Here, I'll show you."

She extracts a sketch book from her portfolio, flipping to a section pasted with color pictures taken from NOD. Rosa's designs range from belle époque confections of satin and lace to fanciful barbarian marmot brassieres. They're good enough to make me want to commission some RL pieces. I give her a soft wolf whistle.

She brightens at the compliment. "Yeah, I like that stuff. But Taboo's new store is on this island where all the *desviados* hang. They spend a lot more money than normal people. So . . ." She fans through several pages. They contain drawings of buxom women wearing unicorn blindfolds, the business ends of which are circumcised to match their dildo-spurred boots. She's got supervillain men with tentacle hands and some animal outfits that flip by too quickly for me to make sense of. Again I see that for fauna fetishists, the beast itself isn't always sufficient. We have to go one better and put Bowser in a latex nun's habit.

I tilt my head at her. She shrugs.

"I'm saving up to go to the Fashion Institute of Technology."

"Your parents know you're here?"

She gives me a hard look. "My dad is in Afghanistan. I've been all over the world. This is no big deal."

Of course she'd be an army brat: Rosette, the daughter of a general. I glance at her as she stares out the window, arms crossed over her chest. A trail of holes runs down the edge of her left ear. Evidence of a rebellious stage? But oddly her ears aren't pierced in the normal place. Instead a short vertical scar notches each lobe, as if she once wore earrings but . . . had them violently jerked out. Then the torn flesh was stitched back together. Maybe this one is a fighter. Or maybe she's been abused. I notice she didn't mention her mother.

I decide to risk trying to slip past the fourth wall. "Ah, this may sound crazy, but let's just say that you weren't really going to a meeting."

"What?"

"Just bear with me. Let's say that someone offered you some money to come up here and pretend like you were going to meet with this company." Her frown deepens. "All I'm saying is I know some people who would pay you a lot more if you could provide any other information about why you're here."

She shifts away from me, her hand inching toward the door handle. "Man, what are you *talking* about?"

I back off. "Nothing. Don't worry about it. I must have you confused with someone else. Forget I said anything."

She eyes me warily. "I thought you said you were just the driver."

"That's right. I am."

"Then why don't you just drive?"

Our arrival at the graveyard goes more smoothly than I expected. While a lot of New Yorkers find Wall Street's emptiness at night spooky, Rosa just sees a bunch of nice buildings, any one of which could be a hotel. I park along Trinity Place across from the Amex building. The church is perched on a knoll right above us. A hoary, now eccentric brick wall lines the embankment. An archway is carved into it midway down the block, and a steep stone stairway leads to an oak door that doesn't look like it's been opened in the church's four-hundred-year history. Tonight we find it unlocked, and the door loudly protests our disrupting its repose. The gloomy climb up into the churchyard finally breaks Rosa's composure.

She jerks on my sleeve. "Hey . . . Where are we? Why'd you take me here?"

I pretend to check something in my cell phone. "This is the address I was given. I think someone is supposed to meet you."

"No. That can't be right. This . . . This place is a *graveyard*."

"It's right. Trust me. Someone's coming to get you. Just sit on that bench over there. It'll be fine."

"Wait. Where are you going?"

"Well, I was just told to bring you here. So now . . . I have to go."

She can't believe what I've just said. "You're leaving?"

I relent. "Look, I have . . . my orders. I'll tell you what." I write my cell number on a twenty-dollar bill. "Stay here for fifteen minutes. If they don't pick you up by then, call me. I'll come get you, and I'll check you into any hotel you want. The Ritz-Carlton is a couple blocks away." I give her the twenty and walk briskly back toward the stairs.

"The Ritz . . . Wait, no, don't leave." She trails after me. "Hey man, don't leave me here." She's on the verge of tears.

But my orders are clear: "Don't look back." I shut the door and hear it latch.

"Come back . . . Please." The last word is a high-pitched cry.

I get into my car and head slowly down the street.

My instructions implied that I would be watched, but I can't see how he'd pull it off. The street around me is empty, no cars, no pedestrians. I make a couple quick turns. Billy could have stationed someone in a building with a view of the churchyard, but there's no way an observer could see to the adjacent streets through the cluster of skyscrapers.

Don't be an idiot. You're buying into his absurd atmospherics. And no matter how well-run his game is, you cannot leave a scared teenage girl alone in that grave-yard at two in the morning.

I swerve right up Liberty Street and then dart the wrong way down

William to head back toward Trinity Place. Turning right, I park on Pine Street two blocks above the church. After slinking down another block among the columns of a temple to commerce, I take refuge in the entry to a Citibank with a good view of the churchyard. I'm hoping Rosa sat on the bench, because then I'll have a perfect view of her through the statuary.

But Rosa is gone.

I survey the area, but there's no trace of her. Other than her bag sitting abandoned on the bench. That doesn't seem good.

Stop it. This is just overproduced street theater. She's gone because Billy can't have his audience follow the actors into the wings.

But I can't help thinking about the awful fate visited upon poor Rosette in *120 Days*.

Come on. She'll be fine. They're probably taking her out for dinner tonight.

All the same, Sade's infernal images have colonized my head.

46

That uneasiness makes me log back into *Savant* as soon as I get home to see if I can discover some clue to clarify what just happened. But I merely wander around the eerie castle battling the creeping, sub-rational feeling that I've done something terrible.

Maybe that's why I start so violently when I hear a familiar voice say, "Congratulations . . . Jacques."

The voice is right behind me, and I spin around so violently that my knees bang into the right trestle of my desk. But there's no one there. Just my rear channel speakers. I realize the voice must have come from *Savant*. Run through my audio system, it sounded like he was in the room with me.

It dawns on me that I didn't have NOD's voice chat feature turned on. For some reason people generally prefer regular text chat to voice. And yet someone just started a session with me without my permission. In NOD, the only person who could do that would be the guy *who owns the sim*.

I mash keys to turn my av, and at last I behold the virtual alter ego of Billy Randall.

But I can tell right away that's not quite right. The av in front of me is a dashing rake in all the finery of a pre-revolutionary aristocrat, and Billy has made him tall, athletic, and extremely fair. A faithful image of his brother Blake. And now I know why the voice was familiar. It's a spot-on impression. Confirmation that Billy's virtually impersonating his brother to place him as a member of his fake Pyrexians.

His NODName, Fedor_Sett, stumps me at first, but eventually I work out "Feed Durcet." Of Château de Silling's four Friends, Curval the judge and Durcet the banker have the most pronounced appetites for ingesting filth. If Billy's assigned Blake the latter role, then I can see why the freelance waiter at Demeter looked surprised when his offering was rejected.

I take a deep breath to settle myself and say into my desktop mic, "Ah, thanks. I'm glad to finally meet you." While speaking, I start a trace on the IP address from which Billy's av is connecting.

But Fedor_Sett doesn't respond. With an impressive flourish of animation, he extracts a card from his jacket pocket. This av is merely a messenger.

I'm surprised Billy hasn't masked the originating IP address for his NoBot, which comes back as 192.0.2.133. The first domestic one I've seen from him. But those numbers feel familiar as well . . .

Because he's spoofing the connection record to appear as though it came from IMP. So Billy's impersonation goes even more than skin deep. When I take the item he's offering, the NoBot rezzes out.

The card reads:

> For the favor you've done
> From our collection here's one
> So to discharge our debt
> Please enjoy this vignette

Fedor_Sett's "vignette" link leads to the first of the videos Billy stole from his sister. A clip that stars him and the twins as young children. Blake sits on top of Billy, force-feeding him a dark mushy substance that sadly does not look like chocolate pudding. Billy repays Blake's culinary exertions by vomiting all over him.

A charming childhood scene that should really appeal to the Sade fans' interest in bodily fluids. The video makes clear where the roots of Billy's rage against his brother were planted.

So this is how Billy's planning to expose his family dirt. He's mixed his awful childhood mementos in with a trove of reward videos for his players. I'll bet he's assembled a record of Blake's crimes that covers everything from youthful cheating at Wiffle ball to his recent indecorous investments. Since the videos have to get progressively worse, he probably intends the climax of these atrocities to be Gina's suicide video and will then detail his reasons for laying her body at his brother's feet. Billy must think that as people start digesting his gumdrops, the pressure on Blake will ratchet to a point where he'll start to envy her.

47

I'm far from the only one helping to pump *Savant*'s poison into the real world. Judging by the series of news reports sent from Red Rook's clipping service, Château de Silling has turned a wave of its inmates loose on the streets.

Several online crime blotters have noted an uptick in sexual misdemeanor cases in certain metro areas. One put together an interesting montage of cuffed men in police cars wearing full powdered wigs.

Sex worker boards are filling with alerts defining archaic terminology. For example, this one on *The Erotic Review*:

> Ladies, if someone asks if you allow "fustigation," the answer is "No," or "Fuck off." It means beating you with a stick. And red-flag him for your sisters. Has there been a full moon this past week, or what?

Then this appeal from a woman posting to the main *Savant* forum:

Thread: Reward for Information

Frantic_Mom	Please help me!!!
Joined:2/01/15	My son has been missing for four days.
Posts: 1	I got into his computer, and I know he
	spent a lot of time playing this game.
Location:	
Los Angeles, CA	

> I don't care what he's been doing, I just
> want him back.
>
> I have $5,000 for anyone who can give me
> information to help find him. No questions
> asked. He is only sixteen.

Attached to the post is a picture split in halves. The left is a yearbook photo of a spindly, nervous-looking teen. The right shows a screen shot of his burly leather-lord NOD avatar.

I guess these days one picture isn't enough.

Blake finally got back to me later that evening.

He left a voicemail asking to meet at an unfamiliar address in Brooklyn, a small bar called Paul's that is more or less the inverse of the Racquet and Tennis. At six PM, the place is dark, dusty, and deserted. Paul must be going through a long-term identity crisis. Woefully maintained Irish accents are muddled by pictures of Mexican national soccer teams from the 1970s.

Blake has secured us a pair of martinis, and he tips his glass as I take the seat next to him. He says, "I didn't suppose the little bastard would ever have the balls to attack my sister. Think this might add some urgency to your efforts?"

"Do you really believe having him committed is going to prevent people from finding out that you're building a virtual sex empire?"

My question was meant to jar him, but it fails miserably. Blake beams a satisfied smile at me, like his prize pupil has just solved a complicated proof. "Virtual sex empire. I like the sound of that."

"Think your board will? What about your sister?"

Blake just shrugs as if the questions, or at least the questioner, are of little consequence. I try a different approach. "You know, my work would have been a lot easier if you'd told me all this at the beginning."

Blake sips his drink and says, "True. But I needed to know what you could find out and how you'd go about it. I won't mention the fact that *your* disclosures on this topic were, shall we say, less than candid?"

"Fair enough. But I'm trying to help you, and you're making that more difficult."

"Okay. Absolute honesty henceforth." But his eyes sparkle mischievously. As if mocking the whole concept of veracity. "What would you like to know?"

There's a lot I'd like to know. Why does Billy blame him for Gina's death? Does he really think his brother is crazy? What's he going to do if he finds him? But all these give way to my real concern: his intentions toward the Dancers.

I ask, "Why are you backing IT? With this huge merger coming up, why give your brother the ammunition? It doesn't make any sense."

"You have any idea why I wanted to meet you at this shithole?"

Exasperated, I shake my head.

"Good. Let's take a walk."

Five minutes later, we've stepped across the street to an anonymous red brick warehouse. Now we sit in a conference room, empty except for a pair of odd contraptions. While I'm used to mechanisms with human orifices, these things look like the open mouths of giant robotic squids. Each has a steel center ring five feet in diameter around which stand a series of eight spiky robot arms. In the center of the ring are two segmented beams bristling with heavy-duty motors. They terminate in what seem to be extraterrestrial ski boots with soles supported by large air cylinders.

"Welcome to Project Holy Duck," says Blake.

He walks up to the first machine, slips off his shoes, and steps carefully into the boots. A rack hanging from the ceiling holds a pair of HMD goggles and a foam maul. Something about its fat cylindrical head attached to a thin plastic handle sets off hazy recognition signals.

Leveling his now sightless gaze at me, he says, "When I said 'let's take a walk,' I hope you didn't think I meant just across the street."

Blake gestures at the other machine, and I climb aboard. A series of bladders inflate around my feet, and I rise a couple inches on what feels like a cloud of air. As if I've strapped on a pair of Mercury's winged sandals. Then the visuals rez up, showing almost the reverse.

I stand in front of a polished brass mirror in an underground burrow. Tree roots meander along the dirt walls. My reflection shows that I've become a garden gnome, complete with bushy white beard and red conical hat. I wiggle to test out the body tracking. It's seamless. I look over to see that Blake's assumed the form of a tiny fluttering fairy.

He says in a voice processed into a squeaky chirp, "Hurry, Gwilligur! Our burrow is under attack!"

With that, he sparkles open the room's door and flies out. Without thinking about it, I follow him. Only as I cross the threshold and enter a long, torch-lit passage do I fully realize what I'm doing.

I'm walking.

Perhaps the most crucial problem with this kind of simulation has been the lack of a natural way to move oneself through space, which tends to ruin the illusion of presence. Here I'm not pushing my av around the screen with a joystick, but actually walking like a normal human through a fantasy world. Just to try it, I turn and walk in the other direction down the hall. Blake's mechanized boots handle this without a hitch.

He's got a working omnimill.

Technically you'd call it an omnidirectional locomotion interface. Most of these have been developed for the army, and various labs have tried everything from motorized roller skates to giant spherical hamster balls, with varying degrees of success. But Blake's system represents a real breakthrough. The complete gestalt.

My thoughts are interrupted by a trickling of dirt down the wall in front of me. A hole opens, and out of it emerges a small but demonic-looking purple mole. Its giant claws and pulsating star nose remind me of something from a fifties creature feature. It calmly steps out onto a nearby root, takes a tiny crossbow off its back, loads a bolt, and fires.

I'm startled almost to the point of panic when I feel a sting on my chest where the arrow hits me—the snap of a rubber band fired from close range.

Can Blake's machine actually be firing BBs at me?

"Ow. That hurts."

His fairy grins at me. "Well, what are you going to do about it?"

Just then I feel another much more painful sting on the left side of my neck. Instinctively, I lash out at the horrible mole with my maul. I'm expecting an airy visual damage metaphor, but instead I get a sharp twinge in my elbow when my mallet impacts with an unbelievably de-lightful crushing sensation. Right then I realize what's familiar about this setup: it's a thirty-years-overdue update of the classic carnival game

Whack-A-Mole. As the most tactilely satisfying game of all time, there's no better app for Blake to show off his next-gen VR system. This game lets the player stroll about and whack moles, not in a restricted little box, but all around him.

And the moles can fight back.

Blake flutters over to inspect the green goo dripping off my war hammer. "I give you Walk-A-Mole." He pronounces its name like the avocado dip that bears a strong resemblance to the remains of the creature I just pulverized.

Suddenly, there's a huge cascade of dirt from the surrounding walls, and a regiment of mutant moles begins unloading on me. Mass slaughter ensues, and three minutes later, after a desperately fought running battle, I stand victorious. Out of breath and sweating, I contemplate the single most compelling digital experience I've ever had—save of course my first date with Ginger. But what Blake has done here is even bigger. He's finally put us all the way into the machine.

I flip up my HMD to see him standing to the side of his omniboots, watching me.

I look him in the eye and say, "Holy fuck."

He bows. "Thus the name. Derived from the word 'holodeck,' but we soon realized it was refreshingly apropos."

"So . . ."

"So my brother's not the only one who swallowed the blue pill." Blake turns his back to me and lifts the hair at the nape of his neck. He uncovers a small tattoo: just a dot with a circle around it.

But clearly a jack.

We're seated in a small chamber behind some one-way glass watching several of Blake's technicians work on the consumer version of the military-grade system I just test-drove.

"Had I known the difficulties," he says, "I would have never started this. But here we are, and now I've got over a hundred engineers worshipping the Duck."

"Shave my head and dress me in robes. That thing is insane. It's also insane that your board was avant-garde enough to back the development effort."

"Ah, well that's just it. They didn't."

"What?"

"Yeah. I pitched them an earlier version of the project, and they barfed all over it. Not a core competency and all that. I decided to do it anyway."

"So you diverted the money? Wait, let me guess . . . From Goblin, which was supposed to be venture capital for squashing future competitors."

"Right. Soon the department will start showing 'material losses,' and the board will start shitting Yorkshire terriers."

"And the Dancers are going to glide in to provide a distraction?"

"Not exactly. When I found out about Olya's opportunity, I knew that, regardless of whether people really want to copulate with machines, the *announcement* would generate a certain amount of heat. And one can profit when the animal spirits are stirred. Now, IMP couldn't invest in IT directly, but I could use some of my personal money to prime the pump. And Goblin could benefit if I bought support companies that might see immediate returns as Money realizes the implications of real virtual sex."

"That's why I'm doing this turbo NOD integration."

"Yeah. And why beforehand we funded the development of LibIA, so that we have a cybersexual ecosystem already in place for when we release the Dancers into the wild. Goblin cashes in on the buzz, and I get time to finish Holy Duck. Once it's a fait accompli, the board will fall in on the marketing." Blake's voice segues into ironic soliloquy. "Holy Duck will be a huge hit, and I become the visionary who is going to lead IMP into the twenty-first century. Then there will be no one to stop my evil plans."

"But in the meantime, you're walking a fine line. If the board finds out about all the money going into Holy Duck, or that you're the one behind our plastic fantastics—"

"They could unravel the whole thing."

"To say nothing about what your sister might do if all this causes the snake handlers in Congress to queer the pitch for her merger."

"She'd take steps to ensure I never experience the kind attentions of your femme bot." He sighs. "I don't want to cross the Princess of Hearts."

"Wait . . . Lady Di?"

"No, Lewis Carroll. Her nickname in the cable division. Comes from her tendency to solve problems by saying, 'Off with their heads!' Very much her father's daughter in that respect. But ultimately she's of a typical 'pipes' person, who wants nothing more than to provide bandwidth efficiently. I prefer to imagine the wondrous things at the end of those pipes."

"Like your father?"

"If he'd shared Blythe's perspective, IMP would never have existed. His empire was built by exploiting novel technology faster than others. New media always lends itself to adult content, and my father had the sack not to shy away from that."

Blake stands to pour himself a cup of coffee. He continues. "My great-grandfather supposedly made a fortune publishing French postcards during the First World War. Lost it all in the Depression, but smut peddling is something of a family tradition. Few people in the world are lucky enough to have a clear sense of destiny. I do. And it's thoroughly informed by my father's legacy. Part of that legacy is the strength not to let the petty prejudices of others prevent you from exerting your will."

"Which is what your brother is threatening to do."

"Right, but we have you to make sure he isn't successful."

I brief Blake on the state of play with Billy. I tell him that, aside from his recent RL provocations, it looks like his brother has set up this Sade-themed file-swapping ring that encourages players to record themselves committing acts of progressing indecency and then share with the group. Given his theft of those awful family videos, I suspect he plans to trickle out the worst material to his players. Who will leak it to the press in this irresistibly lurid context. Which he probably hopes will embarrass IMP's board enough for them to disenfranchise Blake, just as they'd done to him years ago.

Blake agrees that scenario sounds like his brother. While he still favors my pursuing Billy through his game, he's impatient. He wants more action. Billy knows we're stalking him, and his attacking Blythe has soured her twin on stealthy recon as a strategy.

We talk about the brute force option: a herculean program of cracking, bribery, and extortion against several international ISPs in an attempt to trace a physical location from which Billy is connecting to his *Savant* server. He doesn't blink at the price I ballpark him.

I imagine Mercer will kiss me on the mouth at our next meeting.

Which will be sooner than I'd expected, because the next item on Blake's agenda is me.

He says, "So now that you've been initiated into the mysteries, are you ready to take the brand?"

I had a feeling something like this was coming. Now that I know his secrets, Blake wants to bind me more tightly to him. He wants me under his control. A new knave for his suit.

"What did you have in mind?"

"I originally hired you to look into my brother's disappearance. Since then you've proven adept at working your way into some of my most important initiatives. Given the level of trust we've built—"

Except that we haven't. Blake has been evasive from the beginning. He only confirms things I learn independently. And I can sense that there are cavernous pools of information he's still not sharing.

"—I'd like to formalize our relationship. I want you to come and work for me full-time."

He pulls out the contract he's proposing. I let the folder sit on the table between us. I can tell there's something else to this.

Blake searches my face for a while. Then he says, "Were you to join the team, you'd be working for me *exclusively*."

Ah, so that's it.

My stomach sinks.

"So of course there'd be no reason for you to keep meeting with my sister."

Blake has always seen me as strictly servant-class. Like Olya and her robots, he wants only a prince for his sister. So he's asking me to choose between the Dancers and Blythe.

Through the squall in my head, what finally emerges, plangent and raw, is that moment on a gorgeous day in May that Blythe euthanized those few of my hopes still clinging to life.

The Randall twins didn't come back to school until just before exams. I'd left Blythe messages that tried to strike the right note of mournful support, but I received no response. I explained her silence with the notion that such a profound woman would grieve deeply. Without an invitation, pulling the trigger on plane reservations proved impossible. I was plagued by the image of Blake answering the door.

When I finally learned that Blythe was back, it was through a girl who took a bit too much satisfaction in telling me that she was accompanied by a boy.

That "boy" was none other than Graham Welles, then the leading man for a popular twentysomething soap on one of their cable channels. In fairness, they'd starred together in Exeter's production of *The Tempest*. He was an old family friend who'd really "been there for her" during her desolation. He and Blake got on like bandits. And he was hypnotically handsome.

I couldn't even bring myself to blame her. I didn't want a big fight or anything like that. I don't know what I wanted, but I felt like we had to talk. So I staked out her apartment until I caught them coming in.

Welles saw me first, and I had to give the guy credit; he was cool about it all. He shook my hand and smoothly remembered a pressing need for the latest issue of *Variety*. Blythe's soft expression let me cherish a split second of hope that the circumstances were other than what I imagined. Then she said, "You must think I'm completely evil."

"No. Not at all. I just wanted to—"

"I know. I know. I'm sorry. I kind of collapsed. I— I just wish none of this had happened."

"None of it?"

"Oh, honey. You've given me nothing but precious memories. I'm sure you'll hate me now, but—"

"No, Blythe. I'll always—"

As usual, she already knew what I was about to say. So she covered my lips with hers in a gentle, lingering, and even maybe a little passionate kiss. But I could taste the wistful finality of it. Part of me wanted to wrench away in hurt and indignation. But that part was summarily beaten down. I needed to make our last kiss as good as possible.

Any time I'm lying in bed and the episode once again invades my mind, the seething embarrassment of what I said next guarantees I won't sleep until the sun comes up.

As she walked slowly up the stairs outside her apartment, I called out her name. She turned and smiled at me sadly. Then, in my desperation, I said the unthinkable:

"We can still be friends, can't we?"

I think she was surprised that I'd so completely abandoned my dignity. "Oh, James." She shut her eyes and gathered herself. "James, we were never friends. I don't think either of us will be able to settle for that."

A cold and merciless thing to say? Maybe. But she was right. As it was, I could lick my wounds without constantly being faced with the opportunity to create fresh ones. While I spent the summer staring at Blythe's pictures and drinking myself nearly to death, I never even tried to call her. Seeing that person I became in her presence had hurt enough. The drunk that came after wasn't so great either, but at least his pain was endured in private.

And besides all that, she remained in my imagination too perfect to blame. I always absolved her with the refrain that she never made me any promises. She still hasn't.

But her brother, it appears, will.

And really, why pretend you have a choice?

Blake has me cornered. If he removes me from the case, I won't be casually ringing Blythe for cocktails. The whole basis of our reacquaintance is that we're working together to find her crazy brother.

She only invited you to solve a problem for her. She never made you any promises.

The Dancers, however, hold all the promise of the future.

I reach over and place my hand on the folder.

"I accept."

48

Susan Mercer's office is frigid at twilight, suffused with the azure glow of the evening magic hour. I'm exhausted, and nervous about the meeting. Exhausted because I saw little sleep last night while I rattled through a comprehensive proposal for Blake's assault on the internet. Nervous not just because I'm afraid of displeasing Mercer with my news; I'm more worried that she'll amplify my concern that this move is impulsive. That I'm following my testicles into a dicey situation. But with my younger and more beautiful mistresses Olya and Ginger whispering inducements, I gird myself to tangle with the Norn.

At first it seems that she's not there, her desk showing only a vacant circle of orange light streaming from an antique lamp. I hear a faint creak over in the shadows beside the bank of large windows at the far end of the room. She's slowly rocking next to a small table bearing a steaming tea service. Her eyes are fixed on me, her hands, as always, busy with a complex textile.

Eventually she says, "A bittersweet moment."

I try on my own regretful face and take a seat in the weird miniature chair opposite her. "I meant to speak with you about this first, but I see Blake has been impatient."

Mercer shrugs. "Had I known this assignment would be your last, I'd have sent your irritating colleague Mr. Holley."

"I'm sorry. I love it here, it's just—"

Mercer cuts off my apology with a magisterial wave. "Your simple reconnaissance has devolved into a great deal of *unsavory* business." She pats a thick document lying on the table next to the tea. It's bound in red, signifying a services contract. But something in her emphasis bothers me.

Has she found out about the Dancers? Is she aware of my newfound mecha-philia?

If so, she doesn't let on.

She continues. "You know your new employer had the gall to offer us an 'employee referral award,' as if we were an impoverished tribe selling our children for millet."

"You should take it."

"Maybe the partners will. And I shall be forced to blot my tears with ill-gotten specie. Not a position I'm unused to. But what about your tears, dear boy?"

"My eyes are clear and dry."

"Such a hasty marriage . . . What if your groom should disappoint?"

"You assume I'm the wife in this arrangement."

She picks up the invoice and fans through it. "This, while no doubt an amusing expenditure for someone like Mr. Randall, feels like a bride price."

I nod in acknowledgment of the point. At least she's characterizing me as a wife rather than something less charitable. I think about the subtext of my deal with Blake. While returning to a state of Blythelessness may have been the natural result of completing my work for them, he had to make me formally accept it. To choose it.

She offers a wan smile. "I'd just advise you to remember your Tennyson—in general, a sniveling romantic, but wise in writing, 'He will hold thee, when his passion shall have spent its novel force / Something better than his dog, a little dearer than his horse.'"

At this, she stands, and shockingly opens her arms wide, gesturing me inward. Her embrace is awkward—perfunctory and unpracticed. I can feel her gazing past me, at the city, when she says, "Do know that we'll always have a stall here in our stable for you. Remember that before you go trotting off to the glue factory."

49

If I worried over the source of the foreboding Mercer conveyed, she doesn't leave me hanging for long. On my desk sits a thick stack of time sheets for my work to date on the twins' behalf that Billing wants me to initial. The paperwork is generally in order, but someone has "mistakenly" appended a number of forms for various other Red Rook employees from the same client code, but a different case number. I almost just toss them in the burn bin, but one of the entries stops me. Listed among all the opaque acronyms for our shady activities is inventoried six hours for a system penetration of someone code-named E10_Vinyl. Nothing unusual there; we do it every day. But among all the enciphered identifiers is the confirmation line for the computer that got penetrated, which includes its IP: 192.0.2.112.

That's the internet address for *my* home computer.

My brothers in arms have turned their knives on me. Of course one's own medicine always tastes the bitterest. But after taking a panicked inventory of my actions over the past couple weeks, I conclude that they've been mostly innocent with respect to Blake. Since I'll still be working closely with Red Rook in my new position, the philosophical perspective seems best. Besides, leaving a known penetration in place can accord you a stronger position than the person who put it there, since you now have control over a trusted information source.

Perhaps I adhere to some quaint notions of company loyalty, but I'm a little shocked that Red Rook agreed to instrument one of its own employees. Though I guess a cold warrior like Mercer would approve of "watchers watching the watchers" involute security schemes. Since there's no way these papers ended up on my desk by accident, I conclude that at least she had the good grace to give me a heads-up. What motivated her to do that? Occam's razor leaves me with the words: she likes me.

Thank God for that.

An hour later I finally get a message from one of *my* RATs indicating that Nash has logged in to the NYPD's evidence repository. I wait until he signs off for the day before starting my search. Because he was the principal investigator, I have full access to download the file on Gina Delaney's death.

Along with the sundry reports and morgue photos, there's a digital video with a default name from the camera that shot it. Once the transfer finishes, I run a program called MephistoFilese that corrupts the original beyond any hope of redemption. My adding an erroneous storage location entry for the camera's memory card and then switching its status to "item lost" should make retrieving the original nearly impossible. Now I've got the only accessible copy.

I pull up the video on my laptop.

Gina's pale face fills my screen. Tears flow freely past her closed eyelids and down her cheeks. There's a low whirring sound that must be the drill behind her. For a moment, her head sways unsteadily on her neck, and then she opens her eyes. Their sparkling amber is now dilated black, as though she's taken a heavy dose of tranqs. Her gaze rests on a point just above and to the left of the camera. She inhales haltingly and then starts to say something, but her face contorts as she tries not to cry. She jerks her head, the movement restricted by the cords binding her to the garrote. She lets her neck go slack and sobs.

After a few seconds of this, she makes a clear effort to calm herself, taking deep trembling breaths. She closes her eyes. When they open again, she's found a certain stillness.

She says in a nearly inaudible voice made husky by her tears:

I guess you thought
I'd play the daughter of Lot,
But I will not.

The extreme close-up makes it hard to distinguish what happens next. The restraints bite more deeply into the skin of her neck and chin, like she's pressing forward against them.

Then there's the short scraping sound of a cigarette lighter.

The right side of Gina's face receives a warm, flickering light. This seems to wake something inside her. Her eyes become less glassy and start darting around. Maybe she's making a last-minute inspection of her setup. She rotates her head slowly to the right, perhaps testing the tautness of the line. Then back to the left. She repeats the process more quickly, and then I realize:

She's shaking her head.

Her eyes are bright now with panic.

The drill bursts through her mouth, spraying the camera lens with drops of blood. Her body goes limp from the huge hole torn into her spine. I have to close my eyes.

When I open them, Gina's face is still there, mutilated by the razor-toothed hole saw, which spins on with mechanical abandon. The video rolls for another twenty minutes, and by the end of it, I know I'll see that image for the rest of my days.

50

Acquiring Gina's suicide video finally gave me a good card for my hand. But I still need an opportunity to play it. I check in to see where the rest of Billy's gamers are.

Savant's forum has come alive with controversy over a post by someone named Clay_Media proposing that Big Ben Mondano was a member of the Pyrexians. An idea that would unify, as good conspiracy theories do, the two primary strands of speculation concerning the party backing *Savant*. Initially, I assume this is Billy again seeding the story behind his game, but I become unsure, since the post mostly inspired an effort to comb Exotica's back catalog for Pyrexian imagery: black candles, red rings, antique medical equipment, coded messages inscribed on their victims. I suspect this line of inquiry will actually lead them *away* from any kind of connection to Robert Randall.

That said, I'm worried that the *Savant* players' growing numbers and organization will eventually allow them to find their way inside Billy's gingerbread house. And that will complicate my work. I contemplate a subtle disinformation campaign, but before I can solidify any ideas, my duties to the Dancers call.

Olya's discovered a new vibration in Fred's corpus spongiosum, and she and Xan are at loggerheads about whether this is a bug or a feature. I've been called to help Garriott investigate, but perhaps more importantly to procure late-night fuel for the team.

— — —

On my way over, McClaren pulls up and invites me into his Town Car. His news is that Charles Delaney, Gina's father, had called the NYPD out of the blue to demand a copy of his daughter's suicide video. Nash put him off with some claptrap about "evidentiary sequestration" and phoned McClaren. They ran Delaney's bank accounts, which showed two recent deposits of just over nine thousand dollars apiece. The conclusion: Billy is trying to use him to get the video, the "final piece" he mentioned to Blythe. McClaren orders me to Boston to see if he can be bribed into leading us to Billy.

Garriott and I finish our urological procedure on Fred more quickly than I'd anticipated, allowing me to leave GAME at three AM. Needing to sleep on the way, I opt for a train that gets into South Station five hours later.

Somerville is a suburb north of Harvard's Cambridge that's been transformed into a postcollegiate Eden, filled with organic cafés and bars thronged with recent grads. But if you wind up on the wrong side of McGrath Highway, you'll find a neighborhood whose residents didn't all get the "inexorable gentrification" memo: East Somerville. It's only about two miles from the neoclassical halls of MIT, but as with most old Eastern cities, you can span whole galaxies just by crossing a street. I'm amazed Gina made the transition.

The Delaneys' house stands on a blighted block of slumping three-story railcar tenements framed by giant denuded elm trees that look like they were last pruned by WPA employees. Despite the hopeless aspect of the block, there's a yellow Mustang with dealer's plates parked askew at the curb.

Eleven Cross Street is a small rectangle of leprous brown shingles. Its only gesture at decoration is rusting steel bars on the windows, which seem to have been bored into the building's surface at random.

I ring the bell and wait a long time before someone starts wrestling with the warped wooden door. At first there's just a thin gap into the dark of the vestibule, but then the door swings open on a woman who begins the painfully slow process of climbing down a short cement staircase to open the metal security door in front of me. I think she might be in her midsixties, but she has the sick thinness and carriage of a woman well into her eighties. She's draped herself with a worn housedress, and her dull gray hair listlessly crowds her face. Her eyes speak of sleepless nights, and her breath speaks of a seven AM encounter with a gin bottle.

"Mrs. Delaney? Hi—"

"You're here about Geenie?" she asks in a reedy whisper.

"Yes, ma'am."

Before she can continue, a deep voice booms out from behind her. "Ruthie, get your ass back in here. I'll take care of this guy. Go finish your breakfast."

Ugh. I can tell I'd prefer sharing her kind of breakfast to dealing with the owner of that voice. Mrs. Delaney scuttles off without another word.

Charles Delaney is scrawny and unkempt, with a large flat head framed by patchy stubble that in some places aspires to be a beard. He's wearing greasy jeans and a plaid flannel shirt, underneath which a moth-eaten T-shirt proclaims, OBAMANATION: WIPING OUT AMERICA, ONE BABY AT A TIME. He looks me over with a jittery scowl but eventually says in a cigarette-scarred bray, "Well, get yourself in here. It's colder than ass out there."

Against my better judgment, I put out my hand. "James Pryce, it's nice—" But he's already walking away from me down a narrow hallway.

I almost take off. Charles Delaney is disturbing. You see him and think base-head. You smell him and think opossum. His wife's clearly hanging on by her fingernails too. If his daughter suffered from mental instability, the genetic component has certainly been confirmed. The grim abode tells me that her environment wasn't helping anything either.

I follow him down the hall. What I first took for a limp proves to be a stagger. Like his wife, the guy is drunk as a lord at nine AM. He heads straight back to a flimsy door with a Yosemite Sam "Back Off" mud flap stapled to it.

It opens onto a den obviously meant as an off-limits refuge for the man of the house. The room has a sixties basement quality, with artificial wood paneling adorned with outdated Boston sports posters, a beat-up Naugahyde couch, and a giant duct-taped recliner. The low coffee table is covered with Natural Light tallboys dragooned into service as sloppy ashtrays. I'd expect to see an old TV set with a jury-rigged antenna, but instead there's a brand-new sixty-inch Sony LCD inexpertly bolted to the wall. A badass surround-sound system sits in boxes on the floor.

Delaney collapses onto the couch and takes a swig out of a bottle of Midleton Irish Whiskey, which stands in glaring contrast to the dead cans of discount beer. He doesn't offer me any. There's evidence here of an epic Home Shopping Network binge: a lacquer stand of samurai swords, a wall full of valuable Red Sox cards mounted in mahogany frames, and two leather gun cases, which I'm hoping do not contain actual weapons.

I sit on the recliner and start with, "Thank you for taking the time to meet with me."

He snorts as though I've said something idiotic.

"So your wife might have mentioned that I'm working on a documentary that in part deals with the work your daughter—"

"Yeah, I know all about you and your 'documentary.' You want to dig shit up about Geenie. So go ahead and ask your questions. I'm a fucking open book."

"Well, first of all, my condolences on your daughter's death. You must have been shocked—"

"No, I always knew my girl was heading for hell."

"Hell?"

"Suicide is a mortal sin, ain't it? You can't just go picking out the parts of His Holy Word that you happen to like, right? Not like those Episcopal faggots."

"I guess it depends—"

Suddenly heated, he leans toward me. "It don't depend on shit. The Word is the Truth. You better fucking believe that. Yeah, I can tell you don't like me saying that shit about my own daughter. But I don't need you judging me. That's for the Lord, not someone like you." Then he takes a long pull off his bottle and relaxes back into the couch. "But you know . . . I'll probably end up joining her there. Way things have gone for me."

"Faith can certainly be a great comfort. Ah, did your daughter share your commitment to the church?"

"If she did, she wouldn't be burning in the fiery pit right now."

"Did she seem depressed at all before? Did you notice any signs—"

"What I noticed was that she moved to Jew York to be with all those communistic dickheads."

I know there's never been any love lost between New York and Boston, but this is an odd perspective for someone living north of the Mason-Dixon line and in this century. I try, "I understand she went to study at NYU."

"Yeah, all that techy shit. You know computers are the tools of the devil? Once they get their hooks into you, Satan himself can mainline poison directly into your brain."

Here I think he has a point most people would agree with.

He continues. "And those people who went to her school. You wouldn't believe the kind of faggots showed up at her funeral."

Now we're getting somewhere. "Yeah, I was told that one of her classmates created a commotion there."

His enthusiasm at holding forth on the communists and faggots vanishes. "Well, I don't remember much about that. I was dealing with a lot of shit at the time."

"That's understandable. Let me see if I can jog your memory." I pull out an eight-by-ten of Billy. "I heard you might have had words with this gentleman. A friend of your daughter's. That maybe he was taking pictures. That he tried to put something into your daughter's casket. You wouldn't by any chance know what—"

"I don't know that boy from Adam," Delaney says quietly, without looking at the photo.

"Are you sure?" I wait for a while and then push Billy's picture toward him. "Because I was given to believe—"

His earlier rage rushes back. He shoots up and leans over me, poking my chest with his finger. "'Given to believe'? What kind of shit-talk is that? Why don't you just call me a liar to my face?"

I put up my hands to placate him, mentally measuring the distance to all the weapons in the room. "Mr. Delaney, I didn't mean to in any way—"

"Fuck you!" He's still yelling. I feel a fine spray of spittle on my forehead. "Whoever the fuck you are. Yeah, I know you're no fucking filmmaker. He said you'd come sniffing around. Well I'm not telling you shit, so you can get your ass off my chair and get—"

"Mr. Delaney, maybe we could come to some arrangement, if you'd just listen to—"

"No, you listen to me, you shit-sucking—"

Clearly the interview has gone off the rails, so I snatch his finger and roll it back toward his chest until he's forced to subside onto the couch. I don't let go but say softly in his ear, "When you see our friend Billy again, tell him that I have the only copy of that video, and he needs to come to me if he wants it."

I let go and take a step back. Delaney's gaze settles on his new swords. I shake my head. He rubs his sore finger and stares hate at me.

"I'll see myself out."

As I walk back up the hall, I glance into the kitchen. Mrs. Delaney hunches at a battered wooden table with a coffee cup in both hands, letting the steam bathe her face like a child. Her eyes rise to meet mine, and I read in them a nervous question. Her lips open, but she doesn't say anything, and eventually looks back into her mug. I want to walk over to her, but then I hear something crash in her husband's den. I run through the likely consequences of dragging her into this, and my conscience won't sanction the risk. Instead I just take a card out of my pocket and place it on a stack of newspapers sitting against the wall. She makes no acknowledgment.

I slip out into the lacerating Boston wind.

51

Being a dropout, I can't explain why I'm still so attached to my alma mater. But I let the existence of an Acela departure to New York three hours from now convince me that I might as well head toward the river and look in on Fair Harvard. It's after eleven by the time I find parking for my rental car, and I decide that a nice long lunch at the Bat would be a fine antidote to the infectious misery of the Delaney household.

But just as I'm pouring the bourbon over ice, a 617 area code rings my cell.

I answer and hear a small, hoarse voice say, "Can you come back to the house?"

By the time I get there, the yellow Mustang has departed from its place at the Delaneys' curb. I wait through another long pause after knocking, but then Ruth opens the door wearing a worried expression. Without preliminaries, she holds out two items in the palm of her hand. The first is a four-inch figurine of a woman. The second is a Sony memory stick.

She says, "I . . . I saved these. Please take them."

I gently put them inside my jacket pocket. "Thank you, Mrs. Delaney. This is really—"

She puts up a hand. "I thought . . . I thought maybe your film . . . Maybe you could tell me something. She never said anything, and . . ." She stops, at a loss. "I—I just don't know."

With that, she shuts the door firmly in my face.

On the train home, I turn the figure over in my hands. I've seen plenty like it around GAME. One of the touchstones of geek culture is collectible figurines. The ability of 3D printers to crank out custom miniatures of one's online alter egos has only intensified our passion for them. This figure is clearly a NOD avatar. Though representing as a blond, blue-eyed anime vixen, she has Gina's playful elfin features. She's wearing a set of billowing purple robes reminiscent of a kimono, and her hands are joined in front of her at waist level holding a large red gemstone. The only label left on the figure is a name inscribed on the base. It reads: Ines_Idoru.

Could this be another one of Gina's NODNames?

I slip the memory stick into my laptop and see that it contains photos of her funeral. The thumbnails follow a trajectory that confirms Garriott's story. Some introductory shots of the graveyard, then images of a group of maybe forty people gathering around the open grave. Finally a couple of Gina's father stomping over and reaching for the camera.

Running through them again, I see a sequence where Billy focuses on two attendees at the periphery of the group as they're walking in from the parking lot. The first picture shows Blythe Randall extending her hand to Xan. And the next shows Xan taking it.

52

That night I get my chance to ask Xan about the photo.

I slip back into my office under the pretense that I've been "working from home" all day. The team is properly derisive of this excuse, but they don't care to spend the effort scolding me since they want me to put the final touches on the Dancers' voice-recognition abilities. I'm not sure why we're adding this obvious next-rev feature, but Olya demands that the Solo Control mode function without having to balance a keyboard on our chests.

Given the complexity of voice input, all we've been able to implement are simple commands such as "Fuck me" to initiate sexual contact, "Keep going" to prolong it, and of course the ever popular "Faster" and "Harder."

Xan and I are lying in the MetaChairs facing away from each other, both breathing deep from a robust test of the evening's progress.

"I can't believe we get paid to do this," I say with a contented sigh.

She looks over her shoulder. "What, someone's been writing you checks? All this work on my back, and I've yet to see the first shilling."

"You know what I mean."

"Yeah. But our Dancers have yet to prove themselves in front of the public."

"Are you worried? Olya probably told you by now the money's coming from Blake Randall, so—"

"I know. I'm still here, aren't I?"

"What about Blythe?"

"What about her?"

"Do you know her at all?"

"I met her at the same party where Gina met Blake. But no, not really."

"Have you seen her recently?"

"Why do you ask?"

"Just curious."

"You're 'just curious' about Blythe Randall, are you?" She sighs and stretches her back. "Yeah. I saw her at Gina's funeral. We exchanged condolences. I was surprised she was there, but I guess she'd met her through Blake."

"So you were just being polite?"

"James, what are you asking me?"

"Nothing. I remember her from school, and I wanted to see if—"

"Let me suggest that you keep your mind and other body parts on your robot overlords here. You can think about her all you want once we're sailing around Sardinia."

At ten fifty PM, my GAME email gets a message from the spoofed address louis_markey@savant.net. My pulse thumps as I realize that my Boston gambit worked, and Billy wants to meet.

On short notice, it turns out. His message reads:

```
Have a Rabbit Hole at Apothecary by 11pm tonight.
```

Apothecary, a posh downtown bar, publishes a cocktail list so esoteric that it has attracted the attention of both the *New Yorker* and the New York Health Department. A Rabbit Hole must be one of their signature drinks.

As cocktails go, this one sounds treacherous, but if Billy wants to meet for a drink, then he can sure as hell call the round.

53

The bar lies on the border of the Lower East Side and Chinatown. It's unmarked save for the customary mortar-and-pestle glyph molded in wrought iron on the building's side gate. Behind the railing, a steep staircase leads to the basement. Apothecary's interior maxes out the medical history theme with specimen jars of preserved animals, organs, and ambiguous polyps mixed in among the liquor bottles.

A little out of breath from having jogged over, I take a second to text McClaren about this, though I doubt he'll have time to arrange a shadow for me.

Inside I find a man with a stringy beard and beady eyes who has the mien of a Renaissance Faire staffer. Someone who lives by stringing together a patchwork of marginal gigs well on the outskirts of conventional theater. He's polishing the marble bar top with a studied diligence that I've never observed in a real bartender.

Where does Billy find these people?

Of course he'd never make things easy by just meeting me at the bar. Though if I had Blake for a sibling, I would handle one of his agents with a snare pole as well.

I sit down in front of him, and he looks into my eyes with sugary solicitude. "*What* shall it be?"

His delivery makes me want to punch him, but I stick to the script. "I'd like a Rabbit Hole."

I can tell he wants to ad-lib theatrical flourishes but has been warned against improvisation. So much so that he places a beaker in front of me and pours a stream of muddy brown liquid into it from a cocktail shaker. The pre-mixed beverage seems obviously wrong under the circumstances. And Billy is exactly the kind of guy who has a Kool-Aid recipe several lines longer than it should be.

I lean over to smell it. "I don't suppose there's anything unusual in here?"

"Like what?" He makes a visible effort to suppress the phrase "pray tell."

"A sedative would be traditional."

He grins like I've just nailed a Daily Double. "No sedative in there." He reaches into a pocket of his dirty apron, pulls out a large light-blue capsule, and places it on the napkin beside my drink. "There is in this though."

"You want me to take a pill?"

This is too much for him to resist breaking character. He bugs his eyes and smiles. "Just like *The Matrix,* man."

"What if I don't?"

He frowns. "Then I guess we can have a nice talk. May—" He wants to say "mayhap" but stumbles over it. "Mayha-be . . . I can regale you—"

The prospect of being regaled depresses me enough that I pop the pill and wash it down with the suspicious drink. It tastes like a black rum and cider fusion with some odd herbal tones. Delicious really.

The guy tilts his head toward a green velvet couch in the back. "You might want to lie down, sir."

54

As was only to be expected, I wake up in a cage.

A cage packed into a reinforced crate. I'm curled up in a ball, but the space is tall enough for me to sit Indian style in relative comfort. Feeling around in the darkness, I learn I'm surrounded by a grid of iron bars covered over with planks that smell of new lumber. I sense the quiet vibration of motorized transport.

Taking me somewhere.

Also, I'm completely naked. Not that I fear for my safety, though I am concerned about splinters; my nudity just highlights how bizarre my job has become now that I find myself so frequently disrobed in the line of duty.

Those concerns are interrupted as the truck stops and my crate rolls down a steep ramp. I'm wheeled around with teamster brusqueness until I bang gently into a wall. Then I wait for what feels like several hours.

Someone prying off the front side of my crate yanks me back to alertness. I'm in an abandoned construction site well lit by the cool blue glow of an almost full moon. Billy Randall squats before my cage. He's holding the same crowbar with which he attacked Blythe. He raps it against the bars.

I wouldn't have thought it possible, but Billy looks worse than when he was electrocuting himself. His hair has grown longer and now sticks up in greasy dinosaur spikes. The bags under his eyes stand out like makeup, but the eyes themselves reveal a manic fire that makes me start to worry a little. He's sweating profusely.

"I can't believe you actually took the pill. Seems foolish for you to assume I'll be gentle."

"I'm foolish? Your game will have you exchanging your glass house for a concrete cell. When your lunatic horde really hurts someone, it'll be your fault."

"Amazing that my brother's rent boy has the gall to lecture me about morality."

"Rent boy? You've got our relationship all wrong. Think of it more like the one between your marquis and his valet Latour."

Billy coughs out a chuckle. "Really? How's that?"

"It's true I do errands for him. But under the right circumstances, I'm also willing to fuck him."

"And what happens the morning after?"

"He won't know what happened. He's unaware I've got your friend Gina's farewell address. I know you need it. Though I have to ask, would she really want to star in your sophomoric melodrama? Seems like the last project you cast her in had some unfortunate—"

"You better watch your fucking mouth."

"Fine. But if you ever want to see the sequel she made, you'll stop patronizing her demented daddy and deal with me."

"What do you want?"

"A hundred thousand in cash. Delivered by you. In person. No one else and no more games."

Billy considers this for a moment. His lips twist into something resembling a smile. Then he slams the tapered end of his crowbar down into the juncture at the hinges to the door of my cage. Splinters graze my forehead.

"I'll be . . . *in touch*."

He leaves the crowbar, allowing me to begin the long, blistering process of prying my way out.

55

Billy showed unexpected courtesy in also leaving my clothes, so I'm able to ooze home without making an undue spectacle. I arrive at my door exhausted, but assuming that Blake doesn't look kindly upon well-rested employees, I again choose my coffeemaker over my bed.

To follow up on the figurine Ruth Delaney gave me, I check to see if Gina's Ines_Idoru account is still alive. I pull up NOD's sign-in page and enter her NODName, hitting the link for the password hint, which comes back as: d@d.

That seems obvious enough that I should be able to finesse it quickly. I have a program called [p]ass_crack that will spit out intelligent variations on a given string of characters. For example, when I give it "Charles Delaney," it tries "CH@r135 D3!@n3Y," among many other combinations. But none of them are right, so I open up the parameters to include leading and trailing numbers and feed it his birth date, her birth date, and both social security numbers. Still nothing.

Knowing her father's personal deficiencies, I suppose it's unlikely that she'd have wanted to bring him to mind each time she logged in. So let's take the avatar itself: Ines_Idoru. *Idoru* is the title of a William Gibson novel, about a holographic person that a Japanese progressive rocker is planning to marry. Acting out fan fiction is a favorite NOD activity, though most of the energy flows to space opera and X-rated anime. But it makes sense that an intellectual like Gina would name-check a character from one of the classier sci-fi authors. So maybe her hint meant the *idoru*'s father.

The web has only poor plot summaries, so I torrent a copy and start skimming. I gather that Rei Toei, the virtual woman in question, was created by a media conglomerate, not a specific person. I try jamming the corporation name and a number of characters and places from the book into [p]ass_crack. It chugs for a while, but again I get nada.

Frustration warring against fatigue, I check her av name to see if she turns up on any NOD blogs that might give me a clue. Nothing comes back but hits from some Cyrillic language I don't recognize. I'm about to pack it in for the evening when I notice Google asking if, by chance, I might have meant "anesidora" rather than "Ines Idoru."

I didn't, but mindful of NODlings' penchant for wordplay, I click through.

The name, I'm informed, is an alternate spelling for the woman whom Eve displaced as the most significant female ever: Pandora. She of the fabled box that when opened brought everything evil into the world. I pick up Gina's figurine and realize that what I'd blithely assumed was a kimono is actually a stylized ceremonial toga. The jewel-like container's placement over her pelvis refers to a common feminist interpretation of the myth: Pandora's box represents the womb, and the tale is a crude expression of male sexual anxiety.

So who was Pandora's dad? A little reading tells me that while the creation of Pandora was a joint venture, with several deities bestowing various gifts, Hephaestus, that ugly god of fire, blacksmiths, and of course technology, gets the primary credit.

Seconds later, a NOD scene graph is rezzing, and I'm entering the world in Gina's skin.

But Ines_Idoru is a big disappointment. Like a newborn, she's almost completely blank. No inventory, no friends, no favorite places. No evidence of the woman who made her.

Did Gina scrub Ines before she died? But then why would she leave the account alive? Or if this was just a random alt that Gina never really used, why would Billy pick this av to place in her coffin for all eternity?

I'm about to give up in disgust when I notice the box that the av is holding. It doesn't show up in Ines's NObject inventory because she's actually wearing it as an accessory. I select it and bring up the thing's property page. That's where I hit pay dirt. Contained by this box is a list of scripted NObjects. The first lines read:

```
20140203_F0001.215
20140206_M0000.9.3
20140207_F0002.215
20140209_M0000.9.4
20140211_F0003.0
20140213_M0001.0.0
```

They look like successive entries for two objects in an ad hoc version archive, which could be this alt's only purpose. While Gina wanted to obliterate even online traces of *herself,* perhaps she liked the idea of a little bit of her *work* surviving in a forgotten corner of NOD. Maybe this was her last project and held some kind of significance for her, so that she couldn't bear to drag it with her into the void.

I teleport to my private dev sandbox and block-rez a bunch of the NObjects out into the world. When they all finally appear, I'm reminded of that spurious diagram called "The Ascent of Man" that tries to explain how we changed from chimpanzees to Homo sapiens. They're a series of 3D sketches that show a clear evolution from the barest glimmer of a design to two fairly polished mechanisms.

The experience is like seeing baby pictures of your fiancée for the first time. I'm looking at snapshots from the childhood of the Dancers. The last examples show Fred and Ginger very nearly in their current form.

The create dates on all the objects start in early February of last year, and they end four weeks before Gina killed herself.

Five weeks before Olya called the first iTeam meeting.

56

At ten AM, Olya's not in her office or the Orifice. When I call her, I'm surprised to hear that she's working out.

The room on the top floor where I find her is beautiful in the way of ruins. A former dance studio with crumbling brick walls and worn oak flooring. The far side is a huge mirror that has a barre running down its length. The glass is violently cracked, perhaps from the meltdown of a high-strung ballerina. Olya has installed herself in the cool morning rays coming through a mansard window. She's wearing a pale pink halter-style ballet dress and is *en pointe* doing leg lifts. She sees me enter but doesn't stop.

"Zhimbo. What did you want to see me about?"

I watch her for a while, getting lost in her rhythmic movements. Finally I ask, "Our Erotobot operation here was your idea?"

"Idea? They are my children."

"Yeah, but who conceived them?"

One thing I love about Olya is that she catches on quick. You don't have to waste a lot of time with the initial *stupid* lies. She squints at me and snaps out another couple leg lifts. "You know, I wish you'd spend as much time thinking about our glorious future as you do wallowing like a pig in the past."

"Olya, did you steal Fred and Ginger from your dead girlfriend?"

That irritates her. She turns and says, "What is this you're asking? Did

I work with Gina on this? Yes, of course, but it was *our* project, and she's not here anymore. So what do you want me to tell you?"

"Just tell me all of it."

I'm expecting an angry defense, but what comes out is more like an elegy. It's revealing to hear Olya speak without aggression, outside of the imperative case. Her voice is slower and softer; she closes her eyes as if she's really trying to call up the past.

Olya says, "Gina, she is very pretty and nice, and at NYU everyone *likes* her, but she doesn't have any friends. Other than this shit-head Billy, who uses her for his stupid videos. He takes over her apartment for days to make that thing. He forces her to act like this high-tech whore on camera. And then she keeps that horrible torture device afterward to give her dark thoughts. All this because she doesn't know how to say no. I used to see her every day during lunch sitting by herself at this tiny café. I don't know why I care, but it starts to drive me crazy. A woman with these gifts, you know? I decide that we will be friends. I want to help her. So I start sitting with her at boring coffee place."

Olya relates to me how Gina eventually began asking her abstract questions regarding her specialty in exotic materials. Ever direct, Olya soon ferreted out that she was dancing around the idea of simulating flesh, and it became obvious what this inhibited prodigy had in mind. Gina was an *engineer*. She was looking for a material solution to problems residing in her mind. But being a pathologically shy girl overwhelmed with religious guilt, she couldn't take the first step.

Olya sure as hell could, however. When they graduated, she convinced Gina to accept a GAME residency. Their cover project was to create tactile games for blind children, but really they started working in earnest on what would become the Dancers. Gina already had the basic idea and much of the design mapped out. So over the summer, they started prototyping.

She describes how after weeks of searching fruitlessly for a trustworthy source of start-up capital, Gina rolled in and laid a cashier's check for forty thousand dollars on her desk. She said it was from an "anonymous patron," but of course Olya forced Billy's identity from her. She yelled at her that this asshole could not be a partner in their enterprise. But Gina replied, "No, it's a grant. He doesn't even know what the project is." Then she blushed and said that when the Dancers were done, she was going to surprise him with them.

Olya says, "Ginushka goes red as beet. With this silly man she is again acting like a prostitute. But this time for real. I do not like Billy, but this is a lot of money, so I think, *We must be practical.*"

But while Olya couldn't abide the thought of Billy as a long-term partner, she also couldn't help but wonder about the source of his seemingly unlimited wealth. In researching its origins, she figured out who his siblings were and learned from Gina of the estrangement between them. And rumor had it that Blake was an easy touch when it came to new media.

"I think, *Why not?* I have a unique product, maybe he will understand. So I go to his office. You maybe understand that I can get meetings with most men easily. Blake has this very bitchy secretary, so I sit in his waiting room for a long time. Then I see him walk by. She tries to stop me, but for a bitch, she is only a Chi-hua-hua. So I take his arm and say, 'Maybe I know a very good way to torture your little brother.' Blake is interested, so we come to an arrangement."

They worried that Billy knew too much about the project, but they eventually concluded that he probably wouldn't want to mess up their plans out of loyalty to Gina. So he'd be furious he'd been displaced, but impotent—a prospect Blake had found especially appealing. In the end, they decided it didn't matter what Billy did. Blake said, "I can handle my brother."

Everything seemed perfect to Olya.

"So I set up surprise meeting with Gina to tell her this very great news that we finally have a good investor. I think she will be happy, maybe to get rich. She is from poverty, you know. Blake when we meet is smooth, but Gina . . . she is crazy. She says nothing and runs away. I apologize to Blake. He told me before they have this history. Maybe they fuck ten years ago. I tell him I'll talk to her and make everything okay. It's no problem.

"I go back to her place. You know what she is doing? She's in the bath, drunk like a moose. And she is sawing her wrists with a knife. The water is bloody, but they are . . . not deep cuts. She babbles all this religious shit. Verses from the Bible, I think. This is all from her parents, you know. I can understand nothing, so I haul her out and bandage her wrists. I put her in bed . . ."

Olya falters here in her story.

"What?" I ask. But Xan has already told me what's coming.

"And then I make love to her."

She closes her eyes, playing back the evening in her head. Her lips seem to want to tug upward. Then she shrugs. "Ai. It sounds very bad maybe, but I think it works. Gina is not like normal person. She doesn't care about food, clothing, money, where she lives. All she needs is hard problems for her head, and a little love for her heart. But you know, she's so strange, she doesn't get much of that. And she is a wonderful girl. I do love her in certain way."

Olya tells me that in their new relationship, Gina blossomed like a hothouse orchid. She became vivacious, and her newfound energy fed into her work. Gina went from sulking in coffee shops playing *Spore II* to spending all her time in the lab playing Pygmalion.

And Olya knew that her need for Gina was just as strong, because she'd caught the holy fire for teledildonics. "Zhimbo, I think maybe you feel this way, but it's like I was born to do this. When I work, I feel the angels next to me. Maybe they are really devils, but I don't care. So we can't have deal with Blake. Fine. We scrape by until we find someone else."

But while they were building their electrosexual ambitions, Gina's real project morphed into a towering passion for Olya. One that demanded a grand gesture.

"She wants us to move in together. Make all these commitments." She shakes her head at the absurdity. "I find out, the girl, she goes and buys me a ring. She's thinking when our children are ready to be born, we should get married. In Massachusetts." Olya pronounces the state's name as though it's a rarely observed asteroid.

And Olya wasn't the only target for Gina's declarations. Intoxicated with this mad love and resolved to permanent rebellion, she decided to tell her parents. She thought one decisive stroke could free her from a lifetime of resentment against her awful family. Then she could begin building real happiness with her soul mate.

"I don't know what happens when she goes to Boston. I am sure all this seems very unnatural to her parents. But when she comes back, she's like a zombie. She won't work. Doesn't do a thing for a month. She's fucked-up all the time. I try to help her, but she keeps talking all this Bible shit about butt-fucking."

"Sodom?"

"This is butt-fucking, yes?"

"Among other things. So what happened?"

"After weeks of this, I invite her to dinner at this stupid Chuck E. Cheese place she likes. Obsolete video games and rat robots; this is just how she is. I want to try to cheer her up, you know. But she doesn't come. Won't answer her mobile. So I go to her place to look for her."

"And?"

Olya glances down sadly. "And I find her in the bath again. Bleeding." She takes a deep breath and lets it out.

"The cut is again nothing. Used dull scissors. She's not really trying. It's just her craziness. Better if it were like the last time. I make love to her, and everything's all right. But this time she attacked our project. I can't believe it. She cut all the Dancers' wires and then set the laptops on fire."

"What did you do?"

"I took hammer and put a hole in the tub."

I must look dismayed. But Olya doesn't get defensive. Just gives a weak, melancholy shrug.

"Sometimes people need a shock. She's crying like a beaten dog. I don't know half of what she's saying. It's like 'Can you forgive me? Can you forgive me anything?' But I don't want to forgive her for damaging our children. I want her to stop being this crazy bitch. She keeps saying, 'I won't do this anymore. I can't bear it.' I'm tired of her acting so conflicted all the time. So . . ."

At this point in her narrative, Olya pauses for a long time, playing the scene back in her head. Finally she says, "Well, I guess you know I have a very great temper . . . Also, I have not had the easiest life, and . . . I have learned how to hurt people."

She finishes this with a catch in her voice. Her eyes are brimming. I'm astounded that the ice queen is about to melt with only me here to witness. Olya takes a long blink.

I didn't think it was possible to recall tears back into their ducts, but when Olya opens them, her eyes are dry.

"The next night she was dead."

I move to comfort her, but she spurns this and turns back to the barre.

"You can blame me." She shrugs. "Other people do. I knew she was depressed, I put all this pressure on her, I say terrible things to her, and now she's dead. And so it's my fault."

"Olya—"

She puts her hand up. "But I ask, what about her family? I only knew her a year. They had her whole sad fucking life." She flicks her fingers with distaste. "So they tell her she needs Jesus. I say she needs Prozac. But Gina? She decides what she needs is nothing."

"Maybe a little unconditional love would have gone a long way that night."

"Yeah? Or maybe a little less vodka. Or a little less bullshit religion. But too late for that now, is it not?" She slowly rotates back to look at me in the mirror.

I come very close to saying it, but some instinct for self-preservation stops me.

Convenient that she died, isn't it?

But this echo of Billy's question to her sits uneasily. If it's convenient for Olya, it's doubly so for me. If Gina hadn't died, IT might have been in production by now, and I'd just be jerking it at Fleshbot as I wait to find out when I can order one.

I take a different tack. "Thanks for the confession. You have any other revelations about our intellectual property?"

Olya, her face divided crazily by the cracked glass, fixes me with an unreadable expression. "Well, Zhimbo, you think we're being unfair to poor Gina's estate? You should meet her father. Maybe we put him on the board?"

57

My talk with Olya shed some light on Gina's final days. After her death, Olya assembled the iTeam, and of course went back to Blake for money. His initial rejection as a suitor had further piqued his lust. Olya thought she had things under control. "But," she said, "now this *svoloch* Billy is making shit for everybody."

I can also better piece together his state of mind. When Gina dies, he knows enough to have theories about her reasons. And he knows who to blame. He tries to bury with her a figure not of her main av, but rather the one she used to store her Dancer mock-ups. He asks Olya, "Are you happy now?"

Thinking about how I started to unravel this story brings to mind the other party whose grief over Gina seemed as keen as Billy's: her mother. I feel like she deserves to know what I've discovered.

I'm relieved when she picks up the phone, and after thanking her for the figurine and memory stick, I say, "I just wanted to tell you that I acquired the video your daughter recorded of her death. I don't think you'll want to see it."

"No, I guess not." She pauses for a long time, fighting to control her voice. Finally, in a high, plaintive tone, she asks, "But why did she record it? Does she say anything?"

"She says, 'I guess you thought I'd play the daughter of Lot, but I will not.'" I wait to see what she makes of that, but only silence follows. "I could tell you what I believe she meant, to see if it accords with your—"

"No, Mr. Pryce." Hearing her daughter's last words is too much for Ruth Delaney. Her voice breaks as she says, "I've heard enough."

Then she hangs up.

So I'm left to interpret Gina's death for myself. What exactly did she mean by that laconic rhyme? She obviously shared an interest with Billy in Genesis 19: the chronicle of the Lord spending his utmost wrath upon sexual deviants. Lot's virgin daughters were to be sacrifices to a throng of Sodomites. So perhaps Gina identified with them in that she felt she was being forced into serving, through her invention, the lusts of the mob.

But I'm puzzled by her close identification with the Dancers. Why would she have equated Olya's commercialization of them with *her* being savaged by the masses? One hears self-aggrandizing artists talk about the sales process as a form of rape. But that's not a perspective native to engineers. Also, if she truly abhorred pandering to the global umma of perverts, why didn't she just destroy the things? Instead she damaged them superficially and focused on destroying herself.

She knew from previous attempts she didn't have the force of will to drive the blade home. So, like she'd done all her life, she built a mechanism to solve the problem. She looked around for the right materials, and her eyes lit on Billy's garrote. Maybe she recalled the video they made together. Might release from her strangling desperation feel akin to that burst of ecstasy her character achieved when the jack popped into her neck?

Yet the record of her last moments shows the opposite happened.

I doubt I'll ever know all the reasons behind Gina's sad demise, but clearly Billy feels like he understands them well enough. He holds his brother and Olya responsible for her death, and now he wants to put them under the same level of mental strain they placed on her. By making himself the Genghis Khan of cyberbullies with his game.

A game that will be rolling through embarrassing family revelations just as public scrutiny heats up on Blythe's deal. Billy surely knows that in attacking Blake now, the blow will really fall most heavily on Blythe. He would hope the damage then multiplies even further in the pain-reflecting echo chamber of the twins' relationship.

But to complete his oeuvre, he needs the record of his heroine's swan song, something only I can give him. So if Billy wants to play games with it, he's going to have to come to the table.

58

The final words Billy spoke through the slats of my crate were, "I'll be in touch." Thirty-six hours later, I'm driving myself nuts with the worry that I've completely mistaken his need for Gina's death video.

Just as I'm starting to brainstorm new "operational concepts" for a surely unpleasant meeting with Blake, his brother finally deigns to make contact. But he's not reaching out to me; his message comes to Jacques.

In NOD, I find orders for the next *Savant* Degree sent from Madame Martaine. As tired as I am of this nonsense, which has yet to produce any concrete lead, I still open it greedily. The virtual parchment says:

> *Searching for service to the Duc de Blangis?*
> *Please look at my pictures, and soon you will see*
> *Just what you can do to be helpful to me.*

The word "pictures" links to a server hosting a huge library of images.

I zip up all 14,400 and forward them to Red Rook's code quarry. Then I dig in myself.

The unifying theme: women doing violence to other women. Of course, most are lesbian bondage shots, and I'm distressed to see such lovely anatomy so thoroughly abused. Intercalated among all the pinching and probing, I find other categories. Stills from the recent YouTube craze for brawl videos of teenage girls, mothers slapping daughters, soccer harpies dragging opponents to the ground by their hair, and morgue photos of the rare woman murdered by another female. They're Billy's bitter comment on Olya and Gina's relationship I guess.

My cypher-punks return disappointing results: none of the files hold encoded information. So cracking this puzzle won't be as easy as the last one. They're seeking other avenues, but the inquiries will take time. Which leaves me to stew over the images.

I know they carry some kind of message, and Billy probably designed this kind of challenge to frustrate automated analysis. Maybe he wants to force his players to really immerse themselves in his assemblage of gynolence.

They click by for hours as I make detailed notes. But not only do I fail to determine a pattern beyond the obvious, I can't even see a method by which I'd ever find one. How can one be expected to trace all the possible connections among such a mass of complex photographs?

I return to my starting assumption: these files must be telling me something. But what if the individual pictures are relatively meaningless, and their secret resides only in the *collection*? How do you view a series of images collectively? You place them on the table and then stand back.

But that raises the problem of how to arrange them. A linear layout seems unlikely. So how, then? What's the best way to organize 14,400 files? How could one determine the right structure a priori?

I look back at Martaine's message, but there's no hidden verbiage there. Just these thousands of shots mocking me with their intractable quantity.

But that's just it: their *quantity*. The *number* of photos describes the only correct form: a square. 14,400 is the square of a particularly relevant number. Once again, Billy's riddle provides a self-validating solution. The number that multiplied by itself equals 14,400?

120.

A couple minutes using a photomosaic program to make a square of files 120 to a side leaves me with a picture composed of Billy's photos, each one representing a single pixel. Together they reveal the sublime visage of Olya Zhavinskaya.

My new target.

— — —

The crypto department comes back a bit later having determined that if you source Billy's images from the web, you find that the first letters of the file names for each one combine to form an acrostic text.

The message is 165 characters followed by meaningless garbage. It reads:

Our prey resides at 290 Grand second floor
So this evening be sure to keep your eyes on her door
Report when she leaves and observe where she goes
And the Divinest of torments will be mine to impose

Billy's demanding that Jacques assist in his attempt to spoil Olya's evening stroll.

Getting this order right now sets off internal warning bells, but a quick scan of the *Savant* box reassures me that Jacques was probably chosen for his skills, not because Billy's identified me as his player. Assuming he'd select someone from GAME to surveil Olya, he's got forty players to choose from. Only ten of us enjoy Innoculyte status, and six have completed RL missions. Of those, two seem to have quit the game shortly after, and one deleted his NOD profile entirely. With Red Rook's help, I tend to solve puzzles the fastest among the remaining four, so it's no surprise that Billy might call on Jacques if he needed someone to tail Olya.

I'm sorely tempted to ignore the directive, but the last line of the poem implies Billy's going to take a very personal interest in this exploit. Might he even show up himself for the most severe humiliation yet of his favorite target? I can't risk losing a chance at him.

Thinking it through, I realize there's another risk I can't afford:

Telling Olya what's about to happen to her.

I had expected Billy's maniacal minions to do their worst on the way over to GAME. But Olya arrived for her evening work session without incident. Luckily it's cold out, so with sunglasses, a scarf, and my parka hood, I can obscure my face enough to avoid recognition should Billy actually show up. I monitor the exits from the bodega on the opposite corner, sending periodic status updates back to Madame Martaine.

Since my first real break came from following Olya back to her apartment, wouldn't it be just perfect if I finally caught up with Billy after trying it again?

At midnight, she emerges from the rear alley and takes a right. I follow well behind her. Every pedestrian out this evening looks sinister, each glance broadcasting malice until they move past. Twice over the seven-block route I break into a run as some kind of van pulls up next to her.

But nothing happens.

I watch the door to Olya's building shut behind her. What went wrong? While Billy's assets are certainly amateurs, his gross little productions so far have come off quite well for him.

You're missing something.

I pull up her number on my phone but can't quite think of what to say.

A light comes to life in her second-floor apartment. The tall windows are obscured by a translucent shade, but they allow me a view of her silhouette stepping forward to draw together the heavy inner curtains. Only . . .

Only it's not her silhouette.

The contours of Olya's shadow would easily merit an R rating, and I just saw the mundane lines and angles of a skinny man.

I run across the street, dismissing the idea of the police right away. I can't be sure she's in any real danger, and she'll kill me if in trying to help her, I end up getting her deported. I hurtle down the alley on the short side of her L-shaped building and see a rusty fire escape dangling from its back. I have to climb a chain-link fence and carefully navigate a slack coil of razor wire, but from the top of the fence, I can just leap to catch the bottom of the steel walkway.

My first view of her apartment shows a cavernous industrial space held up by exposed brick pylons. The room is layered with luxurious fabrics and filled with low, bed-like furniture.

A motion catches my eye through the window at the far end of the fire escape. I creep over for a better look and see four men in Olya's sitting room arrayed as though on the set of some gonzo porn production.

Two of them are pressing a gagged Olya face-first into a column. A heavyset South Asian with a wolfman beard is trying to handcuff her to a chain thrown over a high wall sconce, but he's only secured one hand. His partner is a grizzled biker wearing a sleeveless leather vest to display his welter of violent Nordic prison tats. He slices at the back of Olya's shirt with a large butterfly knife. Naturally, Olya is *resisting*.

The other men are setting up the gear. A skinny geek with an atrocious grin and Manson bug-eyes has trouble suppressing his excitement as he rigs a hi-def video camera. To his left, a tall guy in a black trench coat with waist-length brown hair done up in a topknot types into a laptop resting on Olya's coffee table. At his studded belt dangles a cat-o'-nine-tails with thick leather straps knotted at the ends. Not the modern prop of safe-and-sane naughtiness but a tool designed to rend flesh.

On the laptop's screen I can see a video feed of a man's face. The window's too small to tell for sure, but I'm distraught to think Billy's decided to witness this via teleconference. Topknot takes out his whip and turns to observe his comrades' struggle with Olya.

Prison Tats has her shirt ripped up its length from the bottom, but the collar has presented difficulties.

Topknot flicks the leather whip against his opposite hand.

Olya wrenches violently, causing Prison Tats to lose patience. He presses his blade hard against her neck. A line of blood smears her throat as she writhes. I have to move.

I charge down the length of the fire escape and pull my jacket up over my face at the last second before I hurl myself into the window. The glass crashes inward, and I'm able to roll as I hit the floor.

Which would be great, except for my Glock jarring loose from my waistband. It flies across the room, caroms off the bottom of a bookshelf, and then slides behind Olya's love seat.

There's no time to mourn its loss. Everyone breaks into furious motion as the split-second shock of my arrival vanishes. Despite seeming the fiercest of the group, Topknot grabs the laptop, tears open the front door, and runs from the room.

I've regained my feet and lunge toward the South Asian guy, slamming my forehead between his eyes. He goes down with a girlish screech.

Prison Tats is a lot faster. He drops into a passable knife-fighting stance and aims an overhand slash at my face. But my first opponent falls awkwardly against his legs, so his swipe gets my jacket, rather than me. He nimbly steps over his colleague while he reverses the stroke.

I'm about to be stabbed to death.

What neither of us anticipated is Olya's right leg arcing up in a perfect roundhouse. Her foot slams into the guy's mouth. That staggers him enough that I'm able to grab his knife hand and ram into him. He drops his blade as he hits the floor, and I kneel on his ribs to drop an elbow into his eye. Olya unhooks her chain from the light fixture.

A piercing, tremulous scream stays my follow-up blow.

"Stop! I'll blow your motherfucking brains out!"

I'd assigned the Geek such a low threat priority, I nearly forgot he was still in the room. Now I'm shocked to see him standing by the couch jerkily pointing my gun at me. Beads of sweat appear on his forehead.

I throw my hands up and stand. Prison Tats rolls over groaning. The South Asian man takes the opportunity to stumble from the room, cupping his broken nose.

The manic glint in the Geek's eye makes me imagine a man who never had the guts to take out his homeroom, but now relishes the feel of a loaded gun in his hand. His chance to take charge.

I say, "Hey, everything's going to be fine here, just—"

He shouts, making an effort to deepen his voice. "Shut up! Who the fuck are you?"

"Eh! Tiny Dick, who the fuck are you? In my home!" Olya yells back. She's leaning against the corner of the column, but I can see her right hand slowly reach for something behind her. Prison Tats spits blood and tries to get to his feet.

"Shoot this fucker," he hisses to the Geek.

I say, "Look, man, I don't know what you've been told, but please listen to me. The police are on their way, and you need to get out of here. This is *not* a game."

Awful choice of words. My last phrase is the very mantra of the Alternate Reality genre.

Prison Tats picks up his knife and advances on Olya. "Now get that shirt off before I have to cut it off. And I ain't going to be so careful about it this time."

The Geek adds, "Do it, bitch!"

Olya glares at him but then slowly tugs at the button to her collar.

Wanting to force the issue, Prison Tats bellies up to her and jerks at the front of her blouse with his free hand. Olya leans in so the tip of his knife is just past her left shoulder. Then she brings her other hand around fast. A liter vodka bottle from the bar cart behind her shatters into the side of his head. He takes two drunken steps back before collapsing.

The Geek twitches the pistol at her, but she pays no heed and marches toward him, brandishing the bottle's jagged neck.

"Shoot me, *goluboi!*"

The Geek considers it.

I place my hand out to stop her while I desperately try to think of the right button to push with him. "You're going to fuck your real life forever if you don't leave now. Things can't be nearly as bad as sharing a cell block with guys like that." I gesture toward Prison Tats lying inert on the floor.

"And also I cut off your balls," Olya adds, pressing closer.

He turns the pistol sideways. Breathing heavy, working himself into a lather.

I step in front of Olya. "This stupid game is not worth it."

Again, probably the wrong thing to say. His face sets as though he's made a decision. He flicks the safety.

A moment of pure terror. His knuckles go white on the trigger.

He's squeezing.

Harder than necessary, I realize. Since I had the safety off when I burst in, the Geek has actually disabled the gun.

I charge at him.

Though the gun failed to fire, I fail to appreciate that it remains a weapon. The Geek throws it hard into my face, nailing me above my left eye. The explosion of pain makes me stumble to one knee. He runs out the door.

Olya goes after him but pulls up lame after leaving several bloody footprints on the way to her door. Glass shards from the broken bottle. I wipe my eye and try to catch up, but the Geek skids down the final stairs and out into the night before I've made the first landing.

Back upstairs, I find Olya ignoring what must be severe pain to stomp on Prison Tats's fingers. He remains unconscious. I embrace her and gently lead her away. She places a hand over her mouth, breathing in deep gasps as the event catches up with her.

I rub her back and whisper soothing nonsense. Olya submits to this for longer than I'd expect. But suddenly she draws back and skewers me with a calculating stare. Her eyes narrow.

"Zhames. Why are you here right now? How did you know to come?"

I don't have a good answer for her.

59

Over coffee the next morning, I cast around for something positive about the events of last night. Since tossing me out after my avowal that I'd happened to drop by in hopes of romance, Olya has ignored all my calls. I have to assume my entrance last night was recorded, so now Billy must know I'm the player behind Jacques_Ynne. Leaving me right back in the tedious position of waiting for him to make a move.

His first sally comes at six PM. I'm about to log off from NOD when Jacques gets a message from Louis_Markey that says:

> I have to conclude that you wanted to see
> What I had in store for the evening's Plan B.

Below that is a NObject link that gives me a short video file titled She Loves Me Not #1.

Rosa stands naked and shivering, her back pressed up against a filthy green-tiled wall. She's bound spread-eagle with rusty chains to a steel framework. A bright light washes out her skin to the tone of a cadaver. She squints, a strip of duct tape across her mouth. From above dangle more chains, each of them terminating in a wicked hook, like something you'd find at the end of an amusement park pirate's arm.

A hissing voice from off camera says, "Let us hear her."

Two men wearing black velvet executioner's masks and long rubber gloves step to either side of her. One rips the tape off her mouth.

Rosa begs. "Please. Please. I'll do anything you want—"

The man on her left kneads the flesh of her shoulder as if seeking to comfort her.

But then the other one sinks in the first hook.

Rosa screams herself hoarse.

I force myself to watch until the end, when they hoist her into the air by the six huge hooks they've stuck in her back. Her flesh pulls into grotesque Vs, and she leaves a trail of blood as she's dragged up the wall.

This can't be real.

But . . . the close-ups on the hooks' insertion. The way she screams. They go out of their way to *demonstrate* that it's real, and I can't see how Billy could fake it.

And if it's real, then Billy truly has gone bug-fuck. That he'd take out his rage at my disrupting his plans for Olya by punishing Rosa in this way defies comprehension. His brother has been constantly talking about how crazy he is, and I'd always put that down to fraternal rancor. But now . . .

Did Gina's death really damage him so much that he's actually drowned his former self in this Sadean cesspool? That he's let his noxious experiment infect his own imagination?

Given Billy's previous manipulations, I can't completely trust what I've just seen. But clearly something awful is happening.

60

Rosa's video demands that I make inquiries to the DC police's missing persons department in a futile attempt to figure out who she is. Though I'm racked with equal measures of guilt, helplessness, and doubt, I cling to the hope that Billy will have no choice but to contact me again.

While trying to think of ways to bait him, I swing by the Orifice to see if Olya's shown up. There I find Garriott head-down on a worktable, a section of his bangs being slowly singed to carbon by a soldering iron he's left on. Perhaps Olya hasn't yet told our partners about last night's events. Which gives me time to get a better story together.

I think to wake him, but he needs his rest and will probably see his style by fire as a badge of geek honor.

On my way out of the building, I get a text from Louis_Markey:

```
Center fountain in Washington Square Park. One hour.
Bring an iPod with the video on it.
```

My fingers nearly spasm with excitement as I put in the call to McClaren.

Fifty minutes later I'm sitting on the edge of the giant circular cement fountain under a gray sky trying to spot either Billy or components of McClaren's "executive" team he's had standing by for the past weeks.

I've just met some of the principals. Three intense, wiry gentlemen in forgettable business casual, but with very expensive sunglasses. McClaren explained that my role was simply to show Billy part of the video and then demand the hundred thousand dollars. They would handle the rest, and one of them even insisted on confiscating my gun as a "potential distraction." When I raised the issue of witnesses—morning commuters crowded the park—the team leader said, "Sir, you will not ever see us. We are very good at this. We could pick him up right in front of the NYPD, and no one would notice."

He was right. Looking around at the mass of humanity traversing the wide plaza, everyone seems suspicious, but no one particularly stands out.

I take a moment to gut-check my role in this "involuntary commitment." At first, I thought that if Billy was crazy, his madness was the high-functioning sociopathic kind, not the delusional "danger to self and others" type normally required to treat someone against their will. But the turns his game has taken lately point to the latter.

Now I'm thinking that if Billy's such a fan of the Marquis de Sade, then an asylum will be the perfect place for him to gain a better understanding of the man's work.

Billy is late. My ass is getting sore from the concrete, so I stand up and stretch. My phone starts vibrating from a text:

```
[C12@192.0.2.117 ProSoap Alert]
Cam 12 - Unrecognized - conf .89
```

I'm about to ignore the message when I remember that camera 12 is the one in the alley at the back of GAME that leads into the POD. The only people it ever sees are GAME residents, and I've only gotten a handful of alerts on it. I pull up a low-res stream.

It's no wonder the face comes up unrecognized. The person standing in front of the doors is wearing large wraparound shades and has a black baseball cap pulled low. But what stand out are the guy's high cheekbones and extreme pallor.

It's Billy. He's decided not to make our meeting. He brandishes a security card at the camera and runs it through the reader. Then he bends down and picks up two items lying beside him. The first is a small gray duffel bag, and the second is a comically large sledgehammer with a short but very fat cylindrical head. He's traded his crowbar for a post maul. I'm sure Billy chose the tool for its aesthetic properties: the proverbial blunt instrument.

He hefts it and then takes a lazy swipe at the camera. The signal goes dead.

Oh no. Our plan is falling apart. Looks like Billy had a different one.

I radio McClaren and tell him the news. There's a brief silence, and then he says, "Okay. Sit tight. We'll get him."

I feel deflated, like the starting quarterback getting unaccountably benched before kickoff. It occurs to me that Garriott is probably still in the Orifice. I'm not sure what Billy's intentions are—though the presence of the post maul provides some insight—but it's worth warning Garriott to lock the room and stay there until we get this under control. I try his cell, but it goes right to voicemail. Concerned, I pull up the bank of camera feeds from one of our tracking systems. Front_Cam_B shows a wide shot of the Orifice. To my dawning terror, Garriott's not there, but Ginger is. She's sitting right in the middle of the worktable. In his sleep-deprived delirium, Garriott must have forgotten to put her in our safe before he stepped out. I picture Billy's hammer coming down hard on her head.

I take off toward the southeast corner of the park, thinking about the odds of getting a cab during rush hour. Then I see a hippie walking toward me with a beat-up ten-speed. I careen up to him and grab the handlebars.

"Buddy. I need your bike. It's a matter of life and death. Take this."

I flip my money clip at him, and he catches it with his free hand. Seeing a hundred-dollar bill wrapping the outside, any thought of resistance leaves him, and he steps back, allowing me to mount up.

I hear him say, *"Vaya con dios,"* as I sprint away.

I'm amazed at the time I make. It's just over a mile from Washington Square Park to GAME, and pedaling furiously, I'm halfway there in less than two minutes. Normally, riding the way I am, I'd have been mowed down by a bus before I hit Lafayette. But as fate would have it, traffic is completely gridlocked the whole way.

I jump off the bike in the alley behind GAME and check myself briefly at the cellar doors Billy left open. The crushed wreckage of the video camera reminds me that I am unarmed, and that it's often best to treat a man with a mallet delicately.

I grab the top lip of the entrance and swing myself down without stepping on the noisy metal staircase. I sink behind a large bank of rusting industrial detritus and listen.

A motor whines along with a high-frequency scraping sound. I see Billy kneeling at the door to the Orifice using a handheld angle grinder on its edge. His choice of tools is commendable, because the noise will cover my approach.

I slink down the hall. Billy doesn't look up until I wrench his grinder away from the door.

I say, "I take it you're going to want to reschedule."

He grins. "Yeah. There's been a change in plans."

Seeing him smile at me in triumph when it's quite clear that I'm going to kick his ass and then hand him over to the dubious care of his brother tells me he really is living in another dimension.

"What did you do with that girl? You little—"

Then I feel something to my right. I don't know if it's a slight shift in the air, but I start turning too late. There's a soft click, and the muscles along my vertebrae seize up in succession like a row of toppling dominos. My entire musculoskeletal system ceases functioning. The sensation is not unlike having your man die in a first-person shooter. You don't always notice the shot that takes your life bar to zero, you just find suddenly that your guy is no longer responding to your input, and then the camera crashes to the ground.

I hit my head hard on the doorjamb on the way down. The last thing I see is the man who gave Olya the necklace sneering at me from above. His lips move in some vindictive epithet, but I can't decipher it. In one hand he's got a sparking stun baton. In the other, a liquid-soaked rag that he's bringing toward my face.

61

McClaren appears above me with a terrifying expression of concern. "Are you all right?"

I run through a system check. My head confirms that it hurts like hell. I can see and hear. Basic mental functions seem to be in order. I can feel my extremities, but—and here's where some triple-distilled horror pours in—I can't move them.

My answer: "No."

McClaren sees me trying to wriggle into a position where I can see what's wrong with my arms. He puts calming hands on my shoulders and says, "Let me untie you, killer."

Before McClaren sent me to the emergency room, I established that Billy made no further attempt to get into the Orifice. So Ginger remained intact. The break-in was just a ruse to get me down there and out from under McClaren's security umbrella, so that he could steal my iPod, and with it, Gina's suicide video. While things are well shy of good, at least the worst case didn't happen.

I'm even able to spare a little admiration for Billy. Since disappearing, he's been hunted by a team of trained professionals, and so far he's run circles around us with his illusionist's ability to make us look the wrong way while he pulls off the trick.

I go home and sleep for a blissful two hours before I'm roughly shaken awake by McClaren. I stutter out a question about why he can't ring my fucking doorbell, but he interrupts. "Get up. Your boss wants a debrief on this morning's tscrewnami."

I've worked with Blake for a month, and this is the first time I've been in his office. He begins with, "Do you want to tell me how the fuck this happened?"

"I'm sorry. Events got out of hand. Your brother engineered everything from the beginning. Our meeting was a ploy." McClaren had filled in the details on the way over. "He used traffic barriers to create a circular detour that snarled traffic all around the Lower East Side just so our team couldn't get down to GAME. Even the guy I got the bike from was probably a plant. We should have been prepared for something like this. Setting up carefully rigged scenes is, after all, what Billy does best. We need to determine how he knew about the team we had in place."

"No, you need to *determine* whether you're capable of doing this job."

So here it finally is. The imperious master lecturing his deficient servant. We're not old college buddies anymore. I want to reply that I was the only one of his underlings who was able to locate his brother in the first place. I'm tempted to offer my resignation, but then I think about the Dancers and stifle the impulse. Luckily, Blake is winding up for a diatribe that doesn't require any input.

"You take off half-cocked into a situation where you're not in control, and without backup? We have a team of ex-SEALs on retainer, and somehow my little brother *subdues* you, and now we've lost the only real leverage we had over him. This is your progress over the last several weeks? Forgive me if I sound less than thrilled."

"Blake, I told you at the outset—"

"You've told me a lot of things, but my brother is still out there fucking with me!"

I'm almost relieved when I hear the strains of a smooth jazz cover of Metallica's "Master of Puppets" issue from my BlackBerry. I'd selected the song for alerts that Billy's av has appeared in *Savant*. "Looks like he wants to join the conversation."

I lean over Blake's laptop and log in to NOD.

Louis_Markey is standing at Château de Silling's gate. He's got audio chat turned on, so we hear him say, "Hello, James. Sorry about our mis-understanding earlier. But these things can happen when you make your-self the plaything of monsters."

"Monsters? Where's Rosa, Billy?"

He ignores my question. "And speaking of which, I take it my brother is there with you?"

How could he know that? Probably tracing our IP to an IMP domain. Or maybe just a good guess after the day's events. I hesitate to answer him.

But Blake presses on. In a faux conciliatory tone he says, "I think it's time we sat down and talked, Billy. Resolved our differences. Let's straighten things out once and for all."

This draws a distorted laugh from the laptop's speakers. Billy adds, "It's too late for that, Blake."

"It's never too late for a new beginning."

"Actually, I think an ending is long overdue. See Blake, I know ev-erything now. I know what you've done. And it's time that you received judgment."

Blake snaps, "Jesus Christ, Billy. You *are* a delusional little poseur. You don't even believe in God."

"But I believe in retribution. And where better to find inspiration than the Good Book? Are you prepared to be judged, Blake? To feel the flames of righteous vengeance?"

"You really played too much Dungeons and Dragons as a child."

"Blake, you're a seeker of strange flesh. Get ready to suffer for it."

"These threats won't look good at your commitment hearing."

I'm not sure Blake should have openly declared his agenda like that, but Billy's already gone.

Blake pushes away from his desk in nearly terminal frustration. He starts making crabbed "You see?" gestures. But then he subsides back into his chair. We stare at each other for what seems like a long time.

He lets out a tired breath. "You have any idea what he's talking about?"

I think about his question. "Well, this is coming just after he saw the video of his friend Gina's suicide. He believes you bear some responsibil-ity for that."

"That's ridiculous."

"Even so. How exactly were you connected with Gina?"

"I'm not."

"Blake, I know she invented the Dancers. So there's no point in hiding the truth here. I'm on your team, remember?"

"Okay. She helped in getting the project off the ground. But I was just brought in as an investor through Olya. Gina was the engineer. I only met with her once."

This is a Blake I never knew in college. This Blake is uncomfortable. On edge. Given his earlier severity, I'm disinclined to make things easier for him. "But you knew her before that. Didn't you?"

He starts to answer, but we're distracted by sudden motion on his laptop. In *Savant*, apparently the world is ending.

The meteors come screaming in from a high angle in the western sky. They're beautiful: startling confections of flame effects and smoky particle systems. His graphics card gives a hitch of admiration as the screen fills with fire.

Then they're upon us. The first clips one of Silling's towers, smashing it and sending stones and masonry into a small group of avs who are watching the spectacle. The meteor buries itself into a nearby mountainside, causing a massive explosion. The ground quakes as two more hit, one much closer to Jacques, and then the whole world vanishes in the inferno.

With the chaos of fire, ash, and airborne earth, visibility shrinks to a few feet. Still, I can see several avs remain standing. All of us are on fire, our avs' clothes and hair incinerated almost instantly. We're treated to the abnormal sight of people watching themselves combust, saying things like "Kewl" and "WTF!?!"

Eventually my avatar freezes. I rotate the camera around him and see that poor Jacques has become a charcoal cinder, now rapidly eroding in the raging winds. Moments later, he's completely gone, and all I can see is the fire and, through an occasional gap in the haze, the ruins of Billy's chamber of horrors.

Quite a show. But what does it mean? Why all the wanton, albeit virtual, destruction?

And more destruction follows. NOD suddenly crashes, but not back to the desktop. Sitting there on a black screen is a lonely blinking cursor.

I try to restore Windows, but Billy seems to have formatted Blake's hard drive as a Parthian shot. And that means he must have compromised his brother's laptop some time ago. Which would be an easy way to monitor Blake's activities. But why would Billy scuttle such a valuable asset? Perhaps, like he said, he really thinks he does "know everything."

I say, "You're going to need a new laptop."

But Billy's just getting started.

Blake's office door opens to reveal Blythe. She looks over her shoulder and then back at us. "What's going on, Blake? What did you do to him?" Her voice is low and freighted with tension.

"What are you talking about?"

"I'm talking about *that*." Her arm shoots out toward the frosted-glass ambient display on Blake's bookcase that indicates movement in IMP's stock by changing colors. It's turned a bloody crimson and has started pulsing ominously. "*That* is our stock collapsing!"

"What? Wait . . . Why do you think it's my fault?"

"It's Billy. He's trying to dump his entire trust into the open market. I've called Ger. He's going to have the NYSE suspend trading for the rest of the day."

The red globe begins flashing more urgently. Blythe closes her eyes.

She says, "We'll discuss it later. Right now, you need to call your bankers and get liquid. You and I are going to step in and absorb some of this or we will have panic selling come Monday."

"Wait, Blythe, I can't really—"

"You can, and you will. I don't need to tell you what this is going to do to our deal with TelAmerica."

"Now, let's just calm down a second."

Blythe makes an exasperated "please the court" gesture at his stock indicator. "Let me ask again, what did you—two—do?"

Blake falls into aphasia. "I . . . I—"

I've never seen Blake at a loss for words. He's rattled. His brother is getting to him.

"I have to testify in front of Congress next month with this shit going on? I can't work while I'm always worrying about one of you exploding a bomb under me. I can't live like this. Blake, please"—here her voice breaks—"is it never going to stop?"

Blake is up like a shot, taking her in his arms. I assume this is my cue to leave. On my way out, I see written on Blake's face a plan to exchange every tear shed by his sister for a liter of Billy's blood.

Blake stops me with a sharp, "James."

"Yes?"

"I'd hate to think you've been subject to conflicting priorities recently."

I squint at him, not sure what he means. Is he talking about the Dancers?

He adds, "Find my brother before the bell on Monday. Or we'll need to find someone who can."

62

Billy still isn't done.

I soon learn that his virtual firestorm was but a fitting prelude to the digital mayhem he's unleashed.

Only a few minutes after I leave Blake's office, an emergency email alert arrives saying that Billy's hacked an IMP server. I have a couple of their tech people pull me a disk image. Live for only minutes before they shut it down, the box is filled with the stuff of IT personnel nightmares.

Billy had reconfigured the server as his own NOD node. I set it up on a clean machine and rez in Jacques to find a duplicate of Château de Silling after the meteor blitz. Only the blackened shell of the castle remains.

However, that leaves the dungeon intact.

And the dungeon has changed. Rebuilt as a prison for the avatars of Billy's players, each of its cells contains the skin of someone who signed on to the game. Since his labyrinth now stretches hundreds of levels into the bowels of Silling's mountain, I gather that nearly a quarter million people have at least dropped in to check out his creation.

I walk through the dank halls, taking in the vast array of avs he's captured. There's something wrong with these skins. Billy has removed all privacy protections on their users' underlying profiles.

Even worse: all of the avs' RL names and addresses appear convincing. I punch a few into the Experian credit bureau database, and they each come back current and accurate. As does phone number, marital status, and occupation. Billy has tied real identities to all these avatars. Looks like *Savant*'s special NOD plug-ins contained some nasty surprises.

Nastier still are their inventories. They're stuffed with way more text, image, and video files than one normally picks up in-world. An aggregation of dirty data that seems to represent anything untoward these people have ever seen online. Billy must have developed some kind of automated system to sift their hard drives for the "naughty bits." Maybe he's reversed one of the flesh-tone and bad-word filters kid-friendly internet companies use to exclude adult content.

Browsing through the videos, I find a mix of *Savant* creations, amateur porn (including some hidden-camera stuff), and genre porn: fetish, bestiality, torture, child. The volume and variety would astonish even the Divine Marquis. I dredge up note cards containing lewd chats with mistresses, employees, and even a babysitter. There's evidence of infidelity, abuse, and some serious crimes.

To refute any claims of innocence, Billy provides links to forensic support, including full hard drive images. He instrumented his hapless victims' computers with all sorts of system monitoring: browsing histories, screen capture, and keystroke logging. The first selection I check shows a Kansas City paramedic logging out of her wedding website. Then she punches in a password to Adultfriendfinder.com. Next I look for my own name, and I'm relieved to see that Red Rook's custom security suite has prevented Billy from completely defiling my system. But many, many others haven't been so fortunate.

Ms. Charlene Sweatmon, of Champagne-Urbana, IL, mother of three, created a series of lush videos of *120 Days* vignettes, including the notorious "sticky toilet seat" interlude. Dave Loeffler's Little League team might like to view his NOD wedding video in which he marries a ten-year-old boy. Glenn Ricardo of Tempe, AZ, is a middle school English teacher who likes commanding (in very colorful language) amputees to coat themselves with tapioca pudding. Ernie Lemuel seems to have a regrettably close relationship with his Labradoodle. Just by dipping my toe in this torrent of twisted video, I can tell that many of the worst offenders are the Pyrexian Innoculytes.

Trusting that I have a pretty good sense of Billy's dramatic instincts at this point, I pilot my av to the bottom of the dungeon.

True to form, he's tricked out the lowest level as a sort of antechamber to hell, complete with stalactites dripping blood and a fiery lake. In the middle is an island on which two avatars are seated in gilded skull thrones. The Duc de Blangis, the leader of Sade's Friends from *120 Days,* is represented by Dr_B_Longey, a handsome re-creation of Robert Randall at his predatory peak. Next to him is Fedor_Sett standing in for Blake.

Dr_B_Longey has a single video file in his inventory. Billy has spliced together a concise summary of his father's dubious business deals along with an account of his many crimes against his family. Among others, there's the clip of Billy's mother displaying the dire effects of their bedroom activity. A kitchen argument that degenerates into his beating her with a spatula and then coming after the cameraman. A particularly harrowing episode of his stuffing Billy's face into a toilet.

Blake's profile contains his personal information (for "occupation," Billy cheekily entered "Malefactor of Great Wealth") but no media. He has a single note card, which reads:

```
One day his plagues will overtake him:
    death, mourning, and famine.
He will be consumed by fire,
    for mighty is the one who judges him.
```

That turns out to be Revelation 18:8 with the gender of the pronouns changed. The original passage refers to the Whore of Babylon, a typically subtle dig at Blake. His use of "one day" implies that, though he seems intent on judging his brother for his crimes, Billy has started the trial by granting him a continuance.

Why would he do that? Is it simple showmanship, building suspense for his audience? Or maybe he believes Blake is liable to commit even greater villainy than his father, and Billy simply wants to wait until all the evidence is in.

My friend Eeyore sees the biblical dimensions of Billy's leak as well. He texts me:

```
Pornaggedon draws nigh.
```

I call him to see what he's learned.

"You think a lot of innocent perverts are going to be spraying their morning coffee all over their computer screens?"

"James, I've just determined that our congressman collects crush videos. Women in high heels mashing insects mostly, which is a relief. The attorney general of Delaware has footage with, ah, various mammals."

"How did you rez in?"

"No, James. Not NOD. I'm using the web database our target has helpfully provided. A nice Flash interface for the casual browser."

I pull up the link he sends me and can't resist trying a few searches to get my head around it. After sorting by occupation, I'm not too surprised to see several state reps, a judge, seven clergy, two semifamous actors, and a child welfare specialist among those indulging some peculiar tastes. Though I'm sure these people *will be* surprised to have their private delights so publicly exposed.

Eeyore says, "He's even got pictures of most people. And linked their addresses to Google Maps."

"I'm glad I finally have some icebreakers for when I see the neighborhood celebrities in the deli."

"If you can fight through the camera scrum."

I check the magnitude of the disclosure. Billy has just shy of a million people pinned to his digital Styrofoam. Like a collection of exotic insects he neglected to suffocate before display, their legs still twitching. That's a far bigger group than just his *Savant* players, and there's something else strange about the data.

"Eeyore, how can this database be *growing*?"

"We don't know yet. Probably some kind of worm. Maybe he's got black hats on the payroll. We have the trawl nets out."

"Money is no object."

"That's true more and more these days."

I sit, remembering the terror I felt the first time I was too reckless online and found my laptop at the mercy of a Czech cracker co-op. When you get infected, you worry first about your bank passwords, then about your files, and finally you deal with the notion that your secrets have been exposed to prying eyes. But most crackers just want your bandwidth and couldn't care less that you spend too much time at MILFmonitor.com. Billy's worm is different, however. Here, exposure is the sole purpose. If his *Hell Is Other People* experiment sought to explore fear, then this turn in *Savant* is clearly meant to explore *shame*.

Anonymity is the lifeblood of the frenzy of raunchiness that followed in the wake of the internet. I can't think of a better way to kill a sex-related business than to start revealing personal details about its clients. What chaos might be created for Blake if his investment in NOD blows up from being implicated in a privacy scandal? He mentioned his board shitting Yorkshire terriers over material losses from his VR project. If Billy's successful here, I think we'll see them trying to pass a mastodon.

Assuming he has one, Billy's larger artistic objective must be to remind *everyone* that while the internet affords us our aliases and avatars, the same technology also makes it feasible to record all our purchases, conversations, and actions with frightening ease. In most cases, our beloved disguises are distressingly fragile, and the volume of secrets that can be disclosed is greater than it's ever been.

McClaren calls me two hours later.

"You have any hot ideas for getting this genie back in its bottle?"

I'd been assessing the possibility of containment just before he called. A couple net-crawlers I sent out searching for sample file names told me Billy already has his NOD shard up on another server. It will only be a matter of hours before his dungeon reconnects to the main grid.

"Well, since he's distributing child porn, I'm sure the ISPs will move fast to shut down his backups. In the meantime, you can have Red Rook hose down sites as they crop up." I'm suggesting he mount a denial-of-service (DOS) attack to cripple any servers found hosting the files. "So if not back in its bottle, maybe we can wash it down the drain."

"Yeah, our guys thought of that. But looks like Billy has alternates in quite a few uncooperative lo-calities. And he's crammed Google's results with pages that link to mirrors. So attacks won't buy us much time before they get impractical."

Billy came prepared. Even if Blake authorizes an internet-scale reprise of his Whack-A-Mole game, I doubt it's one he can win.

McClaren asks, "Anything else?"

I say, "He's probably got a kill switch. If we could find him—"

"Yeah. I'll bet we could talk some sense into the boy. You can imagine the boss is getting a little—"

"I know. I'm doing everything I can."

But I feel a ramping sense of futility. A person with the brains, devious nature, and unlimited resources of Billy Randall can stay hidden from his pursuers too easily. Our only recourse is to track him down, despite that for the past month, the entire Randall security apparatus has failed to do so. They can't expect that I, working more or less alone, will be able to locate him before this stuff storms across the internet.

And yet . . . My mind won't quite let go of the problem. The hallmark of a good hacker is machine-like persistence. The numb commitment to the belief that there is always a way in. You just have to keep swinging your pick.

63

When confronted with what seems like an impenetrable wall, one studies it carefully for even hairline fissures. I bet the faults in Billy's fortifications will radiate from the impact of Gina's suicide. Her death demands this twisted tribute from him. Her memory makes him emotional and precipitate, maybe less careful. Indeed, I first found him through her.

And what do we know about his most recent actions?

Watching that video must have really multiplied his anger at Blake over her death.

But why?

I force myself to endure it several more times. For the life of me, I can't find anything new in that tight head shot. Billy said, "I know everything now." As though watching the video provided some last, essential piece of information. So is there something in the video—a dog-whistle code that only he can hear—that makes him want to train his guns on his brother?

Maybe a dog whistle is a bad metaphor. Maybe it's something that I *could* hear if I just knew what to listen for.

So how do I find out what I'm missing?

Of the two people who could answer that question, one is in hiding and the other is dead. But then I recall something I've learned about Billy's research: the curious way he described his visit to Gina's apartment to her landlord.

Maybe it's time to conduct a séance.

— — —

Virtual world builders are usually very mindful of security since they often have convertible currencies on which their users rely. So they face an economic holocaust if some enterprising cracker finagles himself keys to the mint. NOD keeps their boxes' software locked correspondingly tight.

Breaking in will take a bit of setup. I start by hunting through a bunch of NOD forums for email addresses of company employees. For all but the most senior, they have an enforced "first name underscore last name" convention. I spend a few minutes with Spemtex, a delightful spammer's tool that sends a test email to thousands of combinations of common first and last names at a given organization. This gets me a list of seven people responding with out-of-office emails.

One of these, a database administrator named Zach Levin, is kind enough to provide in his auto-reply the information that he's part of the team at the Massively Metaversal Media conference currently under way in San Jose. Running the names of the subset of other employees whose spam didn't bounce through Dice, the Ladders, Monster, and Career-Builder yields five résumés from active NOD employees. Two of these are low-paid off-hour IT support drudges who are likely to be on duty Saturdays. One of them, Matt Jones, is a recent hire at NOD's satellite office in Austin and simply hasn't yet taken his résumé down. New employees make good targets because they're not as familiar with the company's security policies, they aren't likely to know a lot of their coworkers by voice, and they're generally insecure in their position and eager to comply with well-framed requests. As a final bit of icing, he's included his cell number.

The plan is simple: I pay eight hundred bucks to rent a well-distributed botnet to intermittently DOS the NOD world domains as well as the corporate servers at their main Menlo Park office. One of these boxes is an internet telephony system. Attacking it will cause havoc in their comms. Then I send an email to poor Mr. Jones spoofed to look like it's coming from Zach Levin:

```
Hey,

Sorry to hit you with this out of the blue, but I'm sure
you've heard we've got some problems with the Menlo
```

servers. I'm here at M3 with some guys from Second Life
who say they got nailed last week. They tell me it's just
Chinese script kiddies screwing around. There'll be a
CERT coming out on it soon.

   Anyway, Jack Fisher [VP marketing] is meeting with
IMP about some biz dev stuff, and he needs this report
from the main server for background. Traffic stats,
etc. . . . I tried to log in when the thing was going
down and managed to lock myself out. I can't get ahold of
the Menlo techs, so can you reset my password and leave
the new one on my voicemail? You'd really be saving our
ass up here. Thanks.

—Zach

A key strategy in establishing credibility with a mark is to make predictions that are then confirmed by "independent" sources. So twenty minutes later, I send him a fake report from Carnegie Mellon's Computer Emergency Response Team confirming my story. CERT maintains an email list to which most webmasters subscribe to tell them when giant worm infestations are eating the internet.

I let that marinate for an hour and then lob in a call. I'm counting on the fact that these two people don't know each other well enough for instant voice identification over the phone. I throw on a little cell static just in case. "Jones," he answers.

"Hey, man. Zach Levin. You get my email about the password reset?"

"Yeah. I just put it through."

"Great. Hey, I'm on my cell here. I think there's something wrong with the exchange in Menlo. Can you put me on hold and try one of those lines?"

He clicks off and comes back a minute later.

"Yeah. Seems like it's down. It's not ringing through."

"Right, so I can't get into my voicemail to get my new password. So can you reset it again and tell me what it is?"

"Well . . ." You never give passwords out over the phone.

"I know you're not supposed to. But we're in kind of a bind here. Tell you what, can you put your manager on?"

"He's not here."

"Hmmm . . . Well, I don't know what we should do. It's really starting to hit the fan. Jack is on the warpath, and I'd hate to be one of the Menlo IT guys tomorrow. You could be a real hero by helping us out. I'll write you an email right now authorizing this. Hold on."

I send him another email copying a couple people high in the tech hierarchy. All of whom work in Menlo and don't have access to their server right now.

Finally, he says, "Okay, it's one five bravo tango seven kilo kilo zero four six."

"Thanks, bud. I owe you one."

Five minutes later, I'm deep in their network. I've got some bent Linux libraries on their database server, and I'm silently sucking a copy of the two-terabyte hard disk across their hosting facility's rocking fiber-optic line.

While her physical remains are well beyond my necromantic abilities, perhaps one of Gina's digital selves can be resurrected. I'm hoping this undead Gina will retain some spectral connection to Billy.

Of course no avatar ever really dies to begin with, they just enter a limbo of inaccessibility. Now we can be so carefree with memory that you almost never destroy data, you just redescribe it as "deleted." So I'm betting that Gina's primary av can be exhumed from her plot in the database I've just stolen.

64

ike people, avatars tend to bloat as they age. Rezzed on 9/07/2003, during NOD's beta-testing period, Joanne_Dark had grown gargantuan. Her bulk appears not in the Audrey Hepburn contours of her av, but rather in her possessions. She stores huge amounts of gear for role-playing sims based on *Star Wars, Star Trek, StarCraft*, and *Battlestar Galactica*. J. R. R. Tolkien and George R. R. Martin each get folders. As do C. S. Lewis and Lewis Carroll. But I want to find the places where her NOD life intersected with her real one, and I suspect these fantasy games will only lead me farther afield.

I scroll through her in-world buddy list looking for Billy, feeling my way through her data like a newly blind man trying to recognize a familiar face by touch. If I can find the av Billy uses outside of *Savant*, I may be able to catch him in NOD using a connection I can trace.

Gina has 552 names in her buddy list. A thorough search through all their profile data might take days, but Billy is a kind of artist, and most artists regard anonymity as a deadly poison. He wouldn't neglect to brand his personal avatar. By now, I should be able to spot him from a mile away.

I spend a couple minutes writing code in NOD's scripting language, which they call nVerse. It populates a large area on my server with the primary skins of all of Gina's friends. The assembly looks like a parade formation of the guests from a Halloween party at the Playboy Mansion.

I run through the ranks, first deleting all the Furries. Then the stereotypical fashionistas, stripperellas, goth girls, and superheroines are cashiered along with their male counterparts. Plain Jane animals and their mythical cousins are sent packing as well. I reject a couple avs for their too-obvious monikers, like Ben_Dover or Mike_Hunt.

A couple hours later, I'm left with a company of uglied-up humans, some scary children, a couple clones of famous dictators and serial killers, and monsters of various persuasions, including five renditions of the devil himself. Overrepresented in the top ten of these are what I'd call "freaks of nature." A six-legged Chernobyl horse fetus, an African albino covered with human bite marks, a repulsive sex troll, and a two-headed crow.

I think Billy would rep as something more fearsome than a carrion bird, but there's something about this one's dual black heads and beady crimson eyes that imparts a feeling of menace. Not to mention that its creator has given it a gigantic schlong, which is surely nonstandard equipment for any creature dependent on aerodynamics. Still, I'm about to dispel it when I pause over its handle, A_Ross_Fowles.

I'd initially dismissed "Fowles" as the dumbest possible self-referential name, but the key attribute isn't that the little monster's a bird, but rather that it has two heads. Of course, bicephalic birds have been common symbols throughout world history, used by everyone from the ancient Egyptians to the modern Masons. But I've encountered one of these more recently.

Where was it?

I mentally rehearse everywhere I've been over the past weeks. Finally it dawns on me that since I'm looking at something in NOD, it's not where *I've* been, it's where *Jacques* has been. And he's spent time almost exclusively in one place: the Château de Silling. And a two-headed bird, really an eagle but rendered to look more like a crow, is the first thing you see upon entering. The Sade family crest carved in stone over the castle's gate.

That insight solves the name for me: A_Ross_Fowles reads as Eros Fouls, a natural choice for a man who in real life renamed himself "Coitus Defiles."

But in finding Billy's digital embodiment, I've only uncovered another corpse. My crow's account was closed two days before he disappeared.

I suppose even the dumbest fugitive would abandon his usual online haunts. Or at least he'd use a new avatar.

I can't quite believe that Billy has dropped NOD cold turkey. Since he's forced to keep a low profile while on the lam, what better place to express himself than a virtual world where he's securely armored in a plastic identity?

Beyond that, I've been berating myself that I didn't think of this search strategy before now, but in fairness I'm not sure I could have. I didn't understand until I really got into NOD how attached people become to their virtual world of choice. While players may try on identities like so many party dresses, they often think of the *place* as a sacred homeland. That's why I'd bet my whole stack that Billy is still logging on.

I spend a long time browsing the profiles of A_Ross_Fowles's buddy list. I see that Billy, disagreeable enough in real life, when unburdened of basic social constraints in NOD, becomes intolerable. Almost devoid of "real" avs, his list is populated by corporate mascots and sex workers. More interesting is the series of "friends" that he's made but who have then revoked friendly status within a couple weeks of meeting him. This wall of shame is complemented by an extraordinary number of venues that have banned him, including Fran's Fecal Funhouse.

What could one possibly do to get kicked out of there?

Despite all this information, he's been savvy enough to obliterate any direct trail between his old and new avs. So I face the daunting prospect of having to seek out his new identity in the sea of almost ten million active NODlings.

At least his mutant crow has given me a police sketch to use in my manhunt.

He probably came to life within a week before or after Billy went off the grid. This alone will filter out nearly all of the avs but still leaves me with something on the order of sixty thousand. A couple more filters include avs who have visited servers with *Savant*'s former IP address, NODlings with more than three location bans, and finally people who are registered in any of NOD's developer programs. Sadly, these criteria still yield an army of 7,461 possibilities. Doable, but not on my time-frame. I drum my desk, mulling how to proceed.

I'm resigning myself to just getting on with it when I remember an innovative data-mining package one of the Red Rook librarians was flogging a while back. I find the old email and download the test version of CogneTech's Cut_0.87 data-slicing tool kit.

Once I get it installed and eating from the NOD data trough, the software lets me put in all kinds of free-form search information, including all my previous filters. The algorithm offers to consult the internet to gather data helpful in forming "metaconnections," whatever those might be.

Cut ponders for twenty minutes while I shower. When the software's window resumes focus, I'm presented with a ranked list of avatar handles that it thinks I'll most enjoy meeting.

The results are both amazing and depressing. While I'm nearly floored by the eerie intelligence of the software's choices, I can see immediately that the first results aren't going to be Billy. The top prospect, Tad_A_ LaPhille, lists his real name, and he's a former PiMP classmate of Billy and Gina's. The second is a minor player in the Jackanapes' circle. The third is the av of their dead friend Trevor Rothstein.

After a couple more misses, I find Lillie_Hitchcock, who is unique among Cut's selections in that she's so pedestrian: the off-the-shelf Barbie av of a complete noob with the default T-shirt-and-khaki-pants outfit that everyone ditches immediately upon rezzing in. Her player has only replaced the T-shirt's texture with a set of wide red, white, and blue stripes.

I'm disposed to disregard her, since Billy designs avatars with exacting craft. But what keeps me interested is that I can't tell why Cut selected her in the first place. I flip to the dialogue that explains an item's ranking, and it tells me that her placement was based on a high relevance score for the av's textures to the search term "double eagle." I inspect Lillie for tattoos or anything about her that refers to birds. There's nothing, so I impatiently check the links for an explanation.

Never before have I been so possessed of a desire to kiss a piece of software, my work with the Dancers notwithstanding. And what is the valuable nugget it sifted from a flood of worthless internet nonsense?

The Russian flag. Not the pernicious crimson hammer and sickle. The broad white, blue, and red stripes of the new Russia, which first lived as a flag of the Russian Empire. The other flag in use around that time was yellow, imprinted with a black double eagle from the Romanovs' coat of arms. Nearly identical to the one on the Sade family crest.

Knowing I have my man, I ask Google to unravel her name. Billy's skipped the usual verbal trickery, opting instead for just an obscure reference. "Lillie" and "Hitchcock" are the first two names of the philanthropist who commissioned the famous landmark that looks over the city of San Francisco. Her last name: Coit.

And this av is not only live, but I see she's logged in recently.

I wrap up by inserting a routine in NOD's database scripts that will message me any time Lillie_Hitchcock logs in. So the next time Billy enters NOD, I'll be waiting for him.

I check in with my Red Rook colleagues regarding their suppression efforts. Billy's database had recently propagated enough to stay live for over five hours before they were able to disable the servers, and I sense a growing pessimism among the team. Meanwhile, Eeyore forwards me an entry from the NOD forums describing the Silling firestorm and the poster's subsequent exploration of the dungeon. He details in vehement terms his feeling of betrayal at seeing his hard drive mirrored online and expresses his desire to, appropriately enough, torture Billy to death.

There are nearly a hundred responses, mostly in the same torches-and-pitchforks vein. Though one complains that he found out his daughter's pediatrician had gone pretty far along in the Course of Fever, and he laments the downed server due to the loss of his ability to check his zip code for "shit-eating Sade-freak pedophiles."

The controversy has already been picked up by a couple of the nimbler tech blogs. Blue_Bella renders this verdict: "Such a breach of privacy, some have called it the *Unmasking*, is frightening to closeted exxxplorers, but it could be for the best if it exposes how much we all like this stuff but just refuse to talk about it."

Slashdot is running an article quoting anonymous porn sources saying traffic to their sites has fallen off a cliff. Meanwhile, drive-formatting freeware hosts are currently offline due to unheard-of traffic spikes.

HoseDown has an item headlined:

Netphomaniacs scurry in the glare of sudden sunlight.

Soon I suspect they'll begin to sizzle.

65

Lillie_Hitchcock logs in at four PM the next afternoon.

A short query to the NOD central server gives me what we've been after for over a month now: an honest IP address for Billy Randall.

I'm tempted to send this straight to McClaren's team and go buy myself a bottle of small-batch. But from long experience, I know that I need a solid physical address, or else there's a good chance that they'll wind up SWATing a midtown Starbucks.

I treat the situation gently. A light scan shows his machine is as tight as one might expect from someone with Billy's technical skills. Of course, I've already planned an attack. His Achilles' heel is that he'll have the NOD developer's kit installed on his machine, and I've had plenty of opportunity to assay it for flaws.

There aren't many, but I did find a trapdoor buried in their testing tools. A poorly designed function allows one to load outdated versions for some of the program's components. These contain errors that let me order his current NOD session to silently run any program I might specify. Even if Billy were watching closely, it just looks like NOD has started another of its many processes. But in reality, I've sliced a fatal hole in his system by uploading a tiny RAT designed to mimic a common security application.

Now I have to be circumspect. Not wanting to risk tipping him off, I decide to lie back. In the meantime, I write up a triumphant status report to McClaren and hope that getting into Billy's machine will suffice to prevent Blake from firing me tomorrow.

— — —

I wait until four AM Monday morning to risk firing up my Trojan. I start by creating myself a shadow admin account. After that, I install a program that lets me discreetly spy on his sessions. Then I start copying down his hard drive. I browse through the software he uses: all the Apple media shit, Eclipse . . .

Oh, what's this?

He's running his own remote-access app called Mesmer, which lets you control your desktop from any smartphone.

Billy's phone, that's what I'd really like to crack.

Instrumenting someone's cell used to be a huge pain in the ass. But now that your phone is really a fully functional computer, it's become a perfect surveillance platform. With one program I can listen to your calls, download your texts and email, grab your Facebook password, turn on the mic to listen to your live conversations, take pictures or video, and, most importantly, learn your location from the built-in GPS receivers.

I find several devious hacks in the Red Rook exploits database and rig Billy's system to execute one of them the next time he syncs his phone.

Before signing off, I start his webcam for a quick peep. I'd love the opportunity to spy on Billy at home. But all I can see is an unfocused view out of a large bank of windows, the city lights forming an amorphous constellation.

I set up a script to have the camera wake up periodically, record a couple frames to an external server, and alert me if there's any motion in the images. Then I log off and start poring over my copy of Billy's hard drive. I see immediately that it won't give him up. He's thoroughly stealthed his system. I can hope that by watching his live sessions with it, I'll catch him in a mistake, though that will be chancy and time-consuming—and I suspect Blake won't be satisfied with any kind of long-term digital stakeout.

While things are bad enough now, I'm sure Billy has even more fireworks in store.

Since I left her apartment, Olya has completely ignored me. I decide to check GAME and see if I can find Garriott or Xan to determine what they've heard from her. Neither of them are there.

Actually, almost no one is. Last night, a burst pipe on the third floor caused a team of emergency plumbers to shut off the water for the entire building. This morning they commenced a multimovement symphony of power tools and pipe banging, which has driven away what few of GAME's inhabitants remained. At eight AM, I decide to take my laptop to a coffee shop around the corner on Clinton Street so I can work in peace and avail myself of a functioning bathroom.

I'm still rummaging his files when I get a message from my RAT on Billy's computer. Interestingly, the event wasn't initiated by Billy himself. A server somewhere has stimulated a background program to spawn a window showing a low-res video feed that looks like an abstract photograph. It's all black except for a faint gradient highlighting a square shape in the lower right-hand corner. Nothing happens for a second as I check the title of the program. It's Brimstone. That's an ominous name, so I run through his project files and locate the underlying code.

It begins with simple motion detection on the video feed. When a specific recognition event triggers, it sends a text to a given phone number. Then the program pops up a button that, when pressed, relays a bunch of commands back to the device that's transmitting the video. I skim rapidly through the instructions, until my head almost shorts out as my understanding catches up with my eyes.

The function handler reads:

```
_OnButtonClick (){

   sendCommand(CO_BOX_ADDR, _release_valve1);
   sendCommand(CO_BOX_ADDR, _release_valve2);
   sendCommand(CO_BOX_ADDR, _ flow_accel);
   sendCommand(CO_BOX_ADDR, _ignite);


};
```

The word "ignite" is what grabs me.

What is this? Another one of Billy's faux incendiaries?

Then two things happen in rapid succession. The video image

changes: a wedge of light opens at the bottom, and an arm enters the frame. It flips some switches, which illuminate a familiar space.

It's the Orifice, shot from above. And the arm belongs to Olya.

She enters the room, followed by Blake. A graphics square flashes briefly over his face.

Olya says, ". . . don't know why you want to meet me here. You only should be finding this *govnyuk* brother of yours. You promise me his head. But where—"

"Wait, I wanted to meet? You emailed me."

"I email you yesterday about—ah, never mind. We're here now, so . . . ?"

Blake steps closer to her. "So . . . ?"

They embrace.

Pointless jealousy dilutes my apprehension until I see the Mesmer service awaken. Billy's password scrolls into the key log.

I jump up so fast I upset the table, and my laptop crashes to the floor behind me.

66

I slam into the door of the Orifice, but Olya's got it locked with the inside latch. I bang on it frantically, bruising the meat of my hands. Finally, she jerks it open. Her clothes are disheveled, an irate glare on her face.

"James! What—"

"You need to get out of here. Now!"

Blake steps forward. He looks tired and irritable. "James, get ahold of yourself."

"No. You don't understand." I slide in and grab Olya by the arm. "There's—"

She wrenches it away. "Ai. Don't touch—"

"—a bomb."

Both of their faces go slack as they recall their confusion over who asked for the meeting. I assume Billy wanted them together for this and spoofed their email to that end.

Olya squints. "You think I'd believe anything—"

Behind her, we hear a metallic snap. I flinch away in raw panic. But nothing happens. There's a small sputtering sound coming from above us, where the camera's mounted.

As if to mock my hysteria, the room's sprinkler turns on. Blake and Olya look at each other, negotiating a reaction. Far from a bomb, but something is happening here.

And the water is . . . wrong.

I can't immediately tell what it is. A strange scent. Something like a place I remember . . . or is it, what? Matches. It smells like a box of matches. Then I remember the place that came to mind: Yellowstone National Park. The smell around the hot springs:

Sulfur.

Brimstone.

"We need to get out of here," I say.

The flow from the sprinklers increases, and a new smell wafts in. This one is easy to recognize.

Gasoline.

Blake jumps toward the door. Olya seems transfixed by the sprinkler head. She must have gotten some of the fluid in her eyes, because she blinks them shut and puts her hands up to rub them. I dive to tackle her into the hallway.

Not quite soon enough. As I'm in the air, there's another soft click, but this one is followed by strong wind in my face and a burst of light. Then pain.

First is the shocking collision with Olya, who is not a petite woman. Then the crunch of my kneecaps on the hard cement floor of the hall. I wrench my face away from her hair, which is now on fire, and start batting at it. The heat at my back intensifies. I spastically rip myself out of my jacket, rolling off of Olya, allowing her to flip onto her back and quench the flames licking at her hair. She staggers up and leans against the wall, smothering the flickering fire at her calves before it can ascend her legs. I get my jacket off and glance at her to confirm that she's okay, but she's not looking at me.

She's looking back into the blaze.

Her face has a transcendent focus. A tendril of flame starts climbing again up her leather pants. But she doesn't even twitch.

She steps toward the door.

It takes me a second to understand that she's going back to rescue Ginger. And that with gasoline-soaked clothing, she's not likely to emerge. And that I have to stop her. Suddenly I'm running into the fire as well.

She gets two steps into the room. The Orifice looks as though it's been painted with fire. All the tables, chairs, and computers are still recognizable, but they're outlined in roiling blue and orange flames. The smoke is building, the ceiling now covered by a dense gray cloud. I reach for her arm, but she senses this and pulls it from my grasp. She takes another step forward, grabs Ginger by her neck, and tosses her out the door to skid across the hall into my office. Then she turns to scan the room for other valuables. She pauses long enough for me to get my right arm around her neck. I'm not sure of my ability to wrestle her out.

That's when the real explosion happens. I register a microsecond of surprise when the back of Olya's head impacts my mouth, smashing my lips. Then there's a gap in time, and I find myself lying back in the hall, my head partially buried in the drywall opposite the door. Olya and I have switched positions, with her body now sheltering me from the flames spreading out from the Orifice.

There's a violent cloud of white, and I can't breathe anymore. The last thing I think is:

I can't believe that fucker killed us.

67

I come to in a cool, clean room with luxuriantly breathable air. A hospital room. Things are vague, and I start my "what happened last night" checklist. Then I notice the bandages on my left arm. A beautiful woman sits beside me. It's Xan.

Seeing her makes everything come back, but I can only whisper, "Olya?"

Xan looks at me quickly but then buries her face in her hands, opening in me a black fissure of dread. Tears streaming freely, she says, "She's in the ICU. Surgery."

"Blake?"

Xan tips her head like she might have misheard me. "Blake? What about him?"

This confuses me. I'm not thinking clearly, but I have a specific recollection of his being there. Running back through my traumatized memory, I conclude that the white explosion was a fire extinguisher, and Blake must have discharged it on Olya and me and then disappeared before the firemen showed up. I want to ask Xan about all this, but another question demands precedence.

"Me?" I ask.

This elicits a fragile smile through her tears. She says, "You're going to be all right."

I suspect she might be lying. A body wiggle confirms that my spinal cord is still intact. I'm incredibly stiff, like how a veteran demolition derby driver must feel on the day of his retirement. I gingerly pat myself. Parts of my skin throb like they've been worked on by the Stasi school of cosmetology, but I don't find any stitches, so things can't be too bad. Then I think of Olya and start looking for the morphine button.

Xan is good enough to push it for me.

I wake up alone and in an entirely different frame of mind. I must have slept for long enough for the anesthetics to wear off, through the night probably. The pain from my burns is worse, and I feel unsettled. I reach for the button but can't grasp it. My irritation flares into anger.

Take it easy. You're just coming down from the drugs.

But then I find a target for my fury.

I forget about the button as the feeling crystallizes. This aberrant asshole blew up Olya. The thought of such an unrivalled beauty scarred by one of Billy's dangerous pranks fills me with rage.

How did he even pull it off?

The plumbers of course. He probably flushed a cherry bomb, precipitating the maintenance crisis, and then slipped in with a fake beard and coveralls. I'll bet back at GAME they'll find a storage room directly above the Orifice with its floor ripped up and a remote-controlled flame-thrower resting in the crawlspace, its nozzle disguised as a sprinkler head. Funny that when we upgraded the security of that room, I changed the locks on the big steel door and patched the hole in the wall I came through that first week, but the idea of death from above never occurred to me.

On the chair Xan occupied I see a small duffel bag. In it there's a set of clothes, perhaps pulled from the GAME lost and found. More importantly, in a side pocket, I find my phone.

I rip the bandages off my left hand and start typing.

Minutes later, Blake picks up my call. His voice has an uncertain timbre.

"James. Jesus Christ. I—"

"They say Olya's in intensive care."

"I know. I can't believe . . . I can't believe she—"

"Yeah. Thanks for, uh, extinguishing us."

"Oh. Right. Look, I'm sorry I took off, but it didn't seem like there was much more I could do. And, well, I didn't want . . ."

"I understand."

"You do?"

"Yeah. It will be better if no one knows you were there."

"Uh-huh." Blake's tone is wary; perhaps he was thinking he'd have to sell me harder on the virtues of forgetting his presence. Now he tests how far he can push it. "So I guess the police may want to speak with you. This is very serious, but if I could just—"

"I won't be here."

"Wait. What do you mean?"

"Blake, call McClaren. I know where your fuckhead brother is."

68

Slipping out of the hospital without the normal exit processing is liable to raise some questions, especially when my injuries were sustained in a pretty noteworthy case of arson. And since I was just here after being Tased, maybe I really should stay put to make sure there aren't any parts coming loose. But catching Billy seems more important, so I devise a rickety plan to blame my erratic behavior on PTSD and make my escape.

At first I was puzzled that Billy had holed up in Washington Heights, but on mapping the GPS coordinates spit out from his phone, it made more sense: he's not at a new apartment, he's at the Cloisters.

As good a place as any to contemplate the enormity of one's crimes, the Cloisters is a branch of the Metropolitan Museum of Art dedicated to medieval-period pieces. Set on a hill in Fort Tryon Park and overlooking the Hudson River, it stands as one of the most serene and beautiful places in the city, possessing all the enchantment of an actual medieval abbey. I recall finding in the folder where Gina stored her own NOD models a lovingly detailed replica of the entire complex. Maybe a favorite place of hers. Maybe even the site of a rare RL excursion with Billy.

My GPS fix is good enough to tell me that he's in a gallery in the North Cloister that houses an impressive set of illuminated manuscripts. One of the most famous has a lovely depiction of the destruction of Sodom and Gomorrah.

After a brief stop at home, I hurry uptown. Blake wanted me to wait for instructions from McClaren confirming that his extraction team was in place. But despite having sent two messages, I've yet to hear anything back.

I arrive to find Billy striking a reflective pose on a bench facing the water. His attitude makes me question whether he knows the outcome of his fratricidal attack. A tree on the other side of the path provides a suitable screen as I settle in to wait.

Several minutes pass. I send increasingly shrill messages to McClaren, but they're flying into a void. I get antsy.

Billy fishes his phone out of his jacket pocket, presses some buttons, and reads. He doesn't like what he sees and shakes his phone as if he's going to chuck it into the water. But he restrains himself and just slams his fist into the bench's wooden slats. He then shoots up and casts around as though he's not sure where to go. He elects to return toward the galleries, and I decide I can't take any more of this.

The wind is loud and the clouds prevent any revealing shadows, so I'm able to stalk right up to him and seize him by the shoulder. He freaks, wrenching himself away so hard that he falls down. Gone is the smug hipster who grinned at me when I fell for his tricks at our earlier meeting. Now he's a skinny geek looking up in naked terror. I squat over him, making sure he sees the pistol clipped to my pants. To ensure docility, I hammer my fist down on his nose.

"We're going to start with that," I say.

He yelps, his eyes filling with tears. He takes a second to recover and tries to blow out the blood filling his nasal cavity.

"Where the fuck is Rosa? What did you do to her?"

"No. No, man. She's fine. That's her *job*." This answer is so preposterous I hit him again. But he continues desperately. "Dude, she's a *body modder*. They hang her up like that at tattoo conventions. I swear to God." He starts coughing again while I think about this. Something about it actually seems credible.

Of course: the ripped earlobes. Sewn-up holes from extender plugs.

I can't spare the time to beat myself up for being taken in, since now that I have him, Billy has a whole litany of other crimes for which to answer. I ask, "How do we shut down the *Unmasking*?"

He gasps, "You don't. It's out there. And it's not coming back."

I press my hand over his mouth. "Wrong answer. You're going to fuck with someone you just set on fire?"

He starts coughing blood out his nose. I release my hand.

He says, "Look, man, I didn't know you were going to be there. By the time I saw you, I'd already set it off."

I slap him hard across the face. More blood pools at the corner of his mouth. "You might have killed Olya, you little twat."

"You should thank me. She was—"

I grab him by his shirt and rap his head against the ground. Then I pull his face close to mine. "Are you so nuts as to believe that *they* are responsible for your friend's death? They deserve to die because Gina acted out something from one of *your* sick little movies?"

Billy's eyes had jammed shut on impact, but now they pop open. He gapes at me like I've informed him that headless ogres are rampaging through Central Park.

"Wait . . . You mean . . ." He shakes his head, trying to clear it. "You're telling me you don't know? You *gave* me the video, man."

"You stole it."

"But you've seen it. How can you not know?"

I drop him back to the ground. "Know what?"

He props himself up by his elbows, an incredulous look on his face. "They killed her. G never did that to herself, they tied her up . . ." He trails off, suddenly focused on something behind me.

I twist around for a quick look, see nothing, and turn back to him, thinking he's trying to distract me. But he's still staring north up the pathway. He tries to scramble to his feet, a new sense of panic in his eyes. I let him up but grab him by the hair so he can't run.

Something isn't right. I glance behind me again, and this time I see it: two shadows off to the right of the path moving toward us.

Finally the cavalry show up.

But immediately I know I'm mistaken. These guys aren't McClaren's people. For starters they're both too big: one looks like he's six foot six with a giant head, goatee, and leather Kangol cap, wearing a black Adidas tracksuit, for Christ's sake. The other is shorter but proportioned like a kettle bell. He's got on dark sunglasses and a leather trench coat, underneath which he's carrying something long and unwieldy. Surely not a shotgun.

Who the hell are these guys?

Billy has concluded that whoever they are, they mean him grievous harm. He tries to hurl himself away from me even though this results in a fistful of his hair ripping free. I snatch his right arm and pin it behind his back. Billy is physically weak, but he flails around like a gaffed shark. I wrench his arm upward, which freezes him briefly. He whines, terror-stricken, "Please, not yet. You don't understand . . ."

I only half notice this because my mind is going a mile a minute. I can't escape the conclusion that Goatee and Shades are a hit team. I never had any illusions that Billy was going to be forgiven for trying to kill his brother. He's in for some rough treatment.

But gunning him down in a public park? This was never part of the plan. It's insane.

They're within twenty yards. Goatee is smiling at me. He reaches into his jacket.

Does Blake really want his brother dead? There was a symbolic, mad-scientist quality to the GAME fire. Olya was really only injured because she went *back into* the room. If he'd used a normal bomb, which would have been easier than his napalm sprinkler, all three of us would be dead.

All that aside, could Blake possibly want a police investigation into his brother's public murder?

Shades pulls his coat away from a sawed-off twelve-gauge.

Do I?

No way. This cannot happen.

I push Billy as hard as I can so that he topples over the low wall separating the path from an overgrown slope. I then turn and pray I can clear my Glock before they start shooting. Their reactions are slowed by disbelief, but Shades gets his shotgun trained on me first.

I'm fucked.

Thankfully Goatee has read the situation and swipes his hand under the barrel, knocking it up away from me. I've got my gun out but decide not to risk pointing it at anyone.

Instead, I ask, "Who the hell are you?"

But Goatee ignores me and runs over to the wall, searching for their target. Billy has disappeared into the trees.

Shades has his gun trained on me again, looking like he's dying to use it. But Goatee stares at me with amused contempt, and maybe a little bit of relief. "You just *fucked up*."

69

That turns out to be Blake's perspective as well.

Shades detains me while Goatee converses briefly with an irate Mondano. They then drive me down to Amazone, empty at this hour, and install me at one of the tables near the main bar.

I simmer through twenty minutes of cheek-chewing tension before Mondano and Blake walk in. As he flops down on the seat next to mine, Mondano smirks like he's going to relish this. Blake just looks bewildered. All over he's showing signs of deep strain. Dark bags under blood-shot eyes combine with jerky movements to signal nervous exhaustion. To be expected, I guess, when, while all this is going on, he's trying to run part of a major conglomerate. The effort must be costing him. I'd have given myself over to bourbon and barbiturates long ago.

He shakes his head like he's trying to understand a misbehaving child. "James . . ."

I'm a little bewildered myself. This is the second time I've been responsible for losing his brother, and yet I feel like I've saved Blake from a catastrophe and don't deserve his scorn. I decide on aggression.

"Blake, if you want to murder your brother in cold blood, think maybe you could do it when I'm not standing right next to him in a public park?"

Mondano says to Blake, "I told you this guy was a fucking fruitcake." I notice he's abandoned his world-weary Mafia boss shtick in front of

Blake. Someone who knows him from the old yacht-basin neighbor-hood.

"So your guys were just there to check out the tapestries? And they needed a shotgun in case, what? They were attacked by squirrels?"

"They were there to take control of the situation, which you then in-tentionally fucked up. That little prick offer you more money?"

"Actually, he offered to spare all three of us a twenty-to-life sentence at Sing Sing."

"Already planning to rat on us, Jimmy?"

"Well, Benny, I'll need someone's ass to rent out for cigarettes, and I can't think of anyone better suited to the work than you."

That's too much for Mondano, and he lunges out of his seat. Like many supposed tough guys, he can talk hard but isn't much of a fighter. As I jump up, he aims a looping roundhouse at my head that doesn't have a prayer of connecting. I think, *This is going to feel incredible,* as I pivot to send a debilitating kick into his testicles. I wonder who he'll turn into with his nuts squashed into jelly.

But my kick never gets off the ground. I find McClaren, who's got-ten inside on me before I even know he's there, standing on my foot. He catches Mondano's punch, twists his wrist, and pushes him back into his chair.

He says, "Now, gentlemen, that's no kind of attitude for a team. Ain't any sense trading paint here when we've all got the same color stripes, right?"

I shrug and look down at my foot. He lifts his off of it, and I sit back down. I ask, "Where have *you* been?"

"I've been far afield protecting Ms. Randall, who we can all agree is our first priority. James, I had no idea you'd be so efficient after getting toasted. You seem to have a real knack for locating Billy. It's hanging on to the slippery bastard that's the problem."

"Y'all can handle that without me this time." I point at Mondano. "I'm not working with this clown."

"Oh, you think you can just walk out?" he asks.

"Watch me."

I trudge from the room with Blake calling at my back.

— — —

McClaren sidles up beside me before I get my cigarette lit.

He nudges me with his elbow. "Quite a diva routine you put on in there."

"It's not an act. You weren't there. And *I'm* not going to be there when it all goes tits-up."

McClaren nods sagely. "Yeah, I'll admit it seems our fearless leader might have had a lapse in judgment. Billy's sites are back online. Your boys don't seem to be able to shut them down. So he's under a lot of stress. Sometimes in ex-treem-is we listen to our baser instincts, in this case represented by our Eye-talian-American friend."

"Uh-huh."

"Anyway, I understand you're kind of burnt out. Why don't you spend some time getting your blow-bots back together? That'll be important to the boss pretty soon here. Since you flushed him, we've got some new leads on old Billy we can run down."

Not sure what I'm going to do, I keep quiet. McClaren pats me on the back and continues. "It's been good working with you, Jimmy. You're a real prince."

As always, my conversation with McClaren was troubling. I suppose his grossly premature order to stand down is a sign of Blake's loss of trust in me. But the way he put it sounded like I was due for a medal, and that the whole thing was essentially wrapped up. I try to prevent my frazzled brain from overloading his last comment.

He said prince, but did he mean knave?

In my voicemail, I have messages from a GAME administrator wanting to know what in the world is going on, Officer Aiden Rosedale asking for a statement about the fire, and the hospital trying to determine if I'm planning to pay my bill.

I call Xan.

She's holding vigil at Olya's room with Garriott, whom she puts on speaker.

She says, "James, you didn't see fit to let the poor nurses know you were tired of their care and wanted to go and seek infection for your wounds?"

"Thanks for the concern. But I'm okay. Glad y'all are keeping an eye on Olya."

"While you avoid helping the authorities apprehend the man who did this."

"I'm working on that. What did you tell the police?"

"That Billy was stalking her and finally lost his mind."

"Right. Good. Did they find anything that made them ask what went on in the Orifice?"

"No. Everything melted down to sludge."

Garriott asks, "Do you think it's a good idea to be, uh, messing about with the police? Maybe they'll need the whole story to find that prick."

"Believe me, we'll have Billy in a rubber cell soon enough."

There's silence on the other end of the line. Then Xan asks, "James, what's all this really about?"

A plausible fiction comes to my lips, but I decide my friends have a right to know what's going on. "Billy thinks Olya and his brother killed Gina Delaney. He wants revenge. So for the time being, we need to take some more safety measures. Xan, I want you staying at my apartment for the next couple days . . . Garriott, you can crash there too."

"Hardly, mate. I'm not afraid of that ponce. Just let him come near me."

The idea of Garriott and Billy in a physical altercation is so amusing, I have to bite my tongue. But on the other hand, Billy has almost killed the indomitable Olya, so my levity is short-lived.

At home, I don't have to search much to gauge the level of media hysteria Billy's *Unmasking* has generated. The entire national press corps must be reaching for their Ritalin to help them pump out the necessary yards of coverage. While more financially serious exploits have occurred in the past, the prurient purity of this one has captivated the journalistic tribe:

```
Porn worm spreading rapidly. Experts decry one of the
"greatest privacy breaches in history."
```
                                        —Associated Press

Local archdiocese investigating "computer misconduct" by
several officials revealed by "hacktivist."

—Washington Post

Black sheep Randall heir exposes dark family secrets.
Many others compromised.

—CNN.com

Is your kid's teacher making virtual child porn?

—New York Post

Governor Bryant's spokesperson offers no comment on
allegations concerning the use of office laptop for
"inappropriate chat" with government employees.

—Idaho Statesman

Almost none of Billy's victims are making statements at the moment.
Except Layton Mayfield, an Oakland police officer caught with videos he
made exhibiting some appalling racial bondage scenarios.

He jumped off the Golden Gate Bridge.

70

The stress of the day and the large weeping burn on my forearm convince me to permit myself some painkillers, which in turn convince me to allow myself a few hours of much-needed sleep.

When I wake later that night, McClaren still hasn't left any messages. Changing my bandages, I reflect that Billy has no doubt disappeared back into the ether.

But it's not in his nature to stay totally hidden. Midway through my rewrap, I hear the tone for a critical message on my phone:

```
[Script_Alert: Av_Stalker_07]
Lillie_Hitchcock @NodULE: http://nod.com/ule_find/
dev:143.365.186
```

I would expect Billy to opt for the sterility of a new av, but here he's reusing the very means of my penetration. He must want to talk.

Checking out the IP of his datastream leads to his usual double-buffered open-proxy hell. So I just fire up Jacques_Ynne and teleport to the location in the alert. It's in one of NOD's test sims, and he's left the area in its blank default state, just a flat white plane floating in the perfect blackness of a binary vacuum. Until now, Billy has carefully curated his surroundings, and I'd imagine he's got thousands of dramatic settings, from caves to sky palaces, in which to conduct a meeting. His av stands unmoving in the center of the space.

Though he doesn't turn to face me, he can tell I've rezzed in. A dialogue bubble forms over his head.

Lillie_Hitchcock: Still think my dear brother is innocent of murder?

Jacques_Ynne: With a sibling like you, I'm not surprised that there's domestic violence.

Lillie_Hitchcock: And yet you were an incompetent accomplice to my assassination.

Jacques_Ynne: You're welcome.

Lillie_Hitchcock: Why?

Jacques_Ynne: Why what?

Lillie_Hitchcock: Why did you let me go?

Jacques_Ynne: Practical considerations only.

Lillie_Hitchcock: No. You did it because you believe me.

Jacques_Ynne: I believe that you need a straitjacket.

Lillie_Hitchcock: I can prove my brother and his whore spilled Gina's blood. Just make sure you're not standing next to him when he reaps judgment for his crimes. But then . . . I'm not

	really the one you should worry about.
Jacques_Ynne:	Meaning?
Lillie_Hitchcock:	He knows you know. Do you think he's going to let you live?

Billy disappears with that baleful question literally hanging in the air. I pan around the void surrounding my av. Has the close call in the park stripped away all the baroque effects from his punitive fantasies? Are we now dealing with a more efficient and dangerous Billy, one who's finally stopped playing games?

I write McClaren a short note about this most recent contact, but I don't send it.

What am I waiting for?

Slowly it dawns on me: I'm waiting to see Billy's proof.

71

Though he was masking his NOD connection, Billy most likely logged on from a computer somewhere relatively nearby. I'm sure it will be pointless, but I check the state of my tentacles into his laptop. As I suspected, it's gone dark, probably permanently. Once your machine has been infected by a real hacker, you can't ever trust it again. He'd have figured out we located him through his phone and assumed his computer was compromised as well.

I check my server for the webcam images it was transmitting. The shots are all the same incoherent blur until the final one, taken just before my RAT went offline. The image still shows the view out of a wide bank of windows. But either the lighting has changed or his laptop got moved, because I can see through them now.

And the view makes high-voltage spiders crawl around my scalp.

I grab the image and blow it up as far as it will go. The place must be pretty far south, because you can see a lot of open water in the background. I notice a distant figure emerging from the waves. It's out of focus and yet unmistakable. The stern visage of our Lady Liberty. And there's really only one place in the city from which you get a clean look at her face.

I've seen a similar vista from Gina's former apartment building.

Appropriate that Billy would relocate near the scene of Gina's death to plot his revenge. His sentimentality gives me another chance to find him, but I'm not sure what I'd do with him if I did. He deserves harsh punishment for burning Olya, never mind the lives being shredded by his *Unmasking*. That said, I don't want to be party to a summary execution if I deliver him to Blake and Mondano. At this point, Blythe is probably his only friend, and that's not saying much.

But at least I can rely on her to deal with Billy rationally.

I whiz through the area in Google Maps' Street View until I see the statue from the area I'm targeting. The green space facing Billy's window is too indistinct in the webcam shot to figure out exactly where it is. I find three candidates and select the one whose windows best match the inside framing of Billy's place.

I print out a map and jog downstairs to hail a cab.

The neighborhood around 120 Ferris Street is deserted. Wanting to approach undetected, I tell the cab driver to let me off a block early. Billy's place is three tall stories of corroding brick with an assortment of boarded-up arches for windows. Bits of wire and the crazily sloping remnants of a fire escape decorate its skin, which shows scars where gutters have been stripped off for scrap.

The back of the building, away from the street, will be my safest bet. There's a line of large but sickly trees along the alleyway between the building and the vacant lot next door. One of them has a thick branch leading up to a window whose boards have mostly rotted away. I scramble up the tree, make a hole in the glass with a diamond-tipped cutter, and insert a stiff wire to flip the window's antique lock. I have to climb down a set of empty cable brackets attached to the back of a huge open-air atrium that runs from a deep basement up to the roof.

The interior of the old building is a wreck. The walls down in the basement sprout disused pipe connections and mounting hardware testifying to machinery ripped out when its former occupant was liquidated by creditors. The kind of place that drives architects to suggest "accidental fire" as the best motif for a redesign.

At the far end of the basement is a wide spiral of cast iron stairs, which I follow up to the ground floor. Billy's living room consists of a green velvet couch and a shattered seventy-two-inch LED television. A bachelor kitchen, which appears never to have been used, opens off to the right.

I've been exploring the place in sepulchral silence, but now I become aware of a sound floating just at the limits of my perception. It's a single, unvarying, high-pitched tone, obviously made by an electronic device, but it doesn't have the alternating quality of an alarm.

Another steep spiral staircase leads up to a studio area. As I climb the stairs, the sound gets louder. It confirms my impression that no one is here, since I doubt if any normal human could tolerate the incessant ring.

On gaining the third floor, I see four large workbenches on the left side of the room, each littered with tools, materials, mechanisms, and scraps of clothing. There are three ripped-open workstations and a crushed laptop strewn around. The place looks like a Tokyo gadget market after Godzilla waltzes through.

One of the tables holds what I take to be a severed limb until I see the titanium ball joint projecting from its humerus. Nearby on the floor lies the former owner of that arm, an exceedingly lifelike rendering of a small boy that's been hacked apart. "Drawn and quartered" would be more accurate. Blood from internal bladders, still an artificially bright red, has pooled on the floor around him. I assume this gross display represents a beta version of a prop intended for when Billy reaches the limit of what he can hire body modders to do to themselves. There's a tag on his ankle that reads SAPROPHYTE STUDIOS, which is a Pittsburgh FX operation best known for making fake snuff films so realistic that a Kentucky man spent almost two weeks in jail after police found a copy of one in his apartment.

Toward the back of the room, two more of these mechanized grotesques hang from the wall. One is another little boy, the name "Giton" scrawled in black marker beside him. The other's skin dangles in shreds, as if someone compulsively slashed the latex with a box-cutter. The name beside it, though mostly obscured with blood, seems to be "Augustine."

On either side of the stairwell are small rooms made of pristine drywall. The tone is emanating from the one on my left. I step up to the door and turn the knob. The door catches on its frame at first, and I have to bear down with my shoulder until it pops open with a suffering creak.

Terror starts boiling inside me before I can make sense of what I'm looking at.

It's the smell: once again, brimstone.

Instinct makes me fling myself out of the room. I almost tumble back down the stairs, but my shoulder bangs into the curving iron banister. As

I scramble back to my feet, my mind has a moment to process what I'm seeing.

A bank of monitors surrounds an unmoving human shape seated on a large, high-backed wooden chair. Several plastic blocks rest at his feet. I take a deep breath.

It's just another one of his stupid gore puppets.

I try to get ahold of myself and flip on the light switch by the door. The scene gets worse.

It's a re-creation of the suicide video Billy sent to Blake. But taken to a new level of repulsiveness. The body slumped in the electric chair looks as though his skeleton has been reduced to fragments, held up only by the rusty iron band at his head. Around this are deep lacerations, blackened by the intense current. Below the cuts, one eye has popped out of its socket and dangles to the side of his nose. The other eye is just a red void, the border decorated with a clear jelly. A long, dark stain issues from his mouth, which is shut tight. I refrain from thinking about the state of his tongue.

Finally, there are discolored pockmarks all over his chest and arms, which I can't figure out at first. Then I glance down at the row of car batteries at his feet. Many of them are distended, and a few show cracks in their cases. I guess that would account both for the damage to the body and the smell of brimstone in the air. Many car batteries use lead and sulfuric acid to hold a charge. If one shorts them too quickly, they become very hot and explosive gases can build. Sometimes they rupture, spraying acid everywhere. The last thing I notice is the screen above the body's head. It's a heart monitor, with an unbroken horizontal line traversing its center. The source of the tone I've been hearing.

I don't know what makes me realize it; maybe the barely detectable stench of burnt hair and early decomposition, but suddenly I'm certain: this isn't one of Billy's atrocious mannequins.

This is Billy himself. In the flesh.

72

Back at my apartment, I peer down the neck of a half-empty bottle of Hancock's President's Reserve—a rare treasure I looted from his otherwise indifferent liquor cabinet—and ruminate on William Bennett Randall and his (now vindicated) paranoia. The question that has me slugging it down at three AM:

Do I believe him?

That he was killed in his struggle against his older brother, I have no doubt. His death is obviously rigged for a suicide determination. A verbatim reenactment of his *Jacking Out* video, both continuing the unfortunate Jackanapes suicide rash and making him another victim of his family's yearning for oblivion. I can just see Blake looking despondent, saying to an officer, "We were so worried." True, in its way.

But the Billy I'd come to know this past month was a fighter. He had plans for retaliation, and there's no way he'd fall on his sword without taking another whack at Blake.

My conclusion: Mondano and his goons somehow found him and did this to shut him up forever. I'll bet the batteries were well drained before the lethal jolt from inquiries about how to shit-can his porn worm. Given what he said at the Cloisters, that would have been a bleak exercise. At least whoever planned it came up with a more creative package than a twelve-gauge in broad daylight.

They meant to suppress the climactic reveal in Billy's arcane tour de force: that his brother and Olya murdered Gina Delaney to get control of her invention. I'd love to roll my eyes at his allegations and chalk them up to his deranged game narrative, but he's denied me the easy escape of willful disbelief.

Billy left evidence.

My bourbon bottle now sits next to the lone intact electronics left in the place. And it wasn't easy to find.

From searching the wreckage of all the computers in Billy's studio, I found that each of their hard drives had been meticulously wiped, presumably by whoever had meticulously wiped Billy. They'd even done a careful job destroying the processor boards and flash memory residing in his robotic voodoo dolls. I assume they intended this action to simulate the artist burning his life's work before joining it on the pyre. But after all that, they still missed something. Something only I could see, having been subject to Billy's codes and symbols for the last month.

I'd already completed one round of searching the place. Retossing each room. Pulling open tools. Checking the innards of his electronics. Anywhere he might hide some final communication. I was walking by his animatrons on my way to make a more thorough inspection of the room in which his corpse reposed, something I'd been avoiding for the past couple hours, when the shredded remains of Augustine grabbed my attention. Her silicone body molding had been mostly torn away, but still attached to a small chunk at her left arm socket was a ragged scrap of purple fabric hanging loosely over the shoulder. Something about that particular rich hue, and the way the fabric bunched, brought forth a memory.

That remnant was the same color as the purple toga worn by Gina's av Ines_Idoru.

Despite the thorough dissection, I could tell right away that they'd missed her vital organ. The large gear casing sitting right between the aluminum tubes of her legs. The place at her center of gravity: her womb.

I picked up a screwdriver.

It took quite a bit more surgery to take apart the gearbox. But as I suspected, at its center were the guts of a compact smartphone with a live connection to Verizon's wireless network. I plugged it into my netbook and saw that Billy had a custom script in the scheduler. If he fails to check in for more than 48 hours, it sends a video to a long list of email addresses, including the NYPD, the FBI, and several national news outlets.

This was Billy's version of letting his demons out into the world. As such, the video's a masterpiece.

We begin with Billy's argument for the prosecution in the case of Gina Delaney's murder. It's pithy, well produced, and certain to captivate his audience. Especially when you have the freshly mutilated corpse of the author to add sanguinary interest.

Documentary in style, it starts with a reprise of IT's progress, complete with stills of early versions of the Dancers. He identifies Gina as the real inventor of our system, gives a little background information on her, and then there's a cut to black.

Billy's voice narrates mournfully:

The New York City medical examiner's office ruled Gina Delaney's death a suicide two days after she was found. The primary basis for this determination was a videotape taken of her death, discovered by the responding officers at the scene. Here is the video.

And again I watch Gina's harrowing final minutes. But this time, framed by his forensic inquiry, I'm watching through Billy's eyes. The video takes on the cast of subliminal witchery one finds in the ice cubes of liquor ads.

At the end, we freeze on the shot of Gina's hideous demise, and Billy says, "If you look closely, this video proves beyond a doubt that she was murdered."

Then he starts his assault. His leading elements are reminiscent of those late-seventies Zapruder reconstruction "documentaries," trying to establish that JFK was assassinated by time-traveling Martians. Gina couldn't possibly have lifted the meteorite ballast. The light patterns on her face indicate fire traveling *toward* her. The ME's photos show conclusively that her wrists were recently bound. Some nonsense about the blood spatter being the wrong shape.

The case is meretricious: Gina had plenty of mech-E from MIT and could figure out how to lift anything; there were any number of reflective surfaces in the apartment; her wrists already looked like uncooked funnel cake; and the right combination of model parameters could get Billy's "expected" blood spatter to form a portrait of Mao.

But like a true showman, Billy saves his best for last. And here's where he makes me sit up and take notice. Now he just looks closely at the video itself. A part of it I've seen but never really scrutinized, since it occurs well after Gina is clearly dead.

About three minutes after she dies, her body shifts slightly. Maybe from the drill's vibration. Maybe her muscles relaxing in death. The movement causes her head to tilt slightly to her right. Billy freezes there on a single frame. The video is high def, so he's able to zoom extremely close on Gina's left eye. So close that I can just distinguish the reflections on its glassy surface.

And for me those tiny glimmers have the power of a collapsing star.

There's an old legend that says the eyes of a murder victim will capture the face of his killer. This belief was held widely enough in the early twentieth century that forensic photographers devoted a whole branch of their nascent art to the detailed recording of a corpse's eyeballs, and in some cases even attempted to "develop" images off the deceased's retinas through some rather gruesome means. The idea is lunacy of course, but exactly the sort of thing that would appeal to an artist like Billy. Maybe the concept sprang to mind when he was confronted with Gina's agonized eyes at the time of her death. I can just see him examining them minutely, since that image was the last remaining evidence of the now impassable pathway to her soul and its tragic mysteries. At some point he must have noticed the subtlest motion. Then he realized that in combining a high-res camera with the half-mirror of her eyes, he had a situation where the superstition actually proved true.

They're tiny, picked out in pixels of lightness against the deep black of her pupils. The outline of two figures standing side by side. Her head must have come to rest at just the right angle of reflection from some light in the room. There's not enough detail to get a very clear picture, but one attribute stands out: they both have blond hair. Almost white.

Billy slaps up a frame counter and lets twenty seconds tick by. During this, you can see the couple's heads turn toward each other. The man steps forward until he's directly in front of the body, perhaps touching it.

Then he moves back, and they both walk off to the right until they disappear at the margin of her pupil.

Billy can run all the hypotheticals he wants, and I'm unlikely to pay much heed. Lawyers consistently show that, much like statistics (or people), you can torture models into saying anything. But now he's showing me something I can see with my own eyes. An image recorded on video. And what it means:

Gina wasn't alone when she died.

Not content to rest his case there, Billy wraps up with a seductive reconstruction of his theory of events. There were two people with Gina that night. They drugged her, bound her hands, placed her in the chair, set up the lighter fluid, put a lighter by her hand. She revived slightly and spoke her last words. Not addressing the camera; addressing them. They stood just behind the meteorite and lit the cardboard tube on fire.

When certain she was dead, they unbound her hands and left the room.

As stand-ins for the murderers, he uses these indistinct wisps from Gina's eyes. Then he focuses on them for yet another unmasking.

Gradually, the foggy pixels begin to coalesce into more specific visages. Of course, he chooses his blond bêtes noires. Olya Zhavinskaya stands there directing half-closed bedroom eyes at her accomplice, Blake Randall.

He asks, "And what was their motive for this crime? Why not hear it in their own words?"

An audio loop begins. The sound is slightly muffled, but I can understand the words pretty clearly. Blake must be closer to the mic, since his voice is loud and instantly recognizable.

He says, ". . . why she still feels that way. It's unfortunate. Do you think you'll be able to bring her around?"

Olya's voice is less clear but identifiable from her accent. "She can refuse me nothing. I make things very unpleasant."

"Ah . . . 'The way to a woman's heart is the path of torment. I know of no other.'"

Olya says, "Eh? I don't know. G is very difficult. I think maybe the right path is through her rib cage."

"A bit unsubtle, darling, don't you think?"

"Mmm, but I'm tired of petting her always."

"Well, be patient. I'm sure you'll be irresistible in the end."

Blake's intonation on his line about "a woman's heart" suggests that he's borrowing the words. I guess their source even before searching for it.

So was this conversation what stimulated Billy's whole jihad against his brother? Blake glibly quoting Sade's dating tips?

It explains Billy's use of the marquis's words in his electrocution speech. When did he record this? An early jewel from his surveillance at GAME? Or he could have been listening through the mic on Blake's compromised laptop. Regardless, in the context of all his other evidence, the dialogue plays like a confession.

We fade back in on a shot of Billy himself addressing the camera. He's sitting a few feet away from where I found the video. His face bears a glazed, sorrowful expression. He's wearing the same clothes as yesterday.

Your viewing this video means that I am dead. Murdered. I've never been one to apologize for my art, but I'm afraid this fact may be cast into doubt by my recent endeavors. My death will be seen in the context of suicides both in my family and among my colleagues at GAME. My communications with my brother will be used as evidence to support these lies. I regret that I've given them the weapon. But that cannot be helped now. Here is the truth, for those willing to listen.

Upon receiving evidence of my friend Gina Delaney's murder, I could not proceed any further with my artistic response to her death. I had to take action against the perpetrators. My intention was to finish Savant *with evidence of two final crimes: the one you just saw, and a companion piece showing my revenge against my brother and his whore. But I suppose that has not come to pass.*

I don't argue that my hands are clean. I have never claimed to be innocent. But I cannot abide the idea of my brother standing before the world pretending to virtue. He is a grotesque fiend and must be known as such.

He is aware that I've begun to discover the truth about him, so for the past several days, I have been evading men he has sent to silence me. Abetting him in this have been the pornographer Benito Mondano, Blake's security goon John McClaren, and their mercenary James Pryce. There are others as well, a whole black mob of them, but you will find that these are the principals in my execution.

My only desire now is for the world to hear this shred of the truth I've been able to uncover. The truth about IMP, the truth about my family, and the truth about the horrible murder of at least one innocent young woman. Whether you believe it is up to you. But the facts are there, and I hope that this testament makes it impossible for my brother to keep them from the light.

The screen cuts to black.

I look out my window as I collect my thoughts and notice lights going on across the street. A garbage truck pings as it stops on its way up the block. Billy's case spins through my head. Most of it isn't too compelling: the weight of the rock, the ephemeral light analyses, the marks on her wrists distinguishable only to him . . . Something about that snags my train of thought.

The marks on her wrists.

Billy's phantom binding marks would be hard to detect because of Gina's real scars, put there by her repeated suicide rehearsals. Yet Olya had told me that Gina had cut herself in the bathtub the night before she died. Though the wounds weren't deep enough to be life threatening, there would have been serious cuts that should have shown up in the morgue photos. But they exhibited no recent damage. So why would Olya tell me a story like that?

Unless she was trying to make it seem like Gina was recently suicidal.

I can feel myself start to integrate into Billy's theory all the little dis-continuities and suspicious details one observes in an investigation. I force myself to stop.

I look down at the viscera of Billy's last connection to the outside world. In the dim predawn light filtering into my apartment, I can see re-flected against the wall a blinking glow from the phone's indicator LED. The sedate pulse tells me that it's connected to the net. In ten hours, Billy's orders will send his story into the public domain.

There's a part of me that just wants to let the program run, come what may. It makes me grind my teeth to realize it, but Billy's video has seeped into me. God help me, but I believe him.

But you just had to name me, didn't you?

I bring my bottle down hard on the fragile electronics. The light goes out, leaving the room still and dark.

Billy's created enough bedlam with his *Unmasking* already. A ring of privacy activists have started combing databases and news accounts to assemble a literal postmortem on the incident. The tally so far stands at forty-one arrests (mainly for the people caught with kiddie porn and not fast enough to wipe their drives before the police barged in), fourteen civil lawsuits, eighty-nine divorce filings, seventeen emergency custody hearings, five resignations of public officials, almost a hundred terminations "for cause," three more suicides, and one domestic murder.

Of course, another ghost rattling her chains is Gina. But if Olya and Blake are really guilty, what then?

The police would be one option, but how does that play out?

I walk into Nash's office with the story that one of his suicides was actually a murder, and I know this because of a secret multimedia game created by another dead artist. Billy's death was clearly effected with professional élan, and his killers left nothing incriminating except his video about Gina. While intriguing, it would be pulped into pixel soup by any reasonably sober attorney—never mind the kind of legal firepower Blake Randall could deploy. The video Gina shot is compromised as evidence, since I personally corrupted the official copy. I can't imagine, in a country where Phil Spector remained free for half a decade, that Olya and Blake wouldn't walk. And I suspect neither could a prosecutor with half a brain.

Billy must have made a similar calculation. Is this what pushed him into the role of self-appointed avenger, or failing that, what prompted him to make sure his case reached the public?

And what about his case? If what he says is true, that means, Jimmy, that you're in business with people who murder innocent girls. And, knowing this, maybe your life is in danger as well.

Like Billy said, "He knows you know. Do you think he'll let you live?"

73

"M ate, you realize you sound totally daft." Garriott is looking at me like I just ripped off a *Mission: Impossible* mask.

"I know, Andrew. But I'm completely serious."

Xan's eyes sweep over to mine, and she asks coolly, "You want us to get on a plane?"

"Yeah. Just until I get a better handle on things here."

We're standing in her office up at PiMP an hour after I called them from a brand-new cell phone. I have to assume all my normal comms have been compromised by Red Rook. And it wouldn't do to have Blake apprised of my new plans.

I rolled in tired and just beginning a crushing hangover, not the best state for what I'm trying to sell them. They'd been reluctant to leave the hospital, but Olya was scheduled for a long, delicate skin-graft surgery and wasn't expected to be conscious until the next morning.

Garriott says, "Really, stop fucking about."

"I wish I were."

"So you're telling us you think we're in danger because of some family tiff between the Randalls?"

Xan helps me out. "Garriott, shut up. He's serious. Listen to him." She turns to me and says, "So?"

I sigh, calculating how much I can reveal. "I think we may be at risk. When Olya told me about our partner Mondano, I had some friends in law enforcement check him out, and he is certainly a violent criminal.

I've come by some evidence that . . . well, that Billy's allegations about Gina may not be completely false. Whatever the case, we don't want to be in business with these people. They're dangerous."

"Billy tried to kill us. You can't believe anything from that nutter!"

Xan says to Garriott, "You're telling me you don't think there's been something off about this from the outset?"

He lowers his eyes.

She continues. "I've never worked on a tech project with a casualty rate before."

"But to mothball the Dancers? Flee to California? It's what that dick wants."

Xan ignores him and asks me, "What do you propose?"

"Look, we can debate the merits of our partners later. But I get the idea that they prefer to negotiate with corpses. So right now, we need to take that off the table. Once we're somewhere safe, we can worry about the long term."

Garriott says, "Yeah, let's have ourselves a merry vacation while everything we've worked for goes down the shitter."

Xan asks, "What about the police?"

"We may have to go that route. But first I want to establish exactly what happened. Bear in mind, if all this gets out, it will mean surrendering control of the Dancers to the legal system. We may have to do that, but I think maybe there's another way."

"So where do we go?" she asks.

"We can stay with an old friend of mine at his beach house in L.A. He's actually in the business. If we're nice to him, and introduce him to the Dancers, we may get a new deal out of it."

Xan stares at me for a long moment before nodding. She directs an imploring look at Garriott, who closes his eyes irritably. "Does it have to be L.A.?"

I say, "Garriott, get Fred and Ginger. Xan, maybe you can zip up all our source code and transfer it to a new server. I'll meet you at JFK in two hours."

We stand there looking at each other. Then Xan turns and walks out.

— — —

I hurry from PiMP back toward my apartment and spend the trip on the phone making arrangements with Adrian for us to crash at his place.

I hang up as I'm turning onto Bond from Lafayette. The street is busy with its many construction crews. I'm walking behind a pair of Mexican carpenters, and we have to squeeze past two guys in business casual and hard hats on the way into the wooden passage that takes us under the forest of scaffolding blocking the sidewalk. One of the men in front of me nudges the other and gestures back behind him. The other guy turns to look and shrugs, smiling. I check for an attractive woman or something, but all I see is one of the hard hats putting a radio to his mouth and the other rolling up the plans they were examining.

The Mexican guys I was following duck into their site. Ahead of me now are two men in hard-worn Carhartt overalls carrying tool bags. They're at the end of the block slowly coming toward me. Both are white and clean shaven. On the other side of the street is a pristine gray van with tinted windows. Its engine starts.

I go from hungover plodding to red alert. Just past my left shoulder, another pair of guys walk gradually in my direction on the other side of the street. The two close behind me are still chatting amiably, not making eye contact.

What is it? What's wrong?

There are too many pairs of fat white guys all converging on me right now. I come abreast of my building and notice vague human shapes through the frosted glass of the lobby door. I pause for a second, fishing for my keys.

Hmmm.

The van starts rolling forward now, but it's cut off by a speeding cab coming from the Bowery. This seems like a sign, so I plant my hand and vault over the cement construction barrier into the street right in front of the cab. The driver, a turbaned Sikh, screeches to a stop and lays on the horn. Which gives me time to yank open one of the passenger doors and jump inside. The driver stops yelling when I extract a wad of cash from my pocket.

"Take me to Astor Place fast. A hundred bucks if I'm there in less than a minute. Go!"

He punches it, and we take the corner of Lafayette in a squealing drift.

A number of faces turn to track our progress, and I can see curses forming at some of their lips.

We blaze up Lafayette, fortunately hitting a string of green lights. Looking back, I see the gray van rounding the corner five blocks back. I jump out of the cab and rush into a Kmart across from the main subway entrance. Behind me a black SUV and a beat-up delivery truck pull hastily to the curb.

Christ, that's a lot of people.

Mondano isn't messing around with a skeleton crew. I doubt I'd still be at large if these were McClaren's guys. Either way, how did they know I was planning to bolt?

There's a security guard at the door, so I walk in smooth, but then as I get past the checkout lines, I switch to a light jog. The escalators are clear, and I hustle down to the store's underground exit. I'm hoping that my pursuers won't know that there's this opening directly to the subway. Maybe they'll just cover the aboveground exits and wait, planning to get me quickly into the van rather than contend with store security raising hell. This Kmart's location on St. Mark's demands heavy vigilance against shoplifting punks.

My prayers for a train go unanswered. I hesitate, bouncing on the balls of my feet. The tension is too much, so I check both tunnels for lights and then jump down onto the tracks, nonchalantly, like I've every right to be there. The trip to the other side is a dirty business, but none of the people waiting seem to notice beyond an elderly gentleman pointing out my antics to his grandson. I go to the exit at the extreme end of the station and hide partway up the hallway that leads to the stairs. From here I can still see the entrance to Kmart.

Within seconds, two beefy guys, different from the ones I'd seen before, rush onto the platform where I came in. One pinches his temples and raises a walkie-talkie. I want to break for the surface, but I'm nervous that they would have much of Astor Place covered by now. A beautiful rumbling sound holds me in place. The 6 train comes up the opposite track and stops with its usual squealing protest. The two guys either get on or go back into Kmart, because they're not on the platform when I look again.

I'm still feeling exposed, since it's probably only a matter of time be-fore they check this side of the station. Thankfully, the northbound train arrives before they do. I hop on, careful to check that no one joins me at the last second. Once we hit Union Square, I've lost them.

On arriving there, I race to the L westbound.

Just making that train gives me a chance to think. How did they know to come after me now? I'd have spotted a tail from Mondano's people when I left Billy's. But static surveillance is a lot easier than sticking to a moving target. And Billy's place was fairly isolated on his street. I'd never notice if they were watching with a telescope from half a mile away to see who showed up. After the Cloisters, Mondano would consider my loyalties suspect. So when I didn't go to Blake im-mediately after leaving the murder scene, he'd know something was up. Were I them, I'd want to neutralize me and take control of the Dancers. Which means they're probably going after Xan and Garriott as well.

I get out at the last stop at Fourteenth Street and Eighth Avenue, grab a cab heading downtown, and dial Xan. My call goes straight to voicemail. That scares me, but there could be plenty of reasons for it.

Garriott, however, picks up. "What is it?"

"Hey, they know what's going on. Can you see anyone strange on your street?"

"What?"

"Look out your window and tell me if there's anyone loitering outside. Sitting in a car. I don't know. Someone walking a dog around the block that you've never seen before."

"Um, okay." He pauses for a second. "There's no one on the street."

"What about in the cars?"

"I can't really see from here. But I don't think there was when I came in."

I decide it's worth it to risk a pickup. There's no way Garriott could even spot a tail on his own, much less shake one.

"I'm going to be there in three minutes. When I call you, I want you to run to the corner of Greenwich and Charlton. I'll be in a cab."

"But—"

"Don't worry. We'll get you whatever you need. Just bring the Dancers. Now I gotta call Xan, so just wait for me."

I dial Xan, but it goes to voicemail again.

My driver has a real third-world enthusiasm for urban Formula One, and we barrel down Seventh Avenue at an inordinate rate. Rounding onto Charlton, our starboard side threatening to lose contact with the road, I call Garriott and tell him to go.

Near the corner of Greenwich, I get a jab of panic and yell for the driver to stop. Right in front of me is a tall bearded guy in tinted glasses reaching into his jacket. I burst out of the still-moving cab and blindside him. My elbow explodes in agony as it hits the cement, and I hear metal skittering along the sidewalk as something slides off the curb underneath a parked car. I hope it's his gun.

Garriott is walking toward me from the door to his building. Focused on my dramatic arrival, he doesn't notice the two men who step out from behind another apartment's entrance to his right. A blue van is speeding toward us, its side door sliding open like a raptor's third eyelid. I call out, but the men behind him move fast. Garriott starts running, but doesn't turn until one of the guys tries to torque the handle to Ginger's rolling case out of his hand. The other jams a small pistol into his ribs to encourage cooperation, but Garriott doesn't see it. He just reacts to the pressure by letting go of Fred's case and trying to push away the barrel of the gun.

When people describe moments like this one, they always say that time seems to slow down. It feels to me like the reverse happens. The next thing I know, I'm standing in the gutter dry-firing my pistol at the van now careening up Greenwich.

I turn. Behind me Garriott lies crumpled on the sidewalk, a bloom of crimson growing next to his head.

74

I run as fast as I can down Vandam toward Sixth Avenue, sirens converging behind me. I don't feel too bad for running since the EMTs will be able to do a lot more for him than I could.

Flashing through it in my mind, I think it went like this:

Garriott grabbed at the gun. The other guy saw his partner losing control of it and slammed the butt of his piece down on the back of Garriott's head. He went limp, pulling his assailant down with him. I opened fire at the one still standing. Being a notoriously poor shot, I missed three times before he dropped Ginger's case and brought his own gun to bear. I guess I should be thankful that the bearded man I had just tackled returned the favor by knocking me down into the space between two parked cars. I hit my head hard, but recovered enough to fire at the guy trying to pick up Ginger's case. These gentlemen probably weren't expecting to get shot at, because he abandoned it, and I heard someone shout "Go!" All three piled into the waiting van. I squeezed off my whole clip, and I think I might have hit one of the tires, but that didn't stop it.

I rolled Garriott over. He had a terrible gash almost down to his neck, and blood was pumping out at an alarming rate. I called 911 and spent a second trying to revive him. The pistol in my waistband meant that I couldn't be there when the police arrived, unless I wanted to wind up in jail on a gun charge. I grabbed the Dancers' cases and took off.

— — —

A cab crosses the intersection in front of me at speed, but I whistle loud enough to get it to pull right abruptly. Not knowing exactly where to go, I tell him to keep driving.

Then I call Xan.

Any relief I felt at getting away dissolves instantly when she answers.

"James. So glad you called." She's tentative, completely artificial.

"Xan, what's going on?"

"Yeah. We've had a bit of a change of plans here." Maybe it's the pronoun, or maybe it's the stress saturating her voice that warns me. She's in danger. I picture her with a gun to her head.

"Who's there?"

A shifting sound as if she's put her hand over the phone's mouthpiece. I hear what might be a male voice. Then she says, "I'm not going to be able to make our meeting."

"Right. Okay, what do they want me to do?"

"We all need to get together. I hope you can bring our special friends."

"Fine. Where?"

"There's a warehouse in Secaucus."

New Jersey. One of Exotica's local distribution hubs. Mondano's turf. I don't like it. I say, "How about the McDonald's in Times Square?"

Xan inhales. "Uh. No. It has to be . . . this other place." The terror in her words makes me want to rip someone's face off.

"Fuck. Fine. Tell your friends they need to be careful starting now. And principals only. I see one of these guys from earlier today, things will get very ugly."

"Um . . . Okay, principals only. We, ah, hope things go smoothly."

"When?"

There's a short pause. "Immediately. We'll have a car sent for you."

"No way. I'll be there in ninety minutes." I start to hang up, but she stops me.

"James?"

"Yeah?"

"We may need to demo the products. And we don't want any surprises. Nothing shocking, right? So with Ginger, be sure that you . . . Well, you know how she is. So we'll see you soon."

The line goes dead.

What was Xan's incoherent addendum all about? I can understand that they'd want to confirm that we haven't sabotaged the Dancers. But what does she mean by "nothing shocking"?

"So with Ginger, be sure that you . . ." The words I'd use to complete that sentence are: "Don't come."

She's telling me to bail on the meeting. But I can't bring myself to pull out now.

I have the cab drop me at a twenty-four-hour karaoke place in Korea-town. One of their private lounges serves as an office for twenty minutes while I, taking a cue from Billy, compose an affidavit summarizing recent events. I bundle this with his final testament and attach everything to an email. I set my mail program to send it to my entire address list twelve hours from now.

In less than a day I've gone from suppressing his message to potentially acting as Billy's press agent. The threat of violent death has a way of changing one's perspective. As a cadaver, I suspect I'll be indifferent to being accused of involvement in his murder. So, like a video game paladin, I'll be walking into this engagement clad in armor wrought purely of information.

With that thought weighing on me, I decide to spend my remaining time making sure that the Dancers are ready for a memorable debut.

75

Mondano's warehouse looks like a modest operation from the street. A run-down, one-story brick structure topped by a faded sign whispering EE LOGISTICS. But behind a screen of businesses installed in lots fronting the road hulks an enormous steel-sided warehouse.

I walk through a narrow gap in a chain-link gate topped with a triple-stranded overhang of barbed wire. The tiny parking lot is lit by a pallid green security light. The building looks dark and deserted. As I approach the dented metal door, Blake Randall swings it open. He adopts a rueful expression intimating how sad it is that things have come to this. I just brush right past him.

A reception area holds a bank of cast-off airport chairs opposite a tall counter like you might find at a car rental agency. Fake plants and inspirational posters round out the décor. The banality of this foyer is meant only to camouflage the eruption of carnal oddities beyond.

Blake buzzes me through a security door and into a reprobate's fantasy land. I stand on a thin catwalk overhanging a huge space filled three stories high with pallets of adult novelties sourced from nations spanning the globe. Hanging signs organize the aisles according to some innovative scheme of Dewey Decimal depravity. I can see a section containing enough rainbow-colored dildos to fill every orifice in the tri-state area. A miniature Library of Congress of pornographic DVDs. There's an area where remaindered magazines are collated into "value paks" unlikely to satisfy anyone: *Mature Foxes* with *Barely Legal, Footsie's Petites* with

Rump-A-Dump. Under different circumstances, this place would provide for an amusing couple weeks.

Blake leads me down the catwalk along a series of offices with glass walls commanding views of the warehouse floor. At the end is a long conference room equipped with a ten-seat table. The walls are decorated with promotional posters for storied Exotica releases.

Mondano and Xan sit at the far side of the table. Xan seems unperturbed, but she makes a tsk of exasperation as I walk in and set Fred and Ginger's cases in front of her. Mondano stands slowly. He's got a pistol tucked in the front of his pants.

He catches me looking at it and winks. That little gesture frightens me more than any of his earlier gangster posturing. In contrast to Blake, Mondano's become progressively jolly as events have spun further out of control. He's no longer acting like some kind of Lucky Luciano manqué. Here he's exposing the burbling molten plastic of his unhinged personality. After the Cloisters, I knew I'd underestimated him, but seeing him now makes me think I misinterpreted him entirely.

Slowly, with the exaggerated motions of a street mime, he takes his gun by two fingers and lays it gently on the table. He nods at his piece and grins, inviting me to do the same.

I do, and there's another thud at the end of the table where Blake's positioned himself.

So he came strapped too. Will the wonders never cease?

In front of him lies a U.S. Army standard-issue Colt .45 auto. In service between World War I and Vietnam, if I'm not mistaken. Call it his dad's, or maybe even grandfather's, gun. Reaching for his legacy even now.

Blake assumes the seat at the head of the table and begins. "So this situation is unfortunate. But as long as we all keep ourselves together and stay, ah, courteous, I'm sure we can work this out."

"Is knocking out our partner your idea of courtesy?" I reply.

"Garriott? Is he okay?" asks Xan.

Blake's eyes ignite. He says tightly, "I understand he attempted to disarm one of our employees."

"He was shitting his pants, Blake. He wasn't 'disarming' anyone. I'd be happy to stick my pistol in your ribs and see how you react."

"Now, James, I don't think threats are the way to go here."

"No? How are we supposed to interpret assault and kidnapping?"

Mondano leans forward and levels a spastically wagging finger at me. "If you hadn't started fucking around, he'd be sitting in that chair having a scotch right now."

"Oh. Does the chair have high-voltage lines attached?"

Blake jumps in. "Careful, James. We need to come together to find a—"

I'm about to protest, but Xan saves me the trouble.

"You expect us to 'come together' after you send this shit stain"— she points at Mondano—"to my flat trying to mouth-rape me with his gun?"

Mondano licks his lower lip. "I'll do better than that, *luv*. I've got—"

Everyone jumps as Blake slams his hand against the table. "Enough!" A tortured silence prevails as he collects himself. "Look, we can all walk out of here—"

"I know *we're* walking out of here," I say. "Your roll-up didn't work. So you must know that if Xan and I aren't swilling mojitos at Foo Bar by happy hour, you two are going to be under heat that will melt your skin. Maybe *you* want to try to beat it with an army of lawyers. But maybe cash-poor Benito here doesn't want to spend the prime of his life rimming his ink-faced Latin King cell mate."

Mondano chuckles like that might be a rare delight, but Blake eyeballs him skeptically.

I continue. "And, Blake, I'll bet that if the DA doesn't have your ass, your sweet sister—"

"You say another word about Blythe, and this meeting will end badly."

"I thought you didn't make idle threats, Blake. You're not going to kill us. You have too much to lose. And you won't be able to cover it up this time. I've been more thorough in my preparations than your brother was. So here's how it's going to be. We're going to leave now. You can hang on to the Dancers as insurance. Once we get to a safe place, we'll contact you about the files. It won't be cheap, but maybe we can make a deal. But we're not going to play ball with a gun to our heads. Because we know the gun isn't loaded."

Blake says, "Okay, James. All I ever wanted was for this project to succeed."

And your brother's head on a stick.

Mondano leans forward in his chair. "Wait. These things don't do us any good if dickface here lobotomized them." He leers at Xan. "Maybe our little geisha can show us how they work with a horizontal pussy."

Xan just looks through him.

"Fine," I say.

Is this actually going to work out? Are the Dancers really all they want?

Xan and I configure them in silence for a few minutes until everything is connected. I start up the ErrOS test package on my laptop.

As I'm doing this, my fragile hope that this meeting might remain civil is shattered. From watching Billy's video, I must be sensitized to moving shadows. It's slight and happens very fast, but in the far left corner of the back wall I sense motion. The smallest flicker in the profile of light coming through the glass.

Someone is peering around the corner. I force myself to continue what I'm doing. Then an almost subaudible scuffing sound, this time coming from the right.

Tentacles of acidic fear grip my stomach. There are people surrounding the conference room. Our partners have decided to continue politics by other means. I glance at Mondano, who leans back in his chair with reptilian complacency. Blake, on the other hand, is clearly on edge. Expectant.

I type a few runtime parameters into Fred's system. Xan starts Ginger's software, and we put the Dancers into a test mode that dispenses with the visuals and associated body tracking. The setting makes the machines just a simple sensor/actuator loop, taking them back to their most primitive form.

I say, "Since you're both so excited to see them in action, why don't you guys do the honors?" They both look askance at this suggestion, so I add, "Just use your hands, and you can tell that they're working. We don't have the gear to do full-service here."

Xan is quick on the uptake and grabs Blake's hand to guide two of his fingers into Ginger's opening. This would normally cause Fred to thrust outward a corresponding distance. But he stays in his plastic shell like a frightened turtle.

Mondano smiles up at the ceiling. "What—the—fuck?" he asks in an unnerving singsong.

"Relax," I say. "Maybe he's just having some performance anxiety with our new friends here." I see Mondano catch Blake's eye and shake his head sorrowfully. I take a small Allen wrench out of my bag and open the side flap of Fred's head that allows us access to the hardware. I make a minor adjustment.

"Try it now."

Again Blake slides two digits into Ginger. Again nothing happens. Mondano laughs like we've finally come to the punch line. "You think we can't fix this? You think we need you to make this work?"

I open Fred's hatch again, and while I'm twiddling, I rotate his base slightly counterclockwise.

Blake leans across the table and says, "James, this is very disappointing. What did you think was going to happen here?" Right behind him, I see a flutter in the light from the window. Mondano's men responding to his raised voice. Checking on their boss.

I guess it's now or never.

"Well, Blake, from recent experience, I figured you were going to try to"—I incline my head toward the mic in my laptop—"fuck me."

"Fuck_Me," of course, is the voice prompt that stimulates Fred to action, and so I used it here, but with modified orders.

A soft click sounds as Fred releases the latch restraining his manhood, and there's another louder one as he shifts the cylinder on his primary control valve. During the minute we've been waiting, I let the air pressure build up to over 250 p.s.i., quadruple its normal value. So Fred's plastic member shoots out of his pelvic casing and impacts with the force of a pro fastball into the right side of Mondano's mouth.

He's flung hard to the ground behind the table, so I can't see the exact effect, but I suspect a team of oral surgeons will send their kids to college on the proceeds from repairing the damage.

At the same time, Blake cries out at the surprise I installed for Ginger. All of her internal air muscles inflate to their maximum extent, trapping Blake's fingers in a vise-like grip. Her head then rotates while pulling down hard, hopefully placing his wrist in a painful position.

I dive over the table to knock Xan to the floor. Mondano is screaming, a strangled whistling sound, and his men will be coming in fast.

Xan and I hit hard next to Mondano, who's trying to go fetal under the table. I roll over and thrust my leg up into its underside with enough strength to topple it over so that its opposite edge rests on that side's row of chairs. It forms an incomplete barrier between us and Mondano's men. The giant glass wall explodes from the blast of a sawed-off shotgun. I nearly lose control of myself. Pistols are bad enough. But a shotgun in close quarters is a recipe for slaughter.

Through the gap under the table's edge I can see two sets of legs move into the room. I missed the chance to grab my gun as I vaulted over the table, but Mondano's slid down with me, landing right next to Xan's head. I snatch it and fire at their kneecaps. A startled shout indicates I hit someone, but I know it's not going to be enough.

The men will be on us before I can stand, so in desperation, I grab Mondano by the back of his jacket and turn him so that his body is mostly covering mine. I'm just bringing my pistol up when I see the face of Shades from the Cloisters emerge over the edge of the table. He's looking down past the barrel of his shotgun. He takes in the situation and hesitates. With a handgun it would be an easy shot, but his pellet spread would take a large chunk of his boss along with me. It's just enough time for me to squeeze off two shots into his chest, and he disappears from my view, firing into the ceiling as he falls.

There's still at least another shooter, maybe disabled, but probably not incapacitated. But I can't see him through the table. I roll into a squat and jerk Mondano up onto his knees. He tries to grab at my face, but he's wild with agony and can't mount much of an attack. I lurch forward with him, my adrenaline-saturated muscles just able to propel him up over the lip of the table. I'm right behind him, again using his body as a shield. A muzzle flash from the floor just to my left, and Mondano's head snaps back, spraying my face with gore. I empty my clip in that direction, but I can't see shit with my eyes full of blood. Mondano becomes dead weight and slumps forward onto the edge of the table.

I duck back down, frantic about what I'm going to do now that I'm out of ammo. I listen to try to get a sense of what's happening, but a horrible silence has enveloped the room. Xan levers herself upright beside me, her breath coming in sobs. I put a finger to my lips. She holds her breath. The air is heavy with the acrid smell of burnt gunpowder. Then I hear a muffled thump to my left, maybe against the far wall. Someone is still moving. My brain seizes with terror.

And then I see it. Mondano's lifeless body hanging over the edge of the table has caused his pants to ride up enough to uncover an ankle holster. I grab the gun and rise, looking for targets.

It's Blake leaning against the back wall. One of his hands is bent around at a disgusting angle, the wrist obviously mangled. I suppose that happened when I kicked the table over. Ginger would have come flying off with Blake's hand attached. Despite what has to be unbelievable pain, his other hand is steady. It holds his gun, and is pointed straight at my chest.

On seeing this, I almost start shooting immediately. But something holds me back. Mondano and his help planned violence from the beginning, but throughout, Blake has seemed legitimately shocked by what's happened. He is someone I *know,* and regardless, there shouldn't be any more bodies coming from this. My dreams from the past weeks of a triumphant demo are cruelly mocked by the blood drenching the room's walls. Our unnatural vision of love replaced with this gory nightmare of war.

I have to swallow hard to get my voice to work. "Blake, let's just—"

But then he fires.

I guess I saw in his eyes the hysterical equations he was processing reach a solution. Maybe I noticed him adjusting his aim. Because as I hit the ground, I know that I got off a shot as well, and we both went down.

I can't say it hurts too much, but I know it's bad. Partly because I can't really move my head. In fact, I'm rapidly losing control of my whole body. I see Xan's face swim into my line of sight.

Her mouth opens in what must be a scream.

III

THE QUEEN OF HEARTS

76

My cocoon goes from pleasant darkness to a brighter reddish brown. A light has been turned on, and if I open my eyes, I could find out why. I keep them closed.

Hazy days pass in a swirl of numbness and pain. A surgery I think. I have a dim recollection of being moved onto a rolling stretcher. Some forms thrust at me. McClaren's face close to mine, saying my name. These are only a few among some far more outlandish memories, so they may be nothing but the residue of a fever-fraught, opiate-laced dream.

The next thing that seems definitely real is a soft feminine voice speaking words I can't quite hear. Then an entrancing smell of cigarette smoke. My chest clenches with must-have-right-now urgency. I open my eyes to assess the possibility of getting one.

At first I'm optimistic. The mahogany furniture, impersonal floral wallpaper, and decorative molding place me in a premium hotel suite. But my hopes fall as I take in the adjustable bed, IV stand, and nearby heart monitor, which is reproachfully recording my nic fit. I try to lever myself up, which makes me realize that I've also been shot just over the right hip. Combined with my chest wound, this makes almost any movement excruciating.

I lie still, but a section of my brain is pumping out some sensational anxiety messages. I look around for clues to their cause.

In a sunny alcove off to my right, I see Blythe Randall chatting on her cell. She's wearing a gauzy dark-gray suit. And despite the setting, she's smoking. I'm struck by how beautiful she looks. But then I remember my recent history and conclude that maybe I should be afraid.

Thinking of my email bomb makes me start wishing I hadn't survived. My phone sits on a table next to me just within reach. A few clicks reassure me that it never went out.

Now, how could that be?

I guess Red Rook was farther up my ass than I imagined.

My sigh of relief gets Blythe's attention, and her phone flips shut. I test her attitude by placing two fingers sideways at my lips.

She shakes her head, but the crinkle at her eyes conveys "What are we going to do with you?" not "I'm going to strangle you for shooting my brother." She steps over and places her cigarette between my lips. I inhale deeply, ignoring my suspicion that a coughing spasm might kill me.

Blythe sits next to me and says, "You've had us a bit worried."

I have so many questions, it's hard to know where to begin.

"Where am I?"

"Well, you're not in Secaucus bleeding to death." Her cool tone implies, "Though that could be arranged."

"Good . . . But—"

"We thought after . . . everything, you might need a break. So you're at a private clinic on Long Island. Where you'll receive the best medical care known to man. For the *full duration* of your recovery."

Does that mean I'm effectively a prisoner? Do I care, as long as they keep the Fentanyl flowing?

I'm just amazed Blythe isn't ripping my eyes out.

"What about—" I realize belatedly that I'm heading into dangerous territory.

Blythe is a step ahead of me. She takes some papers off the nightstand and hands them to me. "We're going to need you to confirm this as soon as possible."

I take the pages warily and start skimming.

The document is Xan's statement to the police. She's given them a background précis very close to the truth, but substituting in place of the Dancers some crazy porno NOD build Mondano and Blake wanted to set up. We'd gone to the warehouse to discuss ramping up security on the project due to Billy's attacks. Halfway through the meeting, Blake shows up and starts screaming threats at Mondano about something having to do with his little brother.

The key paragraphs read:

```
In response, Mr. Mondano produced a firearm from his
waistband and pointed it at Mr. Randall. At that point,
the two security personnel [Unknown #1 and Unknown #2]
appeared outside the room, both armed as well. Their
arrival seemed to surprise Mondano, who called them
"worthless traitors" and pointed his gun at them. I
gathered that Randall had co-opted these men and arranged
for them to intervene in case of any altercation. Randall
then drew his own pistol and aimed it at Mondano, who
reacted by pulling Mr. Pryce out of his chair and
stepping behind him. Randall fired his weapon, hitting
Pryce in the chest and hip areas. Mondano shot at
Randall, hitting him in the chest.

     Mondano kicked over the table, blocking my view of
subsequent events. There were a number of shots fired, and
I believe that Mondano shot both Unknown individuals. But
when Mondano moved to inspect the room, one of them shot
him in the head. I then fled the premises.
```

The first thing I realize upon absorbing this is that Xan has lied extravagantly to protect me. In her account, I have been made into an unarmed bystander.

What about my gun? Is it possible that Xan had the presence of mind to get rid of it?

I reach to remember what really happened. No, I never fired it, so there won't be traces for ballistics. The only guns I fired were Mondano's.

But they would have my fingerprints on them, wouldn't they? Is it possible that Xan wiped them and then ran them back through his hands?

What about the Dancers? They're not mentioned, so she must have hidden them as well. Not hard to pull off in a warehouse full of sex toys.

And why would Xan do this anyway?

I think back to that picture Billy took of her shaking hands with Blythe at Gina's funeral. Xan had said she was just offering condolences, but what if it was more than that? What if they struck up an acquaintance? That led to a business arrangement. Could Blythe have asked Xan to "keep her informed" like she did with me?

So when things blow up at the warehouse, Xan calls Blythe, and she sends McClaren to perform triage. They concoct a tale for the police, and the responding officers buy it.

The sickening second insight follows on impatiently: for Xan to have felt free to deliver such a fabrication, there must be no other surviving witnesses. And that means that Blake Randall is dead. I glance cautiously at Blythe, once again wondering if I'm next in line.

She looks at me steadily. "My brother's been laid to rest, James."

I clear my throat. "You seem—"

Her eyes flash. "I am *shattered* with grief for him." She takes a long breath and calms. "But I saw more clearly than anyone how dedicated he was to reliving my father's life. And that couldn't have ended well, could it? I mean, consorting with a psychopath like Mondano?" A hint of bitterness creeps into her voice. "The way Blake would rail about our 'crazy half brother.' When all the time, he was the one losing touch with reality. The Randall family curse." She brushes the corner of her eye with the back of her hand.

"I'm sorry."

"I had hoped you might be able to protect him. Though I'm not sure if anyone could have by that point. He was so bent on . . . Well, anyway, Xan tells me he shot first. And I'm inclined to believe her."

"I'd thought it was over. I don't really remember pulling the trigger."

"I think you'd better forget it. He was a big believer in destiny, and he reached for his fate with both hands. You had the bad fortune to be present at the reckoning."

"And your other brother?"

"After the police found him"—she shudders slightly—"it didn't take them long to piece together what they'd done to him and why."

"Are Xan and Garriott okay?"

"They are. Garriott's here. Recovering nicely. Maybe you two will find yourselves on the shuffleboard court soon. Xan is fine. You are indebted to that woman."

She adds a sharp glance at the papers I'm holding, commanding me to endorse this fantasy for the police. That feels dangerous. There are dead bodies here, and lying about what happened, if it unravels, would be a good way to get a murder jacket rather than a shot at justifiable homicide.

But the tale has already been told.

I'm holding the official version in my hands. If mine should deviate, I not only lash myself to all four corpses, I also make Xan a perjurer. She may not be completely innocent in this affair, but she must have made her statement for my sake.

Easy choice.

"I know. She saved my life."

We sit in silence. Blythe gives me another drag off her cigarette. I watch her smoke for a moment. She French-inhales, which makes me think of someone else.

"And Olya?" I ask.

Blythe's nostrils flare at the name. "That one remains an outstanding issue. She found the strength to check herself out of the hospital well before anyone would have thought her able. Head injuries can be like that, I'm told. We have people looking for her, but she seems adept at covering her tracks. Our best information is that 'Olya Zhavinskaya' isn't even her real name. McClaren tells me there are some unsavory Russian gentlemen trying to locate her as well. Something to do with a previous enterprise. Even so, there's no telling where she went, though I understand statuesque blondes can find all sorts of diverting work in Kuwait. But with the burn scars . . ."

I close my eyes, remembering her.

"No doubt men all over New York are tearing their hair that she's gone. But you'll heal. I'm sure next year's model will be even better."

"So what happens now?"

Blythe waves toward the window framing a priceless view of white sand and sparkling water. "For you? You'll understand that your relationship with IMP can't continue, but I'm prepared to offer generous severance."

I shoot her twin brother, and she's offering me severance?

My surprise lessens as she continues. "After such a tragedy, I'm sure I don't need to say the word '*plomo*'? With all these nasty perforations, I suspect you've had your fill of the heavy metals."

Disconcerting for Blythe to pose a question immortalized by the hall-of-fame kingpin Pablo Escobar: *Plata o plomo?* Silver or lead? A joke, but an edgy one.

She glides a finger just above my chest wound. "What happened was awful, but one day I'm sure you'll treasure these scars. There's something so attractive about a man with the power to stop bullets."

77

After my release from the hospital, I'm tempted to slink back to Red Rook, but that doesn't feel quite right. Blythe bore the cost of patching me up, so I figure the least I can do is spend some of my separation pay to fix the two parties who helped save my life. Ginger's neck is broken in several places, and of course Fred needs to be remasculated.

I try to recruit Garriott and Xan to help, but they seem fairly traumatized by what happened and want no further part of the roborotica business. And they aren't going to have Blythe Randall pulling strings for them forever. We agree that they'll keep their shares of any new company, but otherwise I get free rein.

Though it turns out Blythe is pulling strings for me as well.

Something I find out after fielding a call from my old poker buddy William Coles. He begins by saying, "Dude, I'm totally into fucking robots."

He's taken a page from his father's playbook and gone into currency trading, though his company, Philosopher's Stone Financial, works with virtual currencies. Spinning gold out of silicon. Blythe tipped him off to my new enterprise, thinking he might be an ideal investor. We set up a meeting for a demo.

He closes the call by saying, "And at this meeting I want to fuck

Whitney Houston. Like pre-Bobby? No wait, an octopus! No . . . Uh! All three Olsen twins! Wait, can what I'm fucking change in the middle?"

I then call Adrian to convince him to work with me full-time on bringing Fred and Ginger back to life. He quickly agrees, saying, "The margins on manufacturing virtual snatchola are going to be obscene."

A few weeks later, I pass a newsstand on my way home. The front page of the *Journal* shows a picture of a black-clad blonde emerging from a limo into a crowd of photographers: Blythe Randall returning trium-phant from the closing of her TelAmerica deal. The article lauds her "iron resolve" in getting the transaction done after it was plunged into uncertainty in the "amazingly brief" period of chaos at IMP caused by the deaths of both her brothers. While Blythe has never addressed the press, the article quotes from the statement made by an old Randall fam-ily spokesperson:

```
Ms. Randall is deeply grieved by these developments and
asks that the media respect her privacy in this difficult
time.
```

Of course, the media is not in the business of respecting privacy. From my hospital bed, I'd read some of the coverage in the weeks after Blake's death. You could hear the reporters gnashing their teeth as the police conducted their investigation with unusual dispatch and discipline. They quickly concluded that Billy had been murdered by Mondano's two dead henchmen, and that the warehouse shootings stemmed from a fight that escalated to a lethal pitch. This determination relied on the testimony of two eyewitnesses whose identities had to remain confidential for fear of reprisals. All those suspected of violence were now deceased, so the case was closed without the glorious spectacle of a trial.

The verdict on Blake was, "Rich kid, under too much pressure from an early age, cracks. Tragic consequences ensue."

Two weeks later, Israel reinvaded Lebanon, a photogenic toddler was kidnapped, and an earthquake re-destroyed Port Au Prince. The story dissipated.

Billy's *Unmasking* stayed with us for a bit longer. There were trials to cover, public disgrace to bestow, and tearful confessions to extract. But once the worm was contained and the source of new victims dried up, the sex scandals, being primarily virtual and involving mostly regular folks, lasted no longer than they usually do. Remarkable more for their simultaneous disclosure than anything else.

While there was a short and sharp drop-off in certain online activities, and perhaps a quicker uptake of browsing anonymizers, Lucifer quickly reasserted control over the world's computer screens. I came to agree with Blue_Bella's prediction that Billy's trick would produce more eyes opened in wonder than it did heads hung in shame.

I had little doubt that the Dancers' reception would be a warm one.

78

Ten months later, I'm starting to question whether they'll be received at all. There's a critical bug we can't seem to stamp out.

The problem is that Ginger can have exactly eight orgasms in a session, and then she inexplicably dies. We want to have test units reviewed by a group of influential Sex 2.0 bloggers, and we can't send them out until we squash the bug.

At ArrowTech, our "erotic technology" company, my team has been bickering about it nonstop. Since thirty hours have passed without a solution, I tell them I'll take it over.

Eight hours in, all I can think is that I'm not even supposed to be doing this. Though I'm in charge of our tech efforts, I haven't openly picked up a screwdriver or written a line of code in six months. The last time I tried, it caused a vitriolic argument with Adrian about my wasting time in the weeds. He said that whenever I'm tempted to do anything useful, I need to pick up the phone and tell our HR coordinator to hire someone to do it for me. With the lavish funding from Thrust Capital, Coles's new venture fund, I've already conceded the "get erect fast" argument. But this whole time I've been secretly indulging an urgent need to get my hands dirty. Which is why I'm here at two in the morning hunting this pesky critter.

We started by establishing that the bug exists in the original version of the Dancers' code, in Fred's orgasm-detection routines. So I've been poring over Garriott's old files to see if we missed anything.

After a long time searching, I begin to feel another presence in the code. In a few places, generally the most complicated parts of the program, the ones you can't quite understand upon first seeing them, I find some constructions that don't seem like Garriott. Like someone is speaking with a different voice. A coder whose head is altogether closer to the machine: lots of complex class structures, fancy recursion, and elegant bit manipulation. Garriott is a very good engineer, but his code gives the impression of a rigorous proof. This stuff looks like poetry.

No one would ever write sample code like this, so where did it come from?

The answer's obvious: Gina.

Reading her syntax elicits a welter of emotions. Sadness that I never got to meet this tortured genius mixes with creeping guilt over my exploitation of the project for which she was murdered.

I'm trying to parse a particularly thorny section when I get a feeling of déjà vu. This code is distinctive enough that I must have seen it before. I do a global search and find, in a totally unrelated library, an almost identical function.

My screen-burned eyes finally focus on the difference:

Function 1 is called: `O_fill_packet`
Function 2 is called: `O_fill_packet`

Only a couple of shifted pixels separate the lowercase L from the number 1 in most default programming fonts. A discrepancy so easy to overlook that the names must be intentional. We hackers often use such lettering tricks when trying to disguise files or processes on a target's machine.

The only difference between the two functions is that O_fi11_packet has a single line allocating a variable that creates a huge memory leak.

Someone intentionally put a bug into the system.

I restrain myself from immediately stomping this guy, and instead I check the value of the wayward variable when Ginger goes into her postcoital depression. It reads:

```
This little death I exalt \n
For I'd rather halt \n
```

```
Than make a pillar of salt \n
Gina Delaney \n
03.21.1980 - 10.29.14 \n
```

Gina put in an Easter egg.

The practice of embedding hidden treasures into software has a storied history. There's the Hall of Tortured Souls in Excel '95 wherein, by executing an obscure series of keystrokes, the user can enter a *Doom*-like 3D world. The infamous "Hot Coffee" pornographic cut scene in *Grand Theft Auto* actually prompted Senate hearings, with Hillary Clinton, of all people, acting particularly aggrieved. But generally Easter eggs are credit reels for underappreciated programmers.

Strange for Gina to put hers in a critical bug. This critter has caused enough ill will that any normal coder would remove it immediately. I fix the memory leak but decide to leave her secret memorial. She deserves it.

The word "memorial" sticks in my head. Gina's statement weirdly evokes her final words, and the lifespan notation at the end makes it look more like an epitaph than a signature. Knowing her history, I'm not surprised that she would focus on the connection between death and orgasm. Or that she'd program her bots to actually "die" after experiencing a certain amount of pleasure. But the "halt" she mentions can't mean Ginger, since the next line refers to Genesis 19, just as she did in the video of her death.

Then it hits me.

How could she correctly guess the date on which she would be murdered? And if she didn't put it in, who did?

This section of IT's code base was Garriott's responsibility. But the file history shows he never changed it. So Gina must have added it. Which means the line really was her epitaph, and she hid it in the DNA of the project that came to define her life. If that's true, then she knew the day she would die.

My mind recoils from the logic. I try to clear it by standing up to stretch. But my gaze keeps returning to the verse sitting calmly in my debug window.

If Gina placed these words in her magnum opus, then either she was clairvoyant, or she *selected* the date of her own demise. She could only know it would be October 29 if she chose that date.

And if that's true, then Gina wasn't murdered after all.

79

Her message goes to work on me that night.

Why do I care so much about what happened to this poor girl? I feel like over the past weeks, I've come to know Gina well. In fact, my now gleaming future is really a gift from her.

It was Lot's wife who turned into a pillar of salt, so is she saying here that she'd rather "halt" or die than share the fate of her mother? Billy had assumed Gina's death related to her work on the Dancers, as did I, but here she's invoking her wretched family.

Thinking it might be helpful to review a few details of her case, I lob in a call to Detective Nash, leaving a message that I just want to "tie up some loose ends."

Then I call Ruth Delaney. Having delivered her daughter's last words to her, I guess I owe her these as well. And she may be the only person who can help me decode them.

But the Delaneys are now represented by a "please check your number" message. Charles probably burned through Billy's largesse in a hurry, and now maybe they're having trouble with the bills. I search for an alternate listing but can't find anything.

I know I won't be able to give this up until I talk to her, so the following morning I catch a train to Boston.

— — —

Standing at the corner of Cross Street and Blakeley, I stare with amazement at a vacant lot where the Delaneys' wilted house used to be. Did the city mercifully elect to put it down?

No. A quick look around reveals traces of debris from a fire. Chips from burned timbers still leach black soot onto the sidewalk in the cold Boston drizzle. A few remnants show where the brick chimney fell and fractured across the back of the lot. I find a mud-covered scrap of yellow safety tape from the fire department.

Eventually a neighbor, a balding man with an impressive belly not quite covered by his yellowed T-shirt, shuffles out to get his paper. He darts a suspicious look at me but doesn't retreat when I walk over.

I ask, "When did it burn?"

He replies in thick Bostonian, "Back on the first day of February. Two o'clock in the goddamn morning."

I run this through my mental calendar. That was the night I called Ruth Delaney.

"You know what caused it?"

"Yep."

"What?"

"The wife."

"How do you know that?"

"Well . . . I ain't a fire-ologist, but they can tell stuff by the way the gasoline was spread around, or so they said."

"The fire department said this?"

"Uh-huh. Charlie being stuck to that couch of his with a samurai sword through his gut probably helped them figure it out."

"Wow."

"Yeah. I got the feeling the guy was hard to live with."

"And Mrs. Delaney?"

The neighbor looks a little pained. "I guess she didn't want to live with herself either."

Ruth Delaney burning everything the same night I spoke with her is way too much of a coincidence for my heathen mind to process. So I turn to religion.

She heard something in her daughter's words that I couldn't. I pull up the entire chapter of Genesis 19 on my phone, and this time I read to the end. It details what happens between Lot and his daughters after their mother transforms into a condiment:

> And they made their father drink wine that night also: and the younger arose, and lay with him; and he perceived not when she lay down, nor when she arose.
>
> Thus were both the daughters of Lot with child by their father.

While incest may have been the order of the day in Biblical times, in 2014, being impregnated by your father might start a girl on trying to find a way out.

Is that what Gina meant? Is that why Charles Delaney objected so fervently to an autopsy? Had he received a revelation of what they might find?

I recall Olya's chronology of Gina's final days. She went back to Boston to tell her parents about her new love. She came home depressed and spouting Bible verses about Sodom. Might her grand declaration have set something off in her father? With his frayed sanity, I can imagine Charles deciding that his daughter had surrendered herself to the Sodomites, and that somehow justified him in doing whatever he wanted with her—to her.

So he rapes his girl, maybe reverting to an old habit that Gina thought she'd escaped. Her personality is probably consistent with someone who had been sexually abused growing up. She returns to New York the broken woman Olya observed. Her despair deepens over the following months, enough time to miss two periods. She goes to a doctor and has it confirmed: she's pregnant by her own father.

Like the daughters of Lot.

It stands to reason Ruth Delaney would have a better working knowledge of Old Testament stories than I do. Thus the vacant lot.

Incest would also explain the bloody bathtub the night before Gina died. I'd thought Olya was lying about that incident, but thinking back, she never actually said that Gina slit her wrists again. She just said she cut herself. I pull up Gina's morgue photos from my private server and see it immediately: a ragged scratch moving horizontally between her hips about an inch or so below her belly button. Perhaps she was working up to a freelance hysterectomy the patient was not expected to survive. But Olya finds her first. Gina asks if she can forgive her anything, says she "can't bear it." She looks for redemption through her lover. But Olya lashes out, rather than comforting her.

For a certain breed of computer scientist, symbols are of the utmost importance. So upon learning of her pregnancy, and that Olya cared more for their robot babies than she did for her, Gina might have felt the keystone supporting her life had cracked. That her great project, her Jack of Hearts, had brought her to ruin. I can see how she might want to expunge it.

And so Gina gets busy in her workshop, and the next night she jacks out.

While incest is far more common than people realize, it remains so taboo that even when it's staring one straight in the face, most people won't see it. Social workers have to be specially trained to tweak their antennae. The tragedy here is that if anyone could understand the toxic emotions that spew from a gothic upbringing, it should have been Billy. But he sought an explanation for Gina's misery in his own fucked-up family, instead of hers. Once taken with the idea Blake was responsible, he was predisposed to believe later that he'd actually murdered her.

So did he conjure all his proof out of thin air? Sharpening digital artifacts until they looked like something sinister? Could those two blond apparitions have been summoned by Billy himself?

Whatever the source of his evidence, he was wrong. If there was one person responsible for Gina's fate, I'm now sure it was her father. And Billy ended up dying for his mistake.

I get a call from John McClaren at nine AM the next morning. He's full of his usual hail-fellow irony, but there's an undercurrent of irritation. He wants a meeting. Now.

On the way over, I try to figure out the significance of this appointment. Nash must have informed him about my call. The two had known each other before I ever got involved, and I start to wonder about the basis of their relationship.

— — —

At McClaren's office, I get an overhand shake and a slap on the back. He tells me to sit and spends a moment inspecting me. Finally he says, "So, bud . . . you must be hella busy with your *twatomata*."

"Yeah. It's getting hectic right now."

"Sure, sure." He tilts his head to the side. "That's why I was surprised—I'd say amazed, even—to hear that you've been bothering the local con-stab-ulary with interview requests."

"All work and no play makes Jack a dull boy."

A mirthless chuckle. "So are you planning to blow up the Overlook just for a little excitement?"

"No, I've seen enough fire for the year." I smile back at him and reach for a tone of idle curiosity. "Something came up that muddied my understanding of recent events. Just wanted to mop up a couple details."

"Jim, cleaning is my job. And I just dealt with a very big mess that you were involved in making. Everything's fine now, but what I don't need is you tracking in more shit."

"Things don't look as clean as you might like."

"Uh-huh . . . But remember, you've been read into this situation. So what you see isn't what everyone else sees."

That line pops the bubble of uncertainty that's been swelling in my head. I'd been asking myself: why did Billy see something so different from the police when he watched that video? Most of his voodoo forensics were unconvincing, but what about the pale figures in her pupils? No one who watched the recording, including me, ever saw them before he got it. As if they represented a hidden message intended only for him.

I feel an itch deep in my brain stem. How uncanny that in both *Getting Wet* and her suicide video, Gina's eyes would transmit recondite information. Life imitates art.

Too perfectly, I think. More likely that detail is a product of the same artifice Billy used in *Getting Wet*.

How do I know the copy of Gina's suicide video I took from the NYPD server was anything like the original?

I've been overlooking the crucial attribute of that file: chain of custody. McClaren could easily have gotten Nash to upload a different version. Those tiny ghosts could be the result of a couple hours with After Effects. A capability well within reach of someone who works for one of the biggest media companies on earth.

Relieved by my newfound certainty, I decide to push it. "Is that because you had Nash swap in a doctored recording of Gina Delaney's suicide, knowing that Billy would eventually get ahold of it?"

McClaren laughs. "Buddy, you don't seem to understand that nobody cares anymore about your questions."

"I think after what happened . . . that I deserve to know the whole story."

"You're just killing me here. Look, the only 'story' you should be worried about is your own. Right now you're getting a happy ending. With your line of work, you can probably have as many as you want. Billy? Now, Billy's story is a very, very sad one. You don't want to get caught up again in that kind of story."

"You want to make that threat explicit?"

He watches me, his face shut and barred, bonhomie doused like kids pissing on the coals of a campfire. My mind is still racing.

Why would McClaren want to give Billy a doctored video? To make him believe that Blake murdered Gina? Could it have been a scheme to enrage Billy to the point of recklessness?

If so, I guess it worked, but not before endangering Blake's life and risking that this fraud would be discovered. As a strategy, that would be akin to defusing a live artillery shell with a hammer. I remember the look on Blake's face when Billy started dumping his stock. If that video was a key piece of some plan hatched by his own employee, why did Blake act so surprised when his brother's actions then spiraled into violence?

McClaren sighs as though he expected better of me. "Threat? I'm not making any threats. The only threat we're discussing is the one Ms. Randall might see in you going around trying to dig up the family cemetery for some ridiculous nonsense you got banging around in that head of yours. You should chew over the possibility that maybe things won't go so smoothly for you if she has to withdraw her helping hand. If I was you, the last thing I'd want is for that hand to become a fist. That's just a little friendly advice. Me to you."

Helping hand? My stomach drops as I realize what he's talking about. Blythe called Coles about my new IT enterprise, and I thought that was the end of it. But isn't it interesting how quickly a currency quant was able to raise venture funds? Coles is loaded, but he wouldn't have *that* much just lying around.

Christ, is my company built once again with Randall money?

As the thought settles, it starts to make even more sense. Blake was many things, but he wasn't stupid. Most of the infrastructure he built to profit from IT is still in place. Blythe has already won the contest for control of IMP, so why not appropriate Blake's idea as well?

Which leaves me once again a legionary serving the IMPire. That's a hard thing to swallow right now. But there's nothing to be gained by acting out with McClaren. I need time to think about all this.

I stall. "So that's how it is?"

McClaren makes a hospitable gesture at the space between us, as if to say, "We serve only the finest of fecal foodstuffs. Please enjoy." He looks inquiringly at me.

I have to bite. I'm not prepared to start a rebellion here and now. "I absolutely never meant to cause Ms. Randall any aggravation."

"You haven't yet. That's why we're talking. So that you don't."

"I wouldn't dream of it."

McClaren gets up and puts a hand on my shoulder, giving it an ungentle squeeze. He nods at me solemnly.

"Thanks so much, Jimmy," he says. "You're a real prince."

80

Susan Mercer has lunch by herself at the Sichi Zhilu teahouse in Chinatown at noon nearly every day. Many of my former colleagues believe she secretly owns the place. I find her pouring herself a cup at her regular table.

"Now, James, if you wanted lunch, you could have called my girl. I believe your new vocation is impinging on your sense of decorum." She says this with a smile, but it still throws me.

"I, ah, Susan—" I hadn't expected her to bring up my new job.

"Please, dear boy, no need to blush. Perhaps I'm not the withered old prune you imagine."

"No, of course, I—"

"You came here to discuss something else."

"I just met with John McClaren."

"I know. Johnny and I go way back. I take it you've developed questions that he declined to answer."

"That's right. But he implied that my asking them was dangerous, which leads me to believe there's some truth to their premise."

"You want to know why he set about manipulating certain information."

I nod.

"Let me suggest the traditional follow-on: *cui bono?*" She sits back to let me ponder that.

Who benefits?

There's only one answer to her question: Blythe. She ended up with all the chips.

Supporting evidence: isn't it funny she didn't fire McClaren, despite that for a security specialist, he failed utterly in protecting Blake?

For that matter, Blythe acted suspiciously forgiving of me, the man who *actually killed* her brother. She explained her lack of malice by saying she believes that he brought his fate upon himself. But she can't claim to have done much to stop it. I had always framed the battle of the Randalls in terms of the brothers. I never really placed Blythe in the action.

Mercer sees the light go on in my head. She shrugs. "Consider that while old John is certainly formidable, he's not nearly so formidable as his boss."

"You were working for her. From the beginning."

"We both were. Your Blythe is a student of history. She knows that if you wish to be emperor, you must entice the Praetorians to your side. And we all know the value of picking the right side in a civil war."

A civil war with a faction the other two combatants didn't know they were fighting. The Randall brothers had been openly at odds since Billy had his supervotes yanked. Through it all, Blythe played the appalled bystander to the hilt. But at the same time, she was contending with her twin in the friendly competition for control of IMP. Surely she saw that Billy distracting Blake redounded to her benefit.

"So she planned all of this?"

"I think that would be impossible. But . . . Well, perhaps you know that her twin brother was given to dismissing her as an unimaginative 'pipes' person, while presenting himself as the family visionary. But in my estimation, Blythe is better seen as a *network* person, a weaver of webs. Someone who thinks not only about information itself, but how it's distributed. Someone who understands that you can get a person to accept even the most ridiculous proposition when you present it in the right context."

So how did she ensnare her brothers?

Blythe sets feelers on the shaking strands of their lives. Eventually, she sees this shared pursuit of the male Randalls reemerge: Gina Delaney. Billy's bipolar love interest, and now Blake's conflicted money shot. She watches, pretending to dampen their burning enmity with one hand while secretly mixing nitroglycerin with the other.

Gina's death provides the spark.

Blythe intuits that Billy's terrible grief can, with a judicious reframing, be focused, amplified, and turned to rage aimed straight at Blake. She makes sure he gets a warped view of Gina's last moments and leaves his dark paranoia to do the rest. Like a Soviet spy who only believes information he steals, Billy trusts the video's authenticity because he lifted it from me.

"She used Billy's own puppet-master techniques against him."

Mercer says nothing, but her eyes twinkle with satisfaction that I'm finally getting it.

"And yet she seemed so hurt by everything that happened. After her brother broke into her apartment, she cried . . ."

I think back to that night. Billy knew Blythe was attending that Women in Media panel. Remarkably unlucky that a freak carbon monoxide leak sent her back to the apartment to surprise him. She winds up bleeding in her twin's arms.

Was that the incident that finally did it for Blake? Or was it her sobbing as Billy sold his stock and then asking him, "Is it never going to stop?"

For a woman who supposedly wanted peace between her brothers, she shed quite a few tears in front of Blake. Tears she must have known would inflame his hatred for Billy.

Mercer says softly, "Will no one rid me of this troublesome priest?"

So Blythe wasn't lamenting, she was recruiting. And she found eager volunteers in Blake and Mondano. Then I get stuck again. How did they ever locate Billy? They'd shown no ability in that regard before, and suddenly he winds up dead before I get to his apartment?

Maybe "old John" already knew where he was. That day when he showed up at Amazone after ignoring my calls for over an hour, he told me he was "far afield" protecting Blythe. But I'll bet she adheres to the "good offense" school of security. Let's say she ordered McClaren and his surveillance teams to monitor what Blake and Mondano were going to do at the Cloisters from a safe distance. They see me release Billy, and so McClaren sends a detachment to follow him. Later that day, he "discovers" Billy's whereabouts and passes that information along to her brother. Blake in turn passes it to Mondano's people, who then pass a lethal jolt of current through Billy's brain.

If all this is true, it's a hand well played. Using Mondano, McClaren, and me as the fuel, the brothers incinerate themselves in their feud, leaving Blythe to cool their ashes with her tears.

Weeping, but standing alone on the field.

I say, "Okay, Billy I get. But Blake wound up dead too. Was that just luck?"

"Well, you pulled the trigger. What did it feel like to you?"

I light a cigarette, still thinking. Mercer surprises me by reaching for one as well.

Standing there, facing off amidst all the blood, I remember both of us being dumbfounded that things had gone so haywire.

Mercer continues. "I think we taught you well enough to appreciate that one can never plan everything to the last detail. Chaos will reign. But that doesn't mean you can't devise scenarios that tilt the odds to your advantage. That put others in impossible situations."

So if Blythe was an even better puppet master than Billy, might she also be a better social engineer than I am?

After that initial meeting, I'd asked myself, "Why me?" The answer: Blythe knew I'd be especially easy to beguile into serving her aims. Thinking back through the past weeks, I see how she used each of our encounters to deploy a specific technique we Soshes use to worm our way into the good graces of our victims. *Establishing trust.*

At our Harvard Club chat she delivered the classic *appeal for help,* while providing *privileged information* about her brother Blake. She then offered me *special assistance* with her father's records, at which point she also directly contradicted a few of Blake's lies and evasions. She said he was "slow to trust." The message I took to heart: "You should not trust him. Trust me."

"We both trusted Blythe, but not each other," I say.

"And why didn't he trust you, his faithful janissary?"

"I met with the iTeam instead of going to him after finding Billy's place."

"Why did you do that?"

"I was scared. Seeing the body was upsetting, but I more or less knew that was in the works. I was scared for *myself*. The night he died, Billy warned me. He said, 'He knows you know. Do you think he's going to let you live?'"

"He said that to you?"

Wait . . . No, that's not right. He didn't say it. I read it.

"We were chatting in NOD." Which is odd, since he had used the voice system in our previous meeting. Also wrong was the undecorated blankness of the space. The still, zombie-like avatar, a stark contrast to Billy's previous showy animations.

"Dear boy, that could have been *anyone*."

Who was it then? One of Blythe's people, maybe McClaren, trying to condition my interpretation of events and turn me against Blake.

"But why?"

"Look at what happened," she says.

I freak out and try to take off with Xan and Garriott. Blake and Mondano move to prevent that. Since they've just murdered Billy, it's not unreasonable to conclude that violence could ensue. Blake might be implicated in a crime serious enough to neutralize him. Maybe Blythe had been preparing me for the time when she'd ask me to help her do just that.

If true, then her plan worked better than she might have wished. Blake and I ended up pointing guns at each other. Had he been fed disinformation about me as well? Something that moved him to pull the trigger? Would I have gotten my shot off if I weren't disposed to believe that he really meant me harm? Was it Blythe's whisper in my brain that added just enough pressure on my index finger to see her brother dead?

I'm amazed at how my new picture of Blythe's actions so closely mirrors Billy's game. They both seeded cancerous information about their family within distracting spectacles. In his case, *Savant*; in hers, this break-in at her apartment. He used an avatar to represent as his brother, while she impersonated him. He *tried* to deploy Gina's video to antagonize the twins. She *succeeded* in using it against him. He taunted Blake with a fake electrocution; she made sure that image became a reality. Whatever moves Billy made, she played right back at him. Even the idea to distort the reflections on Gina's pupils derived from Billy's *Getting Wet* video.

I look at Mercer. "So what do I do now?"

"I would recommend a stiff drink to fortify yourself for the realization that the game is over. Please don't indulge the self-important notion that it's your responsibility to ensure 'justice' is served. Indeed, where is the crime here? Maybe something petty like bribing a police officer. Perhaps some flavor of conspiracy. But let's be honest, these are things *we* do every day."

"There are five dead bodies here. Including both her brothers."

"But she didn't fire a weapon. You were the one who did that. James, you must assure me you won't do anything rash. I trust you can see that should you involve anyone else, they may have a less than sympathetic view of your participation in all this. Of course, you remember the cardinal rule of our business?"

"Never make yourself a soft target."

"And don't forget what you've learned about Blythe Randall thus far."

That she is a dangerous woman, to be fucked with at your peril.

Mercer sees the acquiescence form in my eyes before I actually come to a decision. She stands and brushes a lock of hair off my forehead. "Do come see me when you've spent yourself on this new . . . enterprise of yours."

In parting, she plants an adder strike of a kiss on my cheek.

The next day, an invitation arrives.

Blythe is having cocktails at her apartment to celebrate her promotion to CEO of IMP. A little more than a year after her brother's funeral. The minimum decent mourning period.

Written on the embossed cardstock in red pen are the words:

```
Perverse? Perhaps. But I suppose serving the Imp runs
in my family. Anyway, I'll bet nothing shocks you these
days.
```

```
—B
```

81

When I first saw her ridiculous ballroom, I thought it far too large to ever be filled. But tonight Blythe has made a fine effort to do so. The bulk of the crowd consists of executives from IMP with a contingent of up-and-coming actors from their studios to provide the requisite astral element.

I notice Blythe across the room immediately. She's alight with plutocratic joy, laughing and gesturing broadly. Her beloved scarlet pearls gleam at her neck, and I can't help thinking that the strand has grown a bit longer. I'm burning to speak with her, but the conversation will require privacy, so I scuttle out of her line of sight. Biding my time.

Luckily I find a group of old friends from school huddled in a corner of her aircraft carrier of a balcony. I sequester myself among them, as I field questions probing how I've risen in the world enough to score this invite.

I'm astounded at how the night melts away. My watch suddenly reads three thirty AM. When my opponent passes out, I emerge from the billiards room to see that the party has breathed its last gasp. I spare a glance into the ballroom as I pass by. The only signs of the earlier throng are several sticky puddles reflecting the light coming through the windows from a giant moon. Under that moon is a slender figure leaning, hands spread wide, against the balcony's rail.

Blythe.

I can tell from her posture exactly where she is right now. Outside on a perfect night, after a rocking party, celebrating something special. I know the feeling: you want to be by yourself looking down at the sleeping world and take some time to simply *rejoice*. Though Blythe is the kind of person who's probably already making new plans. And I'm afraid some of those plans include me.

I'd agonized about coming tonight. Her sub-rosa investment in ArrowTech meant that I'd have to constantly watch her and worry about her latest agenda. That seemed untenable. So while I may not have the courage to go to the police, at least I want a divorce. The question was: how to serve the papers?

That made me think of the last time I presented her with special papers. Back then my purpose was nearly the opposite, but reprising that motif felt like the right way to close the circle.

I slip through the balcony doors and watch her for a moment. "Blythe . . . Are you starting to feel lonely at all?"

She shuts her eyes and inhales deeply. Then she takes her purse from the balustrade and fishes inside it. I entertain the possibility that she's thumbing a radio that will signal black helicopters to descend and whisk me away, but she merely extracts a pack of Nat Shermans. I light one for her, and she hands it to me. Then I light hers. She sends a long plume of smoke out over the city. I'm about to repeat myself when she looks at me and smiles slyly.

"You ever think about tattoos? As a form of self-expression?"

"I asked you a question."

She ignores it again. "We live in an inspiring age. Human freedom is erupting across the globe. And people embody this by doodling on their skin. Little pictures we use to define ourselves."

"And?"

"So poor Billy and his unfortunate friends decorated their bodies with their obsessions. One of them even crafted her demise around her sacred symbol."

"Billy's demise was 'crafted' that way too."

Blythe nods equably. "You'd seen Blake's right wrist? The Suicide King? He got it shortly after our father passed away. It doesn't take a genius to unravel its meaning. But most people didn't know that he had one on the inside of his left wrist too. His watch band covered it. The Gemini glyph. That was for me, of course. Our birth sign is Aries."

She takes another long drag. "When people looked at us, that's what came to mind: the Gemini. Two, that are in some unnatural way really one. Identical. Copies of each other. Obviously we're fraternal. Male and female. Maybe an even stranger pair for that . . . Did you know that I have a tattoo as well?"

I didn't, though I have studied Blythe closely when permitted. I can definitively say she didn't have one in college and doesn't have one now anywhere that normally sees daylight. She pivots away from me on a heel, her backless dress framing a perfect expanse of white in the moonlight. Her hand brushes slowly down the smooth fabric to the juncture just north of decency. She pulls it down an exquisite inch to reveal two things.

The first is that she has a small Taijitu, the Taoist yin and yang symbol, right over her L5 vertebra. The second: that she has disdained the comfort of even a G-string tonight.

I find myself speechless. Blythe continues. "I know. A silly tramp stamp. How ridiculous, right? I often think of having it lasered away. But that little mark was very important to a confused college girl whose father had just died. And so I never get around to erasing it."

I clear my throat. "It's, ah, fascinating, but—"

She turns back to me, knowing her display had the desired effect. "So to me, Blake and I were more like the poles of a magnet. Bound together, irreducible, but at the same time opposite."

"Blythe, that's a lovely metaphor, but you're evading my question."

She holds up her hand, commanding patience. "I'm not. You want to know about my brothers' sad end, and I'm telling you the way I see it." She looks like she's about to say something cutting to me, but then she purses her lips and peers back out across the park. "Take Billy. Do you know why he chose Sade for his absurd production?" She waits for a response, but I just stare back at her, wanting to see where this is going.

She continues. "Sade was a philosopher of power and its dynamics." Her lips draw a sip of scotch, and her other hand traces a sinuous pattern on the stone in front of her. "To Billy, power was something to be struggled against rather than channeled."

I picture him lying next to his mother, her back a bleeding mess. "I wonder where he got that idea?"

"He was always that way. Unlike Billy, I see Sade as a novelty act. On the subject of power, I prefer Maxwell. His laws of electromagnetism. My little brother lived his life moving through his twin siblings' magnetic field. But he had this quality of *resistance*. If you remember your physics, what happens then?"

"Power is converted to heat."

"And what does heat do?"

"It dissipates."

Blythe nods sadly. "Sometimes, yes. But it can also burn. If the surge is too great, the resistor is destroyed."

"So it was all inevitable. Like clockwork."

"The laws of nature are immutable. Woe unto him that sets himself against them."

"And Blake?"

"Blake died from simple ballistics. Surely I don't have to explain that to *you*."

"He got what was . . . coming to him?"

Blythe shrugs. "I wasn't the one who dreamed of committing my younger brother in a jurisdiction where they still practice electroshock treatment. Remarkable how Billy's demise so closely fulfilled that fantasy. Just far more efficiently. And you certainly don't think such a vulgar display was my idea?"

"Blythe, I can't be in business with someone who has such fine aesthetic sensibilities."

She playfully feigns offense. "You want to abandon me? After all I've done for you?"

"I'm more worried about what you'll do *to* me. So here, I have something for you. A parting gift." I extract from my coat pocket a new bouquet of origami roses. But these I made with images rather than verse.

She seems charmed, but her eyes narrow as she unravels the first one.

A still I isolated from Billy's trove of necrotic family videos. The nasty conclusion of the force-feeding episode.

Continuing the theme, the next flower contains one of freelance photo-pharmacist Pete Novak's least-flattering shots of Blythe in distress.

Her fingers tear violently at the next one: a full nude she let me take of her in perhaps our most tender moment. That's when she really absorbs the pictures' message:

You *can't* trust me. I *will* hurt you.

But the next one puzzles her. A crime scene photo of Billy's disfigured corpse. An inset zooms in on an exposed fingerprint on the batteries' throw switch. Blythe raises an eyebrow at me.

"Amazing the police didn't run down an unidentified print at the crime scene. I guess someone else must have been there when he died . . . Can you account for *your* whereabouts?"

"Tampering with a closed case file? A rather fanciful use of your talents, James."

"Consider it a tribute. Using a technique I learned from you. You think it's *fanciful* because you weren't actually there. You didn't *do* anything, so you couldn't have left fingerprints, right? But you did *play a role,* and you *did* leave fingerprints."

I whip open the last flower for her. This one is not an image, but rather a transcript of my final NOD chat with Billy's avatar. The words are annotated with interstitial numbers denoting detailed timing metrics on each character as it was typed. Together, those measurements, called "keystroke dynamics," can be processed for any given person into a behavioral biometric signature. When I worked for Ravelin during college, they made telecommuting employees use an app that periodically verified your identity this way, and it had recorded Blythe's profile when she sent an email from my laptop. On matching her keyboard signature to Billy's av, at first I couldn't believe she'd risk hijacking it herself. But then Blythe probably didn't even trust McClaren with her most delicate business. Having known Billy from birth, she'd have been the best choice to channel him.

"That's clearly you, Blythe. Your w's and s's are real slow." I wiggle my left ring finger at her to contrast it with the crooked immobility of hers.

"Hardly proof of anything."

"No, just evidence. You think anyone might find it interesting that you were impersonating Billy online just after his death, but before you could have known about it?"

She doesn't make a sound, but her chest rises with a deep breath. She's mastering herself, suppressing rage. She couldn't even abide sharing power with her twin. Now my standing here with this scintilla of leverage must drive her insane. And beyond that, I suppose it will torture her that I found a crack in her masterwork. One that perhaps exposes a structural weakness and portends more cracks to come.

She says, "A very risky move, James."

"My point is, I'm through playing games. So are you."

"Oh, but there's a lot of fun for you and me still to come. You'll see." She casually tosses aside my flowers.

I'm surprised she's insisting on our new partnership. Has Blythe developed the same crush on the Dancers that everyone else did? I suppose to her they're a trophy of her conquest of Blake, or maybe worse: they're part of some dark stratagem I can't yet imagine.

"All I can see is your brothers' blood on your hands," I say, "and I don't want any more on mine."

I try my best at a penetrating stare. And maybe I do all right, because she meets it for a while as though she's deciding whether to argue. She pulls on her cigarette, down to its end, and flicks the butt to the street below.

Softly she says, "Maybe you don't see things as clearly as you think." Then she starts blowing the smoke directly into my eyes. I try to hold her gaze, thinking that this is some kind of test, but the smoke is too much, and I have to close them. Tears flood forth, and one escapes my left eye.

I'm amazed when I feel her lips catch it, as it trails down my cheek. Her hand at the back of my head, her body pressed close. A hint of her perfume induces a trill of vertigo. She makes a soft sound as she tastes it, like an alcoholic relishing her first sip after a decade of abstinence.

She whispers, "James, can't we just be friends again?"

Then she kisses me.

Part of me just wants to dissolve into her. But another, newer facet recoils.

She thinks I'm still so easy to seduce?

A year ago, I was deliriously happy to serve Blythe Randall in any way she might name. I delighted in making myself her creature. What she doesn't realize is that her deposed enemies Billy, Blake, and even Olya have given me a new banner under which to march. I have my own portfolio now, and I will pursue it with all the subtlety and ruthlessness at my disposal, regardless of her belief that she controls it. I am still formally a pawn, but I feel like one who's fought his way up the board to the seventh rank, on the precipice of promotion. Like her brother, she sees me as a knave, but I know that in the relentless shuffling play of the days ahead, I'll come out a king. And I want her to grasp that. To understand how things have changed.

Since that spring day in Cambridge on the steps to her apartment, I've often dreamed of once again kissing Blythe Randall. But I never imagined the touch of her lips would ignite a feeling of righteous rage.

I murmur against her teeth, "We were never friends."

Then my hand that was moving to caress her hair clenches and jerks her head back. My other hand moves to her throat, pressing on her larynx with my thumb. I thrust my tongue into her mouth.

I suppose I was hoping to shock her a little. Force her to take a cautious step back. To say to her:

We can do this, but it won't be like it was.

But Blythe just makes a low hum of appreciation. She steps into me, pressing her thigh hard between my legs. Then she bites down sharply on my tongue. My whole body convulses tightly with pain, bending her farther back. My teeth ram against her lips. I can feel her sucking, not content with my tears, now trying to taste my blood.

There we remain, locked in a farrago of pain and lust, neither willing to relent. And I know this position will define my life in the coming days.

It feels good.

ACKNOWLEDGMENTS

There are a number of people without whom this book would have remained at the far left of the idea/object continuum.

My family. Your boundless love and support have always amazed me.

Dustin Thomason inspired me to pick up my pen. He is an outstanding writer and a matchless friend.

Better writers than me have written encomiums to Jennifer Joel's many virtues as an agent, a word to which they tend to append modifiers like "super" and "über." As a person, she deserves the same prefixes, but to avoid some awkward constructions, I'll just say that she is simply wonderful.

Whatever meager pleasures this volume holds were coaxed to life by my editor, Sarah Knight. Rendering the dross from a manuscript is supposed to be a painful process, but I must admit I found it a rare pleasure to bask in the glow of her coruscating wit and perspicacity.

I'd also like to thank:

The good people at Simon & Schuster: Jessica Abell, Renata Di Biase, Jonathan Evans, Jonathan Karp, Molly Lindley, Aja Pollock, Richard Rhorer, Kelly Welsh, and Jason Heuer.

My early readers: Clay Ezell, Nick Snyder, Mike Fisher, Adam Hootnick, Sam Brown, John Crouch, and David Kanuth.

The faculty, staff, and students at the Interactive Telecommunications Program at NYU's Tisch School of the Arts.

ABOUT THE AUTHOR

Michael Olson, a Harvard graduate, worked in investment banking and software engineering before earning a master's degree from NYU's Interactive Telecommunications Program, where he designed a locomotion interface for virtual environments.